BEHOLD, HE COMETH!

BEHOLD,

HE COMETH!

An Exposition of the Book of Revelation

HERMAN HOEKSEMA

Edited and partially revised by Homer C. Hoeksema

REFORMED FREE PUBLISHING ASSOCIATION
Grand Rapids, Michigan

(Distributed by Kregel Publications)

Copyright © 1969 by the
Reformed Free Publishing Association
Box 2006, Grand Rapids, Michigan 49501

Library of Congress Catalog No. 70-82449
ISBN 0-8254-2809-2

First Edition 1969
Second Printing 1974

Printed in the United States of America

Contents

Page

Editor's Preface

The following pages contain the deceased author's exposition of the Book of Revelation which first appeared serially in the magazine of which he was for many years the editor, **The Standard Bearer**. Tentative plans for publication had been made before the Lord took him to glory. In fact, the title of this volume is of the author's choosing. However, before final preparation of the contents could be completed, the author died. My father and I had consulted on some of the preparations for publishing. Besides, I fell heir to the vast amount of notes and sermon outlines on the Book of Revelation which he had amassed over the years of his long ministry. This made my task of editing much easier. My part in this volume has been mostly editorial. The only exception to this is a few chapters involving parts of Revelation 19-22 which the author himself would have rewritten. Due to various circumstances, as originally written, these chapters were very abbreviated and were not consistent with the others in length, style, and format. On the basis of my father's notes and sermon outlines, I have revised and expanded these few chapters in the hope that this would enhance the value of this commentary.

Perhaps a few biographical notes will not be out of place. The author loved to preach and to teach from the Book of Revelation, perhaps more than from any other book. Twice during his long service as pastor of a large congregation he preached through the entire book. The first series of sermons was shortly after World War I. The second series belonged to the era of World War II. The latter series I remember well from the days of my youth. Besides, more than once the author led his large adult Bible Class through a detailed study of parts or all of the Book of Revelation. His sermons, of which there were two complete sets totalling well over a hundred sermons, were characterized by lucid, simple, and yet thorough exposition; and they were delivered with a warmth and fervor which kept a large congregation at spellbound attention Sunday after Sunday. It is my hope that something of these virtues is reflected in this commentary, which, for the sake of both interest and clarity, was written in essay form, rather than in the form of a verse-by-verse explanation.

May the Lord so bless this effort and sanctify this explanation of the last book of Holy Writ to the hearts of the readers that we may look more earnestly for the coming of our Lord.

—Homer C. Hoeksema

Chapter I

The Revelation Of Jesus Christ

(Revelation 1:1-3)

1 The Revelation of Jesus Christ, which God gave unto him, to shew unto his servants things which must shortly come to pass; and he sent and signified it by his angel unto his servant John:
2 Who bare record of the word of God, and of the testimony of Jesus Christ, and of all things that he saw.
3 Blessed is he that readeth, and they that hear the words of this prophecy, and keep those things which are written therein: for the time is at hand.

Introductory Remarks

"Blessed is he that readeth, and they that hear the words of this prophecy, and keep those things which are written therein: for the time is at hand."

These words should be sufficient justification of the attempt to expound this last book of Holy Writ, if, indeed, the earnest endeavor by a minister of the Word of God to deliver God's message to the church of Christ in the world from any part of the Scriptures ever requires an apology. A satisfactory exposition of the Book of Revelation is considered impossible by many. The book is so full of symbols and allegories, and its true meaning is couched in such mysterious language, that one can never feel sure that he has discovered its real sense. And the history of the interpretation of this book of the Bible apparently corroborates this opinion. Many a commentary has been written on the Book of Revelation; numerous treatises have been published on individual parts of it; and the explanations offered are as numerous and divergent as the scholars who attempted to expound the book. Thus it is alleged. And the conclusion is drawn that it is better to refrain from any attempt at explanation, or, at least, to wait until "the things that must shortly come to pass" are being realized. If, then, an apology would seem to be in order for offering our

1

own interpretation, we would appeal to the last verse of the passage treated in this chapter. The book is intended to convey a blessing to them that endeavor to acquaint themselves with the contents of it and that keep the words of this prophecy. It must be possible, then, "to read and to hear," to understand "what the Spirit saith unto the churches" through this part of the Word of God. It may not be possible to satisfy the spirit of curiosity in which many approach this last book of Holy Writ; but one may surely so understand the "meaning of the Spirit" that he receives the blessing which is here promised.

To obtain this blessing will be more than sufficient reward for our endeavors.

It is quite customary to preface the exposition of the Book of Revelation by a discourse on extraneous matters, such as questions concerning the author of Revelation, the time of its composition, and the proper method of interpretation. We shall not try to add anything to all that has been written on these questions, neither shall we determine upon a definite method of exposition at this stage. Much has been written about the authorship of the book. I presume that all the internal and external evidence that can throw light upon this question has been presented; and opinions are still divided. Some claim that the author is the apostle John; others argue that the John who is mentioned as the author in the book itself cannot possibly have been the apostle "whom Jesus loved." It would be quite useless to repeat the arguments employed in favor of the one or of the other view. One who is interested in the question may consult any commentary on this book. I do not consider the question of any importance. The canonicity of the book does not depend on the apostolic authorship. Nor is the correct understanding of its contents contingent upon the proper solution of this question: if it were, Scripture would surely have given us definite information on this point.

The same is true of the question concerning the time when this book was written. Here also opinions are divided between an earlier and a later date. Although, therefore, it is our personal conviction that the author is the apostle John and that the book was written about the year 95 A.D., we do not consider the matter of sufficient importance to add to the mass of material that has already been written on these questions.

As to the proper method of interpretation, we would rather let the text speak for itself and let it become apparent from our interpretation which method we prefer, instead of announcing such a method beforehand.

Several methods have been applied; and the weakness of them all is exactly that they are **methods**, and that they often have been applied too stringently, so that the contents of the Book of Revelation were forced into their scheme. This is especially true of the church-historical method, according to which the various visions of the book are more or less clearly and definitely traced in the history of the new dispensation. But also the futurist and the praeterist method of interpretation must plead guilty of this. According to the former, almost the entire contents of Revelation must be considered as referring to the distant future, the time immediately preceding the second coming of the Lord. According to the latter, most of the prophecy of this book must be regarded as having been fulfilled in the past, particularly in the fall of the mighty Roman empire. What must be considered the correct method of interpretation must be determined by the contents of the book itself, however; and what method we prefer will become apparent in the course of our explanation.

The first three verses of chapter 1 contain what may be called the superscription of the whole Book of Revelation. It announces the contents of the book: it is a revelation of Jesus Christ and throws light on the things which must shortly come to pass. It informs us how this revelation was received: it was given by God, through Christ, through the instrumentality of an angel, to His servant John, and by John to Christ's servants. And it closes with the beatitude to which we already called attention: "Blessed is he that readeth, and they that hear the words of this prophecy, and keep those things which are written therein: for the time is at hand."

The Revelation Of Jesus Christ

The book, then, presents itself as "revelation of Jesus Christ." The original word for "revelation" is **apokalupsis,** from which our "apocalypse" is derived. It denotes the act of uncovering something that is hid, as, for instance, the unveiling of a statue. In the Biblical sense it denotes that act of God whereby He makes known to us the things concerning Himself and the kingdom of heaven, "the mysteries" of the kingdom of God. For these things are not of this world. They cannot be perceived by our natural senses. Nor can they be conceived by the natural understanding. They belong to another world than ours, to the spiritual and heavenly order of things, "which eye hath not seen, nor ear heard, neither have entered into the heart of man," (I Cor. 2:9). They cannot be apprehended, therefore, unless God reveals them to us, "unveils" them, and unless there be a spiritual eye to see, a spiritual ear to hear, a spiritual mind to understand them. The word "revelation," then, denotes that act of God whereby He discloses to us that other world, the things of His heavenly kingdom and eternal covenant.

Now the text speaks of a "revelation of Jesus Christ." In the original the name "Jesus Christ" stands in the genitive case (apokalupsis Ieesou Christou); and the question is whether this is to be regarded as an objective or as a subjective genitive. If the latter is correct, the meaning is that Jesus Christ is the subject, or author, of this revelation, that He is the revealer of the things contained in this prophecy. If the former is the true interpretation of this genitive, the expression denotes that Jesus Christ is the object of this revelation, that He is the One that is "unveiled," revealed, in this book. The common interpretation takes the genitive in the subjective sense: the revelation which Jesus Christ gave, of which He is the author. In fact, practically all commentators take this sense for granted, and hardly allow for the possibility of taking the genitive in the objective sense.

Yet we believe that there are important objections against this view, objections which are so weighty that we prefer to understand the expression in the objective sense, so that it means that Jesus Christ is revealed to us in this last book of Scripture. In the first place, we call attention to the fact that the expression "revelation of Jesus Christ" usually, if not always, has this sense in Scripture. In I Corinthians 1:7 we read: "So that ye come behind in no gift; waiting for the revelation of our Lord Jesus Christ" (ASV. The KJV has erroneously: "the coming of our Lord Jesus Christ."). It is evident that the meaning here is: "waiting for the day when our Lord Jesus Christ shall be revealed." The genitive, therefore, is objective. The same is true of the expression in II Thessalonians 1:7: "at the revelation of the Lord Jesus" (ASV). The King James Version gives the sense correctly: "when the Lord Jesus shall be revealed." And again, the same expression occurs in I Peter 1:7, and in the same sense, i.e., with reference to the second coming of the Lord: "unto praise and honor and glory at the revelation (KJV: "appearing") of Jesus Christ." And even in II Corinthians 12:1, where the expression is somewhat different in form (the plural "revelations" is used), the objective sense is by no means impossible. And this is the meaning of the genitive in similar expressions, such as "the revelation of the righteous judgment of

God," Romans 2:5; "the revelation of the sons of God," Romans 8:19; "the revelation of the mystery," Romans 16:25. In all these instances the genitive can only be understood in the objective sense. The analogy of Scripture, then, is decidedly in favor of the view that also in Revelation 1:1 the expression "revelation of Jesus Christ" must be understood as indicating that in this last book of Scripture Jesus Christ is the One that is revealed. In the second place, not Christ, but God is the author of all revelation, even though this revelation takes place through Jesus Christ and is concentrated in Him. God is the revealer; Christ is God revealed unto us. In fact, this is even plainly stated in the words of verse 1: God gave this revelation unto Christ. And, in the third place, this is exactly what we have in this book: a revelation which reveals Jesus Christ to us. The revelation of Jesus Christ is the central and all-important theme of this prophecy. For all these reasons, then, we understand the phrase "revelation of Jesus Christ" in the objective sense.

Now this is of importance with a view to the proper interpretation of the Book of Revelation.

We should constantly bear in mind that this prophecy purposes to be a revelation of Jesus Christ. It may be said, of course, that all Scripture is a revelation of the Lord. He it is Who is revealed in the protevangel of Genesis 3:15. And all through the Old Testament, in direct prophecies as well as in types and shadows, the revelation of Jesus Christ is the main theme. Centrally we have the revelation of Jesus Christ in the fulness of time: in His incarnation, public ministry, word and work, death and resurrection, ascension and exaltation at the right hand of God the revelation of Jesus Christ, to which all the prophets and shadows of the old dispensation pointed forward, is become an accomplished fact. And it is that accomplished revelation that is interpreted to us by the Spirit of Christ through the authors of the New Testament Scriptures. Yet the revelation of Jesus Christ is not finished. He appeared from heaven, came in the flesh, died and arose and departed again to the Father. We saw Him for a while, but we see Him no more. He dwelt among us, performed His work upon the stage of this world; but He disappeared again without changing the stage on which He was revealed and accomplished His work. Although He is with us now by His grace and Spirit, yet He is hid from us. His revelation, therefore, is not finished: for in this world we see Him not. And yet, even now, even throughout this dispensation He is operating in this world of our present experience. For He has all power in heaven and on earth; He is even now King of kings and Lord of lords; and He controls all things and governs them unto the perfection of His church and His final appearance in glory. Then, in the day of our Lord Jesus Christ, when He shall be revealed in glory, never to be hid again, when He shall appear never to disappear again,–then shall His revelation be perfected.

Of this final revelation of the Lord Jesus Christ and all that is connected with it, all that leads up to it in this dispensation, this last prophecy of Holy Writ speaks. That is its theme. How the Lord is related to the things that come to pass throughout this dispensation, how through them He is coming all the time, and how He will ultimately come in all the glory the Father hath given unto Him, all this is disclosed to us in this "revelation of Jesus Christ."

This we must remember in our interpretation of the book. It would show us the things which must come to pass in a new light. We can only perceive them from an earthly viewpoint, as mere "history." And from this viewpoint the picture is rather a gloomy and hopeless one. We see wars and hear of more wars, ever widening in scope and increasing in intensity. We see vanity and death, earthquakes and destruction, a creature that is subject to vanity. But this last book of Scripture would show us these same things in the light of the revelation of Jesus Christ. We are asked to look at the history of this dispensation as it were from above. Bearing this in mind we will not approach this book with the purpose of satisfying our idle curiosity, to inquire just what may be the course of events in the history of this world. Why should we be anxious to know the future course of worldly events? What consolation would there be in such knowledge? Did not the Lord teach us that we should take no thought even for tomorrow? Nay, but we shall approach the Book of Revelation in the expectation that it will instruct us with respect to the significance of this present history in the light of the revelation of Jesus Christ, and that it will give us an answer to the question: how must all things lead to the final revelation of our Lord in glory? And if we succeed in thus interpreting the book that "we see Jesus" in all the events of this present time, we shall not fail to receive the blessing that is promised to them that read and hear the words of this prophecy!

The Things Which Must Shortly Come To Pass

In the light of the preceding it will also be possible correctly to understand the text when it informs us that God gave this revelation to

Jesus Christ in order "to shew unto his servants the things which must shortly come to pass."

To "shew" these things does not merely mean to lift the veil that hides the future from our view. If this were the meaning, the Book of Revelation would really present us with a history of this entire dispensation written beforehand. We would then be able to trace the fulfillment of this prophecy step by step in the consecutive events of this present time more or less accurately, and to determine approximately, if not exactly, what time it is on the world-clock. It would follow that we would also be in a position to predict "the day and the hour" of the coming of the Lord. This view really underlies the church-historical method of interpretation of this book. The various visions of this book are directly applied to certain definite historical events which are supposed to be clearly predicted here. The very fact, however, that interpreters of this class differ widely in their choice of the events to which these visions are supposed to refer is sufficient reason to condemn this method. Besides, as we said before, it is not necessary for the believer thus to be able to foretell the future. To be sure, the Book of Revelation shows us in general outlines what will be the course of events in this dispensation with a view to the coming of the Lord and the perfection of His kingdom, but not in the sense that this prophecy is a history written beforehand.

To "shew" the things that must shortly come to pass means to reveal them to us in a new light, in their real significance, as a part of God's own program, as a revelation of the coming Lord! We must "see Jesus" even in the events of the present world. We must have sufficient light to "hold fast that which we have," even in the midst of the confusion and darkness and gloom of the picture presented by the history of the world and of the church in the midst of the world. To enable us to see the events of this present time in the light of Christ's coming, — that is the purpose of this book.

Hence, the things that must shortly come to pass must be shown to Christ's servants. By the term "servants" is not meant a special class or group of believers, such as the apostles, but all the believers in their relation to Christ as their Lord. They are His servants. They were liberated from the dominion of sin and the slavery of the devil in order to serve Christ with a new obedience. His Spirit dwells in them. In Him they are new creatures. His Word they possess and love. They are His friends, because they do whatsoever He has commanded them. And let us note that only His servants can receive the words of this prophecy, and that they alone have need of them. Nay more, it is only in the measure that we are faithful to the Lord in the midst of the present world and walk as His servants that the light of this revelation of Jesus Christ can possibly brighten our pathway. Then, indeed, we shall have tribulation. For as they have hated Him, so they will hate His servants. The servant is not greater than his Lord. Then the things which are below and the events of this present time shall have no comfort for us, until we see all things in the light of this prophecy. But seeing them in this light, we shall be of good cheer, being confident that our Lord hath overcome the world!

Two details we must still consider in connection with these things which come to pass: 1) they **must** come to pass; and, 2) they will come to pass **shortly**.

It is good for us to know, as we look about us in the world, that the things that take place **must** come to pass. This **must** expresses the necessity of all the events of this present time from a two-fold aspect. First of all, it points us to the eternal and perfect and all-wise counsel of the Almighty as the ultimate reason and ground of this necessity. All things are but the unfolding of the eternal good pleasure of the Most High. They are, indeed, determined. All things are determined, large and small, good and evil. But they are determined not by cruel fate or blind force, but by the counsel of the all-wise Creator of all things. When we accept the Word of God and believe that all things **must** come to pass, our hearts find rest because they find rest in Him! And, secondly, this **must** points to the end, the **telos**, the final destination of all things: the perfected kingdom of heaven and its revelation in the day of Christ. This second aspect of the **must** is, of course, inseparably connected with the first. Just because all things have their ultimate reason and necessity in the counsel of God, therefore they must come to pass in order to realize the divine end of all things: the tabernacle of God with men! We may express the same thought thus: all things come to pass because Christ is coming! What a glorious assurance of hope even in the darkest moments of history! Let us declare this truth as His witnesses in the midst of a crooked and perverse nation!

These things must come to pass **shortly**. This expression cannot be used to sustain the view that practically the entire contents of the Book of Revelation must be considered as being fulfilled with the destruction of the Roman Empire. For the idea that all things that must become history before the final coming again of the Lord will be realized shortly is not at all foreign to the New Testament. "The night is far spent; the day is at hand," the apostle Paul writes to the church in Rome (Rom. 13:12). And the apostle Peter exhorts us: "But the end of all things is at hand: be ye therefore sober, and watch unto prayer," (I Peter 4:7). To the church of Philadelphia the Lord Himself declares: "Behold, I come quickly: hold that fast which thou hast, that no one take thy crown," (Rev. 3:11). And again, in Revelation 22:7 we read: "Behold, I come quickly: blessed is he that keepeth the sayings of the prophecy of this book." And in vs. 12 of the same chapter: "And, behold, I come quickly; and my reward is with me, to give every man according as his work shall be." In the last three passages the word translated "quickly" is the same as that which is rendered "shortly" in 1:1. And this is, indeed, the meaning. The Lord comes quickly. He does not tarry. He is not slack concerning the promise. And this implies that the things which must come to pass before that final coming and in the process of that coming must also come to pass shortly, or quickly.

This may not appear so to us. Centuries have elapsed since these words were written, and still they have not been fulfilled. Nineteen centuries to us seems a long time, hardly to be denoted by the term "shortly." But we must remember not only that God's measure of time differs from ours, but also that tremendous things must come to pass before the end shall be. The whole church must be gathered: the fulness of the Gentiles and of the Jews. The measure of iniquity must be filled. Antichrist must reach his culmination and have his day. Gog and Magog must play their own part in the things that must come to pass. If we consider the nature of the things that must come to pass, we begin to see that they do, indeed, occur with astounding rapidity, especially in our own day. However this may be, the Scriptures teach that all things come to pass quickly. There is no delay, so that also the view that God restrains the progress of sin is contrary to this Scriptural teaching. All things hasten unto the end!

Which God Gave Unto Him

This revelation, then, of which Jesus Christ Himself is the object, "God gave unto him," the text informs us.

Of all revelation, and therefore also of this part of it, God is the sole Author. We must think here, of course, of the Triune God, Father, Son, and Holy Ghost, and not merely of the Father as the First Person of the Holy Trinity. We must make a distinction, therefore, between God and Christ as the Mediator in His human nature. Scripture, although clearly teaching that Christ is the eternal Son of God, very God, equal with the Father and the Holy Ghost, nevertheless makes this distinction. This is very evident from those passages which speak of God as "the God and Father of our Lord Jesus Christ." God is the God also of Christ, the Mediator according to His human nature. And this God is the Author of all revelation. Hence we read here: "which God gave unto him."

It is a thoroughly Biblical conception that also Christ in His human nature receives all revelation from God. This is not only taught here, but also in such passages as John 5:19, 20; John 7:16; and John 8:28. There is, of course, a difference between Christ and us with respect to the way in which God's revelation is received. We can receive the revelation of God only indirectly, through Christ, through the "apostles and prophets," through the Scriptures; but Christ, because He is the Son of God in human nature, received that revelation directly and immediately, without the intermediation of other agencies. But this does not alter the fact as such that also Christ receives all revelation from His "God and Father." God gave this revelation to Him. And this particular revelation was given to Christ after His exaltation. It is wholly in harmony with His position at the right hand of God, according to which He has all power in heaven and on earth, stands at the very pinnacle of all creation, that God gave this revelation to Him. For to a position of supreme power and authority belongs the possession of all knowledge and wisdom. Later in the Book of Revelation (chapter 5) somewhat the same thought is presented symbolically in the vision of Christ's taking the book with its seven seals from the hand of Him that sitteth on the throne. But this we hope to explain in the proper place.

And He Sent And Signified It

Having received this revelation from God, Christ communicated it to His servants. He did so by "signifying" it to His servant John through the mediation of "his angel."

The original is somewhat difficult to translate. Instead of the words, "and he sent and signified it by his angel," we read: "and he signified, sending (or: having sent) through an angel." The aorist participle of the Greek verb for "to send" is used; and for this we have no exact equivalent in the English language. Let me just say about it that the aorist in Greek stresses the act as such, rather than any time element.

The idea, therefore, is plain enough. The text emphasizes two elements.

In the first place, it gives us to understand that when Christ communicated the revelation which He received from God to His servant John, He "signified" it. This means that He cast it into the form of signs and symbols derived from our earthly life and experience. The Book of Revelation is a book of visions, full of signs and symbols. And this "signifying" must have been necessary. It seems to imply that the form in which Christ imparted this revelation to His servant John differs from the form in which Christ Himself received it from God. Christ is heavenly, the Lord of heaven, the resurrected Lord in glory. He is able to receive the revelation of heavenly things directly, in heavenly form. But we are still earthy, in our humiliated body. And we cannot receive the revelation of heavenly things in other than earthly forms, signs and symbols. This, then, is one of the truths that must constantly be kept in mind if we would interpret the Book of Revelation, though it is also one of the principles of interpretation which is very frequently violated by many commentators. Christ "signified" the revelation which He had received from God to His servant John.

In the second place, this signification took place through the mediation of "his angel." It appears from the rest of the book that different angels were employed to bring these visions to the perception and mind of John. Yet it is not improbable that one particular angel served as the "interpreting angel," and that the reference here is to this angel particularly. It is **Christ's** angel because the Lord is exalted far above all powers and principalities, and above every name that is named. The angels, too, are His messengers, sent out in His service. Nor is it strange that an angel here mediates to communicate and signify this revelation to John. Angels often appear in Scripture as the medium of revelation, not only directly, when they proclaim the Word of God, as at the incarnation and at the resurrection of the Lord, but also indirectly. We know that the law of Sinai was given by the disposition of angels, Acts 7:53, and that it was ordained by angels in the hand of Moses, Galatians 3:19. And that in some such capacity an angel also mediated in the communication of this revelation to John is reaffirmed in chapter 22:6. Somehow, therefore, an angel was employed as agent to bring the visions of this book before the eye of the seer.

This seer is simply called "his servant John." As was stated before, we believe that this was John the Apostle, although this is often disputed. We do not consider the question of importance for the interpretation of this book. Of many parts of Holy Scripture we do not know the human writers. But it seems to us, apart from all other considerations, that in the light of Scripture there can be no doubt that this "servant John" is the apostle of that name. Who else could thus designate himself without further qualifications and expect that his readers would know who was meant? Surely, one that is acquainted with Scripture can think of no other. That he is not called "the apostle of Jesus Christ" in this passage does not alter the matter. In his First Epistle the apostle John does not introduce himself at all, while in his second and third letters he merely calls himself "the elder." Besides, even Paul does not always introduce himself in his epistles as "the apostle" (cf. I Thessalonians 1:1; II Thessalonians 1:1; Philemon, 1); and he also designates himself as a "servant of Jesus Christ" (Philippians 1:1; Titus 1:1). And on the isle of Patmos, as the recipient of this revelation of Jesus Christ, John is not so much an apostle (one that is sent) as simply the servant of Christ. Although, therefore, we consider the question one of minor importance, we hold that this "servant John" is none other than the apostle "whom Jesus loved," especially on the ground that there was no one who was so well known as the apostle that he could afford to announce himself simply as "his servant John," or "John" (vs. 4), or "I John" (vs. 9).

Through John, therefore, this revelation of Jesus Christ is given to the church, "the servants" of Christ. For he "bare record of the word of God, and of the testimony of Jesus Christ, and of all things that he saw." These words, if taken by themselves, might refer to John's work and calling as an apostle in general. Always it was his calling to witness of the Word of God and of the testimony of Jesus. Yet it is more natural to interpret them as referring to his recording the specific Word of God and testimony of Jesus in this book. And this is certainly demanded by the last part of this second verse: "all things that he saw." "The testimony of Jesus Christ" may be understood either in the objective sense (the testimony concerning Jesus Christ) or in the subjective sense (the testimony of Jesus Christ). In the light of the context, the latter is to be considered as the correct interpretation. It was Jesus Christ Who received this revelation from God and Who communicated it to John. He, therefore, is the prime Witness of it. He it is that bears testimony concerning this revelation, which is the Word of God. And in verse 5 He is called "the faithful witness." Of this Word of God and testimony of Jesus Christ John bare record. The original word for "bare record" does not in itself signify the act of recording the

visions in a book. It merely means "testified." We know, however, that
John was commissioned to write them in a book, verse 19, and that,
therefore, this is the form in which he communicated the things which he
saw to the churches.

Blessed Is He That Readeth

Finally, the Book of Revelation is commended to the recipients by the
promise of a blessing: "Blessed is he that readeth, and they that hear the
words of this prophecy, and keep those things which are written therein:
for the time is at hand."

The blessing here spoken of, no doubt, is in the ultimate sense of the
word the inheritance of the glory of the eternal kingdom in the day of
Jesus Christ, the "inheritance incorruptible, and undefiled, and that fadeth
not away," which is reserved in heaven for the believers, "the salvation
ready to be revealed in the last time," (I Peter 1:4, 5). It is the blessedness
of the New Jerusalem, coming down from God out of heaven, of the new
creation, wherein righteousness shall dwell and where the tabernacle of
God will be with men forever. To this ultimate state of blessedness the
whole Book of Revelation looks forward. Yet this does not necessarily
exclude a blessing for the present time. On the contrary, it rather includes
such a present blessing for them that receive and keep the words of this
prophecy. As long as we contemplate the things of this present time, the
things that come to pass in this world, from a mere earthly, human,
historic viewpoint, there is nothing but darkness and hopeless misery. For
"vanity of vanities, all is vanity" is true of the whole of present existence.
We lie in the midst of death; and there is no way out. In spite of the
optimistic outlook and predictions of the prophets and leaders of this
world, things grow more hopeless as time goes on. And serious men of the
world begin to ask the question anxiously whether our whole civilization
will not totter into ruins. The world is not improving though it is
developing in a cultural sense. It is plainly getting worse. In times like the
present we are strongly reminded of this. Not only do we witness the
horrors of war after war; but every war is worse than the former, and this
in the face of all mere humanitarian efforts to establish a lasting peace.
Besides, the people of God also partake of the "sufferings of this present
time;" and when they are faithful and keep the "word of Christ's
patience," they will be called upon also to suffer with Him. But "blessed
are they that hear and keep the words of this prophecy" even now, even in

the midst of this present darkness and death and hopelessness. For if we may look at these same things in the light of this "revelation of Jesus Christ," and live in the expectation of His coming, there is peace and hope and joy. Then we will be of good cheer, for we know that He has overcome the world!

This blessing is not for all, however. It is not general, but particular, as are all the promises of God. God's blessing is upon His people. His mercy is upon them that fear Him. Hence, this blessing is for him "that readeth" and for them "that hear the words of this prophecy, and keep those things that are written therein." The words "he that readeth, and they that hear" probably refer to the public reader of this book in the church and the listening congregation. We may thus paraphrase them according to their true meaning: "all that receive and understand the words of this prophecy." But this is not sufficient. The mere hearing and natural understanding of this prophecy do not yield for us the promised blessing. We must also **keep** the things that are written therein. This surely signifies that we hear spiritually and receive the word of this prophecy in our heart. But it also signifies more. To keep the Word of God also means to obey it, to be doers of the Word. This is also applicable to this last book of Scripture in general and to many of its special exhortations in particular. Always we are exhorted to keep the Word of Christ's patience; to deny ourselves; to separate ourselves from Babylon; to be faithful unto death; to hold fast that which we have, that no one take our crown; to consider it grace in the cause of Christ, not only that we may believe on Him, but also that we may suffer with Him. These things we must keep! If we seek the things that are below and try to serve God and Mammon, if we receive the mark of the Beast in our forehead or in our right hand, we certainly are excluded from this blessing. He that is seeking to save his life shall surely lose it; but he that is willing to lose it for Christ's sake, shall save it unto life eternal! His is the promise and the blessing, now and forever!

The matter is urgent, and the promise is about to be realized!

For "the time is at hand!"

Chapter II

Salutation And Blessing

(Revelation 1:4-8)

4 John to the seven churches which are in Asia: Grace be unto you, and peace, from him which is, and which was, and which is to come; and from the seven Spirits which are before his throne;
5 And from Jesus Christ, who is the faithful witness, and the first begotten of the dead, and the prince of the kings of the earth. Unto him that loved us, and washed us from our sins in his own blood,
6 And hath made us kings and priests unto God and his Father; to him be glory and dominion for ever and ever. Amen.
7 Behold, he cometh with clouds; and every eye shall see him, and they also which pierced him: and all kindreds of the earth shall wail because of him. Even so, Amen.
8 I am Alpha and Omega, the beginning and the ending, saith the Lord, which is, and which was, and which is to come, the Almighty.

Most of the epistles of the New Testament begin with a salutation of the writer to the readers, a salutation which always assumes the form of a benediction. Such blessings or salutations are not mere pious wishes, but they are the Word of God in Christ actually blessing the people of God who hear and believe them. The blessings which they express and confer on them who so receive them by faith are always spiritual blessings of grace. They are merited by Christ and bestowed by Him, or rather by the Triune God through Christ, by His Spirit upon the church. This is also true of the Book of Revelation. The passage under discussion in this chapter may be considered John's dedication of, or introduction to, the entire book. By it the Book of Revelation is addressed to the "seven churches which are in Asia." About these we shall have something to say in a later connection. Further, our passage contains a most significant salutation, or blessing, in verses 4 and 5a; an ascription of praise by the church to Christ in verses 5b and 6; and, finally, a solemn assurance of Christ's coming, corroborated by a direct Word of the Lord, designating Himself as the Alpha and Omega, the Almighty. These three elements will be the subject material of the present chapter.

Grace And Peace

The blessing is expressed in the following words: "Grace be unto you, and peace, from him which is, and which was, and which is to come; and from the seven Spirits which are before his throne; And from Jesus Christ, who is the faithful witness, and the first begotten of the dead, and the prince of the kings of the earth."

The contents of this blessing are "grace and peace."

Grace, as we know, has a variety of connotations in Scripture. It may refer to a virtue of God: God is gracious. Or it may signify an attitude which God assumes toward the creature, an attitude of favor; or more specifically it may denote that same attitude of favor with respect to the guilty sinner, so that for him it is favor that is forfeited. This last attitude of God is based upon the righteousness of Christ attained through His perfect obedience even unto the death of the cross. But the word "grace" also frequently denotes a power, an operation of the Spirit of Christ within the elect, whereby they become partakers of all the benefits of salvation, and the fruits of this operation or blessings of salvation themselves. It is in this last sense that the word is used in this passage, so that we may paraphrase the meaning as follows: "May God through Christ by the Spirit operate with His grace in your hearts so that the gifts of grace, the benefits of salvation, may become yours."

Of this grace the church is continually in need. For grace is not a blessing which is bestowed upon the believers once for all, so that, having received it, they possess it in themselves. On the contrary, they live only through a constant influx of grace, which blesses them as an ever-refreshing stream out of God, through Christ, in the fellowship of the Spirit. And on their part, they receive this grace of God by faith and through prayer.

One of the chief and first fruits of this grace is peace. Peace is peace with God. It always is. Apart from peace with God there is no peace. This is the fundamental reason why the quest of the ungodly world, outside of Christ, for peace on earth is a vain dream which must ever end in a cruel awakening in the reality of a world of war and unrest. "There is no peace, saith my God, to the wicked," (Isaiah 57:21). But "being justified out of faith, we have peace with God through our Lord Jesus Christ," (Romans 5:1). This peace is, first of all, the blessed tranquility of heart and mind that results from the consciousness that God is at peace with us because our sins are blotted out and we are justified. Secondly, it is also the experience that in principle there is peace in our heart toward God: we are no longer motivated by enmity against Him. And, therefore, they that have this peace are also at peace with one another; they are peacemakers. And, finally, having peace with God, they have peace with all things. For they know that if God is for them, nothing can be against them: "All things work together for good to them that love God, who are the called according to his purpose," (Romans 8:28). This peace, then, is not another blessing in addition to grace, but is the fruit of the latter. It is the peace of grace.

What a wonderful blessing is here pronounced upon the seven churches of Asia and upon the entire church in the world! For the church of all ages is represented by the seven churches in the Book of Revelation. To realize the full significance of this benediction we must bear in mind that, according to the viewpoint of this book of Scripture, the church in the world is always in tribulation. With the church in tribulation we must take our stand. She is in the world. And that world is in darkness. The world in the Book of Revelation is not a world improved and ennobled by "common grace," a tolerably good place for the church to live in; but it is the world under judgment, whose condemnation is an accomplished fact, (John 12:31; Colossians 2:15). It is the anti-christian world, which sets itself against God and His Christ, persecutes His people, and always would force them to adopt the mark of the beast. It is the world of the wicked who "are like the troubled sea, when it cannot rest, whose waters cast up mire and dirt," (Isaiah 57:20); the world as it is full of malice and envy, strife and war and bloodshed, terror and destruction, as we see it today, now the very foundations are shaken and the proud structure of modern civilization threatens to tumble about our heads into ruins! In that world this blessed Word of God in Christ is heard and realized: "Grace be unto you, and peace!"

From Him Which Is . . .

Is it possible that the church in the world may really possess this peace? Indeed it is; and the elaborate and detailed description of the source whence this peace of grace is derived is designed to assure us of the reality of it. The author might simply have written: "Grace unto you, and peace, from God the Father and from the Lord Jesus Christ." But he would assure us of the absolute certainty of this blessing. Hence, he writes: "from him which is, and which was, and which is to come; and from the seven Spirits which are before his throne; And from Jesus Christ, who is the faithful witness, and the first begotten of the dead, and the prince of the kings of the earth."

The words "who is, and who was, and who is to come" refer to God, the Triune. The three-fold description of the Author of the blessing of grace and peace must not be interpreted as if the first part ("which is, and which was, and which is to come") refers to the First Person of the Holy Trinity, the last part ("and from Jesus Christ," etc.) to the Second Person, and the second part ("and from the seven Spirits," etc.) to the Third Person. For although it is, of course, true that Jesus Christ is the very Son of God according to His divine nature, yet here He does not appear as such, but as the Mediator. And although, as we shall see presently, "the seven Spirits which are before his throne" certainly are the Holy Spirit of God, He does not appear here as the Third Person of the Holy Trinity, but as the Spirit of Christ. Hence, the first part, "which is, and which was, and which is to come," does not refer to the Father as the First Person, but to God, the Triune, the God and Father of our Lord Jesus Christ.

This Triune God is revealed here as the One "which is." This has all the emphasis, as is especially evident from the form used in the original. It denotes God, not as existing in the present, but as the absolute Being, the One Who eternally is, the Self-existent, the Uncaused, the ground of Whose Being is in Himself alone, in Whom there is no change nor shadow of turning. The reference is probably to His name Jehovah. But this eternal God, Whose Being cannot be measured or limited by time, revealed Himself in time. To this revelation of Himself in time refer the other two expressions, "who was" and "who is to come," (or: "the coming one," **ho erchomenos**). He was, He did come in the past. He came in creation; and, in the fulness of time, He came in Christ. He is the same God Who made all things in the beginning and Who revealed Himself in His Son. And when He created all things, He did so with a view to His coming in Christ. All His works are known to Him from the beginning. They all are and develop according to His determinate counsel. According to that counsel He is coming, always coming, coming ever since He first came in the beginning.

And still He is the coming One, coming to us as the God of our salvation; and He will not cease to come until He is eternally present with us and His tabernacle shall be with men. This cannot fail. Whatever powers of darkness may rise against Him, the Eternal One is coming in Christ Jesus our Lord. And it is He Who causes His Word of blessing to proceed to His church: "Grace be unto you, and peace!" Surely, in spite of all hell this peace is ours!

And From The Seven Spirits . . .

But, you say, how can this peace from the eternal God be our possession even now? The answer is that it is instilled into our hearts by "the seven Spirits which are before his throne." These seven Spirits must not be degraded into created spirits, or angels, as is done by some, nor abstractly generalized into "seven modes" of God's existence, as others would explain the words. Let it suffice to object against these and similar interpretations that these "seven Spirits" are here presented to us as belonging to the source of the blessings of grace and peace, and that, therefore, they are divine and denote a personal agent. They certainly refer to the Holy Spirit, the Third Person in the blessed Trinity.

And yet we must say more than this. The term does not denote the Holy Spirit as He is in God. Why should He then be called the "seven Spirits?" The Holy Spirit in the Trinity is one. And why should it be said of these seven Spirits that they are "before his throne?" The Holy Spirit as Third Person of the Holy Trinity is very God, co-equal with the Father and with the Son. He is not "before the throne" of God; but He is on the throne, the sovereign ruler of heaven and earth. The words, therefore, must be applied to the Holy Spirit as the Spirit of the exalted Christ and as He is poured out into the church, to make us partakers of the covenant blessings of grace and salvation. We must remember that our Lord Jesus Christ, Who was humiliated and obediently humbled Himself even to the death of the cross, and Who by His perfect obedience obtained for us eternal righteousness and life, was raised from the dead and by the power of God was made exceedingly great and glorious, being exalted to the right hand of the Majesty in heaven. That glorious Lord and Mediator also receives from the Father the power to apply all the blessings of salvation which He merited to those whom the Father gave Him before the foundation of the world. This saving power He possesses through the Spirit that is given Him as Mediator and Head of the church at His exaltation, and Whom He poured forth into the church, that He may dwell in her forever. For He, the Lord Jesus Christ, "being by the right hand of God exalted, and having received of the Father the promise of the Holy Ghost, hath shed forth this which ye now see and hear," (Acts 2:33). This Spirit is "the Spirit of truth; whom the world cannot receive, because it seeth him not, neither knoweth him; but ye know him; for he dwelleth with you and shall be in you," (John 14:17). He is the Comforter, through Whom the Lord Himself came again to His church, and Who abides with us forever, John 14:16, 18. He is the "Spirit of adoption, whereby we cry, Abba, Father," and the Spirit that "beareth witness with our spirit that we are the children of God," (Romans 8:15, 16). He is the Spirit of life in Christ Jesus, by Whom we are liberated from the law of sin and death, Romans 8:2. He is the Spirit of Him that raised up Jesus from the dead, Who will also quicken our mortal bodies by that same Spirit, Romans 8:11.

He is called "the seven Spirits," for the number seven denotes the fulness of God's covenant grace, and the fulness of the church in which He dwells is also indicated by the same number. For there are seven churches in Asia, and there are seven candlesticks and seven stars, Revelation 1:11, 12, 16, 20. And the Lamb, Whose Spirit He is, has seven eyes, which are the seven Spirits of God, Revelation 5:6. He, the exalted Christ, is said to have the seven Spirits of God, Revelation 3:1. And these seven Spirits, or the Spirit of Christ as He dwells in the church with His seven-fold fulness of life and grace, are "before the throne" as "seven lamps of fire burning" to the glory of God, Revelation 4:5. And before the throne is the church, serving God day and night in His temple, and He that sitteth on the throne dwells among them, Revelation 7:15. There can be no question, therefore, that "the seven Spirits which are before his throne" refers to the Holy Spirit as He is given to the exalted Christ and poured out into the church. And it is that Spirit of Christ, the Spirit of life and of truth, the Spirit of adoption and of the fulness of His seven-fold grace, the Spirit Who is given us, dwells in us, never leaves us, Who is the divine agent of this blessing of grace and peace. Can there be any doubt that this peace is and forever will remain ours?

And From Jesus Christ . . .

Again, you may probably complain that you are wholly unworthy of this blessing and that, therefore, you cannot apprehend this word of benediction as addressed to you personally. You lie in the midst of death, and sin cleaves to you and marks your every step on the way you walk. How then can this divine grace and peace be intended for you? But the text removes also this objection when it fastens the eye of faith upon Jesus Christ, the faithful witness, the first begotten of the dead, prince of the kings of the earth. He is the faithful witness. Witness He is, for as the Servant of Jehovah He is God's prophet, Who always bears testimony of the truth of God. He did so during His sojourn on earth, for as He said before Pilate: "To this end was I born, and for this cause came I into the world, that I should bear witness unto the truth," (John 18:37). He still does so in the church, for it is He Who gave us the Scriptures and Who leads us into all the truth by His Spirit. And He is the witness also in this book, Whose Word is quite sufficient for your faith to trust in, when He says, "Grace to you, and peace." For He is the **faithful** witness. For His doctrine is not His, but the Father's which sent Him, John 7:16; and He speaks that which He has seen with His Father, John 8:38. He always acts and speaks in harmony with His position as witness of God: for He does nothing of Himself, but as His Father hath taught Him, He speaks in the world, John 8:28. The Lord God hath opened His ear, and given Him the tongue of the learned that He should know how to speak a word in season, Isaiah 50:4, 5. And no matter what men may do unto Him, though they smite Him and pluck out His beard in their fury, and cover Him with shame and reproach, He never changes His testimony and does not compromise the truth, Isaiah 50:5, 6. He was faithful unto death, even the death of the cross. In life and in death you may rely on His Word: "Grace and peace unto you."

And He is the first begotten of the dead! Let this especially be the object of your contemplation, the ground of your assurance: Jesus Christ is the first begotten of the dead! The resurrection, but then emphatically the resurrection of Jesus Christ, should be the ground of your hope, the object of that faith that fills you with joy and peace. Peace, if ever it is to be ours, cannot be of this world: it must come from the other side of death. Here we lie in the midst of death. How than can we have peace? But hark! this voice that speaks of grace and peace is not of this world. It does not sound from somewhere among the deep death-shadows in which here we grope and find no way out. It is the resurrection-voice! He that speaks stands at the other side of death and the grave as the Risen One! That means that He was dead and is alive again and lives forevermore. He is alive with a new life, a glorious, a victorious life. He was in death, and went through death, and He now lives as never one lived before. And what is more, as He passed through death, He left the way open! By faith we behold Him there, on the other side of death; and looking at His glory from our present darkness, we know by that very token that there is a way out! As a man groping in the black and fearful darkness of a deep cave beholds in the distance the glimmer of glorious sunlight and takes courage to continue his way in the one direction of that light-spot in the distance, assured that there lies his deliverance, so the believer groping in the darkness of the shadow of his present death, beholding by faith the glory of the Risen Lord, knows that there is a way out of death into the glorious liberty of the children of God! For, mark you well, He is not merely risen: He is the first begotten of the dead! And the firstborn is he that "openeth the womb" and prepares the way for all his brethren. Thus Christ was in the womb of death, was born from death, opened the womb of death for all those whom the Father gave Him. And it is He, standing in that spot of glorious light, Whom you see from your present darkness, Who calls to you: "Grace and peace to you!"

No power is able to deprive God's people of that blessing or to prevent the ultimate realization of the peace which is promised them in the day of Christ. For He is Lord. He is Prince, too, of the kings of the earth. This does not mean that Jesus Christ is King also of the state in the sense that worldly magistrates rule by His grace. For in the Book of Revelation the kings of the earth are the antichristian world rulers. They acknowledge not the Christ of the Scriptures as their Lord. They do not delight in doing His will and ruling in harmony with it. On the contrary, they are the rulers that are pictured in the Second Psalm, who set themselves, and take counsel together against the Lord and against His Anointed, saying: "Let us break their bands asunder, and cast away their cords from us," (verses 2, 3). But He that sitteth in the heavens shall laugh and have them in derision. For He hath anointed His King and set Him upon His holy hill of Zion. And this King shall rule the antichristian powers with a rod of iron and break them in pieces like a potter's vessel, Psalm 2:7-9, Revelation 2:27. Christ is the Prince of the rulers of the earth! Though they may rave against Him, yet must they do His will. Even the Neros and Caligulas and Domitians, the Hitlers and Mussolinis and Khrushchevs are His servants in spite of themselves. The church is perfectly safe; her salvation and final victory are sure. "In the world ye shall have tribulation; but be of good cheer; I have overcome the world," (John 16:33). "Grace unto you, and peace!"

The Doxology

Already the church receives this blessing of grace and peace. And she responds in joyful adoration to the pronouncement of this benediction. She confesses this Christ even now, even in the midst of this world and its antichristian rulers; and to Him alone she ascribes all glory and dominion forever and ever. This is the meaning of the doxology which now follows in the text: "Unto him that loved us (or: "loveth us," ARV), and washed us (or: "loosed us," ARV) from our sins in his own blood, and hath made us kings and priests (or: "a kingdom and priests," ARV) unto God and his father (or: "unto his God and Father," ARV); to him be glory and dominion for ever and ever. Amen."

Jesus loved us; or, if the reading of the American Revised Version is the more correct, He loveth us. Essentially there is no difference between these two readings. If we read the past tense, the emphasis falls on the historic fact of the death of Christ on the cross, where He manifested His love once for all; if the present tense is taken as the better reading, the thought of His present and enduring love for us is stressed. But if He loved us on the cross, will He not love us still and forever? And if He loves us now, is it not because He loved us on the accursed tree? The same may be said of the two readings "washed" and "loosed" us from our sins in His own blood. Principally there is no difference between the two. They imply that the blood of Jesus is atoning blood because by His death He fully satisfied for all our sins. They mean that He not merely shed His blood for us on the accursed tree, but that He also applies its atoning power to us. They signify that by the application of that atoning blood to us we are liberated not only from the guilt of sin, but also from its dominion and corruption: the law of the Spirit of life in Christ Jesus hath made us free from the law of sin and death. And thus He made us kings and priests unto God and His Father, or a kingdom and priests unto His God and Father. Christ makes us a royal priesthood, or a priestly kingdom.

The ideas of priesthood and royalty belong together and are inseparable. One who is not a priest unto God can never be a king: the antichristian rulers of this world are mere usurpers and will surely be dethroned. For the deepest notion of priesthood is that of perfect consecration to and love of God, manifested in perfect obedience and willing service. A priest consecrates himself and all things to God. And the idea of the kingly office is that of reign and dominion. A priestly king is a servant-king; a kingdom of priests is a kingdom in which all submit themselves to the living God and reign in His name and under Him over all the works of His hands. Such a royal priesthood Christ makes us through the marvellous power of His grace. By the power of sin we became slaves of the devil, rebel kings, who proposed to rule over God's works apart from Him, against Him. Such is the awful folly of sin. But through the atoning blood of the cross we have been forgiven that folly, we have been perfectly justified, we have obtained the right to be delivered from the slavery of sin and the dominion of the devil, the right to be received into the blessed service of God once more, and in that service to reign over all things. And through the grace of the Lord Jesus, by His indwelling Spirit, we are actually delivered, translated out of darkness into the marvellous light of God, and formed into a kingdom of priests. For indeed, God's people are a kingdom, and not merely a multitude of kings. They are a unity, a kingdom over which Christ rules as the chief Servant of Jehovah, the High Priest according to the order of Melchisedec, Who has a name above all names, and in which His brethren reign with Him, each in his own position and all serving the purpose of the whole, that all may be to the glory of the God and Father of our Lord Jesus Christ.

Such a kingdom of priests the church is even now: for by faith they partake of the victory and royal dominion of their Lord. But not until the day of Christ, when the eternal kingdom of glory shall be ushered in, when all the elect shall have been gathered and the body of the Lord shall be complete, when also our humiliated bodies shall be made like unto His most glorious body, and when all things shall be made new and the tabernacle of God shall be with men in the new heavens and the new earth, shall this kingdom of priests be fully realized.

In the consciousness, then, of this great love wherewith the Lord loved and still loves us, and of the marvellous grace whereby He hath liberated them from the power of sin and death and formed them into a royal priesthood, the believers ascribe glory unto their Lord: "to him be glory and dominion for ever and ever. Amen."

Glory is the radiation of infinite, divine goodness and perfection. God alone is glorious. The creature can only reflect His glory, can never possess any glory of its own. Whatever glory may be seen in creation has its source in God. The highest and fullest revelation of that glory is in Christ. All the divine perfections shine forth through and in Him. For it was the Father's good pleasure that in Him all the fulness should dwell, Colossians 1:19. He is the image of the invisible God, the firstborn of every creature, Colossians 1:15. And in Him dwelleth all the fulness of the Godhead bodily, Colossians 2:9. In the days of His flesh this glory was hid by His humiliated body; only occasionally it flashed through when He spoke with authority or revealed His power in the miracles which He performed. And on the mount of transfiguration the apostles beheld His glory for a moment. But through His resurrection and exaltation at the right hand of God, Christ is glorified with the glory which He had with the Father before the world was, John 17:5. All the divine goodness shines forth through Him, radiates from Him. This is possible, of course, only because He is the very Son of God in human nature. No mere man could possess this glory; and to ascribe this glory to any other than the exalted Christ would be idolatry and blasphemy. But the church knows that He is the Son of God, the final and highest revelation of God the Father, worthy of all glory and honor. She ascribes glory to Him in this doxology.

And she also is taught here to acknowledge Him as the One Who has dominion. Of course, He has dominion, that is, authority and power to reign, to declare His will and to demand obedience, to judge and to execute judgment, in the absolute sense of the word as the Son of God. As God He is sovereign. But the reference in the text is to the dominion, the power and authority, which He received from God as the glorified Christ, in His human nature. All power is given unto Him in heaven and on earth. Christ stands at the pinnacle of all created things. He has received a name which is above all names, that at the name of Jesus every knee should bow, of things in heaven, and things in earth, and things under the earth; and that every tongue should confess that Jesus Christ is Lord, to the glory of God the Father, Philippians 2:9-11. He has dominion over the church, whose King He is; and He has dominion over all things, even over the powers of darkness, which He has overcome and which cannot move against His will. In the church this dominion is a reign by grace through His Spirit and Word: His people are gladly His, and it is their delight to acknowledge His authority and to do His will. Hence, in the words of our text they ascribe this dominion to Him. And in the world and over the powers of darkness He rules by His might, in spite of themselves. And also these, when they shall have been put down finally, and cast into outer darkness, shall acknowledge this dominion; and every tongue shall have to confess that Jesus Christ is Lord! Not Satan, not the servant of the devil, but the Servant of Jehovah alone is Lord forever, that God may be all in all!

Forever shall this dominion be.

Glory and dominion are His even now, and the church acknowledges this in her doxology, according to the text. She means to say: "Glory and dominion are Thine now; let them be ascribed to Thee." But this glory and also this dominion will be His forever. Christ will never abdicate. By some it is argued that the royal power and dominion which Christ now has at the right hand of God will terminate when He shall have finished His work and when His kingdom shall have been completed. The present power and dominion He possesses in order that He may be able to perfect His kingdom. When that shall have been accomplished, He shall reign no more, but be in subjection to the Father. The eternal and sovereign God will then reign directly, without being represented by Christ. This conception is based chiefly on the statement in I Corinthians 15:25, 28: "For he must reign, till he hath put all enemies under his feet... And when all things shall be subdued unto him, then shall the Son also himself be subject unto him that put all things under him, that God may be all in all." But with this view we cannot agree. The text just quoted from I Corinthians 15 does not teach that Christ shall ever cease to reign. That He now reigns **until** He hath put all enemies under His feet merely expresses that this complete subjection of all enemies under His feet is the purpose of His reign, the end that must be attained. And that, when this end shall have been attained and all things shall have been subdued under Him, He Himself will also be subject unto the Father does not mean that He will reign no more, but merely that He will reign as the Servant of God forever, reign under Him. All things shall forever be subject to Christ; with all things Christ shall be subject to the Father; and thus God will be all in all! For all Scripture teaches that Christ's dominion will never cease, that He will reign forever. His dominion is an everlasting dominion, which shall not pass away, and His kingdom that which shall not be destroyed, Daniel 7:14. And the doxology which is put into the mouth of the church in the text under discussion ascribes glory and dominion to Him forever!

Behold, He Cometh

The passage closes with a solemn assurance of the coming of our Lord Jesus Christ: "Behold, he cometh with clouds; and every eye shall see him, and they also which pierced him; and all kindreds of the earth shall wail because of him. Even so, Amen. I am Alpha and Omega, the beginning and the ending, saith the Lord, which is, and which was, and which is to come, the Almighty."

We say that this is a **solemn** assurance, in the first place, because special attention is called to the fact of Christ's coming by the introductory word "behold." It is as if the Word of God here would have the church conceive of this coming as a present fact: always the church must have the eyes of hope fixed upon that final event. Constantly she must stand in the attitude of expectancy and longing, the attitude of the bride looking for the coming of the Bridegroom, with the prayer on her lips: "Come, Lord Jesus!" And, secondly, this is a solemn assurance because of the double corroboration, "Even so, Amen!" The word "amen" is a Hebrew word. It means "it is firm, established, immovable; it shall surely be." Let the church never doubt, never grow faint: the Lord will surely come! The time may seem long, but He cometh. The suffering of the waiting church may be severe, and it may seem sometimes as if the Lord were slack concerning His promise; but He is surely coming. The promise is sealed with a double oath: "Even so, Amen!"

The words refer to the final coming of the Lord Jesus Christ, His literal and personal and visible return, the parousia, which will mark the end of all history and usher in the eternal state of heavenly glory in the new creation. For the history of this world will not reach its consummation by way of a gradual process of development, but by a catastrophe, a final wonder: the appearance in glory of our Lord Jesus Christ. To this final coming the text refers. It is true that the Bible does speak of His coming with the clouds of heaven all through the ages of this dispensation. Did not the Lord Himself thus testify before the high priest in the hour of His condemnation: "Henceforth (ARV) ye shall see the Son of man sitting at the right hand of power, and coming with the clouds of heaven?" All through the ages He is coming. Ever since His exaltation at the right hand of God He has been coming. For He reigns supreme and so directs all the events of this present time that they must lead up to and end in His final coming. He is coming in the sense that He is on the way. And He is hastening! The Lord is not slack concerning His promise. Nevertheless, in the text here the reference is definitely to His final and visible appearance, when "every eye shall see him."

That His coming will be "with clouds" may have a literal fulfillment, so that He shall appear in the clouds of the sky. However, the symbolical significance of these clouds must not be overlooked. Clouds in Scripture are symbols of majesty and judgment. Thus we read in Psalm 18:6-12: "In my distress I called upon the Lord, and cried unto my God: he heard my voice out of his temple, and my cry came before him, even into his ears. Then the earth shook and trembled; the foundations also of the hills moved and were shaken, because he was wroth. There went up smoke out of his nostrils, and fire out of his mouth devoured: coals were kindled by it. He bowed the heavens also, and came down; and darkness was under his feet. And he rode upon a cherub, and did fly: yea, he did fly upon the wings of the wind. He made darkness his secret place; his pavilion round about him were dark waters and thick clouds of the skies. At the brightness that was before him his thick clouds passed, hail stones and coals of fire." And in Psalm 97:2 we read: "Clouds and darkness are round about him: righteousness and judgment are the habitation of his throne." On the mount of transfiguration "there was a cloud that overshadowed them," (Mark 9:7). And when He was taken up from the earth, "a cloud received him out of their sight," (Acts 1:9). He cometh with clouds, not again as the suffering Servant of Jehovah, but in all the glory which the Father hath given Him, in royal majesty and to judge the world in righteousness!

In His coming He will be visible to all. "Every eye shall see him."

His own, who looked for Him with longing, shall see Him; but also the enemies shall see Him. The latter even has the emphasis in the text. They that pierced Him are mentioned particularly. The prophet Zechariah had prophesied that "the house of David and the inhabitants of Jerusalem" would "look upon me whom they have pierced, and they shall mourn for him, as one that is in bitterness for his firstborn." And, no doubt, that prophecy refers to the crucifixion of the Lord, when the Jews literally pierced the Son of God in human nature, though also there the words have a wider significance and may be applied to all the sin and rebellion of the people of Israel throughout their history. This rebellion only culminated in the crucifixion of the Servant of Jehovah. But the looking upon Him and the mourning for Him of which the text in Zechariah speaks are not the same as in the words of our passage from Revelation. There, in Zechariah, they cast upon Him a saving look and mourn for Him in true repentance, as they did, indeed, on the day of Pentecost and ever since, whenever the Spirit of grace touched the hearts of sinful men. For the looking upon Him and the mourning for Him in the prophecy of Zechariah are presented as the result of Jehovah's pouring upon His people the Spirit of grace and of supplications, Zechariah 12:10. Here, however, in Revelation 1:7, they look upon Him in His final coming. They that pierced Him, no doubt, are literally the Jews, and particularly those who crucified Him. But this does not mean that the expression "they that pierced him" is limited to them. It has a wider significance. It includes not only all the Jews who rejected Him, but also all who ever came into contact with Him, despised Him, and crucified the Son of God afresh. They shall be from "all the tribes of the earth." And therefore, seeing Him, all the tribes of the earth shall mourn. They are the hostile tribes, the antichristian forces of the world. They mourn and wail because of Him, or literally, according to the original, "towards" Him. Seeing Him Whom they despised and hated and opposed in His glory and power, they are filled with consternation, realizing that His fierce wrath will strike them down and consume them. But for the church it will be the hour of complete and eternal redemption and deliverance, the realization of all their hope and longing.

All this is steadfast and sure. For it is God Who here speaks, the "Alpha and Omega, the beginning and the ending." He is the "Lord, which is, and which was, and which is to come, the Almighty." His counsel shall stand, and He will do all His good pleasure. Alpha and Omega are the first and last letters respectively of the Greek alphabet. The meaning of these symbols is explained in "the beginning and the ending." He is the Lord, the Lord God (ARV). He is the beginning of all things, and therefore also the ending. He is their sovereign Creator, the Fount out of which are all things. And in Him all things have their purpose. Even as all things are out of Him, so they are also unto Him. From the beginning He made all things with a view to the end: the alpha is connected with the omega, the one must inevitably lead to the other. And whatever lies between the alpha and the omega is through Him. He controls all things in such a way that His counsel is accomplished, His design is fulfilled, His end is reached. And that end is the "revelation of Jesus Christ," the firstborn of every creature and the first begotten of the dead, as the One in Whom all things in heaven and on earth are to be united forever. Then, in the new creation, the tabernacle of God shall be with men; and God shall be all in all, through Jesus Christ our Lord.

And nothing can prevent this Omega. For God is Lord, and He is the Almighty. He is not merely supreme in power, more powerful than all other powers combined; but His is all the power, even the power of the creature, the power also of the forces of darkness. They have no power but from Him. And He uses them, willingly or in spite of themselves, for His sovereign purpose. He is coming, therefore, surely and irresistibly, always coming through the ages of history, coming from the alpha to the omega, from glory to glory, His own glory, until all His glory shall forever shine forth in the perfect revelation of Jesus Christ!

Peace, therefore, unto you who look for the coming of the Lord: the peace of grace, peace in the midst of the conflict and sufferings of this present time!

For behold, He cometh with clouds!

Faith is the victory!

Chapter III

Christ In The Midst Of The Golden Candlesticks

(Revelation 1:9-20)

9 I John, who also am your brother, and companion in tribulation, and in the kingdom and patience of Jesus Christ, was in the isle that is called Patmos, for the word of God, and for the testimony of Jesus Christ.

10 I was in the Spirit on the Lord's day, and heard behind me a great voice, as of a trumpet,

11 Saying, I am Alpha and Omega, the first and the last: and, What thou seest, write in a book, and send it unto the seven churches which are in Asia; unto Ephesus, and unto Smyrna, and unto Pergamos, and unto Thyatira, and unto Sardis, and unto Philadelphia, and unto Laodicea.

12 And I turned to see the voice that spake with me. And being turned, I saw seven golden candlesticks;

13 And in the midst of the seven candlesticks one like unto the Son of man, clothed with a garment down to the foot, and girt about the paps with a golden girdle.

14 His head and his hairs were white like wool, as white as snow; and his eyes were as a flame of fire;

15 And his feet like unto fine brass, as if they burned in a furnace; and his voice as the sound of many waters.

16 And he had in his right hand seven stars: and out of his mouth went a sharp two-edged sword: and his countenance was as the sun shineth in his strength.

17 And when I saw him, I fell at his feet as dead. And he laid his right hand upon me, saying unto me, Fear not; I am the first and the last:

18 I am he that liveth, and was dead; and, behold, I am alive for evermore, Amen; and have the keys of hell and of death.

19 Write the things which thou hast seen, and the things which are, and the things which shall be hereafter;

20 The mystery of the seven stars which thou sawest in my right hand, and the seven golden candlesticks. The seven stars are the angels of the seven churches: and the seven candlesticks which thou sawest are the seven churches.

31

We are now approaching the main body of the Book of Revelation itself and the numerous visions which it presents for our consideration. In the passage we are to discuss in this chapter we have the beginning, the first part, of the first main vision, which extends to the end of Chapter 3. The whole vision may be divided into two main parts. The first part is covered by our passage, which contains the vision of the glorified Christ walking in the midst of the golden candlesticks and commissioning John to write the things which he saw. The second part includes Chapters 2 and 3, which contain the seven-fold message of the Lord which John must deliver to the churches in Asia.

The Circumstances Of The Vision

In this vision, therefore, we deal with the revelation of the exalted Christ in relation to His church, as well as in connection with the things which must shortly come to pass. It is preceded by an explanation of the circumstances under which the vision was received by John. Even as the prophets of the old dispensation were wont to give an account of their calling to the prophetic office, so John in this passage tells us how and under what circumstances he first received the revelation concerning the future contained in this book of Scripture.

He was on the lonely little island of Patmos, a forsaken little isle, rocky and bare in the midst of the sea, not far from the coast of Asia Minor. He calls himself the brother of believers, rather than the apostle, because of the circumstances in which he finds himself. And he adds that he is a companion with them in tribulation and in the kingdom and patience of Jesus Christ. We must note here that all three—tribulation, the kingdom, and patience—are of Jesus Christ. We are partakers of them only if we are in Him. Secondly, we must note that the church is presented as in tribulation. The church was in tribulation then; and, according to the viewpoint of the Book of Revelation, she is always in tribulation in the midst of the world. And if we are to be partakers of the kingdom of Jesus Christ, it is inevitable that we also partake of the tribulation that comes upon the church because of her relation to her Lord and her faithful confession of Him. And, lastly, for that very reason, it is necessary that we partake of the patience of Jesus Christ. For it is only in the power of that patience that we can bear the tribulation and persevere unto the end.

The apostle further informs us that he was on the isle of Patmos for the Word of God and the testimony of Jesus Christ. This may mean that he was sent there to preach the Word of God and be witness of the name of Jesus. Or it may signify that he was there for the very purpose of receiving the Word of God as contained in this Book of Revelation. Or it may denote that he was exiled as a martyr for the sake of the Word of God which he had preached and the testimony of Jesus which he bore. The last-mentioned possibility appears to be the most probable and acceptable sense of the words. In the first place, this is the most natural significance of this phrase, "for the word of God and the testimony of Jesus Christ." Most generally these words convey the idea of true martyrdom. In the second place, this is implied in the manner in which John introduces himself, that is, as the brother and partaker with the church in tribulation. This would seem to imply that at the time of John's receiving this revelation a persecution had broken out for the church, and that John, partaking of the general tribulation and persecution of the church, had been banished to the isle of Patmos. And, in the third place, this would be in accord with the records of secular history, which inform us that about this time the power of the world, represented in the person of the emperor Domitian, raged with fury against the followers of Jesus, the despised sect of the Nazarenes. We conclude, therefore, that John was on the isle of Patmos about the year 95 or 96 A.D. as a martyr for the name and the testimony of Jesus Christ, his Lord.

But the Lord, Who is the prince of the rulers of the earth and Who causes even their counsels to work together for the good of His church, had His own purpose with the banishment of His servant John. And though the worldly power had exiled the aged apostle in order forever to silence his faithful testimony, the Lord transformed this lonely and secluded isle into a spot which served as an oracle for the revelation of one of the most beautiful and important parts of Holy Writ. Without any doubt, the abode of the apostle's exile, where nothing but wild nature surrounded him from day to day, where he was separated from the tumult and bustle of the world, where he could witness the terrible symbolism of the restless sea, listen to the monotonous roar of the powerful waves beating against the rocky shores of his abode, where, moreover, he had an unobstructed view of the heavens, and where his observation of the four corners of the earth was arrested only by the horizon where sky and water met,—this forsaken abode was undoubtedly naturally adapted to be the scene of the prophet's visions and revelations, offering as it did a natural background for them and being conducive to making the apostle spiritually capable of receiving them.

There, then, John was exiled; and he tells us that he was in the Spirit on the Lord's day. By the day of the Lord in this connection we must not understand the final day of judgment. For although that may be the meaning of the term, this interpretation is by no means in accord with what immediately follows. Much more natural it is to explain that by the Lord's day John refers to the day of the Lord's resurrection, the first day of the week, set aside by the church under the direction of the apostles as a day of special worship and consecration to take the place of the seventh day Sabbath of the old dispensation. The expression "in the Spirit" does not merely mean that he was profoundly meditating on spiritual things, but rather that he was in a state of prophetic, spiritual ecstasy, so that he was separated from the world of sense and experience, and prepared to receive visions of spiritual things. We believe that in the visions which the apostle is privileged to see there is, indeed, something objectively real. They were not merely subjective, so that they consisted only of the spiritual states of the seer; but the object that was presented to his view was of such a nature that the mere natural eye could not perceive it, and therefore a translation in the Spirit was necessary to prepare John to receive the visions.

In this state, then, John heard a great voice, mighty and clear as a trumpet call. And as he hears the voice behind him, and therefore turns about, he beholds the vision which is recorded in our passage: the glorified Christ in the midst of the golden candlesticks.

It will be observed immediately that in this vision there are two elements. In the first place, there is the element of the golden candlesticks, of which it is most natural to assume that they were standing in a circle around the Savior. And, in the second place, there is the appearance of the glorified Redeemer Whom John describes in detail.

The Glorified Christ

To begin with the latter, what a wonderful appearance He is! In general, He made the impression of a being overwhelming in glory and brightness of appearance: for He was as the sun shineth in his strength. It is only after John has become somewhat accustomed to the glory of this marvellous vision that he is able to note some of His details. Gradually he begins to notice that this being bears the general resemblance and appearance of a son of man, of a human being. His head and His hair, so he notices further, were white as wool, white as snow. Out of His mouth proceeded a sharp two-edged sword; and in His right hand He held seven stars. His feet were like unto burnished brass. His eyes reminded one of flames of fire, while His voice was like the roar of mighty waves beating against the rocks when the storm sweeps them into fury. His garments consisted of a long robe, stately and majestic, flowing down to His feet; and about the breast He wore a golden girdle, glittering in the general brightness and glory of His appearance.

Such is the general description of the vision. And we naturally ask: what is its significance?

In order to arrive at a correct interpretation of the whole, it will be necessary, first of all, to make a careful study of the details of the vision, in order that then we may combine them into their proper synthesis and thus obtain a conception of their essential meaning. Certain it is from the outset that here we have the appearance of the Savior from a certain definite point of view. The vision has a specific meaning, purposes to present the Son of Man in a definite light; and every detail of the vision must undoubtedly serve to emphasize that one particular idea.

We may take the outstanding features as our starting-point in explaining the vision.

First of all, it draws our attention that this glorious being is described as "one like unto the son of man." The expression is familiar to us all: for Jesus was fond of using that name with application to Himself during His public ministry on earth. The name is most probably derived from Daniel 7:13, 14. There we read: "And behold, one like the Son of man came with the clouds of heaven, and came to the Ancient of days, and they brought him near before him. And there was given him dominion, and glory, and a kingdom, that all people, nations, and languages, should serve him: his dominion is an everlasting dominion, which shall not pass away, and his kingdom that which shall not be destroyed."

If we compare this passage from Daniel with the passage we are discussing, the following inferences would seem to be justified. First of all, in the phrase "one like unto the Son of man" we have a reference to the Lord in His human nature. He was truly man, and as such He is called the Son of Man. That in the vision He is not directly called by that name, but described as "one like unto the Son of man" makes no difference. The form of the expression certainly does not mean to deny His true and real manhood and only to affirm that He bore resemblance to the human form. Rather must the indefiniteness of the phrase be attributed to the impression of the overwhelming glory His appearance made upon John. In the halo of glory John beholds the form of a son of man. In this phrase, then, we have a special reference to Christ as the Son of Man, as the human Servant of Jehovah. However, He does not appear here as the suffering Servant, but as the glorified Lord. If it is correct to assume that the name Son of Man is derived from the prophecy of Daniel quoted above, it is evident that it does not refer to His humiliation only, but rather to Christ as He was destined to inherit the kingdom: to the Son of Man in His humiliation, indeed, but only as a necessary way to His exaltation and Messianic glory. It is to this glory and dominion that the passage from Daniel refers with emphasis. There the "one like unto the Son of man" is presented as approaching the Ancient of Days, God, to receive His everlasting kingdom. Naturally, in the prophecy of the Old Testament His glory is presented as to be expected in the future. But at the time John is favored with this vision of the glorified Christ, the prophecy of Daniel was already fulfilled. The "one like unto the Son of man" had approached the Ancient of Days, through His suffering and death, His resurrection and exaltation at the right hand of God; and He had already received His everlasting dominion. And as such, as the glorified Lord Who received His kingdom and dominion from the Ancient of Days, He appears in this vision. And, thirdly, from a comparison with the text in Daniel we may draw the inference that He here appears as being authorized and empowered to function as Judge. When Daniel beholds Him, thrones are set and judgment is about to take place; it is just before the judgment is begun that the "one like unto the Son of man" receives His power and dominion. A comparison of the two passages, therefore, leads us to the general conclusion that the glorified Savior here appears as the mighty King-Judge.

As a second striking feature in the vision, we may point to the whiteness of His head and hair. Also in this detail there is an unmistakable reference to the passage from Daniel 7. In the ninth verse of that chapter we read: "I beheld till thrones were placed, and one that was an Ancient of Days did sit: his raiment was white as snow, and the hair of his head was like pure wool." The reference is clear. The whiteness of the hair refers to the age of the Ancient of Days; and it is a symbol of His divinity, because it describes Him as the Eternal One. In our passage, therefore, the whiteness of His hair pictures the Savior in His divine nature, as very God: for only as such He is the Eternal One, "whose goings forth have been from of old, from everlasting," (Micah 5:2). In Daniel it is the hair of the

Ancient of Days, not that of the "one like unto the Son of man," which is white. Here, however, it is the glorified Son of Man Who is thus described. In Daniel, therefore, the Ancient of Days and the Son of Man are two distinct persons; in our passage they are presented as one. And again, this difference is in harmony with the distinction between the two dispensations: when Daniel wrote his prophecy, the Word had not yet become flesh; when John received his vision, the incarnation had been accomplished. God and man, the divine and the human natures, had become united in the one person of Immanuel, God with us; and the Ancient of Days could therefore appear in the vision as being at the same time the "one like unto the Son of man." The glorified Christ, the Son of Man, but also the very Son of God, appears here in the vision on Patmos as the glorious King Who has entered into His inheritance from Jehovah, has received His dominion, is authorized and mighty to execute judgment and to realize the consummation of His kingdom.

Most of the rest of the symbolic details of the vision serve to strengthen this general appearance of Christ as the powerful King-Judge.

This is true, for instance, of the eyes like flames of fire. This denotes both His holy anger and His power of omniscience. The eyes of this mighty Judge penetrate into the deepest recesses of the hearts of men; they discover hidden things. Before them all things are an open book, even the secret thoughts and intents of men. Under the glare of those eyes every evil thought or deed, every wicked device, is exposed. And He comes to judge and inflict punishment upon the forces of evil, whether they be found in His church in the world, or in that world itself. Without compromise He will expose the evil, wherever it is found, in the church first (for judgment must needs begin at the house of God), and then also in the world. And having exposed it in its true character and worth, He will visit it with a just retribution. For those flaming eyes also express holiness and righteous indignation and wrath.

Somewhat the same idea is expressed in the symbolism of the feet "like unto burnished brass." They are like white hot, shining brass, burning in a furnace; and with them He will tread down the powers of darkness, all His enemies, until they are consumed.

We may notice here, too, that His voice is as the voice of many waters, that is, as the roaring tumult of the storm-swept deep, when wave after wave breaks against the rocks. It is the voice of thunder, the voice of power, the awe-inspiring voice of the mighty King Who is come to execute judgment in righteousness.

And, lastly, this general impression of Christ as the glorious King-Judge is also corroborated by the feature of the sharp two-edged sword that proceeds out of His mouth. The sword in Scripture is symbol of authority, of power to punish evil-doers. In Romans 13 the apostle Paul says of the powers that be: "But if thou do that which is evil, be afraid, for he beareth not the sword in vain: for he is the minister of God, a revenger to execute wrath upon him that doeth evil," (vs. 4). This sharp two-edged sword that proceeds out of the mouth of Christ is a symbol of that power to take revenge and execute wrath upon all the workers of iniquity. It proceeds out of Christ's mouth, indicating that it is by the power of His mighty Word that He will execute wrath and vengeance. All these details, therefore, corroborate the general impression that the glorified Savior appears here to John as the great and mighty King, Who is coming to judge His church and the world, till all the powers of darkness shall be destroyed forever.

However, it is not only as King and Judge that He reveals Himself in this vision. He is also the great High Priest, Who is busy for His church in the sanctuary of God. This is indicated by His apparel: for He is clothed with a garment down to the foot, and girt about the breasts with a golden girdle. The high priest of Israel in the old dispensation wore a long robe, or upper coat, called the robe of the ephod. It is evidently in this long high-priestly garb that the Lord reveals Himself here to John in the vision. The fact that the garment is pictured as hanging down to the foot indicates that He is not now functioning in the offering of sacrifices of blood, for in that case the garment would have been taken up by means of the girdle. The great and final sacrifice has been offered. It is finished. On the other hand, the fact that He still wears the golden girdle shows that, although the bloody sacrifice is finished, yet this High Priest is still engaged in active ministration in the sanctuary: for the old dispensational high priest would wear this girdle only as long as he was busy in the temple, and immediately after his ministrations were accomplished would lay it aside. And thus we have here a beautiful picture of the Savior as He has finished His sacrificial work on the accursed tree of Golgotha but is still engaged as our High Priest and Intercessor with the Father in the sanctuary above. There He prays for us, and from thence He blesses us with all spiritual blessings in heavenly places.

Some think that there is a point of difference with the appearance of the Old Testament high priest in the fact that the Lord here wears the girdle about the breasts. But this does not seem to be based upon fact. The high priests, as well as the common priests, wore their girdles about the breasts, and not about the loins. But a real point of distinction may be seen in the fact that our High Priest in this vision wears a girdle of gold, while the ordinary girdles of the priests were of fine twined linen and purple and scarlet. This reminds us once more of the royal character and dignity of this High Priest after the order of Melchisedec.

Finally, it is evident that the Lord in this vision also reveals Himself in His prophetic office. This cannot be deduced from His appearance as such, unless it be implied in the detail of the sharp two-edged sword that proceeds out of His mouth. For although it is true that this sword denotes chiefly His authority and power to execute judgment, it may very well also refer to His power as prophet. For, as we have seen, that sword is the Word which He speaks; and that Word is "quick and powerful, and sharper than any two-edged sword, piercing even to the dividing asunder of soul and spirit, and of the joints and marrow, and is a discerner of the thoughts and intents of the heart." Also as prophet He speaks His efficacious Word. Besides, the offices of Christ may be distinguished, but they can never be separated. However, apart from any detail in His appearance, He reveals Himself as prophet by the Word which He speaks. First of all, He addresses John in the vision and enjoins him to write. He must write all that he sees in a book and send it unto the seven churches which are in Asia; and particularly he must write what he has seen, and the things which are, and the things which shall be hereafter. Besides, He appears as the prophet in the consolation which He gives to John and to the church, verses 17 and 18. And in the chapters which follow He certainly functions as the Prophet of His church, addressing to the seven churches of Asia words of instruction, of consolation and encouragement, of exhortation and rebuke. We conclude, therefore, that in the vision the glorified Lord appears in His three-fold office of prophet, priest, and king. And as such He stands here in the midst of the seven golden candlesticks.

In The Midst Of The Golden Candlesticks

These seven candlesticks are a symbol of the church in her ideal existence and relation to her Lord, as a light shining to the glory of God in Christ. They represent the church in perfect holiness and righteousness, as she is in the counsel of God, and as she once shall be when the Lord shall present her as His perfected and glorified bride, without spot or blemish. The symbolism reminds us, of course, of the seven-armed candlestick, or lamp, which once stood in the holy place of the temple in Jerusalem. In that sanctuary there were the altar of incense, the table of shewbread, and the golden candlestick. The last-mentioned piece of temple furniture consisted of a perpendicular shaft from each side of which three arms branched out, so curving that their tops were level with that of the central shaft. The lamps had to be kept burning continuously, and they symbolized the truth that Israel was the light of God shining in the darkness of the world to the glory of Jehovah their God. In our vision the seven candlesticks represent not Israel of the old dispensation, but the church of all ages in her ideal perfection. They convey the truth that the church is a light, even as God is a light and there is no darkness in Him. She is a light, not of herself, but, as is clearly indicated by the fact that Christ stands, or walks, in the midst of the seven golden candlesticks, only through her fellowship with Christ in the Spirit. The Lord is her light, and apart from Christ she is in darkness and lies in the midst of death.

We may notice, however, that there are two points of difference between the candlestick as it stood in the temple and the seven candlesticks as they appear in this vision. First of all, it may be observed that the former consisted of one lamp whose arms all stood in a straight line, while in our vision the seven candlesticks evidently stand in a circle around the Savior: for we read that Christ stood in the midst of them, and in the first verse of the next chapter we even read that He "walketh in the midst of the seven golden candlesticks." This distinction is in harmony with the difference between the church of the old dispensation and the church in her ideal perfection, or as she is already being realized in the new dispensation. In Israel the church was confined to a single nation: the covenant line ran in the generations of Abraham according to the flesh. But the church is gathered from every nation and tongue and tribe. And already this is being realized, for the church is gathered from Jew and Gentile both. And, secondly, we may notice that the candlestick in the temple was one piece of furniture, so that there was a material and visible connection between the seven shafts, while in our vision there are seven separate lamps without any visible connection. The significance of this is plain. Among Israel the church was united by the physical bond of the nation and the theocracy; but the true and eternal connection between the church and her Lord and between believers mutually is a purely spiritual one. It is in the Spirit and through faith that we are connected as one church with Christ our Head in the communion of saints. That these candlesticks are golden denotes the perfection and purity, the incorruptibleness and the preciousness of the church of Christ, which He has purchased with His own precious blood. The church is more precious than the finest gold. She is pure and holy and more glorious than the noblest of metals. And she is incorruptible and imperishable because of her union with her Lord, the Son of God in the flesh, Who died and was raised and lives forevermore: death hath no more dominion over Him!

In the seven stars which Jesus holds in His right hand a transition is made to the church as she exists in the world, represented by the seven churches of Asia. For indirectly these seven stars also represent the church. The Savior's own interpretation is that they are the angels of the seven churches, verse 20.

Interpreters differ, however, with respect to the question just what is meant by these seven angels. Some would explain the term as denoting real angels, heavenly spirits, and think that they are the guardian angels of the several churches. But this would not seem to be a very plausible explanation: for John is commissioned to address letters to these angels, and it is rather difficult to conceive of the possibility of writing letters to such guardian angels. Others would spiritualize and idealize the term, and maintain that the expression refers to the peculiar and distinctive "spirit" of each congregation, to its individual disposition, in some such sense as even now we speak of "the spirit of the age." But also this interpretation must be rejected as impossible, in view of the fact that one could not very well address a letter to such a "spirit of the church." And still others, more correctly, have applied the words to the officebearers, or overseers, of the churches, especially to those who were busy in "the word and doctrine."

Let us bear in mind, first of all, that the symbol of the star refers to a light which is conspicuous and yet dependent and subordinate. Further, we should also remember that in the Word of God the original term for angel (**malakh** in the Hebrew, **anggelos** in the Greek) does not always refer to one of God's spiritual servants in heaven, but may also simply denote a messenger or servant from among men who is called to fulfill some important mission in God's church or kingdom. With reference to John the Baptist, Malachi prophesied: "Behold, I send my messenger, and he shall prepare the way before me," (Malachi 3:1). And, finally, as we already remarked, we must remember that John is ordered to write to these seven angels of the seven churches of Asia. All these considerations establish it beyond doubt that the angel of the church in this case is a human servant of God, the overseer or elder that is busy in the Word and doctrine, the minister of the Word of God. They are called "angels" simply because they are God's servants and messengers. And they are symbolized in stars, not because the churches receive their light only and absolutely from them, but because it is the Lord's good pleasure to enlighten and instruct His church in the world through their ministry. Through them especially it pleases Christ to preach and to preserve His Word.

And yet by these stars that are held in the right hand of the glorified Lord the churches themselves are also indirectly indicated. On the one hand, you cannot separate these "stars" from Christ. He holds them in His right hand. Without Him they are nothing. Unless Christ Himself works through them, they cannot function. Only when Christ, as the Chief Prophet, speaks His Word, can there be preaching. But, on the other hand, they cannot be separated from the churches. They represent the churches. The churches function through them. This close connection between the stars and the churches is evident from the seven letters which follow in the next two chapters. For it is evident that in these John does not merely address the angels, but through them writes to the churches which they represent and serve. The glorified Lord holds the seven stars in His right hand. This symbolizes not merely that He controls and holds in His power the angels of the seven churches, but also indirectly that the entire church is held and preserved by His power alone. No one can pluck His own out of His hand!

The Seven Churches

And thus, finally, we come to consider the church as she is represented by the seven churches of Asia.

That there is an essential connection between these and the seven candlesticks is evident from the number seven. Repeatedly this number occurs. There are seven churches to which John must write; there are seven candlesticks in the midst of which the Lord appears; there are seven stars in the right hand of the Savior; and, as we have seen before, there are also seven Spirits before the throne of God, seven lamps of fire burning before that throne, seven eyes of the Lamb, (4:5; 5:6). Seven denotes a fulness and perfection of grace. It contains the numbers **three** and **four**, and it is also the sum of **six** and **one**. In the latter sense it denotes the perfection of all that God does in time with a view to and including the eternal sabbath, the rest that remaineth for the people of God, the consummation of all things in the eternal kingdom and tabernacle of God. In the former sense it symbolizes the perfected communion of God (three) and the cosmos (four), the perfected covenant of God's friendship in Christ, God's dwelling with men. And for the same reason it denotes the fulness of the Spirit that dwells in the church, the fulness of grace and spiritual blessings, and the fulness of the church itself as the body of Christ. This is the essential connection between the seven candlesticks and the seven churches in Asia. They are not the same. The former denote the church in her ideal existence and eternal perfection, her essence, as she appears in the eternal counsel of God, and as she once will appear in the eternal kingdom. The latter represent the church as she is in the world, essentially the same as the church as represented by the seven candlesticks, but an earthly manifestation of the latter, the historic church on earth with its essential holiness and actual imperfections and infirmities: the church of Christ, indeed, but as she is still in constant need of consolation and encouragement, of exhortation and rebuke, the house of God from which judgment must needs begin.

That, therefore, exactly seven churches are selected indicates that in these the whole church, as she exists in the world at any time of the present dispensation, is represented. They no doubt actually existed at the time. They are no mere fiction, but historical churches. And they are mentioned here in the order of their geographical position in Asia Minor: from Ephesus north to Pergamos, and thence south to Laodicea. However, these churches were chosen because they were prepared by God through Christ in order that they might together constitute a picture of the entire church in the world, with its perfections and defects, its strength and its weaknesses, its trials and temptations. And thus it happens that in the seven-fold message to these churches in Asia Minor we have the Word of Christ to His church in the world at any time and in all lands, even until the coming again of the Lord. These messages, therefore, concern us as directly as they concerned the first seven churches to which they are addressed.

Now let us try to view the whole significant picture. Christ, Who walks in the midst of the seven golden candlesticks, the Head of His ideal church, given Him by the Father, also is in the midst of His church in the world. He is her light and life. Without Him she is nothing and can do nothing. He is in her midst as her merciful High Priest, praying in her behalf and blessing her with all the blessings of salvation. He is with her as her mighty King, ruling over her by His grace and Spirit, protecting her in the midst of hateful enemies, and leading her unto victory and glory. He comes to her also as her righteous Judge, commending whatever good there is found in her, rebuking and admonishing her for her sins and weaknesses, calling her to repentance and threatening her with His wrath and judgments. It is because Christ is in the midst of His church in the world as her Judge that the church must ever reform, even though separation from a certain manifestation of her is the result. And He is in her midst as her only Prophet, giving her the stars, instructing her through His Word and Spirit, and causing her to know the things that must shortly come to pass. Look on Him, and be filled with that fear and trembling in which you must work out your own salvation! Behold Him, and be assured that the church can never perish; she is safe though all hell come raving against her!

A Word of Comfort

The appearance of the glorified Lord has a terrifying effect upon John. He tells us, verse 17: "And when I saw him, I fell at his feet as dead." The sight of so much majesty and glory fills him with awe. Some understand this as indicating that John had not recognized the Lord, and that he does not know Him until the Savior addresses him in the words that follow. But in the light of the preceding verses this is very improbable. For he had already received his commission to write, and he had seen Him as the "one like unto the Son of man." But although he knows it is the Lord, he is filled with fear by the awe-inspiring glory of His appearance. Once he had seen a shadow of this power and glory when he and Peter and James were with Him in the holy mount; but now "in the Spirit" he beholds the reality of that awful majesty, and he is stupefied and falls at his feet as dead. All this must be understood as belonging to the vision, and it takes place "in the Spirit." This becomes the occasion for the Lord's comforting words, addressed to John, but also to the church of all ages. For also we tremble at His glory. When, like John, we stand face to face with this mighty and righteous Judge of heaven and earth, we realize the sinfulness of our own condition, and we are impelled to fall down before Him and cry out with the prophet of old: "Woe is me, for I am undone!" Even as we are discussing the vision of this glorious and majestic Judge, we realize that we would not be able to stand in His presence. We are inclined to fear at His coming, rather than hope for it. And therefore both now and in the day of His coming we have need of His comforting words: "Fear not!"

It is, of course, also in the vision and "in the Spirit" that Jesus laid His right hand upon John, and that He addressed him: "Fear not; I am the first and the last: I am he that liveth, and was dead; and, behold, I am alive for evermore, Amen; and have the keys of hell and of death." This is the message of comfort in all our fears, and how perfect a comfort it conveys! Let us notice that it consists entirely in calling our attention to Christ and to what He now is. And what else could possibly be our comfort in life and in death than that Christ, our Lord, in Whom we believe, to Whom we belong with body and soul, is the first and the last, the One that liveth and He was dead, the One that holds the keys of death and of hell? He is the Alpha and the Omega (vs. 11), the first and the last (vss. 11, 17). In verse 8 this was said of God; here it is attributed by Christ unto Himself. Nor is there any conflict here. For Christ is not only very God; but also as the Mediator, the Son of God come in the flesh, the first begotten of the dead, He is the firstborn of every creature, through Whom and unto Whom all things were made. And He is the Risen One! Note the order of the words. He does not say: "I was dead and am alive again;" but, "I am he that liveth, and was dead!" He is the Living One! This clause should stand by itself. It is first. It is the cause and reason of all that follows. He is the life! He has life in Himself, for He is the eternal God come in the flesh! And He became dead! The Living One entered into death, into our death, in the human nature, in order that as the great High Priest He might finish the sacrifice for sins. But death could have no dominion over Him: for He is the Living One! And so He issued forth out of death into the glorious resurrection, and now He is alive forevermore! And the keys of death and hell are His. "Hell" here is "Hades," the abode of the dead, the grave, the place of corruption. It is presented here as a mighty fortress: the power of all death. And Jesus has the keys, the power to open and no one shutteth, and to shut and no one openeth. He has the power and authority to open the jaws of death, the gates of darkness, in order that His own may come forth into the glory of eternal life! Fear not! Ah, the essence, the real cause of all our fears is death. But for them that trust in this glorious Lord, this fear is not only removed, but is changed into the sure hope of eternal life and glory in God's everlasting tabernacle with men! Blessed are they that put their trust in Him!

Christ's Commission To John To Write

Having thus quieted the fear of His servant John, the Lord gives him his commission: "Write the things which thou hast seen, and the things which are, and the things which shall be hereafter." These words, no doubt, characterize in general the contents of the whole Book of Revelation. John must write "the things which he has seen," that is, the vision which we have been discussing. "The things which are" refer to the things then present as a basis for the things to come, and, therefore, to the things which are always present. And "the things which shall be hereafter" are the future things as they develop according to God's counsel from "the things that are." From this it will be evident that we do not believe that any mechanical division of the Book of Revelation can properly be deduced from this passage, as if "the things that are" must be found in the next two chapters, while "the things which shall be hereafter" are recorded in all that follows Chapter 3. For, even if the "things which are" would be applied exclusively to the seven churches in Asia **in the first place,** it cannot be denied that those churches and the seven-fold message they receive also look toward the future of the church in the world. For those seven churches, as we have seen, represent the church in the world throughout this whole dispensation. The contents of the first three chapters deal, therefore, with both, "the things that are" and "the things which shall be hereafter." And the same holds true for the rest of the book. Throughout, until we come to the vision of New Jerusalem in the new creation, the whole book sheds light from above, the light of the coming Lord upon the things which are and upon the things which shall be hereafter in their organic historical development. We will find that in the chapters that follow there is repetition, but that in the repetition there is progress. The same forces are at work throughout the ages of this dispensation; the same events occur in the world of men, in the universe, in the church; but they increase in scope and intensity as time progresses. And always the end in view is the coming of the Lord in glory and the perfect redemption of the church, the tabernacle of God with men. All things progress from the Alpha to the Omega in a straight line, without any retrogression or restraint. For the moving force behind and in all things is the counsel of the only Potentate of potentates, Who is in the heavens and doeth all His good pleasure!

Chapter IV
The Beginning Of Decline
(Revelation 2:1-7)

1 Unto the angel of the church of Ephesus write; These things saith he that holdeth the seven stars in his right hand, who walketh in the midst of the seven golden candlesticks;
2 I know thy works, and thy labour, and thy patience, and how thou canst not bear them which are evil: and thou hast tried them which say they are apostles, and are not, and hast found them liars:
3 And hast borne, and hast patience, and for my name's sake hast laboured, and hast not fainted.
4 Nevertheless I have somewhat against thee, because thou hast left thy first love.
5 Remember therefore from whence thou art fallen, and repent, and do the first works; or else I will come unto thee quickly, and will remove thy candlestick out of his place, except thou repent.
6 But this thou hast, that thou hatest the deeds of the Nicolaitanes, which I also hate.
7 He that hath an ear, let him hear what the Spirit saith unto the churches; To him that overcometh will I give to eat of the tree of life, which is in the midst of the paradise of God.

In Chapters 2 and 3 of the Book of Revelation we have the seven letters addressed by the Lord to the seven churches in Asia. In order to understand these messages we must bear in mind the relation of these seven churches to the seven golden candlesticks in the vision of 1:9-20. The latter are symbolic of the church from an ideal viewpoint, perfect and holy, as it has its light and life in Christ. It can never perish. None of them can ever be removed from its place. Were the church on earth identical with, perfectly like that which is symbolized in the candlesticks, messages like those that are contained in these two chapters of Revelation would neither be necessary nor appropriate. But the seven churches of Asia

47

represent the church on earth, essentially holy, but still imperfect, earthy, and characterized by many infirmities and sins. Hence, they are subject to rebuke and exhortation, and even to threats of judgment and utter extinction. The candlestick of a local church may, indeed, be removed out of its place. A church on earth may cease to be a manifestation of the church as she appears in the symbolism of the seven golden candlesticks.

The Idea Of The Letters To The Seven Churches

Before we enter upon a discussion of the seven letters, a word must still be said about the general significance of the seven churches to which they are addressed. They were really existing churches at the time when John is commissioned to write to them; but at the same time they present a seven-fold picture of the church on earth throughout this dispensation. They were not the only churches existing at the time, but they are selected because in them was found the clearest and most complete picture of the church of all ages. The question is raised, however, whether the completeness of the church as represented by these seven churches must be understood as referring to a simultaneous or to a successive totality. Do these seven churches represent the church on earth as she exists at any period of this dispensation, or must we see in them seven phases in the development of the church in history? Both views have been and still are championed by interpreters of the Book of Revelation.

There are those who advocate the view that in these seven messages, picturing seven different manifestations of the church on earth, we must discover a portraiture of seven distinct phases in the history of the church in the world. According to this view, it is possible to discern in the development of the church the same order of different dominant conditions as is found in these seven letters to the seven churches of Asia. Each of these seven messages must, accordingly, be applied to a more or less definite period in the history of this dispensation, from the time of John to the second coming of Christ, or, according to others, to the "rapture," the moment when the church shall be taken up to Christ in the air.

However, this view is plainly untenable. Already the fact that at the time when these letters were written the church did not present one dominant feature, but rather a seven-fold picture, – in other words, the fact that the seven churches certainly existed simultaneously, – would contradict this view. Laodicea existed side by side with Ephesus; Sardis existed in the same period as Philadelphia; and Smyrna, Pergamos, and Thyatira were simultaneous. Besides, the history of this method of interpretation certainly justifies the remark of Godet: "One may doubtless, by taking up this latter standpoint, succeed in bringing out some ingeniously conceived points of harmony, but they always have a somewhat arbitrary character." We must, therefore, reject this view.

Yet there is, no doubt, an element of truth in this interpretation. Although it is our conviction that the seven churches must be understood as representative of the church in the world as it exists in any period of this dispensation, so that at any time these seven types may be observed in the church, nevertheless these seven types are not always equally prominent in every period of the history of the church on earth. Sometimes it is the characteristics of the church of Ephesus which predominate in the church; at other times it is the picture of the church of Smyrna that is most vividly reflected. In some periods of history the church is characterized by intellectualism, dogmatism, confessionalism; in other periods by emotionalism, revivalism, pietism; in still other periods by practicism, indifferentism with respect to principles and doctrines. Now the church is cast into the crucible of tribulation and persecution, to be refined as by fire; then she enjoys a period of peace and rest. Always all the features presented by the seven churches in Asia are observable in the church in the world, yet so that now one, then another of these features appears on the foreground. On this basis we may well assume that in the order in which these churches are mentioned, though it is, indeed, the geographical order, there is also an indication of the course of development the church will follow: the direction of this development will be from Ephesus to Laodicea. At the end of this dispensation the church will present the likeness of the church of Laodicea. Maintaining, therefore, that these seven churches are representative of the whole church as she is in the world at any period of history, and rejecting the view that each of them represents a limited period in the history of the church of the new dispensation, we nevertheless believe that in a general way there is in the order in which these seven churches are addressed an indication of the trend of development the church in the world will follow.

With respect to the formal side of the seven letters addressed to the churches in Asia, we may note that they all present much the same characteristics. Each epistle begins by addressing the angel of the church to which the letter is sent, which address is immediately followed by the

Self-designation of Him that sends these messages to the various congregations, the Lord of His church. Characteristic of these Self-designations is that they are clothed in terms derived from or suggested by the vision of Christ in the midst of the seven golden candlesticks in 1:9-20. In every one of these Self-designations those terms are chosen which bear relation to the particular condition of the church addressed. For instance, to the church which lost its first love and which is threatened with the judgment that its candlestick will be removed from its place, the Lord introduces Himself as the One that walketh in the midst of the golden candlesticks. To the church in tribulation, which is encouraged by the promise of a crown of life, He announces Himself as the first and the last, Who was dead and is alive again. Thus it is in all the letters. Following this Self-designation of the Lord comes the description of the peculiar condition of each congregation, usually headed by the enumeration of the commendable traits wherever this is possible. To this general rule the churches of Sardis and Laodicea are exceptions: nothing good is to be recorded of them. On the other hand, the churches of Smyrna and Philadelphia are distinguished by the fact that they receive only praise and encouragement; nothing worthy of rebuke is found in them. And, finally, each letter closes with an exhortation, containing a promise or a threat of judgment, or both, depending upon the condition of the church addressed.

The Church Of Ephesus

We now turn our attention to the first of these seven messages, which is addressed to the church of Ephesus.

The city of Ephesus was situated on the west coast of Asia Minor, some forty miles to the northeast of Patmos. It was an important city, rich in trade and commerce, famous, too, for its culture. But it was also notorious because of its shameful idolatry, its well-known temple in honor of the goddess Diana, its frivolity and worldly-mindedness in general. It may be compared to one of our modern metropolitan cities, with all their wealth and luxury and amusement-seeking, their carelessness and levity of heart and life, their vices and social evils. We may well note that in such a world-city the Lord had established a church. The church in the big city occupies a difficult position, more so than the country church. In the metropolis pulsates the life of the world. There the antithesis is sharpest.

Nevertheless, no church needs to shun the big city and seek the seclusion of the country. The Lord would have His church in the world, though never may she be of the world. In the midst of the world she is called to be a manifestation of His grace, that she may let her light shine and show forth the praises of Him that called her out of darkness into His marvellous light.

There is every reason to believe that the church of Ephesus used to be one of the strongest and most flourishing churches of that early period of the new dispensation. It had enjoyed the labors of some of the greatest, most devoted, ablest servants of the Lord. Paul had been there three times: first only for a brief period, but during his second missionary journey he abode with the Ephesian church for almost three years, during which time, as he himself testifies, he labored night and day with tears, declaring unto them the whole counsel of God. Timothy, too, the spiritual son of the great apostle to the Gentiles, had labored there, building upon the foundation laid by his spiritual father. And the apostle whom Jesus loved had spent many a year among the believers in Ephesus in hard and faithful labor. To speak in terms of our own time, the church there had enjoyed the labors of the best and most excellent preachers of the time. He Who holds the seven stars in His right hand had blessed the church abundantly.

Strong In Doctrine

Nor had the labors of these ministers of Christ been without effect upon the church. On the contrary, even at the time when John is commissioned to write this message to her the influence of their work is still plainly noticeable.

For we may observe, first of all, that the church of Ephesus was strong in doctrine. This is evident from the description which the Lord Himself gives of her in this letter. The Lord testifies that the church had "tried them that call themselves apostles, and are not," and that she had "found them false." These words suggest, first of all, the doctrinal soundness and strength of the Ephesian believers. True, they also indicate disciplinary action; but notice that it was discipline exercised over those that called themselves apostles, which implies that the discipline concerned a matter of doctrine. True apostles were men with authority, infallibly guided by the Spirit of Christ into all the truth. They were direct witnesses of Christ, of His suffering and resurrection. Their word was gospel. It possessed infallible authority, the authority of the King of the church Himself. Of this the church at that time was conscious, as is evident from more than one passage of the New Testament. They made a clear distinction between the word of an apostle and the word of others. For that reason the apostle Paul deems it necessary sometimes to defend his apostleship in the churches. Whenever false teachers purposed to neutralize his influence in the church, they attacked his apostolic authority, aware that only in this way they could oppose the contents of his teaching. Now this letter to the church of Ephesus informs us that men had appeared in their midst who called themselves apostles. Evidently they made this claim and defended the right to this title for the purpose of exercising doctrinal authority in the church. They claimed to be divinely inspired and therefore demanded unconditional acceptance of their teaching. They taught a false doctrine, and for it they claimed apostolic authority. Fundamentally, therefore, the case which the Ephesian church had tried concerned a matter of doctrine. Who these would-be apostles were the text does not inform us; but we are inclined to believe that they were the same as the Nicolaitanes mentioned in this same letter. However this may be, certain it is that they taught a doctrine which differed from that of the apostles. But the church had tried them, had put their doctrine to the test. Probably there had been an official trial of these "apostles," and in spite of their claim to the apostleship the church had found them liars and had rejected their doctrine.

The conclusion, therefore, is justified that the church of Ephesus was sound in doctrine, well-founded in the truth of the gospel. How otherwise could they have exposed the lie of these false apostles? Only those who are themselves sound in the truth can expose the error wherever it presents itself and with whatever claim of authority it may come. But where knowledge of truth is lacking, the church is helplessly exposed to every wind of doctrine. This is one of the main reasons why the church of today is in such a miserable condition. There is no knowledge of the truth, no love for true doctrine, no instruction in the Word of God. Hence, the church of today is easily seduced, tossed about by all kinds of false doctrines. In Ephesus this was different. There was knowledge of the truth. And if there was knowledge of the truth, there must have been study of the Scriptures, instruction in the principles of true doctrine. For without continual instruction through preaching and teaching, knowledge of the truth cannot be maintained. Hence, all these were found in the church of Ephesus. They were able to discern between the truth and false doctrine, and thus they could pass judgment upon them that claimed to be apostles and were not. Ephesus was a church sound in doctrine.

The same inference may be drawn from the statement in verse 6: "But this thou hast, that thou hatest the deeds of the Nicolaitanes, which I also hate." About the origin of this sect nothing definite is known. Their name is probably derived from their leader, one Nicolaus, who must not be identified, however, with the deacon mentioned in Acts 6:5. The Lord here speaks of their works, but these works were based on false doctrine. This is evident from verses 14 and 15 of this same chapter, where the church of Pergamos is addressed as follows: "But I have a few things against thee, because thou hast there them that hold the doctrine of Balaam, who taught Balac to cast a stumblingblock before the children of Israel, to eat things sacrificed unto idols, and to commit fornication. So hast thou also them that hold the doctrine of the Nicolaitanes, which thing I hate." It is evident that these Nicolaitanes, about whom we shall have more to say in connection with the letter to Pergamos, were false teachers, men who disseminated evil doctrines and thus seduced the church to spiritual fornication and apostasy. Now the Lord gives the Ephesian church testimony that they hated the works of the Nicolaitanes. This implies that their false doctrines were clearly discerned and rejected. This also leads to the conclusion that the believers of Ephesus were sound in doctrine, well-founded in the knowledge of the Word of God.

Faithful In Discipline

From what we discussed thus far it will also have become evident that the church at Ephesus was faithful in discipline. This is usually connected with doctrinal soundness. Where the one is present, the other usually is also found. Where the church is lax in discipline, soundness in doctrine cannot maintain itself very long. Christian discipline is the reaction of the church against every form of evil, both in doctrine and life, through the preaching of the Word of God as well as through personal admonition and, ultimately, through excommunication. Also in this respect the church of today is miserably weak and wanting. The keys of the kingdom of heaven are practically forgotten. But about this we shall have more to say in our discussion of the letter to Pergamos. The church in Ephesus was faithful in the exercise of discipline. This is evident from their trial of the false apostles. Nothing can be urged against the view that they tried these false teachers officially and finally excommunicated them from the church. But besides, the Lord writes to that church: "...thou canst not bear them which are evil," (vs. 2). The thought is that men who wrought wickedness in doctrine or life were not tolerated in that congregation. Evil workers usually could not find a place among the believers in Ephesus; and if they did find a place for a time, they usually did not feel themselves at home there because of the sound preaching of the Word and the general testimony of the members. But if they persisted in their attempt to perform their evil work in the church, they were expelled from the communion of the saints by the application of the keys of the kingdom of heaven. The church was not only sound in doctrine; she was also faithful in the exercise of Christian discipline.

Abounding In The Work Of The Lord

Nor is this all. The commendable features of the church of Ephesus are not limited to soundness in doctrine and discipline; the believers there were also abounding in the work of the Lord. It was not a church, at least not at the time when this letter was addressed to her, that was characterized by dead orthodoxy, that had an intellectual grasp of the truth but was loath to apply this knowledge to life. On the contrary, the Lord gives her the testimony: "I know thy works, and thy labour, and thy patience... and (thou) hast patience, and for my name's sake hast laboured, and hast not fainted," (vss. 2, 3). This is a beautiful testimony indeed, especially if it is taken in connection with the fact that the church was also sound in doctrine and in the exercise of discipline. In our day there are many, indeed, who clamor for a so-called practical Christianity, who would have the church do nothing but labor and toil in the world "to make the world better," but who are absolutely indifferent in regard to doctrine. What one knows about doctrine and believes matters little or nothing if he is only willing to work and to serve. This was not the case in Ephesus; they kept the gospel that was delivered them. But, on the other hand, there are also churches which are characterized by cold and dead intellectualism and orthodoxy, which emphasize the necessity of soundness in doctrine, but which are lacking in the application of the truth to actual life and in zeal for the work of the Lord. But also this could not be said of the church in Ephesus. She did not take it easy in the kingdom of God. She did not follow the line of least resistance. She labored and toiled; and she did so for Christ's name's sake. This does not refer to all kinds of work, but to the work that is in harmony with the calling of the church to hold forth the Word of life, the preaching of the gospel, within the church and without. They bore testimony of Christ in word and deed. Their conversation sealed their profession. And even if their faithful confession caused them inconvenience, required them to take up the cross and suffer with Christ, even if the reproach and contempt of the world was their reward, they remained faithful. For the Lord bears them testimony that they have patience. Repeatedly this is stated. In verse 2 it is mentioned; in verse 3 it is repeated, "and hast patience;" and it is added, "and didst bear for my name's sake," (ARV). And patience is the spiritual virtue and power to endure suffering and tribulation for Christ's sake. And do not infer from the rest of the epistle that this testimony refers to the past, and that the church manifested this patience and faithfulness in doctrine and conversation no longer. For this would be a mistake, as is evident from what the Lord adds, "and hast not fainted." They still were strong in doctrine, faithful in the exercise of discipline, zealous in the work of the Lord, and willing to bear the cross and to suffer with Christ patiently.

Without Her First Love

From all the foregoing we would, perhaps, be inclined to draw the conclusion that the church of Ephesus was well-nigh perfect. But in this we would be mistaken. The church of Ephesus receives a very serious rebuke. There was something lacking in the church of Ephesus. There was a certain defect in her inner life, hidden, perhaps, from the eyes of men, but known to the Lord Who tries the reins and the hearts: a defect so serious that it would lead the church to utter ruin unless she repented. Something was gnawing at the very life-roots of the church which would cause her to die if it were not removed. The very life of the church was ebbing away.

The Lord points to this serious weakness in the words: "Nevertheless I have somewhat against thee, because thou hast left thy first love," (vs. 4). The condition described in these words has frequently been compared to a similar condition in the life of an individual Christian. Perhaps we are acquainted by experience with such a loss of first love. Immediately after our conversion, especially if that conversion was rather marked and sudden, we were filled with a fervent spirit and ardent love of the Lord. Our heart throbbed with a holy zeal. The experience of our salvation caused us to abound in gratitude. We loved to speak of Jesus and to witness of His love. It was our sincere desire to consecrate our life, our all, to Him Who loved us even unto death and by Whose power we were translated from darkness unto light, from death to life. Nothing seemed too difficult for our faith. It seemed impossible that we would ever become unfaithful to Him with Whom our hearts were united in love. But another period began. The first zeal and enthusiasm cooled down. We were not so fervent in spirit any more as in the period of our first love. It became evident that we had not reached perfection, that sin still operated in our members, that we often did evil when we would do good. Perhaps we grew anxious about our own condition and began to wonder whether our conversion had been real. We left our first love! This experience of the individual Christian has often been used as an illustration to explain the meaning of the Lord's words to the church of Ephesus, "I have against thee that thou didst leave thy first love." Yet this comparison is not entirely correct. There is something very normal in the experience of the individual believer which we just described. In it there is really nothing to be alarmed about. Fact is that the first experience of the love of Christ by that believer was largely a matter of emotion. He was in a state of spiritual tension which could not last. His real condition was not up to the level of his feelings. Sooner or later reality was bound to assert itself. And then it became evident that he was not so near to perfection as he first imagined. The glow of his first enthusiasm died down. And this change, while it was a cause of grief to the consciousness of the believer, was nevertheless very likely accompanied by a deepening of spiritual life and love. With the passing of that first experience of love which was sustained mostly by feeling, another, firmer, deeper love appeared, rooted in the heart, the expression of a sanctified will. And in as far as this experience of the individual child of God is normal, it cannot be compared with the abnormal condition of the church in Ephesus which is here rebuked by the Lord.

Nor may the church in Ephesus be compared to those churches in our own country which need periodic revivals to keep them emotionally alive. A church of this kind is weak, spiritually anemic, needs always stronger stimulants of spiritual sensationalism to keep her on her feet. She is not instructed in the truth and not used to sound doctrine, and, therefore, is not firmly rooted in Christ. She lives on religious emotions. When her pastor has exhausted his own resources of sensationalism, the emotional interest of his congregation dies down; and then the church is in need of a stronger blast of sensational preaching by some outsider who travels the country with some "soul-stirring" messages which serve like a "shot in the arm" for the churches in whose midst he appears. But this not a true picture of the church of Ephesus. It was not a weak church which lived on emotions. It was sound and well-founded in the truth, and it certainly would have tried many a revivalist preacher of today and found them liars.

No, when Jesus brings against the church of Ephesus the indictment that she had left her first love, He refers to love in the deepest sense, to the true love of God in Christ as the very life of the church. And of this love, as it first had filled the church of Ephesus, the Lord states that it had been left, forsaken. This was a very serious matter. If it was not remedied, the church would die. For the love of God in Christ is the deepest root of all our spiritual life. If a church leaves that love, the spiritual fountain of her life will dry up.

This is the reason why we characterize the church of Ephesus as the church in the beginning of her decline.

In the abandoning of her first love we must recognize the beginning of all apostasy of the church in the world. It is not true that the beginning of corruption must be sought in departure from the truth, or in laxity in discipline, or in a tendency to worldly-mindedness. These may all be manifestations, first symptoms of spiritual decline; but they are not the root. That the church of Ephesus is the first in the series of seven churches which are addressed in these letters is not incidental or irrelevant. It is significant. From Ephesus to Laodicea may seem a long way, but it is an inevitable way. The church which abandons its first love ultimately loses all her spiritual treasures.

This is a very serious lesson for the church of today! How many complaints are registered against the present day church on earth! How indifferent she reveals herself to be with regard to doctrine! How ignorant she is in the things pertaining to the kingdom of God! How utterly she neglects the keys of the kingdom of heaven! How adulterous she is become in her alliance with the world, her seeking of the things that are below rather than the things that are above! Yes, but if all these wretched diseases of the church, or of what still calls itself church, could be traced to their beginning, you would discover that their source is the abandoning of their first love. How can a church which keeps her first love possibly apostatize? How can she become indifferent with respect to the truth as it is in Jesus? How could she become so miserable that she can tolerate evil men in her midst? How could such things as worldly amusements, worldly associations, seeking of worldly treasures and pleasures even become a "problem" in a church which clings to her first love? It is well for us to understand this clearly and to bear it constantly in mind. A good thing it is, indeed, to watch over purity in doctrine: for the church which forsakes the truth has no foundation. But let us remember that outward purity in doctrine is not enough, and that it must itself be rooted in the love of Christ. Let us watch, therefore, and pray that, while we preserve the purity of the truth, we may remain rooted in the love of God in Christ!

There are questions, of course, which arise in your mind as you read these things. The first is this: but how is it possible that a church abandons her first love? Is not love a matter of grace? Is not the love of God poured forth and shed abroad by the irresistible operation of the Holy Spirit? How then can this love be abandoned? Is there then a falling away from grace? In answer to this question we remark, first of all, that we must make a distinction between the church and the individual believer. Surely, there is no falling away from grace. We are saved by grace once for all. Once a believer is always a believer. Once united with the Lord in the bond of love is always thus to be united with Him. Our conscious faith may sometimes be weak; our conscious love may often be wanting in fervency; our prayer for the grace of the Holy Spirit may frequently be mere lip-work. But we certainly cannot be separated from the love of God which is in Christ Jesus our Lord. The reason for this is simply that His love is and remains always first, the never-failing source of our love to God. No one can pluck us out of His hands. But what is impossible for the individual believer may happen to a church as she appears in the world.

Let us try to visualize the development of the church in Ephesus. The Lord speaks of her first love. By this He refers to the love which filled her when first she came into contact with the gospel and was called out of darkness into the marvellous light of God. Then she had been filled with the love of Christ. All had been living members of the body of Christ. All could profess their personal faith and testify of their part with the Savior. This was true of the angel of the church; it was equally true of the members. The love of Christ was experienced. It permeated and glowed through all their activity as a church. It characterized the preaching, which was more than cold doctrine. And it marked the life and conversation of the members. If you had visited the families of the church at that time, you would have found no difficulty to converse with them about the experiential aspect of the Christian life. The whole church was rooted in and motivated by the love of God in Christ Jesus. But all this had changed. That first love had been left by the church of Ephesus. Not as if the real love of God had died out in the hearts in which it once glowed. No, but the constituency of the congregation had changed. Many years had passed since the time of that first love. A new element had been added to the church. Some had joined themselves to the congregation from without; others had been added from within by the organic growth of the church. And the church had not been watching. It had emphasized the necessity of soundness in doctrine, faithfulness in discipline, diligence in the work proper to a church of Christ; but it had neglected to stress the necessity of personal faith and love in the Lord. Outwardly the church had grown; inwardly it had become weak. Many of those that were added to the church were not Israelites in the spiritual sense of the word, possessed not the love of the Lord. They could speak of the truth objectively, but they knew nothing of its spiritual experience in the heart. And this element had increased. It gained in influence in the church. It had become predominant. There were still those, indeed, who knew the love of Christ. But they no longer were the predominating element in the church. And thus the church had left its first love. What could never be said of an individual believer was certainly true of the church of Ephesus: "I have somewhat against thee, because thou hast left thy first love!"

But you ask another question: how, if the church had left her first love, could the Lord bear such a beautiful testimony concerning her as is contained in this letter? How could she still be sound in doctrine, faithful in discipline, zealous in the work of the Lord without growing weary?

We must remember that the Lord writes this warning to the church in the first stages of her spiritual decadence. Her apostasy was as yet not in an advanced stage. In close connection with this, we must bear in mind that there were still those who possessed the love of the Lord in their hearts, that had not forgotten the days of the church's first love. No doubt, the fact that the Lord could speak so well of the church was in a large measure due to the influence of these living members. But, thirdly, it must not be forgotten that a church may, for a time, drift onward on the current of tradition. This, no doubt, was also the case with the church of Ephesus. When the church was in the period of her first love, it had labored to keep the Word of Jesus, to know the truth, to instruct young and old, to expel evil from their midst; and it had been zealous in the work of the Lord. Now the original motive power which had impelled the church had decreased in force. But as a steamer in the ocean will continue for a while with apparently undiminished speed after the engine has been shut down, so the church in Ephesus apparently lost none of its energy, lived and labored by virtue of the momentum of that first love which had motivated her in the beginning. Partly because of the love which was still present in the church, partly by virtue of the momentum of tradition, the church of Ephesus was still active in the work of the Lord and did not grow weary. And thus you have the phenomenon of a church which is sound in doctrine, faithful in discipline, active in all the work of the Lord, but without the motive power of her first love!

It is the church in the beginning of her decline!

Rebuke And Admonition

In view of this very serious defect of the church of Ephesus, we are not surprised that the Lord sharply rebukes her and approaches her with an urgent admonition to repent. No doubt this admonition is addressed first of all to the angel of the church and to its office-bearers, whose calling it is to watch over the flock. But in and through them the Lord also admonishes the church as a whole.

We may distinguish three elements in this exhortation: the call to repent, the admonition to do the first works, and the exhortation to remember whence she was fallen.

The last element shows the church the way in which she may come to true repentance. The church must remember whence she has fallen. She must recall former days, the days of her first love. Oh, it is altogether possible that the influence of the dead, carnal element in any church may become so strong and overwhelming that for a time even the spiritual succumb to it and fall asleep. They deplore a condition of dead orthodoxy and dead works. For a time they raise their voices in protest against the tendency to emphasize mere doctrine and external activity at the expense of true faith and love. But gradually they become more or less accustomed to the situation. Their voices are silenced. They grow passive. Gradually they forget the days of the church's first love. The past does not live in their consciousness any more. And now they fail to notice the lack of spirituality in all the activity of the church. It was missing everywhere. It was wanting in the preaching of the Word, in the instruction of the youth, in the pastoral work. If I may speak for a moment in terms of our own church-life, when the angel of the church or the elders went through the congregation to visit the families, the subject of spiritual growth in the knowledge and grace of the Lord Jesus Christ was hardly broached. Such routine questions were asked as whether the services were faithfully attended, the sacraments were used, the church-papers were read, the budget was paid,—questions, in short, that all pertained to the external life and activity of the church. Everywhere the spiritual note was now missing. And the true spiritual element of the church had grown accustomed to this situation, had forgotten the former days. Hence, the Lord shows them the way to repentance. They must awake out of their slumbers. The angel and elders and members of the church must bring back to their minds those former days, when all were filled with the love of Christ, when all the activity of the church was aglow with real spiritual life. And recalling that former condition, they must be filled with an earnest longing to restore the church to that former state.

They must repent. Their backsliding must become sin unto them, which they confess before the Lord and before one another. And they must do the former works. Things must change. In preaching and teaching, as well as in the personal communion of the saints, the spiritual note must be struck once more. While remaining sound in doctrine, faithful in discipline, and zealous in good works, she must return also to her first love and do the first works. Once again the life of the church must spring forth from the root of true love in Christ Jesus her Lord!

An Urgent Word

This call to repentance is urgent. The church must heed it. So urgent is the matter that the Lord threatens the church with complete extinction if she does not repent.

Significant in this connection is the way in which the Lord introduces Himself to this church: "These things saith he that holdeth the seven stars in his right hand, who walketh in the midst of the seven golden candlesticks." He holds the seven stars, the angels of the seven churches. They are His gifts to the church. Only when He gives them are they truly ministers of the Word. Only by His Spirit can they be equipped with light and understanding and life to minister the Word of God. Only when the Lord Himself speaks through them is there preaching of the Word. This is a truth which the church in the world must always remember. Training of those who are to serve in the ministry of the gospel is certainly indispensable. But there is no seminary that can furnish the church with ministers of the Word. The Lord alone holds the seven stars in His right hand. If the minister of the Word is not one of those stars which Christ holds in His power and bestows on His church on earth, he may be a false teacher, a carnal seeker of self and the world; but he cannot preach the Word. Besides, Christ walks in the midst of the golden candlesticks. The church has her life in Him only. It can be a light in darkness only through His Spirit and grace. Without Him she is nothing and can do nothing. Very essential, therefore, it is for any church to stand in living fellowship with Him. She must not leave her love. She must understand that there is no life for her in separation from Him. A mere human society can never be church. This Self-designation of the Lord already contains a solemn warning to the church which left her first love. If she does not repent, but continues in the direction in which she is developing, death and darkness can be the only result.

But this same inevitable end is directly expressed in the threat of judgment: "...or else I will come unto thee quickly, and will remove thy candlestick out of his place, except thou repent," (vs. 5). The Lord here addresses the church as her King and Judge. When in this connection He speaks of His coming, it is evident that He does not refer to His final coming to judge the quick and the dead, but of His coming for judgment upon the historical church of Ephesus. Out of that place will He remove the candlestick. The meaning of this is evident. The church of Ephesus will cease to be a manifestation of the body of Christ on earth. She will become extinct. Outwardly, as a mere human fellowship and gathering, she may probably continue to exist for some time; but she will no longer be a representation of one of the candlesticks in the midst of which Christ walks. If she continues, she will be one of those dead churches of which we may notice so many round about us in the world of today. They are bearing the name of Christ's church falsely. They are no more than mere human associations, without the light of the truth, without the life of Christ. Thus the church of Ephesus will die. In the way of leaving the love of Christ, she will lose every spiritual virtue. The judgment threatened is, therefore, wholly in harmony with the defect and sin of the church.

Let us take it to heart! He that hath an ear, let him hear what the Spirit saith unto the churches!

An Encouraging Promise

But the Lord does not close this letter with this threat of judgment, but rather with an encouraging word of promise to those that overcome and fight the good fight even unto the end.

He introduces this word of comfort with the well-known, "He that hath an ear, let him hear what the Spirit saith unto the churches." This admonition, therefore, is addressed not only to the church of Ephesus, but to all the churches, to the whole church of all ages. Not all have ears to hear, even in the church visible on earth. Only they that were efficaciously called out of darkness into His marvellous light can spiritually hear and discern and heed the Word of Christ. To these the Lord now addresses Himself. He did address them, too, in the preceding, though the whole church must hear the call to repent. For only they that have an ear will obey His Word and repent and do the first works. They must assert themselves in the church of Ephesus, and insist upon repentance. They must fight, even within the church, in order that she may reform and return to her first love. This will not be easy. They must expect opposition, even from the carnal element in the church. A bitter fight it may become for them, in which they will have to bear the reproach of Christ and suffer for His name's sake. For worse and more bitter enemies than carnal Israel the church has none in all the world. They must expect scorn and derision, hatred and contempt and persecution. Perhaps they will be expelled, cast out of the synagogue. Outwardly they may suffer defeat. But if they only will be faithful to the end, they will surely overcome. And to him that overcometh the Lord will give to eat of the tree of life, which is in the midst of the paradise of God, vs. 7.

In the original paradise there stood the tree of life. It stood in the midst of the garden. The garden of Eden was God's house, His dwelling-place with man on earth. It was His tabernacle, in which God blessed man with the fellowship of His friendship. And the midst of the garden might be called the "holy of holies." There God dwelled. There Adam could meet his God as a friend meets his friend. There he had life in the true sense of the word. There also stood the tree of life. It was a sacred symbol to man that he could have life only in God's blessed fellowship. Surely, the tree was more than that. It was a means of life. By eating of that tree man could perpetuate his earthly existence. But it was also a sign of God's covenant with Adam. He could eat of that tree only as long as he stood right with his God. He could not reach the tree unless he could meet his God. And he could not meet his God except in righteousness and holiness and truth.

And that same tree of life was also an image of better things to come. For the earthy is an image of the heavenly. Paradise the first is an image of the better paradise of God which is to come, when all the weary night of sin and death shall have passed away, and all things shall have been made new. Then the tabernacle of God shall be with men forever! The perfected tabernacle of God in heavenly glory, in the new creation, is the ultimate realization of the first paradise. It will be far more blessed and glorious than the first paradise could ever be. For the first paradise was of the earth, earthy; but the final realization of it shall be heavenly. When that better day dawns, we shall walk as bearing the image of the heavenly Lord, in everlasting perfection, as friends of God.

In that new paradise there shall also be a tree of life, planted by the river of life that flows from the throne of God and of the Lamb. We shall have more to say about this tree in our discussion of the last chapter of this Book of Revelation. Suffice it to say now that it is not quite correct to identify the tree of life with Christ. It is evidently a means in the new creation through which the perfect and eternal life of the redeemed and resurrected saints shall be sustained, as well as a symbol of their everlasting covenant with God in Christ. In a sense, indeed, we may say that the believer has a foretaste even now of what it will mean to eat of that tree of life. But the promise refers to the glory of the eternal kingdom that is to come. Soon the dark night of suffering and battle is past. Presently the eternal morning dawns, the morning of a day of everlasting victory and joy. Then we shall be perfected, and we shall behold the beauty of the Lord in His temple. And forever we shall be satisfied with the pleasures which are at His right hand, eating of the tree of life which is in the midst of the paradise of God.

Hear, then, what the Spirit saith unto the churches!

The promise is for him that overcometh, that fights the battle even unto the end, and that is willing to suffer with Him, that we may be also glorified together!

And He that promised is faithful!

Chapter V

The Church Strong In Tribulation

(Revelation 2:8-11)

8 And unto the angel of the church in Smyrna write; These things saith the first and the last, which was dead, and is alive;
9 I know thy works, and tribulation, and poverty, (but thou art rich) and I know the blasphemy of them which say they are Jews, and are not, but are the synagogue of Satan.
10 Fear none of those things which thou shalt suffer: behold, the devil shall cast some of you into prison, that ye may be tried; and ye shall have tribulation ten days: be thou faithful unto death, and I will give thee a crown of life.
11 He that hath an ear, let him hear what the Spirit saith unto the churches; He that overcometh shall not be hurt of the second death.

The church in Ephesus represents the church in the beginning of her decline, though she is still strong in doctrine and in discipline. The church in Smyrna, in distinction from that of Ephesus, represents the church in the midst of tribulation, but rich and strong in every respect, as may be gathered from the fact that the Lord evidently has nothing to complain about her.

The Church In Smyrna

The city of Smyrna was a beautiful city, situated north of Ephesus on a bay of the Aegean Sea. In respect to business and industry it might well rival Ephesus for the honor of being considered the first city of that time. Perhaps it must be largely attributed to this fact that there were many Jews living in Smyrna, who, as usual, belonged to the well-to-do and influential class of people in the city. Also in Smyrna there had been founded a church of Jesus Christ, just as in the city of Ephesus. But as we already suggested, a comparison of the two letters which are written to

65

these congregations respectively will show that there was considerable difference between them.

In the first place, there was a difference outwardly, as to their relation to the outside world. Of Ephesus we receive the impression that also in an external sense it was a rather strong congregation, large and flourishing and even able to assert itself over against the world from without to a certain extent. It is true that also in its case the Lord suggested that it was subject to the ill will and mockery of the world: for He speaks of their patience and power to bear. But we do not get the impression that it was persecuted at the time by an overwhelming power of the world. In respect to the church in Smyrna, however, this is quite different. Of this church we are told that it is poor and in tribulation, that the people of God in the city were slandered and falsely accused, that they were persecuted and killed all the day long.

In the second place, however, there evidently was also a marked spiritual difference which is worthy of our attention. Of Smyrna we read that it was rich though it was poor; of Ephesus, that it had left its first love. In the case of Ephesus we read that the Lord has something against it; nothing of the kind is found in the epistle to Smyrna. Ephesus is warned with a threat that the candlestick will be removed out of its place if she does not repent. Smyrna receives nothing but the most beautiful and comforting promises and commendation. Hence, we may characterize the church in Smyrna as the church that is strong and rich in tribulation.

Smyrna's External Condition

The external position of the church in Smyrna and her relation to the world is indicated, first of all, in the words: "I know thy works, and tribulation." The ARV, correctly, does not have the term "works." The word employed in the original for "tribulation" denotes a condition of oppression, of being hard pressed, of being in narrow straits. It indicates that the world from without exerted a pressure upon the little congregation which was well-nigh unbearable, which threatened to leave it no standing room in the city. The world hated the little church, and pressed down upon it from every side with a view to its ultimate destruction. It persecuted her, revealed its hatred and contempt in many ways, and caused the members of the congregation to suffer because of the Word of God and the testimony of Jesus. It appears that at the time when this epistle was written to Smyrna, this persecution assumed chiefly a social aspect. It does not seem that at the time the people of God in Smyrna were already brought to the scaffold and to the stake. This form of persecution still lay in the future. At the present they were the objects of social persecution, so that they had no standing room in the midst of the world.

That this is true is indicated, first of all, by the phrase, "and thy poverty." The church of Smyrna was poor, not spiritually, but materially and socially. Spiritually they were rich, as the Lord informs us. But in a social sense they were poor. Perhaps they had already experienced a foretaste of that form of persecution which will be dominant at the time of the supreme and ultimate manifestation of Antichrist, when the people who refuse to receive the mark of the beast and the number of his name shall be allowed neither to buy nor to sell. It is not impossible to imagine that especially under the influence of the influential Jews they were deprived of many privileges which others enjoyed. They could not do business as others did. They could not make headway in the world from a material and social standpoint, as could the Jews. Perhaps they were even directly deprived of some of their property: their goods were confiscated because of their testimony of Jesus. At any rate, the church of Smyrna was poor. They had no social standing. They were not rich in earthly possessions. Perhaps they gathered for public worship in a miserable little shanty of a church. Perhaps they could not even decently provide for the necessity of the angel of the church, who, according to some, at this time was Polycarp, who also suffered martyrdom in Smyrna. It was undoubtedly with great difficulty that they could maintain themselves as a church in the city.

This social form of their tribulation is indicated still further in the words, "and the blasphemy of them which say they are Jews, and are not, but are the synagogue of Satan." The believers in Smyrna were slandered, blasphemed, reproached, reviled. The Jews, who, no doubt, could exercise a very subtle and powerful influence in the city, utilized every opportunity to revile the name of the members of the little congregation. Exactly what was the nature of their slander we are not directly informed in this epistle of the Lord to the church of Smyrna. Yet we may easily surmise the character of their reproach. For the Lord describes these blasphemers, first of all, as those who call themselves Jews, and are not. No doubt they belonged to the nation of the Jews. In a national sense they were children of Abraham. And, as usual, they were proud of this prerogative. They made it a special claim that they were the children of God because they were children of Abraham according to the flesh. The Christians, who made the same claim, were, of course, considered to be and branded as impostors. From this it may be inferred what was the nature of their slander. They publicly called themselves Jews, though in the true sense of the word they were not. They insisted openly that they were the only people of God, that they still expected the Messiah, and that therefore the Christians, who claimed that the Messiah had already come, and who proclaimed Him as their King, were nothing but a dangerous sect, dangerous to the state because they might easily incite the people of Smyrna to rebellion against the proper authorities and persuade them to acknowledge no other king than Jesus of Nazareth. At the same time, they must have slandered the little church in the very name of their professed King. The Messiah of the Christians was nothing but a crucified criminal,–something which must have been extremely horrifying and repulsive to the rest of Smyrna's population: for the cross was foolishness to the Greeks. However this may have been, it is certain that the slander of those Jews was directed against the believers of Smyrna because of their testimony of Jesus. Principally they slandered the Christians in Smyrna because of the bitter hatred of the Jews toward the Christ Who had come. For although they called themselves Jews, they were not. Not the national Jews, not the natural descendants of the father of believers, are Jews in this dispensation, but only they that are partakers of the faith of Abraham and that are justified by faith in Christ Jesus.

This faith in Christ and justification in His blood these so-called Jews simply despised with their whole heart. They did not believe in Christ. They rejected Him and crucified Him again. They trampled under foot the blood of the new covenant. And therefore they were no Jews in reality. On the contrary, they were a synagogue of Satan, as the Lord informs us. No doubt the Jews possessed a synagogue in the city of Smyrna. Literally the word "synagogue" signifies an assembly, a gathering. And therefore the Lord characterizes these men who call themselves Jews, and are not, as a gathering under the leadership of the devil. Satan is their chief, and he inspires all that they do. He therefore is also the instigator of their slander. We may also infer from this description what was the nature and the contents of their slander and blasphemy. For the name Satan means "opponent, adversary." He is the opponent of God and of Christ and of His people in the world. And as he had gained the leadership in the synagogue of the Jews in Smyrna and instigated their malignant and pernicious blasphemy, we may easily understand what sort of reproach was cast into the teeth of the little flock. The slander of these Jews was decidedly antichristian. They were reviled for Christ's sake. As Christians, followers of the despised Jesus of Nazareth, they had to bear the reproach and hatred of the world about them. They became for the sake of Christ objects of most bitter hatred and invidious contempt.

However, this could not be the end. More tribulation and persecution were yet to come. The deepest stage of their suffering had not yet been reached. Now they were poor and slandered, social outcasts in the city of Smyrna for Christ's sake. But the malignity of the synagogue of Satan could not be satisfied by mere slander and words of reproach. Even as this malevolent slander had its root in their bitter hatred against Christ and His church, so it could not cease before it had manifested itself in actual persecution of these Christians. Of this the Lord forewarns them in the words: "Fear none of those things which thou shalt suffer." And He continues: "Behold, the devil shall cast some of you into prison, that ye may be tried; and ye shall have tribulation ten days." It is more than probable that the poor Christians of Smyrna themselves already had a presentiment of the fierce persecution which was presently to break loose over their heads. Hardly could it be different. Persecutions of the church generally do not break out all of a sudden, without any precursory signs and warnings. When we hear the distant rumbling of thunder and see the dark clouds gather threateningly, we know that presently the storm will break forth in all its fury. Thus it is with the persecution of the church. It may come very quickly, but hardly without any premonitions on the part of those who are persecuted. Thus it must have been in the congregation of Smyrna; and they must have understood that the evil slander of the Jews must finally develop into actual persecution. Dark clouds must have been gathering at the horizon at this time. The very form in which the Lord sends His message indicates clearly that this persecution is not far off, that the days of trouble and tribulation are nigh at hand. For the Lord writes that they are **about** to suffer some things, and that the devil is **about** to cast some of them into prison. The very atmosphere must have been pregnant with indications that persecution was about to break out. And the hearts of the poor believers in Smyrna may well have been filled with fear and gloomy forebodings of the near future.

Cheer And Encouragement

Just because of this the Lord sends them the message of cheer and encouragement. He surely does not comfort them by assuring them that persecution shall not come, that suffering and trouble shall not touch them. But, while predicting that suffering will be their lot, He encourages them and writes: "Fear none of those things." Do not forget! This is the Word of Him which was dead, and, behold, He liveth!

Fear not! This is the positive message of the Lord to the church in tribulation. He not only cautions them in advance, so that they may be fully prepared; but He also comforts them and encourages them to face the future without fear. He does so, in the first place, by assuring them that it will be Satan who is the prime author of their tribulation. They will be cast into prison, and for ten days they will have tribulation. But they need not be ashamed of their reproach and suffering, nor need they fear. On the contrary, they may deem it an honor to be in oppression, for the simple reason that it is the devil who causes it all. Indeed, it is a glorious comfort to know that the devil is persecuting us. To suffer persecution from the hand of the righteous and just is unbearable; but to be an object of the devil's hatred is principally a cause for rejoicing. Perhaps these Christians in Smyrna will be treated by the civil powers in the city as criminals and rebels, and be branded as such before all the world; but nevertheless, they must be mindful of the fact that behind these municipal authorities and behind these malignant Jews is the devil, inciting his agents to do their hellish work. It might be grievous to them to be publicly exposed and treated as dangerous criminals; but to know that the devil was behind it must be for them a cause of serene satisfaction. For to be an enemy of the devil is to be a friend of Christ. To be persecuted by the adversary is the best proof of our belonging to God's party in the world.

Moreover, the Lord encourages them by informing them concerning the essential character of their future suffering. They will be cast into prison in order to be **tried**. This, indeed, was not the devil's purpose: for his highest aim was their apostasy from the truth. But above the devil stands the almighty God. And the powerful Priest-King walks in the midst of the seven golden candlesticks. His purpose will, after all, be reached. And therefore, also by this explanation of the character of their future suffering the Lord encourages His church. In the fact that the character of their suffering will be a trial they have the assurance that they are not unconditionally delivered to the power of the devil, but that they are safe in the hands of their Lord. It is He that employs even the devil to reach His own divine purpose. Besides, this is a source of comfort to them because it assures them that they shall be faithful to the end through the grace of their Lord. It will not be their downfall. In their own strength they would never be able to stand persecution; but by the grace of Christ they will certainly persevere even unto the end. As they consider themselves, fear, no doubt, fills their hearts: the fear that they shall become unfaithful and deny Him Whom their soul loves. But now they are informed that this will not be the ultimate outcome of their persecution. It will assume the nature of a trial. God will try His people, in order that the strength of His grace may become manifest to the world and to the devil, and that thus His own name will be glorified. To be worthy to be thus tried, to be deemed worthy of being a manifestation of God's grace over against the devil and the wicked world, is a cause of joy and a source of mighty comfort!

Finally, the Lord encourages His church with a view to the coming suffering by informing them as to the time of its duration. They shall be in tribulation ten days. This measure of time, no doubt, has symbolic significance. For even though this period should be understood in the literal sense of the word as applied to the congregation of Smyrna, the symbolical significance would by no means be excluded, no more than the recognition of the historical existence of the seven churches prevents us from considering them in their typical character in relation to the church of all times. But besides, it may safely be adopted as a general rule that the indications of time and space in the Book of Revelation are to be taken in the symbolical sense of the word. Not all the numbers occurring in the book can possibly be taken in the literal sense; but on the general basis that they are symbolic of some higher spiritual reality, they can all be interpreted. And therefore, also these "ten days" we take in the symbolical sense. And then we agree with interpreters in understanding this expression as being indicative, in the first place, of only a short period. But the brevity of the period is not to be found in the number ten: for in itself this number may indicate a long as well as a short period of time. No, that the time of their persecution will be comparatively short, though severe, is expressed rather by the fact that it is measured not by years, or months, but by days. In comparison with the glory that shall be revealed in us, the apostle Paul has it, the suffering of this present time is not worthy of consideration, Romans 8:18. When viewed in the light of the

ages, the tribulation of the church in this dispensation is always
insignificantly short. So also in respect to the tribulation of the church in
Smyrna: it will last but ten days.

The figure ten, however, implies a far greater comfort: for it is symbolic
of a far higher reality than the mere fact of brevity. Ten is a number which
is very frequently employed in Scripture, and it often occurs in the Book
of Revelation. The antediluvian period was comprised of the lifetime of
ten patriarchs. Before the heart of the king of Egypt is inclined to let the
children of Israel go to serve their God, ten great plagues are sent upon the
country. Life in its totality is measured by ten great spheres, indicated by
the division of the law into ten commandments. The Lord in His parable
speaks of ten virgins, and of servants entrusted with ten pounds whom He
will place over ten cities. In the Book of Revelation we read of the ten
horns of the great red dragon, of the ten horns of the beast and of his ten
royal diadems, of the ten kings who shall hate the harlot with whom they
first commit fornication, (chapters 13 and 17). Now if we consider this
number in the abstract, there can be no question of the fact that it is a
round number, that whatever other number is multiplied by it must also
be a round number. As such it beautifully serves as a symbol of
completeness and fulness.

But if we consider the passages in which the number ten is employed,
we soon find that there is still a more specific significance attached to the
number ten. The general idea that lies at the basis of its employment in
Scripture seems to be that of a fulness, completion, totality, of the
measure of anything, whether it be of time or power or action, of reward
or punishment, determined solely by the fixed plan of God Almighty. And
therefore, in our text it denotes neither that the time shall be either long
or short, nor that the Evil One shall be permitted to develop his full power
in persecuting the church of Smyrna; but it indicates that a certain definite
period is allotted to the devil during which he may persecute the church of
Christ, a period which is determined not by himself, but by the will and
counsel of the Lord. The devil possesses no power of himself, nor can he
sovereignly decide upon the persecution of the church. His power and
authority are characterized and symbolized by the number ten. It is both
limited and meted out to him by God. It is always the same with the devil
as in the case of the history of Job. The devil must approach God for
permission to afflict God's servant. And when Satan fails to induce Job to
apostasy by depriving him of all that he has in the world, he must again

turn to the Most High for permission to continue and to aggravate his attack upon Job. The devil, therefore, can never proceed beyond the limits set him by the Almighty; neither can he reach any other end than the purpose of God in the affliction of His people in the world.

Thus it is with the church in Smyrna. And this is applicable to the persecution and suffering of the church of all ages. The devil possesses power to oppress the church, no doubt. He will make life hard for the faithful in the world. He will rage against them in all his fury. We must expect this. But the blessed comfort for the church lies in the fact that the power of darkness is under the absolute control and sovereignty of Him that walketh in the midst of the seven golden candlesticks. The King of the church has received all power in heaven and on earth: power, too, to control the devil, the mighty adversary of Christ and His cause and His people in the world. And when the full measure of his time and power has been meted out to him according to the will of God, the Lord bids him stop, and he can stir no more against the church. What mighty comfort for the church in tribulation! The devil can do her no harm, but must serve the purpose of God in Christ. The gates of hell cannot prevail against us. Under the mighty protection and care of her great King the church has nothing to fear. "In the world ye shall have tribulation; but be of good cheer; I have overcome the world."

Smyrna's Spiritual Condition

It is evident from all this that tribulation can never harm the church. It is simply a trial, by which the church is sanctified and purified and strengthened in the faith. This is also evident from the epistle of the Lord to the church in Smyrna. Does the tribulation of the church in Smyrna, present or future, cause weakness and fear and trembling in the church? Does it lead the church away from its Lord and cause it to enter into the camp of the enemy? Exactly the opposite is true. The condition of the congregation in Smyrna was as good as possible. The church was in as flourishing a condition as might be expected in this dispensation. In proof of this there is, in the first place, the negative observation that the Lord in this letter mentions no cause for rebuke. This is surely sufficient to justify the inference that there was nothing worthy of blame in the congregation of Smyrna. If there had been, the Lord would have called the attention of the church to it. He was thoroughly acquainted with the condition of the church. And if there had been any reason to reprove, He surely would have known and expressed it.

Nor must we entertain the erroneous idea that the Lord would have overlooked the weakness of this specific congregation and passed it in silence in view of the fact that in its tribulation it had need of encouragement rather than of rebuke. This would have been fatal and detrimental to the church.

No, there is nothing to criticize. There is no reason to reprimand the church in any respect. And again, also here we must remember that it is not the individual believer, but the church as a whole that Jesus is addressing. It is not so that the members of the congregation in Smyrna had already reached perfection, and that they sinned no more. But addressing the congregation as a whole, the Lord finds no weakness, mentions no cause for rebuke, for the simple reason that it did not exist. The church at Smyrna possesses all the favorable features of the church in this dispensation. It does not present any of the weaknesses and signs of degeneration found in others.

But, further, this sound condition of the congregation is positively expressed by the Lord when He says, "But thou art rich." Its condition is exactly the opposite of the church in Laodicea. The latter was rich and luxurious, filled to the full and in need of nothing, suffered no tribulation; yet it was poor and naked in the consideration of Him Who walketh in the midst of the golden candlesticks. But the church of Smyrna is outwardly destitute, poor and despised, a social outcast, in the midst of tribulation, and with more severe persecution to be expected in the near future. In this respect it offers a complete contrast to the church of Laodicea. But although the church in Smyrna was outwardly poor and in miserable condition, nevertheless she was spiritually rich, rich in the grace of our Lord Jesus Christ.

There is no reason to limit this assertion of the Lord as to the condition of the church in Smyrna. It implies that it is rich in all the treasures and blessings of grace. She was rich in the knowledge of the truth. She was rich in works and patience. She was rich in bearing the cross and revealed a strong spiritual life in the midst of tribulations. The church in Smyrna had not lost its first love, as was the case with the church in Ephesus. Strong the church was in the faith, firm in hope, ardent in love, abounding in works, patient in affliction, and in the midst of tribulation expecting the day of the Lord, the day of perfect deliverance. Rich the church was, undoubtedly, in sound, experiential knowledge of the truth. The members of that church were prepared to give testimony of the hope that was within them at all times. They were rich in actual fact. Though the world hated them, deprived them of their possessions, made them poor and naked and miserable from the temporal point of view, yet they knew that their King was the Lord of heaven and earth, and by faith they were saved in hope. Indeed, the church in tribulation is rich!

This is always true. It is not only applicable to the church of Smyrna, but equally so to the church in tribulation in all ages. It has even become proverbial that the blood of the martyrs has become the seed of the church in history. Never does the church offer a more miserable and pitiable aspect than in times of prosperity from a worldly point of view, times of peace and abundance. Never is its condition more precarious than when it caters to the good pleasure of the world and craves for wealth and glory and honor after the measure of the world. The church of Laodicea is a warning example. But, on the other hand, it is equally true that the church is never more nearly perfect in this dispensation than when it is called upon to fight the battle of faith, to suffer and endure affliction for the Word of God and the testimony of Jesus.

This is but natural. The question might be asked: why is it that the church of Smyrna, and the church in tribulation generally, is strong and rich? The answer is not difficult to find. In the first place, there is, no doubt, a theological reason. Scripture reveals to us that among the elect of God there are not many wise and noble and rich in the world. The reason for this is very evident. The church does not exist for its own glory, but for the glory of God in Christ Jesus our Lord. And therefore the church does not exist for the purpose of showing forth its own strength and abundance from a natural point of view, but of manifesting the grace and power of the Lord her God. This it can do no more clearly than in times of tribulation, when it becomes manifest that it possesses no resources, no strength, no faith, no hope, outside of Christ; that its all is in Him; that from Him it receives its strength to stand and to be faithful.

Besides, there is also a spiritual reason why the church in tribulation flourishes and is strong. The root of its life is faith. For by faith it is connected with Him Who walks in the midst of the golden candlesticks. By faith only it receives all the treasures of salvation. The stronger and the more conscious this faith is, the more the church will grow in grace and increase in all spiritual riches in Christ. But what is more conducive to the exercise and strengthening of faith than a period of outward poverty and tribulation? It is when the storm howls in the woods that the oak strikes its roots more deeply and firmly into the soil and is strengthened. So it is when the storm of persecution sweeps through the church that the latter strikes the roots of its faith more deeply into Christ and draws from Him more consciously the very strength of its life. And therefore, it is especially in times of trouble that the church flourishes: for at such times it is taught to cling to its powerful King, and seeks its all in Him.

Finally, there is also a historical reason for this concurrence of tribulation and spiritual strength and prosperity in the church of Smyrna and with regard to the church of Christ in tribulation in all ages. In times of prosperity and wealth and peace, when the church is honored rather than despised in the world, there is a grave danger that many an Israelite who is not spiritually of Israel becomes member of the church in the world from carnal motives and for selfish reasons. It becomes a matter of honor, or even of common decency, to be a church member. Hence, many join the church. These carnal members are a veritable danger to the church of Christ. They often become dominant, and assume the leadership in the church. They impose their carnal desires upon the church. They lead her into the world, and, of course, to destruction. They are of the world, and they would make the church a part of the world. In times of persecution, however, when church membership and the reproach of Christ are inseparable, this danger does not exist. On the contrary, when the faithful must suffer persecution and reproach for Christ's sake, the church is cleansed of these hypocrites. They are exposed in their carnal nature. If he must lose his life because of it, there is no danger that the hypocrite will join himself to the church or that he will remain in her midst. And therefore, also from this point of view it is not difficult to understand that in times of persecution and tribulation the church is spiritually blessed.

What then? Shall we wilfully incite the malignity and enmity of the world, and strive for the martyr's crown?

Our answer is: there is absolutely no occasion for any such thing. If the church is truly faithful, faithful in its confession and in its walk, unfurling the banner of its King, and walking in the light in the midst of a world that is in darkness, the latter will naturally hate her, and the reproach and suffering from the side of Antichristendom are inevitable. But in all this we need not be afraid. For especially the sufferings for Christ's sake work together for good to them that love God, to them who are called according to His purpose. Besides, the sufferings of this present time are not worthy to be compared to the glory which shall be revealed in us.

Admonition And Promise

Now let us see how the Lord comforts the church in Smyrna.

First of all, we call your attention to the manner in which the Lord announces Himself to the church of Smyrna. We observed in connection with the former letter that these announcements, these Self-introductions of the Lord to the churches, are in harmony with the condition of the church which is addressed. Thus it was with regard to the church of Ephesus, where the Lord introduced Himself as the One that walketh in the midst of the seven golden candlesticks and that holdeth the seven stars in His right hand. This is also the case in regard to the church of Smyrna.

Here He introduces Himself as the One Who was dead and lives again, as the first and the last.

It is scarcely necessary to point to the appropriateness of this announcement, especially with a view to the condition of the church in tribulation. It is certainly adapted to fill the members of the faithful church with courage and hope in the midst of suffering. Christ is the first and the last. He was before all things and before all history, and He will be when this dispensation shall have come to its finish. He is the principle of all that is, and its purpose. He stands above all time and controls all history. He will be the last also in the sense that He shall prevail in the battle against the devil and against the power of Antichrist. Not the devil, not the powers of evil, shall be the last on the battlefield; but Christ shall be the victor! Even with death He was in battle, and He remained victor. For He was dead, and He lives again. He stands, as it were, before the congregation in tribulation, holding the keys of death and of hades in His right hand, and saying: "Behold, my people: I have overcome death, and have the power to open and to close, to condemn and to deliver! I, even I alone, am He that controlleth all these things!" And therefore, with that powerful victor as their Savior and their King, they need not fear the enemy. The devil may cast them into prison, and terrible tribulation may come in the near future. What of it? Christ has overcome the devil, and he is subject to Him alone. Yea, even death may threaten them, as is implied in the admonition which follows. Nothing can harm them. Christ has power even over death. And in due time He shall deliver them and give them life and glory.

This latter assurance the Lord gives them directly in the admonition, "Be thou faithful unto death, and I will give thee a crown of life." Faithfulness surely is one of the most beautiful virtues that exists, even from a natural point of view. It implies, in the first place, that there exists an established relation between two persons, or parties, whether it be a relation of friendship or of mutual contract and agreement. It implies, in the second place, that this definite relation is put to the test, whether it be by a long period of time or by adverse circumstances, which make it difficult to keep the agreement or the bond of friendship. And, in the third place, it implies that in spite of these adverse circumstances the relation remains as it always was. A friend in times of prosperity is nothing special; but in adversity the faithfulness of a friend is put to the test.

In the spiritual sense, faithfulness is the chief virtue of the covenant people. They belong to God's party in the world. They confess Christ as their King. The question is whether at all times they will be loyal to their King in the midst of a world which hates Him. There exists a certain definite relation between the King and themselves. And the question is whether they shall publicly confess that relation, never deny their King or be ashamed of His name, no matter what happens. Thus it was in the congregation of Smyrna. In times of prosperity it is not so difficult to confess Christ as their King. When He scores victory upon victory, it is an honor to belong to His church. Our faithfulness is not manifest. But when because of His name we are subject to persecution, the objects of the mockery and reproach of the world, when the confession of His name is the cause of trouble and much tribulation, then to confess that name is faithfulness. The church in Smyrna was in tribulation. It could expect a still more severe form of persecution in the future. Yea, according to this very admonition, they might expect that their lives would be demanded as a toll for their faithful confession. And therefore, to them comes the exhortation: "Be thou faithful unto death..." For this last phrase does not merely exhort to a faithfulness unto the hour of death. It is not merely a phrase denoting the extent in time. But it indicates a causal relation between faithfulness and death. It means: be faithful even if confession of My name should cause physical death.

As we have already suggested, history informs us that this exhortation was literally heeded by the gray-haired angel of the church in Smyrna. He was placed before the very alternative of denying the Lord or of being put to death. And, placed before this definite choice, he answered: "Eighty-six years have I known and confessed my Master, and He has never done me any harm. Shall I then now deny Him? Never!" And he died the martyr's death. History also speaks of thousands and thousands who have followed old Polycarp in this path of martyrdom. But they have become partakers of the beautiful promise which the Lord adds to this exhortation: "And I will give thee a crown of life!"

By "crown" in this connection you must not understand the royal diadem: for the original indicates that a wreath of victory is meant. Evidently the meaning is: I will give thee eternal life as a crown of victory. And do not imagine now that this is merely a meaningless form of expression. Surely, we all shall inherit eternal life. Nor is the relation such that we shall merit that eternal life in our own strength or even by our own faithfulness. It is because of Christ's obedience that this eternal life is ours. But if once we shall stand in glory among the one hundred forty-four thousand of the elect of God, we shall notice that the glory of that throng is varied according to the different degrees of reward each shall receive. And among them shall also be those who wear the crown of life, those whom eternal life adorns as a crown of victory in a special sense of the word. They are those who have been in special tribulation, who have not loved their lives unto death, who have been faithful unto death in the most literal sense of the word. More than others, they shall appear as victors and shall occupy a victor's place of honor in the new creation.

Finally, the Lord closes also this letter to the church of Smyrna with a general admonition and promise: "He that overcometh shall not be hurt of the second death."

We all are in the midst of the battle of faith. We may not all be called to sacrifice our lives upon the altar of faithful confession. We surely all must fight. And in the battle against sin, the world, and the devil and his whole dominion, we must overcome. Not in our own strength, not by sword and cannon, but spiritually, in the power of our Lord Jesus Christ, we must overcome. And to him that thus overcometh the Lord promises that he shall not be hurt of the second death. From our point of view, the first death is the separation of body and soul, or physical death. The Lord does not promise His church that they shall not be hurt of it. Surely, also His people die that death, and often die it violently. But though they may experience temporal suffering and want, though they may be called upon voluntarily to descend into the valley of death for the Word of God and the testimony of Jesus, they shall not be hurt in the real sense of the word.

The second death does not touch them. And therefore, the first death is merely a transition to everlasting life. This second death is eternal death, absolute separation from the Fount of all good in everlasting woe. Of that death the fornicators and the unfaithful shall be hurt. But he that overcometh shall pass through the first death into glory everlasting!

"He that hath an ear, let him hear what the Spirit saith unto the churches."

What doth the Spirit say?

Be faithful unto death! Seek not the things of this world. For the things of this world pass away, and behind them lurks the second death. Be faithful, O church of God, in the midst of the world, no matter what happens. In serious times we are living, indeed: serious, because we hear of wars and rumors of war as never before; but serious still more, because of the rather general apostasy from the truth and from the God of our salvation in Jesus Christ our Lord. And therefore, be faithful, and confess Him Who is your King. And if the struggle should become hard, and the battle well-nigh impossible to endure, then look upon Him Who walketh in the midst of the golden candlesticks, Who is your guard and protector at all times. He is the first and the last, Who was dead, and is alive! And He holds the keys of death and of hades forevermore!

Be, therefore, faithful unto death; and receive the promise, "I will give you the crown of life!"

Chapter VI

The Church Lax In Discipline

(Revelation 2:12-17)

12 And to the angel of the church in Pergamos write;
These things saith he which hath the sharp sword with two
edges;
13 I know thy works, and where thou dwellest, even
where Satan's seat is: and thou holdest fast my name, and
hast not denied my faith, even in those days wherein
Antipas was my faithful martyr, who was slain among you,
where Satan dwelleth.
14 But I have a few things against thee, because thou hast
there them that hold the doctrine of Balaam, who taught
Balac to cast a stumblingblock before the children of Israel,
to eat things sacrificed unto idols, and to commit fornication.
15 So hast thou also them that hold the doctrine of the
Nicolaitanes, which thing I hate.
16 Repent; or else I will come unto thee quickly, and will
fight against them with the sword of my mouth.
17 He that hath an ear, let him hear what the Spirit saith
unto the churches; To him that overcometh will I give to
eat of the hidden manna, and will give him a white stone,
and in the stone a new name written, which no man
knoweth saving he that receiveth it.

In this particular letter of the Lord to the church in the world we have
a picture of the church which differs considerably from that of the two
churches we have already discussed. The church of Ephesus was
characterized by many good features, but also by a falling away from its
first love, so that it was in grave danger of ultimately seeing its candlestick
removed out of its place. The church in Smyrna presents the picture of the
church faithful in tribulation: poor and despised, yet rich in all the
spiritual blessings of grace in Christ Jesus. Also the church in Pergamos
occupies a dangerous position in the midst of the world: for the text tells
us that Pergamos is the place where Satan dwells and where the very

throne of Satan is established. But that church in Pergamos has one characteristic which distinguishes it from the former two congregations which we have discussed. It is this: the church in Pergamos bears with evil men, and therefore is the church which is growing lax in discipline.

The Church In Pergamos

It is evident from the outset that in this letter to the church of Pergamos all the emphasis is placed upon the position which that church occupies in the midst of the world. It is the church that is situated where Satan dwells and where he has established his throne in a very special sense of the word. Pergamos was a rather large city, situated somewhat farther north from Smyrna than the latter was distant from Ephesus. If Smyrna was the competitor of Ephesus, Pergamos emulated both of the former in striving for the honor of being the foremost city of Asia Minor. Commerce and industry found in Pergamos a center. Science and art found their home there. Also in this city the church of Christ, which certainly is not called to retreat into the smaller towns and villages or to hide in the outskirts of the larger cities, had come to manifestation and was established.

Judging by the contents of this letter, addressed to them by the Lord, Pergamos had a very difficult time of it. The city is called the throne of Satan, and the very dwelling-place of the devil. What is meant by these expressions in the general sense of the word is not difficult to understand. A throne in the Book of Revelation occurs frequently as the symbol of dominion, as the center whence the authority of the king emanates throughout his entire kingdom. Satan is the adversary of God and the great opponent of our Lord Jesus Christ and of His kingdom in the world. He is forevermore endeavoring to organize and to bring to development the power of opposition against God's Anointed in the world, and therefore against His church. Throughout this dispensation he is the instigator of all opposition which manifests itself against the church of Christ. And therefore, if we read in this letter that Pergamos was a place where Satan had his throne, the city is pictured to us as being dominated by this power of opposition, as being dominated by the prince of darkness, as being a stronghold of the devil, where he could have full and undisputed sway, except for the little bulwark of Christ which had been built in the city.

This must be taken with special emphasis in regard to Pergamos. In general, it is true of this entire dispensation that the world is under the dominion of the prince of darkness. The whole world, John tells us, lies in the Evil One; and the kingdoms of this world belong to his dominion. But it is also true that in one place this dominion of the devil becomes more clearly manifest than in another. In our own time, it is generally evident that in the larger cities, like London and Paris, New York, Chicago, and San Francisco, sin comes to a higher and bolder form of development, and the devil exercises more absolute and undisputed sway than in the smaller towns or rural communities. At any rate, of Pergamos it might be asserted that in a special sense it was the seat, or throne, of Satan. He dwelled there. While in other places he also manifested his presence occasionally, Pergamos was his continual abode. If he would go out as a roaring lion, seeking whom he might devour, he would always return to Pergamos. There you could always find him at home. There he had his headquarters. There was his permanent abode. There was the center and seat of his authority and power.

If we inquire more especially, and ask the question in what sense this dubious prerogative could be claimed for the city of Pergamos, the text does not supply the answer. But from history we know two things.

First of all, we are informed that among other forms of idolatry practiced in the town, Pergamos was famous for its worship of Aesculapius as its chief god. Characteristic of this god was that its chief symbol, representing him, was that of the serpent, – the symbol also of the devil. The special power attributed to this god was that he could save people from the miserable effects of sin, from disease and sicknesses of all kinds. People from the city and from all the surrounding country flocked to his temple for help and recovery. And because of this imaginary power of this god, he was generally known as Soter, that is, Savior. Thus we obtain indeed a striking symbolism of the power of Antichrist and the dominion of Satan, consisting ultimately of this, that the serpent, the symbol of the devil, was hailed as the savior of men and was worshipped as such.

In the second place, we are informed, too, that the city of Pergamos was one of the first centers of worship of the Caesars, the emperors of Rome. As we may know, the emperors of Rome had themselves deified and worshipped as gods. And in the city of Pergamos there was a temple erected in honor of Caesar and dedicated to his worship. In short, it may be said that in Pergamos we meet with a rather striking manifestation of the Antichristian power and dominion: not, indeed, in the same form as Antichrist rules today, or as he shall come in his manifestation in the future; but nevertheless, the similarity is striking. Satan, the serpent, is honored and worshipped as the savior of men instead of Christ; and Caesar, man, is worshipped as lord of all instead of Him to Whom all power is given in heaven and on earth. Truly, Pergamos was the throne of Satan, the place where the prince of darkness had his permanent abode.

Of course, in principle the position of the church in Pergamos in relation to that city is the position of the church of all ages in relation to the world. As we have remarked, the prince of darkness is the ruler of this age. And he still exercises dominion over the kingdoms of the world. He is, in principle, hailed as the savior wherever the Christ is rejected; and the divinity of man is proclaimed wherever the divinity of the Son of Man is not acknowledged.

But this relation to the world is not always equally vivid, nor does it manifest itself in the same form in every period of history. During the period of the early church Rome, with its emperors, raging against the little flock of the Good Shepherd, was, no doubt, the throne of Satan and his abode. In the age of the Reformation the Roman Catholic Church might suitably be designated as the throne of Satan,—more specifically so, the seat of the pope and all connected therewith. And when finally the Reformation was initiated, it soon became evident that the little church of Protestantism dwelled where Satan had his abode.

But again, a sad and fatal mistake we would make, if we would imagine that also today the center of Satan's authority must be sought in the Roman Catholic Church, as some interpreters have it. It would blind us to the tremendous movement of Modernism, of Humanism, of Man-worship, which is sweeping over the world of Christendom and developing with astounding rapidity. Today man is his own savior. Man is the savior of humanity. Man is today his own god: not, indeed, because he worships any particular human being, be it Caesar or some other, but because he has generalized his worship of man in the worship of humanity.

Also today Satan has his throne and dwelling-place. He has it in many a school and college and university, where Christ is humanized and man is deified, where the worship of humanity is preached and taught in its boldest and rankest aspect, and where the blood of Christ is trampled under foot. Nay, still stronger, the devil has succeeded in ousting the true Savior from many a Christian church. The revelation of Christ is proclaimed and maintained from many a modern pulpit no more. Or, if it is, its features are so distorted that you can recognize the Christ no more.

Surely, also today the prince of darkness has his throne and dwelling-place. He has them in the midst of the Christian world; and he has succeeded in charming the minds and the imagination of men by upholding before them the image of the modern Aesculapius, called Humanity! Also today the church is established where Satan has his throne; and its relation to the world is not so much different from that of the church in Pergamos. May she be found faithful, as was that congregation of the early church.

Commendable Features Of The Church In Pergamos

For this may be said of that little church in Pergamos, in the first place: she was faithful. Read: "...and thou holdest fast my name." Such is the testimony which Jesus gives of the church in this particular letter.

The question might be raised whether it were not advisable for the little church to migrate out of that wicked city where the devil had his throne and dwelling-place. It might be more safe for it in other cities in the vicinity. But that is not the message John must deliver to the church, nor is it the attitude of Scripture in general. Mark, we are dealing with the church as a whole, not with the individual Christian. The Word of God does not approve of the dangerous worldly-mindedness of many a Christian who, for material advantages and gain, separates himself from the communion of saints and lives in isolation from the church of Christ in the midst of the world. Much rather does it call our attention to the sad history of Lot's family in such cases. On the other hand, the Scriptures never tell us that the church of Christ as such must emigrate from the world and live in literal and local isolation. This were, indeed, impossible. No, "In the world, though not of the world" is the rule which holds for the church of all ages. And therefore, the church of Pergamos is not commanded to leave its wicked and devilish surroundings, but rather to be faithful to the name of its King and Savior. And faithful the church had been in the past. It had kept the faith and held fast the name of Jesus.

Naturally, this must be understood in contrast with the environment of the little church. In the city the name of Jesus was not honored and confessed. It was the name of Aesculapius and of Caesar that was on the lips of all. And in the midst of these idolatrous surroundings they held fast to the only name that is given under heaven for salvation: they confessed the name of Jesus Christ. They kept the faith. They were not seduced. They were not shaken in their faith and hope and love, but they clung to the name of Him Who walketh in the midst of the golden candlesticks.

Still more the Lord witnesses of them in their favor. They were not only a believing church, but they also publicly confessed the name of their King and Lord. It were conceivable that they kept the faith and clung to the name of Jesus, but that they kept it all for themselves, that they lived in seclusion, and that they carefully avoided an open clash with their wicked environment. But once more, this is not the calling of the church of Christ. Christ does not establish His church in the world in order that it should exist in oblivion, hiding itself in some secluded little corner of the world, or seeking refuge on some solitary little island, far from society. It is in the world to let its light shine, to witness of the grace and the glory of its King. It may not hold its peace, even when the world threatens with devilish fury. The church must confess; and not to confess is to deny. And also in this respect the church of Pergamos had been faithful. For the Lord testifies of it: "...and hast not denied my faith." They confessed, therefore; they were not silent. How could they be? There they lived, in the midst of an environment which proclaimed a false god as savior and a man as their lord and god. Would it not have been unfaithful of the church, had they been silent and kept their peace? Would it not have been a dishonor of the name of their Lord and King if they had left the impression that they lacked the courage to confess Him? No, this they could never do. Over against the cry of the town, "Aesculapius is savior," they boldly maintained: "There is no other name than that of Jesus." When the world proclaimed that Caesar was god, and as such was to be worshipped by all, they could not submit; but, opposing the world also in this respect, they confessed that Christ was King, that the Lord God, and He alone, is worthy of worship and adoration. And thus it is also the calling of the church today to let the testimony go forth over against the Man-worship of Humanism and Modernism: "Jesus Christ is King, and He alone is the Savior of the world!"

But still more is implied in this faithful confession of the name of Jesus over against the world on the part of the church in Pergamos. For the Lord speaks of days of tribulation and persecution which the church had already experienced in the past, in the days of Antipas, one of Christ's faithful witnesses, who had been killed among them, where Satan dwelled. Nor does it cause us surprise that the world could not tolerate the witnesses of Christ in the city. Surely, the church may escape the bitter hatred of the world and persecution from its side for a long time, as long as it will only be silent and unfaithful and hide its light under a bushel, as long as it does not condemn the world in its self-made religion and Man-worship, and as long as it does not boldly confess the name of Jesus. But no sooner does the church realize its calling and faithfully unfurl the banner of its King, than the hatred of the world against that detestable Jesus of Nazareth and His "blood theology" will manifest itself in bitter persecution. Thus it had been in Pergamos in the past. Nothing else is known of Antipas, mentioned in this letter, than that he was a faithful witness and had been killed for the testimony he had given. But surely, this incident is proof of the fact that the church had experienced dark and evil days, days of tribulation, even as the church in Smyrna experienced. And in all this they had been faithful, and had not denied the name of Jesus.

Pergamos Defective In Discipline

From what we have considered of the church in Pergamos thus far, we would be inclined to draw the conclusion that it was a beautiful and most perfect specimen of a church, in no respect inferior to the congregation of Smyrna. And we would surely not anticipate any form of rebuke in this epistle which is addressed to it. Also here we have the picture of a church in tribulation in the midst of a world which cannot tolerate its existence, yet flourishing spiritually and faithful to the Lord their King.

Yet the Lord holds a few things against the church of Pergamos.

In order to understand how this is possible, we must notice, in the first place, that there is a noticeable difference between this church and the one in Smyrna. The latter was right in the midst of tribulation; in fact, the darkest days for it were still in the future. But with Pergamos this is somewhat different: the Lord refers to the days of Antipas as belonging to the past. The church still lived in the midst of a hostile world, to be sure. It had experienced the hatred of that world and had been persecuted for the testimony they had given. But evidently the first wave of fury had passed. Pergamos had lived through its attack from Satan and the world. Now it was a time of relief for the church. And history plainly shows that such times are dangerous for the church of Christ.

In close connection with this fact stands another, namely, that the church in Pergamos was defective in discipline, the discipline of its own members. This is a feature not mentioned of the church in Smyrna. In fact, I imagine that there was not much occasion for discipline in that congregation, for the simple reason that it was a church in tribulation. But in Pergamos discipline had become lax, while there was abundant occasion that called for strictness in this respect. No, the situation in Pergamos was not as serious as that in Ephesus. But the defect was of such a nature, nevertheless, as to call for a rebuke from the Lord. Discipline is the Christ-ordained guard in the church of Jesus. It is the sentinel, standing watch by the purity of doctrine according to the Word of God and by the holiness of the sacraments, as well as by the walk of believers. Where that sentinel is not placed on guard, or where he is sleeping while on duty, the church is exposed to the evil, seducing influence of false doctrine, as well as to the degenerating influence of the world upon the life of its individual members.

In Pergamos that sentinel was fast asleep. For the Lord reprovingly calls its attention to the fact that it has there "them that hold the doctrine of Balaam, who taught Balac to cast a stumblingblock before the children of Israel, to eat things sacrificed unto idols, and to commit fornication," and "them that hold the doctrine of the Nicolaitanes," in like manner. There were, therefore, evil men in the church of Pergamos, men who did not belong to the church in Spirit and in truth; and they were allowed in the midst of the congregation.

The reason why the church was lax in disciplining these men is not revealed. Hardly would it seem conceivable that the church was not aware of their existence in its midst: for they must have labored for the spread of their evil influence. Perhaps it was afraid that since the congregation already had to cope with so many difficulties and had a hard battle to fight against the world, the disciplining of its own members would weaken it still more. Perhaps the excuse was given which is so often offered for laxity of discipline in our own time, namely, that the church must not cast out, but save. "The church must save, and not reject," thus we often hear in our own time. Who knows whether these evil members, if they are borne with patience and longsuffering, will not come to repentance. On the basis of such false excuses evil men are tolerated within the church of Christ. Some churches defend the membership of those who belong to secret societies on that very basis. If only they are in the church once, they may be persuaded to sever their connection with the lodge. Men who hold a false doctrine are tolerated, and the church which does not exercise discipline over them is excused, because, so they say, true faith is after all not a matter of doctrine, but of the heart, and it would be cruel and indicative of a "holier-than-thou" spirit of intolerance if such men would be excommunicated from the church of Christ. We are perhaps acquainted with the flimsy arguments which are used in defense of laxity of discipline. Jesus, however, will not have it so. And whatever may have been the cause of this laxity of discipline in the church of Pergamos, the Lord holds it against them, and in His letter speaks of it rebukingly.

Exactly in what manner these evil men in the church of Pergamos had made themselves proper objects of discipline the letter does not tell us. There were Nicolaitanes here, as in Ephesus, where they were hated and not tolerated. In this letter, however, we receive some more definite information about them. They are compared with Balaam, that most abominable of all false prophets pictured in the Old Testament. Second to Judas, who betrayed the Savior for thirty pieces of silver, it is perhaps difficult to think of a meaner, more abominable and debased creature mentioned in Scripture than this Balaam, this agent of the devil.

You are acquainted, of course, with the history of this man. Sent for by Balak, king of the Moabites, to curse the children of Israel that are encamped in the plains of Moab, Balaam is attracted by the prospect, though he knows it is wicked and against the will of Jehovah, for the simple reason that there is money in it. Repeatedly the hypocrite implores the Lord to let him go with the king's ambassadors, till finally because of his importunity Jehovah grants him the wish of his heart and lets him walk in his evil way. On the way thither he receives another warning through his mute beast, but without effect. He travels on, arriving at the place of his destination; and beholding from the heights the children of Israel, he cannot but pronounce upon them the blessing of Jehovah which the Spirit gives him to speak. And in spite of his own miserly soul and the provocation of the king of Moab, he must confess that he cannot curse whom the Lord Jehovah would bless. And what now does this debased instrument of Satan do? He gives the king some practical advice; and, according to Numbers 31:16, he counsels him how he may shrewdly bring destruction upon the people of God. And through his counsel he causes the people of Israel to commit fornication in the service of Baal-peor and to sacrifice to Moab's idols. That was the advice of Balaam. And its immediate object was the obliteration of the distinctive character of the people of God, their amalgamation with the people of Moab.

In the text these Nicolaitanes are compared to that wicked Balaam of the Old Testament, who offended the people of God. It is not impossible that these Nicolaitanes were antinomians, people who deliberately taught that it mattered not how the Christian lived here upon earth since Christ fulfilled the law and the old Adam was doomed to destruction anyway. They were not very scrupulous as to their own lives. They would feast with the heathen and eat of their sacrifices. In a word, they were a class of people that threatened by their doctrine and life to obliterate the distinction between the church and the world in Pergamos, even as the counsel of Balaam was calculated to wipe out the characteristic difference between the people of Israel and the Moabites.

Thus, the church of Pergamos, by allowing these Nicolaitanes to exist in the church, was in grave danger of losing its distinctive character as a church of Christ. The purpose and subtilty of the devil in this scheme is transparent. In the recent past he had made an attempt to wipe out the church and make it unfaithful to its Lord by subjecting it to bloody persecution. But in this he had failed. For the time being he now abandoned this course of action, in order to try the method of corrupting the church and thus wiping out the distinction between the church and the world.

I think that in this respect the epistle of Christ to the church in Pergamos has a great lesson to teach us. Is not obliteration of all distinction and amalgamation of the church and the world characteristic of all that the devil does today? Are we not told that it matters not what form of doctrine we embrace, if only we will all be brothers? Is the devil not busily engaged in socializing and secularizing the church of Christ? And, on the other hand, is not the church of Christ growing more lax in discipline and weaker in its hold upon the truth of the Word every year? I am convinced that such are the conditions indeed. And therefore the church in Pergamos in this respect, at least, is a true picture of the church of today.

Exhortation And Threat

The message which the Lord instructs John to write to that congregation may also be applied to us: "Repent; or else I will come unto thee quickly, and will fight against them with the sword of my mouth."

This sword had already been mentioned in the Self-announcement with which the Lord introduces this letter to Pergamos. Of this we read in verse 12: "And to the angel of the church in Pergamos write; These things saith he which hath the sharp sword with two edges." It is evident, therefore, that the threat of judgment which the church in Pergamos receives is in harmony with that Self-announcement of the Lord. He presents Himself as the One out of Whose mouth proceeds the sharp two-edged sword.

The significance of this sword we pointed out in a former discussion. In brief, it denotes the power and authority of the One Who walks in the midst of the golden candlesticks to execute judgment and destroy the evil-doers by the Word of His mouth. He is Judge supreme, and He rules also against the evil men in His own church, destroying them by the sword that proceeds out of His mouth. That sword is His sovereign and powerful Word, executing judgment. An earthly judge can pronounce a verdict of guilty and announce the sentence of punishment; but his word has no power; it has not the power to inflict that punishment and to enforce his sentence. Not so, however, with the Word of Jesus. If He, as the mighty King-Judge, expresses a sentence upon anyone, the very word of the sentence is the power that inflicts the punishment and realizes the judgment expressed. It is the sword that executes the sentence. In this light, then, as the King-Judge in the midst of the church, He announces Himself to the congregation in Pergamos. She has in her midst evil men, who aim at the destruction of the church by their evil doctrine and practice. And these men must be rooted out from her midst. Hence, His appearance with the sharp two-edged sword proceeding from His mouth is in accord with the condition of the congregation.

Before the Lord comes to exercise the power and authority of that sharp sword, however, He sends the message to the church: "Repent!"

These words are not primarily intended for the evil men who held the doctrine of the Nicolaitanes. It is not they, but the congregation that is addressed through its angel. It is the church as a whole that is guilty and worthy of rebuke because of her laxity in discipline. And therefore of this she must repent. She may not make light of the glory of her King and be careless in regard to the well-being of the church by tolerating these Nicolaitanes continuing in her midst. The call to repentance in this case is equivalent to the call to exercise proper discipline over the Nicolaitanes in the bosom of the church.

And if they do not repent and cut off these evil members, the Lord threatens that He Himself will come, and that too, quickly, to make war with them. Let us notice, in the first place, that the church is not threatened with the removal of the candlestick, as was the case with Ephesus. Her condition was not as precarious as that of the church which was losing her first love. The congregation is to be saved even though the

Lord must come with His judgment. Exactly what would be implied in this coming of the Lord to the church in Pergamos, the text does not indicate. Most probably we may think in this case of temporal judgments with which the Lord will visit the church in order to chastise them for their laxity in discipline and to cut out the evil men from their midst. An analogous case we may find in the congregation of Corinth. She also was loath to banish evil men from her midst, and permitted the desecration of the Lord's Supper. And she too was visited by the Lord with many a temporal chastisement. Where the true church still exists and is as strong as the congregation in Pergamos, her sole defect being a weakness in discipline, the Lord visits His church with temporal judgment, in order that she may repent and excommunicate the impenitent evil-doer.

Comfort And Encouragement

But this is not the last word. On the contrary, many were the faithful in the church of Pergamos. And for them the Lord closes with a word of comfort and encouragement. To them that overcome the Lord has a two-fold promise.

In the first place, He promises them that they shall be fed with the hidden manna. And, secondly, He promises that they shall receive a white stone, and upon the stone a new name written, which no man can read except he that receiveth it.

The figure of the hidden manna is not difficult to understand. We all are acquainted with the history of God's people from which this symbol is derived. In the desert during their long journey to the promised land, Jehovah fed His people miraculously with bread from heaven. Every day, except on the sabbath, He rained His manna from heaven. And in the Gospel according to John we are told that this manna which rained from heaven in the wilderness was not the real manna, but that Christ is the true bread of life, of which the manna in the desert was only typical. But even as the people of God in the old dispensation were fed with the material manna, raining from heaven, so the people of God are spiritually nourished with the true manna, the bread of life, which nourishes them unto everlasting life. In Christ is their all: their justification, their sanctification, and their complete redemption. All the grace they need to be delivered from the power of sin and death and to appear finally before the Father in everlasting glory, to serve Him in perfection, is only in Christ Jesus their Lord. He is the hidden manna. By the Spirit, through the medium of faith,

Christ imparts Himself unto His people who have become one plant with Him. And therefore, to the faithful in Pergamos the Lord promises a full supply of the hidden manna, which will strengthen them in their battle against Satan and his throne and which will finally lead them on to perfection, when they shall have appropriated all the blessings of salvation completely. Because of their mystical union with Him Who walketh in the midst of the golden candlesticks, they shall be fed with the hidden manna; and eternally their souls shall be satisfied.

As to the symbol of the white stone, we can perhaps interpret it most correctly by recalling the ancient custom of expressing a verdict upon him that was arraigned in court by means of two stones, a white and a black. Each one of the jury members would be given a white and a black stone. In case he deemed the accused guilty, he would cast the black stone in a vessel; if judged innocent, the defendant would have a white stone cast in his favor. The black stone, then, was a symbol of guilt and condemnation, the white stone of innocence and justification. By promising the faithful in Pergamos a white stone, the Lord assures them of their final justification and purification in the day of the Lord. They need not be alarmed by the appearance of that two-edged sword: for they shall receive the white stone in proof of their perfect justification and glorification; and they shall be presented to the Father without blemish, without spot or wrinkle, shining forth in the perfection of their new being.

In close connection with this white stone is the new name written upon it, which they only shall be able to read who receive it. The name in Scripture is expressive of one's being and individual nature. That peculiar character of each person that causes him to differ from his fellow human being is his name. It is therefore but natural that in perfection the children of God shall receive a new name, in harmony with the perfect renewal of their being. In this dispensation their name so frequently spells imperfection and misery, imperfection both physically and spiritually. In principle, indeed, they already possess their new name in Christ. But the glory of that new name is so largely covered up by the darkness of their old name of sin that frequently it hardly becomes manifest. Sin controls them often. Besides, the world hates them and adds to their outward misery in this dispensation. But in the eternal kingdom this shall be different. If they persevere and overcome and are faithful unto death, they shall once enter into glory everlasting. And in that perfect state the glory of their new being shall shine forth in all its splendor uninterruptedly. Still more: not all the saints shall be alike, so that there should be an endless monotony of identically the same beings. The difference between one individual and another shall not be obliterated in perfection. On the contrary, there shall be an infinitely rich variety of individuals. Personality shall also be in heaven. Individual character shall even be emphasized to perfection. That is why the text has it that only he who receives the name shall know it. Even here, on the earth, it is true that after all a person knows himself only; and never shall we be able to penetrate into the hidden depths of another's individuality. The greater and deeper the person, the more difficult it becomes fully to explain him. The shallower and more insignificant a person, the more easily he is scrutinized. In perfection personality shall be emphasized and developed to its highest glory, so that each saint shall know his own name only. Thus God shall be glorified in the new humanity, in which the image of God shall shine forth in all its divine fulness and beauty, radiating, as it were, from the Lord Jesus Christ into all the members of His body, and reaching its full realization and manifestation not in each individual saint, but rather in the harmony of the whole. Each one only knows his own name. Each particular child of God shall then manifest his own peculiar shade of God's image. And together with the new creation, they shall all reveal in one grand and most beautiful harmony the wonders of God's image.

He that hath an ear, let him hear what the Spirit saith unto the churches.

What doth the Spirit say?

Watch, and do not remove the sentinel of discipline, allowing evil men in the midst of the church of Christ. Never allow them to obliterate the distinction between the church and the world, as Balaam tried to erase the line of demarcation between Israel and Moab. For the rest, in the midst of the world, where Satan has his throne and dwelling-place, the faithful must always uphold the honor of their King.

For he that overcometh shall be given to eat of the hidden manna, so that he shall be satisfied with the blessings of salvation in eternal life. He that overcometh shall be given a white stone, the stone of his justification and purification in the blood of the Lamb. He shall be given a new name, expressive of his new and eternal being, a name which he alone shall be able to know, a name that determines exactly his personal place in that blessed throng that shall once gather around the throne of God and the Lamb and reveal in all its fulness and splendor the image of our God.

Chapter VII

The Church With A Mystic Tendency

(Revelation 2:18-29)

18 And unto the angel of the church in Thyatira write; These things saith the Son of God, who hath his eyes like unto a flame of fire, and his feet are like fine brass;

19 I know thy works, and charity, and service, and faith, and thy patience, and thy works; and the last to be more than the first.

20 Notwithstanding I have a few things against thee, because thou sufferest that woman Jezebel, which calleth herself a prophetess, to teach and to seduce my servants to commit fornication, and to eat things sacrificed unto idols.

21 And I gave her space to repent of her fornication; and she repented not.

22 Behold, I will cast her into a bed, and them that commit adultery with her into great tribulation, except they repent of their deeds.

23 And I will kill her children with death; and all the churches shall know that I am he which searcheth the reins and hearts: and I will give unto every one of you according to your works.

24 But unto you I say, and unto the rest in Thyatira, as many as have not this doctrine, and which have not known the depths of Satan, as they speak; I will put upon you none other burden.

25 But that which ye have already hold fast till I come.

26 And he that overcometh, and keepeth my works unto the end, to him will I give power over the nations:

27 And he shall rule them with a rod of iron; as the vessels of a potter shall they be broken to shivers: even as I received of my Father.

28 And I will give him the morning star.

29 He that hath an ear, let him hear what the Spirit saith unto the churches.

The Church At Thyatira

Thyatira was a city in Asia Minor southeast from Pergamos, on the road to Sardis. It was known for the art of dyeing. And, as we know, Lydia, the seller of purple, was from that city, Acts 16:14. It was not a large city, like Pergamos; and it was not exactly a place where Satan would naturally establish his throne and where he dwelt. For that reason the church in Thyatira might enjoy a comparatively peaceful existence; and although the letter of the Lord to this church suggests that there also the believers had suffered for Christ's sake, yet this congregation did not have to suffer tribulation and persecution as did the churches of Smyrna and Pergamos.

For the rest, at first glance the letter addressed to the church in Thyatira would leave the impression that her condition was almost identically the same as that of Pergamos. The resemblance is indeed striking. Also the church in Thyatira was faithful to the Lord, as the text plainly indicates. Her weakness, or defect, seems to be that she suffered evil men, — in this case, an evil woman with her following, — in her midst. And hence, we would be inclined to draw the conclusion that also in Thyatira we are presented with the picture of a church weak in discipline. Still more, even the nature of the heresies which were being propagated in the two churches appears to be the same: for also in Thyatira the Nicolaitanes had their influence.

However, there must have been a difference between the two churches. For if in the seven churches of Asia Minor we correctly discerned a picture of the church in its totality from seven different aspects, it is plain that the church of Thyatira and the church of Pergamos each presents a different aspect of the church as a whole; and each adds its own peculiar detail to the picture of the church in its totality. This distinctive feature we try to express in the subject of this chapter, "The Church With A Mystic Tendency."

It is undoubtedly not superfluous, first of all, to ask and answer the question: what is meant by this phrase, "the church with a mystic tendency?"

By mysticism, in the sense in which the term is employed by us now, sometimes designated as "false mysticism," we denote a condition or tendency in the church of Christ characterized by ardent and abundant spiritual life, rather of the experiential or emotional type, but more or less severed from the objective criterion and test of the Word of God. Perhaps you will be able to gain some conception of this condition if we say that it represents the direct opposite of the condition of the church of Ephesus. The latter was strong in respect to whatever is purely objective: strong in doctrine and the knowledge of the truth; faithful, too, in works; and strict in discipline. But she was weak in regard to the life of the Spirit and had lost her first love. She was poor in warm, inward, devotional spiritual life. With a church of mystic inclination it is exactly the reverse. She is generally rich in spiritual devotion, abundant in that part of our spiritual life which cannot be explained and expressed in words, and often claims a direct intercourse with the Spirit. But she most frequently manifests an accompanying tendency to separate herself from the objective standard of the Word. She is usually poor in knowledge and, in general, in regard to things which can be grasped and analysed by the intellect.

Or, to prevent any possible misunderstanding, it is perhaps expedient to call your attention to three possible conditions in the church of Christ on earth.

In the first place, we may mention the correct, the healthy and normal, the most perfect condition of the church on earth, namely, that condition which is characterized by a correct and constant equilibrium of the subjective and objective. It is the condition of the church which is both strong in knowledge and maintenance of the truth, emphasizing the necessity of the Word properly, but which at the same time is not devoid of true, devotional, ardent spiritual life, and in which the latter is continually guided and tested by the former. Of course, in any form of true Christian religion there is a mystic element, resulting from our spiritual communion with Christ our head. And any true child of God will be able to speak of the fact that he experiences moments of sweet communion with the Savior that transcend all analysis and expression in human language. To speak in terms often employed by children of God, there are moments when they have "good times" with the Lord, moments in which we experience the mystical feeling of the bride who is near the bridegroom. Such moments are perfectly normal, and they should constitute an element of our life with God. There is no danger in such mystical communion, if only it is continually subjected to the objective test of the Word of God. And if such a condition is peculiar of an entire church, that church enjoys what may be called a state of healthy mysticism.

A second condition, however, also met with in the church of Christ on earth, is that which results when the value of pure doctrine and the function of the intellect in religion is over-rated and exclusively emphasized, while the inward life of the Spirit is forgotten. Then all the emphasis is placed exclusively on cold doctrine. The congregation never receives a taste of sweet mystical communion of the Spirit, and religion becomes cold and dead intellectualism, — a body without a soul. Such a condition is, of course, to be condemned; indeed, it is very dangerous!

But there is still another form that reveals itself from time to time in the history of the church as the dominant form, a form, in fact, which never vanishes out of sight entirely. That is the condition of what we call false mysticism. If dead orthodoxy over-rates the value of doctrine, false mysticism undervalues sound knowledge of the truth altogether. If the intellectual church does not sufficiently emphasize the life of the Spirit and mystical communion, the church which is mystically inclined places all the emphasis on the subjective experience of the soul. The mystical element is there, exists, in fact, in an abundant measure; and many in the church can testify of the "good times" they experience with the Savior. But this mystic life is from the start not guided by the objective testimony of the Word. Such a congregation makes the experience of its members the test and guide of all spiritual life. She is in danger of running wild with devotion. And if this mystical tendency continues and develops, she will attach significance to all kinds of feelings and sentiments, perhaps even to visions and dreams. And, finally, being cut loose from the Word of God, she becomes a fit object of Satan's seductive influence, exposed to any and every error of the kingdom of darkness.

There was, I think, a clear tendency towards this false and dangerous form of mysticism to be discovered in the church of Thyatira.

Commendable Features Of Thyatira

Let us notice, in the first place, that the Lord in His letter to the church of Thyatira first enumerates some of the most excellent qualities which a church may possibly possess. Writes He: "I know thy works, and charity, and service, and faith, and thy patience, and thy works; and the last to be more than the first." It is evident that the term "works" in the first part of this description must be taken in the general sense of the word, as referring not merely to external works of faith, but just as well to the internal, spiritual condition of the church, while this all-comprehensive term is further analysed and specified in the words "thy charity, and service, and faith, and thy patience." The meaning, therefore, is: I know thy works, namely, thy charity and service and faith and patience.

The church, according to this description, was in an enviable condition.

Notice, however, from the start, that love is mentioned first: not because love is first, for that is not the case. Love in the sense in which it evidently occurs in the text is not the root of our spiritual life, but faith is. It is by faith that we are grafted into Christ, by faith that we draw from Him the treasure of our salvation, by faith that we grow in the knowledge and grace of our Lord. Not love is the root of faith, but faith is the root also of love. And the latter flourishes and blooms only on the root of faith. But in this letter love is mentioned first because it was the most apparent, the most eminent, the most prominent quality of the church in Thyatira. It was a congregation overflowing with real, warm, spiritual love of the Lord: exactly the opposite of the church in Ephesus. In Ephesus love was wanting to a large extent; in Thyatira it is abundant. In Ephesus, I think, one could be found only with difficulty who would consciously speak of the love of Jesus; here in Thyatira almost every member would be able to give a testimony in a prayer meeting. There, in Ephesus, the hearts were cold; here, in Thyatira, they were glowing with ardent love.

Surely, there was also faith. For how otherwise could love exist? But faith is mentioned in the second place. The congregation was characterized not so much by the firm strength of conscious faith as by the attractive warmth of true and ardent love. This also became manifest in their actual life. It was again love revealing itself in works which appeared on the foreground. For in the text their ministry, or service, is mentioned first of all. This term "ministry" may be taken in a general sense, as applied to all kinds of service in the kingdom. All the members in Thyatira exerted themselves to do something for the kingdom of God. I imagine that if anyone was taken sick in the church, the angel would have to be on the alert if he desired to be the first one who called on that sick person. If anyone was in suffering or want, the church was sure to know it; and all would help to alleviate the suffering or to provide in case of need. The ladies of the church perhaps often came together in the afternoon, not to gossip or to expose the sins and weaknesses of the brethren and sisters, but to work for the relief of the poor, — if not in their own church, then for the benefit of the poor in other parts of the church. All this they performed from the motive of love, not in order to be seen by men and to receive the praise of the world: for also they were subject to reproach and malevolent slander. But with patience they bore and labored and ministered in the kingdom of God. Nor were they in a condition of gradual degeneration. On the contrary, the congregation was spiritually growing, increasing in their love and faith and service and patience. For the Lord testifies of them that their last works were more than the first. Indeed, a beautiful picture this aspect of the congregation presents to our view. It is, perhaps, not a picture which necessarily impresses one by its strength of features or staunchness of expression, but one which is attractive because of its sweetness, which appeals because of its beauty.

Reproved For Tolerating Jezebel

But there is another side to this picture, a side which is as horrible and repulsive as the former was beautiful and attractive. The Lord turns this side to our view when He continues in His letter: "Notwithstanding I have a few things against thee, because thou sufferest that woman Jezebel, which calleth herself a prophetess, to teach and to seduce my servants to commit fornication, and to eat things sacrificed to idols."

These words reveal the existence in the church of Thyatira of a most horrible heresy which had already obtained a foothold and which was evidently gaining ground. There is no reason to conceive of this fornication and eating of things sacrificed to idols in any other than in the literal sense of the word, especially since it is a well-known fact that immoral practices, sometimes adultery of the worst sort, were intimately connected with idolatry in those times, especially in connection with the sacrificial feasts. Hence, in this congregation, so filled with love and so busy in the ministry of the kingdom, presenting such an attractive and sweet picture, we meet with one of the worst forms of degeneration conceivable in the church of Christ. The impression is, in fact, that at this time there were already a comparatively large number who lived in open adultery and who participated in the heathen sacrificial feasts. And, what is far worse, this departure from the way of sanctification was evidently defended by an appeal to principle. Clearly, in the church of Thyatira we meet once more with the Nicolaitanes, people who boasted in wanton profanity that it mattered not at all how the Christian lived here upon earth, Christians who sinned that grace might abound the more. The old Adam was doomed to destruction anyway; and Christ had fulfilled the law. The argument that was adduced to defend such a life in sin was, as we shall see presently, that a descent into the very depths of Satan caused the child of God to appreciate the glory of Christ's gracious deliverance all the more. But in reality the protagonists of this view made of their so-called Christian liberty a pretext for the flesh. And therefore, there is no question about it:

the church of Thyatira, viewed from this angle, offered as horrible an aspect as the first view was sweet and attractive.

You remark, perhaps, that this recalls to our mind exactly the condition of the church in Pergamos. There also these evil Nicolaitanes were found. And there, as here, they were allowed to exert their evil influence upon the church without being disciplined. And in so far you are correct. But there was nevertheless an important difference between the two congregations with respect to the reason why these dangerous heretics were allowed in the church and were tolerated. In Pergamos it is a case of mere laxity in discipline. We are simply told that the Nicolaitanes existed in that church and that they had not been disturbed before the Lord addressed His letter to them. That they were allowed to teach and to seduce others we do not read. But this is entirely different in the church of Thyatira. Notice, in the first place, that in Thyatira the propagator who disseminated the seed of this horrible heresy was a woman, Jezebel. There is no reason to allegorize and make this woman a fictitious character, symbolizing something entirely different, though the name calls to our mind one of the most despicable female characters of the Old Testament. No, there was a real woman in the church of Thyatira. And we receive the impression that she was allowed to teach her contemptible doctrine regardless of the fact that the woman was not allowed to teach in the church, but was enjoined to be silent. Regardless of the further fact that this particular woman taught a most horrible doctrine, seduced many of the servants of God from the path of righteousness, this Jezebel was nevertheless allowed to teach. If we add to this the fact that her teaching is characterized as a sort of mystic gnosticism by the words which evidently designate the slogan of her and of all who followed after her, "who know the deep things of Satan," I can suggest but one possible explanation of this toleration on the part of the Thyatiran church: she was mystically inclined and was in danger of severing her beautiful spiritual life from the infallible Word of God.

If I may be allowed to cast a modern hue over the ancient church, and to present to you in a concrete picture my conception of the congregation in Thyatira, I would offer the following. It is Wednesday evening. The church holds a midweek prayer meeting. Let us attend one of these. The angel of the church opens with a fervent prayer and offers a few words of introduction glowing with the love of his heart toward the Lord Jesus. He speaks of it, how in the past few days he realized his sinful condition, but also how clearly he had experienced the all-sufficiency of the grace of Jesus Christ. Speaking evidently with all his heart in it and with tears of gratitude glistening in his eyes, he praises the Lord for the abundance of His grace. After him an old man arises who also testifies in the same manner. Of years ago he speaks, when first he became acquainted with the gospel of redemption. And he emphasizes that this gospel has been sweet unto his soul, a power of love ever since. A third, and a fourth, and a fifth give their testimonies; and all witness of their personal participation in the grace of Christ Jesus and of their love to Him. But finally a strange figure attracts our attention. It is a woman of a weird and repulsive appearance. Her large, protruding eyes, sensuous lips, and morbid complexion witness of a life of sin and dissipation. She also speaks. And with a voice which sounds as if it comes from the nether world, she tells the congregation of a vision which she had in a by-gone night, and how the Lord appeared to her to reveal His truth in a dream. For she claims to be a prophetess. In her dream, so she continues, the Lord showed unto her the horrible depths of Satan, the abyss of sin and iniquity. And as they both stood on the brink of that dark and horrible abyss, the Lord said unto her: "If anyone would truly taste my grace and infinite mercy, he must actually descend into these depths, and learn to know them by experience. For the more he is able to realize the depths of Satan by actual experience, the more he will be in a condition to appreciate my salvation." She still continues to explain that she has personally obeyed, that she did descend into those depths of Satan. She committed fornication. She feasted with the heathen in their sacrificial meals. She subjected her body to the vilest service of sin. And she concludes by testifying that to her there was a great blessing in this descent into the abyss of sin. For the more clearly she realized the awful depths from which the grace of Christ redeemed and delivered her, the more fully could she gratefully appreciate the wonders of His mercy. Thus this instrument of the devil speaks in the midst of the congregation.

But what now does the congregation do? Does she cast this vile woman out, admonishing her to repent of her horrible sin? On the contrary, she listens. She is silent. She admits the possibility that this woman is actually a prophetess, though her speech directly contradicts the objective revelation of the Word of God. And many even follow her, and in harmony with her teaching they descend into the depths of Satan. Many servants of the Lord are seduced by her teaching.

How must this be explained? How is it possible that this ardent little congregation of Thyatira listens patiently to the dark testimony of this instrument of hell? In but one way: this sweet and lovable little church had gradually forgotten to apply the objective standard of God's revelation and had allowed personal experience to be the chief criterion of the truth. If they had at all made an attempt to apply the test of the Word of God to the speech and life of this woman Jezebel, they would have detected her heresy immediately and would have cast her out if she did not repent. But they are inclined to false mysticism. And Satan, aware of this tendency in the congregation, employs a woman, who largely lives by intuition, is more easily inclined to drift away on subjective feeling and experience, and is of a stronger and more ardent emotional nature than man, to appeal to the mystic tendency in the church of Thyatira, in order to seduce her from the truth. For the same reason Scripture calls this woman Jezebel, which may be considered a symbolic name, to remind the church of her real nature. For even as Jezebel seduced the people of God of the old dispensation to the service of Baal, so does this woman lead the people of Thyatira astray in paths of fornication and vilest sin.

In short, we discover in the congregation of Thyatira a church with a tendency to false mysticism, a church which is strong in warm devotional life, but which has enthroned personal experience as the criterion for the truth.

Frequently this aspect of the church has become prominent in history. In the Middle Ages, when the death-chill of scholasticism and Roman Catholicism began to cause a reaction, this mystic tendency became manifest before long. At the time of the Reformation there was also a mystic strain mingled with the otherwise healthy movement of Protestantism. After exclusive stress had been laid on dead orthodoxy in the eighteenth century the same inclination became manifest. And every time, when the church has passed through a period of intellectualism, the right of the more emotional and mystic element of our religion to assert itself is maintained, and by reaction the church swings to the opposite extreme of false mysticism. Moreover, just as often this mystic strain became the occasion for the flesh and ended in sin and dissipation, simply because of its licentious separation from the objective testimony of the Word of God.

The church, therefore, should be on her guard against both extremes. She should watch against the danger of cold intellectualism, but at the same time refuse to enthrone subjective experience as supreme lord. Our personal experience must be subjected constantly to the test of the Word of God. And if anyone would experience anything not in harmony with that objective revelation, he should draw the conclusion that it is of the Evil One. And again, if on the basis of his experience any member would spread a doctrine not in harmony with the Scriptures, he should be corrected; and, if he will not repent, he should be excommunicated without improper delay.

The Lord's Judgment On Jezebel

It is only if we bear in mind this peculiar condition of the church in Thyatira that we will also be able to discern the reason for the particular message which is sent unto her through John. Notice that the customary admonition to repent is lacking in this message. The Lord does not enjoin on the church to discipline the wicked Jezebel and her followers and to excommunicate them if they do not repent. They would not be in a condition to obey this command. Discipline can only be exercised on the basis of the objective Word of God; and in regard to the knowledge and application of this Word the church of Thyatira was weak. They were not able to distinguish the true from the false. They lacked the power to discern and test the spirits. And for that reason the Lord Himself will mark the evil-doers in the congregation and clearly point them out as the objects of His sore displeasure. In person He will exercise discipline Himself.

He announced Himself in such terms as are suitable to reveal Himself as the One Who is able to search the hearts. He is the Son of God. And especially in connection with what follows, it is plain that this appellation must serve to bring Him before the consciousness of the congregation as the Omniscient One, before Whose eyes nothing is concealed. For He continues to announce Himself as the One Who has eyes like a flame of fire, Who possesses power to penetrate into the innermost parts of man and scrutinize the deepest depths of a man's heart. This woman Jezebel and her followers might hide a horrible nature of sin behind a mask of piety and devotion. To Him that mask does not conceal a thing. He is able to expose to view all the darkness of sin that is hidden behind this mask of godliness. Still more: not only does He possess the power to penetrate and to know the hearts of Jezebel and her followers, but He is also able to execute terrible judgment. For His feet are like unto burnished brass. If His eyes detect iniquity, with those feet He is able to tread down the enemy and consume him. In short, the Lord announces Himself to the congregation as the omniscient and omnipotent Judge of the evil-doers in His church.

In harmony with this Self-manifestation of the Lord is the message which He delivers to the congregation. He not only appears as Judge, but He will act as such in the midst of the church. By His own judgments He intends to expose the evil-doers. "Behold," thus He speaks, "I will cast her into a bed." Behold! The Lord wants to draw the attention of the church. For it is primarily for her sake that He will come with His judgments upon the wicked. They themselves were not able to exercise proper discipline, and they allowed the wicked Jezebel to teach and to seduce the church. They were not in a condition to discern the spirits and lacked the courage to assert that Jezebel was not a prophetess of the Lord, but an instrument of Satan. Now the Lord will plainly expose her and reveal that she is nothing but an agent of the devil to seduce the congregation of Jesus Christ. But then the church must pay attention. Hence, "Behold, I will cast her into a bed." The judgment of Christ will strike the woman, first of all. Her case is hopeless. She has descended into the depths of Satan voluntarily and consciously so often that she will come to repentance no more. And therefore, the measure of her iniquity is full, and the time for judgment is come. That the Lord will cast her into a bed must, of course, not be understood as if He would cause her to be an instrument of adultery still more. He will not cast her into the bed of prostitution. This she had been doing herself. But it is most natural to assume that the Lord would send unto her those horrible and repulsive diseases which are inevitably the result of a life of dissipation and prostitution. For in this way the Lord would reveal by His judgment most plainly that all impurity is despised by Him and that it is not His will that we descend into the depths of Satan that grace may abound.

But also upon her children the sin of the mother would be visited. Perhaps she had many children. Perhaps they were all children of adultery. However this may be, the sin of their mother will become manifest also in them. Not as if the children were considered guilty of the sins of their mother; but, in the first place, to reveal the effects of her sin also in her children, and, in the second place, to add to the severity of her own judgment. And for the children it may have been a blessing that they were killed with death.

Finally, also those who have been seduced by her and who will follow in her steps, who commit adultery with her, are mentioned in this message.

For them the time of repentance is not past; and therefore their judgment is presented as conditional upon their attitude to this message. If they do not repent, the Lord will send unto them great affliction. If they continue to follow in Jezebel's steps even though they behold how the Lord despises her works, the Lord will also visit them. And no doubt also their affliction will stand in close connection with the nature of their sin.

The purpose of these judgments is that the churches may know that the Lord is He Who searcheth the reins and hearts, and that He will give to each one according to his works. Again, this avowed purpose is clearly in full harmony with the condition of the church in Thyatira. She could not test the spirits and distinguish the true from the false and exercise discipline wherever necessary. The Lord, Who searches the hearts, would do it for them. Again, the church of Thyatira allowed a doctrine of licentiousness to be taught in her midst, a doctrine which boldly advocated a life of sin, a descent into the dark depths of Satan, in order that grace might be more abundant. Jesus will appear as the rewarder of each one according to his works, and thus expose the devilish nature of such a heresy. The church of Thyatira shall see the works of the Lord, and at the same time become a warning example to the churches round about, in as far as they also were endangered by the heresy of the Nicolaitanes.

And not only is the church of Thyatira a warning example to the churches of that time, but to those of all ages as well. The devil even in the present day goeth about like a roaring lion; and his object is always again to sever the church from the basis of the Word of God, and thus to set her adrift on the seductive current of human imagination. The church of Thyatira, therefore, may also be our warning example. For the Lord searches the reins and the hearts, and He will finish a just work upon the earth!

Exhortation And Promise

However, also the message to the church of Thyatira does not conclude with threats of judgment, but closes with most glorious promises to them that are faithful and overcome in the battle. In the first place, the Lord tenderly comforts them, and at the same time warns them against the danger of falling into an opposite extreme, when He says: "But unto you I say, and unto the rest in Thyatira, as many as have not this doctrine, and which have not known the depths of Satan, as they speak; I will put upon you none other burden." These last words are referred by some to a

burden of judgment. The meaning then would be that the Lord would
indeed visit the congregation with His judgments by afflicting and
punishing the evil-doers, but that outside of the culprits He would not
afflict any other in the church. But this view appears less than probable.
More natural, it would seem to be, that these words refer to a burden of
law and precepts. As the undefiled would witness the judgments upon the
wicked Jezebel and her following because of their fornication, they might
be inclined to the opposite extreme and imagine that the complete
fulfillment of the law was still incumbent upon them and necessary for
their salvation. From antinomism they might swing to phariseeism and
nomism. And against this the Lord warns them by saying that He will put
upon them none other burden.

The latter interpretation would seem the more probable because there
is an unmistakable reference in these words to the passage of Acts 15:28,
29. We remember that the question of circumcision and of the entire
Mosaic law had been a burning one in the early churches, and that it had
been discussed and settled by the "Synod" of Jerusalem in approximately
50 A.D. And the well-known decision for that important gathering had
been: "For it seemed good to the Holy Ghost, and to us, to lay upon you
no greater burden than these necessary things; That ye abstain from meats
offered to idols, and from blood, and from things strangled, and from
fornication: from which if ye keep yourselves, ye shall do well." This,
then, was the burden that had been laid upon them heretofore. And if
they only had adhered to these precepts, they would undoubtedly have
kept themselves undefiled from the vile sins of Jezebel and her wicked
brood. But now the danger was more than imaginary that the faithful, at
the sight of the judgments inflicted upon the wicked woman in their
midst, would turn to the other extreme; and, not intimately acquainted
with the doctrine of the church, they would timidly subject themselves
once more to the bondage of fear. This must be prevented. Hence, the
Lord comes with the definite message: "I will lay upon you none other
burden. Just keep what you have till I come."

To these faithful, then, to those who keep what they have and are pure
from the defilement of Jezebel's teaching, the Lord comes with a most
beautiful promise. Says He: "And he that overcometh, and keepeth my
works unto the end, to him will I give power over the nations: And he
shall rule them with a rod of iron; as the vessels of a potter shall they be
broken to shivers: even as I received of my Father."

To see in these words anything but a promise of final victory in the day of our Lord Jesus Christ is to do violence to the plain words of Scripture. Plainly Jesus promises in this passage that He will give to the faithful the same power He has received from His Father. In the day of His coming they shall share in His power and glory of victory. Evidently the reference is to Psalm 2. There we are presented, first of all, with a picture of the powers and the might of the world raging and striving to obtain the world dominion which properly belongs to the kingdom of God's Anointed. This dominion the Father gave to His Son. He has been anointed King over God's holy hill, over Zion. And when that Son declares the decree of Jehovah, He says: "The Lord hath said unto me, Thou art my Son, this day have I begotten thee. Ask of me, and I will give thee the heathen for thine inheritance, and the uttermost parts of the earth for thy possession. Thou shalt break them with a rod of iron; thou shalt dash them in pieces like a potter's vessel." Evidently the dominant thought is that the powers of the world strive to break the dominion of Christ and rebel against the Most High, but that the Son shall have the ultimate victory in the day of His coming and shall execute vengeance upon all His enemies. This is the power which He has received of His Father. And in this power the faithful of the church of Thyatira shall share, according to this glorious promise. In a later connection we shall have occasion to explain this promise more definitely. Now it must suffice that we state as our conviction that this promise is to be literally fulfilled. Literally the enemies rage against the kingdom and dominion of the Son. Literally the Christ shall come to break the power of His enemies. But these enemies which rise against the kingdom of God also oppose the subjects of that kingdom while they are still on earth. They reproach and slander them. They persecute them and cause them to suffer for the sake of Christ. But even as they share in His reproach, so shall they also participate in the glory of His victory in the day when He shall have the final victory over all His enemies. They shall come with Him. With Him they shall judge the nations. And with Him they shall enter into His dominion when the nations are broken to shivers like a potter's vessel and when all the power of opposition shall have an end.

In the second place, the Lord gives to the faithful the beautiful and suggestive promise of the morning star. Mention of the fact that the righteous shall shine with radiant glory, as the bodies in the firmament, is not foreign to Scripture. In Daniel 12:4 we read: "And they that be wise shall shine as the brightness of the firmament, and they that turn many to righteousness as the stars for ever and ever." And in Matthew 13:43 the Lord says: "Then shall the righteous shine forth as the sun in the kingdom of their Father." All the righteous, therefore, shall shine. That is the glory of their perfected new being in Christ. Cleansed and purified in the blood of the Lamb, they shall forevermore reveal themselves in eternal luster and resplendent glory. To that eternal glory also the symbol of our text refers. But evidently there is this difference, that the morning star shines with greater splendor, is more obvious in brightness, than the other stars in the firmament. It is a star of special luster and glory. Thus also they who keep themselves pure in the midst of great temptation, who remain faithful in times of special stress and danger, shall shine forth with distinguished glory in the eternal kingdom of God. Even as the morning star shines with special glory in the firmament of heaven, so shall they that have kept themselves pure from the defilement of Jezebel, and who in the midst of great temptations have been faithful unto the end reveal themselves in the eternal kingdom with distinct glory and splendor.

He that hath an ear, let him hear what the Spirit saith unto the churches!

What doth the Spirit say?

Do not drift away on subjective experience, ignoring the objective principle of the Word of God. Cling to the Word. For only that Word is our safe guide and firm basis in the midst of strong currents of human theories. And if false prophets arise, who would lead you astray with their own imaginations, test the spirits, and reject them without hesitation. This false doctrine may sometimes appear under a very beautiful mask. In Thyatira it was a mask of super-piety. In our day it is the mask of service to humanity. Surely, service is good if it is service not merely of man, but, above all, service of God. Service is good if it is based not upon the vain theories of human philosophy, but on the eternal principle of the Word of God. Cling, then, to that Word. Keep yourselves pure from the wicked Jezebel.

For the faithful to the end shall receive the same power as Christ has received of His Father!

And they shall shine as the morning star in the kingdom of heaven!

Chapter VIII

The Church About To Die

(Revelation 3:1-6)

1 And unto the angel of the church in Sardis write; These things saith he that hath the seven Spirits of God, and the seven stars; I know thy works, that thou hast a name that thou livest, and art dead.

2 Be watchful, and strengthen the things which remain, that are ready to die; for I have not found thy works perfect before God.

3 Remember therefore how thou hast received and heard, and hold fast, and repent. If therefore thou shalt not watch, I will come on thee as a thief, and thou shalt not know what hour I will come upon thee.

4 Thou hast a few names even in Sardis which have not defiled their garments; and they shall walk with me in white: for they are worthy.

5 He that overcometh, the same shall be clothed in white raiment; and I will not blot out his name out of the book of life, but I will confess his name before my Father, and before his angels.

6 He that hath an ear, let him hear what the Spirit saith unto the churches.

An Increasingly Dark Picture

On the whole, the picture of the church of Christ in the world which we have been studying thus far in connection with the seven letters addressed by the Lord to the seven churches in Asia Minor is not a very bright one. There is, indeed, some light; there is a bright side to the picture. But there is also a good deal of darkness; in fact, we receive the impression that there is more darkness than light.

Ephesus was, indeed, a beautiful church from every outward aspect. She was strong in the knowledge of the truth, faithful in discipline, abounding in works. Yet there was at the same time a very fundamental defect in the congregation. It was a defect which was bound to bring her to destruction as a church of Jesus Christ: she lost her first love. Smyrna, the second church addressed by the Lord, presented us with a picture of the church as perfect as we may ever expect to meet her in this world: she receives no rebuke from the Lord. She was spiritually rich. Her dark side consisted in this, that she was the church in tribulation: she was poor and held in disrepute by the world about her. Pergamos, evidently, had been a very faithful church in the past; but now she was weakening and had become lax in discipline, as was evident from the fact that she allowed the evil Nicolaitanes to exist in her midst. Thyatira, so we found, was a beautiful little church, warm in spiritual life, ardent in respect to the works of faith. But her weakness was that she was strongly characterized by a tendency to false mysticism, so that she even permitted wicked Jezebel to teach in the church and to seduce its members from the truth as it is in Christ Jesus our Lord.

We may say indeed, therefore, that there is a good deal of light in the picture of the church as we have studied her thus far, but also much darkness. And one who expects the church to be perfect in the world may well learn a lesson from the seven-fold picture of the church which we find in the Book of Revelation.

We must still call attention to three more of the churches in Asia Minor to whom the Lord addressed letters. Nor does the picture of the church in the world become brighter in these three last letters. If we would expect, perhaps, that the Lord so arranged the order of these letters to the seven churches that the picture gradually becomes brighter, we will certainly meet with disappointment. The two most miserable representations of the church in the world are still to be considered. First comes the church in Sardis, a most wretched representation and manifestation of the church in the world. For a moment we may find some comfort and joy in the letter of the Lord to the church in Philadelphia, a church small and of little strength from the viewpoint of the world, but true and faithful and abounding in spiritual strength. But then the series closes with the most miserable picture of the church in Laodicea, a church which was rich in her own estimation, but devoid of every manifestation of spiritual riches.

Also in this order and arrangement of the seven letters, which is, of course, intentional, we see the purpose of the Lord to warn His church in the world not to expect great things in this world as the end of this present age approaches. It is true, as we have remarked before, that in these seven letters to the seven churches of Asia Minor we do not and may not discern seven successive periods in the history of the church in the world, as some would have it. Nevertheless, there is reason for this arrangement in which the series closes with the most miserable picture of the church in the world. Nor can this reason be found only in the geographical situation of the seven churches. On the contrary, although it is true that the order of the seven letters follows the geographical location of the seven churches, yet the order of these letters is intentionally such that, with two exceptions, the trend of development of the church in the world is downward. It steadily points to the false church as represented by the church in Laodicea.

A Dead Minister And A Dead Church

Sardis was a city located in a rich plain, mostly south of Thyatira and east from Ephesus. The city was noted for its wealth. This may have had something to do with the condition of the church there. The general description of the church is contained in these words: "Thou hast a name that thou livest, and art dead." And we receive the impression that these words, as well as the entire letter, are addressed, indeed, to the entire church in Sardis, though they refer, first of all, to its angel, or minister.

To the pastor of this flock, therefore, must be applied that he had a name that he lived, and was dead.

Commentators have surmised that this angel of the church in Sardis had a proper name which signified "life" or "living." But there is no need of such an ingenious invention. Rather do we understand the Savior's words as meaning that he had a reputation that he was living, but that he did not live up to this reputation. Nor do we have to read these words as if they suggested that this particular minister was especially famous as a preacher and as an active pastor: for the facts would seem to contradict this. It is quite sufficient to remember that this man not only had the name that he was a Christian, but also that of a minister of the Word of God. As such, he naturally had a name that he was living, full of the new life in Christ, manifested in ardent zeal and devotion to the Lord, diligent in his calling, abounding in good works. If anyone is expected to be living and to reveal his life in diligent service, in constantly seeking the kingdom of God, in walking in holiness, and in thus being an example unto the flock, it is the minister. And there is nothing more disgusting than the sight of a dead minister! O, indeed, we may well remind ourselves that also the pastor is but a sinful man and that it cannot be expected of him any more than of the members of his church that his walk and conversation are perfect and without sin. Fact is, nevertheless, that he is a minister of the Word of God, that as such he has an holy calling, the most exalted there is in this world, and that therefore he has a name that he lives. A living minister is zealous in his work, devotes himself wholeheartedly and with all his power to the study of the Scriptures, the preaching of the Word, the instruction of young and old in the truth, to his pastoral work, to meditation and prayer. And he is doubly careful to be an example to the flock and to adorn his work of the ministry by a walk in all good works.

But in all these respects the minister of the church in Sardis was dead.

The meaning is not that he was personally devoid of the life of the new birth, but that his life and walk as a minister of the Word of God was characterized by lack of consecration. He was a dead **preacher**. He did not give himself to the study of the Scriptures and to prayer. His word was not a living testimony. He was unfaithful as a pastor. He failed to watch over the flock, to bring consolation to them that mourned, to admonish the wayward, to comfort the sick and afflicted, to instruct the young in the fear of the Lord. Where there should have been fervor, there was apathy. Instead of zeal in the work of the Lord, there was a manifestation of cold indifferentism. Instead of diligence, there was indolence. His work was a burden to him. And you may depend on it: he loved the things of the flesh,—leisure, worldly comfort and pleasure, the luxuries for which the city of Sardis was noted.

But enough of this dead preacher. The church was just like him. For although the angel of the church is addressed in the first place, the church is rebuked at the same time.

Also the church has a name that she lives. Is she not the body of Christ? Does not Christ her head live in her? And her life becomes manifest in her confession and walk as a life of faith and hope, of confidence and love, of holiness and righteousness. She fights the battle of faith and keeps her garments clean in the midst of an ungodly world. She lets her light shine, that men may see her good works and glorify her Father which is in heaven. But the church in Sardis was dead. It is true that there were a few who had not defiled their garments; but of the majority this could not be said. The flesh dominated in the church of Sardis. The Lord accuses her that her works were not perfect before God. This does not mean that her works were defiled with sin: for this is always the case, even with the very best of our works. But the church as such, and believers individually, failed to walk in those works which were required of them. There was no interest in Sardis in the things of the kingdom of God, no searching of the Scriptures, no daily prayer, no confession of the name of Christ, no testimony for the truth, no zeal in proclaiming the gospel, no instruction of the youth, no battle of faith, no patience and suffering for Christ's sake, no manifestation of sorrow after God, of true repentance, of the love of God and of the brethren. Instead, there was a seeking of the things of this world, friendship with the world, a striving after the treasures and pleasures of Sardis. The church, exactly because she was church, had a name that she lived; but she was dead!

The church of Sardis presents, indeed, a most miserable picture!

A dead minister, and a dead church!

Let us inquire a little more into this situation. The Lord says that the minister, and the church too, have a name that they live, but in reality are dead.

We understand that this is not to be interpreted in the strict and absolute sense of the word, either of the minister or of the congregation. In respect to the minister, it undoubtedly refers to him only as the angel of the church, in his capacity as officebearer. It does not mean that there was no life in him as a personal saint: for then the Lord, it seems to us, would not have admonished him as He does in this letter. He still comes to him, in the first place, with the admonition to wake up out of his indolent slumbers and to repent. In the second place, he admonishes him to strengthen and to establish that which is about to die. Hence, the statement that he is dead can hardly refer to him personally. He may very well have had the principle of the new life in his heart. But although he may have been a regenerated child of God, as we rather suppose he was, nevertheless that life appeared to be dead, did not come to manifestation in his life, especially in his life and labors as a minister and shepherd of the flock of Jesus Christ. Just as you sometimes meet with persons in the natural sense of the word of whom you say that they are dead because they seem to have no ambition and reveal no interest in anything, so it was in the spiritual sense with the angel of the church in Sardis. In his entire manifestation as minister of the Word he acted as if there were no life in him. No spark of life flashed from him to the congregation.

In all he did as minister and pastor of the church in Sardis he appeared to be dead. Dead was his preaching; dead was his catechetical instruction; dead was he in his pastoral work. During the week he had no ambition to study the Word of God from which he must feed the flock on the Sabbath.

He would sit with his wife or with his friends and idle away his time. The result was that when he came to his pulpit on Sunday, he really had no message for the flock which was congregated. There was no content to his brief sermon, and even what he said was without the fire of the conviction of faith. When he finished his sermon and said "Amen," it was with a sigh of relief: he was glad that it was over again. In catechism it was the same story. He would quickly have his pupils recite their lessons and dismiss them as soon as possible. In Sardis they had finally only one service on Sunday, and the sermon lasted just long enough for the congregation to fall fast asleep. In his pastoral work the angel of the church in Sardis was most negligent of all. He hated to go out and visit the flock. Family visitation was never done by him. Sick visiting he did very rarely; and when he did visit the sick, he knew not what to say to them: the word of life and comfort he could not find. In a word, in the entire manifestation of his life and work the angel of the church in Sardis was dead. He shamefully neglected his calling.

Such was the angel of the church in Sardis: he had a name that he was living, but was dead.

Such was their spiritual leader, who had to feed them with the bread of life, who was supposed to be their example, admonish them to be awake, strengthen them in their faith, be their captain in the battle of faith, and lead them on to victory!

Do you wonder that the whole congregation was virtually dead? This was evidently the case. The Lord comes to them with the admonition, "Be watchful!" It is true that these words are first of all addressed, undoubtedly, to the minister of the flock; but they are also intended for the whole congregation. The church in Sardis was fallen into a deep spiritual slumber. There was but little activity in the church, little manifestation of spiritual life. They were not concerned about doctrine and the truth of the Word of God. They were too far gone to be interested in maintaining the truth. In the church as a whole there was very little expression of spiritual life. The service on Sunday was poorly attended, and those who did attend revealed in their whole attitude that they were not interested. The whole congregation was about to die. Their general condition is expressed in the words, "Thou art dead." If you would peruse the congregational record, you would discover that there were a number on the membership list whom no one knew any more. No one, either in the congregation or in the consistory, would be able to give you any information about them. Another number you would find who never attended the church service. There were also some who still showed some signs of life, but who were already fast falling asleep. True, there were also the faithful in Sardis; but of them we must speak presently. On the whole, the congregation was about to die. Hence, the Lord comes to them with the admonition: "Be watchful, wake up! And strengthen that which is about to die!"

And how about their works?

Was it, perhaps, thus in the church of Sardis, that they were not doctrinally but practically inclined?

Also this was not the case, as we have already remarked. Nor was this to be expected of a church which was about to die. The very contrary is true. For the Lord adds in His admonition that He had not found their works perfect, or full, before God. No, this does not mean that the church in Sardis had not as yet attained to the state of perfection in regard to their works. In this respect all the churches would have to confess that their works were not full before God. Believers in this present time have but a small beginning of the new obedience, and their works are never perfect. No, but, in the first place, this implies that some works which the church in the world is always called to perform were entirely neglected. The church did not let her testimony go forth in the midst of the world: it was no shining light in the midst of the darkness of this present world at all. The world hardly knew that there was a church of Jesus Christ in Sardis. Her influence was not felt. Besides, even in her own midst her works were not full. Works like that of taking care of the poor and indigent, the work of mercy, the work of instructing the children in and according to the Word of God,—these were almost, or even entirely, neglected. And what the church in Sardis still did was done so half-heartedly that there was no manifestation of life in it.

But there was still more. If we consider that the Lord praises the few faithful in the congregation of Sardis because they had not defiled their garments, we may certainly draw the conclusion that the other members had defiled them and that they lived in open sin in the midst of the world. How could it be different? A church which was about to die, most of whose members were already dead, a church which cared no longer for the truth of the gospel and which did not perform the works a church is called to perform, was but naturally inclined to seek the things of the world and to live in sin. They enjoyed the pleasures of the world. In their actual walk they could not be distinguished from the world. And those of the flock who did walk after the precepts of the gospel they despised and considered narrow-minded. Hence, it certainly was not true that with a view to their practical life and walk they appeared to be alive. On the contrary, they were dead in the entire manifestation of their life.

Admonition And Threat Of Judgment

A most miserable church indeed is that of Sardis! A church about to die! A dead minister and a dead congregation: a minister and a church which have a name that they live, but they are dead! Most of the members had already fallen sound asleep; the rest were about to die. Conformed, they were, in their life and walk, to the world in the midst of which they lived. For this the responsibility rested, in the first place, on the angel of the church, but not in such a way that the congregation was without guilt. And therefore it is also to the church as a whole that the admonition is addressed: "Remember therefore how thou hast received and heard, and hold fast, and repent. If therefore thou shalt not watch, I will come on thee as a thief, and thou shalt not know what hour I will come upon thee."

We may see, therefore, that although the condition of the church in Sardis is as miserable as we have described her, nevertheless it is not yet hopeless. The congregation as such may still be changed and repent. For, in the first place, there are in the midst of the congregation a few faithful who have not defiled their garments; and, secondly, there are also those who are not devoid of spiritual life, though it is far from bright and flourishing and though they are fast asleep. And therefore the Lord comes to them with this admonition to repent.

We may notice there is a similarity between this admonition and the one which is addressed to the church of Ephesus. The latter the Lord admonished in the words, "Remember therefore whence thou art fallen." To the church in Sardis the Lord writes, "Remember therefore how thou hast received and heard." In principle there was, no doubt, a good deal of similarity between the two churches. The one had lost her first love; the other had a name that she lived, but was dead. The latter might be considered a further development of the former: for the church which has lost its first love is about to die. This is the reason also for the striking similarity in the admonitions to the two churches. Both must remember something which they had possessed in the past and had now lost. The

memory of their former estate may appeal to them in as far as they are
still alive, and may be an inducement to repent.

Sardis must recall how they had received and heard in the beginning.
The reference is, of course, to the gospel and all that is contained in the
gospel of Jesus Christ. The congregation must recall how, that is, in what
manner, they had received and heard that gospel when it first had been
proclaimed unto them. What a profound joy it had wrought in their
hearts! What ardent and true spiritual enthusiasm it had caused in their
inmost soul! How they had received it with joy and had witnessed to all
about them of the grace of God and of the glorious salvation there is in
Christ! How, through the power of that gospel, they had fought the good
fight and had walked in a new and holy life! That former state they must
now recall. They have fallen from it. They can experience it only in their
memory. If there is still a spark of life in them, even though they are fallen
into a deep slumber, the recollection of their former state will appeal to
their inmost heart. Remembering that former state, they will see how
deeply they have fallen; and, through the power of the Word of the Lord,
they will wake up, repent, and return to their former state. Sardis must
have a revival: not, indeed, a revival which must be repeated every few
months, but a true spiritual revival, a revival of abiding value. They must
remember how they have received and heard the gospel, and must repent
in true sorrow of heart and mind.

But although there still seems to be hope for the church in Sardis, the
future does not look very bright. Hence, the Lord immediately follows up
this admonition to remember and to repent by a threat of His coming for
judgment: "If therefore thou shalt not watch, I will come on thee as a
thief, and thou shalt not know what hour I will come upon thee."

These words have been explained as referring to the sudden coming of
the Lord for judgment. All of a sudden, according to this interpretation,
when it is too late, the Lord will come upon the congregation, and they
shall realize that the Lord has visited them as Judge while they were still
sleeping. With a view to the final coming of the Lord, this is, of course,
true. If they do not heed the admonition of the Lord, but continue
sleeping, death will come; and in their death the Lord will come upon
them as their Judge. Nevertheless, there is, I think, another idea in this
coming of the Lord as a thief upon the church in Sardis. A thief's aim is
not to come upon you all of a sudden and inspire you with fear, but rather
to sneak into your house without your being aware of it, do his work,

remove your valuables, and disappear without your having noticed him. So the Lord will come upon this church which is sleeping and about to die. He will come as a thief. The church shall never be aware of His coming. He will do His work as Judge, remove the candlestick out of its place, and the church shall have died in her sleep, without waking up even for a moment. The condition here is just the reverse from that of Thyatira. That church is called to attention in regard to the judgments the Lord will execute in her midst. But to Sardis the Lord writes that He shall come as a thief. Entirely in harmony with their deadness and spiritual slumber, He will come upon them without their being aware of His coming. He shall execute His judgments before they know it.

That this is true is plainly indicated by the Lord in His Self-announcement. He says: "These things saith he that hath the seven Spirits of God, and the seven stars." We remember that also in the first chapter both these expressions occur. The first expression, referring to the seven Spirits, does not occur in the vision of the Savior in Chapter 1, but it is used in connection with the salutation of John and his benediction. The seven Spirits are not presented there as the Spirits which are held by Jesus, but simply as the Spirits that are before the throne of God. We remarked in that connection that these seven Spirits are not simply a reference to the Holy Spirit as the Third Person of the Trinity, but rather that they refer to the Spirit of Christ as He received Him from the Father. He now has that Spirit as the head of the church and the Mediator of the new covenant. And while that Spirit dwells in Him as the head of the body, He also poured Him out into the church. It is the Spirit Who establishes the unity between the head and the body, between the church and her King. It is as the One Who has the seven Spirits of God that the Lord announces Himself to the church of Sardis, first of all, in order to inspire them with hope in case they repent: for He has the seven Spirits, and through these He dwells in the church, so that they may expect from Him life and strength to keep what they have, that no one take their crown. But, secondly, with a view to their spiritual condition, the mention of the seven Spirits must serve as a reminder to them of what will surely happen if they do not repent. If He withholds the seven Spirits, the church will be dead even though they may still have a name that they live. The same is true of the seven stars. It was especially due to the angel of the church in Sardis that they were dead. Now the Lord holds the seven stars. It is He Who gives them to the church; it is also He Who withdraws them. If He does the latter, the light of the Word shall, at least through them, shine no more. Thus the Lord will come with His judgment upon the church. He shall come as a thief. Before they are aware of it, the Spirit shall have departed out of their midst, and they shall be without the light of the Word that shines through their star. The church shall cease to exist as the church of Jesus Christ.

The Lord's Promise To The Faithful

But there are still a few who are faithful in the church of Sardis. The Lord concludes this letter with beautiful promises to them and to those that overcome in general.

These faithful, first of all, are described. They are those who have not defiled their garments. The Lord knows them by name. The fact that the Lord describes them as those who had not defiled their garments implies, of course, that the rest of the congregation in Sardis had defiled them. The question is: what is meant by the garments of the members of the church in this connection? It is evident that they do not refer to the righteousness of Christ: for all the members had these garments, and some, or many of them, had defiled them. Rather, therefore, we must understand that these garments refer to their outward membership in the church. They were all baptized in the name of the Triune God. They were all members of the church in an external sense of the word, and they were known as such in Sardis. They all outwardly professed the name of Christ. They all wore the garments of the church. Even as the soldiers of the same army wear the garments, or uniform, of the army, so all the members of the church in Sardis wore the uniform of Christ. But all had not lived in harmony with the garments which they wore. They were dead. They had dishonored the name of their King. They did not distinguish themselves from the soldiers of Satan in the midst of the world. They had defiled their garments by a walk in sin. Hence, the expression that the few who were faithful in Sardis had not defiled their garments does not and cannot mean that they were without sin and that they had already reached perfection, but simply that they had been faithful to their profession both in their confession and walk. They had been faithful to the name of Jesus their Lord, and they had refused to walk in the sins of the world as did the others.

A difficult position they must have occupied in the church of Sardis. The others were dead and asleep. These were alive and awake, loving the truth and busy in the things of the kingdom of God. The others were enjoying a walk in the sins of the world and did not manifest themselves as scrupulous in regard to their life and walk in the midst of the world. These, however, refused to become conformed according to the life and standards of the world in the midst of which they lived. How it must have troubled them that their angel was dead and that he could not and did not bring them the Word of life! How it must have grieved them to see that the church was so dead and that she was becoming more and more apostate! And above all, how it must have pierced their soul like a sword that they had to bear the reproach and shame and mockery of their fellow-members in the church of Sardis! For that was naturally the result. The worldly-minded members of the church filled the faithful few with reproach and shame and called them narrow-minded. It is hard, indeed, to bear the reproach of the world. But this you cannot avoid. You expect this of the world. But a thousand times more grievous it is that you must bear the reproach of them that wear the garments of Jesus and that profess to belong to the church of Christ. Such was the position of the few names in Sardis. In the midst of all these difficulties they had not become unfaithful, but had refused to defile their garments with sin.

To them and to all who are victorious the Lord gives a most beautiful promise in a three-fold form. They shall all walk with Him in white garments; their names shall not be blotted out of the book of life; and Jesus shall confess their names before God, His Father.

In general, it is evident that the Lord here promises them eternal life and glory. The three-fold form of this promise is in harmony with the position of these faithful ones in the midst of the church in Sardis.

There is, in the first place, the promise that they shall walk with the Lord in white garments. In Scripture, white garments are a symbol of righteousness and holiness and purity, of perfect deliverance from sin and corruption. Hence, in this beautiful promise the Lord assures the faithful in Sardis that they once shall be delivered perfectly from sin and death and that in their entire life and walk they shall be as the Lord. With Him and as Him they shall live and walk, without any imperfection; and never they shall defile their garments any more. It needs no mention that this was exactly the deepest desire and longing of these faithful ones. While many in the congregation lived in sin, they fought the battle of faith and strove to keep their garments pure. How this promise that in the future they would be perfectly holy and pure must have appealed to their inmost heart and must have spurred them on to be faithful even unto death!

Secondly, the Lord gives them the assurance that their names shall not be blotted out of the book of life. Scripture speaks more often of books. There are before God's countenance books of remembrance; they shall be opened in the day of judgment so that all the works of men which are done in time may be revealed. Then there is also the book of life. In that book, written before the foundation of the world, the names are written of those who are chosen unto everlasting life and glory. The names that are written in that book will, of course, never be blotted out. Nor does the Lord say that this is possible. He merely assures the faithful in Sardis that their names shall **not** be erased from the roll of God's elect. Fact is that once upon a time also the unfaithful ones in Sardis had appeared as if they had been written in that book of life too: for their names had appeared on the roll of the church. Now, however, their apostasy and their walk in sin prove that their names had never been written in the book of life. Hence, not to be blotted out from the book of life represents the assurance that they had from all eternity been written in it and that the believers in Sardis may be confident that they shall find their names are written therein in the day of judgment. A glorious promise this is, indeed! If we are faithful and do not defile our garments, we may have the assurance in our hearts that in the day when "the roll is called up yonder," the roll of those who inherit eternal life, also our names shall be called. In that day there shall be no fear or anxiety on the part of those who were faithful in the midst of the world and who by grace have overcome in the battle of faith. They shall stand in the assurance that their names are written in the book of life.

Finally, in close connection with the assurance that their names shall not be blotted out of the book of life stands the third form of the promise, that the Lord will confess the names of these faithful ones before His Father in heaven. As the names are being called from the book of life, Jesus shall say: "Yes, these are also of my sheep which Thou, Father, hast given me; they have been faithful and have not defiled their garments; they are worthy to enter with me into Thy everlasting glory!"

Hear what the Spirit saith unto the churches!

What does the Spirit say?

Watch!

Many a church has fallen asleep in our day. Many are the churches and ministers which have a name that they live, but are dead. Shall we remain faithful? Many have defiled their garments. Shall we keep them clean? We shall, if, by the power of the grace of God, we fight the good fight even unto the end.

Watch, therefore, that no one take your crown!

Chapter IX

The Church With The Promise Of An Open Door

(Revelation 3:7-13)

7 And to the angel of the church in Philadelphia write; These things saith he that is holy, he that is true, he that hath the key of David, he that openeth, and no man shutteth; and shutteth, and no man openeth;

8 I know thy works: behold, I have set before thee an open door, and no man can shut it: for thou hast a little strength, and hast kept my word, and hast not denied my name.

9 Behold, I will make them of the synagogue of Satan, which say they are Jews, and are not, but do lie; behold, I will make them to come and worship before thy feet, and to know that I have loved thee.

10 Because thou hast kept the word of my patience, I also will keep thee from the hour of temptation, which shall come upon all the world, to try them that dwell upon the earth.

11 Behold, I come quickly: hold that fast which thou hast, that no man take thy crown.

12 Him that overcometh will I make a pillar in the temple of my God, and he shall go no more out: and I will write upon him the name of my God, and the name of the city of my God, which is new Jerusalem, which cometh down out of heaven from my God: and I will write upon him my new name.

13 He that hath an ear, let him hear what the Spirit saith unto the churches.

It is certainly remarkable that there are but two churches of all the seven churches addressed in these letters to the churches in Asia Minor who receive no rebuke, but only praise and consolation. These two churches, as we know, are the congregation of Smyrna and that of Philadelphia. The latter is the subject of our discussion in the present chapter.

124

It cannot escape our notice that these two churches reveal a marked similarity in regard to their general description and characterization by the Lord Jesus. Especially may we notice that of both churches it is true that they are small and of little strength. Evidently they have but little standing room in the world in which they live. Of the church in Smyrna it is said that she is poor and despised and that she exists in the midst of a world which hates and persecutes her. The same is true of the church in Philadelphia. The Lord in this letter describes her as a church which has but little strength. Moreover, the same enemies who lived near the church of Smyrna and were a source of trouble to her, those who say they are Jews and are not, but are a synagogue of Satan, are also mentioned in the epistle to Philadelphia. Hence, there is not only spiritual similarity between the two congregations, but also in an outward respect they are nearly alike. Only there seems to be this difference, that the church of Smyrna evidently must spend all its spiritual strength in the bearing of the cross for Christ's sake, while the church in Philadelphia still has the opportunity to spread the gospel of Jesus Christ, to gain converts especially from among the Jews in the city, and thus to increase and extend the church and the kingdom of God. Moreover, although until that time her labors appear to have been without fruit, the Lord promises her such fruit in the future when He writes to her that He will give her an open door, which evidently means an effective entrance for the preaching of the gospel into the hearts of others.

The Outward Condition Of Philadelphia

One of the chief characteristics of the church in Philadelphia is undoubtedly expressed in the words of the Savior, "Thou hast a little strength." This describes her outward condition in the world. The meaning is that the church was small. This was one of her most emphatic traits.

We understand, of course, that this does not imply that the other churches were outwardly great and strong: for this was not the case. In fact, we may undoubtedly say that the church in general, the true church of Jesus Christ, is always of little power if compared with the strength of the world. It is always comparatively small in numbers. It usually is financially poor. It does not count among its numbers the rich and the great of the world. And therefore, it is evident that in a general sense what the Savior here writes about the church in Philadelphia may be said of all the churches addressed thus far. Ephesus, Smyrna, Pergamos, Thyatira, and Sardis,—all were small and poor and of little strength according to the measure of the world. Nevertheless, of the church in Philadelphia this was especially and emphatically true. It was not the chief characteristic of the other churches, but it was one of the main features of the church in Philadelphia. We may take it, therefore, that in this little sentence the Lord gives a brief description of the peculiar situation in the church of Philadelphia from an external point of view.

The Spiritual Condition Of Philadelphia

However, when the Lord addresses the church in Philadelphia thus, and remarks that she has but little strength, this refers only to her outward position in the world. It does not describe her spiritual condition. Spiritually the little church in Philadelphia was not weak, but strong indeed. That this is true is evident from rest of the letter addressed to her.

The Lord commends her for having kept His Word, which implies that the church remained faithful to the truth of the gospel. And thus to keep the Word of Jesus certainly requires spiritual strength. The church that is spiritually weak certainly will not keep the Word of Jesus. Always the enemies encompass the church of Jesus Christ in the world; and always those enemies attack her especially from the viewpoint of the truth. It requires strength, spiritual strength, the exercise of the power of faith, to be faithful to the truth and to keep the Word of the Lord. This is emphasized in what follows immediately. It is evident that the church had not only kept the Word of Jesus, but also confessed His name. For the Lord writes to her: "Thou hast not denied my name." The negative form of this expression implies that the enemies, perhaps especially the Jews of Philadelphia, had exerted all their influence to make the church deny the name of Christ. They persecuted her and left her but little standing room in the midst of the world. But this negative expression also implies, by way of contrast, that the church in Philadelphia had openly confessed the name of the Lord Jesus Christ. They could not and did not keep still about that name of their glorious Lord and Redeemer, in Whom they believed and Whom they loved, Who had delivered them from sin and death and merited for them everlasting life and glory. Of course, all this points to real spiritual strength. To confess the name of the Lord is from a natural point of view by no means an easy matter, especially over against the enemy and especially when the confession of that name instigates persecution and hatred on the part of the world. This certainly had been the case in

Philadelphia. This is evident from what the Lord continues to write to her: "Thou hast kept the word of my patience." Patience, in the Scriptural sense of the word, always presupposes suffering for Christ's sake, the bearing of His cross. The confession of the name of Jesus, the preaching of His Word, had caused the saints in Philadelphia suffering and persecution. But they had been faithful in the midst of the suffering of this present time and had not denied His name. They had kept and proclaimed the Word of Jesus Christ, and for it they had suffered affliction and persecution; and thus they had kept the Word of Christ's patience, the Word which always exhorted them to be patient and to suffer and bear the cross for Christ's sake.

It must not be said, therefore, that the little church in Philadelphia had little strength spiritually. No, in grace she was strong, very strong indeed. But outwardly, according to the measure of the world, the little church was weak in every respect of the word. She was small in numbers, no doubt. Perhaps the church was hardly known in the city; she counted but few members. Neither did this small band belong to the great of the world. The financial resources of the congregation were practically none. She had no wealth. She possessed little property. The little band did not belong to the wealthy and influential in the city. According to the standard of the world, the church in Philadelphia had indeed but little strength. From an outward aspect one would judge that the church could exert no influence at all. If Philadelphia existed in our day, she would no doubt receive the advice to unite with some other church as soon as possible. In her small and isolated condition, so we would judge, she can be of no influence and power in the world. The sooner she becomes member of a larger body, the better it will be for her.

But Philadelphia did not think so. At least, from the letter we receive the impression that the church had been busy preaching the gospel and witnessing for Christ. No doubt, they had witnessed for the name of the Lord also with a view to gaining converts, and that especially among the powerful and influential Jews in the city. That this is true is evident from the entire letter. In the first place, the Lord in this letter announces Himself as the One that has the key of David, that openeth, and no man shutteth; and shutteth, and no man openeth. The expression "key of David" is derived from Isaiah 22:22. The prophet there pronounces judgment upon Shebna, the king's treasurer and most important officer over his house. This office shall be taken away from him and shall be given to Eliakim, the son of Hilkiah, who was found to be more worthy than Shebna. And it is in this connection that Isaiah uses the expression "key of David." Says he: "And the key of the house of David will I lay upon his shoulder; so he shall open, and none shall shut; and he shall shut, and none shall open." This power of the key, therefore, symbolized general supervision over the king's business, and included specifically the authority to determine who were allowed to enter into the king's presence and into his service. Now then, Christ possesses the key of David. That is, He has the authority to open and shut the door of the Father's kingdom. He, and He alone, determines who shall enter into that kingdom and who shall remain without. It is He, therefore, Who adds to the church. And this announcement, no doubt, points to the hope and the desire of the little congregation in Philadelphia, as well as to her activity in regard to witnessing for Jesus and in respect to the proclamation of the gospel, that the little church may increase in numbers and that converts may be gained. In that respect she was a true missionary church. True, the congregation was of little strength; yet they had been very active. And though they had remained small, and though their labors had been crowned with but little success, yet the Lord reminds them that He is the One from Whom alone the growth of the church must be expected. They must be faithful, and they must preach, and they must witness. But the Lord holds the key of David. He alone opens and shuts the door of His Father's kingdom.

The Promise Of An Open Door

In the second place, the Lord tells the congregation: "Behold, I have set before thee an open door, and no man can shut it."

Different interpretations have been given of this figurative expression; yet, in the light of Scripture in general, the meaning can hardly be dubious. When Paul and Barnabas return from their missionary journey and report to the church of their labors and the fruit upon these labors, we read that the church rejoiced because the Lord had given an open door unto the Gentiles, Acts 14:27. In II Corinthians 16:9 the apostle writes: "For a great door and effectual is opened unto me, and there are many adversaries." And again, in II Corinthians 2:12 he writes: "Furthermore, when I came to Troas to preach Christ's gospel, and a door was opened unto me of the Lord, I had no rest in my spirit, because I found not Titus, my brother: but taking leave of them, I went from thence into Macedonia." And once more, in Colossians 4:3 the apostle writes: "Withal praying also for us, that God would open unto us a door of utterance, to speak the mystery of Christ, for which I am also in bonds." The meaning of the open door, therefore, is evidently that the Lord would create an opportunity and a receptivity for the preaching and the hearing of the gospel of Christ. And if we may conclude, as certainly we may, that this promise is in harmony with the desire and longing of the congregation, we see that also this expression points to the fact that the church in Philadelphia was characterized by zeal for the Lord's cause and was bent upon the extension of the kingdom of God. They were small, but faithful, and purposed to add to their little band by means of preaching of the gospel.

This picture is of great significance for the church today. For it tells us that the Lord fulfills His strength in weakness. The church of today seems to be quite forgetful of the fact that she is in herself of little strength. The talk of the day is of money and funds and men and organizations. The church is united into a powerful army. Long, so it is said, the church has been forgetful of her great task to bring the world to Christ. But now she will accomplish that tremendous task. But what we need is organization. What we need is men and means. What we need is sound business methods. And surely, we do not oppose all these. We surely may employ the very best methods, even in the extension of the kingdom of God. We surely need men who will preach the gospel. We surely need funds, even for the extension of the kingdom. But we fear that the expectation is more and more from these than from Him Who holds the keys of David. After all, let us never forget that we do not open and shut, but the Lord only. He will use His church as an instrument; but that church must always be mindful of the saying of Jesus, "Thou art of little strength."

Secondly, the picture of the little church in Philadelphia reminds us that the church must not force the fruits when they do not immediately become evident. Today this is often the case. In her anxiety to force men into the kingdom the church not so infrequently compromises on the gospel of Jesus Christ and the truth of the Word of God. It does no longer emphasize the essential truths. It feels that perhaps men are repelled by the preaching of sin and total depravity, of wrath and condemnation, not to speak of the fundamental truths of election and reprobation. These truths, therefore, are no longer preached. Instead, a certain shallow gospel of love takes its place, in order to attract men and to force them into the church. Gradually the gospel loses its strength and its true content. And the result is that rather than bringing the world to Christ, we bring the church into the world. Philadelphia had not adopted this method. She had labored faithfully and seen no fruit. For still she was small. But she had kept the Word of Christ's patience and had in no wise denied His name. And therefore, finally, in Philadelphia we have the true picture of the faithful mission church. Mindful of her smallness and of her dependence on Christ, mindful that He must open the door, she remains a faithful witness and does not deny the truth.

Glorious promises are given unto this church for the present as well as for the future.

First of all, the Lord promises that she shall see fruit upon her labors. This promise is already suggested in the manner in which Christ appears to the church of Philadelphia. He is the holy and true One, upon Whose Word the congregation may rely. He holds the key of David, and has the authority to open and to shut. In these words there is already a faint suggestion that presently the Lord will open the gate of the kingdom and cause some of them among whom they had witnessed and labored to enter in. This inference becomes practically a certainty when the Lord tells them: "Behold, I have set before thee an open door, which no man can shut." Hitherto it had seemed as if with all their activity they had only aroused enmity and bitter hatred against the Lord and His church. The enemy appeared not even to be approachable. The hearts were closed. But now the Lord would open the door. They would find entrance. They would henceforth experience that the attitude of the enemy had changed. Their witnessing would meet with a certain eagerness to listen to the truth of the gospel. The Lord would prepare the field for them. And, finally, this fact is raised beyond all doubt, and is at the same time stated more definitely, when the Lord adds: "Behold, I will make them of the synagogue of Satan, of them that say they are Jews, but are not, but do lie; behold, I will make them to come and worship before thy feet, and to know that I have loved thee." There was in Philadelphia a synagogue of the Jews. They were filled with bitter hatred against Christ and His people. They had no doubt slandered the congregation. From them the church had suffered much. But over against them the little church had witnessed faithfully. Only, hitherto it had all seemed to be in vain. The door was closed. They could not be approached. They did not appear open to conviction. They met their gospel with bitterness and scorn. But now, behold, the Lord would finally crown their labors with blessing unexpected. Some of those very Jews who hated them and persecuted them would be converted. These very enemies would come and worship before the feet of the church, that is, in all humility; expressing in their attitude that the church is the beloved, the bride of the Messiah, these Jews would come and take their place among the followers of Jesus of Nazareth. Long, therefore, they may have labored in vain; but glorious is the victory.

And the same is true today. Long all our labors may appear to be fruitless and without result. Let us never forget that the Lord will surely bring His own, and that also through our labors.

The Promise Of Being Kept From The Hour Of Temptation

Neither is this the only promise the Lord gives to the church of Philadelphia for the present time. Troublous times were approaching for the church, also for the faithful in Philadelphia. They must have been filled with apprehension of this fact even at this very time. The clouds of persecution appeared at the historical horizon. Presently they would cover the firmament and burst forth their black darkness over the church. The Lord speaks of those times that are about to come when He writes: "I also will keep thee from the hour of temptation, which shall come upon all the world, to try them that dwell upon the earth." The hour of trial, or of temptation, here mentioned refers, of course, in the first place, to a wave of persecution which swept over the church of Christ at that time. Likely it was the same hour of persecution which would come over the church of Smyrna. It would sweep over the entire then-known world, and try men with a view to their loyalty to Christ Jesus.

But although this hour of temptation refers, in the first place, in the literal sense of the word to a time of persecution which would arrive for the church of Philadelphia, yet it remains true that this same hour of temptation was repeated several times in the history of the world. It was repeated when the Mohammedan half-moon rode high over the Christian world. It was repeated when the harlot church, as represented by Roman Catholicism, sent the sons of the Reformation to scaffold and stake. And after all, it will find its complete fulfillment no sooner than the time of Antichrist, when days so terrible are still to arrive for the church that even the elect would not endure if they were not shortened. All these hours of temptation, repeated several times in history wherever the church was persecuted, are after all but faint types and forebodings of what will come when the Man of Sin shall reach his full development and power. The hour of tribulation will come, will surely come, perhaps will come soon.

And what now is the promise to the church of Philadelphia and also to the church of the present time? This: that she will be kept from the hour of temptation that shall come upon the whole world.

Does that mean that the church will not be subjected to that hour of trial? Does it mean with regard to the church of Philadelphia that she will be kept by the Lord and in some wonderful manner remain unmolested when that hour of temptation sweeps the world? And does it mean with a view to the final period of suffering that the Lord will first receive His faithful church up to heaven, before that final suffering comes? Thus is the view of many. If the church is faithful and keeps the Word of Christ's patience, she shall meet the Lord in the air before the persecution by the Man of Sin breaks loose in all its fury.

But I do not believe that this is the meaning of these words. In the first place, the question arises: why should the church of Smyrna be cast into the midst of that tribulation and the church of Philadelphia be excused? In the second place, we may notice that the entire conception that the faithful church shall be delivered before the persecution of Antichrist comes is false and dangerous. It is false, for it is not in harmony with Scripture. Christ warns His people more than once that this hour shall come, and that they must remain faithful unto the end. Why all these warnings of tribulation, with which Scripture abounds, if they that are faithful shall not be in the hour of temptation? And dangerous this conception is, because it puts the church to sleep. The church which expects to be received in the air before the great tribulation comes does not prepare itself for the battle and for the hour of temptation. That hour shall catch her unexpectedly. And therefore, we must not labor under this illusion, but must expect to be in tribulation, and must prepare for the evil day, putting on the whole armor of God. In the third place, the tribulation which is mentioned here is pictured as coming over the whole earth; and it is not likely that the faithful little church of Philadelphia would escape the attention of the enemy. It is exactly the faithful church which must endure persecution. In the fourth place, the original may very well be interpreted to signify that the little church of Philadelphia would indeed be cast into the midst of temptation and be tried with all the world, but that in that tribulation the Lord would keep her, so that she would come out of it unharmed.

The latter is indeed the meaning. Not that the church shall be kept from tribulation is her glory and comfort. Not that she shall not meet with tribulation must be her assurance: for it would be false. But that in the midst of suffering and persecution, when the enemy rages and the temptation to deny the Lord is strong and fierce, the Lord by His grace will be sufficient to keep the church, so that she endures to the very end,—that is the meaning of the text. That is the assurance the church may have. That is the comfort which the church needs. Also with a view to the great tribulation which is still to come, the church is in need of that consolation. Who does never tremble at the thought of what must still come to pass? Who of God's children, when he thinks of the terrible suffering that is connected with the persecution of the church in the last days, never asks himself the anxious and all-important question whether he shall be faithful even unto death? The church, therefore, has need of that comfort, the comfort that the grace of God will be sufficient even in the hour of trial.

Finally, this interpretation is in harmony with the admonition which immediately follows this announcement: "Behold, I come quickly: hold that fast which thou hast, that no man take thy crown."

It is exactly in times of tribulation and persecution that the church has need of the comforting assurance that the Lord is coming quickly. For the coming of the Lord will mean her victory and final deliverance. And again, it is not when the church escapes persecution, but when she is in the midst of it that she needs the admonition, coming directly from the Lord: "Hold fast that which thou hast, that no man take thy crown."

And therefore, this, we take it, is the meaning of this assurance. The church of Philadelphia, and the church of all ages, and the church of the latter days especially, may expect the hour of temptation which shall come over all the world. She will be cast right into the midst of it. But in the midst of suffering and trial, the vision of the Lord may always be before her, holding the keys of David, calling Himself the faithful and true, and giving the church the assurance that she need not be afraid, for His grace will be sufficient to keep His faithful ones out of the hour of temptation, so that no one shall take their crown.

The Promise Of Future Blessing

But the Lord has still more promises. He does not only come with promises for the present time, but also with promises of glorious blessings for the future: "Him that overcometh will I make a pillar in the temple of my God, and he shall go no more out: and I will write upon him the name of my God, and the name of the city of my God, which is new Jerusalem, which cometh down out of heaven from my God: and I will write upon him my new name."

Let us notice, first of all, the important fact that this promise is given in general to him that overcometh. The glory of the Messianic kingdom is preceded by the suffering of this present time. And the rule remains without exception that we must suffer with Christ in order to be glorified together. Christ and His people have a common cause. They are inseparably united. But they also suffer a common lot in the world. If they have hated Him, they shall also hate us. And if they have persecuted Him, they shall also persecute those that are His. Hence, only for him that overcometh is this future promise. Not for him who is defeated; not for him who falls by the wayside; not for him who succumbs to the devil; not for him who does not keep the Word of Christ's patience; not for him who denies the name of Jesus; but only for him that overcometh is this promise. For the unfaithful the Word of the Lord has no promises. But he that overcometh shall be made a pillar in the temple of Christ's God.

Is it necessary to mention in this connection that there is no reference here to a literal temple, made with hands? If temple is taken literally, pillars must also be taken in the same sense. And it would be a poor consolation indeed for the people of God to learn that they all will be changed into pillars in the future. No, the sense is symbolical. Temple is symbolic of the dwelling of God with man, of His most intimate communion, of the full realization of God's covenant of friendship. God's temple is His people, living in most intimate communion and union with Himself. The pillar is figure of abiding firmness. The Lord Himself supplies the commentary on this expression when He adds: "and he shall go out no more." To be made pillars in the temple of God, therefore, is to enter lastingly and abidingly into the eternal covenant communion with God, the God of Jesus Christ our Lord. They that overcome in the present struggle, they that are firm in the hour of trial, shall finally enter into that eternal covenant communion with God which is life eternal.

The Lord further makes mention of a three-fold name which they shall bear who thus overcome. They shall bear the name of God; they shall bear the name of the city of God; and they shall bear the new name of Jesus.

The name is the manifestation of their being. It is the expression of what they are. If, therefore, the Lord here promises that the faithful shall receive the name of God, He expresses that the image of God shall have reached its highest possible development. There shall be the highest possible degree of likeness between God's people and Himself, so that true and perfect covenant communion is possible, and they shall see Him as He is. We shall bear His name. We shall be like Him. No, we shall not be God; but the highest possible affinity that is conceivable in the creature shall exist between God and His people. And in that relation they shall see Him face to face, and He shall speak to them as a friend with his friends.

They shall bear the name of the city of God. It is not necessary to go into detail as to the reality and the meaning of this new Jerusalem. Suffice it to say that it represents the society of the elect in glory, the body of Christ, the complete assembly of all the saints. In that society every individual shall have his own name. Individuality shall not be lost. Yet his name shall always be the name of that city, that is, his individual being and manifestation shall be in harmony with the general society of all the saints, so that all together they shall form one grand harmony, manifesting the glory of God's grace. Besides, the communion of saints shall there be perfect, when they shall all bear that common name of the city of God, the new Jerusalem that cometh down out of heaven. Now that city is being prepared, and one by one the company of the elect are being gathered in heaven. But once it shall come down out of heaven from God into the new creation, there to live forever to the glory of the grace of the Almighty.

Lastly, the Lord mentions His own new name. It is the name which was given Him at His exaltation at the right hand of God, a name of glory and power and strength and majesty. It denotes our Lord Jesus Christ as the Lord of all! For in the new creation He shall be King forever. That name shall also be bestowed upon His saints, that is, they shall share in His glory. With Him they shall reign. With Him they shall walk in the light of God. With Him they shall be prophets, priests, and kings of God forevermore!

Hear what the Spirit saith unto the churches!

What doth the Spirit say?

In the first place, that the church is of little strength outwardly. This is true today as it was at the time of the early church. In the task she is called to perform, in the tribulation she will have to suffer, she may continually bear in mind that she is of little strength. She need not, she may not, rely on that strength. In the second place, the Lord is faithful and powerful. He has the key of David. He opens, and no one shuts; He shuts, and no one opens. No one shall pluck us out of His hand. No one shall root us out of His kingdom. And in all our work in the kingdom of

God, our reliance should be on Him alone. Of little strength itself, the church is mighty in her mighty Lord, faithful and true. In the third place, tribulation shall come; and temptation the church must expect. But in the midst of tribulation and suffering for Christ's sake, the vision of the mighty King of kings may always be before us! He shall keep us, so that we shall never fall. And with our eyes on Him we may be sure of the victory!

That victory may surely be our consolation!

It shall be the victory of eternal glory in the new Jerusalem, in the temple of God and His tabernacle with men, where we shall see Him face to face and love Him forever, as He hath loved us!

Chapter X

The Church Nauseating To The Lord

(Revelation 3:14-22)

14 And unto the angel of the church of the Laodiceans write; These things saith the Amen, the faithful and true witness, the beginning of the creation of God;

15 I know thy works, that thou art neither cold nor hot: I would thou wert cold or hot.

16 So then because thou art lukewarm, and neither cold nor hot, I will spue thee out of my mouth.

17 Because thou sayest, I am rich, and increased with goods, and have need of nothing; and knowest not that thou art wretched, and miserable, and poor, and blind, and naked:

18 I counsel thee to buy of me gold tried in the fire, that thou mayest be rich; and white raiment, that thou mayest be clothed, and that the shame of thy nakedness do not appear; and anoint thine eyes with eyesalve, that thou mayest see.

19 As many as I love, I rebuke and chasten: be zealous therefore, and repent.

20 Behold, I stand at the door, and knock: if any man hear my voice, and open the door, I will come in to him, and will sup with him, and he with me.

21 To him that overcometh will I grant to sit with me in my throne, even as I also overcame, and am set down with my Father in his throne.

22 He that hath an ear, let him hear what the Spirit saith unto the churches.

The Church Of Laodicea

Laodicea was an important city in Phrygia, southeast of Philadelphia, on the river Lycus. It was noted especially for its industry and commerce, and therefore it was very prosperous. The letter addressed by the apostle Paul to the Colossians was also intended for the church in Laodicea. For in Colossians 2:1 we read: "For I would that ye knew what great conflict I

137

have for you, and for them at Laodicea." At the time when Paul addressed his letter to them, the church at Laodicea had been in danger of being led astray by ascetic, Judaizing philosophers. Against them the apostle warns in Colossians 2:8: "Beware lest any man spoil you through philosophy and vain deceit, after the tradition of men, after the rudiments of the world, and not after Christ." And this is further expressed in Colossians 2:16-23: "Let no man therefore judge you in meat, or in drink, or in respect to an holy day, or of the new moon, or of the sabbath days," etc. This philosophy did not only concern the question of meat and drink and holy days, but was also an emphasis on voluntary humility and worshipping of angels, (verse 18). All these things, according to the apostle, have a show of wisdom in will worship, and humility, and neglecting of the body; but after all they have nothing to do with the service of Christ. For the saints are no longer subject to such ordinances, seeing they are dead with Christ, (verse 20). At the time, however, when the Lord Jesus addressed this letter to the church of Laodicea, its outstanding sin was no longer this refraining from meat and drink and this voluntary humility; but it consisted rather in spiritual self-complacency, accompanied, no doubt, by a spirit of worldliness.

This letter closes the series of the seven epistles written to the churches of Asia Minor, and with it our discussion of the seven-fold picture of the church in general comes to an end. We emphasized as our view that we may not consider these seven letters as so many historical predictions concerning seven consecutive periods in the history of the church, so that we will be able with tolerable accuracy to point out which period of history is presented in each of the seven epistles. On the contrary, these letters rather picture the seven-fold aspect of the church in general at any period of her history in the world. Taken in general, the church always presents this seven-fold aspect, and appears with a mixture of light and darkness, good and evil qualities, attractive and repulsive features. The good qualities of the church ascribed to her in the seven-fold picture are soundness in doctrine, faithfulness in regard to discipline, an abounding in the work of the Lord, warmth and fulness of spiritual life, love, hope, confidence, and patience in suffering and persecution for Christ's sake. These features the Lord Jesus praises and strengthens. On the other hand, there are the evil features of the church in the world: coolness of spiritual life, lack of love, laxity in discipline, a tendency to false mysticism, lack of zeal in the work of the Lord, and, as we shall see in connection with the letter to the Laodiceans, a combination of all these evil features, manifesting itself as miserable lukewarmness. These evil features the Lord strongly rebukes, and in regard to them He admonishes to repent. In connection with the evil which He found in the churches the Lord always approaches them with His threatening judgments and coming. But at the same time, He never fails to promise life and glory to those who are faithful and who overcome in the battle of faith.

Yet, although we strongly repudiate the idea of seven definite periods being represented in these letters, it must not be overlooked, as we said in the last chapter, that there is a certain intentional arrangement in the order in which the seven letters appear. The last church to be discussed is that of Laodicea, a church most miserable in every respect. There is in this purposely arranged order an indication as to what we may expect in the future. From a human point of view, the Word of God pictures that future as not too bright. And those who live under the impression that toward the end of time and the coming of our Lord Jesus Christ the church will appear in a most flourishing condition certainly find no support in Scripture. The order in which these letters occur seems to indicate that we rather may expect a gradual decline, till the church presents the aspect of the congregation of the Laodiceans. From Ephesus to Laodicea appears to be the path the church will follow in her outward development. The evil element in the church will assert itself and develop more and more, till the general aspect is such that the Lord is ready to spue the church out of His mouth.

The Condition Of Laodicea

The general description of the Laodicean church you may find in the words, "...thou art neither cold nor hot...So then because thou art lukewarm, and neither cold nor hot, I will spue thee out of my mouth." This characterization applies, no doubt, not only to the works of the church in the outward sense, but to her entire condition, internal as well as external.

It is useless to make the attempt to analyse this description and give an interpretation of the various elements, spiritualizing each one of them. This has frequently been done, but exactly by such a procedure the point of the figure that is here employed is lost sight of. To be hot was then interpreted as being zealous in the work of the Lord and filled with true spiritual life. Naturally, to be cold was then understood in the opposite sense of the word and applied to a condition of absolute spiritual deadness, to a complete lack of spiritual life. But, in the first place, the conclusion would then seem to be quite inevitable that in the light of such an interpretation the condition of lukewarmness would always seem preferable to the state of being cold. But Jesus evidently prefers the latter above the former: for He says in this letter, "I would thou wert either cold or hot." Either of these is preferable to lukewarmness. Hence, such an interpretation seems in the nature of the case excluded and impossible. In the second place, as we have stated already, the point of the figure is entirely overlooked in that interpretation. The Lord employs a figure to describe the condition of the church in Laodicea. It is the figure of a drink of water. A hot drink is pleasing to the taste and recuperating in its effect. A cold drink is refreshing and delicious. But a lukewarm drink is disgusting to him who swallows it. It turns the stomach. It is sickening. It has a nauseating effect. Well, then, by this figure the Lord describes the general condition of the church and the impression she makes upon Him. He simply says: "Your condition is such that you are nauseating to me." That this is the meaning is emphasized by the form in which the Lord puts the threatening judgment, "I will spue thee out of my mouth." Literally the Lord says in these words, "I am about to vomit thee out." The meaning, therefore, is very plain. We must not attempt to find a spiritual signification for every one of the terms employed in the figure, but rather understand the figure in its general meaning. And then it is plain that the Lord means to say: "The church of Laodicea is so miserable that I cannot tolerate her any more. I am about to reject her in disgust!"

The question arises, however: what is the condition of this church which makes her so nauseating to the Lord?

Christ Himself gives the answer. He tells us that the church is "wretched, and miserable, and poor, and blind, and naked," first of all.

Of course, all these terms refer to the spiritual condition of the church. Hardly could we find a more emphatic description of miserableness in Scripture than the one here presented of Laodicea. The word used here in the original for "wretched" is the same as that employed by the apostle Paul when, at the close of Romans 7, he exclaims: "O wretched man that I am! Who shall deliver me from the body of this death?" There is no reason why we should not understand the word here in the same sense. Laodicea was wretched in herself. She was sinful and condemned. In herself she was nothing but the object of the wrath of God. In the day of judgment she would never be able to make both ends meet. That is why she was at the same time miserable, that is, according to the original, "an object of pity." She was to be pitied. Unless the mercy of God had compassion on her, she would be utterly lost. The wretchedness of the condition of the church in Laodicea is emphasized still more when the Lord says that she is "poor, blind, naked." She is the very opposite of the church in Smyrna. The latter was rich; Laodicea is poor. She does not possess the riches of grace. Faith, love, hope, patience, understanding of the truth, watchfulness, and a fighting of the battle of faith,—all these were sought in vain in the church of Laodicea. She was blind. Instead of being able to see the wretchedness of her condition, she was wanting even in the knowledge of self. She could not see her own misery. She was naked. In all the wretchedness of her condition, in all her sin and shame, in all her misery and poverty, in all her blindness and condemnation, the church of Laodicea stood without a cover for her shame. In her bare misery she stood before the eyes of Him Who pierces and scrutinizes the darkest corners of the human soul. In a word, Laodicea was simply the picture of misery!

Nor is this all. Perhaps you would make the remark that there is nothing strange and extraordinary in this description of the church. Is it then not true of every church that she is wretched and miserable and poor and blind and naked in herself? Does not the Christian daily apply this very description to himself? This, of course, is true. But the nauseating condition and attitude of Laodicea consisted exactly in this, that she did not apply this to her own state and condition. She did not admit that she was wretched. Never would she recognize her own picture in this description by the Lord. The very opposite is true. The testimony of the church regarding herself was exactly the opposite from the picture which Jesus drew of her. Jesus said that she was wretched and miserable; the church in Laodicea maintained that she had need of nothing. Jesus said that she was poor; Laodicea's idea of herself was that she was rich. Jesus described her as being blind and naked; the church's opinion of herself was that she was increased with goods. Of course, all these expressions are to be taken in the spiritual sense of the word. It may be true that Laodicea was also rich in goods according to the world. It may very well be true that she had many possessions, and that her goods increased in the material sense of the word. Earthly riches and spiritual poverty often accompany one another. And also in the spiritual sphere it is true that it is very difficult to remain strong in faith and rich in spiritual life at the same time that we increase in riches in the material sense, in the riches of the world. Nevertheless, in these words the church of Laodicea is described in her state of spiritual self-satisfaction. They were well satisfied with their own condition. They thought themselves to be a strong church. Such followed exactly from their blindness: they never saw their own misery and their lack of every spiritual good. They formed quite an opinion of themselves. Spiritual poverty and spiritual pride went together.

I take it that here, as in the church of Sardis, the angel of the church was chiefly and principally at fault, in the first place. The development of the church is often thus, that the leader, the angel, the minister of the church, becomes lax and unfaithful and falls away first of all; and the congregation gradually follows. I imagine that the angel of Laodicea was a well-satisfied, easy-going, good-for-nothing sort of man. He must have been a man who always spoke of peace where there was no peace. He lacked the courage to lay his finger on the sore spots. He was no fighter. He attempted to find out what the opinion of his people was before he expressed his own. And so he gradually flattered them into their self-satisfied condition. He preached no sin and condemnation; or, if he did, he knew how to do it in such a way that nobody could possibly be offended. He left the people blind and poor and naked; and he told them that they were rich and that their goods increased. Thus, I imagine, did the angel of the church in Laodicea behave. Small wonder, then, that the congregation followed! But however this may be, it was exactly this awful contrast between their actual condition and the opinion which they had of themselves that made them perfectly nauseating and that at the same time made their condition so hopeless. For indeed, the publican, who knows and confesses his wretchedness, is justified; but what hope is there for the miserable Pharisee, who thanks God for his own goodness?

It may, perhaps, seem a severe indictment; but personally we have not the slightest doubt that the church of today begins to reveal an alarming degree of similarity with the church of Laodicea. Also in the church of today there is a goodly measure of self-satisfaction and self-righteousness. The church cries out more loudly than ever: "We are rich and increased with goods, and have need of nothing." I am speaking of what calls itself the church in the modern world. Christianity of today boasts that she is waking up to the great task of the church of all ages. We speak of big things. We are going to bring righteousness and peace in society and state, and thus usher in the kingdom of God. It appears that man intends to do so in his own power, which, by the way, already miserably fails. The word spoken to the church in Philadelphia, "Thou hast a little strength," is no more understood. In the second place, our age is characterized by a sad, but very emphatic lack of the knowledge of sin and misery. The church knows not that she is wretched and miserable and poor and naked. And also today, we take it that the leaders, the ministers of the gospel, are to be blamed primarily. Sin is no more preached. Of depravity and misery, of sin and guilt, we hear no more. And the result is that also the gospel of the cross, the gospel of the righteousness of Christ by faith in Him alone, is fast disappearing from our pulpits. Christ of Galilee, not of Calvary, is preached. The Christ Who loved and did well, the social Christ, is held up as our example. But the Servant of Jehovah, the suffering Servant, Who was punished for our transgressions and bruised for our iniquities, is lost out of sight. I am speaking, I repeat, of the church in the modern world in general. Is it a wonder that the church is asleep, that she imagines that she is rich and in need of nothing, while in actual fact she is poor and blind and naked, wretched and miserable? A terrible blow it must have been to that profoundly self-satisfied church of Laodicea when the message came to her: "I will spue thee out of my mouth." But would to God that the church of today might hear this same message, that she might be stirred up from her self-satisfied condition and stung to the quick.

The Lord's Self-Announcement

Let us learn what message must be brought to such a church as that of Laodicea. First of all, we may notice that the Lord Jesus emphasizes strongly that not their opinion of self, but His opinion of them is true and reliable. This He does in His Self-announcement. Says He: "These things saith the Amen, the faithful and true witness." "Amen" denotes that which is firm, abiding, true. It is that on which one may rely. Hence, the latter phrase, "the faithful and true witness," may be considered as a sort of commentary and explanation of the name "Amen." Just because the Lord is the Amen in Himself, He is also such in His testimony. His witness is true and faithful. He never makes a mistake. Error is out of the question with Him. Neither must it be expected that He will become unfaithful and cater to the good-will of men. And the result is that His testimony is perfectly in harmony with the condition of the church in Laodicea. The members of the church may certainly rely upon it, that if His testimony concerning them clashes with their own opinion of self, it is because the latter, and not the former, is erroneous. This the Laodiceans must hear, in the first place. They were filled with conceit. They had been flattered into the delusion that they were rich and in need of nothing. Not easily would they exchange this view for that of someone else. If their minister had preached this gospel of wretchedness and misery and poverty and blindness and nakedness to them at this time, likely it is that they would have deposed him. And therefore, Jesus comes first of all with the gentle reminder that it is the faithful and true witness speaking, the Amen, upon Whom they may rely. And the same method holds true for the church of today. The church must again hear the Word of God. She must again understand that from her pulpit it is not a private and personal opinion, but the authoritative voice of the Amen that is speaking. If she does not, there is no hope for her.

In the second place, the Lord reveals Himself as the rich and all-sufficient One. Already in the expression, "the beginning of the creation of God," this truth is suggested. The meaning of this phrase is, of course, not that Jesus is the first of the creatures, and therefore Himself a creature: for this would conflict with all that the Word of God reveals of Immanuel. He is from eternity to eternity God. But the meaning is rather that He is the principle of all that was created. In that sense He is the firstborn of every creature. All things were made by Him and through Him, the eternal Word. He is the fountain of all that exists. And because He is the beginning of all things that are made, they all subsist in Him and by Him. Now the purpose is that in these words Jesus might reveal Himself in His divine fulness. That He is the beginning of the creation of God points Him out to us as the eternal and all-sufficient One, Who possesses and controls all things in heaven and on earth, and at the same time as the One by Whom and for Whom all things are created in heaven and on earth. He alone, therefore, and that too, as the Christ, is the beginning of all riches. He alone is the fount of all good for the church.

But also in the counsel Jesus gives to the church of Laodicea He introduces Himself as having in His possession exactly those things the church so sorely needed. She was wretched and miserable, and her misery consisted in this, that she was poor and blind and naked. But the Lord possesses gold tried by fire, spiritual riches and glory, which make the possessor truly rich. The Lord has eyesalve which will open the eyes of the blind: spiritual eyesalve, which will cause him that applies it to see the true light in Christ. The Lord has garments, spiritual garments of righteousness

and sanctification, which will truly cover them that buy them of Him
before God Almighty. He, therefore, is the fulness of the church. The
church must rid herself of the notion that she is rich in self, and she must
confess that Jesus Christ alone is her riches and fulness.

The Lord's Counsel To Laodicea

In the third place, we notice that Jesus approaches them with the
advice, the earnest appeal, to come to Him and buy these precious articles
of gold and eyesalve and garments. Of course, we cannot and do not
interpret these words as if the blessings of grace could be bought with a
price which we have in our possession. That would be an absolutely false
and unscriptural interpretation and conclusion. It is true, gold and eyesalve
and garments here represent the riches of grace as they are all in Christ
Jesus our Lord. They represent those riches which the church of Laodicea
so sorely needed and lacked. And they are blessings of **grace** in the most
absolute sense of the word. The sinner has nothing wherewith he would be
able to buy them. How could anyone who is poor buy gold and garments
and eyesalve? Hence, when Jesus speaks here of buying, He simply
employs the figure of the merchant consistently. There is in the very
contradiction that is implied in these words a certain irony. Laodicea
thought that she was rich. Well, then, let her buy what she needs mostly.
Who that is rich and increased with goods walks about without garments?
What wealthy man is without gold? Who that is blind and has the
opportunity to buy eyesalve would be without it? But above all, Jesus
expresses here also in this counsel that they are in need of all these things,
that they do not possess them although they so sorely need them, that
they ought to realize their need first of all. He that imagines that he
possesses all a merchant offers does not buy. As long as Laodicea imagines
that she is rich, she will not buy gold. As long as she imagines that she is
clothed, she will not buy garments. As long as she lives in the delusion that
she can see, she will not buy eyesalve to anoint her eyes. Hence, in this
admonition the Lord presses the thought upon them that she is wanting in
all these things, that she must come to the realization of this want, and
that in the consciousness of it she must come to Him who possesses what
can fulfill her needs, in order that she might receive all from Him.

Truly, this counsel may well be presented to the church of today. As
we have said, the church in general is growing more and more
self-sufficient, and feels that she has need of nothing. All she feels is that

the world is in need of many things; and she is bent upon increasing the whole world with goods, but herself is satisfied. She does not feel the need of gold and eyesalve and garments; yet she is poor and blind and naked. Well may her attention be called to this fact emphatically. The testimony must be heard again and again, that only in Christ is all grace and fulness of blessing, and that outside of Him we lie in the midst of death. The testimony of the rich Christ and the poor sinner must go forth loudly and emphatically, in order that the church may buy gold and eyesalve and garments to cover her nakedness. If she does not hear this counsel, the church will turn to destruction and be swallowed up by the world.

Judgment, Exhortation, And Promise

But will the church of Laodicea listen and heed this counsel of her Lord?

We do not receive the impression that she will. Of course, she would return only by the power of the grace of her Lord Who is writing this letter unto her. But there seems to be very little hope. Time and again in the history of the church we find that there is a return from apostasy and a quickening by the power of the grace of Christ. But naturally, the time will come that the church will repent no more and when only judgment can be expected. Throughout the letter we get the impression that such is the condition of the church in Laodicea.

Notice, in the first place, that the announcement of judgment upon the church as a whole is unconditional and absolute. In other letters the threat of judgment was always contingent upon impenitence. If they would not repent, the Lord would visit them with His punishment. But here the judgment and punishment seem inevitable. The Lord simply says: "Because thou art lukewarm, and neither cold nor hot, I will spue thee out of my mouth." He will utterly reject, cast out, this miserable church. There seems to be no hope for her. The impression, therefore, is that the church will not repent.

In the second place, we may notice that the admonition to repent and the promise in case of repentance and faithfulness is addressed to individuals in the church, rather than to the church as a whole. Of course, there will always be a faithful remnant in the church of Christ. Even to the end of the world there will be the elect of God, even though the church outwardly may apostatize and become unfaithful and miserable. And it is to these that the Lord evidently addresses Himself. In the first place, this is plain from the expression, "As many as I love, I rebuke and chasten: be zealous therefore, and repent." The thought evidently is that even in the most miserable church of Laodicea there are still some of Christ's true people. They have perhaps fallen asleep, overcome by the deadening atmosphere which is prevailing in the church of Laodicea. And the Lord comes to them with His admonition to wake up to new zeal and to repent. They must manifest themselves as His people. They must wake up to the situation. And being zealous for their Lord, they must witness against the unfaithfulness of the church. They must not remain asleep with the rest of the church. Hence, the Lord rebukes and chastens them, that they may come to repentance. This is even more evident when the Lord adds: "Behold, I stand at the door, and knock: if any man hear my voice, and open the door, I will come in to him, and will sup with him, and he with me." There certainly is no need to change the manner and object of the address here, as if Jesus were now standing at the door of the heart of the sinner. We are undoubtedly well aware as to how this interpretation is quite popular. Jesus is presented here as standing at the door of the sinner's heart, begging that the sinner may open the door, to let Jesus in. But this representation of the matter finds no support in the text.

Evidently Jesus is standing not at the door of the heart, but at the door of the church in Laodicea. That church had become unfaithful. That church had cast Him out. He was now standing outside. Within, however, there are those whom He loves and whom He would rebuke and chasten, that they may come to repentance and wake up to a new zeal. Therefore He addresses them from without. He admonishes them to wake up. And He promises them who would hear His voice and let Him in that He will sup with them. Once more, the church as a whole seems hopelessly lost. It is miserable beyond redemption. He will spue her out of His mouth. But His own beloved, the elect of God, must not perish with the rest. Hence, He calls them. And He promises them that they shall have communion with Him, the communion of the covenant. That communion they now miss. For in their present condition they cannot exercise conscious communion with their Lord. But if they repent and wake up to a new zeal, they shall again be receptive for all the blessings of His grace. And wake up the remnant according to the election of grace surely will, when the Lord applies by His powerful grace His Word of admonition to their hearts. The supper is symbol of friendly communion. When therefore the Lord promises that He will sup with His people, He assures them of that most intimate communion of friendship which is the central, the most essential idea of the covenant. He will sup with them! In Him they will sup with the Father and the Son through the Spirit. They shall be restored to that intimate communion with the Triune God which is life. From all this, however, it is quite apparent that the church as a whole is lost, and that only the individual faithful, the individual people of God within the church, shall be saved.

Finally, the Lord concludes also this letter with a promise for him that overcometh and is faithful unto the end: "To him that overcometh will I grant to sit with me in my throne, even as I also overcame, and am set down with my Father in his throne."

If in the former promise the Lord assured His people of the communion of the covenant, symbolized in supping with Him, in this passage He promises the faithful that they will enter into the kingdom eternal and reign with Him forever. Closely are these two truths related. Man was created a covenant being, destined as the image-bearer of God to have most intimate communion with Him. In that relation of friendship of man to God, however, he was at the same time to have dominion over all things. In communion with God, standing in relation to Him as a friend to his Friend, man was to reign over the works of God. But through his sin and fall in Adam as the head of the race, man fell out of that relation to God, became God's enemy, and at the same time was consigned to slavery, the slavery of sin. In Christ Jesus, however, the relation of the covenant is restored and elevated to the highest possible level. He comes to suffer and bear our condemnation. He overcomes as the suffering Servant, being faithful unto death. He restores our human nature to that height of glory and perfection where the perfect communion of the covenant is again possible and is realized in the highest possible sense of the word. At the same time, in Christ the dominion over all things is again restored to man. He overcame and was exalted. So shall all who overcome with Him be exalted. And all who overcome shall participate in that glory at the moment they pass from the church militant into the church triumphant.

True, the final glory still abides until the day of the Lord Jesus Christ. Nevertheless, it remains true that even as Christ now reigns in glory, so principally the believers in Christ also reign with Him through faith even in the present world. And it is also true that even immediately after death they shall be given part of that glory of our Lord and reign with Him as kings. That glory and that reign and that dominion shall be perfected in the new creation, after Christ has come to judge the quick and the dead. What a tremendous difference! Here the people of God belong to the despised, to the poor, to those who are persecuted, to those who are without glory. There they shall share in Christ's own glory, there they shall reign as kings, there they shall shine as the sun in the kingdom of their Father; and all creation shall be subject unto them through Christ Jesus their Lord.

Hear, then, what the Spirit saith unto the churches!

What doth the Spirit say?

Watch and fight; overcome and be faithful unto the end! Have no part with the church that lives in self-sufficiency and has no need of anything. Only in our Lord Jesus Christ is the fulness of grace. Only going out to Him shall we be satisfied with His friendship. Watch, therefore, and be zealous! Be faithful unto the end!

Chapter XI
The Vision Of The Throne Of God
(Revelation 4)

1 After this I looked, and, behold, a door was opened in heaven: and the first voice which I heard was as it were of a trumpet talking with me; which said, Come up hither, and I will shew thee things which must be hereafter.

2 And immediately I was in the spirit: and, behold, a throne was set in heaven, and one sat on the throne.

3 And he that sat was to look upon like a jasper and a sardine stone: and there was a rainbow round about the throne, in sight like unto an emerald.

4 And round about the throne were four and twenty seats: and upon the seats I saw four and twenty elders sitting, clothed in white raiment; and they had on their heads crowns of gold.

5 And out of the throne proceeded lightnings and thunderings and voices: and there were seven lamps of fire burning before the throne, which are the seven Spirits of God.

6 And before the throne there was a sea of glass like unto crystal: and in the midst of the throne, were four beasts full of eyes before and behind.

7 And the first beast was like a lion, and the second beast like a calf, and the third beast had a face as a man, and the fourth beast was like a flying eagle.

8 And the four beasts had each of them six wings about him; and they were full of eyes within: and they rest not day and night, saying, Holy, holy, holy, Lord God Almighty, which was, and is, and is to come.

9 And when those beasts give glory and honour and thanks to him that sat on the throne, who liveth for ever and ever,

10 The four and twenty elders fall down before him that sat on the throne, and worship him that liveth for ever and ever, and cast their crowns before the throne, saying,

11 Thou art worthy, O Lord, to receive glory and honour and power: for thou hast created all things, and for thy pleasure they are and were created.

The Theme Of This Section Of Revelation

The Book of Revelation may most conveniently be divided into two main parts. The first part we have thus far treated; it includes the vision of Christ and the seven churches. The second part embraces all that is still to come and pictures the displacement of the kingdom of Satan by the kingdom of God in Christ. Or, if you please, in 1:19 John had been commissioned to write the things which are and the things which shall come to pass hereafter. In the previous chapters we have discussed the things which are. We saw Christ in the midst of the seven golden candlesticks. We obtained the description of the seven churches as they manifest themselves upon earth. In the part which is still to be discussed we are called upon to consider the things which shall come to pass hereafter, that is, the future from John's vantage point. In the part we have discussed thus far there were, besides the superscription and introduction, two parts: the first containing the revelation of the glorified Christ as the great King and Priest, ready for judgment and walking in the midst of the seven golden candlesticks, as well as holding the seven stars in His right hand; and the second part containing a seven-fold picture of the church of all ages as she becomes manifest in the midst of the world in this dispensation with all her weaknesses and strength, the good and evil properties.

It is well, before we enter upon a discussion of the rest of the book, which is often difficult and which requires diligent and prayerful study, to have the main theme of this portion of the Apocalypse clearly before your mind. Also in the part which is still before us there are numerous separate visions, in which you will perhaps get lost, as in a labyrinth, if you do not hold before your mind's eye continually the main theme of the book. That main theme is the certain displacement of the kingdom of Satan by the kingdom of God in Jesus Christ, a displacement which in its process will follow the line of historical development, but which will find its final consummation in the great world-catastrophe which will accompany the second coming of our Lord Jesus Christ to judge the quick and the dead. The displacement of the old and sinful order by the new and perfect one, the displacement of the satanic kingdom of darkness by the glorious kingdom of our Lord Jesus Christ,—such is the main theme of the rest of the book. All the visions which are recorded in the second part of the book bear upon this theme, serve to throw light upon this general subject. There are in this world two orders, two kingdoms, between which there is continual warfare, even though the kingdom of God in Jesus Christ already has gained the victory in the exaltation of the Lord at the right hand of God.

On the one hand, therefore, we shall find in the battle which is pictured to us in the Book of Revelation the force of the devil, Satan, the Antichrist, the beast and the false prophet, Babylon, and Gog and Magog. On the other hand, we shall find the Almighty God revealed in Jesus Christ our Lord, the Lamb, the holy angels, the church, and the new creation, with all its powers battling for victory, even though on the part of Christ the victory is not only sure but is also already won. Hence, the ultimate result will be that the force of the kingdom of Satan is hopelessly and definitely defeated forever, while the glorious kingdom of our God has the eternal victory.

One thing we must be warned against as we follow the discussion of this most intricate, but at the same time most beautiful, part of the Word of God. That is that we have in the Book of Revelation, no more than in any prophecy of Scripture, not a mere history written beforehand. If such were the character of the book we are studying, the matter would be quite simple indeed. In that case you would simply be able to turn page after page, just as you peruse the pages of history, in order then to find scene after scene of the world's history depicted in this book, and that too, just in the order in which they will take place. In that case you would, of course, also be able to identify the fulfillment of every portion in actual history, and point out very definitely how far we have already advanced on the road which leads to the end of time and to the victory of the kingdom of God. Even though many interpreters of the Book of Revelation entertain this notion and insist that only in this way can we properly understand the book, this conception is nevertheless very false.

We must rather present the whole book to your attention as a picture of all that must still come to pass, a picture thrown on the screen of symbolism. No attempt is made at all at following the historical order of things. At no time does the book present the chronological order. The element of time is wanting. John merely perceives different scenes, and he relates those scenes as they are held before his vision. No attempt is made in the book to point out historical causes and effects, so essential in the record of any history worthy of the name. John merely presents to us the scenes which are presented to his vision and which picture the future as they are all connected with their main cause, the Almighty God and His eternal decree as revealed in Jesus Christ our Lord.

This, therefore, you must remember as we shall study in the chapters which follow the gradual displacement of the sinful order by the perfect one as pictured to us in the seven seals, the seven trumpets, and the seven vials which represent the general outline of the second part of the book. Even as we have already maintained in connection with our discussion of the seven churches, so also in relation to the second part of the Book of Revelation we must remember that what is pictured in this part is both contemporaneous and consecutive. History repeats itself. And in that ever-repeating history you will see the recurrence of the scenes pictured on this screen. Only you must remember this, that they develop and repeat themselves with ever increasing force and vehemence, till finally Christ shall come to establish His own kingdom forever and in perfect righteousness.

There is a parallel noticeable between the first part of the book, which we have already discussed, and this second part. You will remember that in the first part, before the letters to the seven churches were written, we found the vision of the Christ, the head and the very life of the church. Thus it is also here, in the second part. Before the Lord shows John the actual battle between the two opposing kingdoms in history, He reveals to him in Chapters 4 and 5 the eternal and unconquerable power which shall surely have the victory. In these two chapters He gives us the picture of the battling force of the kingdom of God from its ideal point of view. In these two chapters, therefore, there occurs as yet nothing which relates to the battle as such. But they give us the picture of the eternal power and control of the world's history as it will display itself in the new dispensation. We shall find that they give us a picture of the new order of the kingdom as it must surely battle on to victory throughout this dispensation, even unto the end. In Chapter 4 we have the vision of the throne of God, an ideal representation of the new order which is to come at the parousia, in the day of the Lord, the realization of which is the efficient cause of all that is revealed in the rest of the book.

A New Vision Introduced

"After this," so John tells us, "I looked, and, behold, a door was opened in heaven: and the first voice which I heard was as it were of a trumpet talking with me; which said, Come up hither, and I will shew thee things which must be hereafter."

There is no reason to believe, as some have it, that there was a long interval between the time that the first vision was finished and the time that the second vision began. However, John was conscious of a change, as is evident from the entire description, and especially from the words of verse 2, "And immediately I was in the spirit..." We remember that he told us with respect to the first vision that he was in the spirit on the Lord's day. It seems that after that first vision was finished he returned to the natural state. And now, at the call of the same voice he had heard before, the voice as of a trumpet, he again is translated in the spirit, so that he can behold the things which natural eye cannot perceive. Although, therefore, we must not suppose that there was a long interval of time between the first and the second visions, there is nevertheless a decided transition from the first vision to the second, a transition of which John is very definitely conscious. The difference between the first and the second vision is characterized especially by the change of scene. The first vision was on earth, and for that reason had a very definite historical background, which made it rather easy for John and also for us to understand and comprehend its meaning. John was acquainted with the seven churches. And those seven churches, as we know, were a picture of the whole church as it exists throughout the ages, as it also exists today. But in the second vision John is called to heaven. Heaven is opened to his spiritual eye, and a voice calls to him, "Come up hither." Of course, we do not understand this to have been a literal and bodily translation; but it was a translation only in the spirit. It was a being called to heaven in the vision; and it was for that same reason also that the obedience to the call was visionary, or, if you please, in the spirit. The door, the voice that called him up hither, and the obedience to that call, — all were visionary. Nevertheless, we must remember that what we are to see and to study in the future is shown from the viewpoint of heaven, and especially from the point of view of Him that sitteth on the throne. In harmony with this, all that is recorded in the future is more idealistic and symbolic than that which we have studied in the past.

The things revealed in this second part are things which must come to pass hereafter. This "must," you understand, is a divine must. It implies the necessity of God's counsel. God has decreed the entire course of history, and because of that decree things must necessarily come to pass, and that also, exactly as decreed, and not otherwise. It is because of this fact of the decree of God that only the Almighty possesses the power to reveal what must come to pass in the future. Nothing that is revealed in this book can fail to come to pass, because behind it all stands the unchangeable counsel of the Almighty which has determined the end from the beginning. And when these things are further described as things which must come to pass hereafter, and, therefore, in the future, we must in no wise understand this to mean **after the church has finished its history**. Thus, indeed, some would have it. They present the course of events and the outline of the Book of Revelation as follows. First there is the history of the church in the world, as pictured in the first three chapters of this book. Then follows the rapture of the church, the church's being caught up into heaven. This is supposed to be described in Chapters 4 and 5. After this, according to these interpreters, follows the period of the great tribulation for the world, when all the woes and afflictions which are predicted in the main body of this book shall be realized. But the church shall have no part in this great tribulation. For from the time that is pictured in Chapters 4 and 5 the church is no more in the world, but in heaven. Thus these interpreters picture the order of this second part of the Book of Revelation. Evidently, however, this is a mistaken notion. The church is spoken of several times, also in the remaining portion of the Book of Revelation. Besides, John never tells us that the church is caught up into heaven. He merely informs us that he himself was translated, and that too, only in the spirit. But above all, if that were the case, if the church from this time forth would have no part in all the tribulations which the world must suffer, what would be the use and the purpose of the rest of this book, which is plainly written for the comfort of the church in the midst of the tribulation of this present time?

Hence, we will have nothing of this interpretation, but maintain that all that is recorded in the rest of the book concerns the whole church in the world and is written for the joy and comfort and hope of the church of Christ in this present time. And when the text says that these things must come to pass hereafter, it does not mean after the church has finished her course, but simply **after the present time from John's point of view**. John was to record the things which are and the things which will be in the future, according to 1:19. The things which are he has recorded with a view to the seven churches of Asia. In the rest of the book he is to receive the revelation of the things which must come to pass in the future, and then again, not merely things which happen only toward the end of time but in the entire future, in this entire new dispensation, from the time that

John receives his vision even unto the end. But again, we must remember that these things shall come to pass in this dispensation with increasing force as the day of the Lord draws nigh.

The Throne In Heaven

Having thus introduced the vision and prepared our minds and hearts to receive it, John informs us about the things which he saw in heaven. The first object which draws his attention is a throne. It is indeed the central figure in the whole vision, the chief element of it. It, above all, draws his attention. All the rest is grouped around that throne.

A throne, as we have had occasion to remark before, is the symbol of royal sovereignty and majesty, and therefore, at the same time, of the supreme power of judgment. Here, of course, as we learn from the rest of the vision, it stands for the highest sovereignty of heaven and earth. For He Who sits on the throne is none other than the Triune God. It is true that John simply speaks of one sitting on that throne. He does not attempt to describe Him. And this is perfectly appropriate: no one has ever seen God, and John could not definitely describe His form. He merely states the general impression which he received of His holiness and righteousness and glory and majesty in general, when he tells us: "He was to look upon like a jasper and a sardine stone." A sardius is a stone of bright red color, and therefore is representative here of the fire of God's holiness and wrath. Exactly what was the appearance of the jasper which John here mentions cannot be ascertained. But in connection with elements of other visions of God, in Ezekiel and Daniel, we may probably think of a bright, crystal-white stone, something like the diamond, thus indicating the righteousness and purity of God, as well as His glory and victory. These stones, shining together and their glittering view intermingling, present a beautiful picture of the righteousness and holiness of God in themselves, as well as in their action against a sinful world, shining forth in their majesty and sovereignty, and therefore also in His holy wrath.

But there are still more elements to be considered.

Round about the throne John saw a rainbow. It calls to our mind every time it stretches forth its beauty in the heavens the gracious covenant which God made with Noah, promising him that the world should no more be destroyed as in the flood. In general, therefore, the rainbow is a symbol of God's grace with a view to all His works. And if we read, as we do in this section, that this rainbow round about the throne of God was like an emerald to look upon, we find in it especially the symbol of hope. The emerald is green. It is the symbol of nature budding forth and renewing itself in the time of spring, the symbol also of the new creation, and therefore the symbol of hope with respect to the coming of the day of the Lord. Together, therefore, the vision of the throne, with God to look upon as a jasper and sardius, and with the rainbow round about the throne, represents God in His righteousness, holiness, purity, grace, and majesty, and at the same time in His wrath against sin and Satan, and as promising the coming of the new and sinless order in the new heavens and the new earth. It is a throne of righteousness and grace, holiness and purity, wrath against the world and hope for the people of God.

Still more. Out of the throne proceed lightnings and thunderings and voices. Voices here does not stand for anything definite, as if the voice of God or the voice of any creature were meant, but simply indicates the impression John received over and above that of the lightnings and the thunders. They were accompanied, no doubt, by the roaring noise of the stormy sea, which John calls the voices. They are as the voices of many waters. What is more important is that in this description we find once more a symbol of the majesty of God, both in itself and in its terrible activity against the sinful world as the Judge of all. When we read of these lightnings and thunders, we naturally think of Mt. Horeb, where God appeared in His majesty as the King of Israel and its Lawgiver. We may also think of the many psalms which describe the Lord in His majesty and coming for judgment in lightnings and thunder.

But there is still more. Before the throne are seven lamps burning, which are the seven Spirits of God. These seven Spirits, as we have already explained in connection with 1:4, are indeed the Holy Spirit, but then as the Spirit of Christ as He dwells in the church of God forever. The Triune God sits on the throne. The Father, the Son, and the Holy Ghost in their essential divinity are enthroned as the Lord God Almighty, thrice holy. But here, before the throne stands the Spirit of Christ. It is the Holy Spirit as He dwells in Christ as the head of His church, and therefore, the Spirit Who dwells also in the church. It is also the Spirit of God in Christ through Whom the kingdom of God will be perfected and in its perfection will exist forever. This, therefore, is the place of the seven Spirits in this beautiful vision which is symbolic of the new order that is to come.

There is still more. Before the throne John beholds as it were a sea of glass like unto crystal. Some have made of this sea of glass the realization of the brazen sea in the temple, connected with the altar of burnt offering in the court. Others are of the opinion that this sea of glass represents the sea of nations, because in the Book of Revelation the term **sea** always refers to the nations of the world. However, neither of these explanations can satisfy us. For the brazen sea there is in this scene no place, no more than for the altar of burnt offering. For it is plainly the picture of the ideal new order, as it will ultimately have the victory. And although it be true that the term **sea** in the Book of Revelation generally symbolizes the nations, it must be remembered that for such nations there is no room here. Nor is the picture of the crystal sea very appropriate to indicate the sea of the rebellious nations. Secondly, John does not say that he saw a sea, but **as it were a sea,** something like it. We therefore rather fasten our attention on the glass and crystal, and explain that this sea is a symbol of the splendor, as well as of the transparency, of the entire new creation. In the sea of glass and crystal before the throne the new creation in all its glory and beauty must have been reflected. So in the new creation all things shall reflect the glory and beauty, the holiness and righteousness and grace of Him Who sits on the throne. In that creation there shall be no more darkness. There nothing shall hinder the beauty of God from shining forth gloriously. And there all things shall reflect His glory, where we shall know even as we are known.

The Twenty-Four Elders

John in his vision, however, beholds still more. Round about the throne of God he beholds twenty-four different thrones. On those twenty-four different thrones he perceives twenty-four elders.

It is not difficult to understand the symbolism of all this and to be convinced as to the identity of these twenty-four elders. Literally, the term **elders** refers to older men, and therefore to the heads of tribes and families. Here, in the words of our text, it is to be understood in that sense. It does not mean elders as officebearers of the church, or elders in any official meaning of the word; but it simply refers to older people, first of all,—heads of the tribes, heads of families, heads of a certain people.

And as far as the number twenty-four is concerned, immediately you observe that it is twice twelve, and that as such the number will have to be explained. Twelve tribes, there were, of the people of Israel. And in the church of the new dispensation there were also twelve apostles. There can be no shadow of doubt that these twenty-four elders here must be taken as representatives of the church and of the people of God of all ages, both of the old and of the new dispensation, of Jew and Gentile. How, in the face of this symbolism, people can possibly maintain that there was no church in the old dispensation, how, in the light of this symbol, people can possibly maintain that Jew and Gentile shall not be one in the kingdom of heaven that is to come, we confess is a mystery to us. Evidently these twenty-four elders represent the entire church of the old and of the new dispensation, the church as she was redeemed and washed in the blood of the Lamb throughout the ages of history.

For notice, further, that these twenty-four elders sit on thrones surrounding the great throne in the midst of them. This symbolism, which means that also they possess royal glory and dominion, at the same time makes it very plain that their royal dominion, the royal dominion of the church, is dependent upon the throne which they surround. Moreover, wreaths, or crowns of victory, they wear. For the church is, of course, here pictured from its ideal point of view: not as the church in tribulation, but as it exists in the decree of God, looked at from the point of view of eternal glory in heaven, and therefore as having already overcome. And garments of white these elders wear: for they are washed in the blood of the Lamb, Who is still to appear on the scene of this vision. Round about the throne, therefore, the church, washed in the blood of Christ, having overcome in the battle of faith, and being set in royal dominion and glory in dependence on God Almighty, appears here in the vision which John beholds.

The Four Living Creatures

More difficult it may seem to explain the appearance of the four living creatures. John informs us that he saw "in the midst of the throne, and round about the throne, four beasts ("living creatures," ARV) full of eyes before and behind. And the first beast was like a lion, and the second beast like a calf, and the third beast had a face as a man, and the fourth beast was like a flying eagle. And the four beasts had each of them six wings about him; and they were full of eyes within."

Innumerable explanations have been given of these four living creatures. We shall not consider them all here. Only two of them deserve our consideration. In the first place, there is the interpretation which explains these four creatures to be mere cherubs, heavenly beings, angels of a specific class. And in the second place, there is also the interpretation which refers these four creatures to all living creation and its powers.

It appears to us that we must rather combine these two as they are in the vision and say that they are cherubim which, however, in the vision are made to represent the entire fulness of creation in all its various powers from an ideal point of view. When the kingdom of Christ shall once be completed, the sigh and groan of the brute creation which is mentioned in the eighth chapter of the Epistle to the Romans shall also cease; and all creation, with all its powers and with all its forces, shall be delivered actually from the bondage of corruption and shall share in the glorious liberty of the children of God. This ideal creation, with all its fulness of life, with all its powers and gifts, these four cherubim represent in the vision. Especially if we compare this vision with that in Ezekiel 1, this is clear. The prophet there also has a vision of four cherubim with faces of a lion, a calf, a man, and an eagle. The two visions, therefore, are strikingly similar. It will not do to interpret the one without the other. What is the purpose of the vision in Ezekiel? It forms the basis of the entire prophecy. Ezekiel was commissioned especially to prophesy the destruction of the old temple and the rebuilding of the new, that is, of the ideal temple of God. Or, if you please, he was to predict the displacement of the old temple which was made with hands by the new temple which would consist of the new creation, of the new heavens and the new earth. Just as John must prophesy the displacement of the sinful order by that of the perfect order of the new creation, so also Ezekiel. And even as John, so also Ezekiel at the outset receives a vision of the perfect order which is to replace the old and where God shall dwell among His people in all the new creation. In Ezekiel, therefore, as well as in John, you may call the beings, the four living creatures, cherubim. But in both these visions the cherubim are made to represent the fulness of the life of creation as it will shine forth in the new heavens and the new earth.

If we bear this in mind, we shall be able also to explain their appearance.

In the first place, we must consider their number. John saw four of these creatures. Four is the number that is symbolic of creation in all its fulness. Think of the four winds of heaven, and the four corners of the earth. In their number they therefore represent the entire creation. Then we can also explain their appearance. These four creatures present the appearance of a lion, of an ox, of a man, and of an eagle. They are therefore four royal representatives of the animate powers of creation.

What the lion is among the beasts of the field, the ox is among the cattle, man among the intelligent creatures, and the eagle among the birds. They represent, therefore, the powers of creation in their physical strength, in their daring courage, in their keen intelligence and intuition, in their freedom of movement and development with majestic flight. In a word, once more, they represent creation in all the fulness of its power and talents, as once it shall develop to the glory of Him Who sits on the throne.

Then we can also understand the symbolism of the eyes and of the six wings. As to the latter, the wing is the symbol of free flight and movement, as well as of ascent and development. Six is the number of the creation as it originally received its power from God. The six wings of every creature indicate its power of development to its full extent, unhindered and unhampered. In the new world all creation shall mount up with its six wings and reach the fulness of its development to the glory of God. And as to the former, namely, that these creatures were full of eyes, we must not refer this symbol to their ability of looking and moving in every direction, but much rather as revealing plainly their inmost nature and being. All creation is to reveal itself plainly and openly to God's glory, and the nature of creation shall no more be under the veil of sin. That this is the meaning of the symbol is plain to us from the following chapter, where we read of the Lamb that has seven eyes, which are the seven Spirits. In the eye the creature reveals his spirit, his nature, and, therefore, his name, above all other features. In the seven eyes the seven Spirits that dwell in the Lamb shine forth. In the eyes of these creatures their real nature, their spirit of life, under the influence of the Spirit of all creation, is revealed. Once more, therefore: in these four creatures, cherubic though they be, we see a representation of all the fulness of power and glory of the new world as it shall be completed when the kingdom of God shall have come in all its perfection.

Thus the symbolism is complete. In this vision of the fourth chapter of the Book of Revelation we have an ideal picture of the kingdom which is to displace in history the kingdom of Satan and sin and which is to have the complete victory in the end. We may even say that in this vision we have a picture of the battling force which will come up against Satan and his host. In that kingdom God and His throne of righteousness and holiness and majesty and grace shall be the central figure. For He shall be all in all. In that kingdom the church shall be enthroned forever, delivered from all the power of sin and darkness, washed in the blood of the Lamb, and crowned with wreaths of victory. For the elders are clothed in white raiment and have golden wreaths upon their heads. In that kingdom all creation shall be delivered, and shall be allowed to exist and to develop in unhampered flight of development and to reveal itself in all the fulness of its life to the glory of Him Who sits on the throne. In that new creation all things shall reflect the glory of the Most High God through Jesus Christ our Lord and in the seven Spirits which are before His throne. All shall be glory and life and bliss. And all shall reflect the holiness and righteousness and glory of Him Who sitteth upon the throne forevermore. That kingdom exists ideally in God's decree. That kingdom must go through a process of battle before it can reach its historical realization. But that kingdom shall surely come! For God Almighty is on our side, and the Lamb is our King! For that kingdom of light and glory and bliss we long, we hope, we fight. For that kingdom we gladly sacrifice all, and glorify the Lord our God, also in the present dispensation of spiritual realization.

The Praise Of The Creatures And The Elders

That this explanation of the vision is no mere philosophy or human fancy, but the actual interpretation of the text in Revelation 4 is for us, at least, corroborated by what the text tells us of the activity of the creatures and of the elders. We read: "And they rest not day and night, saying, Holy, holy, holy, Lord God Almighty, which was, and is, and is to come. And when those beasts give glory and honour and thanks to him that sat on the throne, who liveth for ever and ever, The four and twenty elders fall down before him that sat on the throne, and worship him that liveth for ever and ever, and cast their crowns before the throne, saying, Thou art worthy, O Lord, to receive glory and honour and power: for thou hast created all things, and for thy pleasure they are and were created."

Here we have what we consider the song of the new creation, anticipated in the vision, and that too, in the most beautiful symbolism. Remember, as we have emphasized repeatedly, the purpose of all things is the glory of God. For that glory all the world exists. All the world, and all the fulness of the world, and all the powers of the world, and all the beauty of the world,—all exists to reflect the glory and the majesty of Him Who sitteth upon the throne. In brute creation, as well as in man, God is to be glorified. But there is a difference. Brute creation glorifies God unconsciously. It is as such a reflection of the majesty and power and glory of God. But man stands in the midst of this silently adoring creation and consciously takes note of God's glory. He knows that all creation has been made by Him. He knows that it all is a reflection of God's glory. He knows that they and he were created for the purpose of being a name unto the Most High God. And therefore, he understands creation round about him. He sees how the creatures glorify God. And standing in the midst of this glorifying creation, and beholding the beauty of the Lord his God in all the creatures, he falls down in adoration, and exclaims, "O my Lord and my God!" Such is the original intent and purpose of the existence of all things.

And what now do you see in the vision? The same thing. The creatures give glory and honor and thanks to God in the highest, to Him that sitteth on the throne and liveth forever and ever. That is, all creation here gives praise to God. The fulness of creation ascribes glory to Him. It all sings of the holiness of the Most High: "Holy, holy, holy," thrice repeated to express the divine fulness of the holiness of God, of the Triune. But in this connection we must remember that also the power of sin and the whole sinful order still exists. And that power of sin and Satan must be opposed and overcome before the kingdom of God and of Christ can be perfectly realized. In the vision the creatures and the elders sing of this power. All creation shall presently show forth the power of God. But again, we hear also a battle cry in this song of the creatures and of the elders. The Lord God is almighty; and therefore, His is the victory over all sin and over all the power of darkness. They sing of His eternity. For He is the One Who was, and is, and is to come. And also in this we hear the battle cry, announcing a sure victory. For it tells us that God is eternal, that therefore His kingdom ruleth forever and ever, while the powers of darkness shall surely suffer defeat. And as all creation thus sings of God's glory, the redeemed shall look and listen and see the beauty of their God, and worship and adore. For the elders fall down at the voice of the creatures. And acknowledging that their royal power and glory are but a reflection of the sovereignty of Him Who sitteth upon the throne, they cast their diadems before Him, descend from their thrones, fall in the dust, worship, and say: "To Thee, O Lord our God, belongeth the honour and the glory and the power: for thou hast made all these things because and on account of Thine own will." Thus shall they glorify their God in all His works. And God shall be all in all!

Chapter XII

The Vision Of The Sealed Book

(Revelation 5)

1 And I saw in the right hand of him that sat on the throne a book written within and on the backside, sealed with seven seals.

2 And I saw a strong angel proclaiming with a loud voice, Who is worthy to open the book, and to loose the seals thereof?

3 And no man in heaven, nor in earth, neither under the earth, was able to open the book, neither to look thereon.

4 And I wept much, because no man was found worthy to open and to read the book, neither to look thereon.

5 And one of the elders saith unto me, Weep not: behold, the Lion of the tribe of Juda, the Root of David, hath prevailed to open the book, and to loose the seven seals thereof.

6 And I beheld, and, lo, in the midst of the throne, and of the four beasts, and in the midst of the elders, stood a Lamb as it had been slain, having seven horns and seven eyes, which are the seven Spirits of God sent forth into all the earth.

7 And he came and took the book out of the right hand of him that sat upon the throne.

8 And when he had taken the book, the four beasts and four and twenty elders fell down before the Lamb, having every one of them harps, and golden vials full of odours, which are the prayers of the saints.

9 And they sung a new song, saying, Thou art worthy to take the book, and to open the seals thereof: for thou wast slain, and hast redeemed us to God by thy blood out of every kindred, and tongue, and people, and nation;

10 And hast made us unto our God kings and priests: and we shall reign on the earth.

11 And I beheld, and I heard the voice of many angels round about the throne and the beasts and the elders: and the number of them was ten thousand times ten thousand, and thousands of thousands;

12 Saying with a loud voice, Worthy is the Lamb that was slain to receive power, and riches, and wisdom, and strength, and honour, and glory, and blessing.
13 And every creature which is in heaven, and on the earth, and under the earth, and such as are in the sea, and all that are in them, heard I saying, Blessing, and honour, and glory, and power, be unto him that sitteth upon the throne, and unto the Lamb for ever and ever.
14 And the four beasts said, Amen. And the four and twenty elders fell down and worshipped him that liveth for ever and ever.

Even the casual reader will notice immediately that this grand vision is a continuation of the vision which was begun to be revealed to John in Chapter 4. Chapters 4 and 5 belong together. They are one whole. They constitute one vision. What is told us in Chapter 5 simply adds a few new elements to the vision which was begun in Chapter 4. It reveals to us above all Him Who is next to the One Who sitteth upon the throne, the most important figure of the entire scene: the Lamb that standeth as though it hath been slain, the Lion of Juda's tribe, the Root of David, Who has overcome to open the book and to loose its seven seals. Jesus Christ is here shown as receiving the power from God to do what no one in all creation was worthy and able to do, namely, to bring and complete the glorious kingdom of God in all creation. Hence, the chief thought of the chapter is that the Lamb is found worthy to open the book.

We must, for a correct understanding of this entire passage, bear continually in mind that in it we have no revelation as yet of the things which must come to pass hereafter. It pictures, rather, the new order of things, the order of the new kingdom, as it exists perfectly in God's counsel and as it was in principle realized in the exaltation of the Lord Jesus Christ, and as it will give battle in the new dispensation to the still existing power of the prince of darkness on earth, and as also it shall finally have the complete victory and be the realization and manifestation of the kingdom in all the glory of its ultimate perfection in the new heavens and the new earth. It is, from a certain point of view, a picture of the battle-force on the side of God opposing the serpent and his armies. Now in our chapter we receive a vision of the **general** of this battle-force of the Almighty, of Him Who will lead the armies of God on to victory and Who will finally gain complete victory at the time of His second coming, our Lord Jesus Christ, the Lamb that standeth as though it had been slain.

He is the chief figure of this entire chapter. Let us, then, from this central point of view consider the new elements John introduces into the vision.

The Sealed Book

It is plain that if the apostle did not notice any definite figure on the central throne before, he now does. For he speaks of the right hand of Him that sat on the throne. The right hand, in general, is the symbol of power and sovereign authority. And therefore we have here mention made of the power and sovereign authority of the Most High. On that right hand John perceived a book. For literally we read in the original that the book is **on** the right hand of Him that sat on the throne. That it is **on** the right hand of God indicates evidently that the book is safely kept by the power of the Most High and rests on His own authority. The fact that it is presented as being **on** the hand calls to mind the picture of one who offers something to another. God, therefore, is ready to present, to give, this book to someone else.

The book itself is described to us in detail. Many interpreters have attempted to give a graphic and definite description of this book. They have tried to visualize it. Especially have they discussed the question whether here we must picture to ourselves a book as we know it, a number of separate pages bound up in two covers, or whether it was the ancient roll of a book which John saw in the vision. To us this question appears to be of little importance. In our discussion of the Book of Revelation in the future we shall often meet with visions which cannot be visualized concretely whatsoever, of which we cannot draw a graphic picture before our minds. Neither is this necessary. What we must attempt is to ascertain the central significance of each vision, and explain the details of each scene in the light of this central idea, more or less as a parable is explained. Thus also with this book. It is, in the first place, a book. And this causes us to think of the thought that is expressed in its contents, in this case the thought and plan of Him Who sitteth upon the throne, the eternal thought of the living God. This book, so we are told, was written within and on the back, that is, it was completely covered. This symbolizes the fact that the thoughts of God in this book are complete and constitute one whole. Nothing can be added to this book, and nothing may be subtracted from it. Just as the two stone tables of the Decalogue were covered on both sides, symbolizing the completeness of the Law of God, so this book is complete in itself.

Further, we notice that the book is sealed. A seal serves to safeguard the contents of any manuscript or book against a possible intruder, for whom the contents of a certain letter or book were not intended. Thus, the fact that the book on the right hand of Him Who sitteth upon the throne is sealed and that its seals have never been broken signifies that the contents are as yet secret. They are not known to anyone outside of Him Who sitteth upon the throne and Who is the author of the book. Yet the manner in which it is sealed causes us to surmise something in regard to the nature of its contents. For it is sealed with **seven** seals. And seven is a symbolic number. Seven is the symbol of completion, and as such it indicates in this instance that the book is completely and safely sealed. But in distinction from the number ten, which also denotes completion, seven has generally to do with the kingdom of God. And thus the number seven, often indicating the completion of God's work in the coming of His kingdom, makes us immediately conjecture that this book is somehow connected with the perfecting of the kingdom of our Lord Jesus Christ.

The question which is of supreme importance in this instance is: what is the significance of this book? This must be answered. And in connection with this first question there is another: what is the meaning of the opening of the book and the breaking of its seals? On this question hinges, more or less, our entire view of the chapter.

And then we remark that there can be little doubt about the fact that this book is symbolic of the living and powerful decree of God with regard to the things which must shortly come to pass. Let us clearly understand the implication of this statement. We do not mean to assert that this book is a copy, a dead copy, of that decree, or the symbol of such a copy. In that case the opening of the book would imply nothing more than that the hidden things of God's counsel were prophetically revealed to us. But that is not so. The book is the symbol of the decree itself, of the living, irresistible, powerful decree of God, Whose chief purpose it is to realize the kingdom of God, which He planned from before the foundation of the world. The breaking of the seals does not simply open the hidden things of God's counsel. Its idea is not simply that of revelation. But the opening of the book signifies the very realization of that powerful, all-comprehensive decree of God. It signifies, therefore, the very realization of the kingdom. He who receives the book and may open the seals receives the living decree of God itself and the power to realize it. He who is honored with the distinction of breaking the seals receives therefore the power to establish and to complete the kingdom, actually to bring to pass all that is written in the book.

That the book signifies the plan of the Almighty is evident, first of all, from the fact that it is found on His right hand, indicating undoubtedly also that He alone is its author. That is shown, in the second place, by the fact that it is sealed with seven seals. The seal is symbol of its secrecy, and seven is connected with the kingdom of God. When all of these seals shall have been loosed, the counsel of God shall have been realized and the kingdom shall have been established in glory. This is evident, in the third place, from Revelation 4:1 in connection with this book. There John was called to heaven to see the things which must shortly come to pass hereafter. It is plain from all that follows in the Book of Revelation that these things are contained in the book on the right hand of Him that sat on the throne. And that this book is not a mere dead copy of the decree of God, but symbol of the living decree itself, so that the breaking of its seals involves the realization of God's counsel, is plain from all that follows. For when seal after seal is broken, we are not simply served with some information read from the book in regard to the things that must come to pass hereafter; but we see these very things being realized before our eyes. We conclude, therefore, that the book is symbol of the irresistible decree of God with regard to the things which must come to pass in this dispensation, and that the opening of the book, the loosing of the seals, implies the power to realize that decree and bring the eternal kingdom to perfection.

The Challenge

If we accept this as the correct interpretation of the book and of the breaking of its seals, it will not be difficult to understand what follows. First of all, a challenge is sent forth to every creature in all the world to open the book: "And I saw a strong angel proclaiming with a loud voice, Who is worthy to open the book, and to loose the seals thereof?" In general, we find in these words of the angel a challenge sent to every creature to open the book if he is able.

John beholds a strong angel. Strong the angel is, not because he holds any special office. It is not necessary to make various conjectures as to the identity of this angel. Scripture tells us nothing about him. He must be strong for the simple reason that his present task requires that strength. He must shout with a strong, with a great voice. His message must resound throughout all creation. It must reach every possible creature in the whole world. It must rebound over the earth; it must echo through all the heavens; it must penetrate into the deepest realms of darkness. All must receive the message. A strong angel, then, with a great voice, causes the challenge to go forth: "Who is worthy to open the book and to loose the seals thereof?"

The meaning of this invitation is plain. The angel does not merely invite everyone that will make an attempt to take the book and break the seals. No, the question is whether there is any creature that is worthy, that possesses the legal right and the power to receive and open the book. And if we now remember that the loosing of the seals of the book implies really the bringing and completion of the kingdom of righteousness and peace and bliss, the kingdom of God in all the world, the question amounts to a challenge, sent forth to all creation, to bring that kingdom and to realize it if they are able.

Thus the passage becomes pregnant with significance. It is by no means irrelevant to the character of the Book of Revelation as a whole. The book pictures to us the coming of the kingdom of God in its battle against the kingdom of darkness. It must become very plain that this kingdom is a kingdom of God indeed. It is a kingdom of God, divinely conceived in His eternal counsel. It is a kingdom God did establish in the blood of the Lamb. It is a kingdom God Himself does historically realize and complete and lead on to its final manifestation in glory. It is a kingdom of God from beginning to end. It must become very plain that there is no creature that could possibly establish a kingdom like it. It must become evident that all the world could not produce the creature that could bring to the world the kingdom of peace and righteousness and everlasting glory. All the attempts of the creature must publicly fail, in order that the power and grace of the Most High may become plainly evident.

Hence, the creature receives the opportunity first. Before the Lamb that stands as though it had been slain steps forward and takes the book out of the hand of Him Who sat on the throne, every creature must receive the invitation. Hence, the message goes forth. It goes forth to the angels in heaven: "Can ye open that book, ye myriads of holy spirits, who day and night surround the throne of God? Can ye save the world? Can ye bring peace and bliss to a world of sin?" The challenge also comes to the earth, particularly, of course, to man. "Man, here is your opportunity. If you are worthy, take the book, and bring the kingdom. Send righteousness and bliss to all the world. Ye wise men of the world, ye giants of thought, hear the message resound. Do you know how to open the book? Can you suggest the way of salvation for the world? Ye rulers and mighty ones, can ye open the book? Can ye by your laws and institutions, by your armies and power, inaugurate the kingdom of peace? All ye that speak so highly of the regeneration of society, of a better world to live in, of social righteousness, here is the challenge! Are ye important enough to take the book, and are ye able to break the seals? Come on, now, human wisdom and power, riches and wealth, science and invention, come and take now the book, and open its seals." The message goes forth under the earth. It resounds even to the depth of hell. It trembles in the ears of the prince of darkness and his angels. O, surely, he is shrewd, he is powerful and mighty! He once proposed to take the place of God and sang the deceitful siren-song that man would be like God if he only would obey him, the devil, instead of his divine Friend and rightful Sovereign. Since then all the promises of the devil proved empty and deceiving. Sin, evil, suffering, and black death he brought to the world. Here then is the opportunity. If he is able, let him come! That book possesses the secret of power necessary to bring the kingdom. Let him now take the book and bring bliss and righteousness if he is worthy!

The Silent Answer To The Challenge

All creation is silent. "And no man in heaven, nor in earth, neither under the earth, was able to open the book, neither to look thereon."

The angels stand in breathless silence; and their profound silence is the testimony of their unworthiness. The devil shrinks back into the remotest corner of the regions of darkness and fails to respond; he and all his devils must confess that they are not able and that they are not worthy to open the book. All the earth confesses mutely that no one is able to break the seals and therefore to bring in the kingdom of God.

Neither must you receive the impression that this entire scene merely belongs to the embellishment of the vision and that there is nothing in history that presents us with the realization of this challenge. On the contrary, this message of the angel and the profound silence with which it is met symbolize the vain efforts which are always being put forth by the creature, outside of the Lamb that standeth as though it had been slain, to restore peace and bliss to the world. Men have repeatedly exerted themselves to work out their own salvation and the salvation of the world.

Systems of thought, world-systems of philosophy, have been built up by human minds one after another, to show the true way to peace and righteousness and to establish an imitation of the kingdom of bliss. But they have all met with utter failure and disaster. No human wisdom has been able to call back the paradise lost. The might of the world, kings and rulers, have throughout history attempted to realize the world-kingdom, embracing all the earth. If only they would attain their end, if only such a universal kingdom could be realized, they would surely bring peace to the world. Nebuchadnezzar, Alexander the Great, Caesar, Charlemagne, Napoleon, William of Hohenzollern, and Hitler are their names. But they have failed. Their glory is faded. Their power is broken. Their name is trampled under foot. Today we are told that the glorious dawn of a new day is faintly seen at the horizon of history. Democracy will perform what autocracy failed to bring. Crowns must be removed. Thrones must tumble in the dust. We must have the rule of the people. Besides, all the nations of the world must combine in this great movement for universal peace and righteousness. A league of nations is what we need and what has already been established. In this way righteousness shall come to dwell on earth, and peace shall reign undisturbedly. But already it may safely be predicted that also this ideal shall never be realized. Never shall it bring the much longed for kingdom of peace. Also in our day men of social service assure us that society must undergo a radical transformation. It must itself be regenerated. It must have new laws, new institutions, new customs, new relationships between capital and labor, shorter working days and better living conditions for the workingman, the abolishment of liquor and other evils of society. If thus we labor, so they say, for the regeneration of society, we shall bring in the kingdom of God. All these human efforts, put forth by mere human strength and ingenuity, present the historical realization of the challenge of the angel: "Who is worthy to open the book and to loose the seals thereof?" And the ultimate failure of all these attempts constitutes the historical realization of the statement: "And no man in heaven, nor in earth, neither under the earth, was able to open the book, neither to look thereon." History must reveal the failure of all attempt to bring the kingdom of God without the Lamb, and that simply because of the great fundamental truth entirely ignored by the men of the world, that at the basis of all trouble and confusion and war and destruction lies the guilt of sin and the corruption of the nature of man.

We further read in the text: "And I wept much, because no man was found worthy to open and to read the book, neither to look thereon."

These words picture to us the effect which the silence of all creation in answer to the challenge that had been sounded by the strong angel had upon John himself. He was very sorely disappointed. He was filled with bitter sorrow. And it seems to us that this weeping and wailing on the part of John corroborates the view that the book on the hand of Him Who sitteth on the throne is not a mere copy of the decree, but a symbol of the decree itself, and therefore that the opening of the book does not merely involve a revelation of the things which must come to pass hereafter, but the realization of them and the bringing of the kingdom of heaven. It hardly seems possible to us that John would have wept so sorely and would have wept so bitterly if the keeping closed of the book merely meant to him that he would not have received a vision of the future. Hidden or revealed, John certainly would know that the future was in safe hands, and that the Almighty would bring it to pass, whether or not it was revealed to him. But now the book stands for the bringing of the kingdom itself. If that book is not opened, if it must remain sealed, the kingdom will never come. John evidently realizes this. Hence, he weeps sorely. This book is the testament of the kingdom, still sealed, but waiting for the heir that may receive and open it. And therefore that there is in all creation evidently none that is found worthy to open the book and to look thereon is to him nothing less than a terrible disaster.

Hence, in the vision all are silent. No answer is given. No one appears to take the book. In the vision John has not yet seen the Lamb, for otherwise he would have fixed his hope on Him. In the vision John feels as if that book must remain closed. And in the vision he weeps.

The Lamb Worthy To Open The Book

But he is also immediately comforted and bade not to weep: "And one of the elders saith unto me, Weep not: behold, the Lion of the tribe of Juda, the Root of David, hath prevailed to open the book, and to loose the seven seals thereof."

This is indeed a beautiful picture. The elder is representative of the church, of the church triumphant, while John is still in the church militant. And the church triumphant here comforts the church militant in her grief by assuring her of victory. Not as if there is an actual contact between the church triumphant and the church militant, except, of course, in the Spirit Who dwells in them both. No, but who in the entire scene would be more worthy and more qualified to comfort the weeping apostle than this elder? John here is weeping because he cannot see how the victory will be won and the kingdom for which he hopes and longs will ever be perfected, since no one appears worthy to open the book and to break the seals thereof. And there is the elder, already enjoying the victory of the kingdom. And therefore, by actual experience he is acquainted with the power of the Lamb to win the victory. He knows that the victory is certain. He also knows who is the Victor. And therefore, it is his privilege and honor to announce to John the Victor, Who is worthy to open the book.

As to the announcement itself, the one who is here proclaimed as being worthy to open the book and to loose the seven seals is presented as the Lion of Juda's tribe and the Root of David.

The Lion in nature is the king of all the beasts of the field. As such he appears time and again in the Word of God. As such he is also mentioned in our text. He is the symbol of royal majesty and power, of the power to conquer and to subdue, as well as to reign and to be acknowledged as sovereign. Here we may remark in anticipation that he serves as the symbol of Jesus Christ, the glorious and victorious King. As such he stands directly over against His antagonist. The devil's symbol and ensign is the serpent, the type and symbol of sneaky subtlety. There is nothing royal about the serpent, crawling in the dust, stealthily coming for an attack in the back of his opponent and biting his heel. There is nothing servile about the lion. Conscious of his superiority, he is ready to stare his enemy in the face, meet him without fear, and battle in the open. Thus is also the difference between Christ and the devil. Christ is the Lion; the devil is the serpent. The very onlook of them will assure you that not the serpent, but the Lion shall have the victory. He is further called the Lion of Juda's tribe. The source of this expression we find in Genesis 49:9, 10. There we read of Jacob's blessing his sons, the heads of the future tribes of the people of God. And it is of Juda that he says: "Judah is a lion's whelp; from the prey, my son, thou art gone up: He stooped down, he couched like a lion, who shall rouse him up? The sceptre shall not depart from Judah, nor the ruler's staff from between his feet, until Shiloh come, and unto him shall the obedience of the people be." Here we have mention made of Juda under the symbol of a lion. And rabbinical writings inform us that as the children of Israel encamped in four divisions in the desert, each under a leading tribe, and that leading tribe with its tribal ensign, the symbol of

Juda was a lion. Juda, therefore, was the royal tribe: he should rule over his brethren. His would be the dominion over the people of God. From him would come forth the king that would lead the people of God on to victory and defend them against their enemies. But all this was bestowed on Juda because on him the blessing and privilege was conferred to bring forth **the** King, Who would have dominion forever and reign over the people of God without end. Juda carried in his loins the Lion. All the kings who might come forth from him were after all but types of the Lion, of the Lion Who would finally be brought forth, the Shiloh, after which Juda as the royal tribe and earthly type of Christ might disappear. And therefore, if you ask who is the Lion of Juda's tribe, because of whose presence in Juda's loins he might be called a lion, the answer can be but one: Christ Jesus, and He alone.

In the second place, He is announced as the Root of David. Also this expression occurs in other places of Scripture. In the first place, we find it in this same Book of Revelation, 22:16, where the Lord announces Himself and says, "I am the Root and offspring of David." And for its Old Testament source we must turn to Isaiah 11:1, 10: "And there shall come forth a rod out of the stem of Jesse, and a Branch shall grow out of his roots. And in that day, there shall be a root of Jesse, which shall stand for an ensign of the people; to it shall the Gentiles seek: and his rest shall be glorious."

The general meaning of this is perfectly clear. It refers to the Christ as the off-spring of David, as being the seed of David. Yet it seems to us that we lose exactly the beauty and the power of the figure if we would say no more than this. Jesus is not called the off-spring of David without anything further. But He is named the Root of David. And no doubt, when the Savior in Revelation 22 says, "I am the Root and the off-spring of David," the meaning is: "I am the off-spring of David because I was his Root. The very fact that I was the Root of David made it possible that I am his off-spring." A brief consideration of the symbol here used will make this perfectly evident. A root bears the tree, and not the tree the root. From the root the tree sprouts forth and develops. From and through that root it derives its life and strength. And the picture which is implied in the symbolism of the text here is this, that you may level a tree to the ground; but leave its root, and the tree will again sprout forth, and that in a more glorious manifestation than before.

In that sense Christ is the Root of David. David was king; and God had made a covenant with him that on his throne, on the throne of Israel, his seed should sit forever. But the essence, the root, the life, of that covenant and everlasting kingdom was not David, nor was it Jesse, nor was it Judah. It was David because he was the type of his own Root. The essence of David and of his kingdom was Christ Jesus. That is the Root. Because he carried in his loins the Seed Who was to sit on the spiritual throne of Israel in the future, therefore that everlasting covenant could be made with him. From that root of Christ, the typical manifestation of the spiritual kingdom sprouted forth in David's time and for some years thereafter. But this typical manifestation might disappear. It was levelled to the very ground. At the time when Jesus was born it had almost been destroyed. No one would be able to point you to the Davidic kingdom at that time. Nevertheless, it still existed: for the Root was still there. And that Root was Christ. That Root blossomed forth anew. It sprouted. A shoot came forth out of it. And that shoot will continue to develop until the tree is completed and the kingdom of David shall appear glorious and beautiful, everlasting and without a possibility of destruction, in the day of the Lord. The Lion of Juda's tribe is at the same time the Root of David. But this symbol pictures in unmistakable language the unity of the old and the new dispensations. The kingdom of David from its spiritual side is no other than the kingdom of Christ in the new dispensation. The one kingdom is in its outward manifestation only typical of the other. In essence it was the same. For that same Root that sprouted and brought forth a shoot which will develop into the new and everlasting kingdom of Christ Jesus was present also in the loins of David. Israel and the congregation, the old and the new kingdom, are not two, but one.

Of Him the elder says that He has overcome to open the book. The opening of the book, we remember, is the bringing and completion of the kingdom through the breaking of the seven seals. And therefore, that the Lion has overcome to open the book implies that He has already gained that particular victory which was required to complete the kingdom of God. In what capacity He has gained this victory becomes clear when He Himself appears on the scene before the wondering eyes of John.

"And I beheld, and, lo, in the midst of the throne, and of the four beasts, and in the midst of the elders, stood a Lamb as it had been slain, having seven horns and seven eyes, which are the seven Spirits of God sent forth into all the earth." Thus we read in the text.

Also in regard to this wonderful Lamb interpreters have exhausted their ingenuity to picture to their minds its image, and artists have tried to the utmost of their creative genius to present its picture on canvas, but with little result. Evidently if you read the text, it seems quite impossible to picture a Lamb with seven horns and seven eyes. And even though this were possible, so that a graphic presentation might be given of this Lamb, certainly the fact that the Lamb stands as though it had been slain can never be concretely represented. Neither is this at all essential to the interpretation of the symbolism.

Rather than this, we should pay attention to all the details which are mentioned, in order to obtain a true interpretation.

We note, therefore, in the first place, what also John must have noticed with surprise, that here stands a **Lamb**. The one who would be able to take and to open the book had been announced as a Lion. But if John now also expects that he will see a Lion in all his royal majesty appearing before his vision, he is utterly mistaken. And yet it is perfectly in order that the Savior should appear in the vision as the Lamb, though He had been announced as the Lion of Juda's tribe. You see, the assurance has been given that the Lion has overcome. But the question that is now answered by the appearance of this Lamb is: how and in what capacity has He overcome? Has He gone forth like a roaring Lion, to conquer the enemy by His royal power? No, the answer to this question is: the Lion of Juda's tribe has overcome in the capacity of a Lamb. In fact, He has done so in the capacity of a Lamb for the slaughter. Perhaps if it had required the mere power of the Lion, the creature could have fought the battle that would make him worthy to open the book. But it required something far different. And that something is pictured in the symbolism of the Lamb. The lamb in Scripture is the symbol of most perfect submission, and therefore of absolute obedience. As we read in Isaiah 53: "As a lamb that is led to the slaughter, so he opened not his mouth." And for that reason it is the symbol of the most perfect sacrifice to God, brought in absolute submission and obedience, without rebellion and murmuring.

In the second place, note that the Lamb stands as though He had been slain. That means, of course, that the Lamb bears the marks of having been led to the slaughter, of having been sacrificed. But it also brings out very forcibly that this Lamb did not succumb, but stands even after it has been slain. Although it was already sacrificed, yet it stands and lives.

Thirdly, we note about this Lamb that it has seven eyes, which the text interprets as being the seven Spirits of God. The Lamb has received the

Spirit of God in all His fulness. And that Spirit dwells in Him, but is also sent forth into all the kingdom, so that He is the life of that kingdom.

Then, too, note that the Lamb also has seven horns. The horn is the symbol of royal power and dominion in Scripture. Seven is the number of completeness with a view to the kingdom of God. Especially is this the case when it is compared with the power of the beast. The beast receives ten horns, and therefore he also possesses a complete dominion. But the dominion of the beast is limited by the decree of God, and therefore his number is ten. Whenever you see the beast appear with the mark of ten, you may depend on it that it is the kingdom of the devil. Even though he tries to imitate this number seven, you must never believe him. This, indeed, is what he tries to do: he continually makes an attempt to change the number of his horns, as Daniel tells us. When he receives ten, he destroys three of them and tries to appear, therefore, under the symbol of the number seven. But never believe him! Seven is the number of the Lamb. And this number seven you find only there, where the marks of the Lamb that has been slain also appear. If therefore the devil appears with beautiful imitations of the kingdom of Christ and tries to have us enlist in the service of his kingdom, ask immediately for his marks of sacrifice. It is the only thing which he cannot show. The Lamb has seven horns, and therefore He is King over the entire kingdom, and King everlasting.

Finally, note also that this Lamb stands in the midst of the throne and of the four living creatures and of the four and twenty elders. He is the life and center of them all, and His seven Spirits pervade them all.

It is not difficult to understand the meaning of all this. This Lamb is Christ Jesus, and that in His humiliation and exaltation. It shows how He has overcome and that He has overcome to open the book. He has overcome like a Lamb, that is, as the Servant of God, ready to perform the will of the Father to perfection. He was ready to bear His wrath. He was ready to suffer under that wrath. He was ready to walk the dark and difficult way of the cross. He was ready to give His life and to fulfill all the righteousness of God. There is only one way in which the kingdom of God can ever be established. That is the way of obedience even unto death. Hence, if one can be found who is able to bear the wrath of God and the penalty of sin, able to suffer and die, and who can satisfy the unchangeable righteousness of God, He, and He only, will be worthy and able to open the book. That Lamb is Christ. But not only in His humiliation, also in His exaltation He stands there. He stands there, and therefore He lives. He died; but He arose and lives forever. He stands there, but only as the Victor. He has already received His glory and possesses the power of the kingdom. He possesses the Spirit Who dwells in Him and Who must complete the kingdom for the Father. In a word, that Lamb is Christ crucified; but at the same time it is Christ glorified.

The Lamb Takes The Book

This Lamb, then, takes the book: "And he came and took the book out of the right hand of him that sat upon the throne."

We need not dwell on this at great length any more, after all that has been said. The general meaning of this action is perfectly clear. Only a few words we must add to this. We are here almost immediately reminded of that beautiful portion in the Book of Daniel where he describes how the one like unto the Son of Man approaches the Ancient of days, Who sitteth on the throne. There we read, Daniel 7:13, 14: "I saw in the night visions, and, behold, one like the Son of man came with the clouds of heaven, and came to the Ancient of days, and they brought him near before him. And there was given him dominion, and glory, and a kingdom, that all people, nations, and languages, should serve him: his dominion is an everlasting dominion, which shall not pass away, and his kingdom that which shall not be destroyed."

In principle we have the same vision here in the Book of Revelation. Of course, in harmony with the difference in point of view, Daniel sees the transaction in a little different light than John. In Daniel's time none of these things were as yet fulfilled; in John's time they had principally become reality. In Daniel's time the prophet could not realize the distinction between the first and the second advent of the Messiah; John plainly realized this distinction. Daniel, therefore, sees the entire transaction all in one vision. He sees the approach of the Son of Man to the Ancient of days; that is, in vision he sees the Christ approach the Father along the path of humiliation and exaltation, along the way of obedience. He sees that this Son of Man receives the power and the kingdom, the authority to bring and realize the kingdom. But he also sees that this kingdom is actually given Him and completed, so that all nations bow before Him. The first of these had already been realized, so that John merely beholds the Lamb as standing as though it had been slain. The third of these must still be realized in the future, so that John does not as yet see the completion of the dominion. What John here beholds is that second element, namely, that the power and authority is given to Christ to bring the kingdom of God. The Lamb takes the book. It does not say that the book is given Him: He takes it, in answer to the challenge. He waits till all creation acknowledges that it cannot bring the kingdom, that it is not worthy to receive the book from Him that sitteth on the throne. Then He steps forward, silently, majestically, fully conscious of His being worthy to open the book and its seven seals, and takes it out of the hand of Him Who sitteth upon the throne.

We may ask: when was this realized? When did Christ receive the book from the hand of Him Who sits on the throne?

In order to understand this, we must be careful, and not bring the time element into the vision. The Lamb receives the book not at the time when John sees it, in the last decade of the first century. Nor can it be said that the Lamb receives the book after He has received what is symbolized by the horns and the eyes. On the contrary, the whole is symbolic, to picture to us forcibly that Christ Jesus has received all power in heaven and on earth and in hell. After He has been slain and is risen from the dead, after He has ascended to the Father, He is exalted to the highest position, and that in the capacity of the Lamb that has been slain. Exalted, He is, to the right hand of God. And this being seated at the right hand of God simply means that to Him all dominion is given in principle, that all power in heaven and on earth is surrendered into His hands. Christ rules His church and His kingdom as it has been spiritually established on earth in the new dispensation. Christ rules the world also: the world, that is, from its evil point of view. He controls all history in the name of Him Who sitteth on the throne. And therefore it is literally true that the Almighty has given to the Lamb the decree that is powerful to its own fulfillment. Christ now controls all history. He is busy in the preaching of the gospel, busy in wars and bloodshed of the world, busy in pestilence and famine, busy in all the social relations of our time. And through them all He works out the decree. He breaks seal after seal, as we shall see, and brings to pass all that must come to pass in this present dispensation, and all this with a view to the bringing of the glorious kingdom of God. When that kingdom shall have been completed, and the power of opposition shall have been broken, then He shall surrender His absolute power and subject Himself and reign over the completed kingdom under God forever and ever.

Praise And Adoration

So, then, the Lamb is found worthy to open the book. That means that Christ received all power to develop and to complete the kingdom, and to control all forces that rise against it in this present dispensation. Is it a wonder that the entire new economy of things as they are pictured in heaven breaks out in praise and adoration of Him Who sits on the throne and of the Lamb? "And when he had taken the book, the four beasts and four and twenty elders fell down before the Lamb, having every one of them harps, and golden vials full of odours, which are the prayers of saints. And they sung a new song, saying, Thou art worthy to take the book, and to open the seals thereof: for thou wast slain, and hast redeemed us to God by thy blood out of every kindred, and tongue, and people, and nation; And hast made us unto our God kings and priests: and we shall reign on the earth."

The creatures and the elders, that is, the representatives of the church and of the redeemed creation, take the lead in this heavenly choir. They come to acknowledge the dominion of Christ Jesus and the worthiness on His part to open the book, to bring the kingdom of God to perfection. They do so, in the first place, by falling down before Him. Just as the elders fell down before Him Who sits on the throne in the preceding chapter, in order to acknowledge that He is absolutely sovereign and that they had no independent dominion, so now the representatives of the church and of all the redeemed world acknowledge that Christ is King by falling down before Him because He has taken the book. They come and fall down before the Lamb, having harps and golden bowls of incense, representing the prayers of the saints. The harp in Scripture is the instrument that is symbolic of the prophetic office. In I Samuel 10:5 we read that Samuel informs Saul that he will meet a band of prophets carrying harps. When, in II Kings 3, we are told about the request of the kings of Israel, Judah, and Edom, warring against the Moabites, that Elisha the prophet may give them counsel, we read that the prophet calls for a minstrel to play for him. In I Chronicles 25:1-3 we read that David set apart the sons of Asaph, Heman, and Jeduthun, who should prophesy with the harp and other instruments. And in Psalm 49:4 we read: "I will open my dark sayings upon the harp." The harp, therefore, is symbolic of the prophetic office in the highest sense of the word, namely, to adore and glorify God Almighty with our lips. The golden bowls of incense are explained by the text itself. Incense is the symbol of the priestly office. It was the priest above all who burned incense before Jehovah on the altar of incense and when he appeared in the holy place. This is again in full harmony with the symbolical significance of the incense. It symbolizes the prayers of the saints, to present which was the office of the priests. And these prayers are, of course, especially the expression of devotion and consecration to God. The highest purpose and the highest idea of prayer is not that it is an expression of our needs, but rather in the highest sense of the word it is the expression of our devotion and consecration to the Lord our God,—the laying of ourselves in love upon His altar, even as sweet incense, pleasing unto Him. So these creatures and elders come here to acknowledge the kingly dominion of Christ. And therefore they fall down and glorify His name with their lips. Hence, they each have a harp; and they come to express their consecration to Him. And for the same reason they have golden bowls of incense, filled with the prayers of the saints.

And they sing a new song. This song is new because it is different in kind from any song ever sung before. Its subject is different. The object of its adoration is different. The original song of creation sang the glory of the Triune God because He had made all things and was worthy to receive the honor and glory and the power forever. But this song is new. It is also a song of adoration, but not to God immediately and directly, but to the Lamb, and through the Lamb to Him. The Lamb that has been slain now holds the book with its seven seals. It means, therefore, that He will do battle and that He will have the ultimate victory, to establish the kingdom of God in glory. For this all creation gives Him glory and honor. They sing: "Thou art worthy to open the book." What a contrast! A moment ago all creation was silent, and John lay weeping because no one could open the book. Here the Lamb is praised and glorified, for He is found worthy to open the book. Thus it is in reality. The world in all its struggles, outside of the Lamb that was slain, is bound to suffer defeat and will ultimately have to acknowledge that the Lamb only has the victory. A new song, therefore, this is: for the object of adoration is the Lamb.

But a new song it is also because of the contents. It does not merely speak of creation; it speaks of glorious redemption: "For thou wast slain, and hast redeemed us to God by thy blood out of every kindred, and tongue, and people, and nation." It is the song that glorifies the Lamb for His work of redemption. But at the same time, and through this glorification of the Lamb, it adores the incomprehensible grace of God, Who gave His only begotten Son that He might bear our sins on the accursed tree. It is a song of victory. For it mentions that the Lamb has made the saints to be kings and priests unto God, and that they reign upon the earth. Now they are already a kingdom in principle: for the kingdom of God has been established spiritually even in this dispensation. But the completion of the kingdom is assured. For the book has been taken out of the hand of Him that sitteth on the throne. When that book shall be opened by Him that is worthy, the kingdom shall be perfected. And therefore, after the book has been taken and the future of the kingdom secured, after it has been ascertained that the Lamb shall bring the kingdom to final perfection, these creatures and elders speak as if the whole were already accomplished. Once more, it is the picture of the perfected creation which we see here. Already Christ has made them priests and a kingdom. Already they reign with Him on the earth.

But this song resounds and rebounds through creation, so that more and still more creatures appear to give glory to Christ Jesus. They are myriads of angels: ten thousand times ten thousand, and thousands of thousands. And they also join in the song of the creatures and elders. With seven-fold glory adoring the Lamb, they sing: "Worthy is the Lamb that was slain to receive power, and riches, and wisdom, and strength, and honour, and glory, and blessing." Seven-fold is this adoration. The Lamb is worthy to receive all the power and the glory of the kingdom over which He shall reign forevermore. But even this is not all. Finally all creation joins together. No creature can keep silence at this glorious occasion, now that the victory is assured and the coming of the kingdom safely rests in the hand of the Lion of Juda's tribe. Wider and wider the circles become, and the voices and shouts and music, all of adoration, join together and blend into one great harmonious song, the song of the new creation, the new song glorifying God and the Lamb, and saying: "Blessing, and honour, and glory, and power, be unto him that sitteth upon the throne, and unto the Lamb for ever and ever." Glory to God and the Lamb! Such is the contents of the new song. For we are of Christ, and Christ is God's. God shall be all and in all through the Lamb that was slain. God through the Lamb shall in the eternal and glorious future, when the book shall have been completely opened to its last leaf and seal, be the song of creation. Because the Lamb was slain, and in the slain Lamb the eternal and incomprehensible grace, holiness, and righteousness of Him Who sitteth upon the throne was revealed in the highest sense of the word, God and the Lamb, – God through the Lamb, – is therefore the subject of this new song. At this song all the creatures represented by the four living creatures shall say, "Amen, even so." And at this song the elders shall fall down, and all the redeemed of God shall worship.

Such is the picture, a picture of overwhelming beauty and glory. It is a picture which we can but very inadequately represent in words. But it is a picture the reality of which will still surpass our boldest expectation. That kingdom shall surely come! Seal after seal shall be broken, till the kingdom shall have been perfected. But it will come only through the power of the Lamb that was slain. In the church, therefore, only the crucified Jesus will be known and recognized. And only those that believe in Him shall never be ashamed!

Chapter XIII

The Four Horsemen

(Revelation 6:1-8)

1 And I saw when the Lamb opened one of the seals, and I heard, as it were the noise of thunder, one of the four beasts saying, Come and see.

2 And I saw, and behold a white horse: and he that sat on him had a bow; and a crown was given unto him: and he went forth conquering, and to conquer.

3 And when he had opened the second seal, I heard the second beast say, Come and see.

4 And there went out another horse that was red: and power was given to him that sat thereon to take peace from the earth, and that they should kill one another: and there was given unto him a great sword.

5 And when he had opened the third seal, I heard the third beast say, Come and see. And I beheld, and lo a black horse; and he that sat on him had a pair of balances in his hand.

6 And I heard a voice in the midst of the four beasts say, A measure of wheat for a penny, and three measures of barley for a penny; and see thou hurt not the oil and the wine.

7 And when he had opened the fourth seal, I heard the voice of the fourth beast say, Come and see.

8 And I looked, and behold a pale horse: and his name that sat on him was Death, and Hell followed with him. And power was given unto them over the fourth part of the earth, to kill with sword, and with hunger, and with death, and with the beasts of the earth.

The Seals In General

Now the Lamb is in possession of the book with its seven seals and commences to open it, breaking the seals one after another.

In the opening of the seven seals we have approached the discussion of the things that were designated in the first chapter of the Book of

Revelation as "the things that must come to pass hereafter." We are perhaps aware of the fact that the phenomenon of the seven seals and the record of their being opened by the Lamb constitutes at the same time all that is contained in the rest of the Book of Revelation, except for the fact that we meet with several interludes which have been inserted for various reasons. We are perhaps also acquainted with the further fact that the seven seals do not retain throughout their character as seals, but that the seventh seal is revealed as seven trumpets, the seventh of which later again dissolves and becomes manifest as the seven vials of the wrath of God.

At first we intended to treat these seals separately, one by one. But a study of the first four seals soon led us to the conclusion that such a method would be both impossible and impracticable. For, in the first place, it soon becomes evident, as one investigates the contents of the first four seals, that they really belong together, are very closely allied, and therefore ought to be discussed in their relation to one another and in their combined effect upon the history of this dispensation. And, in the second place, a method which would discuss these seals one by one would be in danger of calling attention to all kinds of doctrines and truths which are undoubtedly implied in the text but of which the discussion would be irrelevant to the main purpose of the Book of Revelation, that is, to reveal the coming Christ in glory. Therefore, we now enter upon a discussion of the first four seals, which contain the vision of the four horsemen.

Before we begin the discussion of the significance of each of these four horsemen, it will not be superfluous to give a word of general introduction both in regard to the general character of the seven seals and the proper mode of their interpretation.

As to the first question, there seems to be a rather general impression that all of the seven seals can be classified in the category of judgment-acts of Christ over a sinful and antagonistic world in the special and narrow sense of the word. Now it is very well possible to consider all that Christ performs in the world in this dispensation as being acts of judgment in a general sense of the word, either for good or for evil, namely, in as far as He is the King of glory Who works for the establishment and final perfection of His kingdom, and as such appears always as the great opponent of Satan and his dominion. But if we take the word "judgment" in its specific and narrower sense, namely, as a calamity sent by Jesus Christ for the purpose of chastizing the world, or by way of recompense for wrong committed, it will soon become evident that the most general idea of all the seals cannot be expressed by that one term. To begin with, it is rather difficult to discover the idea of judgment in the sense designated in the first horse and its rider, going forth conquering and to conquer, and symbolizing, — as a superficial consideration of the text will assure us, — the victorious progress of the cause of the kingdom of God in this dispensation. The same conclusion must be reached in regard to the fifth seal. As it is opened, the souls under the altar appeal to the Judge of heaven and earth for vengeance because their blood has been shed by the enemies of the kingdom of God on earth. Also in this case it is difficult to detect any act of judgment whatsoever. The martyred saints are simply told to be patient yet a little while; and white robes are given them as a symbol of their anticipatory glory and righteousness.

And therefore we must arrive at a more general, comprehensive conception of the nature of these seven seals, and consider them rather as symbolizing the history of this present dispensation from its main aspects, the chief currents of events as they all flow toward the one great goal of all history, the perfection of the glorious kingdom of God in Christ Jesus. The history of this dispensation has only one possible purpose and consummation: the coming of the glorious kingdom of God. All the events of history, all the factors and agencies which combine to make history must be conducive to that one great purpose. And any event in the world's history possesses its own peculiar significance for the coming of the kingdom in glory. Taking into consideration, therefore, that the one important theme of the Book of Revelation is the coming King and the completion of the kingdom, and that the book of the seven seals must be taken as symbolic of the living and powerful decree of the Almighty, the ultimate purpose of which is the glory of God's name through the coming of God's kingdom, we are safe in drawing the conclusion that these seven seals are intended to reveal to us the main aspects and larger currents of the history of this dispensation as they cooperate to bring the kingdom of Christ to its perfect consummation.

In regard to the second question raised, pertaining to the proper mode of interpretation, we would remark that we cannot agree with those interpreters who explain these seals in the temporal, historical sense, as if we must consider them as revealing the successive events of history in their exact chronological order, each seal extending over a rather definitely designated period of history, till finally the climax of this dispensation is reached in the kingdom of God. Concerning this mode of interpretation we would make the practical observation, in the first place, that it not infrequently has been conducive to the wildest speculations with respect to the exact date of the coming of Christ for final judgment. Naturally, if the different seals are indicative of seven successive periods of the history of the church and of the world, and if, moreover, it is possible to identify these periods in actual history with any approach to definiteness, we must surely be able to ascertain rather reliably exactly how far we have advanced in our day on the road to the second advent and make at least some calculation as to the length of the way still before us. This, however, is an impossibility if we may believe that the Word of Jesus in relation to the exact day and hour of His coming is true today as well as at the time when it was spoken. Besides, such an interpretation is based on an altogether too mechanical view of history and is not at all in harmony with reality. It is, for instance, not true that the first four seals,—call them, if you please, the victorious progress of the kingdom, war, famine, and pestilence,—find their corresponding realization in definitely marked periods of history. On the contrary, history much rather presents such an aspect as to make a surmise from the outset that these four riders are simultaneously upon earth, although with this exception, that now the one, now the other, appears emphatically on the foreground. And therefore, this mode of interpretation cannot be accepted as the proper one.

On the other hand, we must also dissent from those who would refer the realization of the prophecy contained in all the seven seals entirely to the future, preferably to a period immediately preceding the coming of our Lord. Among these we may especially note that class of interpreters which would place all the seals in the period of the great tribulation. The church has already been taken up into heaven; the rapture has taken place, when these seals shall be realized. Against this view may rightly be urged that in that case the book loses its value and purpose. For it undoubtedly means to be a source of instruction and consolation for the church of Christ in general, which she scarcely needs if all these things shall be realized after she has been taken up into glory. Against this may be urged, in the second place, that heretofore the book has not spoken of a rapture of the church whatsoever. The slender ground which is supposed to be found in Chapter 4, verse 1, where the seer is called "up hither," is altogether too feeble to support this theory. And, finally, against this may also be urged the fact that history plainly reveals that the things symbolized in the seals to a certain extent actually do come to pass and are realized day by day.

Hence, we must rather combine the two theories mentioned into one, and maintain that although the realization of the seals undoubtedly must be looked upon as to a certain extent still future, and although there is a certain succession noticeable in the fulfillment of their prophecy in actual history, so that new elements enter in occasionally which have not been witnessed in the past, and, besides, there is an increase in clearness and vividness of their realization, nevertheless to a large extent the seals,— especially the first six,—are being realized simultaneously, so that, as we have remarked, the four horsemen are making their drive through the earth all at the same time, and that throughout the period spanned by this dispensation many of these things have come to pass in days gone by, are being realized in the present day, repeat themselves in the history of the world from time to time with increasing vehemence and clearness, till all the different streams and currents of history shall converge in the final goal, the completed kingdom of our God.

The First Four Seals

Turning our attention now to the first four seals, we may remark, in the first place, that they belong together and form a group of seals distinct from the rest. First of all, they are plainly distinguished by their allegorical figures, the horses and their riders, which occur in connection with all the first four seals, and with them only. In the second place, they are distinct by the fact that in the issuing forth of each one of them one of the four living creatures which surround the throne of the Almighty sounds the command, or invitation, "Come!" This is evidently the correct rendering. The KJV has it that in each case one of the living creatures bids, "Come and see." And the impression might be that every time it is John who is addressed, rather than the horse and its rider. However, this is not the case. John is already in the spirit in heaven, and does not need the invitation to come and see. And if such an invitation should have been necessary at the rushing forth of the first horse, it certainly would have been superfluous to repeat it with the other three horses. Besides, it may be supposed that John is wide awake, stirred to the depths of his soul, profoundly interested in the vision he receives, and therefore does not need the invitation, "Come and see." Not to him, but to the horseman that is about to rush forward on his impetuous drive through the earth, comes the simple command, "Come!" And if now we remember that in these four living creatures we have the symbols of the fulness of all earthly creation, we understand immediately that the suggestion is given in this four-fold command that all the world is deeply interested in the work of these four horses with their riders. However this may be, certain it is that also in this repeated bid we have an indication that the first four seals evidently belong together, and form a distinct group.

In regard to the symbolism implied in these seals, in general we have our attention called, in the first place, to the figure of the horses and their riders.

Even in our day the horse is an animal employed in battle. But especially in Scripture does the horse occur pre-eminently as an animal of war. Already from Psalm 33:17 this becomes evident, where we read: "An horse is a vain thing for safety, neither shall he deliver any by his great strength." Here the horse is evidently referred to in connection with the battle. And then it is also plain that he is pictured in Scripture, even by implication in the text quoted, as symbolic of undaunted courage and vehement, irrepressible onslaught in battle. Beautiful is, from this point of view, the description we have of the horse in Job 39:19-25: "Hast thou given the horse strength? hast thou clothed his neck with thunder? Canst thou make him afraid as a grasshopper? the glory of his nostrils is terrible. He paweth in the valley, and rejoiceth in his strength; he goeth on to meet the armed men. He mocketh at fear, and is not affrighted; neither turneth he back from the sword. The quiver rattleth against him, the glittering spear and the shield. He swalloweth the ground with fierceness and rage: neither believeth he that it is the sound of the trumpet. He saith among the trumpets, Ha, ha; and he smelleth the battle afar off, the thunder of the captains, and the shouting." This is surely a most beautiful and masterful picture of the horse from a literary point of view. But for our purpose it is sufficient to observe that the Word of God knows the horse as the animal for battle **par excellence**, the picture of strength and undaunted courage, of irrepressible onslaught and vehement eagerness for the battle. Hence, when we see these horses go forth into the earth, we may be assured that there is to be war and battle, and that the power of these seals cannot be checked or successfully opposed.

However, they do not symbolize wild and undirected forces. On the contrary, these horses all have a rider who directs the horse according to his will. This shows in general that the powers and forces symbolized by these horses can do nothing more than they are supposed to do. They are forces directed and limited by intelligent will to a definite goal. Already the fact that they proceed from the book with its seven seals and that they therefore are liberated to do their work at the bidding of the Lamb inspires us with confidence that they cannot run at random, that they are not blind powers or independent forces. But especially the fact that each of these horses has a rider, directing them intelligently, is symbolic of the fact that they cannot run wild, that the forces symbolized by the horses are well controlled and directed to their proper destination. We must not ask the irrelevant question as to whom the rider represents on every horse, for the simple reason that he does not symbolize any particular person definitely. Horse and rider belong together. They constitute one whole. They represent one idea. And that idea is an irrepressibly strong and vehement force, ready for battle, completely controlled by intelligent will. Or, if you please, it reveals to us that history in this dispensation is completely under the control of the Lamb that standeth as though it hath been slain, to Whom all power is given in heaven and on earth, and that events on this earth are definitely and intelligently directed by His Spirit, sent forth into all the earth.

The Four Horses Individually Considered

Our next observation in regard to the symbolism of these four seals concerns the color of each horse, and in harmony with their respective colors the other details of description.

The color of the first horse is white, which is symbolic of victory. Repeatedly this color appears as such in Scripture. Those who are faithful and overcome shall ultimately appear in white robes. In Chapter 19:11 ff., where we have a final description of the battle of Armageddon, the Lord Jesus appears as the victor, seated upon a white horse, in all the glory of His power and victory. Thus it was also customary in the Roman army that the victors should return riding on white horses. Hence, it may be deemed rather evident that the white horse is symbol of a victorious power. In harmony with this color of the horse are the other features pictured in the text. First of all, we are told that the rider has a bow, which is symbolic of righteous and victorious warfare. In Psalm 45:5 we read of the king who is typical of Christ: "Thine arrows are sharp in the heart of the king's enemies; whereby the people fall under thee." In the second place, the rider receives a crown: not the royal diadem in this case, but the garland, the wreath of victory. And finally, this idea of victory is definitely expressed in the last clause, that the rider goes forth "conquering and to conquer," which by its peculiar repetition assures us of the certainty of the victory this rider will win. Therefore, we have in the first seal the picture of an armed warrior, going forth to battle, whose victory is assured him beforehand.

The color of the second horse is red, or, as the original indicates, a color glowing like fire. It is the color of wrath and anger, of heated passion and violent emotion, such as causes a man's blood to rush to his countenance, of lust and gain, of envy and revenge, of blood and war. The man that cometh from Bozrah, with sprinkled garments, who has trodden the winepress of Jehovah's anger alone, is red in his apparel. And when the Lord is described in all the holy zeal of His heated anger, He is pictured in Scripture as a consuming fire. This horse bears the color of a glowing fire, of heated passion and revenge and bloodshed and war, of which it is also symbolic. Again, the other details mentioned of this second horse and its rider serve to corroborate and enforce this idea. For, in the first place, we read that he receives a great sword, symbolic of war and death and destruction. And, in the second place, the definite information is given us that this horse receives the power to take peace from the earth. In general, therefore, the second horse and his rider are the picture of heated passion and wrath going forth to do its work in the earth.

The third horse is black. Occurring in the Word of God, this color is the symbol of scarcity and famine. In referring to a drought in the land of Judah in his own time, the prophet Jeremiah writes: "Judah mourneth, and the gates thereof languish; they are black unto the ground; and the cry of Jerusalem is gone up," (Jeremiah 14:2). And in his Lamentations (5:10) we hear the same prophet complain: "Our skin was black like an oven because of the terrible famine." Black, then, is the color of scarcity and want, of drought and famine. The rest of the description of this horse is again in harmony with this idea of the black color, although at the same time we should not fail to notice that by it the idea of famine is somewhat modified and mitigated. The rider is pictured as one who holds a balance and who does some careful weighing. And as he weighs, the voice is heard: "A measure of wheat for a penny, and three measures of barley for a penny." A measure of wheat (about one and one-half pints of our measure) constitutes the equivalent of one man's subsistence for one day.

And the same is true of three measures of barley. If in connection with this we also bear in mind that a penny, or shilling, constituted just about a day's wages of the common laborer, we come to the conclusion that this third rider represents scarcity and dearth, rather than downright famine. The relation between the wages of the common people and the cost of the necessities of life is such that the latter devour the former every day. But this is not all. The voice continues, and says, "The oil and the wine hurt not." Oil and wine are symbols of plenty and luxury, of merriment and feasting. These may not be hurt, but must continue to exist. And hence, the complete portraiture of this third horse and its rider presents a remarkable contrast: a contrast between poverty and riches, between a bare subsistence and luxurious living.

The fourth and last horse is of a pale green, such as is the color of death. Here we cannot be left in doubt as to the meaning of this fourth horseman. The horse represents the color of a corpse, of death itself. And in harmony with the color of the animal is the name of its rider, which is Death, while Hades, the abode of the dead, follows him, ready to receive the victims killed by this terrible horseman. The definite commission which this fourth horseman receives is to kill and destroy one fourth part of the earth's inhabitants with the sword, with pestilence, with the wild beasts of the earth, and with death in general. If four is generally the number representing the completeness of the world, one-fourth represents such a fraction as is in harmony with the present existence in the world throughout this present dispensation. The symbolism of the last horse and its rider makes us think of death in all its various forms.

After the general significance of the symbolism presented by these four horses and their riders has been ascertained, it cannot be difficult to grasp the meaning of each one of them and to discover what they represent in the history of this dispensation.

The victorious warrior on the white horse evidently stands for the triumphant progress of the cause of Christ's kingdom in this dispensation. As we have said before, we must not attempt to personify and interpret the details of the picture. We must not maintain that the rider is in this case Christ: for then we would have to apply the same method to each of the four riders, which is impossible. Horse and rider represent just one idea; and together they picture the victory of the cross in the world of sin. The world lies in darkness, is the dominion of the prince of darkness, stands inimical over against the kingdom of Christ which is to come. And therefore, if that world is to be transformed into a kingdom of God, it is not sufficient that the evil-doers be destroyed, but spiritual victories must be won. The power of the new kingdom must go forth into this inimical world and make subjects for the kingdom of heaven. For this purpose Christ sends forth His Spirit and Word to regenerate and call and bring to a conscious faith, to cause men to fall down before the great King and worship Him instead of the Evil One. And it is this combined effort of the Spirit and Word and all that is connected with their work which is portrayed under the symbolism of the white horse and its rider.

That victorious warrior, going forth conquering and to conquer, shoots his sharp arrows into the hearts of the enemies, and thus brings them into subjection to the Lord of lords and King of kings. Up to the present day this rider has pursued in the main a very definite course. He did not ride at random and roam in every direction, all over the earth; but clearly he had his course prescribed and definitely mapped out. Starting from Jerusalem, he drove to Antioch and through the various cities of Asia Minor. From thence he crossed over into Europe, first scoring his victories in Macedonia and Greece, then boldly striking for the very heart of the mighty Roman Empire, in order from there on to sweep over the mountains and plains of Europe, and finally cross over into the western hemisphere when the time was ripe. Surely, today he also rides in other parts of the world, and the inhabitants of Asia and Africa must bow before his power. But there is a distinct difference between his work in Europe and America and that among the nations of the Far East and the south. In the former countries his victories were so pronounced that outwardly entire peoples have been christianized, while in the latter the result of his drive is noticeable only in the conversion of individuals. And thus the ultimate result of the drive of the first warrior is that the tremendous contrast is called into existence between the so-called Christian world and the world of heathendom, Israel and Gog and Magog.

The second horse and its rider together are the symbol of war. It is because of the drive of this horse on the earth that the slumbering passions of men and nations are aroused and called into action, so that nation rises against nation all through history. We must not fail to notice that also in the case of this second horse and its rider it is Christ Who opens the seal, and He sends forth the horse and its rider. Also in this case the horse does not run at random, but is directed by its rider. It assures us that in the deepest sense of the word also the wars of the world are sent forth and controlled by Jesus Christ, the Lamb that holds the book with its seven seals, through the Spirit Who goes forth into all the earth. Well controlled the red horse goes forth. Is it necessary to call your attention to its presence and impetuous drive all through the ages of history? Nation rises against nation in every period of history. It is Rome against Greece, the powerful hordes from the dark north against the declining Roman Empire, the various nations of Europe warring among one another or against the New World. Does it need special proof to show that wars have increased rather than decreased in power and vehemence, as well as in number, as time went on and civilization developed, and that exactly because of the presence and drive of this red horse the ideal of universal peace in a sinful world is a mere dream? Riding upon the glowing passions of lust and greed, of power and conquest, of hatred and revenge and jealousy, this second horse and its rider go forth to slay individuals and conquer nations. Fiercer and redder than ever, it is driving over the world today. But remembering that also this horse is sent forth and controlled by the Lamb, we may rest assured that it must perform its own part for the bringing of the kingdom of God to its completion.

The third horseman has the sphere of social life assigned to him and maintains the tremendous contrast between scarcity and plenty. Of this contrast, always existing, the third rider is especially the symbol. I do not pretend to say that the special famines are for that reason excluded, especially not as they often follow in the wake of war. In our own day the black horse stalks about threateningly, especially in war-ridden countries, where a measure of wheat can be sold for a penny no more. But although this is true, we would be mistaken if we would discern this third rider only in special periods of war and famine. He is always among us, and continually he does his work. The symbolism of the picture does not indicate what may be called downright famine, but much rather a striking contrast. On the one hand, it points to a living by the day; on the other hand, to luxury and abundance. This horse it is that causes all our social problems, because through its work the contrast is maintained between rich and poor, between plenty and scarcity, between wealth and miserable poverty. Always the masses live by the day. Always their wages are sufficient to provide a bare subsistence. Always the oil and the wine remain untouched, and the few live in wealth and splendor and royal ease, in distinction from the masses. Very emphatically this condition appears in Europe and in other countries; but also in our own country it is developing with alarming rapidity. A very small percentage of our population possesses and controls more than seventy-five per cent of all the wealth of the country, while the masses may divide the remaining twenty-five per cent of the nation's gold among themselves. Always the black horse and its rider maintain this contrast in the social world, a contrast that in turn is the cause of many events in history. It is the cause of feasting and riotous living, on the one hand; of the dissatisfaction, misery, protest, rebellion, revolution, and bloodshed, on the other. But in all these things the children of the kingdom see the black horse and its rider, sent forth by the Lamb that holds the book, performing its own part for the bringing of the kingdom of glory.

Finally, the fourth horse and its terrible rider present the picture of death in all its various forms and manifestations. A horrible picture indeed this horse calls before our imagination. A horse of a pale green, ghastly color, ridden by Death in person, swinging with powerful fist his awful sword, followed by Hades, ready to swallow up the victims that may fall in the path of this merciless monster. It is death in all its forms as he enters your home to slay your dear ones by death, as he steals through the streets of our cities in order violently to kill by dagger and pistol, as he stalks over the battlefield to reap his greatest harvest. Not merely, therefore, as you see his work on special occasions, but as he may be watched day by day in all parts of the world, he is presented to us in our text. For it is especially mentioned that this horse also kills by death. Surely, also by the sword, by pestilence, by the wild beasts of the earth, and by all kinds of accidents this rider performs his awful work. By homicide and suicide, in wars and revolutions, in pestilence and epidemic, by storm and flood and fire, by the beasts of the field, but also by the infinitesimally small wild beasts we are wont to call germs, this rider mows away millions and millions in a short period. But for the rest, he simply kills by death in all its regular appearance. For in all he kills just one-fourth of the inhabitants of the earth: just as many as is in harmony with the history of the world and as will maintain the equilibrium among the peoples of the earth, according to the divine plan. In short, the sum-total of all death-cases in the world, according to regular statistics, is the effect of the drive of this pale horse and its rider.

We come, then, to the conclusion that these horses and their riders symbolically proclaim that all the different phases of human life in particular and of the nations of the earth in the broadest sense are under the absolute control of Jesus Christ, the Lamb that was slain. He it is Who controls the progress of His kingdom as symbolized in the white horse. He it is Who holds the reins of history when nations rise against nations. He it is Who fixes price lists and wages, and maintains the social contrast between poverty and riches. He it is, finally, Who sends death into all the world in order to mow down His victims, the proper persons at the proper time. To Him is given all power in heaven and on earth, and He executes the will of Him Who sitteth upon the throne.

The Reason For The Horses

Even so, however, we cannot be satisfied and we may not stop at this stage of our investigation. We do not merely want to know that these horses are making their drive over the earth; nor are we satisfied to know what each of them separately signifies. But we must, first of all, learn to understand the reason for their presence, and place ourselves before the question: why is it necessary that all these four horses perform their peculiar tasks, exert their peculiar influence upon the various phases of human life? Why is it that the white horse is not sent forth alone? Why is it that he makes his drive over the earth accompanied by the red and the black and the pale horses? All the more this question is urged upon us in view of the fact that it is from the book of the seven seals, symbolic of the living decree of God Almighty, that these horses issue forth to do their work, that they are liberated for their drive by our Lord Jesus Christ, and that they are under the evident control of the Spirit. Proceeding from the faith that there is wisdom in all the decrees of the Almighty and that the Lord does nothing without a sound reason, we take courage to investigate whether we may perhaps discover the wisdom of the Lord our God and His glorious design in all these things. Besides, there is also a practical reason for this question. Especially in the times in which we are privileged to live,—times so pregnant with meaning,—there are all sorts of theories in the air that mean to explain the tremendous events in history, especially in the history of today. Interpretations are offered, also of the conflicts in the world of our present time, which are far from Scriptural and often thoroughly humanistic. And it requires not merely a strong faith implicitly, but also a clear vision of the truth as revealed to us in the Word of God, in order to stand immovably and to resist the strong currents of humanistic philosophy that tend to sweep us off our feet. Hence, we must clearly see and understand why there is not only a victorious progress of the kingdom of Christ in the world, but why there is also war and social trouble and revolution and bloodshed and death. Why are all these calamities necessary? These are questions which naturally arise in times like ours, and which demand an answer.

In order, then, to arrive at a satisfactory answer to this question, we must proceed from the truth which is to faith self-evident, and therefore needs no further proof or elucidation, namely, that all the events of history occur in order to bring in the kingdom of God. There is but one reality, and that is the kingdom of heaven. There is but one possible terminal for all history, and that is the completed kingdom of Christ. This needs no proof. And therefore I say that in our discussion of the question raised we must start from the firm faith that all things in this dispensation must be conducive to the bringing of that glorious kingdom, either directly or indirectly, in a positive or in a negative manner. If you ask me, "Why that white horse?" I answer: to bring the kingdom. If the question is asked, "Why must there be war?" I say without hesitation: for the sake of the kingdom of God. If you inquire, "Why is this tremendous social contrast between luxury and poverty necessary in the world?" I say again: this is necessary to lead to that one goal, the completed kingdom of glory. If you should ask, "Why does that terrible rider on the last horse massacre one-fourth of men?" I would offer the same general solution: it is all for the completion of the kingdom of God. That this is the general purpose of all these four horses is also evident from the fact that the purpose of the entire Book of Revelation is to picture the Christ coming to His glorious kingdom.

This, therefore, being established, we have really but one question to answer, namely: how do the forces symbolized by the four horsemen work together for the good of the kingdom of God and its completion? To find the correct answer to this question we must first of all recall a few facts concerning this kingdom of God and clear away some rubbish which nowadays is thrown on the market of spiritual realities.

First of all, then, it will be necessary clearly to grasp the truth that originally God created the world His kingdom. I take the world now in an all-comprehensive sense of the word, including all creation, the spiritual world not excepted. It includes the world of simple matter with all its elements and powers, hidden or already revealed: the wood and the stone, the silver and the gold, all inanimate creation. It embraces the seas and the oceans, the rivers and the lakes, the running streams and quiet waters, with all that they contain and with all their laws and ordinances and powers. Thus it was originally; and thus we still conceive of the world as created by the Almighty, even though it is at present under the curse. When the sea roars, you ought to listen by faith to a sound in the kingdom of God. And when the brook murmurs over its cobbled bed, you may again listen to a sound in that same kingdom. To that kingdom belongs the atmosphere that envelops our globe, the air with all its wonderful powers. When the storm rages, you may know that a part of the kingdom of God is disturbed. When by steam-power you are moved from one place to another at the speed of many miles per hour, or when by pushing a small button you suddenly create light in your living-room, or when you are carried aloft thousands of feet in the air upon the wings of an airplane, you remember by faith that you are employing but powers in that kingdom which God originally created. To that kingdom belong the beasts of the forest and the cattle of your meadows, the creeping things and flying birds, woods and fields, trees and flowers. All things, in a word, belong to that kingdom of God. To that same kingdom, finally, belong God's rational creatures, man and angel, and these with all their talents and powers, with their entire being. Man's body and his soul, his intellect and will, all that he possesses has originally been given him as a subject of the kingdom of God. In one word, as we speak of the kingdom of God in this connection, we refer to all creation in its widest conceivable sense, with earth and sky, animate and inanimate creation, matter, plant, animal, and man, as well as the angels in heaven, with all the hidden and revealed powers which the Almighty Creator has stored from the beginning in this mighty product of His omnipotent will.

Secondly, we must understand what is implied in the assertion that God Almighty created that entire world a kingdom. Of course, the main idea in this connection is that there is a king, who issues his laws and ordinances and demands obedience. Hence, in regard to the kingdom of the world it should be remembered above all that God is King supreme, that He is King in the absolute sense of the word. It is this which makes of the world a kingdom of God. All the world must obey His will and His ordinances. The stars run their courses as He has ordained. The earth follows its path according to His will. The trees grow in harmony with His law. The flowers blossom according to the ordinances of the Almighty King. Steam and electricity are bound by His law. All is subject to His will. All things must obey Him. And in it all the name of the King supreme is glorified. For if you ask, "What may be the common purpose of all that exists?" the answer is, of course, that all the world reveals and must reveal the glory of its Creator. But there is a difference. Just as in any kingdom, so also in the kingdom of the world as God created it there is order and gradation. In a kingdom there are not simply the king and the common people who must obey. But between them there are various officials who represent the will of the king in all the kingdom. Thus it is also in the kingdom of God. There is order and gradation. It would be interesting to study this order in detail; but this would lead us too far from our main purpose. Suffice it simply to remind you of the fact as such that there actually is order and gradation also in the world as a kingdom of God. There is the order of lifeless matter, the order of plant life, the animal world, and, finally, the order of God's rational creatures, men and angels. And of all these man is created as the highest creature, destined to rule over all things in the name of God.

For it is true that, according to Psalm 8, man was made a little lower than the angels; but if we would see man in the reality of his power and glory, you must consider him as he is in Christ Jesus his Lord. Being related to both the material and the spiritual world, he is naturally destined to rule all things, to have dominion, to bring to light the hidden powers of creation, and thus lead all that kingdom on to the full realization of its highest purpose, the glory of God. Man is king. But even as king he remains servant. He is not, he may not be, he never can be king in the absolute sense of the word. But always he is king under God. With relation to the world, man is ruler: for God gave him dominion over every creature. But with respect to God, man is servant: for to obey from free and willing love was his great calling. Hence, when we speak of the world as a kingdom of God, we refer to all creation as it finds its climax in man, who rules over all things according to the will of the Almighty and consecrates himself and all things to the glory of his Maker.

In the third place, we must remember that sin and the devil could never essentially change this God-ordained order of creation. What we mean is that Satan could never change the works of God in such a way that creation was a kingdom no more. No more than Satan could change man into another being, no more could he so change the order of the world that it was no more a kingdom. The world remained a kingdom, whatever the devil might do. Neither,—and this must be remembered as well,—could the devil create another kingdom, next to the kingdom of God. Satan also is a mere creature; and however powerful a creature he may be, the fact remains that he is nothing but a creature, and that a creature can never create. All the creature,—the devil too,—can do is to accept creation as God made it.

But what he naturally might do and what he was allowed to do and what he actually did do was to subject that entire kingdom of the world to himself. It is evident, then, that it was Adam's obedience that connected all the world as a kingdom with its God. As long as Adam would be servant of God in the world, creation was God's kingdom. But the moment Adam rebelled, the world stood in rebellion against the Sovereign of heaven and earth. If Adam, instead of kneeling in the dust as the king-servant before his highest Sovereign, would subject himself to the will of Satan, the kingdom of God would be changed into a kingdom of the prince of darkness. And this is exactly what took place. Not a new kingdom was created. Neither was the essential order which made the world a kingdom changed at all. But the kingdom of the world was subjected to the will of the devil and became a kingdom of Satan. Adam fell. In his capacity of king of the world he rebelled against his rightful Sovereign, refused obedience to Him, in order to surrender himself and his kingdom to the arch-enemy of God. Man did not cease to be king; even though through sin he became a creature under the curse, nevertheless God preserved man and the human race for the sake of His own covenant and kingdom. And therefore, even in his sinful state man still reveals that originally he stood in royal power. Even though he lost much of his original power and glory, in relation to the world he still rules, Even though he is extremely limited, he still attempts to subdue the earth. Even in his sinful condition he reigns over air and water and brings the powers of creation into subjection. Hence, he did not through sin suddenly lose all of his royal power and position. If that had been the case, the devil would never have been able to realize a kingdom of darkness in the world, as he now does. But what happened was this, that man, the king of creation, delivered himself and his kingdom into the power of Satan; and instead of remaining obedient to the God of his life, he served the devil, became an ally of Satan against God. Not another world was created, but the world as kingdom was delivered to Satan, had become a kingdom of darkness. In this sense the devil was right when he pretended before Jesus that all the kingdoms of the world were his.

In the fourth place, we must understand the most significant truth that this entire kingdom, all the world in the most comprehensive sense of the word, is given unto Christ, to be saved by Him, to be put into complete subjection under God once more, and to bring it to its highest possible glory in the kingdom of heaven. Unless we accept this cosmological view of salvation, we shall never be able to understand Scripture, least of all, perhaps, the Book of Revelation.

We are, alas, accustomed to run in the narrow track of our individual salvation, preferably in the rut of the salvation of our soul. We must be regenerated. We must come to faith in Christ Jesus. We must be sanctified and delivered from sin. We must go to heaven. This is, in brief, the entire story of our salvation as it lodges in the minds of many of us. Even the redemption of our body often recedes into the background. If only our immortal soul is saved! And no doubt all this is very significant. I do not underestimate the salvation of man. Surely, we must be regenerated; we must come to conscious faith in Christ; we must be justified and sanctified. And we must surely emphasize that here we have no continuing city, but that we seek the city that hath foundations. All this is perfectly true. Nevertheless, it is only part of the truth, not the whole of it. Neither is it the truth conceived in its proper light. It is not the truth as Scripture presents it, not the truth as we must necessarily conceive of it in order to understand the Book of Revelation.

Instead, we must again emphasize the Biblical truth that all the world, the entire kingdom which God originally created and which fell into the power of sin and the devil and lies at present under the curse, will again be restored and even raised to a far higher glory than it originally possessed. We must understand that after all sin and the devil can never do more than serve the realization of the plan of Almighty God to lead His kingdom to glory and to realize His everlasting covenant in Christ Jesus. This is plain from the fact that the very world is a revelation of the name of God and is created to reveal the glory of that name. If there were nothing more, the conclusion would be fully warranted that the Lord of heaven and earth will lead that world to final glory: for He cannot give His glory to another. But this is also the general teaching of Scripture. God loves the **world,** John 3:16. Because He loves the world, He sent His Son, that in Him all things might be united. And in the meantime it is all creation that groaneth and travaileth together in pain. And all creation shall be delivered from the bondage of corruption into the glorious liberty of the children of God, Romans 8:19-22.

If we understand this situation, we shall be able to grasp why there must necessarily be continual war in this world between God and the devil, between Christ and Antichrist, until the kingdom of God shall have been completed and shall have appeared in perfect glory. There are not two worlds; there is only one. If God and the devil could each have a kingdom, there would be no war. But this is impossible; and this, of course, is certainly not the case. There is but one world-kingdom. But in this historical dispensation there are two powers that fight for dominion over that one kingdom of the world. Or rather, there is one power that fights for that dominion while God, Who never fights, simply rules over all, even over the powers of darkness. On the one hand, there is the dominion of Satan, who apparently gained the victory in paradise; on the other hand, there is the dominion of Christ, the representative of the Father, to Whom God gave all things, and Who is called to restore the kingdom to God and to bring that kingdom to everlasting glory. Hence, in the world there is a continual war of the devil against Christ and His church for the dominion and possession of all things. This is the war of the ages.

This war of all the ages may be traced from the earliest periods of history.

The beginning of it we have in the declaration of war on the part of God in Genesis 3:15: "And I will put enmity between thee and the woman, and between thy seed and her seed; it shall bruise thy head, and thou shalt bruise his heel." This putting of enmity is nothing less than the beginning of the awful warfare of the devil and the powers of darkness against Christ and His church and the kingdom of heaven. Man has become the friend of the devil, his ally. And God here declares that He will break that alliance. He did so by putting enmity into the heart of man against his very ally, or, if you please, by immediately regenerating Adam and Eve. I think there can be no doubt about the fact that our first parents were both regenerated, and that they were regenerated right on the spot in paradise. Since they were the natural root of the entire human race, the operation of grace should commence right there, and the enmity against Satan be instilled in their hearts.

But as soon as they bring forth children, the conflict appears. For God follows the line of election and reprobation in all the history of the world. Before the flood this conflict is evidently of an individual character. We read nothing of kingdom against kingdom, but of the sons of God and daughters of men, of Cain and Abel, of Lamech and Enoch, till through the amalgamation of the sons of God and the daughters of men the seed of the serpent threatens to exterminate the seed of the woman, and God saves His kingdom through the flood.

Soon after the flood we notice a new stage of development. We read of mighty Nimrod and of the attempt to realize a world-kingdom of darkness with the tower of Babel as its center. And when the Lord frustrates the attempt and separates the human family into nations, the same tendency to realize the ideal of a world-kingdom becomes apparent in individual kingdoms that strive to subdue every other kingdom under them. In the meantime God separates Abraham and his seed, and in them establishes His own kingdom, even presently in national form. Israel becomes the typical kingdom of God in the old dispensation. Hence, after the flood the struggle begins to assume the character of a battle, not between individuals but between different kingdoms. On the one hand are the heathen nations with their gods; on the other hand stands Israel with Jehovah as its King. Thus the struggle continues, first up to the captivity, when it seems as if the kingdom of God suffers disastrous defeat; then, after Israel reappears from captivity, the struggle still continues up to the first coming of Christ.

In the new dispensation the battle again reaches a higher stage of development and assumes a different form. Principally the devil and his powers are already defeated, and Christ through His cross and resurrection has the final victory. Nevertheless, also in the new dispensation the devil still attempts to maintain his own kingdom of darkness. The kingdom of God in the new dispensation breaks the bounds of Israel's national existence and becomes international, but at the same time it becomes also purely spiritual. Christ has received the kingdom and now gathers His subjects from all parts of the world and out of every nation and tongue and tribe. It is no more a battle between the nations. We must therefore never compare our dispensation with the dispensation of Israel in the Old Testament as if they were principally the same. The battles Israel fought must not for a moment be thought of as similar to the battles of the world in our day. No war can ever be Messianic in the new dispensation. No war today can be called a war for the kingdom of God. The kingdom of God fights a spiritual battle, and cannon and sword cannot destroy her enemies. But although the battle is now chiefly spiritual, it is nonetheless very real. Essentially the battle between the children of light and the subjects of the kingdom of darkness is still the same as in the old dispensation. The form has changed; the essential character nevertheless remains the same. On the one hand, there is still the power of darkness, aiming at nothing less than the establishment of his own kingdom and the subjection of the whole world under the devil in all the different spheres of life. And, on the other hand, there is the power of grace through Christ, fighting the battle of the kingdom and claiming that all things are God's and His Christ's. Side by side these two powers exist in the same world, developing under the same outward influences, principally radically different from each other, agreeing in no respect, fighting inch for inch in every sphere of the life of the world. They never meet; they never agree. They are always in conflict; and compromise is impossible. Thus is reality in our own dispensation.

Lastly, we must also understand that these two powers in the world make use of all the outward means and powers and of all the institutions God gives to the world in this entire dispensation. They live in the same world. They enjoy the same rain and sunshine. They receive outwardly the same benefits. They develop along the same lines in the purely formal sense of the word. It is here that our view often becomes obscure. Yet also at this point we must be clear. In this historical dispensation, in which the principles of sin and grace both operate in the world, God created various institutions in order to maintain the possibility of orderly life and development of the human race as far as possible in spite of the fact of sin, and thus to make room, to form a basis in the world, for the establishment and realization of His own kingdom and covenant. All these institutions are employed as well by the power of darkness and of Antichrist for the realization of his own kingdom as they are by the power of the kingdom of light. There is the institution of the state. Government was instituted by God and equipped with the sword to maintain order in society and to punish the evil-doer, in order that the kingdom of God might have a place and develop. Without this outward check upon the development of sin the principle of evil would develop prematurely, and life on earth would soon prove impossible. But ever since the attempt at Babel the same institution of the state is also employed by the power of Antichrist to realize his kingdom. And especially in recent times the tendency of history is again in the same direction as was indicated in the attempt to establish the world-power of Babylon. There is even the institution of the church, established in the world for the upbuilding and edification of the saints and for the establishment and extension of the kingdom and covenant of God. But especially in our time the attempt is made again to employ that institution of the church for the advancement of the kingdom of darkness.

There is the institution of society in general,—the home, the school, business and industry,—in a word, the entire many-sided development of social life in our day. No doubt all of these institutions must be subservient to the kingdom of Christ and to the realization of God's eternal covenant. But one by one they are also employed by the power of darkness for the establishment and development of the kingdom of Antichrist. And if you understand this clearly, you will be able to observe that the battle rages along the whole line. The two powers fight for nothing less ultimately than the possession of the whole world. And in this fight they both make use of all the institutions which God has established for this dispensation. Nevertheless, once more: God never fights! God in Christ already has the victory. God simply makes use of the powers of the kingdom of darkness for the realization of His own everlasting decree and for the establishment of His own kingdom.

The Combined Effect Of The Four Horses On History

We are now prepared to discuss the answer to the question: what is the combined effect of these four horses on the history of the world?

In this connection, however, and before we point out this effect specifically, we must remember this one truth, that the same causes do not produce necessarily the same effect. Fact is, of course, that the forces represented by these four horses are sent into the world in general, and that they also exert their influence upon that entire world. On the face of it, we might perhaps expect that this would not be the case. We might imagine such an arrangement of things that, since there are two powers in the world that aim at the complete dominion over the whole world, the Lord would separate His people and kingdom already in the present time from the kingdom and people of the devil in such a way that only the latter were affected by the evil forces of history, such as war, famine, death, etc., while only the benevolent influences of His power would be felt by His people. Or, to speak in terms of this particular passage of Revelation, we might conceive of such a dispensation that the white horse would come into the world and have contact only with the people of God, with those whom He would call out of the world, while the last three horses would affect the evil world only. However, this is evidently not the meaning and is not the situation.

On the contrary, all these forces are sent into the world in general; and they affect men without distinction. The white horse, for instance, we explained to stand for the positive progress of the cause of God's kingdom in the world through the influence of the Word and the Spirit. Does this imply now that as this white horse makes its drive through the world it affects the people of God, the elect, alone, and leaves no impression whatever upon the subjects of the kingdom of darkness? Does it mean that this white horse represents a certain secret power in the world, to be noticed and felt exclusively by the people of God? We know better. The influence of this white horse is by no means limited to the elect children of God. You will realize the truth of this statement immediately if only you remember that there is such a thing as an outward Christianity, and that in the external sense of the word we can speak of a Christian world in distinction from the world of heathendom. This is not to say that every individual in this so-called Christian world is actually a child of God and a child of the kingdom of heaven; for that is certainly not the case. But there is a general influence of the Word and of the Spirit, so that in some way even those who do not belong to God's elect are influenced. Christianity has become the religion of the nations, at least in Europe and in our own country. The Word is preached publicly, not in secret. And there is even a general influence of the Spirit that is not unto repentance. Hence, with regard to the white horse, at least, it must be remarked that its influence is not limited to the citizens of the kingdom, but is much rather general.

Still more evident this is in regard to the last three horses. It is very plain that the people of God are not exempt when the evil forces of war, social upheavals, revolution, scarcity and famine, and death are sent into the world. When the red horse makes its drive through the nations, the seed of the woman fight side by side with the seed of the serpent. Also the people of God belong to a certain nation. Also they are subject to authority. Also they must go when the call to arms comes. They, as well as the children of evil, see their sons go to battle. They, as well as the children of darkness, must see their homes destroyed and their fields devastated, and must in general suffer the evil effects of war. The same is true of the black horse. When it appears, the people of God are not exempt from its influence. They live in the same society as the children of evil. And in general it may even be stated that they belong to the poorer class of people. The pale horse, too, knows of no distinction, but enters into the homes of the righteous and wicked alike. Death mows away young and old, rich and poor, from the midst of the godly and the ungodly. And in respect to Hades, it might indeed be said by the wise man that they all go to one place. Hence, once more: there is no distinction. These four horses have their influence upon all men without discrimination.

On the face of it, this fact might lead us to the conclusion that in this way the kingdom of Christ will never reach its completion. We are inclined to reason that the same causes have the same effect, and that what must be a blessing to the one must also be a blessing to the other, while what is destructive and injurious to the one must be equally harmful to the other. If this were actually the case, nothing could possibly be accomplished by these four riders, except that either both powers in the world are strengthened, or that both are ultimately destroyed.

This, however, will not be the outcome. We may state this from the very start as an established fact. Not both kingdoms, that of Christ and that of Satan, will be perpetuated; but the former will have the complete victory in the end, and the latter will be uprooted.

But in order to understand how this is possible, we must learn to see that the same causes do not have the same effect, and that what is beneficial to the one is harmful to the other in the world.

As the first rider, the one on the white horse, passes through the world and comes into contact with men in general, he has an entirely different effect upon the children of God than upon the subjects of the devil. To the former he is, of course, a benevolent power, through which they are called to new life and translated from darkness into light. But to the latter he becomes a curse, through which they develop in evil and ripen for the day of judgment. The same two-fold influence proceeds from the last three horses and their riders. They are injurious to the children of evil, but work together for good to those that love God, who are the called according to His purpose. The powers or forces represented by the horses are the same in each case, but the objects upon which they exert their influence are different from each other. The receptivity of the objects is not the same every time. Beautifully this is explained, at least with regard to the causes themselves beneficent, in Hebrews 6:4-8. There we read: "For it is impossible for those who were once enlightened, and have tasted of the heavenly gift, and were made partakers of the Holy Ghost, And have tasted the good word of God, and the powers of the world to come, If they shall fall away, to renew them again unto repentance; seeing they crucify to themselves the Son of God afresh, and put him to an open shame. For the earth which drinketh in the rain that cometh oft upon it, and bringeth forth herbs meet for them by whom it is dressed, receiveth blessing from God: But that which beareth thorns and briers is rejected, and is nigh unto cursing; whose end is to be burned."

This is indeed a powerful passage of Holy Writ.

Many are of the opinion that they may refer to this passage as a clear proof that Scripture teaches the possibility of a falling away from grace. But rather than accept this view of the text, we must maintain, first of all, that Scripture throughout militates against the falling away from grace and upholds the perseverance of the saints. That there is a falling away from grace is untenable on the basis of the truth of election and reprobation. God knows those that are His from all eternity, and no one shall ever pluck them out of His hands. They are securely sealed by the Spirit of grace, and every one of the one hundred forty-four thousand shall surely be saved. Salvation is of the Lord; and that He should first regenerate a person, in order then to allow him to fall away from grace, is inconceivable. "For whom he did foreknow, he also did predestinate to be conformed to the image of his Son, that he might be the firstborn among many brethren. Moreover whom he did predestinate, them he also called: and whom he called, them he also justified: and whom he justified, them he also glorified," (Romans 8:29, 30). No one shall pluck God's people out of His hands. There is, then, no falling away from grace. And this certainly is not what the author of Hebrews 6:4-8 intends to teach.

Yet we are told that it is possible that a man may once be enlightened, that he may taste the good Word of God, and the powers of the age to come, yea, that in a sense he becomes partaker of the Holy Spirit of grace. It is possible, therefore, that men come into very close contact with the Word of God and with the blessings of God's kingdom and covenant. Or, to speak in terms of our passage from Revelation, men may sometimes come into very intimate contact with that first rider on the white horse, so that they see the beauty of the kingdom of God and to a certain extent enjoy the outward blessings of that kingdom. Yet they may fall away so deeply that they become hopelessly lost and that they become the bitterest enemies of the kingdom of God, so that they crucify again the Son of God and put Him to an open shame. Or, if you please, the very same power that makes subjects of the kingdom of Christ also accentuates the enmity in the hearts of its opponents, also makes most bitter enemies of God and of His cause in the world.

And the author explains this fact by the illustration of a field. A field is blessed by abundant rain,—a blessing which is, of course, essential to the development of the good seed and the raising of the crops. But under the influence of that same benevolent rain, which in itself is a blessing, the thorn and the thistle also develop. If no rain descended upon the field, the thorn and the thistle could never grow. But the more abundant the outward blessings of rain and sunshine, the more luxuriantly also the thorn and the thistle will grow. Hence, under the same influence of identically the same blessings, the good seed sprouts and the grain ripens in the ear, but also the thorn and the thistle prosper. The same fact is true of the spiritual blessings of the kingdom of God.

We must remember, therefore, that this white horse and its rider have a two-fold effect as they make their drive through the world of men.

Nor is it difficult to see that the same general truth is applicable to the influence of the last three horses. Also these have a two-fold effect, according as they meet with different objects. What is evil to the world is by no means evil to the children of God. The same adversity causes the one to rise in rebellion and curse God, the other to humble himself and be patient. The same affliction hardens the one and brings the other to repentance and sanctifies him. The same tribulation that brings despair to the one causes the other to glorify his God.

As people of God, therefore, we may be comforted from the outset. All these horses come into contact with all men, without discrimination. But they all will be beneficent in their influence and effect upon the people of God, while they are harmful to the children of evil. And thus we can already in a general way discern how they must ultimately bring the kingdom of Jesus Christ while at the same time they will lead to the defeat of the power of Satan and Antichrist in the world. All things work together for good to them that love God, to them who are called according to His purpose.

What then is the effect of the first horse and its rider in the world?

In general, we may answer that it causes separation. This is not difficult to understand. If there never had been any operation of the power of grace in the hearts of men, if there never had been any influence of the Word and of the Spirit, it is evident that never a separation would have been accomplished between the seed of the woman and the seed of the serpent. It has been alleged sometimes that sin is the factor that causes separation between man and man. And in a certain sense this is, of course, true. But we should never forget that without the power of grace operating in the world there would be no fundamental separation, would be no split in the ranks of humanity, after all. Grace is the wedge that in this sinful world makes separation and divides all men into two principally different and opposing camps. This, then, is the general effect of the work of this first rider upon the world of men.

On the one hand, a people of God is called into conscious existence in the midst of the world. The Spirit of God regenerates, so that the inmost being of man is placed in a new relationship to God and to the entire world. The Christian is a new man. Principally he has become a friend of God and belongs to His party in the midst of the world. The Word calls and brings that new man to consciousness of his new life, of his new relationship to God and to the world, so that he begins to live and to manifest himself as a subject of the kingdom of God and a member of His covenant. The people who are thus formed in the midst of the world acknowledge again the highest sovereignty of the God of heaven and earth, and that too, in every sphere of life. They begin by recognizing the righteousness and holiness of God. They are conscious of their sins and transgressions and confess them before the face of Him Who sitteth upon the throne. And they acknowledge Jesus Christ as the representative of the righteousness of God, but also as their Savior and Redeemer in His atoning power.

Hence, they stand in an entirely new relation to God and also to the world. Formerly they stood over against Him in rebellion, hating Him with all their heart and mind and soul and strength. Now they humbly bow before His throne, asking, "Lord, what wilt Thou have us do?" Formerly they imagined in the wickedness of their corrupt nature that all things existed for them, for man; and man, to them, was god. Now they realize that all things exist for the glory of God and that the Lord of heaven and earth is God alone. Formerly they emphasized that all things should exist and be arranged according to their own evil imagination, and they did not ask for the ordinances of the Most High. Now they insist that all things must be based on the principles of God's Word, and that Christ is King. The result is that they come to the world with a principally different life-view and with a new demand. All things must be made subservient to the glory of God and His kingdom, and in every sphere of life the precepts of their King must be maintained. For all of life they have their own demands. The state, according to them, is an institution of God, established for the maintenance of justice and righteousness in the world, for the punishment of evil-doers and for the protection of the good, in order that God's people may have room to develop in the midst of a sin-cursed world. The church is essentially the body of Christ, and, as instituted, it exists for the upbuilding of the saints, a witness of God in the world for the extension and establishment of His kingdom. It must needs remain separate from the state. The two differ in character. They differ in purpose. And they must never amalgamate. The church is universal; the state is national. The church is eternal; the state is temporal. The church stands for the eternal and absolute righteousness of God in the world; the state maintains, or rather is called to maintain, the righteousness of God in the present dispensation. The state fights with the sword; the church never does so. Surely, her members in this dispensation are citizens of a certain country, and they are subject to authority. Neither do they refuse as such to go out and meet the enemy in battle. But the church as such does not fight the battles of the world. She has a spiritual warfare to accomplish. The church as such sings no national songs; but she sings of the country beyond, of the city that hath foundations. The church as such has no national emblem, but unfurls the banner of the cross.

And thus the people of God have their own life-view with regard to every sphere of life and every institution of the world. The home is an institution existing primarily for the perpetuation of God's covenant in the world. The school is an institution for the purpose of instructing the covenant children according to the principles of Holy Writ for every sphere of life. Society, with business and industry, art and science, and all things that exist, must, according to them, be controlled by the principles of the Word of God and be made subservient to the idea of God's kingdom in the world. In a word, they have a new life-view. They are members of God's covenant, His friends in the world, subjects of His kingdom. And, in principle at least, they want to live the life of that kingdom also in the present world.

But this is not all. This, in fact, is only one side of the influence of the white horse and its rider in the midst of the world.

That white horse also has influence upon the ungodly and the reprobate. Upon the enemies of the kingdom it inevitably has this effect, that it enlightens them with regard to the idea of the kingdom, but at the same time it accentuates their hostility and embitters them all the more. They also learn to taste the powers of the age to come and to see the beauty of the kingdom of God. That this is true will be evident the moment you compare the Christian world in general with the world of heathendom. The Word of God has a general enlightening influence. There is what might be called even a civilizing influence of the Word and Spirit. Intellectually the children of evil understand the truth. But the principle of enmity against God remains unchanged. They do not come to repentance. They refuse to acknowledge the righteousness of God. They refuse to bow before Him as their Sovereign. They deny Christ, not indeed as a good man, but certainly as the representative of God's righteousness. They deny that Jesus is the Christ, the Son of God. They remain antichristian in their deepest principle. And thus they naturally come to this, that they also will establish a kingdom, in form like the kingdom of God, whose beauty they have learned to see. But it is a kingdom without Christ and without His atoning sacrifice. Instead of God, man is absolute sovereign in this kingdom. In that kingdom it is emphasized that the powers of this world must be brought to complete development and that man must have dominion over all things. Progress in business and industry and commerce, in art and science, is characteristic of this kingdom,—all without God and without His Christ. Still more: also in this kingdom they speak of righteousness and brotherly love, and only clean men and women can enter into it. They demand outward righteousness, and they insist upon brotherly love. They strive to realize the universal brotherhood of man. They struggle to arrive at the realization of a great international confederacy. And they want to establish universal peace. They want to abolish the effects of sin and bring universal bliss to the world. In a word, they aim at nothing less than the consummation of what they call the kingdom of God in the world.

For they are enlightened and have come into external contact with the white horse and its rider. But the principal trouble with them is that they deny that Jesus is the Christ. The old enmity, instilled in the hearts of men by the serpent in paradise, constitutes the principal motive of all their aspirations. They are not regenerated. They are children of evil. They do not stand in a new relation to God. And the result is that their so-called kingdom is after all no kingdom of God, but a kingdom of man, by man, and for man. The state must legislate men into this kingdom, and by force of law they are made to practice temperance and to manifest their love to the brother. The state, in combination with other states, will enforce universal peace. All the nations must unite. A great world-power must soon be established, controlled by a central committee, in order that war may be abolished and the kingdom of peace may presently be ushered in.

For the establishment of this kingdom the cooperation of the church is also invited. The church must preach a social gospel. The old message of sin and guilt, of total depravity, of righteousness and holiness, of the necessity of atonement through blood and of regeneration by the Spirit of Christ, has become antiquated, is no more adapted to the needs of the present time. Instead, a new gospel has come to the forefront, the gospel of love and peace for all men, without Christ. Not that man is spiritually impotent, but rather that he is divine; not that he is guilty and condemned, but rather that he is by nature good and a child of God, must be emphasized with a view to the new era we are about to enter upon. And the church must allow herself to become a powerful agency for the establishment of this universal kingdom of peace and righteousness.

The school must serve the same purpose. It must not be separate. It must not be sectarian. It may not teach a definite religion. For that would not be in harmony with the idea of the universal brotherhood. But it must be general in its instruction and inculcate the general principles of love to humanity. Society must be transformed according to the same principles. Differences must be removed. Competition must cease. The socialistic state of things must be established, to cover up the sore spots of covetousness and greed. And in as far as family life would obstruct the development and the ultimate realization of this idea, it also must be transformed. Free love will perhaps never be advocated on a large scale; and the **form** of the family will remain unchanged. But if the murder of children or the destruction of seed is advantageous to the establishment of this kingdom, its practice must be encouraged. Thus is the tendency of the present age. You may verify it with your own observation. The great aim is to establish a kingdom that is in outward form like the kingdom of God as it is pictured in Holy Writ. But the principal motive is enmity against God and against His Christ.

In a word, under the influence of the same white horse that calls to life the covenant people of God in the world, also the kingdom of Antichrist reaches its development and consummation.

But if the case is thus, you will have no difficulty to understand that this white horse cannot run alone with its rider through the world of men. Just ask the question: what would be the result if this first horse were not followed by the red and the black and the pale? In other words, what would be the result if there were no war, no social struggle, no death in all its forms? The answer is evidently: the result would be that the kingdom of Antichrist would reach the height of its development prematurely. The sinful world, striving to establish a world-kingdom, would soon succeed in organizing into an international federation of nations, and thus constitute the formidable world-power that is pictured in the thirteenth chapter of this Book of Revelation. Peace and happiness would reign supreme, and no more bloody wars would be fought. All things would be under the control of this world-power. It would employ by main force the powers of church and state, of home and school, of business and industry and commerce, and establish the antichristian order of things. Social contrast would cease to appear. All would enjoy equally much, or at least approximately so, all the products of the earth; and all competition, strife, and revolution would have an end. But this tremendous world-power, with all things under its own control in the most complete sense of the word, would naturally leave no standing room for the true church of God on earth. It would persecute and, if possible, destroy the kingdom of God in the world.

But this may not be as yet. The time will come, indeed, when Christ will allow a partial realization of this antichristian world-power to maintain itself for a time. And that time will be most terrible for the children of the kingdom. They shall, according to Scripture, be able to buy and sell no more; that is, they shall be social outcasts. And so terrible will be those latter days, that even the elect would not persevere, were it not that those days were shortened. But as yet this order of things may not be realized. For these events the time is not yet ripe. The days may not yet be shortened.

The formation of this tremendous world-power, therefore, must be checked, must be prevented for the time being. And therefore, Christ, Who possesses all power in heaven and on earth and Who opens the book with its seven seals, sends war, sends the red horse into all the earth. It is not as if Christ were the sinful cause of war. No, thus we never conceive of the matter. But the principle of sin must manifest itself in some way. And Christ so controls the sinful passions of individuals and nations that war ensues. He does this through historical factors. If you peruse the pages of history, you may observe that never any great and powerful nation was allowed to exist for any length of time as sole lord of the universe. No sooner has one nation ascended to the zenith of its power and apparently become undisputed lord of all the world, but another nation develops and

becomes its competitor for world power. There are always two or more
nations which rival one another for the control of the world. It is Assyria
and Babylonia, Babylonia and Persia, Persia and Greece, Greece and Rome,
the latter and the dark hordes from the north of Europe, the Netherlands
and Spain, France and England, or, as it is today, alliance against alliance.
All through history things are so controlled that the situation is thus, the
end cannot come. There are, indeed, those who have expressed the
expectation that this war will not end. But this expectation is erroneous.
The present conflict will surely end again. For nation must rise against
nation; but the end is not yet. For as long as nation rises against nation,
the world-power cannot realize itself, for the simple reason that it labors
continually for its own destruction. A time will come when wars shall
apparently cease and the great world-confederacy whose principle is
enmity against Christ shall be realized. And that time of world-peace will
be the most dangerous period of history for the church of God in the
world. But that time is not yet; and therefore wars must come.

The same purpose is served by the black horse and its rider. Just as
nation rises against nation, so also one element rises against the other in
the midst of these nations, in society, because of the tremendous contrast
between rich and poor. Whatever men may do, this contrast cannot be
eliminated. As soon as the wages increase, the prices of all commodities are
raised; and the relation remains as it always was. Rich and poor, labor and
capital will remain. And it is this continual contrast between poverty and
luxury which causes society to be a house divided against itself and is the
source of strikes and social convulsions and panics, of insurrections and
revolutions many a time. Just recall the bloody scenes of the French
Revolution, and you will be able to understand how the drive of this black
horse prevents the establishment of the kingdom of outward peace and
righteousness. Also to this there will come an end for some time. We know
not how. Not impossible does it seem at present that this social contrast
will find its final solution in the socialistic state of things. For Socialism is
advancing with tremendous strides in our own day. But true it is that also
socially the kingdom of Antichrist will be allowed to realize itself for a
time. As yet, however, this may not be. And therefore the presence of the
black horse is required, and the sin of covetousness and greed is controlled
by the Lord that always and again this social contrast appears with all that
is implied in it.

Lastly, also the pale horse must serve the same purpose. Clearly you will realize this if you consider the significant addition that this horse and its horseman have power over one-fourth part of the earth. That is, death always mows away the proper persons at the proper place and at the proper time. Whenever a person has served God's purpose in the economy of this dispensation, he is mowed away and is no more. At the moment when Pharaoh and his powerful army become really perilous to the children of Israel in their exodus from Egypt, this pale horse appears on the scene and destroys the army of Pharaoh together with its king. When the enemy endangers the gates of Jerusalem, this horseman with his pale horse removes an entire force of 185,000 from the scene of action. He enters the palace of Alexander the Great and kills him by fever at the moment when he would be lord of all the world, that his kingdom may be divided. And when Antiochus Epiphanes would become too perilous to the little remnant of Israel, this awful horseman makes the cruel monarch a prey of Hades in a moment. Always this formidable rider selects the proper persons at the proper time and place. And whenever a person's purpose is served and he would perhaps become too powerful or dangerous to the people of the kingdom, the pale horse appears on the scene and snatches him away.

If, therefore, you ask: "Why these horses? Why war? Why social contrast? Why death in all its forms?" my answer is: to prevent the premature establishment of the imitation-kingdom of Antichrist, that kingdom which resembles in outward form the kingdom of Christ but which is based on the principle of enmity against God and His Anointed. All these three horses check the development of the world-kingdom in this dispensation. They all make the world-power too busy with itself to launch its final attack upon the children of the kingdom.

It is not difficult, then, to understand that these last three horses are not harmful, but must be beneficent in their effect upon the children of the kingdom. Wars and revolutions, famines and pestilences and death cannot injure the kingdom of God for the simple reason that as yet it exists purely spiritually. War does not hurt the people of God **qua talis**. Surely, they also suffer according to the flesh. They also are grieved when their sons die on the battle-field. They too are troubled when their homes are destroyed and their fields are devastated. But all things work together for good to them that love God. In trouble and affliction, in tribulation and sorrow, in the midst of ruin and terror, they are spiritually never harmed: for by faith they cling to God. And as they experience the troubles and trials of this present time, the eyes of their faith are fastened more and more on the glory that awaits them in the future, their hope is quickened. Here it is war; soon it will be peace. Here it is misery; soon it will be glory. Here it is sin and imperfection, rebellion against the God Whom they love; and the power of Antichrist comes more and more to its full manifestation. But presently it will be righteousness and holiness, peace and splendor, when the kingdom of Christ shall have been completed and shall appear in finest glory in the new heaven and the new earth. And therefore the contemplation of this tremendous contrast between what is and what will be strengthens and quickens their hope, and with all creation they begin to groan with longing for the glory that shall be revealed in them. And as far as death is concerned, to their faith the pale horse is no terror, but merely an instrument to transfer them to the anticipatory state of glory in the house of many mansions.

Be not afraid, therefore, ye people of the kingdom! All these things must needs come to pass. In times of war and trouble, famine and pestilence, when the red horse drives through the earth and the black horse appears in your streets, or the pale horse enters into your homes, let your hearts rest in the power of our Lord Jesus Christ, Who holds the book with the seven seals and controls all things in heaven and on earth unto the ultimate completion of His glorious kingdom!

Chapter XIV

The Slain Witnesses And Their Outcry

(Revelation 6:9-11)

9 And when he had opened the fifth seal, I saw under the altar the souls of them that were slain for the word of God, and for the testimony which they held:

10 And they cried with a loud voice, saying, How long, O Lord, holy and true, dost thou not judge and avenge our blood on them that dwell on the earth?

11 And white robes were given unto every one of them; and it was said unto them, that they should rest yet for a little season, until their fellowservants also and their brethren, that should be killed as they were, should be fulfilled.

The Idea Of The Fifth Seal

This passage speaks of the fifth seal. The first four seals we have already discussed. They revealed the four horsemen, the white horse representing the victorious march of the gospel throughout the world, the red horse representing war, the black horse revealing social contrast, and the last horse (the pale) representing death in all its forms. Now we have the fifth seal, which speaks of the souls under the altar, or the slain witnesses and their outcry.

It is, in my opinion, impossible to explain the seals in such a way that they refer to the future only, or especially to a period of tribulation after the church has been taken to heaven, or as referring to special periods in the past, as others do maintain. This was difficult already, as we have explained, in respect to the first four seals. But this becomes still more absurd as soon as we come to the consideration of the fifth seal. True, there is indeed a certain progress in history and also in the order of these seals. Also this fifth seal, and still more plainly the sixth, shall be most clearly and definitely realized towards the end of this dispensation. But it is not true that these seals have either already been fulfilled or that they all belong to the future in all their effect. It is evident on the very face of it that this fifth seal speaks of martyrdom, of a being slain for the Word of God and the testimony which the saints proclaim in the midst of the world. But this does not refer to any specific period in the history of the church in the past, as, for instance, the period of the Waldenses or Albigenses or the period of the Reformation. It is true that also in those days this fifth seal was plainly manifested and realized. But it was not only in those times but also in various other periods throughout the new dispensation that the operation of this seal was seen. Was not John exiled to the Isle of Patmos for the Word of God and the testimony which he held? Did not most of the apostles suffer violent death because of the same fact? Did not the church suffer one of the most terrible persecutions under the Roman Emperor Domitian? And thus it is and was all through the new dispensation. Nor can it be true that this part of the Book of Revelation must be referred to the future only. To be sure, also in the future the saints will suffer for the Word of God and the testimony which they hold. Most violently the people of God shall suffer martyrdom towards the end of this dispensation. But also in the past they have suffered as severely as one can possibly conceive.

Hence, also this fifth seal we understand to refer to the entire history of the present dispensation, though we may, no doubt, expect that it will increase in force and that at the same time there is a certain logical sequence and connection between the first four seals and this fifth one. Nor is it difficult to discover that connection. The tremendous contrast caused by the white horse naturally causes martyrdom for the loyal subjects of the kingdom of Christ. The real spiritual kingdom employs no physical force or means, and its subjects merely testify of the name of our Lord Jesus Christ and of the God of our salvation in the midst of the world. But this is not true of the kingdom of darkness. That kingdom, in order to maintain itself, is bound to employ force and fights those who oppose it with scaffold and stake. The result is martyrdom for those who are faithful. Besides, it must also clearly be discerned that as far as the material of this fifth seal is concerned, it is in a way already implied in the fourth seal, which represented, as we saw, the power of death mowing away the righteous and the wicked and doing so in all manner of ways, killing also by means of violent death the faithful witnesses of the truth.

This fifth seal, therefore, does not mean to emphasize the martyrdom of the saints as they are being slain and persecuted. This the fifth seal rather presupposes. The saints who are mentioned in this fifth seal have already fought the good fight and are evidently in heaven, waiting for their full adoption and the final glory. And one of the chief purposes of this special seal is undoubtedly to show clearly that also the martyrdom of the saints is controlled by Christ Jesus and that the world avails nothing unless the Lord wills it. For it is only when He opens the seal that there are martyrs crying for vengeance. And it was also only when He opened the seal that they were slain. We may add to this that also the purpose of this seal is to assure us that the martyrdom of the saints is an element in the progress toward the completion of the kingdom of Christ.

The Souls Under The Altar

Let us, then, look more closely for a moment at the description of these martyrs. We must not lose ourselves in the contemplation of all kinds of non-essential details. Nor must we forget that the whole is symbolical and visionary. If we do, we are likely to ask and find an answer to all kinds of foolish questions. Thus, the question has been indeed asked whether it were possible to see souls, which are spiritual. For John in this passage tells us that when the fifth seal was opened, he saw souls beneath the altar. But is it possible to see souls, it is asked. But the question is absurd. We must not forget that John is in the spirit; and in the spirit he is in heaven. All that he beholds he sees in the spirit and in a vision, so that the question whether in our present state we would also be able to see souls may indeed be considered absurd. Then too, the use of this passage in order to picture the abode of the dead after this present life and before the resurrection is equally absurd for the same reason, namely, that the whole is visionary and symbolical. And as to use made of this passage to prove that the souls after death are conscious, since they cry for vengeance, we may indeed conclude from other parts of Scripture that the souls after death and before the final resurrection live consciously in glory; and perhaps we may also admit that there is some proof in the words of this particular passage from the Book of Revelation. Yet we must guard against the danger of making too much of a passage which is in itself visionary and symbolical. Besides, we cannot tarry here to make a lengthy discourse on this particular question. Our purpose in the study of the Book of Revelation is not the establishment of all kinds of different doctrines, but rather to obtain as clear a view as possible of the coming of Christ. And although it is undoubtedly true that there are many portions in the Book of

Revelation which afford beautiful material for building up of dogma, nevertheless we must at this time pass that by with a mere mention.

The chief purpose, therefore, is that we learn to understand the meaning of the symbolism.

John, in the first place, sees an altar. There can be little question that the altar which he here sees is the altar of burnt offering, which originally stood in the temple court. First of all, it may be said that the original word for "altar" points us in that direction, and not to the altar of incense. Secondly, the souls that are under this altar point to the shedding of blood, as was characteristic and essential to the altar of burnt offering, and not to the altar of incense. Also the fact that John saw the altar makes us think that it was the altar of burnt offering, which stood in the outer court and which, in distinction from the altar of incense, could be seen by the people. To that altar, therefore, the text evidently refers. On this altar the bloody sacrifices were made. Under this altar, we are told, was a large basin, into which the blood of the sacrificial animals was poured. And the sacrifices which were brought on this altar were symbolic of reconciliation and consecration to God the Lord. If we bear this in mind and find that in the vision John does not see the blood of animals under the altar, but the souls of men, the souls of the saints, we may from the outset draw the conclusion that the whole is symbolical of the fact that witnesses of Christ Jesus have laid their lives upon the altar of consecration to their God and Savior in Christ Jesus their Lord. These souls are men who have literally been slain, who have been butchered, on the altar of consecration to God in Christ. The opening of the fifth seal, therefore, shows us the martyrs in the church after they have fought the good fight and have been faithful even unto the end.

All this is corroborated by the further description of these souls under the altar. For we read that they had been slain for the Word of God and for the testimony which they held. Literally it says here that they had been butchered, and therefore that they had suffered violent death at the hand of the enemies of Christ and His church. And the occasion and reason for this violent treatment by the enemies of Christ is also clearly stated in the text. It was the fact that they clung to the Word of God and that they openly testified for the truth of that Word.

They were men, therefore, who had been touched by the rider on the first horse, so that they had ben changed from darkness into God's marvellous light. By nature they belonged to the kingdom of darkness, and

they were subject to the power and dominion of the devil. But the white
horse had approached, and the rider on that horse had touched them. The
result was that their inner being had been turned about. They had been
regenerated by the Spirit of our Lord Jesus Christ. They had been called
by His Word. They had obtained a vision of the glorious kingdom which
was to be established by Jesus Christ, the Servant of God, their Mediator
and Intercessor. Thus the Word had become their subjective possession.
They were dominated by that Word of God. They knew the truth, and
they loved it with all their heart. Hence, for and according to that Word
they lived in the midst of the world. On the basis of that Word they stood
and manifested themselves in the present world. They claimed that in
every sphere Christ Jesus is Lord, that He is King over all the world and
over all the hidden powers of that world. They firmly believed that there
was hope for that world only in the blood of their Redeemer, and that
only when a man was touched by the Spirit of Christ and was regenerated,
so that he had a new life, could he possibly be called a subject of Christ.
Such was the Word. And thus they believed. And the truth had struck root
more and more in their inmost heart.

But there is more.

They did not hide their light under a bushel, but they testified of it.
The Word as they appropriated it was burning in their hearts, and they
were bound to express it. They could not possibly keep silent. And they
felt that over against the world in the midst of which they lived they were
bound to witness of the name of Jesus Christ their Lord. Such is the
meaning of the words "...and the testimony which they held."

There are interpreters indeed who maintain that this must be
understood as a testimony which Christ gave of them before the Father
which is in heaven. But it is rather difficult to understand how for such a
testimony they could ever suffer martyrdom on earth. Hence, it must be
understood as referring to the testimony which they gave, which they
expressed before all the world. They were obedient to the injunction of
Jesus: "He that confesseth me before men, him will I confess before my
Father which is in heaven." Thus they were witnesses.

The central idea and the chief contents of their testimony was that
Jesus is the Christ, the Son of the living God. Constantly they must have
spoken of the cross as the only hope for sinners. They witnessed that man
was lost in himself because of his fallen and sinful state, and that therefore
there was no hope for him outside of Christ Jesus and His cross. They

witnessed undoubtedly also of the necessity of regeneration in order to enter into the true kingdom of God. And they boldly maintained that all that was not in harmony with the principle of the sovereignty of Christ in the present world did not and could not belong to the kingdom of God. In the blood of Jesus was the only righteousness of sinners. For at the bottom of all questions and problems in the world lies the guilt of man. Thus they testified.

We can easily understand that as they bore this testimony in the world they came into conflict with worldly men. For as we have seen before, even the world is touched by the white horse. But the only possible result of this is that it aims at the establishment of what they conceive to be the kingdom of God, but which is in reality a kingdom of man. O yes, also the world wants peace and righteousness, bliss and happiness. But that world never confesses its guilt and its impotence to do any good. And therefore they must have nothing of the blood of Jesus Christ as the propitiation for their sins, and of the truth that the sinner must be regenerated by the Spirit of God in Christ Jesus. They establish an imitation kingdom, a kingdom without Christ as He is revealed in Holy Writ. And the faithful witnesses of Christ condemned this kingdom of man and predicted its utter destruction. Thus they principally incurred the displeasure and hatred of the world, because they confessed that Jesus is the Son of God, the only Sovereign and King over all even in the present dispensation. They came into conflict with this world because they testified of the principle that God is the highest and only Sovereign of heaven and earth and that all men must bow before Him, something they will never do apart from Christ Jesus, His cross and His Spirit. And this hatred of the world became so bitter, and the attitude of the world toward those who are of Christ became so hateful and intolerant that they finally cast themselves upon these faithful witnesses and butchered them, killed them because of the testimony which they had. And thus they were slain because of the Word of God and the testimony of Jesus Christ.

Is it necessary that I point to the history of the world, and particularly to the history of this present dispensation, to prove that this seal is actually opened? A long list of names could indeed be mentioned of them that are slain for the name and the truth of God in Christ Jesus our Lord. Even in the old dispensation the history of these faithful witnesses was written in blood. There is the name of Abel, killed, no doubt, because of his faithfulness to God and to His service. There is the name of Enoch and

the name of Noah, who truly were not killed, but who must have endured
the reproach of the world for the name of the God they confessed. There
are, as you know, the names of all the prophets, most of whom have been
killed because of their faithful testimony, so that Jesus might indeed say:
"Jerusalem, Jerusalem, thou that stonest the prophets and killest them
that are sent against thee..." Or, if you please, read the latter part of that
memorable chapter of Hebrews 11, and you will be surprised that even in
the author's time there were so many of these souls under the altar of
consecration to God who had been butchered for the Word of God and the
testimony which they held.

However, this seal does not refer to the old, but to the new dispensation.
Christ has received the book with its seven seals. And He is opening the
seals. It is under His administration that His saints, His servants, His
witnesses, are slain. And also here it is evident from all the history of this
dispensation that this fifth seal is constantly being realized. Think of the
apostles, who first bore the testimony of Christ into the world. How they
suffered and were persecuted, how they were hated and finally killed by a
world which would not receive their testimony! Think also of the churches
which are pictured in the first part of the Book of Revelation, of Smyrna,
Pergamos, and Philadelphia. They were persecuted and hated, and the
saints in Christ Jesus were killed. Think of the terrible persecutions under
the Roman emperors, how they who confessed the name of Christ Jesus
were literally butchered and tortured to death! Think also of the
forerunners of the Reformation and of the thousands of martyrs at the
time of the Reformation who did not wish to return to the mother church,
to the harlot church of the sixteenth century. How they all suffered! How
they all were persecuted! How they were driven from place to place! How
they were put on the rack and tortured in every conceivable way! How
they were brought to the scaffold and burned at the stake! In a word, as
you go through history from its very dawn to the present time, you will
find a host innumerable under the altar, slain for the Word of God and the
testimony which they held.

And what is the reason for all this? It is simply the tremendous contrast
between the kingdom of Christ and the kingdom of the devil, the kingdom
of light and the kingdom of darkness, striving for the possession of the
same world.

The Prayer Of The Saints

Now these souls under the altar make a loud outcry. Thus we read in verse 10: "And they cried with a loud voice, saying, How long, O Lord, holy and true, dost thou not judge and avenge our blood on them that dwell on the earth?"

We must constantly remember that also this fifth seal, as well as all the others, represents a vision. And therefore we have symbolism in the text. As soon as we lose sight of this fact, we are apt to raise all kinds of objections and questions. Forgetting the fact that we have a vision here, we might simply conceive of these souls under the altar as glorified souls in heaven, and no more. Then, of course, the question arises: do these souls in heaven still suffer? Are the saints in glory still impatient, as is evident from the outcry? And are they still unhappy after death? Does not this outcry represent a very deep need that is not as yet fulfilled? Are not the souls especially of those who have suffered for the name of Jesus in this world perfectly blessed after this present life? But this question is not essential, and it should never be asked. We will understand this as soon as we remember that the text represents indeed a very important truth, but that nevertheless it is a vision, and that therefore in the outcry of the souls under the altar we have symbolism. Again, the question might be raised: do these souls in the state of perfection in glory cry out for vengeance? Is it not true that while they were still in this present world they prayed for their enemies, according to the injunction of the Lord Jesus that they should love their enemies, do good to them that hate them, and pray for them that despitefully use them? How then is it possible that now they invoke the wrath of God on them, and that too, while they are in the state of perfection in heaven? Is there then still sin in the state of glory in the hearts of the saints? But also this is not essential and has nothing to do with the idea of this outcry of the saints under the altar. As we shall see, they do not cry for sinful vengeance, but for the final manifestation of righteousness and justice and for the glory of their God. Hence, we must constantly bear in mind that we have also in this outcry symbolism in the highest sense of the word. This is in harmony with the whole Book of Revelation; and it is also in accord with the passage we are now discussing. For the entire passage is visionary and symbolic. It is only in the vision that John is able to see the souls. The altar under which they are found is visionary and symbolic. And the same must be applied to the outcry of these souls under the altar.

The question we must ask is this: what is really the meaning, what is the reality of the outcry of these souls under the altar? What is the essential idea of this symbolism?

The answer is not difficult to find. The outcry is symbolic of the necessity of ultimate justice, of the final manifestation of the righteousness of God which is to be revealed in the just vengeance upon the heads of those who have killed and persecuted the saints in Christ Jesus. It is an outcry which ascends to the throne of God throughout all the history of the church in the world. It represents the longing of the saints for the day of their final justification and of just retribution for all who have hated and persecuted them in the present world. This must be perfectly evident from the contents of this outcry. The saints under the altar address Christ Jesus, Who is exalted at the right hand of God, the King over His church and the Sovereign over the whole world. This is evident from the expression used in this address, which in the original means "despot,"—not in the evil, but in the good and favorable sense of the word. It means "master, lord, absolute sovereign." Some would have it that in this expression the Triune God is addressed. With this, however, we cannot agree. Not to God directly, but to Christ their Lord these saints address the outcry. This may also be gathered from the addition, "thou holy and true one." The same expression occurs in 3:5, where the Lord Jesus refers to Himself in these same words when He addresses the church of Philadelphia. Not the Triune God, therefore, but Christ is addressed. For to Him is given all power in heaven and on earth; and the Father also has delivered all judgment to Him Who sits at His right hand. That this outcry is not the expression of sinful longing for vengeance, but of just and necessary judgment, is plain from the fact that the judge in this case is called "holy and true." According to His holiness, He cannot allow sin to have the victory. He must execute wrath against all the iniquity, injustice, and oppression of men. And according to His truth, He must reveal Himself as He is, in harmony with His holiness and with His justice against all sin and unrighteousness. These souls under the altar, therefore, do not cry for a mere human and sinful vengeance. On the contrary, they long and cry for nothing less than the perfect manifestation of the holiness and truth of their King and Master. For His glory they have suffered in the midst of the world at the hands of those that hate their Christ.

We must remember that these souls under the altar have suffered because of the Word of God and the testimony which they held. They have suffered for the name of Christ Jesus and because they represented Christ's cause in the midst of the world. The enemies that have caused them to suffer have done so not because any unrighteousness was found in these souls under the altar as they lived in the world, but only because they hated the very name of Jesus and were opposed to the cause He represented, the cause of God Himself. Hence, when Jesus Himself was in the world, they manifested this enmity directly against Him. They caused Him to suffer and die on the accursed tree, and they cast Him out of the world. But He has been exalted to glory, and they can never touch Him personally any more. But the saints are still on earth. And they follow in His steps and represent His cause. They do so by bearing faithful testimony of Him as shining lights in the midst of the darkness of this present world. And because of this testimony concerning Him, they must needs also bear His reproach. What the enemies of Christ can no longer do against Him personally they now do against His people, against the saints who represent Him. And the principle of this persecution of the saints in the midst of the world is the same as that which motivated them in casting out the Christ. To harass and persecute and butcher the saints who are still in the world is a manifestation of their hatred against Jesus the Christ, the holy and true One. The holiness and truth of Christ is trampled under foot when the world kills His saints.

Moreover, in the present world this hatred and enmity appears to be quite victorious. It seems as if the enemy can kill and persecute the people of God in Christ Jesus their Lord with impunity. As far as the present history is concerned, Christ does not avenge the blood of His saints. Many years and centuries already have elapsed, and in these centuries rivers of blood have flowed. And the souls under the altar have always been crowded out of the world. The world still goes on. And the enemies of Christ, trampling under foot His saints, and thereby also trampling under foot the truth and holiness of their Lord, have never been punished. The saints have never been avenged. This, therefore, is the essential meaning of this outcry of the saints under the altar. It is the blood of the saints that cries out. And it cries out with a great voice. If only you will listen closely to the voice of all history in this new dispensation, you can very plainly hear this cry of the souls under the altar. There are the cries, first of all, of the apostles, butchered for the testimony of Jesus which they proclaimed in the midst of the world. They were butchered relentlessly, but they were never avenged. And there is also the blood of all the saints who followed the apostles throughout the history of the church. Many of them were tortured to death for the sake of Jesus and the testimony which they held. They were butchered for their faithful witness of the name of Christ. In fact, all the saints of the new dispensation as they have suffered in the world for the sake of Christ their Lord are represented by the souls under the altar. Their blood must be revenged. The holiness and truth of their Lord are at stake. And therefore, all history cries as do these souls under the altar for revenge and for the final manifestation of the holiness and truth of their Lord and Master.

Such, then, is the meaning of the outcry of these souls under the altar. It is the expression, the historic expression, of longing for a day of vengeance which swells and grows louder and stronger as time goes on, a longing for the final day of judgment and the coming of our Lord Jesus Christ.

Thus it also must be plain that this fifth seal is of importance for the completion of the kingdom of God and His Christ. That kingdom cannot come by way of gradual development, but can only appear in a public day of judgment and destruction of the world. Those who have it that the kingdom of God will come without this day, that it must come along lines of gradual development here upon earth, are cruelly unjust in respect to the past and the history of the saints in the world. Hundreds of thousands, yea, millions of Christ's saints have suffered martyrdom; and the world has rejoiced over their death. Shall their suffering and death be passed by in silence? Shall the justice of God in Christ never be revealed at all? God forbid! These souls under the altar would cry unto all eternity if the Lord would not come and if He would not avenge them publicly, if He would hide His name of truth and holiness and justice so that it was never publicly manifest. In a final day of judgment the righteousness of Christ, the King of His people and the Lord of all the world, must be made very plain; and it must become manifest that He is holy and true indeed.

Hence, the fact that this fifth seal is opened and that the witnesses of Christ who are slain cry out for vengeance certainly implies that the kingdom of God will be completed by a final day of judgment. He must judge in righteousness. In that day it must become perfectly plain that the world actually hates Christ Jesus and that in this hatred of Him they hated the Father. This hatred they also reveal in the slaying of the saints who witness for the Word of God and the name of Christ. Hence, it is because these souls have been slain that the perfect revelation of the righteousness of God must be revealed in a day of Judgment, so that it will become perfectly manifest to all the world, as well as to all the church, that Christ is holy and true and that He represents God in His perfect righteousness and justice.

The Answer To The Saints' Prayer

What answer do these souls under the altar receive to their outcry?

It is found in verse 11 of this same chapter: "And white robes were given unto every one of them; and it was said unto them, that they should rest yet for a little season, until their fellowservants also and their brethren, that should be killed as they were, should be fulfilled."

The answer, therefore, is two-fold.

In the first place, they receive a white robe. And this white robe is, of course, symbolic of their glorified nature. A long white robe it is which they receive. As we have said before, white is, first of all, the symbol of their justification in the blood of the cross, of the fact, therefore, that Christ Jesus does not condemn them and that they are justified in Him. In the second place, these white robes are also the symbol of their holiness. They are now perfectly cleansed from sin, and they are holy before God in Christ. They are perfectly pure, and they can sin nevermore. In the third place, white is also the symbol of victory in the battle. Even as the white of the first horse is the symbol of victory of the cause of Jesus Christ, so also is the white of these robes which are given to the souls under the altar symbolic of the fact that they have conquered in battle, in the battle of faith.

And thus the meaning is perfectly clear. These saints have suffered for the cause of Christ. They have been put to death violently. They have been butchered innocently. They have suffered crying injustice. And therefore, here upon earth their blood cries out for just revenge and for the manifestation of the holiness and truth of Christ Jesus. Nevertheless, these saints under the altar have gone on to glory. They are perfectly blessed from the very moment that they entered into the state of glory. And as they entered into the blessed abode, they immediately received their white robes, their perfect and glorified nature, robes of justification and holiness and purity and victory. In these white robes they are blessed forevermore. In the world they were despised; in heaven they are glorified. In the world they were treated unjustly and trampled under foot; in heaven they are justified from the very moment of their entrance. In the world they seemed to be wrong, and the world appeared right in persecuting them; in heaven they are immediately given the symbols of their justification and victory.

In the second place, however, they are told that they must wait just a little while. Their question in the outcry was, "How long, O Lord?" And the answer is: "Not yet, but within a short time." This little while which the souls under the altar must still wait may seem a long time from our present point of view. Centuries already have elapsed since this was written, and yet these souls under the altar cry upon the earth. Still they must wait a little while. We must remember, as it is always in the Word of God, that the day of the Lord is always represented as being very near. It is the last hour. And in the Book of Revelation we are assured by the Lord Himself that He will come quickly. Therefore, although to us it may seem a long time, the Lord actually comes very quickly. He comes as quickly as possible. In view of all the tremendous events which must take place in the present dispensation before the time is ripe for the coming of the Lord and His kingdom, it is indeed but a little while that the Lord waits. And besides, in view of the fact that the souls under the altar are already glorified, and that they have received their white robes of justification and holiness and victory, they can afford to wait. To them the time cannot seem long, for they have already entered into eternal glory.

However, this time that these souls must wait before their blood shall be avenged in the day of judgment publicly is also further defined, and defined materially. How long must they wait? The answer is: until their fellowservants and brethren, that should be killed even as they were, should have fulfilled their course. This is plain language. It simply means that the time is as yet not ripe for judgment. The world has not yet shown its real character in all the hatred of its corruption. And before the world is ripe for that day of judgment, the Lord cannot and will not come. We find this phenomenon time and again in Holy Writ. The prediluvian period lasted about sixteen hundred years before the measure of their iniquity was full. And even when the climax was almost reached, the Lord still gave them one hundred twenty years in which they might hear the testimony of God through Noah, so that it might become fully evident that the day of judgment was a day of righteousness and justice. The same is true of the history of Israel. That history shows us that they had killed the prophets and stoned the messengers of God who had been sent against them. And it seemed as if the Lord would never visit them for their iniquity. But the time was not yet ripe. Not until they had revealed their hatred to the full, not until they had clearly shown that they rejected the Son of God, could the day of judgment come and Jerusalem be destroyed. These judgments, so the Bible tells us, are but typical of the great day of the Lord that is to come. And therefore, also for that day the time must be ripe and the measure of iniquity must be filled. The witnesses of Christ also in the future must let their testimony go forth. They must witness of the Christ. They must witness of the blood of the cross. They must witness against all that rises up against Him. And over against this testimony the world must reveal its hatred still more plainly than already it has done in the past. In the past all these things were mere local affairs. In the future the Christian world in general, so-called, will rise up against the church. In the past the witnesses of Christ were butchered, but the enemy was not so directly conscious that they rose up against the name of Jesus Christ. In the future the enemy will do so fully conscious that it is the hateful name of Jesus Christ that is the great obstacle to all their plans for the world. And thus the world becomes ripe for judgment. There are still a certain number who must be killed for the Word of God and for the testimony which they hold. And when they are killed, then the Lord will come and avenge His holiness and truth and establish His kingdom forever.

Hence, we also must bear testimony for the name of Christ in the midst of the world. No, we do not have to seek martyrdom. We may not seek it purposely, just for the sake of dying and suffering for Christ. Nevertheless, we must bear testimony for the Word of God and for the name of Jesus as children of the kingdom. And if we do, we may have the hope in our hearts that presently we shall receive the white robes of justification and holiness and victory. And let us never forget that the enemy who persecutes us merely serves as an instrument to bring us to that state in which we shall enjoy the glory of the kingdom of Christ forevermore. The Lord rules! He opens the seals, also the fifth. And not a hair of your head shall ever be touched against His will!

Chapter XV

The Shake-up Of The Physical Universe

(Revelation 6:12-17)

12 And I beheld when he had opened the sixth seal, and, lo, there was a great earthquake; and the sun became black as sackcloth of hair, and the moon as blood;

13 And the stars of heaven fell unto the earth, even as a fig tree casteth her untimely figs, when she is shaken of a mighty wind.

14 And the heaven departed as a scroll when it is rolled together; and every mountain and island were moved out of their places.

15 And the kings of the earth, and the great men, and the rich men, and the chief captains, and the mighty men, and every bondman, and every free man, hid themselves in the dens and in the rocks of the mountains;

16 And said to the mountains and rocks, Fall on us, and hide us from the face of him that sitteth on the throne, and from the wrath of the Lamb:

17 For the great day of his wrath is come; and who shall be able to stand?

The General Meaning Of The Sixth Seal

The fifth and sixth seals belong together. They are closely related although there is also a significant difference between the two. The difference is that while the fifth seal deals with men, particularly with the suffering saints in the world, the sixth seal does not deal directly with the world of men, but with the physical universe. And in as far as it does mention men, it refers only to the effect of the shake-up of the world upon the unrighteous.

But these seals are alike in this respect, that they both will be most fully revealed and realized in the time immediately preceding the end of this age. And the order is that the tribulation of the saints, which is mentioned in the fifth seal, is first; and the shake-up of the physical universe follows. This order is not only apparent in the Book of Revelation

232

but also in the sermons of our Lord and Savior Jesus Christ. There, too, we frequently find the same order in picturing things to come. First there is the great tribulation; immediately thereafter come the signs in the heavens and on earth. For instance, in Matthew 24:29 we read the clear statement: "Immediately after the tribulation of those days shall the sun be darkened, and the moon shall not give her light, and the stars shall fall from heaven, and the powers of the heavens shall be shaken." The same order may be observed in Luke 21, where Jesus first speaks of these signs and wonders in heaven (vs. 11), and then continues and says (vs. 12): "But before all these, they shall lay their hands on you, and persecute you, delivering you up to the synagogues, and into prisons, being brought before kings and rulers for my name's sake."

Thus it is also the order in the chapter we are now discussing. The seals which we have thus far discussed all liberated powers upon the world of men. All the four horses and their riders had their field of action among men in the world. The first horse had reference to their spiritual life and their relation to the kingdom of heaven. The second horse had reference to their political and national life and the attitude of nation over against nation. The third horse had respect to the social life of men in the world and to their relation to things material. And the fourth horse had reference to their physical life and their passing away from the scene of history at the proper time in death. All had this in common, that they applied directly to the world of men only. This, as we have seen, was also true of the fifth seal. For this seal revealed to us the souls under the altar crying out for vengeance upon those that lived on the earth because their blood had been shed for the holiness and truth of the Lord, for the Word of God and for the testimony which they held. The wickedness of the world as such and its rebellion against the Anointed of God must be fully revealed; and this becomes manifest when that world rises against the testimony of His Word and the witness of His name. For this reason the tribulation and persecution of the saints must in the future become still more general; it must become universal in its character, and must involve all the historic world. That world must attack the church of Christ in the full consciousness that it makes an attack upon the holiness and truth of the Master. From all these five seals the sixth differs, as we said, in this respect, that it does not deal with the world of men directly, but rather with the shake-up of the physical universe.

Of this, therefore, we must speak in the present chapter.

The Interpretation Of The Sixth Seal

The text speaks indeed of tremendous and terrible things. In the vision John feels a tremendous earthquake, causing the very foundations of the entire earth to tremble and wiping mountains and islands out of existence. At the same time he beholds wonders in heaven. The sun is darkened as sackcloth of hair, and the moon' spreads a weird light, flooding the earth with a color that speaks of blood, while the stars fall from heaven to the earth, and the firmament seems to pass away and roll together as a book.

The question which arises, in the first place, is, of course: how must all this be interpreted? Must the text be explained in the literal sense of the word, so that it refers here to physical reality? Does heaven refer to the firmament as we see it? And does star refer to a luminous body in heaven? Is a mountain literally a mountain, and an island an island in this passage? Or must all this be understood in the symbolical sense of the word?

There are, indeed, many interpreters who do not understand the text literally, but rather symbolically. They argue that the entire Book of Revelation is symbolic. For instance, in Chapter 1 a star is not one of the luminous bodies in the firmament, but has reference to the angel of the church, as the Lord Himself explains. Besides, the Lord informs us Himself in that same chapter that all things written in the Book of Revelation are "signified," that is, given in signs and symbols. And therefore also the things mentioned in the text we are now discussing must not be understood as representing reality but as being signs and symbols of other events in the history of this present dispensation. Especially those who are of the opinion that in these seven seals we have reference to things which already happened in the past, reference to definite historical periods, are bound to apply this principle also to the sixth seal. All kinds of different interpretations have been presented. We will not tire your attention with all of these explanations of the sixth seal. Just one of them we will mention in this connection, just to give you an idea as to how the Word of God has strangely been interpreted in the past and how it is sometimes interpreted even in the present time. According to the interpretation to which we are now referring, the earth is the Roman Empire. And the shaking of the earth by the earthquake is the shaking up of that empire at the time of Constantine the Great, about the year 313 A.D. The sun, according to this interpretation, is the chief ruler of the empire, the person of the emperor. And the moon represents his fellow ruler on the throne, while the stars are symbols of important personages throughout the provinces of the Roman Empire. Again, according to that interpretation, the eclipse of the sun and moon and the falling of the stars stand for the eclipse of the glory of the rulers of the empire and their falling from office through the conquering power of Constantine the Great. The heaven, according to this explanation, is the place of the Roman deities, which also fell from their place of glory at this time since the Christian religion replaced the pagan worship at the period here referred to. And the mountains and islands represent the territorial divisions of the Roman dominion, while their being moved out of their place symbolizes that they are wrested from the power of Rome. Such is a fair example of the symbolic interpretations, with which we cannot possibly agree.

Even though you may not be able to point out the fundamental error of such modes of interpreting Scripture, and particularly the Book of Revelation, you must nevertheless spontaneously feel that there is something radically wrong with such explanations. The very fact that those explanations are so numerous and that in detail they all differ from one another would, at the very best, leave the church fundamentally in doubt, wondering whether perhaps they cannot add many interpretations to those already offered. Besides, you all would realize that if such were the true meaning of this particular passage, the church of today would have no interest in this entire portion, except in as far as it would show how in the past prophecy has been fulfilled. But the fundamental mistake of such a way of interpreting Scripture, and particularly the passage now under discussion, can also very easily be pointed out, so that you can all see what is its error. The trouble with such interpreters is that they do not and cannot distinguish symbolism from reality.

When, for instance, we explained the four horses as being symbols of different forces in history, no one can possibly question the truth of this interpretation. And why not? Simply because the very representation of these horses immediately left you with the impression that they could not possibly be explained literally, but that the interpretation must be symbolical. When, for instance, we read of the fourth horse, we feel immediately that the power of death does not ride upon a real horse, and that real hell, or hades, does not follow such a horse. Hence, the whole is clearly symbolical. The same is true of the fifth seal. When we interpreted the souls under the altar as being symbolical of a higher historical reality, no one of us could possibly object. Why not? Because we realized at once that spiritual souls and material altars do not belong together, except in a symbolical way. The same is true of other portions of the Book of Revelation. When we read in the first chapter of stars, no one thinks at all that they are real bodies in the universe or in the firmament of heaven. Why not? Because of the simple fact that these stars are found in the hand of Jesus, and therefore, if we would take the term literally, we would run into impossibilities. When we read in 8:8 of a great mountain cast into the sea, we certainly do not think of a real mountain. Why not? In the first place, because the text there does not say "a mountain," but "as it were a great mountain." Not only this, but that we cannot think of a literal mountain is also evident from the effect that this mountain has upon the sea into which it is cast. When in the thirteenth verse of the same chapter we read of an eagle in mid-air, we do not think of that mighty bird in the literal sense of the word, and there is no danger at all of such an interpretation. Why not? Simply because it cries with a human voice, "Woe, woe, woe!" The locusts out of the abyss, the beast with the horns, the woman with the moon on her head, and many other things are all immediately conceived as symbolical, simply because the connection in which they all occur makes a literal explanation an impossibility.

But how is this in the portion now under discussion?

The answer is: it is just the opposite. Here the literal interpretation is the only explanation possible.

In the first place, let me call your attention to the fact that the whole text is very natural from this viewpoint and that no symbolical interpretation is necessary whatsoever. It is very evident that in the text the earth is the earth as we see it and know it, and nothing else. And when it quakes, real mountains and real islands are removed out of their place. The stars fall from heaven, that is, from the firmament; and in the firmament they are. And therefore, also in regard to this there is nothing inconceivable or impossible. The sun mentioned in the text is evidently the luminary in the firmament as we know it; and there is nothing in the context or in the text itself to indicate the contrary. The same may be said of the moon: also it is simply the luminary in the firmament as we see it at night. In a word, it can only be by a method of putting our own thoughts into the text that we can possibly conceive of this part of the Book of Revelation as symbolical.

But there is more. If we attempt to impose the symbolical interpretation upon the text, we run into serious difficulties. For in the second part of this passage we are told that because of this shake-up of the physical universe, kings and princes and chiefs and free men and bondmen are struck with fear and consternation. Now it stands to reason that if you take the first part of this passage as being symbolical and as referring to kings and princes and emperors and great men in the earth, you are obliged also to apply the symbolical interpretation to this second part of the text. However, this is never done even by those who wish to apply the symbolical interpretation to the passage. They interpret kings as referring to real kings in the world; and the same is true of the rest of the great men mentioned in the text, and even of free men and bondmen. They are all interpreted as referring to real men, and to nothing else. Such an interpretation, however, is completely arbitrary. And even if we would grant that such arbitrariness of interpretation is allowable, which it certainly is not, the result is a strange contradiction. For then you come to the conclusion that the text pictures the effect of kings and chiefs and princes upon themselves, which, of course, is impossible.

Finally, we must remember that it would be an impossibility to describe things which happen in the physical universe in terms of symbolism. The physical universe and elements of it may be used as symbols of things spiritual and historical, but how shall the shake-up of the physical universe be symbolized?

The Signs In The Physical Universe

Hence, there is nothing strange in the fact that, though heretofore we have had nothing but symbolism in this part of the Book of Revelation, John beholds in vision physical realities here. Thus, at least, we understand the passage. Just as in the second part of the text real kings and real princes and captains and bondmen and free men are indicated, so in the first part nothing but real stars and real sun and moon and real mountains and islands are beheld by John in the vision as all being shaken up. What we have in the sixth seal is very plainly the shake-up of the physical universe. When that seal is opened, the stars fall from heaven, the sun is black as sackcloth of hair, the moon is weird with a color as of blood, the mountains tremble, and the islands are removed out of their place. Nothing in all the physical world remains stable and secure. All seems to turn to chaos. The whole world is passing away.

Perhaps we raise the objection that the literal interpretation of this passage does not fit in with the interpretation of the other seals. Concerning the other seals we explained that they have occurred in the past, that they still occur, and will occur in the future. But can this also be said of the sixth seal? In my opinion this is very well possible. Limited realizations of the sixth seal have frequently occurred in the past, although the complete realization of this seal carries us to the time immediately before the coming of the Lord. This latter fact is but natural. The effects of the coming of Christ upon the physical universe are naturally last. Just as in our individual redemption the spiritual precedes the physical, so also in the redemption of the universe all the spiritual factors must first be ready and prepared. After that the physical universe will begin to show the full signs of its coming redemption. Nevertheless, also the sixth seal has been opened ever since the time that John received this revelation.

Earthquakes have occurred very frequently in the past, as we all know. Of them we read already in Holy Writ. Just after Christ had been crucified and killed, the earth quaked. Also when Paul and Silas were about to be delivered from prison, an earthquake occurred. Innumerable earthquakes have occurred ever since, some of them in alarming force and proportions. In the year 1875, so we are told by the science of seismology, as many as ninety-seven earthquakes occurred; and in the following year one hundred four. The same science informs us of the fact that between the years 1600 and 1850 there were as many as six thousand or seven thousand earthquakes in various parts of the earth. Surely, this is sufficient proof that in this respect also the sixth seal is opened throughout this dispensation in a limited way.

The same is true of the darkening of the sun and moon. They also have occurred more than once. We do not now refer to the regular eclipses of sun and moon, as are recorded in our calendars, but to extraordinary obscurations of the heavenly bodies. Thus, we are told that in the year 1780 a strangely dark day has been witnessed in the northeastern part of America, so strange that it has gone down in the annals of history as supernatural, at least as unaccountable. Also the red appearances of the moon have been frequently witnessed. When the text speaks of the falling of the stars, we must not think of those bodies in the heavens that are larger than our earth: for then it were impossible that they should fall on the earth. Rather do we think of those atmospheric phenomena which are called meteors, or shooting stars. One of these shooting stars, a large ball of fire, thus we are told, is able to light up an entire landscape in the night. It is very bright and light for a moment; then suddenly it is extinguished and disappears. And soon after its disappearance a loud detonation is heard in all the surrounding region. These meteors have frequently fallen in such large numbers as to strike fear and consternation into the hearts of all who were witnesses. In some instances they have fallen very thickly. In 1872 some observers counted as many as ten thousand of these shooting stars falling within two hours' time. In regard to such a shower of stars happening in the tenth century one witness testifies that it had lasted "from midnight until morning; flaming stars struck one against another violently, while being borne eastward and westward, northward and southward, and no one could bear to look toward the heavens on account of this phenomenon." One of these showers we have on record with the testimony of a witness who informs us that people were thrown into consternation and cried out to God the Most High with confused clamor. From the year 900 to about 1850 there occurred as many as sixteen of such extraordinary star showers, in as far as we have them on record. Hence, also this element has occurred time and again in the present dispensation. The same is true, as we know, of the removal of the mountains and the islands. It is a well-known fact that mountains have been blown to pieces or entirely wiped out, and that many an island that has once existed can be found no more. In a word, it cannot be said that this seal has not become manifest throughout the history of the present dispensation.

All these phenomena, however, must increase in force and generalness of manifestation. The sixth seal will not be completely realized till all these natural phenomena have become completely universal, so that all men will be able to witness them. Earthquakes will occur which affect the entire surface of the earth. Darkening of the sun and a bloody appearance of the moon will be seen which will be lasting and not again be changed to normal conditions. And a universal storm of these fiery balls will occur which will affect the whole earthly world. To be sure, the world laughs at this; and the people of God are called fools to believe this coming catastrophe. But the wisdom of the world is foolishness; and the louder their laughter and mockery now, the wilder will be their consternation when all this shall appear. For the time will surely come when, according to the writer of the Epistle to the Hebrews, the earth and the heavens shall shake, and when the sun shall be darkened and shall refuse to shed her comforting light upon the scene of wickedness, so that men shall move about in darkness, only horrified all the more by the deluge of bloody light shed by the moon, and when the stars shall fall to the earth without ceasing and the heavens shall appear to be rolled together as a scroll. Our Lord Jesus Christ is King, King also over the physical universe. He is mighty to fulfill all His Word. Hence, fools may laugh at all this; the children of God look forward in earnest expectation to the time when all these things will come to pass. To be sure, the time is not yet. First the great tribulation must come. First the number of the souls under the altar must become full. But after this, surely, also this sixth seal shall reach its full reality and spread horror and consternation upon all who have trampled under foot the blood of Christ.

Even before we answer the question as to the significance of these occurrences, we must first of all refer you to Scripture. For the Word of God is full of assurances that these things will actually come to pass. When Joel pictures the coming of the Lord for judgment, he says (2:10, 11): "The earth shall quake before them; the heavens shall tremble: the sun and the moon shall be dark, and the stars shall withdraw their shining: And the Lord shall utter his voice before his army: for his camp is very great: for he is strong that executeth his word: for the day of the Lord is great and very terrible; and who can abide it?" Again, he speaks of that terrible day of Jehovah when he says (2:30, 31): "And I will shew wonders in the heavens and in the earth, blood, and fire, and pillars of smoke. The sun shall be turned into darkness, and the moon into blood, before the great and the terrible day of the Lord come." Thus also, in the prophecy of Haggai we read (2:6, 7): "For thus saith the Lord of hosts; Yet once, it is a little while, and I will shake the heavens, and the earth, and the sea, and the dry land; And I will shake all nations, and the desire of all nations shall come: and I will fill this house with glory, saith the Lord of hosts."

Of the same shake-up of the physical universe we read in the New Testament also. In Matthew 24:29 we read, in connection with the coming of the Lord for judgment: "Immediately after the tribulation of those days shall the sun be darkened, and the moon shall not give her light, and the stars shall fall from heaven, and the powers of the heavens shall be shaken: And then shall appear the sign of the Son of man in heaven: and then shall all the tribes of the earth mourn, and they shall see the Son of man coming in the clouds of heaven with power and great glory." The same we read in the Gospel according to Luke, 21:9-11: "But when ye shall hear of wars and commotions, be not terrified: for these things must first come to pass; but the end is not by and by. Then said he unto them, Nation shall rise against nation, and kingdom against kingdom: And great earthquakes shall be in divers places, and famines, and pestilences; and fearful sights and great signs shall there be from heaven." And in verses 25 and 26 the Lord speaks of the same things: "And there shall be signs in the sun, and in the moon, and in the stars; and upon the earth distress of nations, with perplexity; the sea and the waves roaring; Men's hearts failing them for fear, and for looking after those things which are coming on the earth: for the powers of heaven shall be shaken."

All these portions of Scripture speak evidently of the same events which are coming in the future, and that too, in the same connection, in connection with the coming of the Lord for judgment. In general, therefore, we may say that the sixth seal brings upon the earth the signs which immediately precede the coming of the Lord. Then these signs shall be realized in all their fulness.

In order that you may be able fully to understand the meaning of these signs and their connection with the coming of the Lord, it is probably expedient for me to employ an illustration. Imagine that you stand at a railroad station, waiting for the train. At first all is quiet: nothing tells you that in the next half hour a train will come roaring into the station. Only now and then a passenger arrives at the station to purchase a ticket. But gradually the scene changes. More passengers arrive, and the environment becomes a busy scene. The employees in the station begin to hustle. Baggage, trunks, and suitcases are piled up and put in a convenient place for loading them in the baggage car attached to the coming train. People begin to be restless. All these are signs to you that the train is coming. But other signs presently appear. The block signal changes, and reveals that the train is approaching. Smoke from the locomotive is seen in the distance. The shrill yell of the whistle is presently heard. And you are certain that the train is coming. These last signs are inevitable manifestations, the unavoidable signs, of the coming train.

Thus it is also with respect to the coming of our Lord Jesus Christ and the signs which are connected with this coming. These signs are not arbitrary, not signs which might just as well have been omitted. But they are signs which are inevitably connected with the final coming of the Lord itself. Jesus is coming! That is the message of the Book of Revelation in brief. It reveals the coming of the Lord. He is coming into a sinful and miserable world, into a world which has fallen into the power of sin and death and which is subjected to the dominion of Satan. Man and beast and all creation is subject to this bondage. The Lord, however, is coming to redeem that entire world, with His elect people at the center, from the dominion of sin and death and hell, and to establish the reign of righteousness and everlasting perfection in glory, to subject that entire world again to His God. He is coming, coming throughout this dispensation, coming all through the present history of the world. All through this dispensation, therefore, the signs and signals of that coming, signs which are inevitably connected with that coming, are plainly visible.

When He comes on the white horse, He appears in the spiritual world, and you can see His signs in repentance and faith and confession and obedience and a walk in newness of life. When He comes on the red horse, you can see Him in war and in nation rising against nation, as a sign of His coming for judgment in the end. When you see the black horse, you see the signs of His coming in the social world and in all the struggles of that world. And when the power of death mows away thousands upon thousands at the proper time and place, you see the signs of His coming in the physical world of man. So it is also with the blood of the martyrs. And thus it is also with the signs in the physical universe. You see Him come in the earthquakes and volcanic outbursts, in storms and floods, in the signs which appear in the heavens throughout the history of this present time. For also the physical universe is in the power of sin and death, in the bondage of corruption. And therefore you must not be surprised that the coming of Jesus causes strange signs also in this physical world. They are signs that our redemption and also the redemption of the universe is nigh. But the redemption of that physical universe is last of all. And therefore, the full reality of these signs will be seen only toward the last of the present dispensation. They are the changing of the block signals, the rising of the smoke from the engine in the distance, the blowing of the whistle. When these signs shall occur,—and they surely shall occur, as the Scriptures everywhere testify,—then lift up your head! For then your redemption draweth nigh! The Lord cometh, and all the universe will be affected by His coming! Hence, all the universe will also reveal the signs of that coming.

The Effect Of These Signs Upon The World

The effect of these signs upon the world is most terrible. To be sure, it will also have its effect upon the people of God that these signs shall appear in the heavens and upon the earth. From a mere natural point of view these signs will also be terrible and alarming for them. I cannot understand how expositors of Holy Writ, particularly on prophecy, can deny that during these days the church, at least part of the church of God, will still be on earth. I fail to understand how they can deny that they shall experience at least the great tribulation in full. For Scripture testifies of this very plainly and emphatically. Whenever the Lord speaks of these things, He speaks of them as signs of His coming, as signs of comfort to His people in the midst of the world, and especially in the midst of the great tribulation of the last times. He speaks to them of the fact that they shall be in great tribulation especially when the fifth seal shall be fully realized. And He also declares that after this great tribulation the signs which are pictured in this sixth seal shall reach their fulfillment. And in connection with this, He tells His disciples and all His people: "And when these things begin to come to pass, then look up, and lift up your heads; for your redemption draweth nigh" (Luke 21:28). And it stands to reason that also for the people of God the beginning of these signs shall be dreadful from a mere natural point of view. But it does not fill them with fear and consternation. This will be impossible. They have suffered persecution. They have been in awful tribulation. Such is undoubtedly the course of events in the future, shortly before the coming of the Lord. The fear of the people of God, their suffering, their anxiety, their persecution, has been terrible, most terrible indeed. Thousands of them have been killed and tortured because of the Word of God and the testimony which they held. And the spiritual result of all this was, naturally, that they longed for the coming of Christ and for their final redemption. Now these signs appear. And though these signs will also fill them with horror from a natural point of view, yet they fill them at the same time with a great hope. They begin to see in them that Jesus draweth nigh when these things begin to come to pass. Thus the Lord had told them: "Then lift up your heads, for your redemption draweth nigh."

Now He is still tarrying, but only for a little while. Already they see His signs. Already they hear Him come for Whom their soul longeth. And lifting up their heads in expectation, they look for the sign of the Son of man in the heavens.

But of this we must speak in a later connection.

Our text speaks now of the effect of these natural phenomena, or rather, of these supernatural phenomena, upon the wicked world. And what is the effect? Of this we are told in the last part of the passage we are now discussing, in verses 15 to 17: "And the kings of the earth, and the great men, and the rich men, and the chief captains, and the mighty men, and every bondman, and every free man, hid themselves in the dens and in the rocks of the mountains; And said to the mountains and rocks, Fall on us, and hide us from the face of him that sitteth on the throne, and from the wrath of the Lamb: For the great day of his wrath is come; and who shall be able to stand?"

Notice here, in the first place, that all classes of men are included, but that the strong and mighty and rich are emphatically mentioned first and are predominating to a large degree. They are predominating, not necessarily in number,—for that is probably not the case,—but because it is exactly in their capacity as strong and rich according to the standard of the world that here they reveal their consternation. All classes, from kings and princes to bondmen and servants, are included in this crowd struck with fear. What they have all in common is that they hated the Lord Jesus Christ. They certainly have never loved Him, as is evident in their fear. For according to the apostle John, love driveth out fear. They hated Him. They have rebelled against Him and against His Word. They have opposed Him. They have persecuted Him and His flock. And as such they were the kings and the mighty ones of the world, those who were rich in money, who dominated the social world, the strong in physical power and strong in authority, who dominated the political world. They are the ones who used to win victories in battle in the earth. They are also the strong in wisdom and learning, who denied the Christ in their worldly philosophy and who in their imagined strength have always laughed at the folly of the people of the Lord, who believed the gospel. These all,—the mighty and the wise and the rich according to the measure of this world,—are now filled with terror. They are filled with a terror so strong that they seek death. They are filled with consternation. They know not what they are doing. They flee to the caves; but there is no help and no protection there. They flee to the mountains and to the rocks; but behold, they find no refuge in them. Wherever they flee they see the signs of the Lord Who is coming. And these signs do not cause them to repent. There is no forgiveness for them any more. The measure of their iniquity is full. They call to the rocks and to the mountains, "Fall on us, and hide us from the face of him that sitteth on the throne, and from the wrath of the Lamb." The day of wrath and judgment has come, and they realize it. And because they have not kissed the Son, but continued in their wild rebellion, they are now struck with terror, and they seek death, but find it not. Terrible in that day is the position of the ungodly! Terrible indeed is the day of the Lord for them who have not feared His name!

How is it to be explained, you ask perhaps, that now they are so completely struck with consternation and fear?

The answer is: because the stability of the material universe was the presupposition of the kingdom of the world which they intended to establish. They were to build up an imitation kingdom, a kingdom of bliss and righteousness and justice and peace and of material blessedness. That was their purpose, and that was their striving. And they attempted to accomplish all this without Christ Jesus. They never believed that Christ was King. They never knew that He had the principle of His spiritual kingdom already realized in the world and in the hearts of His people. They laughed at the idea that this world was principally wicked and that heaven and earth would pass away. And therefore the supposed eternal stability of the material universe was the basis of their hope. This hope was now frustrated completely and in a moment. The whole universe seems to pass away. The heavens and the earth are shaking. They cannot account for it. Human wisdom is too small, and human science cannot explain the shake-up of the physical universe. It is beyond their comprehension. Human strength now avails nothing. They have been able to do great things. They ruled over the elements, and they were in power over the sea and the land and the air. But all these things are beyond them now. Nothing can avail. They are overcome. And therefore, two facts are now powerfully impressed upon their unbelieving minds, namely: that the very basis of their imitation kingdom is going to destruction, and, secondly, that the kingdom of Christ shall prevail. And therefore, they realize that their bitterest enemy, the King of heaven and earth, He Whom they have pierced, is about to have the complete victory. Therefore they fear. In their folly and impotence they pray to the rocks and mountains, and the Word of God is literally fulfilled: "I will destroy the wisdom of the wise, and I will bring to nought the discernment of the discerner."

Blessed are they who in that day belong to the Lord and are in Zion! For Joel, after he has finished his description of that day, says: "And it shall come to pass, that whosoever shall call upon the name of the Lord shall be delivered; for in Mount Zion and in Jerusalem shall there be those that escape, as the Lord hath said, and among the remnant whom the Lord shall call." It is in full harmony with this that the Lord our Savior has foretold us: "When these things begin to come to pass, lift up your head; for your redemption draweth nigh. In the world ye shall have tribulation; but be of good cheer, I have overcome the world."

Chapter XVI

The Sealing Of The One Hundred Forty-Four Thousand

(Revelation 7:1-8)

1 And after these things I saw four angels standing on the four corners of the earth, holding the four winds of the earth, that the wind should not blow on the earth, nor on the sea, nor on any tree.

2 And I saw another angel ascending from the east, having the seal of the living God: and he cried with a loud voice to the four angels, to whom it was given to hurt the earth and the sea,

3 Saying, Hurt not the earth, neither the sea, nor the trees, till we have sealed the servants of our God in their foreheads.

4 And I heard the number of them which were sealed: and there were sealed an hundred and forty and four thousand of all the tribes of the children of Israel.

5 Of the tribe of Juda were sealed twelve thousand. Of the tribe of Reuben were sealed twelve thousand. Of the tribe of Gad were sealed twelve thousand.

6 Of the tribe of Aser were sealed twelve thousand. Of the tribe of Nepthalim were sealed twelve thousand. Of the tribe of Manasses were sealed twelve thousand.

7 Of the tribe of Simeon were sealed twelve thousand. Of the tribe of Levi were sealed twelve thousand. Of the tribe of Issachar were sealed twelve thousand.

8 Of the tribe of Zabulon were sealed twelve thousand. Of the tribe of Joseph were sealed twelve thousand. Of the tribe of Benjamin were sealed twelve thousand.

A New Vision Introduced

At this stage of our discussion of the Book of Revelation it seems necessary to remind you of the plan of the second part of this book, beginning with Chapter 4, verse 1.

That plan is, as you will remember, dominated entirely by the number seven, the number of the completion of the kingdom of God. There are seven seals to be opened; and these seven seals cover the whole of the Book of Revelation. When the last part of the seventh seal shall have been realized, the kingdom shall have come, and the works of the devil and of the Antichrist shall have been completely destroyed. The seventh seal, however, when it is opened, reveals itself as seven trumpets. And the seventh trumpet is presented as seven vials of the wrath of God. Undoubtedly this implies that as time goes on the judgments of the Lord upon the wicked world will increase; His activity to bring the kingdom of God will become more pronounced and emphatic. Of course, it also implies that the seventh seal is revealed to the church in greater detail than any of the preceding six seals.

Six of these seven seals we have thus far discussed. These, as we have noticed, formed two main groups, the first four belonging together and the last two also being closely allied.

In the first four seals we noticed the powers that were let loose upon the world of men in general in this dispensation. There is, first of all, the power of the spiritual kingdom, symbolized in the white horse. Secondly, there is the power of war, symbolized in the red horse. Thirdly, there is the power of social strife, in the black horse. And, finally, there is the power of death, in the pale horse.

As to the second group, seals five and six, we found that the first of these concerned the saints and pictured to us the people of God that have been slain for the Word of God and the testimony which they had. And we found that the blood of these saints becomes one awful testimony against the world that hates and rejects the Christ, the world which rises in rebellion against His holiness and truth. This means also that the fifth seal furnishes the spiritual, ethical basis for the destruction of the world in the day of judgment. And thus, finally, the sixth seal affects the physical world. All creation belongs to the kingdom of Christ. And therefore as the Messiah begins to establish His world-kingdom and reconquers it from the usurpation of the devil and his host, it is no wonder at all that also the physical world shows the signs of the kingdom of our Lord. This shake-up of the physical world, however, has the effect upon the world of evil that they begin to realize the coming of the great Judge, begin to realize that their imitation kingdom is after all vanity. However, they do not come to repentance. On the other hand, we also remarked that according to the words of Jesus our Savior, it is exactly these signs which may cause the people of God to lift up their heads in hopeful expectation that their suffering and tribulation will soon have an end, and that the Lord will come to redeem them completely.

We might expect, perhaps, that now the Book of Revelation would continue to reveal to us the contents of the seventh seal. Evidently, however, this is not the case. The opening of the seventh seal is not recorded before we come to the eighth chapter of this book. On the other hand, however, it is also evident that this seventh chapter does no more belong to the sixth seal. For, in the first place, that sixth seal is very plainly completely revealed in Chapter 6, verses 12 to 17. That portion is complete by itself, as is plain from the entire form of the section. And, in the second place, the manner in which this seventh chapter is introduced also shows plainly that here we have something new. For John tells us clearly, "After this I saw..." This seventh chapter, therefore, is neither the opening of the seventh seal nor the continuation of the sixth. It is something between the two. It forms an interlude.

Before the opening of the seventh seal is revealed, the Lord deems it necessary to come to His people with a message of a different nature. Terrible things have already been revealed in connection with the six seals which have thus far been opened. And the question which is asked by the world of unbelief when the sixth seal is opened has undoubtedly by this time also arisen in the midst of the people of God, namely: "Who shall be able to stand?" Still more awful occurrences will be revealed when the opening of the seventh seal is realized. The Lord, therefore, before He proceeds to reveal the opening of this seal, answers the question which might so easily escape from the worried souls of the faithful, "Who shall stand?" It is the answer to this question which we find in this chapter.

This answer contains two parts: the first consists of verses 1 to 8, and the second of verses 9 to 17. And the passage we are now discussing speaks of the sealing of the one hundred forty-four thousand.

The One Hundred Forty-Four Thousand

The first question which naturally arises in our minds when we read these words is: who are these one hundred forty-four thousand of whom the text informs us that they are sealed?

Judging by the numerous interpretations which have been offered, it would seem as if it were indeed an impossibility to come to a satisfactory conclusion.

The explanations which have been given may, in the main, be divided

into two classes. In the first place, there are those authors who take it that
Israel means the people of the Jews in the literal sense of the word, and
that the names of the twelve tribes actually point to the people who used
to be the people of God as a nation in the days of the old dispensation.
These, therefore, take this indication of the sealed ones in the literal sense
of the word. They inform us that here we have the record of the sealing of
the people of Israel. But among them there are different shades of
interpretation. First of all, there are those who believe that the nation as
such, the nation of Jews, shall be saved and shall occupy a special place in
the economy of redemption in the future. Israel as a nation shall in the
future accept their Redeemer, Whom they have first rejected; and in our
text we have the indication of the fact that the greatest destruction of the
world may not be initiated before this has been realized. Secondly, there
are also those who believe that in the future a time will come in which
every individual Israelite will believe in Christ. Not only the nation as a
whole, but every individual Jew who exists at that period will call upon
the name of the Lord. And the sealing of the one hundred forty-four
thousand foreshadows this glorious event. In the third place, there are
those who do not believe in the restoration of the nation of Israel in any
manner, but who see in these sealed ones the salvation of the remnant of
the elect of the Jews, who will be and must be graffed in into their own
olive tree, from which they are cut out. Thus, the one hundred forty-four
thousand indicate the elect from among the Jews of all ages and countries
into which they have been scattered. Finally, there are also those who take
it that these one hundred forty-four thousand must be referred to the elect
Jews, not of all ages, but only of the period of the great tribulation. That,
in general, is the interpretation of the first class which we mentioned.

The second class consists of those who explain these one hundred
forty-four thousand sealed ones as referring to true, spiritual Israel of the
new dispensation. Israel, even in this portion of the book, must not be
taken in the literal sense, but in the symbolic, or typical, sense of the
word. And therefore, these sealed ones simply refer to God's own people
of all ages. But then there is a difference of opinion even among these.
There are, in the first place, those who think that we have here a reference
to a special class of people of God who have either escaped from or
experienced the great tribulation; and, in the second place, there are those
who simply take it that these one hundred forty-four thousand refer to all
the people of God at any time.

I must confess that for some time I was rather inclined to cast my lot with the first class of interpreters and to explain that these one hundred forty-four thousand sealed ones had reference to Israel in the literal sense of the word. I did not believe that we have any reference here to the Jewish nation as such, so that the text would mean that there would be a restoration of the Israelitish nation. Nor did I ever think that there would be a special kind of salvation for the Jews. Nevertheless, I thought that these one hundred forty-four thousand symbolized the remnant according to the election of grace, all the elect of Israel, who are to be saved in Christ Jesus. If ever, therefore, I was inclined to find a reference in Revelation literally to Israel as such, it was in this passage.

However, reflection and further study of this particular portion changed my mind. I am now firmly convinced not only that this section does not speak of Israel as a nation, nor of the Jews only, but that Scripture in general absolutely teaches that there is no more a national Israel with special spiritual privileges and with a special way of salvation. And since the subject of Israel as a nation is very frequently discussed, especially in our day, and since the error is often made of maintaining that the Jews as a nation still have special privileges, and still will have a great future as such, I must dwell for just a moment on the teaching of Scripture in this respect.

The portion of Scripture to which I naturally must call your attention for light on this subject is that which we find in the Epistle to the Romans, Chapters 9 to 11. There Paul begins in Chapter 9 by expressing his heartfelt grief over his brethren according to the flesh because of the pitiful condition in which they are found at this time, after they have rejected their own Messiah. But he continues to argue that if anyone would think that the promises of God had failed, and that He had rejected His people, and that the promises of a great seed, as the sand on the seashore and as the stars of heaven, would not now be realized, since Israel as a nation was evidently rejected, he would be sorely mistaken. On the contrary, that promise never was fulfilled as it now is, in the days of the New Testament, if only we make the true distinction between Israel and Israel. "They are not all Israel that are of Israel," says the apostle. Not the fact that they are children of Abraham made them true Israelites. For Ishmael and the children of Keturah also were children of Abraham in that same sense. Yet Isaac was the only child of the covenant. The same was true of Esau. If Israel according to the flesh had been the true Israel, then surely Esau was a child of Abraham as well as Jacob. Yet Esau was rejected according to the election of grace. But what made anyone a true Israelite was the fact of election. Spiritual Israel, and not Israel as a nation, must be considered the true Israel, Romans 9:6-12. And therefore, we must distinguish also in the days of the Old Testament between Israel as a nation and the true, spiritual Israel. Not all the national Jews were true Israelites. But all true Israelites in the Old Testament were also Jews, belonging to the nation. True Israel, that is, the true, spiritual people of God, were enclosed in Israel as a nation. Now, however, this has been changed. The nation as such has been rejected in the days of the new dispensation; and spiritual Israel, the elect of God, are now gathered from Jew and Gentile alike, as also Moses had already prophesied, Romans 9:24-29. The result is this, that the Gentiles, who did not seek after the righteousness of the law, have obtained the righteousness which is by faith, while Israel, who was seeking in its national blindness after the righteousness of the law and of works, failed to obtain the righteousness in Christ Jesus by faith, Romans 9:30-33.

This righteousness, which is by faith in Christ Jesus,—so Paul continues in Chapter 10,—is the main and the only true blessing and characteristic of the people of God in the old as well as in the new dispensation. There is, therefore, in the days of the New Testament no difference between Jew and Gentile: "For there is no difference between the Jew and the Greek: for the same Lord over all is rich unto all that call upon him," (Romans 10:12). It was in that righteousness of faith that the true Israelites of the Old Testament were saved. But the nation as such sought after the righteousness of the law, the righteousness of works. They did not subject themselves to this righteousness which is by faith in Christ Jesus, and therefore as a nation they were rejected from that time forth. And this rejection of Israel as a nation simply meant that salvation from now on was no more confined within the limits of Israel as a nation, but that it became the common property of Jew and Gentile both. If the true people of God in the days of the Old Testament were found only among the Jews, the rejection of the Jews as a nation became the occasion of a universality of salvation.

Finally, the apostle in Chapter 11 approaches the question whether Israel is then rejected of God in such a way that there is no salvation for them, either for them as a nation or for any individual among them. This idea the apostle refutes very strongly. No, Israel is not rejected in that absolute sense, that no Jew can be saved. On the contrary, the apostle argues that he too is a real Jew, and yet he is saved. And he quotes from the time of Elijah to prove that even then there was a remnant according to the election of grace, the seven thousand who did not bow before Baal. And thus it is also now. Even in the days of the New Testament there is undoubtedly a remnant also among the Jews which certainly will be saved. But they will be saved in no other way than the Gentiles are saved, that is, by the righteousness which is by faith in Christ Jesus. And therefore, though Israel as a nation failed, that remnant according to the election of grace will certainly be saved in Christ.

Hence, in the New Testament day this is the relation. If Israel is likened unto an olive tree, then many branches have been cut out of the olive tree. For a hardening in part has come over Israel. But instead of those branches which have been cut out of the olive tree, other branches are graffed in, and that from Jew and Gentile both. And thus, the apostle concludes, all Israel, namely, the true, spiritual Israel, shall be saved. When the fulness of the Gentiles has been ingrafted upon the olive tree of Israel in the spiritual sense, and the fulness of Israel also have been ingrafted upon that same olive tree, then all Israel shall have been saved. Thus is the reasoning of the apostle. In brief, therefore, we may conclude these principles:

1) In the first place, that true Israel, in the old as well as in the new dispensation, is spiritual, not carnal, Israel.

2) In the second place, that the nation as such has served its purpose, and that true, spiritual Israel in the present dispensation is gathered from Jew and Gentile both.

3) In the third place, that there is no difference between the two in the present dispensation. They can be saved only in the same Christ and by the same righteousness which is by faith. In Christ there is no Jew or Greek.

If, therefore, you would be Scriptural, then the only conclusion is that there is no such thing in the new dispensation as a special nation with special privileges over and above the Gentiles, and perhaps with a special future. This certainly is not the case.

Let us now return to the Book of Revelation and to the words of our text.

If, in the light of Scripture, as was indicated above, we study this wonderful book, we soon find that it never speaks of Israel in the literal and carnal sense of the word. Thus, when it speaks of Jerusalem, it either refers to apostate Christendom, which crucifies the Christ, or it refers to

Jerusalem which is above, the bride of Christ in glory. Jerusalem, Israel, the names of Israel, Zion,—all these are not used in the literal sense of the word, but always in the symbolical sense. And the book goes even so far that it speaks of those who claim that they are Jews merely because of their physical relation to Abraham as a synagogue of Satan, 2:9. And if you say that in this portion we have nevertheless a reference to the Jews as a nation, then let me call your attention to the following clear facts:

1) In Chapter 9, verse 4, we meet these sealed ones again. The locusts out of the abyss have been let loose, and they are about to begin their destructive work. And what is the commission which they receive? Whom may they hurt? Only such men as have not the seal of God on their foreheads. Now if these sealed ones in this chapter are only Jews, then the portion in Chapter 9 would mean that the locusts might indeed hurt the Christians from the Gentiles, but that only the saved ones from the Jews are immune. The absurdity of such a position is very plain. No, only on the basis that with Israel in this chapter both Jews and Gentiles are meant, the spiritual Israel of the New Testament, can that portion be explained. As such, therefore, we accept it.

2) Let us look at the portion itself. First of all, let me call your attention to the fact that in verse 3 these sealed ones are called the servants of God. The servants of God must receive the seal. Are then the Jews only the servants of God, or also the Christians from the Gentiles. The answer is, of course: also the latter. Further, notice the haphazard way in which the twelve tribes are mentioned. Ephraim is not mentioned here, nor is Dan. Have they then forfeited all right to salvation? Must we then assume that there will be no saved ones at all from these tribes? Secondly, Joseph is mentioned, who as such never formed a tribe among Israel. And if you would argue that this name takes the place of his two sons, then you are again mistaken: for Manasseh, one of the sons of Joseph, is mentioned indeed by name. In the third place, they are mentioned without any arrangement as to order. Judah is first, and then Reuben, while also Levi has a portion here as one of the tribes of Israel, though in actual fact he never did have a heritage among them. Now whatever else this may be found to indicate, it certainly tells us that we may not think here of the literal tribes of the nation of Israel, but of the spiritual Israel here upon earth, or rather, of the church of the new dispensation gathered from Jew and Gentile both.

3) Finally, I also insist that if one part of this portion is taken literally,

consistent interpretation of the Word of God demands that we take the whole in the same sense. Then we must dare to assume that this text literally tells us that there will be exactly one hundred forty-four thousand Jews in the future, or in this entire dispensation, that will be saved. No one will accept such an interpretation.

Hence, we maintain that also this portion of the Book of Revelation must be understood in the symbolical sense of the word. Israel is the church of the new dispensation. And the only question that is still to be answered is this: how must we conceive of this church according to the passage?

It is evident that the number must give us the answer to this question. One hundred forty-four thousand is the number John heard, twelve thousand out of every tribe. It needs no argument that, in the first place, we have here the symbol of completion. Dominant in the number is the number **ten**. Moreover, it is the number of completion also because of the fact that one hundred forty-four contains the number **twelve** multiplied by itself. It makes us think of a square, even as the perfected Jerusalem is also represented as a perfect square, just as long as it is wide, and just as the holy of holies was ten times ten. It is therefore the number of completion and the number of perfection. But the second question arises: complete in what sense? If one hundred forty-four thousand indicates a complete number of the people of God, does it indicate the number of God's people of all ages, or does it rather indicate those that exist during a definite period? In order to answer this question we must look at the number a little more closely. The basic numbers of one hundred forty-four thousand are evidently **ten** and **twelve**. Now twelve is the number of God's people on earth from the point of view of their free salvation. It is like the number seven in that it contains both three and four, but with an important difference. As we know, the number seven is also employed in Scripture as a symbol of the church and of the completed kingdom of Christ. And so also is the number twelve. But Scripture does not simply employ these different numbers for the sake of variety, but to express a different thought. The difference between the number seven and the number twelve is evidently this, that seven is the mere union of three and four, while twelve is obtained by the process of multiplication of four by three, thus representing the influence of three upon four. If you bear this in mind, the thought is clear. Seven is employed with a view to the church where the union of the church and their head, the union of four and three, is to be indicated, as, for instance, in the first chapter of Revelation. But twelve is the number of God's people from the point of view that they are the ones who are saved by grace, by the free grace of God. It points to the influence of God upon the world, three being the number of the Trinity, four being the number of the world. Hence, we have in this number twelve an indication of the people of God from the point of view of their reconciliation to God through the influence of divine grace. In the second place, twelve is also the number of the people of God from the viewpoint of their earthly existence in any period of time. In the Old Testament there were twelve patriarchs and twelve tribes of Israel; and in the New Testament there are twelve apostles and twelve elders. In the state of perfection they are combined, and you obtain the number **twenty-four**. But here upon earth the church, both in the Old and in the New Testament, appears under the symbol of the number twelve. And thus we come to this conclusion, that this number, twelve times twelve, is the symbol of the church of God from the viewpoint of their reconciliation to God through His free grace, and that too, during any period of their existence. And since, as we found, ten is the number of God's decree, and this number is contained in the one hundred forty-four thousand three times, we evidently have here the complete number of God's elect people, reconciled by grace, as they are upon earth in any period of this present dispensation.

The Sealing

This rather intricate interpretation was necessary, first of all, in order to understand correctly the portion which we are now discussing. For now we can ask the second question: what is implied in the sealing of these one hundred forty-four thousand?

The symbol of the seal is very often used in Scripture, both in the Old and in the New Testament. Its general significance is clear to us all. It is a mark impressed upon something. And its most general idea seems to have been that of security and safe-guarding. A proprietor would seal a certain part of his property, for instance, to mark his ownership and safe-guard it against robbery. A book was sealed when its contents had to be kept secret, to safe-guard it against being opened by improper parties. And so we read also in the New Testament more than once of the sealing of the saints. In II Corinthians 1:21, 22 we read: "Now he which stablisheth us with you in Christ, and hath anointed us, is God; Who hath also sealed us, and given the earnest of the Spirit in our hearts." Again, in Ephesians 1:13 the apostle writes: "In whom also after that ye believed, ye were sealed with the Holy Spirit of promise."And once more, in 4:30 of the same epistle, we read: "And grieve not the Holy Spirit of God, whereby ye are sealed unto the day of redemption." In all these portions of Scripture we read that the saints are sealed, and that they are sealed by the Holy Spirit. It is, therefore, a mark which is placed upon them which safe-guards them against attack, which makes them invulnerable. It is a seal which will remain upon them till the day of redemption, a seal which makes them immune from a certain point of view.

We cannot go into detail with this idea at this point, but certain it seems that the Holy Spirit is represented as placing a mark upon them which immediately characterizes them as belonging to the Lord, as being sheep of His flock, as being subjects of His kingdom, members of His church. And it is undoubtedly safest that in our interpretation of this part of Scripture we closely adhere to the Word of God in general. The Holy Spirit changes the subjects of Satan into subjects of Christ. He it is Who brings them to regeneration, to faith, to justification, and to sanctification. He it is Who works within them, so that they also confess the truth. They bear the stamp, the mark, of the Holy Spirit. When the Word of God calls this change of the people of God, this impress made upon them by the Holy Spirit, a sealing of the saints, the idea simply is that their ownership can never be changed again. This mark placed upon them by the Holy Spirit is not to be obliterated. These people who are thus sealed by the Holy Spirit can never be changed again into subjects of Satan. In short, the idea of this sealing is the same as that of perseverance of the saints.

Thus it is also in the words of our text. When we read that these people of God, these one hundred forty-four thousand of God's elect, are sealed, all that is indicated is that they belong to God, that they are the possession of Jesus Christ, bought by His precious blood; that this same Jesus Christ also in this present dispensation places His own seal upon them, makes His impress upon them through His Holy Spirit, and that by all the work through which they are changed from subjects of Satan into subjects of Christ; and, finally, that this work cannot be changed again, but that these saints will remain His, that they are as subjects of His kingdom immune from any attack from without. There is no power on earth or in heaven or in hell, there is no tribulation or affliction, which can possibly erase this seal, which can make the work of the Holy Spirit undone. Once regenerated is always regenerated. Once having come to the faith, one remains a believer. Once being justified is always to stand in the conviction that God forgives us our sins and calls us perfectly righteous. Once having surrendered ourselves to the Savior implies that we shall always belong to Him. He is ours, and we are His, not because we are so faithful and because we are so strong in ourselves, but because the work He has begun for us and within us, in our hearts, partakes of the nature of a seal which can never be erased.

The Significance Of This Sealing

If we understand this clearly, then we will also understand the significance of this portion. For this seal of the living God which is placed upon the foreheads of the people of God is impressed under peculiar conditions. It is a time of tribulation in which these people must bear that seal. The representation of our text is that it is on the eve of tribulation and great affliction that this seal is impressed upon their foreheads. Four angels stand on the four corners of the earth, and they hold the four winds of the earth. And another angel ascends from the east and warns these four angels not to let the winds go until the servants of God shall have received the seal of the living God on their foreheads.

The meaning of all this is plain. The angels are here the servants of God who must execute the judgment of Christ. And the winds which they hold are the evil powers which will presently be let loose upon all the earth. That they are four, standing on the four corners of the earth and holding the four winds of heaven, shows plainly that these evil forces will affect all the universe ultimately. It is on the eve of tribulation and affliction. The earth and the sea, that is, all that is level upon earth, but also the trees, that is, all that stands upright, will be hurt by these evil winds. And now the angel ascending from the sun-rising comes,—perhaps the Angel of the Lord, our Lord Jesus Christ Himself, the Sun of righteousness; at any rate, another angel comes,—and warns them that they may not let those winds go till the one hundred forty-four thousand shall have been sealed, that is, till they have been made immune against the evils which shall come upon the earth. Hence, the general idea of this portion of the Book of Revelation is that the people of God in the midst of tribulation and affliction are safe, and that the upheavals of the world shall not touch them, because the Lord their God has sealed them as His own possession.

One more question must be answered: how must we understand this being safe, this security of the people of God on earth, in the midst of trouble and affliction, in the midst of persecution and plagues? Must we take it in the sense that these plagues shall not touch them in the natural sense of the word? Must we understand this sealing in the sense that the people of God shall be exempted when the storms of trouble lower over the world, even as the people of Israel in the midst of Egypt were exempt from plagues which struck that country?

Evidently this cannot be the meaning. Also the people of God are subject to these plagues which shall come upon the whole earth. With a view to the six seals which we have thus far discussed this has become perfectly plain. Surely, the people of God are touched when the ravages of war devastate the whole world. Surely, the people of God partake of the suffering from a natural point of view which follows from the social contrast. Also the people of God fight the awful battle against death. They also partake of the evil forces which shall be on the earth when the seventh seal is opened. They shall be on earth when the plagues connected with that seal shall be inflicted upon the world. Still more, they shall be subjected to a suffering which the world shall not know, the suffering for Christ's sake. They shall be persecuted. The world shall more and more oppose them, shall kill them, because of the Word of God and the testimony which they hold. And therefore it may be said indeed that the people of God shall suffer more than the children of the world before the time of the end shall come. In this sense they are not immune; and the sealing of the one hundred forty-four thousand does not at all mean that the people of God shall not suffer.

No, but they are immune as children of the kingdom. From a spiritual point of view they are immune indeed. Spiritually they are sealed. Spiritually they are the subjects of Christ Jesus. And spiritually they shall not be touched or hurt by the plagues and persecutions which shall come upon the earth.

This, then, is the meaning and also the comfort of this particular portion of Revelation.

Six seals have already been opened. Those six seals implied the suffering of the people of God in the world. The seventh seal, which is still to be opened, will reveal still greater suffering and more terrible times. Hence, the question may arise: shall we be able to stand? The answer is in this part of the Book of Revelation in the sealing of the one hundred forty-four thousand by the Spirit of our Lord Jesus Christ. It means that you are sealed in the book of God's decree, that you are elect. It means that you are marked as one of the flock of our Lord, that you are His possession, His peculiar people. It means that you are sealed unto the day of redemption, and that you shall never fall away.

Be not afraid of all that is still to come!

The Lord is our possessor, and He has sealed us also against the evil day!

Chapter XVII

The Numberless Throng

(Revelation 7:9, 13-17)

9 After this I beheld, and, lo, a great multitude, which no
man could number, of all nations, and kindreds, and
people, and tongues, stood before the throne, and before
the Lamb, clothed with white robes, and palms in their
hands;
13 And one of the elders answered, saying unto me, What
are these which are arrayed in white robes? and whence
came they?
14 And I said unto him, Sir, thou knowest. And he said to
me, These are they which came out of great tribulation, and
have washed their robes, and made them white in the blood
of the Lamb.
15 Therefore are they before the throne of God, and serve
him day and night in his temple: and he that sitteth on the
throne shall dwell among them.
16 They shall hunger no more, neither thirst any more;
neither shall the sun light on them, nor any heat.
17 For the Lamb which is in the midst of the throne shall
feed them, and shall lead them unto living fountains of
waters: and God shall wipe away all tears from their eyes.

In this chapter we consider briefly the numberless throng pictured in
Revelation 7. We will leave the song of the redeemed and of the angels,
found in verses 10-12, for a separate chapter.

The Identity Of The Throng

Who are these people who are pictured to John and to the church in
this second vision of Revelation 7? What is their relation to the one
hundred forty-four thousand who are mentioned in the first part of this
chapter?

In order to answer these questions we must, of course, first of all study
our text and discover what it tells us about them.

Then we find, in the first place, that they are a throng without number:

261

"After this I beheld, and, lo, a great multitude, which no man could number..." In these words it is indicated at the same time that the apostle now beholds a different vision. It is not a mere continuation of the vision in the first part of the chapter, but it is something new. And when he says that he beheld a multitude which no man could number, he does not mean to say that in actual fact there was not a definite number, or that the multitude was actually infinite. That, of course, would be impossible. But he means to impress upon us that the throng which he beheld was so immense that the very attempt to count them seemed folly and impossible. There is an end to man's capacity of expressing things in number and of counting a certain number of objects. Thus it is, of course, with the stars of heaven. Who would deny that there are a definite number of stars in the sky, so that they surely can be counted, the number of which is also known, yea, the names of all of which are known to God Almighty? But the number of the stars is so immense that it is folly for man even to attempt to count them. This is also true of the sand which is on the seashore. There is a definite number of grains of sand on the shore; but to count these grains is beyond our human capacity. This, then, is also the case with this great multitude which John beheld. It is numberless, that is, the creature cannot count them. It is so immense that the very attempt to number them and to express their number is foolishness. And immediately we are reminded of the promise to Abraham concerning his seed. To Abraham a seed is promised as multitudinous as the stars of heaven, and as the sand which is by the seashore innumerable. This promise certainly is not completely fulfilled in the children of Israel: they always could be numbered. Nor is it completely fulfilled in the spiritual Israel of the new dispensation: for also their number is within our reach, and they may be expressed in the definite number, one hundred forty-four thousand. But here, in this particular vision, we see for the first time the fulfillment of that glorious promise to Abraham. For John beholds a numberless throng.

Secondly, we must also note that this throng is universal in character. It is a multitude "of all nations, and kindreds, and people, and tongues." This implies, in the first place, that the Lord has His people among all nations. For there is no reason not to take these words in their full and literal meaning. There is no nation whatsoever that is excluded from this throng. The chosen people of God's grace are in this dispensation hid among all the nations of the earth. Hence, we have the suggestion here that it is incumbent upon the church to preach the gospel to all nations and tongues. Fully in harmony with the great commission which the Lord left to His church before He ascended to heaven, "Go ye therefore, into all the world, and preach the gospel to every creature," or, "Make disciples of all nations," is the presentation in the words of this passage. Among all the nations of the earth are the people of God who shall once be gathered in glory. Since, therefore, these must be called by the Word of the gospel, that Word must be preached to all without distinction. In the second place, it seems to me that we have an indication here that even in the new economy of things there shall not be an endless monotony of men, all the same, the one the exact picture of the other, but that national and tribal characteristics shall be plainly visible and represented in the numberless throng. It is the Lord's will that the human race should develop into many nations. Not one nation forms the organism of the human race all by itself, but all together compose that organism. Not one nation can be missed. And therefore, the beauty of that organism shines forth in the combination of all the characteristics of each and every nation combined. This is implied in this present vision. Hence, there is a throng from all nations, and in the vision John immediately recognizes that every nation of the globe is represented. In the third place, we may remark in passing that also the Jews are included in this very throng. They do not live separately from it, but are included in this multitude: for it is a throng of all nations. Besides, of a separate Jewish multitude we read nowhere in the Word of God. It is, therefore, a universal throng, a glorious harmony of all nations, each with its peculiar characteristics, but each also with one great characteristic in common: they are all of Christ, and they are all in glory everlasting.

That the latter is true, namely, that this multitude is conceived as being in glory, is evident from the entire text.

The text describes these people as being arrayed in white robes, and as having palm branches in their hands, and as standing before the throne and before the Lamb. Now that they are arrayed in white robes indicates that they are purified of sin and of all the effects of sin, as is also indicated in the latter part of verse 14. This undoubtedly is their chief characteristic at this moment. That this is actually true is also evident from the latter part of this portion. John stands amazed at the sight of this multitude and is wondering as to their identity. And one of the elders who stand around the throne, seeing that he is wondering, places him before the question,

"What are these which are arrayed in white robes? and whence came they?" And John, acknowledging his ignorance in regard to them, answers, "Sir, thou knowest." And the elder explains that they come out of great tribulation. So much concerning their origin. But as to their chief characteristic, the elder says that they are those who washed their robes and made them white in the blood of the Lamb. Very strikingly we read here that they have done so themselves. They themselves washed their robes in the blood of Christ. You understand, of course, from all Scripture that this must not be understood as if they had saved themselves: for this certainly is not the case, and the throng do not conceive of it in that light themselves, as is plain from the song which they sing. The people of God certainly do not save themselves, and they do not obtain the forgiveness of sin and deliverance from corruption through their own efforts. For salvation belongs unto the Lord. He washed them in His own redeeming blood. Yet we must not imagine that this is a mere form and that this indicates identically the same thing as if the text had read, "They are those whose robes are washed in the blood of the Lamb." There certainly is a point of view from which we may say that the saints wash their robes in the blood of Christ. For, do not forget, through the Holy Spirit they receive the power of faith; and through that power of faith they consciously cling to Christ, are rooted in Him, draw from Him all they need, all the blessings of salvation. Through faith the Christian becomes active in his own salvation. Through faith he appropriates Christ and all His benefits. Through faith he consciously goes to the blood of Christ to wash his robes. And this throng consists of those who have thus washed their robes in the blood of the Lamb. They are now delivered. Every spot of sin has been washed away. They are pure and holy, and they have gained the victory in the battle of faith. They stand here as having overcome already, as being victors in the battle.

The same truth is indicated by the palm branches which they hold in their hands. By these we are referred, no doubt, to the celebration of the Feast of Tabernacles, when the children of Israel commemorated how they had been in the desert and joyously thought of their being led out of bondage into the land of promise. So also this multitude: they have been in the wilderness of life, of sin and imperfection, of suffering and want and death. But they are all through; they are now in the land of promise. They celebrate their final deliverance and entrance into the land of glory.

Finally, this is also indicated by the place where they are now found.

They stand before the throne and the Lamb. They are in the place where the glory of Almighty God and of the Lamb shines forth, where the elders worship, and where all creation, with the mighty angels, praises the name of the God of their salvation. They are in that new economy of things which has been pictured to us in the fourth chapter of this book, that new economy which was to replace the old dispensation of imperfection, the new economy of the perfected kingdom of glory. And there they **stand**, that is, they are ready for worship and service and praise. To sum it up, this portion permits us to cast a glance into the future, to see what will be the portion of the people of God when all shall have been accomplished and when the new heavens and the new earth shall have been realized. This numberless throng is the multitude of the people of God after they shall have been gathered in eternal glory in the new creation.

Finally, it is of importance that we notice their origin. For also this is expressly indicated in the text: the elder tells John that they have all come out of the great tribulation.

To understand this clause fully, we must remember the general viewpoint of the Book of Revelation. We have seen time and again that it pictures to us the events of this entire dispensation as they, under the control of Christ, must lead to the completion of the kingdom of God. These events cover this entire dispensation, as we have stated repeatedly. Nevertheless, they will increase in force and in number as the time draws near that the Lord shall return to establish the kingdom of glory forever. This must be remembered also with regard to this great tribulation. In the narrowest sense of the word this phrase calls to our mind the period immediately before the coming of Christ. There is no doubt in the light of Scripture that there shall be a period of persecution of the church, a period of great tribulation for the people of God, such as has never been before. When the power of the Antichrist shall develop and reach its climax, when the great apostasy shall take place and the few faithful shall stand over against a world which is filled with enmity against Christ and His people, then shall they be hated of all nations and shall be subjected to terrible persecution. To this particular period the phrase refers in its narrowest sense.

Nevertheless, we must never conceive of this great tribulation as standing all by itself. For that is not the case. It is merely the climax, the ultimate manifestation of the power which always was filled with bitter hatred against the church of Christ in the world. We must, therefore, not forget that this great tribulation is in process of formation all the time, throughout this entire dispensation. In a wider sense, it includes also those minor persecutions, terrible enough in themselves, but minor in comparison to the final tribulation, to which the people of God have already been subjected. There was the persecution under the Roman emperors, – under Nero, under Domitian, – the persecution in the period immediately preceding the Reformation, as well as during the time of the Reformation. All these were in principle the same tribulation as that which is still to come shortly before the coming of Christ. Only, they were not such fierce manifestations of it as the last one will be, according to the words of Jesus. We may understand this term, therefore, in the broadest sense, namely, as including the tribulation of the people of God of all ages. Principally the people of God from the spiritual point of view are always in this great tribulation. The power of Antichrist was in the world already in the time of John, has been in the world ever since, and is never out of the world. That power of Antichrist always is filled with enmity against God and His Christ and His people, always plans to hurt the children of God and to destroy the kingdom of Christ, – now in one form, now in another. And therefore the children of God always have a battle to fight if they are faithful: the battle against sin within and the power of evil without. And always the Word of Jesus is true, that we must take up our cross, deny ourselves, and follow Him in the path of tribulation if we would be His disciples.

Hence, the picture which we may form of this great tribulation is that of a great ocean, involving all history and every age. But in this great ocean there are higher and lower waves, while the great tribulation which is still to come is the highest of all and the most threatening to the church of Christ and the people of God. Hence, when our text speaks of great tribulation, it does no doubt refer especially to those times of persecution when the blood of the saints shall be shed for the testimony which they have and for the Word of God. Yet in general it implies this entire dispensation to a greater or smaller degree.

We are now ready also to answer the further question: what is the relation between the one hundred forty-four thousand, those who were sealed, according to the first part of this chapter, and those who are in the numberless throng, standing before the throne of God and the Lamb, who have already entered into everlasting glory?

There are, of course, various possibilities and also different interpretations. These different interpretations vary according to the explanation which is given of the first passage of this chapter. Those who claim that the first one hundred forty-four thousand are Jews in the national sense of the word also maintain that in our text there is a reference to an entirely different class of people. In support of this assertion, they point, in the first place, to the fact that in the former portion mention is made only of Israel, while this part speaks of people from all nations and peoples and tongues and tribes. In the second place, they point to the fact that in the first portion the people referred to are still in the midst of the battle, while this numberless throng in white robes and with palm branches in their hands evidently have already gained the victory. And, in the third place, they especially point to the proof that the former consists of a definite number, while here there is mention made of a numberless throng. For all these reasons they claim that we must accept the idea that these are not the same as the one hundred forty-four thousand, but are a radically different throng.

We will not enter into detail in regard to these interpretations. All we wish to do now is to make clear that essentially the numberless throng and the one hundred forty-four thousand are not a different class of people, but principally the same. This is shown in the first place, by the fact that the great tribulation is one of the main ideas in both passages, that which speaks of the one hundred forty-four thousand and that which is now under discussion. In fact, both passages find their reason, the reason why they are revealed, in the coming of that great tribulation upon the church. The purpose of both passages evidently is to reveal to the church their precarious position in the world, and nevertheless their safety over against that great tribulation. The only difference is that the one hundred forty-four thousand still confront that tribulation, while the numberless throng have already passed through it. It is very evident that it is the same throng: the one pictured as in the midst of the great tribulation, or rather, as standing on the verge of passing through it, and the other pictured as already having experienced it and having overcome. It is, therefore, the same multitude, only in different states, at different periods, and therefore from different points of view. In the first part they are upon the earth; in the second part they are already in glory in the new economy of the kingdom which is completed. In the first they are in tribulation; in the second they are already passed through that tribulation.

And if you ask, then, how the difference in number must be explained, then I ask you to recall our explanation of the one hundred forty-four thousand who were sealed. We found that they represented the people of God as they were upon earth at any period of history. One hundred forty-four thousand is the number of God's elect as they are in the world at any time. But the numberless throng represents the people of God of all ages added together. At the time of John the one hundred forty-four thousand existed. During the period of the early church there were the one hundred forty-four thousand of God's people. At the time of the Reformation they were there. And they are there today. Hence, remember: the one hundred forty-four thousand are all the elect existing at any time in the world. In every generation there are the complete number of God's elect on earth, as symbolized by the number one hundred forty-four thousand. But this numberless throng represents all these one hundred forty-four thousands added together, from every generation. From the beginning to the end of the world Christ Jesus gathers His church. Part of that church is always in the world; and that part is represented by the number one hundred forty-four thousand. It is the church militant. But at the end of time all these parts shall be gathered together before the throne and the Lamb. Is it surprising, then, that at the end of time we find no more than one hundred forty-four thousand, but nothing less than a numberless throng? Who then are these people? They are the people of God of all ages and climes and nations and tribes, gathered together in the new economy of things in the new creation.

The Blessed State Of The Numberless Throng

If you ask why it was necessary that also this vision was revealed at this time, what the purpose of this passage is, what is the comfort implied in it for the people of God in the world, we must place ourselves for a moment before the important question: what is the state of these people, and what is their present condition?

Regarding this question, we read in the text, in the first place, that they are in the temple of their God. Thus we read in verse 15: "Therefore are they before the throne of God, and serve him day and night in his temple: and he that sitteth on the throne shall dwell among them."

A moment's reflection will make it plain that in both parts of this verse the same idea is expressed: they shall serve Him in His temple, and He shall spread His tabernacle over them. The central idea of the temple, in the first place, is that it is the place where God dwells, the place where He makes His abode. And, in the second place, it is the sanctuary of His holiness, where He is worshipped and served in the true sense of the word. In the old dispensation this was the building in Jerusalem, the type of the true temple which was in heaven, especially in the most holy place. The idea was, of course, that since sin came into the world, God's temple was no longer found everywhere, as it was in the beginning, before the fall; but the place where He dwelled was limited to a definite building. In the beginning, before the fall, all creation was His temple: in all creation He dwelled, and in all creation He was worshipped and praised and glorified. But through the fact of sin this was changed. God no longer dwelt in all creation. In the old dispensation He dwelled typically among His people in a definite, limited place, to the exclusion of the rest of creation. That was the meaning of the temple in Jerusalem. In the new dispensation, however, there is this development, that the idea of a definite place is removed, and that since the Spirit is poured out, God now dwells in His people and makes His abode in their hearts. He tabernacles among them and with them. However, still He does not dwell in all creation; and still all creation is not His temple. His temple in the new dispensation is the church of the living God in Christ Jesus our Lord; and with His people He dwells in the spiritual sense of the word. But this is not the end, and this is not the ideal situation. It is a step in advance of the old dispensation, and there is evidently progress. But although it is true that the time has come that the people of God worship no more at Jerusalem, but in Spirit and in truth, nevertheless, the ideal is not reached before all the world and all creation has again become the temple of the living God, and God not only tabernacles and dwells with His people, but spreads His tabernacle over them. This is the condition which is pictured in verse 15 of this chapter.

In that new economy they are before the throne of God, and they serve Him day and night in His temple. God's temple shall again be all creation, heaven and earth. And wherever the redeemed in eternity shall turn, whether they shall rise up to heaven or shall dwell on the earth, whether they shall sit down at the streams of living water and dwell in all the glorified creation,—everywhere they shall see their God and be aware of His presence. All creation shall again spell the name of their God and reveal His glory, even as it was in the typical temple of Jerusalem. Thus God shall widen His tabernacle. He shall spread His tabernacle over them. He shall spread His tent over all the world. And in Him and in His presence we shall be in the literal sense of the word. In all creation He shall be revealed. By all creation He shall be glorified. In all creation shall be His temple. And the redeemed, walking constantly in the presence of God and in His fellowship through the Spirit of Christ in their heart, constantly enlightened by that Spirit, shall serve Him day and night in the new creation. Surely, day and night in the literal sense of the word: not only in the sense of always and continually, but literally day and night they shall serve Him in the new creation. The old creation shall again shine forth in all its beauty and purity, and the night as well as the day shall sing of the glory and of the power and wisdom of God Almighty.

In the second place, we read something about the personal condition of these saints of the numberless throng. Several details are mentioned here which all find their central idea in this, that they shall be perfectly delivered also from all the effects of sin. Thus we read in verse 16: "They shall hunger no more, neither thirst any more; neither shall the sun light on them, nor any heat." This implies, in the first place, that the saints of this numberless throng shall never know any want. They shall lack nothing, absolutely nothing. Hunger and thirst are the most emphatic manifestations and expressions of dire need and want. When one has no bread wherewith to feed himself and no water to quench his thirst, he is in dire want and lacks the very necessities of his existence. Hunger and thirst, therefore, are here taken as the symbols of all need and want. Notice, it does not say that we shall have no more desires and no more needs; them we shall surely have, even in glory. A life and existence without needs and without wants is inconceivable, and, in fact, would be no life at all. But this is the condition of the numberless throng in glory, that all their desires shall be completely satisfied. There shall be no more any vain desire; there shall be no more any need which is not immediately and completely fulfilled. No more hunger and thirst shall there be in the new creation. There shall be no hunger and thirst either in the physical or in the spiritual sense of the word.

Oh, what a glorious contrast there is between this numberless throng as they are now in glory and that same throng as they existed throughout the ages of the world! These people came out of the great tribulation. They were in a state of imperfection. Often they were in suffering and tribulation. Often they were in want, physically and spiritually. Often their soul thirsted after God. Often they were in trouble and in affliction because of their many wants, spiritually as well as physically. Still more: they were the despised, the hated and persecuted in the world. They were chased all over the world, homeless, breadless, miserable. They were shut up in dingy cells, behind prison bars. They were brought to the scaffold, and they were burned alive at the stake. They were poor, naked, hungry, despised. And no one there seemed to be who took pity on them in the whole world. But now, behold, they suffer no more want! There is no more lack of anything. But they dwell in the temple of their God, without fear and without any unfulfilled desire. They now serve Him perfectly and have perfect fellowship with Him, according to the desire of their heart, and that too, constantly, day and night. The heat of the sun, nor any heat, shall strike them no more. There shall be nothing outside of them, not in nature nor in the world of men, which shall ever do them any harm. Nature shall be perfectly redeemed. All the evil forces of nature shall have disappeared. All that harms us now and that causes sickness and pain and suffering and death because of the disharmony in nature shall be forever removed. At the same time, all that harms and inspires us with fear and causes trouble and tribulation from the world of men shall also be removed, so that all is perfect and all adds to their bliss, both physical and spiritual. Their body and their soul and their spirit shall be in perfect harmony also with the world about them. And all together they shall be in harmonious relation to the Lord God Almighty in Christ Jesus their Lord.

The Source Of Their Bliss

The reason for all this is expressed in the last words of the passage: "For the Lamb which is in the midst of the throne shall feed them, and shall lead them unto living fountains of waters: and God shall wipe away all tears from their eyes."

Is not this glorious and beautiful in the highest sense of the word? Does not this fulfill all the desires of our hearts even in the present world? Are there among the people of God to whom this does not appeal in the highest sense of the word?

Human language could never say it more beautifully than it is expressed in this beautiful and rich symbolism of the Book of Revelation. But a few words of explanation we must nevertheless stammer. We often forget, perhaps, that Christ will be our head and our all even in eternity. He is not a Savior Who serves only in this dispensation, unto the end of this present time, and Who will leave us again as soon as we are perfectly redeemed. No, Christ is now our head in the absolute sense of the word, our Lord and our King. He now sits at the right hand of God and rules over us in perfection. The time shall come indeed when He will deliver His kingdom, deliver it to the Father, and He Himself shall also be subject. This, however, does not mean that then He shall disappear as our Savior, lay aside, perhaps, His human nature, or abdicate entirely and occupy no place in the new creation. On the contrary, then He shall occupy the place of our head and of our King under God as the second Adam, and that too, forevermore. Also in eternity we shall be organically one with Christ. Also then He shall be our head. He shall be our King, our leader, in the new creation. Also then we shall have our all in Him, and our life we shall draw from Him forevermore, and through Him from God. He is now our redemption and our sanctification: and all we receive in the line of grace we receive by faith from Him. But also then He shall be the fount of our life, through which we shall draw the living water of eternal life from the Lord our God. That is the meaning of the expression that He shall lead us to fountains of waters, of the water of life. No more suffering and no more want shall there be. And why not? Because the Lord Jesus Christ shall forevermore be with us and shall forevermore give us the true life, the abundant, perfect, eternal life, life without the taste of death in it, life of everlasting satisfaction and glory. And God shall remove all the causes of suffering and sorrow from our body and from our soul and from the entire creation; and thus He shall wipe away all the tears from our eyes.

Thus we also understand the meaning of this particular portion, and that too, in distinction from the immediately preceding. The first portion contained for us the comfort that the Lord keeps us in the midst of tribulation and that we shall not be harmed, however high the billows of affliction may go over our heads. For we are sealed, and the Lord through His Spirit keeps us and always gives us strength according to the tribulation. But this second portion pictures before our eyes what will be the outcome of the tribulation, in order to inspire us with confidence and courage, and to cause us not to be afraid of the tribulation of this present time. The glory which is pictured to us is so great, so beautiful, so all-comprehensively abundant, that for it we are willing to give our all, our life and our possessions. And with a view to it, in the strength of our Lord Jesus Christ, we can well afford to suffer a little persecution and a little pain for a little while. For it quickly passes away; and then the glory, everlasting glory, is awaiting us. Then our dear Lord Jesus Christ will forevermore be with us, and in Him our God and our Father shall have perfect communion with us! Surely, then we shall serve Him day and night!

What will be the expression of our service we hope to see in our next chapter. Let it now be sufficient that we have again by faith grasped a glimpse of that everlasting bliss, and that we have learned to understand the words of the apostle: "For the suffering of this present time is not worthy to be compared with the glory which shall be revealed in us!"

Chapter XVIII

The Song Of The Redeemed And Of The Angels

(Revelation 7:10-12)

10 And cried with a loud voice, saying, Salvation to our God which sitteth upon the throne, and unto the Lamb.
11 And all the angels stood round about the throne, and about the elders and the four beasts, and fell before the throne on their faces, and worshipped God,
12 Saying, Amen: Blessing, and glory, and wisdom, and thanksgiving, and honour, and power, and might, be unto our God for ever and ever. Amen.

A Heavenly Song

I think that we have a perfect right to call this outcry of the numberless throng and of the angels who surround the throne and the elders and the four living creatures a **song**. For, in the first place, it is safe to say that in the perfected economy of all things all our expressions shall be in the form of a song in a certain sense of the word. If we take "song" now as a higher and fuller and more beautiful, harmonious expression of all our conscious life in glory, then indeed it may be asserted that in heaven and in the state of perfection and glory we shall always sing. There our human language shall have reached the height of perfection. There the human voice shall sound in all the fulness of its perfect beauty. And there we shall be able to give the most harmonious expression to what we think and feel, to all our conscious life and experience. In that sense we shall always sing in heaven.

But also the text itself indicates that we should think here of a song, a song which these redeemed of God and the angels sing together to the glory of the Most High and of the Lamb. This is not so apparent as long as we take these expressions separately and look upon them as two separate expressions, the first of the redeemed and the second of the angels. But that is evidently not the case. It is true that in our text they are separated by a few clauses; besides, they are expressions of different beings and with apparently different contents. And yet, if we look a little more closely and

274

consider these two expressions of the redeemed and of the angels more carefully, we will soon find that they belong together both in form and in contents. As far as the form is concerned, let us notice that the part which the angels sing is really a reply to the shout of the redeemed throng. This is clear from the fact that they begin their song with the corroborative "Amen." This "Amen" evidently means to be an answer to the outcry of the redeemed. The redeemed cry out, "Salvation to our God which sitteth upon the throne, and unto the Lamb." And the angels take up their song and answer: "Amen. So be it. So it certainly is forever and ever." Even as in olden times the daughters of Zion would meet one another in courses and in their song respond to one another, so also in this heavenly choir the angels respond to the song of the redeemed. The latter sing that salvation belongeth to God; and the angels meet them and respond with their solemn adoration and ascription of glory to the Most High. And therefore the form plainly indicates that the two expressions belong together and must not be separated.

The same is true also of the contents of this song. It is essential that a song must have unity of thought and theme. This is certainly true of the song of the redeemed and the angels. The theme is the same in both. That theme is the glory of God as it has become revealed in the mighty work of salvation. The redeemed throng sing of the fact that of this salvation God and the Lamb are the authors: they have wrought it; they have planned it; they have completed that salvation. And the angels conclude by pointing out that therefore all praise and glory and honor and thanksgiving and wisdom and power and might belong to the Most High, and that all the powers of creation unite in ascribing glory to Him Who sitteth upon the throne.

Hence, we repeat: in the theme and form and outcries of angels and redeemed we have the record of a heavenly song, sung by all the moral and rational creatures in God's glorious creation.

The Singers

Let us fasten our attention for a moment upon these singers.

We do not mean to determine now who they are: that has been settled in our previous chapter, at least in as far as the numberless throng is concerned. This throng consists of the redeemed and glorified and perfected children of God who have passed through the great tribulation and have now been gathered from all peoples and nations and tongues and tribes into everlasting glory. And those who reply to their outcry are the mighty angels, ten thousand times ten thousand and thousands of thousands in number.

But we must watch and consider them for a few moments as singers of this wonderful song. And then we shall find that there never was a better qualified chorus upon earth than this mixed choir of men and angels. A song is chiefly a matter of perfect and harmonious expression. The clearer our consciousness and knowledge of the contents of our song, the fuller and more beautiful our song will be. The more deeply we feel and realize the depth of meaning which there is in the song we sing, the more impressive will be the song we are singing. It must be admitted that from these points of view the chorus which is here singing in the new heavens and the new earth, according to the words of the text we are now discussing, is perfectly qualified. They have, in the first place, arrived in the state of perfect knowledge. Their consciousness has been cleared; and the cloud of sin which here overshadows and bedims our knowledge, the knowledge of the people of God, has been dispersed.

It is true that also here on earth we often sing, but our song is as imperfect as ourselves. Our minds are still darkened by the influence of sin; our consciousness is beclouded by the effects of sin. We do not fully understand the truth of God and the contents of that of which we sing. As the apostle Paul has it, "We behold a dim image, as in a dark glass; but we do not as yet see face to face." Sometimes the darkness seems to break, and there are moments when we see more clearly than at other times. There are moments when we behold more clearly the beauty of God's plan and of the work of salvation. In such times we sing rather consciously with the inspired poet of old, "O how love I Thy law; it is my meditation all the day." But even at those best moments of our present life upon earth, the darkness of sin has not been fully dispersed; and we do not see face to face. And as it is with our knowledge, so also it is with our will, with our feeling and with our desires. Our will is still under the influence of sinful perversion. The lust of the flesh often still dominates and controls us to a certain extent, and we do not live the fulness of our spiritual life in the present dispensation. We are by no means perfect. There is, in fact, but a small beginning of the new obedience. There is but a small principle of the new life within us. And the result is that here we cannot sing in the perfect and true sense of the word. How often we even sing merely from an aesthetic point of view, merely for the enjoyment of the sound of the trained human voice. How often we sing mechanically, without realizing the depth of meaning there is in the songs of Zion. How often we sing without our heart being expressed in the song which we are singing. The best of our songs is under the influence of the power of sin and imperfection.

This, we understand, is not true of the song of the redeemed throng and of the angels who respond to their song. The redeemed are now perfectly delivered from the power of sin. Their minds have been cleared. They see no more a dim image in a dark glass, but now they see face to face. The cloud of sin has been dissipated. They know as they are known. Their consciousness has been purified. Fully they understand the implication of their song. With all their clearest consciousness they understand the full implication of the words which they sing: "Salvation to our God which sitteth upon the throne, and unto the Lamb." All the more do they realize the depth of meaning which is hidden in their song, and all the more fully can they express their inmost heart in this song because it is a song of their own perfected experience. They do not sing of something which does not and never did concern them. It is not a song which, for instance, has been composed for them by one of the great masters of music among them, the meaning of which is foreign to them and the tune of which is strange until they have learned it by heart. On the contrary, they themselves are the authors of this song; and they simply sing of what they have experienced, in the light of their glorified consciousness. Here upon earth they often did not understand themselves when they sang. They could not fully interpret their own experience. They could not understand their own feelings and desires. They could not see the reason of the way in which they had to walk, in which they were led here in the world by the God of their salvation. But now all is different. Clearly they understand their own experience. Here upon earth they often sang, "Sometime, sometime we'll understand," because they realized that they did not understand themselves. But now that "sometime" has been changed into the everlasting present. Now they know!

And their own experience, that which has been realized in and for and through them by the Lord their God, the God of their salvation, in the light of their redeemed consciousness, is the subject of their song. They were sinners. They used to be in the power of sin and death. And while they were in this life in the midst of the world, they sometimes felt the horrible implication of the truth that they were in the power of corruption. But the full reality of this terrible fact we really never feel in this present life. We do not know what it means to live the life of perfection. We do not know what it implies to be entirely perfect, without sin and corruption, in mind, in heart, in will, in all our feelings and emotions. We do not know what it means to be completely free from the effects of sin. We only faintly feel sometimes that it must be unspeakably blessed to live the full and abundant, eternal life of perfection. But in perfection and glory we shall realize it all. Then, looking back, we shall certainly be conscious of our former state in the midst of the world. O, this shall not be the case in the sense that the sins of this present life shall still be a cause for sorrow and repentance. In heaven, in eternity and glory, in the new creation, God shall wipe all tears from our eyes, also the tears of repentance and sorrow over sin. But it shall certainly be true in this sense, that we shall recollect the depth of misery from which we are saved. Now we cannot know the contrast; then we shall see it clearly. Now we can only faintly feel what it means that we are still in the power of sin and death; then we shall clearly understand how deeply we had fallen and from what depth of misery we are saved.

Still more: in this present life the saints of God were in tribulation. The enemy,—Satan, sin, the power of the Antichrist,—left them no rest. Some of this numberless throng have been in the hottest of the battle. They were poor and despised. They were persecuted and subjected to the most awful suffering. They were bearers of the cross. But now they are perfectly delivered. They live in the new heavens and the new earth. Wherever they turn, there is fullest freedom. Wherever they go, the Lord their God spreads His tabernacle over them. Wherever they go, there is their God and their Savior. Wherever they turn, there they see the beauty of their God, and they may serve Him day and night in His temple. They do nothing else. Constantly they serve Him Who sitteth upon the throne. They are now perfectly redeemed. They therefore can realize now the contrast fully and clearly between what they were and what they are now, between their former and their present condition. And it is small wonder that they altogether cry out in their song with a tremendous shout of deliverance: "Salvation belongeth unto the Lord that sitteth upon the throne, and unto the Lamb." It is the song of their deepest conviction. It is the song of their fullest knowledge, their clearest consciousness. It is the song of their own deepest personal experience.

The same is true of the angels.

We know, of course, that it is not true in the same sense as of the redeemed throng who constitute the new humanity. However, we must never forget that also the angels are interested in the plan of God with regard to the salvation of the world. Personally they were not affected by sin and misery. They are and remained in the state of perfection. God had created the angel world differently from the world of man. Man was created an organism. A man, therefore, could not sin and fall away from God as a mere individual. Man was created under one head. Adam was the head of the whole human race, the head both in a legal and in an organic sense of the word. Hence, when that one head fell, all the members of the human race were involved and dragged down to the abyss of sin and death. This, however, was not the case with the world of the angels. It is true, of course, as we know, that sin did not have its origin in the world of man, but in that of the angels. Satan, the prince of the devils, was the first one to fall away from and to rebel against his God. But that fall and rebellion of the devil affected only part of the world of angels, and the rest remained perfect and upright. Nevertheless, it cannot be denied that the angels are deeply interested in the redemption of God's people and of the entire universe.

In the first place, this is true because in their state of perfection they must have a far clearer view and deeper insight into the meaning of all that happens in the present world than we do. They know the mighty Satan far better than we do. They have had fellowship with him while still he was perfect. They knew that he was one of the mightiest among the mighty, yea, perhaps we can say that Satan was the very mightiest of all. They also clearly and fully realize the awful power of his rebellion. On the other hand, they live for the glory of the Most High, Who sitteth upon the throne. They long to see His glory fully realized historically. They know that this glory of their God shall not be fully realized before the redeemed have all been gathered and perfected, the world shall have been renewed, and the mighty Satan shall have been forever subjected and cast out into outer darkness along with all who took his side in his rebellion against the Most High. Hence, the angels long to see that day of universal perfection. They are even eager to catch a glimpse of it. They rejoice over every sinner that cometh to repentance. They are always ready to serve in the bringing of that glorious kingdom.

Besides, we must not forget that because of sin also the harmony between heaven and earth has been disturbed, even the harmony in the

world of the angels. That world has been broken up by the fall and
rebellion of the devil. There is disharmony everywhere, a disharmony
which is to be removed and to be replaced by perfect harmony under
Christ Jesus, the eternal King, under God, over all creation,—King also over
the angels. In that eternal kingdom, in which heaven and earth shall be
reunited, they also shall have a place, a definite place, a place which they
cannot occupy till all shall have been accomplished. But now, at the
moment when these angels respond to the song of the redeemed, all is
accomplished and perfected. Satan has now been cast out and destroyed
forever. Now all the works of darkness have come to an end. Now heaven
and earth are the temple of God, in which angels and men, under Christ
Jesus as their everlasting head, serve God forever, day and night. And
therefore also they are perfectly qualified as singers in this heavenly choir;
and they sing with perfect consciousness and from deepest emotion when
they respond to the outcry of the redeemed: "Amen: Blessing, and glory,
and wisdom, and thanksgiving, and honour, and power, and might, be unto
our God for ever and ever. Amen."

The Contents Of The Song Of The Redeemed

Let us pay attention for a moment to the contents of their song. The
redeemed throng sing: "Salvation to our God which sitteth upon the
throne, and unto the Lamb."

In order to understand this song we must make an attempt to place
ourselves on the vantage-point of the redeemed in the glorified creation.
Only then can we fully understand what they mean by salvation. The
meaning of the entire sentence of this song is rather clear: these people out
of all nations and tongues and tribes mean to say, "Salvation belongeth
unto our God; salvation is entirely out of our God; God is the only author
of salvation; and salvation therefore can only be to the glory of the Triune
God."

It is plain that this is not a preaching of the gospel: for the gospel
cannot be preached in perfection. There is no more an audience to whom
the gospel can be preached. The saints in this throng do not mean to
proclaim the glad tidings that there is salvation with God and that the
Most High is willing and able to save. For the work of salvation is at an
end. There is no salvation to be accomplished any more. All that had to be
performed is now fully finished.

Hence, these redeemed and these angels can only think of the complete wonder of the work of salvation. Just as we can speak of creation in more than one sense of the word, so also these redeemed now employ the word "salvation" in the sense that all is now finished. I can imagine that Adam in Paradise, when he beheld the wondrous works of God round about him, when he was still standing in perfect knowledge and was conscious of his Creator in all things, would sing, "Creation unto our God." The meaning naturally would be that Adam recognized that the works round about him were the finished product of the Almighty Creator, Who had wrought all these things and through all of them glorified Himself. So it is also with the song of these redeemed. Salvation has now been realized. It is a completed work. And when they sing of it, they take it as they see it, as they have it before their very eyes, and as they experience it and enjoy it.

They sing of it in its all-comprehensive sense. By it they refer, in the first place, to their own condition and state, as well as to all that was necessary to lead them to this state of glory. They were guilty and miserable. They were in the power of sin and death. They were condemned, as far as they were concerned, to everlasting corruption. And they were subject to the just wrath of the righteous God. They might sing with the poet of old, "Cords of death compassed me about." And now they are delivered from all sin and death and corruption, and they enjoy the fulness of eternal life and glory. There is no guilt, nor any consciousness of guilt, that oppresses them any more. There is no power of sin any more that corrupts them and rules over them. There is no darkness that beclouds their minds. There is no transgression that perverts their will. There is no hatred that causes them to rise in rebellion against their God. There is but one life, but one desire, but one constant longing: that is to enjoy the full communion of Him Who sitteth upon the throne, and of the Lamb. They do not look for it in vain. Their every desire is now satisfied. They hunger no more, neither thirst any more. Wherever they go, they find themselves in the temple of their God, and they find themselves covered by His tabernacle. They find that they dwell with Him, and He with them, and that they serve Him day and night. For not only they personally have been saved; but also all creation has been completely redeemed, according to their present perfect state. All things have now been brought into subjection to man in Christ Jesus their Lord. All creation has become a kingdom under man, in Christ, a kingdom with its King standing before the throne of the Most High, serving Him day and night. In a word, when these redeemed sing of their salvation, they understand it in its all-comprehensive sense; and they refer to the redemption of all the world in its fulness and to the restoration of perfect harmony in the new heaven and the new earth. In a word, salvation is the state of universal perfection.

What do they sing of this salvation? The answer is that it is unto God and unto the Lamb. This implies that they ascribe to God and to the Lamb all the authority, all the authorship and power, all the perfection and completion of what they behold in the new creation and of what they now experience in everlasting glory.

This implies, in the first place, by way of contrast, that it is in no sense of the word the work of creature, that it is not at all the work of man, and that man has no part in it whatsoever. Salvation belongeth unto God and unto the Lamb, and to no one else.

This is a song which, it would seem, is often difficult to sing in the present world and in the present dispensation. There seem to be even among the people of God in this world who cannot accept this truth now which once they hope to sing with the throng in the new creation, "Salvation is of our God and of the Lamb." To be sure, they probably will go a good way along with you and Scripture in confessing that salvation is of the Lord. They admit with us that Christ has performed all the work which needed to be done for our salvation. He has paid the debt. He has fulfilled the law. He is our all. And we come empty-handed. And with us they will confess, "Surely, He hath borne our sin and our transgressions. The chastisement of our peace was upon Him. And by His stripes we were healed." But for the rest, they make salvation, − in part, at least, − dependent upon man. Christ has opened the way, but that is all He could possibly do. If man now refuses to walk in that Christ-opened way, then God stands impotent, and His kingdom will be a failure. And it is, after all, due to a large extent to this willingness of man to believe in Christ and to accept Him that God is successful in the realization of His kingdom. Or, what is worse, and what is surely impossible for a Christian to maintain, according to the modern view, Christ has simply taught us the principle of His kingdom; and He has by His life shown how to realize it; and now it is up to us. We must bring the kingdom of God in the world. We must be up and doing. And if we do not bring the kingdom, it will never come and be perfected. Man is powerful, man is willing, man is essentially good and is by nature a fit subject of that kingdom of God in Christ. Hence, we must simply believe in the power and the goodness of man, and must set to

work to realize the kingdom and to redeem the world from the curse and
the effects of imperfection.

Over against this stands the song of the redeemed in the new world.
They do not sing, "Salvation is unto our God and unto man." But they
sing, "Salvation unto our God which sitteth upon the throne, and unto the
Lamb." No doubt, among this throng there are many who did not confess
this in all its fulness while they were still in the midst of the world. But
now, in perfection, now that their minds have been delivered from the
darkness of sin and imperfection, now that they know as they are
known,—now they have changed their conception. Now they confess in all
its fulness and in all its meaning that the entire work of salvation is the
work of God and of Christ as the Lamb Who was led to the slaughter and
Who overcame and was raised from the dead. It is God Who from all
eternity gave unto Christ a people whom He chose in order to show forth
His virtues and His power of salvation. It was God, the Triune God, Who
ordained the Mediator, Jesus Christ the righteous, to redeem that people
of His choice and to reveal the love and grace of their God. It was God
Who sent that Mediator, His only begotten Son, into the flesh at the
appointed time as the Lamb Who would be slain. It was the Lamb Who
obeyed. It was the Lamb Who bore the wrath of God, Who took upon
Himself all the sins of all His people and carried them upon the accursed
tree. It was the Lamb Who fulfilled the law and all righteousness. It was
the Lamb Who blotted out all our sins and transgressions and Who, having
fulfilled all, rose to glory on the third day. It was the Lamb Who ascended
into highest heaven and received all power in heaven and on earth, Who
realized His kingdom spiritually by pouring out the Spirit of grace. It was
the Lamb Who through that Spirit regenerated His people, called them out
of darkness into His marvellous light, Who gave them the true and saving
faith, Who justified them and sanctified them, Who protected them and
led them in the way of life in this present dispensation. It is the Lamb Who
receives the book with its seven seals and Who opens seal after seal, Who
controls all things in this present world. It is the Lamb Who will overcome
the last manifestation of the Antichrist, Who will judge the world in
righteousness, Who will by His Spirit cause the people whom the Father
gave Him to rise to glory. It is the Lamb Who thus completes the kingdom
of God. And when all shall have been completed, then the Lamb shall
deliver that kingdom to the Father, and, subjecting Himself, shall eternally
be at the head of all His people, leading them unto fountains of living

water forever and ever. Such is salvation! Man and the world are the **object**, never the subject of it. Is it a wonder that in the new world, when all this shall be clearly understood, there shall be no more controversy about these truths, but all shall sing with all their heart and mind, "Salvation,—this completed work of salvation,—is unto our God which sitteth upon the throne, and is unto the Lamb for ever and ever?"

The Angels' Response

The angels respond in one grand eulogy. They fall before the throne on their faces, and they worship.

And what is the expression of their hearts in this worship? "Amen: Blessing, and glory, and wisdom, and thanksgiving, and honour, and power, and might, be unto our God for ever and ever. Amen." This is a seven-fold ascription of glory to the Most High.

To the relation between their song and that of the redeemed we have already called your attention. It is a corroboration, and at the same time a more detailed explanation, of what the redeemed have sung. The latter have shouted that salvation, that is, the completed work of salvation as it shines forth in the new world, in the new heavens and the new earth, is the work of God and of the Lamb forevermore. These angels now sing in brief that therefore all the glory and praise and honor and wisdom and thanksgiving and power and might which shine forth from this new creation are of our God and shall be ascribed to Him forever and ever.

As in His temple you listen to the songs and sounds of the new creation, you will find that notes of praise reach your ear. And who is the object of all this praise that rises from the new kingdom, from man and angel and from every creature? God, and God alone! As you look about you in this new creation, you find that a wonderful glory shines forth and is reflected in and through it all. Whose glory is it that thus shines forth from the new world? It is God's, and God's alone! As you walk about in His temple, in this temple of your God, you will more and more notice how all speaks of wisdom and highest intelligence. Whose is this wisdom? It is the wisdom of God, and of Him alone! You will notice that under the leadership of the Lamb all creation serves one and only one, day and night, and gives honor to just one. Who is that one before whom all bow in humble worship? It is God, and God alone! From the bosom of creation rises a note of thanksgiving and heart-felt gratitude, speaking of love and of grace and of mercy revealed. For whom is that note of thanksgiving? It has its object in the Most High God, and in Him alone! Power and talent and mighty strength are now beautifully revealed and shine forth harmoniously from all the new creation. It is the power and strength and the glorious virtue which belong to the Almighty God, Who sitteth upon the throne. Thus it is and will be in the new and eternal economy of all things.

Thus shines forth the new world!

And God's conscious and rational creatures take notice of it all. They find in it all a reflection of the glory of God. And being conscious of this, they sing. They sing the new song. They sing in heavenly notes of music, sing with all their heart and mind enraptured by so much glory: "Salvation is of the Lord Who sitteth upon the throne, and unto the Lamb." And all the mighty angels join in the song of the redeemed as they shout: "Amen, yea, Amen. Praise, and glory, and wisdom, and honour, and thanksgiving, and power, and might be unto our God for ever and ever. Amen."

Chapter XIX

The Presentation Of The Prayers Of The Saints

(Revelation 8:1-6)

1 And when he had opened the seventh seal, there was silence in heaven about the space of half an hour.

2 And I saw the seven angels which stood before God; and to them were given seven trumpets.

3 And another angel came and stood at the altar, having a golden censer; and there was given unto him much incense, that he should offer it with the prayers of all saints upon the golden altar which was before the throne.

4 And the smoke of the incense, which came with the prayers of the saints, ascended up before God out of the angel's hand.

5 And the angel took the censer, and filled it with fire of the altar, and cast it into the earth: and there were voices, and thunderings, and lightnings, and an earthquake.

6 And the seven angels which had the seven trumpets prepared themselves to sound.

The Place Of This Vision In The Plan Of The Book

What we have in the words of the text quoted above is indeed a most beautiful and also a most significant passage of the Book of Revelation. At the same time it is a portion which is not so easy to understand and which will require our closest and most prayerful attention.

It is necessary, first of all, that we understand the connection of this part with the preceding. If you will refer to the preceding part of our exposition, you will find that we explained the former chapter in general as an interlude, as something which is inserted. From the end of the sixth chapter the book does not merely continue its course of thought, but, before continuing it, presents a separate vision. This was Chapter 7. In that chapter we had the vision which showed us the safety of the people of God in the midst of trouble and tribulation and judgment, as these are to come into the world, in the sealing of the one hundred forty-four

286

thousand. In the second part of that chapter we were shown the glory of those who had been faithful even in the midst of the great tribulation and who had their garments washed in the blood of the Lamb. Because, however, this seventh chapter is an interlude, we must now again interpret as if that chapter had not been written; and we must connect the eighth chapter with the last part of Chapter 6. The opening of the seals was interrupted for a moment, but now it is continued. You will remember that we explained the first six seals as already reaching the very end of time. These seals showed us, first of all, the four horses, or horsemen, which were let loose upon the earth for the completion of the kingdom of God. The first horse presents the progress of the kingdom as it is completely victorious over all things. The second horse presents the discord and war of nations. The third horse represents disharmony in the social world because of the tremendous contrast between rich and poor. And the fourth horse portrays the terrible effect of death. The fifth seal revealed to us the cry of the saints who have been slain for the Word of God as they cry and long for the day of judgment. And the sixth seal, finally, showed us the tremendous upheaval in the entire physical universe. With this last seal the seventh now connects itself immediately.

It may be observed that those interpreters who take the seals as being strictly successive, so that the one is not opened before the preceding one has been finished, must run into serious difficulty as soon as they come to the interpretation of the seventh seal. It cannot be denied that the sixth seal already took us to the very eve of the final judgment, to the end of time. For it is evident that it meant nothing less than that the entire physical universe was subjected to tremendous changes which immediately precede the coming of the Lord. Now for those who interpret the seals as strictly successive this sixth seal in its fullest realization places us before the very day of judgment. But how then can the seventh seal picture events which merely follow the things revealed in the sixth? In the latter seal heaven and earth have already been shaken, the sun has been darkened, and the moon has been changed to blood. How can that which is revealed in connection with the seventh seal still take place if it is supposed to follow in time upon the sixth seal? As we know, this seventh seal is revealed as seven trumpets. And again, the last of these trumpets is dissolved into seven vials, or bowls, of wrath. But the first six of these seven trumpets speak of things which take place on earth, in the physical universe as well as in the world of men. Therefore the seventh seal does not and cannot presuppose that all that has been revealed in connection with the sixth seal has been finished. There is but one possible explanation. The seals do not present a successive order of events merely, but they overlap. They are at the same time contemporaneous and successive. All the seals are upon the earth from the very beginning of this dispensation. But there is this difference, that as time advances, the trumpets and the vials shall force themselves more and more to the foreground and draw the attention of men. The seven trumpets, therefore, do not begin where the sixth seal ended, but rather have begun already with the first seal, only revealing to us different forces at work more in detail, and that too, according to the symbolism of the trumpets. The blast of the trumpet forces our attention especially upon the fact that judgment is coming.

However, this seventh seal does not only reveal to us the seven trumpets, but also something else. And to this we must call your attention first of all.

The Attending Circumstances

First of all, let us take a close look at the passage under discussion, so that we may have a clear idea of the symbolism involved. For that we have symbolism in this passage is very plain; it needs no proof. The passage speaks of the opening of the seventh seal. It calls us, in the first place, to heaven, to see what takes place there. In heaven we find an altar, and trumpets given to angels, and incense, and smoke, and a golden censer, and fire. When the fire is thrown upon the earth, it creates voices and thunders and lightnings and an earthquake. Hence, the presentation of the matter is pictured in such a way that we need not guess whether the language is symbolical or real. And this is always the case in the Book of Revelation.

The text, then, speaks, in the first place, of a silence in heaven for the space of about half an hour. That is the first thing which strikes John's attention. In the second place, he sees that there are seven angels standing before the throne of God and that they receive seven trumpets. But they do not blow these trumpets immediately; on the contrary, they reverently keep silence until something else has been finished. Another angel comes and approaches the golden altar which stands before the throne of God. He bends over it, as it were for the purpose of serving. He carries a golden censer in his hand, but as yet the censer is without contents. Presently, however, he receives much incense in that censer; and the commission is given him that he add the incense to the prayers of all the saints, and, kindling the incense with the fire from the altar, to cause it to ascend with the prayers of the saints to Him Who sitteth upon the throne. The angel obeys. And having caused the perfume of the incense to rise to Him Who sitteth upon the throne, he takes fire from the same altar and casts it upon the earth. The result is voices and thunderings and lightnings and an earthquake, while at the same time the seven angels prepare themselves to blow the trumpets.

Such is the scene portrayed in the text under discussion.

It is evident on the very face of it that the main theme of this passage is the presentation of the prayers of all the saints. All the rest belongs to the attending circumstances as far as this present scene is concerned.

To the prayers of all the saints belongs, in the first place, the half hour of silence in heaven. About this half hour of silence all kinds of different interpretations have been offered, some even going the length of explaining that this silence exhausts the contents of the entire seventh seal and that it simply teaches us that the seventh seal must remain a mystery to us until the day of judgment. But we will not tire your attention by all these different interpretations. To us it seems that if we merely allow the scene to impress our minds, the silence is very easily explained. It is connected with the main theme, namely, with the fact that the prayers of the saints are offered with the incense from the altar to God. If we take this into consideration, it seems to us that the explanation of this silence must not be sought in the importance of the events which are now to follow, so that the angels and all who are in heaven stand spell-bound and, as it were, dumbfounded and holding their breath because of what will happen. If that were the case, we can see no reason why they have not been spell-bound and why they did not hold their breath before. For the events pictured in all the seals and all the trumpets are of sufficient importance and significance for all the inhabitants of heaven to stand amazed. Instead, therefore, we explain this silence as standing in immediate connection with the specific nature of the scene here pictured to us. It simply means that it is the silence of reverence, occasioned by the solemnity of the scene. It is an hour of prayer in heaven. The prayers of the saints are to be offered to Him Who sitteth upon the throne. And the solemnity of the occasion so impresses all who stand by that they are silent for half an hour. Hence, the half hour of silence has no further symbolical significance than that it befits the scene of the offering up of the prayers of all the saints and all that is connected with it. The transactions here pictured, the commission to the seven angels and to the one angel who offers the prayers of the saints and who casts fire to the earth would take about the space of half an hour. And during this entire transaction there was profound and reverent silence.

In the second place, we must pay attention for a moment to the seven angels with their seven trumpets. We shall, of course, have occasion to refer to these again. But since these angels stand by reverently while the prayers of the saints are being offered and wait with the execution of the commission given unto them till this heavenly hour of worship is finished, we must also now take a look at them. They are described to us as the seven angels that stand before God. Mark you well, they are not merely seven angels who **now came** before God; but they are evidently **the** seven angels who always stand before the throne of God, the well-known seven angels whose special place is before God. We know, of course, that also in the angel world there is order and gradation, so that there are different classes of angels. Scripture speaks of archangels as well as common angels; and Paul speaks concerning the angel world of dominions, principalities, and powers. So, evidently, there is a special class of angels who always stand before God. We know that Gabriel is one of them. For, according to Luke 1:19, he says to Zacharias: "I am Gabriel, that stand in the presence of God; and am sent to speak unto thee, and to shew thee these glad tidings." It is not impossible that Michael is another of these angels, but this is not specifically stated in Scripture. Moreover, that they are seven in number shows that they have to do with the covenant and kingdom of God, of which Christ is the head. That they stand before the throne indicates that they are called and always are ready for special service with a view to the completion of the kingdom of God.

To these seven angels, then, there are given seven trumpets. The trumpet occurs frequently in the Word of God. The people of Israel were instructed to use the trumpet in time of war. Before they went to war against the enemy that oppressed them in their land, they had to blow the trumpet. It seems, therefore, that the trumpet is a symbol of war for the kingdom of God. In the second place, it also indicates the downfall and the destruction of the enemy of the kingdom, as is evident from the downfall of Jericho. For thus we read in Joshua 6:2-5: "And the Lord said unto Joshua, See, I have given into thine hand Jericho, and the king thereof, and the mighty men of valor. And ye shall compass the city, all ye men of war, and go round about the city once. Thus shalt thou do six days. And seven priests shall bear before the ark seven trumpets of rams' horns: and the seventh day ye shall compass the city seven times, and the priests shall blow with the trumpets. And it shall come to pass, that when they make a long blast with the ram's horn, and when ye hear the sound of the trumpet, all the people shall shout with a great shout; and the wall of the city shall fall down flat, and the people shall ascend up every man straight before him." It also indicates evidently judgment and authority, as is plain from God's appearing with the law under the sound of a trumpet on Sinai. For thus we read in Exodus 20:18: "And all the people saw the thunderings, and the lightnings, and the noise of the trumpet, and the mountain smoking: and when the people saw it, they removed and stood afar off." Further, the trumpet was used with the people of Israel for the convocation of the assembly in connection with their sacrifices and festivals and for the crowning of the theocratic king, as, for instance, in the case of Jehu and of Solomon. And therefore it also denotes, in general, any activity in the kingdom of God proclaiming God's gracious presence over His people, but at the same time destruction and judgment over the enemy.

In connection with the seven trumpets mentioned in our passage it is especially the latter element that is on the foreground, as we shall observe later. The trumpets signify especially that God through Christ Jesus is coming to inflict judgment and destruction upon the enemy of the kingdom of God. When our text informs us, therefore, that the angels who stand before the throne receive the seven trumpets, it thereby indicates that these servants of the Most High receive power to execute judgment over the world of evil.

The Prayers Of The Saints

However, before these angels sound their trumpets or even prepare to sound, they stand in silence, watching what takes place in heaven, namely, the presentation of the prayers of the saints. For we read in our passage: "And another angel came and stood at the altar, having a golden censer; and there was given unto him much incense, that he should offer it with the prayers of all saints upon the golden altar which was before the throne. And the smoke of the incense, which came with the prayers of the saints, ascended up before God out of the angel's hand."

It is very evident that the all-important element here is the prayers of the saints.

To understand the entire scene it is undoubtedly necessary to understand and to emphasize that these prayers which are here presented with the incense to God are the prayers of **saints**. They are not presented as mere men, nor even as believers; but they are pictured from the point of view of their being saints.

Who are these saints? They are not merely people who are already in heaven, as is the view of those who make the church of God go to heaven at the time that is mentioned in the first verse of the fourth chapter. They claim that the people of Christ have gone to heaven before the seals are opened, and that henceforth the Book of Revelation speaks no more of a church on earth. Hence, when our text nevertheless speaks of saints, they claim that naturally they are people who are already in heaven, and that the prayers of these people are also actually made from heaven. However, we cannot agree with this. Saints are not only those who are already in glory, but just as well the people of God on earth. Scripture calls believers saints time and again. Only think of the manner in which the apostle Paul is accustomed to address the church in his epistles. All the people of God are saints because they are members of the body of Christ. They are of Christ, and they are in Him. They are in Him as their head, first of all in a juridical sense of the word, so that all their sins are forgiven them and they are justified. And therefore, from this viewpoint they are saints in the most perfect sense of the word. They have in Christ Jesus no sin whatsoever. But they are also in Christ Jesus in the organic sense, that is, they are ingrafted into Him. They are living members of His body. The life that is in Him is also in them. There is one body, with one head, and with one and the same Spirit of life. That one body is the body of the church. All believers are members of that body. Or, if you please, in the strictest sense of the word, all that are regenerated by the Spirit of God are members of the body of our Lord Jesus Christ. Of that body Christ is the head, and the Spirit given to Him is the life of that body. That Spirit dwells in Christ as the head, and in the saints as members of His body, and causes their faith and hope and love,—in fact, causes all their life to be one, one in Christ. By that Spirit of Christ they are controlled. By that Spirit of Christ they are sanctified and walk in newness of life. When our text, therefore, speaks of saints, it refers to that entire body of Christ and to all its members.

We must remember, in the second place, that they pray exactly in their capacity of saints. Not every prayer which rises from the lips of believers is here referred to, but merely the prayer which rises from their hearts as saints of Christ. Here upon earth our prayers, or so-called prayers, are often very imperfect. We do not always pray as members of Christ's body. Our requests are often sinful. We often send petitions to the throne of grace which are never heard because our prayers are often controlled by the lust of the flesh. But of those prayers our text does not speak whatsoever. They pray only in the capacity of saints. It speaks of prayers which actually rise to the throne of God in Christ Jesus our Lord and which are surely heard. Perhaps they arise to the throne of grace only in the form of the groanings of the Spirit which are mentioned in Romans 8:26, 27. When we do not pray, or cannot pray, as we ought to, the Spirit of Christ Who dwells within the body of Christ and in the hearts of all the saints prays for them with groanings that cannot be uttered. The Spirit knows the needs of the saints. That Spirit also knows their deepest longings as members of the body of Christ. And that Spirit presents these longings now through their own consciousness, teaching them how to pray, and now praying within them, outside of their consciousness, with groanings which cannot be uttered. And it is of these prayers of the saints, as they rise from their hearts, controlled by the Spirit of Christ Who is in them, that our text speaks.

Thus conceived, it is not difficult to guess what these saints pray for. What is their highest purpose? And what is the deepest longing of the saints in Christ? It is the perfect fellowship with the God of their salvation, the Sovereign of heaven and earth; and it is their desire that He may be glorified. And as they know that this God of their life shall never reach His glory except through the completion and perfecting of the kingdom of Christ, the prayer of the saints is that the kingdom may come and quickly be completed. Moreover, since they also know that the glory of God and the kingdom of Christ cannot come otherwise than through the judgments that must come upon the wicked world, their prayers include also these judgments. Not only the saints whose blood has been shed for the Word of God and the testimony which they had, but all the saints, the entire body of Christ, pray for judgment upon the world. The saints whose blood was shed pray for that particular form of judgment that is connected so closely with the shedding of their own blood. But all the saints nevertheless through the Spirit of Christ Who is in them, waiting and longing for the glory of God and the perfect fellowship of His covenant through the coming and completion of the kingdom of Christ, pray for judgment, that God may be vindicated and that the everlasting economy of glory may be established.

That this is actually the correct view of the matter is also clear from the fact that the text speaks of the prayers of **all** the saints: not of the prayers of a few, but of the prayers of all. This implies all the saints in the strict sense of the word. It implies, in the first place, the saints of all ages, the saints that have ever appeared in the history of the world. This prayer of the saints is heard at any one time. We must not make the mistake of imagining that there is one definite period in history in which these prayers of the saints rise. For then they could not be the prayers of **all** the saints. And yet this is emphatically stated. Hence, also this scene of the seventh seal, as all the other seals, evidently covers the entire period of this dispensation. It refers to all the saints of all lands and from among all nations of the earth. It implies the saints who have already entered into glory everlasting. But, in the second place, this word "all" indicates that we may not think here of the particular prayer of the individual saints, but exactly of those prayers which they all have in common. As saints they have common needs and common desires. As saints, under the control of the Spirit of Christ, they utter but one great prayer, to which all the rest of their life and their prayer is subservient: "Hallowed be Thy name. Thy kingdom come. Thy will be done on earth as it is in heaven." All the saints, as members of the body of Christ, pray for the coming and the perfecting of that kingdom of Christ. And it is that prayer that is here presented to the Almighty. That prayer is always heard from the lips of the saints. But that prayer, under the influence of the Spirit of Christ, will grow more fervent and more powerful as the time draws near when the Lord shall come, until it really becomes the prayer of the longing quoted at the close of the Book of Revelation: "Come, Lord Jesus; yea, come quickly."

The Presentation Of The Prayers

It is those prayers of the saints which are here presented as being offered to the throne of God. As the seven angels who stand before God are still reverently waiting, another angel comes with a golden censer and stoops over the altar that is before the throne of God, in order to offer the incense which he receives with the prayers of the saints to the Most High. As he does so, the sweet vapor rises to Him Who sitteth upon the throne and evidently is well-pleasing and acceptable to Him. Such is the presentation of the text.

The question is often asked whether the altar which is mentioned in the text is the altar of incense, which stood in the holy place, or the altar of burnt offering as it stood in the outer court. According to some, it is even interpreted as being the ark of the covenant, which stood before Jehovah in the most holy place. Moreover, the suggestion is even made that the angel who comes with the incense is the Lord Jesus Christ Himself, since He alone makes our prayers well-pleasing in the sight of God Almighty. It is our opinion, however, that all these detailed explanations are unnecessary and that they raise questions which cannot possibly be answered. It really makes no difference whether the altar here is the altar of incense or of burnt offering. As far as the fire mentioned in the text is concerned, it seems to have been the altar of burnt offering. And as far as the incense is mentioned, it seems to refer to the altar of incense. And as far as it stood in the presence of God, it may have been the ark of the covenant. But all these questions are immaterial to the explanation of the passage. The essential idea is that prayers are upon the altar before God, and that incense is added to the prayers, thus symbolizing that the prayers now rise to God Almighty. The same applies to the question concerning the angel that is mentioned in the text. The question as to the identity of this angel is altogether irrelevant to the essential idea. That it was not Christ Himself would seem to be implied in the fact that he **receives** the incense: it is given to him. At any rate, what is revealed here is simply this: in heaven the prayers of all the saints are made acceptable unto God, so that they rise before Him and are well-pleasing in His sight, even as the vapor of the incense is sweet and well-pleasing in His nostrils.

This is the symbolism.

What is the reality corresponding to this?

We must remember that the Lamb has received the book with the seven seals. And the Lamb opens that book: seal after seal is broken by Him. This book with its seals represents, as we have seen, the decree of God Almighty as a living force, completing the kingdom which He has given to Christ. And therefore, as Christ opens seal after seal, He thereby completes and perfects the kingdom of heaven. Thus it was with the other seals, as we have seen before. All these seals became forces, living forces in the history of the world which would ultimately lead to the perfecting of the kingdom of Christ. Thus Christ uses the gospel. Thus He employs war.

Thus He uses the social contrast in the world. Thus He employs the very power of death. Thus He energizes the outcry of the souls under the altar. And thus He causes the shake-up of the physical universe. To that end He also sends forth the angels with the seven trumpets presently, who constitute the second part of this seventh seal. But thus it is also with the prayers of the saints. These prayers are, in the first place, included in the book of God's decree. God Himself has from eternity decreed that the saints should pray. Before the kingdom can come, their prayers must be full according to the measure of that decree. Hence, Christ Himself, as the head of His body, employs these prayers of the saints as forces to bring the kingdom of heaven unto perfection. Of these prayers He is the author: for we do not pray of ourselves, but through the Spirit of Christ Who dwells in us. Christ therefore prays within us through His Spirit. He teaches us; He causes us to pray for the coming of the kingdom. And thus the prayers of these saints rise to God Almighty, crying for the perfection of the kingdom of heaven. He adds to them the sweet incense of His atoning blood. And on the basis of that atoning blood He presents them to the Father, and says: "Father, I will that these prayers be heard." When these prayers are full, according to the measure of the decree of God, they will be one great outcry of longing, rising from the body of the Savior: "Thy kingdom come, O Lord."

The Answer To Their Prayer

Is that prayer answered?

It certainly is!

It is sad enough that we so often fail to see the answer of the Almighty to His praying people. But the answer is there.

This answer is indicated in the last part of our text. For we read: "And the angel took the censer, and filled it with fire of the altar, and cast it into the earth: and there were voices, and thunderings, and lightnings, and an earthquake."

The idea evidently is this, that the saints, praying for the kingdom of God, receive a preliminary answer even before the kingdom cometh. That is the entire purpose of this passage, to show us that our prayers are not lost in space, but that we can see their answer already here upon earth. O, we do not see this if we are blind for these effects of our prayers. We certainly cannot see this if we have never learned to pray as the saints of Christ pray. We do not see this if our prayers still concentrate around ourselves and around our earthly and carnal needs, and if we have identified ourselves with the present world. Then indeed we pray wrongly, and we understand wrongly, and we judge the present history of the world in a wrong light, and we cannot see the fulfillment of our prayers. Of course not! If Israel had identified itself with Egypt, do you think that it would have seen an answer to its prayer in the plagues which were sent upon the land? I tell you: Nay, but it would have prayed the Lord that these judgments might be taken away. It would not have understood that the fire had been taken from the altar in heaven and cast upon the land because their prayers for deliverance had risen to the Lord Sabaoth. And the same is still true. It is because we identify ourselves with the world that we do not recognize the answer to the prayers of all the saints and do not see that God is bringing the kingdom according to His promise.

Yet, so it is. The saints pray for the coming of the kingdom. And these prayers are presented as forces with sweet-smelling incense to God Who sitteth upon the throne. And the answer which is sent to the earth is the fire of God's wrath, taken from the same altar before His throne. That fire cast upon earth reveals itself in omens of judgment and destruction. It reveals the presence of the Judge. Voices, and thunderings, and lightnings, and earthquakes are symbols of judgment. And therefore, the passage means to teach us that in answer to the prayers of all the saints for the perfecting of the kingdom the judgments of the King are sent to the earth. It is through these judgments, it is through great upheavals,—through war and bloodshed and changes in the physical world,—that the everlasting kingdom will surely come. And for that very reason these judgments are an answer to the prayers of the saints, assuring them: "My kingdom will surely come. It is coming now. It will come till all shall be completed. And My name shall receive the honor and the power and the glory and the wisdom forevermore."

The same answer the saints who prayed in heaven receive. For we read in the closing sentence of our passage: "And the seven angels which had the seven trumpets prepared themselves to sound." In what this preparation consists the text does not tell us; and this is of minor importance. Sufficient it is to notice that they prepare themselves visibly, so that John in the vision, and therefore also the saints in heaven, can see their preparation.

Again, this preparation is an answer to their prayer. When these angels sound the trumpets, they know that judgments will come. And along the way of judgments the kingdom of God will be perfected. And therefore their preparation immediately after the prayers of the saints assures them that their prayers are heard and accepted by the Most High, and that presently their inmost desires shall be granted. Such is the picture.

This, therefore, is the practical lesson of our passage. In the first place, it teaches us that we shall not be disturbed about the judgments of Christ which come upon the world. These judgments are upon the earth now; and they shall increase. They must increase. For in no other way can the kingdom of God come. Sin and unrighteousness will develop, and must develop. And this sin and unrighteousness must be destroyed. And the glory of Christ must be revealed and vindicated, and can be vindicated only by the judgments upon the world. Be not disturbed, therefore, and by no means implore God that He may stop bringing His kingdom in the way of judgments. And if you should feel that your prayers are not answered, then know that there is something wrong with your conscious life. The prayers of all the saints are certainly answered. And the beginning of their fulfillment you may see in the judgments of Christ upon earth. Bring your prayers, therefore, into harmony with the revealed will of your God. And, spiritually separating yourselves from the world, let your prayers be in the true sense of the word: "Hallowed be Thy name. Thy kingdom come. Thy will be done on earth as it is in heaven."

Chapter XX
The First Four Trumpets
(Revelation 8:7-12)

7 The first angel sounded, and there followed hail and fire mingled with blood, and they were cast upon the earth: and the third part of trees was burnt up, and all green grass was burnt up.

8 And the second angel sounded, and as it were a great mountain burning with fire was cast into the sea: and the third part of the sea became blood;

9 And the third part of the creatures which were in the sea, and had life, died; and the third part of the ships were destroyed.

10 And the third angel sounded, and there fell a great star from heaven, burning as it were a lamp, and it fell upon the third part of the rivers, and upon the fountains of waters;

11 And the name of the star is called Wormwood: and the third part of the waters became wormwood; and many men died of the waters, because they were made bitter.

12 And the fourth angel sounded, and the third part of the sun was smitten, and the third part of the moon, and the third part of the stars; so as the third part of them was darkened, and the day shone not for a third part of it, and the night likewise.

The seventh seal, so we found, is revealed as seven trumpets. The first four of these trumpets we shall discuss in the present chapter.

We must constantly bear in mind the fact that we are discussing the last of the seven seals. Because this seventh seal reveals itself as seven trumpets, we are likely to lose sight of the fact that after all we are discussing the seven seals. But it is necessary that we keep this in mind for a correct understanding of the entire book. The whole history of this dispensation is implied in these seven seals. But the seventh seal is divided into seven trumpets, while the seventh trumpet is again divided into seven vials of wrath. We must also remember that the relation between the seals and the trumpets is not to be conceived of as strictly successive, but rather as contemporaneous, while we bear this in mind, however, that the judgments and the forces that are thus represented by the seals and the trumpets become more emphatic and more severe as the time draws near for the coming of the Lord Jesus, and that they finally assume the character of clear signs, to be witnessed by all that live upon the earth.

All Refer To The Visible Universe

Coming now to the discussion of the passage we quoted above, it is not difficult to see that the first four trumpets, even as was the case with the first four seals, form one group and belong together. The first four seals, we saw, were very clearly distinguished from the last three especially by the fact that they all came with the figure of the four horses. The same is true of the first four trumpets. There can be no doubt about it that they form a distinct group. This is clear, in the first place, from their very contents. As we hope to see more clearly presently, they all refer to the visible universe, and that too, to the world outside of man, to creation, to nature, though it stands to reason that man, standing in close touch with this visible universe, is also affected. But in the second place, that these first four trumpets form a separate, distinct group is also plain from the fact that in the text they are separated from the last three by the outcry of the eagle in mid-heaven, announcing a three-fold woe upon the inhabitants of the earth because of the three trumpets which are still to be sounded. Hence, also in regard to the trumpets it is to be noted that there is a division into four and three. This division and distinction is undoubtedly intentional, plainly indicating that the number seven does symbolize the union between the world and God, between the human and the divine,—if you please, the covenant relationship between God and His people.

We will readily admit that the interpretation of the trumpets in the Book of Revelation is very difficult. That this is true is not because the text itself is difficult to read, that there are many dark sayings in it: for that is not the case. If we had nothing else to do than merely to explain the words of the text, it would be rather easy. Little explanation would then indeed be required. But that is not the purpose of the Book of Revelation, nor of our interpretation of the book. We must not merely try to understand the text as such, but we also must try to learn the historical reality represented by and referred to in the text. If we do not attempt to do this, the book does not become real to the church of Christ and can offer little or no consolation. Yet this is evidently the chief purpose of the book. Two questions, therefore, must always be before our minds when we interpret the Book of Revelation, namely: first, what is the literal meaning of the text? And, secondly, where do I find the things that are thus revealed in the history of our present dispensation?

To find the answer to these questions it may be well to limit from the outset the sphere of our investigation by first of all discarding the results of many allegorical interpretations also in connection with the first four trumpets. You understand that the question is: must we conceive of the facts mentioned in the text quoted above as real, or symbolical, or allegorical? Does the earth mean the earth, or something else? Do hail and fire mean hail and fire literally, or do they represent something spiritual? Do the sun and moon and stars which are mentioned in the text mean the heavenly luminaries, or do they represent realities in the spiritual world?

Those who prefer the allegorical method of interpretation apply this method throughout. For instance, this allegorical method comes to the conclusion that the first trumpet reveals upheavals either in the church or in the Roman Empire. According as interpreters adhere to the one or to the other explanation, they make of the hail and fire erroneous teachings, while the trees that are hurt by them are preachers and teachers in the church, and the grass represents the common Christians; or they interpret that the earth represents the Roman Empire, and the hail and fire destructive forces of enemies who destroyed a third part of that empire immediately after Constantine the Great. According to the same method of interpretation, the burning mass which falls into the sea according to the second trumpet is allegorized into the devil, raging with fury because of the progress of the church and the kingdom of God in the world. Or again, the whole is referred to great naval exploits and battles at the time when the Vandals devastated Rome. The star falling from heaven, which is mentioned in connection with the third trumpet, represents either heretics, apostatized from the church and poisoning the fountains of the truth and thereby killing many spiritually; or again, it is made the symbol of Attila, the Hun, invading the Roman Empire. The darkening of the sun and the moon and the stars, mentioned in connection with the fourth trumpet, is very readily spiritualized into the apostasy of the false teachers and the preachers of the church. Or again, by those who think of the Roman Empire, it is made to refer to the rulers whose glory was eclipsed at the time of its downfall.

Such are a few examples of the interpretations which have been offered by those who are of the opinion that they must always spiritualize, that the allegorical method must be applied to the Book of Revelation. It would seem, then, that the Book of Revelation was purposely written in such unintelligible form that the church could never understand its real meaning.

We cannot accept this mode of interpretation.

We believe that whenever the text is to be taken in the symbolical, or allegorical, sense of the word, the context or even the very contents of the verses will plainly indicate this. When, for instance, John is said to swallow a book, it is evident in itself that this is not reality, but symbolism. But in this connection there is absolutely nothing that compels us to such an interpretation. It is true that there are portions in the text which may be taken in the symbolical sense. There is one part in which John himself plainly indicates that it cannot be taken in the literal sense, namely, when he says that a burning mass, as it were a great mountain, fell from heaven. But this gives us no reason to depart so radically from its literal interpretation as to spiritualize and allegorize everything. There is nothing strange in hail and fire falling from heaven, or in the disturbance caused by the mass from heaven in the sea, or in the poisoning of the waters, or the partial darkening of the heavenly bodies, sun, moon, and stars. In fact, the text is plainly in favor of the literal interpretation. For you will notice that by these four trumpets the whole physical universe is involved,—the earth, and the sea, and the rivers, and the heavens, — thus presenting one whole, which can never be obtained by any allegorical interpretation. Even as the first four seals refer to every sphere of human activity and relationship in the present dispensation, so the four trumpets evidently refer to every sphere of the visible universe, together constituting the whole of the world, as is also indicated by the number **four**. In the second place, the allegorical interpretation gives no satisfaction. It is conducive to all kinds of arbitrary questions, demanding just as arbitrary an answer. And the result is that after all is said, you are not sure whether you have attained to the right interpretation or not. If hail and fire may mean heresies, and may also mean political disturbances in the world of the Roman Empire, why may they not refer to a thousand other things in the world? All certainty is thus removed, and Scripture becomes a source of speculation. Thirdly, I refuse to go along with this mode of interpretation because the reference to definite historical facts and periods, as is implied in such a method, has always led to disappointment, and still does. Perhaps you remember, — to mention just one example, — how the first world war in the early part of this century was explained as meaning that it referred to Revelation 13. The German Kaiser, so they had it, was the beast that is there pictured. And this war was to end in February, 1918, according to the exact calculation based upon the forty-two months which are mentioned in that chapter. Of course, that theory was exploded. And I suppose that other theories of the same kind can be built up. For it seems impossible that people learn by experience in this respect. But we will not be seduced by any such methods to interpret Scripture in this wise.

I wish it to be understood from the outset, therefore, that in general the text means just exactly what it expresses. Hail and fire mingled with blood refer to the destructive forces in nature with a view to the vegetable world. The sea is nothing else but the sea; and the creatures referred to are the inhabitants of that sea, while a ship means literally a ship. Rivers and fountains of water refer to inland waters in distinction from the oceans and seas; and their poisoning means exactly what it says. And sun and moon and stars are the heavenly luminaries with which we are acquainted, and not some mysterious reality either in the political or in the Roman world. We have here, in a word, a picture of the effects of the four trumpets on the physical universe in the history of the present dispensation.

All Represent Evil Phenomena In Nature

However, if this be established, we still confront the further question: what do these trumpets mean? To what exactly do they refer?

Our answer is, first of all, that they all refer to natural phenomena. If we see this, it will bring the vision much nearer home. As I have emphasized repeatedly, the seals and the trumpets principally all refer to events which take place throughout this dispensation. True, they will increase in force in an alarming measure as time goes on and as the completion of the kingdom draws near. Some of the phenomena here mentioned, as, for instance, the blood with which the hail is mingled, are to be revealed in the future, perhaps, in the literal sense of the word. But for the rest, they all refer to mere natural phenomena that take place and may be observed in our own time.

All the four trumpets, then, refer to phenomena in nature outside of man. This does not mean that man is not affected or involved. On the contrary, man is very plainly interested in all these natural phenomena.

The individual as well as the nations are affected by these four trumpets. Man is dependent upon the world in which he lives. He is dependent upon the soil which he cultivates, upon the crops which are raised. He is dependent upon the condition of the climate, upon rain and sunshine. He is dependent upon the water which he drinks. And through it all he is dependent upon the condition of the heavenly luminaries. This also the text indicates very plainly. And of course, what is true of the individual is also true of the nations and the relation between them. By the influence of these four trumpets the history of the nations is controlled and directed. Never has this been more plainly understood than in our own time. I remember that in the war in the early part of the present century it was emphasized that food would win it. And by this expression a deep truth is expressed. If food will win a war,—and to a large extent it will,—then the further truth, which is most often overlooked, is also very evident, that Christ, Who rules over the elements, over sunshine and rain, over hail and fire, after all determines who will be victorious in any war. And what is true with regard to the land is also true in respect to the sea and to the inland waters and to the sun, moon, and stars. By these four trumpets the physical universe is affected, but through it all the world of men and the relation of nation over against nation is largely determined.

Let us also notice, in the second place, that these four trumpets have this in common, that they all refer to what we may call **evil** phenomena in nature. On the whole they picture destructive forces which become active and affect the whole of the natural world.

Hail and fire from heaven are the representatives of all the destructive forces in nature with a view to the world of vegetation. As such I understand them. In the first trumpet we have the picture of a mighty thunderstorm bursting forth over the land and accompanied by the fall of heavy hail. That this can actually be a tremendous force we may plainly perceive when sometimes hailstones as large as hen eggs fall in great number in our own vicinity, destroying property and leaving large holes in the ground where they dropped. Thus it is in the vision. Tremendous thunder and hail storms are pictured, destroying trees and grass, in general the representatives of the vegetable world. Crops are therefore destroyed in a moment by this first trumpet. As far as the blood is concerned, I take it, in the first place, as having reference to the accompanying destruction. And we may take it in the literal sense of the word. In fact, history speaks more than once of a bloody snow and hail which fell in various places.

And with a view to the future, this blood mingled with the hail and fire will be so general and real that it becomes a sign to all that witness it.

Thus it is also with the second trumpet. It pictures to us a destructive force upon the oceans and the seas. John does not tell us that a great burning mountain was cast into the sea, but that in the vision he saw as it were a great mountain burning with fire and cast into the sea. It matters little, evidently, what this particularly stands for. But in general it is plain that it simply represents a destructive force with regard to the sea. The sea is represented as becoming a pool of blood, so that the creatures which live in it die. And at the same time it is represented as being swept by a tempest, or at least as being greatly disturbed, so that the ships are destroyed and caught in the storm.

The same is true of the third trumpet. The picture is either that of a star shattered to pieces and strewn over the waters outside of the ocean, or that of a comet leaving behind its poisonous gases and embittering the waters which must be drunk by men. Perhaps we may think in the literal sense of the word of a star. For it is not impossible that the stars influence our world far more than we know just now. However this may be, the main thing is that we remember that by this force of the third trumpet the waters and the fountains of waters are made bitter and poisonous, so that many die because they drink of them. Wormwood is, properly speaking, a plant that is noted because of its very bitter taste and because of the poisonous nature of its volatile oil. Here the name is given to the star because of its embittering and poisoning effect upon the waters.

Finally, the same is also true of the last of these four trumpets. It speaks of a change of the heavenly luminaries. They are smitten for a third part, so the text speaks, so that they do not shine to that extent upon the earth. What this would mean with respect to the sun ought to be plain to us all. A third less sunshine than necessary to ripen the crops would be determinately detrimental to any land. And although we know less of the influence of the other heavenly bodies upon our planet, we may believe that they all affect us to a sufficient extent to become destructive when their relation to us is changed.

Now picture, if you can, the combined effect of these four forces, and you will understand the first four trumpets, and feel them rather near. A decided cooling down of the atmosphere and lack of sunshine, caused by the darkening of the sun, and added to that the less known effect of the darkening of the other luminaries at night; a poisoning of the rivers and lakes and fountains of waters, so that not only men die because they drink of them, but undoubtedly the creatures which live in them also die because of the poison; a great disturbance in the sea and the ocean, so that the fish of the sea die and the ships are destroyed; and, last but not least, tremendous thunderstorms and falling of hail, so that the crops are destroyed and there is no grass for the cattle, nor any fruit. That is the meaning of the first four trumpets. It would mean that on the land there would be nothing to eat, neither for man or beast, that when men turn to the waters to live on the creatures of the sea and rivers and lakes, they find them vacated, while at the same time they themselves die because of all kinds of epidemics caused by the poison waters. Surely, if this were universal there would be no creature left alive in all the universe. But evidently universal and absolute these trumpets are not yet. Only what aggravates the condition for the stricken lands is that one of the main means of transportation is also cut off, for the ships are destroyed, so that nothing can be transported from one nation to another.

The "One-Third" Characteristic Of The Trumpets

It is, however, to the partial character of the trumpets and the forces which they represent that we must call your attention finally. In fact, I consider this one of the chief elements in the explanation of the text itself. Very emphatically it tells us several times that only one-third of the elements are affected by these trumpets. The expression "a third part" occurs even as many as twelve times in this particular passage, surely indicating that the Lord would have us pay special attention to this particular feature. A third part of the earth, a third part of the trees is burnt up. And though it literally reads that all the green grass is burnt up, we take it to mean all the green grass that grows on the third part of the earth, as is most natural. The third part of the sea is turned into blood; and the third part of the creatures die, and the third part of the ships is destroyed. The third part of the waters and fountains of waters are smitten by the star called Wormwood and are made bitter. The third part of the sun, and the third part of the moon, and the third part of the stars is smitten, so that they do not shine for the third part of the day and of the night. Surely, there is reason for the question: what is indicated by this "third part" occurring so often in the text?

There are some who interpret this third part as meaning the smallest half. One-third is destroyed; two-thirds are still left intact. And then these interpreters have it that the judgments are not as yet absolute: there is still time left for repentance. The mercy and grace of God are still greater in their effects than His wrath. Soon, when the vials are poured out, there is an advance over the trumpets in this respect, that they are universal and absolute in their effect. They speak no more of a third part. Mercy is now still predominant. We do not deny that there is an element of truth in that interpretation. Surely, there is an advance in judgment. And gradually the tokens of God's general providence are withdrawn from the world. And as the power of that general providence of God is withdrawn, the judgments pictured in the words of our text will become more absolute and universal. In so far it is possible that also this idea is implied in the repeated mention of a third part.

Nevertheless we do not think that this is the only idea, or that it is even the main idea, that is expressed. On the contrary, rather than saying that one-third means the smaller part over against two-thirds which are not affected, I would say that one-third signifies just a little more than the one-fourth which is always affected.

You will remember that we explained the meaning of one-fourth in connection with the fourth seal. That fourth horse and its rider traverse the earth and kill one-fourth part of all men. We then said that one-fourth signifies just as many as is in harmony with the history of this dispensation; or, if you please,—to speak concretely,—one-fourth indicates the ordinary death-rate of the world. Four is the number of the world. And one-fourth is that part which is in harmony with the present existence of the world of men. One-fourth therefore indicates the ordinary rate in which men die. But the same is true with hail and fire, with storms and upheavals in the sea, with the poisoning of the waters, and with the cooling of the atmosphere. There is always one-fourth part of the earth affected by hail and fire. There is always one-fourth part of the earth and the trees and the grass and all the crops that is destroyed. Every year this happens again. The same is true of the sea. One-fourth of the fishes always die. That is the ordinary number of them. One-fourth of the ships always perish. That is the ordinary number of ships that are destroyed by the ordinary number of storms. There is never a year that no fish die, and there is never a year that no ships are destroyed. One-fourth part of the waters is always struck with the star which is called Wormwood. One-fourth part of them always causes epidemics, so that some die.

One-fourth part of the earth is always affected by the lack of sufficient sunshine.

In a word, these same things always recur, only, according to the measure of this dispensation, one-fourth part of the universe being affected. But as long as this is not increased, the earth does not consider them judgments. There is nothing strange in this. We have become accustomed to this. In general, all the world figures with this part of the crop being destroyed by hail and fire and by cold weather. In general, all the world figures on just so many ships being destroyed on an average, and just so many people dying because of the poisonous waters.

But now, in connection with the first four trumpets, this is increased just a little. Not much, it is true; only the next fraction is taken, instead of one-fourth, one-third. Just a little more hail and fire, just a little more cooling of the atmosphere, just a little more death to the creatures of the sea, just a few more ships destroyed, just a few more people die because of the waters, and just a little more cooling off of the sun. This is meant by the four trumpets.

You know the effect of this just-a-little-more: it upsets all the calculations of men. Just a little cooler atmosphere during the summer, and the crops do not ripen. Just a little more hail and fire than usual, and another part of the crop on which men had figured is destroyed. Just a few more storms and disturbances in the sea, and the number of ships on which we depended is greatly lessened. And thus it is with the supply of fish and with the waters of the earth.

In a word, by the just-a-little-more of these trumpets Christ controls all the world, and determines absolutely the relations which must ensue so as to complete His kingdom and ultimately destroy the power of the Antichrist. By these very natural causes it is Christ, blowing the trumpets through the seven angels, Who determines the development of the nations and so directs all things that exactly that constellation is called into existence which He desires. It is by controlling these natural phenomena that Christ ultimately will also destroy the Antichrist and Gog and Magog. In a word, it is Christ Who in this dispensation controls the fate of the nations also through these elements of the universe, Who gives victory and deals defeat, Who sets up and dethrones powers and dominions, and thus controls the history of all the world with a view to the bringing of His own kingdom.

Forces Directly From Heaven

Thus you will also clearly understand the words of our text in relation to all history. All the forces which cause these things come directly from heaven. It indicates that Christ, Who holds the book of the seven seals and opens it seal after seal, also determines crops and crop failure, plenty and lack of everything, and through all these determines the coming of His kingdom.

Be not afraid, therefore! These things must surely come to pass. They will come ever more forcefully and plainly. And in them all you may see the judgment that is coming upon the world and the answer to your own prayers.

Be not afraid! For even though by these judgments you will undoubtedly be touched as far as your present existence and life in the world is concerned, the spiritual kingdom of Christ is invulnerable and immune from the spiritual point of view. In the midst of these times as they are pictured in the text, the people of God are sealed, and they are sealed securely; that is, spiritually they shall surely conquer. And finally they shall through all these things enter into the economy of things where God shall spread His tabernacle over them, and they shall serve Him in His temple day and night forevermore.

Chapter XXI

The Locusts Out Of The Abyss

(Revelation 9:1-12)

1 And the fifth angel sounded, and I saw a star fall from heaven unto the earth: and to him was given the key of the bottomless pit.

2 And he opened the bottomless pit; and there arose a smoke out of the pit, as the smoke of a great furnace; and the sun and the air were darkened by reason of the smoke of the pit.

3 And there came out of the smoke locusts upon the earth: and unto them was given power, as the scorpions of the earth have power.

4 And it was commanded them that they should not hurt the grass of the earth, neither any green thing, neither any tree; but only those men which have not the seal of God in their foreheads.

5 And to them it was given that they should not kill them, but that they should be tormented five months: and their torment was as the torment of a scorpion, when he striketh a man.

6 And in those days shall men seek death, and shall not find it; and shall desire to die, and death shall flee from them.

7 And the shapes of the locusts were like unto horses prepared unto battle; and on their heads were as it were crowns like gold, and their faces were as the faces of men.

8 And they had hair as the hair of women, and their teeth were as the teeth of lions.

9 And they had breastplates, as it were breastplates of iron; and the sound of their wings was as the sound of chariots of many horses running to battle.

10 And they had tails like unto scorpions, and there were stings in their tails: and their power was to hurt men five months.

11 And they had a king over them, which is the angel of the bottomless pit, whose name in the Hebrew tongue is Abaddon, but in the Greek tongue hath his name Apollyon.

12 One woe is past; and, behold, there come two woes more hereafter.

310

In verse 13 of the preceding chapter we have a little parenthetical scene. An eagle flies in mid-heaven and announces a three-fold woe upon them that dwell on the earth by reason of the voices of the trumpets that are still to sound. Much has been made of this eagle, and people have speculated as to what this eagle might be. Some reach the conclusion that it is a member of the church triumphant who has already been taken to heaven, according to these interpreters, before these trumpets are sounded. We, on our part, cannot attach special significance to the identity of this eagle. We rather accept that it merely belongs to the symbolism of the entire scene that John, before the last three trumpets are sounded, beholds this eagle, the bird with its penetrating look, flying in mid-heaven and calling, "Woe, woe, woe, for them that dwell on the earth." In the meantime, it indicates that we may expect that the three trumpets which are still to sound will bring events which are quite different from those revealed thus far. The element of vengeance and suffering in them will be more pronounced. They will be most plainly visible as the day draws near when the Lord shall return in His final appearance. They indicate that the world gradually becomes ripe for judgment. Accordingly, we expect also that it will be more difficult to point out the exact historical realization of these last trumpets, seeing that they point to events which must for the most part still be fulfilled in the future.

The Description Of The Locusts

Our text speaks of the locusts out of the abyss.

First of all, we note that as the fifth angel sounds, John beholds a star fallen from heaven. It will be well to call your attention from the outset to two things. In the first place, there is the fact that this star does not fall from heaven at the moment when John hears the sound of the fifth trumpet. He does not say that he saw a star falling from heaven, but simply that his eye beholds a star that had already fallen from heaven at the moment when the trumpet sounds. John merely beholds that star now though the star had been cast out of heaven before. He beholds it at this particular moment because at the sound of the fifth trumpet that star begins to operate. This brings us to our second remark, namely, that this star is surely no star in the literal sense of the word, for the simple reason that the things which are told us of this star cannot be true of one of the heavenly luminaries that shine in the firmament of heaven. In the first place, it would already be an inconceivability that a star would fall from heaven and simply lie on the earth without any further effect. But above all, it would be impossible to maintain that this is a real star in the light of the fact that the star acts like a person with intellect and will. We read of this strange star that the key of the pit, of the abyss, was given him, and that as the key was received by him, he went and opened the pit of the abyss.

Whoever may be represented by this star, therefore, so much is certain from the outset, that it is not a real heavenly luminary, but some being who is able to receive and understand commands and to act accordingly. In harmony with what follows in the text, the supposition is not without grounds, as we shall see, that this star represents no one else but Satan himself. He is called in the Word of God the prince of the powers of the air (Ephesians 2:2), the prince of the demons (Mark 3:22). Of him the Savior speaks in language remarkably similar to this passage, namely, that He saw him fall as lightning out of heaven (Luke 10:18). And, as we hope to see presently, it is in that very capacity that he occurs also in the words of this particular passage.

This star, this prince of the devils, — or as he appears here, this prince of the abyss, — opens the pit of the abyss. The picture here given is that the abyss is a place beneath the surface of the earth, evidently widening according as it extends deeper below the surface, and therefore narrowest at the top, until it narrows down to a simple shaft, or, as it is called in our passage, a pit. This pit is locked, indicating that for the inhabitants it forms a prison from which they cannot at will escape. Nor is it thus, that they can attain their freedom merely at the command of their prince, the star. For evidently, according to the words of the passage we are now discussing, he does not hold the key of this abyss. It is not in his power, but it is **given** to him. In ordinary circumstances he does not have this key; but it is now given to him. And therewith he receives the power, and also the liberty evidently, to open the abyss over which he is prince.

He does so. And the result is terrible. Out of this abyss issues forth, in the first place, a terrible cloud of smoke, darkening the sun and the air. And out of the smoke gradually a tremendous host of locusts becomes visible.

Of locusts we read several times in Holy Writ. They are, whether literally or symbolically, the harbingers of the judgments of the Lord. Thus we read of them as constituting one of the ten plagues which fall on the land of Egypt by reason of its stubborn resistance and oppression of the people of God. Thus we also read of a plague of locusts which threatened the people of Israel in the second chapter of the prophecy of Joel. And a plague they certainly were. In the eastern countries an army of these locusts would sweep over an entire country that was rich in vegetation and would leave no green thing behind it.

But the locusts mentioned here are of a very peculiar description. In general, indeed, their description is somewhat derived from the general appearance of the locust. Nevertheless, their appearance is entirely peculiar. They are in shape like horses that are prepared for war. Crowns of gold, or at least something that makes one think of crowns of gold, they wear on their heads. And they are protected with breastplates as it were of iron. Their faces are as the faces of men. And they have long hair, as the hair of women. But in contrast again with this human and even feminine appearance, they show teeth as the teeth of lions, and tails like the tails of scorpions. They come in orderly array, with a king by the name of Abaddon, or Apollyon, at their head. And as they pass, the sound of their wings makes one think of a tremendous army, with horses and chariots, rushing for war. Thus is their description.

Still more strange is their monstrous power. One might think, perhaps, that their description is merely an overdrawn picture of the imagination though the general traits of the ordinary locust are maintained. But this cannot be said of their power. In the first place, it is strange that these locusts have their power of destruction in their tails instead of in their mouth. And in the second place, it is also strange that they do not touch the grass or the crops or the trees or any green thing. Thirdly, it is peculiar that their power is limited to men, and that to those who have not the seal of God on their foreheads. And fourthly, it is also peculiar that they may not kill these men, but merely torture them, so that life becomes an awful burden to those who are struck by the locusts.

The Identity Of The Locusts

In answer to the question who these locusts are, we may limit the field of our investigation in two ways.

In the first place, we may deem it an established fact that they are not real locusts. We have always emphasized that in the Book of Revelation the text always plainly indicates whether we must take a certain passage literally or in the symbolical sense of the word. And surely, in this case the text is sufficiently clear to make us feel safe in asserting that real locusts are out of the question. In the first place, of course, there is their description. True, as we have already said, real locusts might be described in terms of a strong imagination as horses running to battle, because indeed the locust resembles the horse, especially as to the shape of its head, and also because in the second chapter of Joel we find a somewhat similar description. But it is not true that the locust also has the face as of a man, that it possesses teeth like the teeth of a lion, that it has hair like the hair of women, and that it has a tail like that of a scorpion, in which its terrible power lies. But, secondly, there are clearer indications that Scripture does not intend to have us think here of real locusts. First of all, we must call your attention to their origin. They arise from the abyss, over which Satan is king. And they have as a king another angel, whose name is Abaddon, or Apollyon, the first of which is Hebrew, and the second Greek. Both of these names mean "Destroyer." Ordinary locusts surely do not have their dwelling-place in the abyss, whatever that abyss may be. Besides, their work is entirely different from that of ordinary locusts. They do not touch the grass and the trees or any green thing. But that is exactly what the locust devours. In an inconceivably short time the locust knows how to make a barren desert out of the most fruitful country, abounding in vegetation. These locusts, on the other hand, touch only men, and touch them not with their mouth but with their tails. And they cause these men to suffer the most fearful agony, pain comparable only to the pain caused by the sting of a scorpion, which, as travellers assure us, is well-nigh unbearable. All these things, therefore, establish it beyond a shadow of doubt that we would violate the purpose of the text if still we would maintain that they were real locusts. No, they are not real locusts, but they must be taken as symbols of something else. That they are described as monstrous locusts, infernal in their appearance and in their power, is merely because the locust actually constitutes one of the scourges wherewith the Lord visits the earth in His judgments.

Besides, and in the second place, we may also from the outset discard the interpretation which finds in these locusts the symbol of an army of men. This explanation constitutes, indeed, one of the favorite interpretations, especially of those interpreters who explain the Book of Revelation as being historically and successively fulfilled in the course of time. These locusts, so they say, are the symbols of the hordes of the Mohammedans that flooded parts of Asia, North Africa, and southern Europe in the seventh and eighth centuries of our era. In detail, these interpreters find in the description given of these locusts the picture of these Saracens as they rose from the East and swept the entire northern part of Africa, as well as the southern part of Europe, constituting an awful scourge upon the countries which they conquered.

But there are elements in the words of our text which simply make such an interpretation an impossibility, – elements which I find that these interpreters simply ignore and overlook. First of all, what does it mean that these locusts have their power in their tails? That seems to constitute an essential element in the passage we are now discussing. Yet this cannot be sufficiently explained on the supposition that they are the symbols of the Moslem army, or, in fact, of any army of human beings. Still more, the text makes the important statement that the people who have the seal of God on their foreheads must be left untouched. But was it not especially against the Christians that the fury of the Mohammedans raged? Or can it be said of any army in the world that they ever make a distinction between the people of God and the people of the world, and refuse to do the former any hurt? Still more: these locusts receive the command that they may not kill, but simply hurt men for five months. Granted now, for a moment, that it is permissible to take these five months in the symbolical sense, every day of them constituting one year, so that the entire period might be calculated as being one hundred fifty years, was it ever beheld of an army, – that of the Moslems surely not excluded, – that they did not kill, but merely hurt the enemy? Surely, all these objections, – facts so plainly and so emphatically mentioned in the passage, – are simply insurmountable. These locusts are not the symbol of an army of men.

Both these possibilities being ruled out, there is practically but one possibility left. And that one is indeed in harmony with the entire passage, as well as with the Scriptures in general, namely, that these locusts form an infernal army of demons let loose by Satan for a certain definite purpose. We know from the Word of God that Satan was not the only person who fell in the spiritual world, but that with him a veritable host of angels fell away from God into rebellion. We know not how many of the angels fell with their prince; nor is this important. But we certainly receive the impression that there were indeed thousands upon thousands who fell with Satan. Now what became of these evil angels? Plain it is that they have not yet received their final judgment and punishment. Also the angel world is still to be judged; and it shall not be judged until the great day of our Lord

Jesus Christ, when we shall judge them with Him. Satan still goeth about like a roaring lion. And also the evil spirits, direct subjects of his kingdom, are not confined to the place of their eternal torture. It may safely be said, therefore, of all these evil angels that although they have been cast out of heaven and no more enjoy the light of life in the presence of the Holy One, – which, of course, would be impossible, – yet they have not received their final sentence, and still must be made subject to their eternal punishment. In other words, in the literal sense of the word the devil and his angels are not yet in hell.

Where then are they?

It seems to us that Scripture makes a distinction. Also the lot of these fallen angels is not the same for all, and according to their different state they accomplish a different purpose in the economy of the present dispensation. In the first place, we read of evil spirits roaming about in desert places or being bound by the river Euphrates. In the second place, we learn from Scripture that there are a number of these evil spirits in aerial places, – perhaps the main army of them, Satan included. Paul calls the devil the "prince of the power of the air" (Ephesians 2:2). And he warns the Ephesians that they shall put on the whole armor of God: "For we wrestle not against flesh and blood, but against principalities, against powers, against the rulers of the darkness of this world, against spiritual wickedness in high places," (Ephesians 6:12). They seem to be at the disposal of Satan continually, and constantly to fight the battle with him against the realization of the kingdom of Christ. But in distinction from these devils, or demons, in the air, there is another division of the army of Satan. They are in the abyss. They are shut up. They do not have the liberty to roam about, except on special occasions. At the time of Jesus' public ministry, for instance, we find mention of one legion of them. And when they are cast out, they beseech the Lord that He may not send them back into the abyss. Peter also speaks of angels that have sinned and that have been committed unto pits of darkness, to be reserved unto judgment (II Peter 2:4). And Jude, verse 6, makes mention of "angels that kept not their first estate, but left their own habitation," which "he hath reserved in everlasting chains under darkness unto the judgment of the great day." And of these latter evil spirits our text also makes mention. It tells us of them that they are in the pit. And the smoke which issues out of the abyss as it is opened evidently speaks to us of the fact that their proper habitation, the sphere in which they exist, is darkness. It tells us that the pit of this abyss is locked, so that they cannot issue forth from it at will. And since even the prince of this abyss must receive the key, it also tells us that these evil spirits are ultimately at the disposal of Christ. They cannot leave their prison except at His bidding. They cannot perform their infernal purposes except when He deems it the proper time. Then He blows the trumpet and hands the key of the abyss to the prince, that he may let his armies go forth to battle.

What we have, therefore, in the words of the passage we are now discussing is nothing but the picture of the letting loose of one of the reserve forces of hell over the world of men.

Satan has his regular troops. They are the powers of the air, the spiritual host of wickedness in high places. With them he always works. With them he always offers battle against the Christ and His people. And against them we must be armed with the whole armor of God. With these he always stands in close contact with his human servants on earth. Through them Satan influences the minds and hearts, the thoughts and the affections of men, so that he may be able to maintain his position as the prince of this world. And over against them Christ also has His angels, strengthening and protecting His people. Through this regular army of Satan, under the influence of them, develops what we call "the spirit of the age." If we say that the spirit of the present age is humanistic, we must not imagine that the development of the same has nothing to do with the regular hellish troops of the devil. On the contrary, also that spirit is come to the consciousness of the wicked world under the influence of the powers of the air. They are everywhere. They stand behind the throne of kings and emperors, as we learn, for instance, from the tenth chapter of the prophecy of Daniel. They control the minds of the leaders of the people. They influence the thoughts and the teachings of the infidel professors in our universities. And in a thousand ways they are influential in causing to develop the so-called "spirit of the age."

But of these our text does not speak. No, it speaks of special forces, of the reserve troops of hell, of the army of maneuver of the devil. Not of the powers of the air, but of the spirits of the abyss, who are commonly bound and imprisoned but who are let loose at the command of Christ over the wicked world, does the text speak.

The Work Of The Locusts

And what is the teaching of the Word with regard to these wicked spirits? When are they to be let loose? Whenever the world is ripening for judgment.

The sinner and the sinful world in general chooses to do the works of Satan and his kingdom. They choose to trample under foot the precepts of the Most High and to walk in ways of darkness. And therefore, entirely in harmony with their own choice the Lord surrenders them to the devil and his host. And as they continue and reach the stage of sin and evil in which they have fully surrendered themselves to the powers of darkness, He sends them more devils and more demons, that they may actually increase their sin and become ripe for the great day of the Lord. This we read time and again in Scripture. When the leaders of the Jews blaspheme the work of Jesus and prove that they love darkness rather than light, we find that Jesus begins to teach in parables for the very purpose that the things of the kingdom of heaven may remain hid to them. After Paul has given a description of the idolatry and foolishness of the heathen world, he continues to say: "Wherefore God also gave them up to uncleanness through the lusts of their own hearts." And again: "For this cause God gave them up unto vile affections." Hence we find this relation in Scripture. Man has surrendered himself to the service of the devil. In this service he stands in the power and under the influence of Satan and his host generally, and the powers of the air have dominion over him. The more he serves sin and Satan, the more this power of the evil hosts in high places is emphasized, until, when gradually the world becomes ripe for the judgments of God, this power is made stronger by the letting loose of the reserve forces of Satan, the evil spirits out of the abyss. And it is that emphasis of the power of Satan over the wicked world that is pictured in the words of our passage. Again, therefore, in harmony with the character of the trumpets, there is just a little emphasis of the general conditions. If the general influence of the powers of the air may be compared to one-fourth, the influence is now increased to one-third by the liberation of these locusts, of this infernal army of the reserve forces of the devil.

But what is the special work of these infernal spirits?

The text emphasizes that it is their task to torment men. With emphasis this is stated. Their power is as the power of scorpions. This power is in their tails. Their torment is as the torment of a scorpion when it strikes a man. They are not allowed to kill, but only to torment such as have not the seal of God in their foreheads. And the effect of this torment is such that in those days men seek death, but shall not be able to find it. They desire to die, but death fleeth from them. And they may torment these men who have not the seal of God on their foreheads for five months.

From the outset we may say that these five months have no other symbolical significance than this, that these infernal spirits may serve their full time. The five months are evidently in harmony with the picture that is given of the locusts. We are told that the time during which locusts may be expected is generally five months of the summer. Not as if any swarm of locusts would continually remain in a country for that length of time: for their work is generally finished much more quickly. But five months is the period of time during which they may be expected. And the meaning, therefore, is that these spirits may serve their full time and do as much harm as they possibly can.

But the question is: what is meant by this torment, and what is its nature?

The answer to this question we must seek, first of all, in the description of the locusts themselves. There is evidently a marked contrast between their front and their tails. Their appearance in front makes us think of war and victory, of power and glory, of intelligence and invention, of charm and fascination. For they look like horses prepared for battle. They wear crowns as of gold. They have teeth as the teeth of lions. They wear breastplates as it were breastplates of iron. They have faces as the faces of men. And they have hair like the hair of women. In a word, these spirits represent all that attracts the wicked world, all that which the world of sin considers the source of bliss and salvation. They are the spirits who play on the passions of men. Already the world has sought its happiness in power and dominion, in war and victory. These spirits emphasize these passions. Already the wicked world has sought help in vain philosophy, in following the lie, in science and invention, − all without God. These spirits simply must emphasize this passion, so that they seek their bliss still more exclusively in these things. Already the world has sought salvation in the satisfaction of its lion-like greed. These spirits must emphasize this sinful passion and cause it to glow still more. Already the sinful world has thrown itself in the arms of a sinful art, yea, in the charming pleasures of vile sin. These spirits must incite men to do still more, and to give themselves up to all the pleasures of sin. Such is their appearance: they appeal to the sinful passions of an already wicked world.

But this is not their final, and therefore, not their real task. It is not their essential characteristic. On the contrary, these evil spirits, whether they like it or not, have power to hurt men, such men as have not the seal of God on their forehead. Their tail-end is their real nature. These same spirits who have incited the wicked world to plunge still more deeply in sin and vile transgression fill the hearts of men with the darkness of despair. They are the spirits of pessimism. And after men have followed their inspiration, they find that their end is more bitter than death itself. Just as the children of God have sometimes a foretaste of the pleasures of heavenly glory because they walk in the way of God's covenant and of His precepts, so the children of the world, under the influence of these infernal locusts, are given a foretaste of the despair of hell. They follow their sinful ambition for power and victory to its very end. But despair follows in its wake. They give themselves to the satisfaction of their lion-like greed; but also this is immediately followed by a gloomy pessimism. The path of philosophy they tread to the end, only to look into the mocking eyes of the devil of despair and dissatisfaction. Art and pleasure and vile lust are worshipped as the saviors, until the dissatisfaction of them is proved and a gloomy pessimism is the result. Thus the purpose of these demons is to emphasize sin and all its pleasures and all its evil passions so that men follow them to the full, only to be tortured by them in the end by these same demons on the rack of pessimism and despair.

That this is actually the case is also evident from verse 6. The nature of their torment is, of course, purely spiritual; and it consists in a being tired of life, in a seeking of death: "And in those days men shall seek death, and shall not find it; and shall desire to die, and death shall flee from them."

Literally the state of these men, therefore, is one of the most gloomy pessimism.

Do not say that such a condition is inconceivable, for that would be beside the truth. Do not say that if men really seek death, they can find it in suicide: for then you do not know the heart of men. The meaning of this text is simply this, that the pessimism of men in those times is so great that they cannot even find the courage and the incentive to take their own lives. Not the suicide, who hastens to take his own life when all of life is despair, but he who desires to die and cannot find the courage to commit suicide is the living illustration of the most terrible pessimism in this world. These same spirits that torture them have not the power to kill them. They have power to hurt them, but nothing more.

Time and again such waves of pessimism have swept in limited proportions over the world. It swept over the world of Grecian civilization when all the efforts of sinful men to find the way to happiness along the road of sin and idolatry and vain philosophy and lusts failed absolutely. It swept the Roman world when it had cast itself into the arms of conquest and power, into the arms of luxury and dissipation. Gloomy pessimism was the result. It also has swept the modern world more than once whenever it has had to confess failure to find the road to happiness. What else is the spirit that prevails in the spheres of Spiritualism and Christian Science and Theosophy, yea, even of Buddhism and heathen religions, than the black smoke that is rising from the abyss?

But all these things are only a limited fulfillment of what is still to come upon the world. As the time draws near for the coming of our Lord Jesus Christ, as the world once more exhausts itself to work out its own salvation without Christ and without God, as it exerts itself to find this way in paths of war and conquest, in ways of philosophy and vain lies, in ways of lusts and vile pleasures, it will also become prepared more and more for the influence of these infernal locusts. And literally also this part of Revelation is still to be fulfilled, so that the state of utter despair will come upon the world of sin, and men will continue to follow the paths of sin and transgression and of blasphemy against the name of Jesus Christ. Then again men will seek death, but will not be able to find it. Not as if this state of universal pessimism will be the final state. On the contrary, the power of the locusts is limited to five months. It is only a preparation for still greater efforts and for the final public worship of the beast that comes out of the abyss. But surely, it will come; and the children of the world will then have a foretaste of the torments of hell.

Blessed is the comfort that is implied in these words. For those who have the seal of God on their forehead in those days, who do not follow the ways of the world and sin and lust and the lie, are protected by Christ Himself. From Him these locusts receive their power and authority. And that power is limited to the world of sin only. These sealed ones have put on the whole armor of God, and they are not generally under the influence of the powers of the air. Christ and all His holy angels protect them, so that they are not hurt. And though they more and more may have to fear the gloomy despair of the sinful world, it will remain literally true that the gates of hell shall never prevail against them.

Chapter XXII
The Sixth Trumpet
(Revelation 9:13-21)

13 And the sixth angel sounded, and I heard a voice from the four horns of the golden altar which is before God,

14 Saying to the sixth angel which had the trumpet, Loose the four angels which are bound in the great river Euphrates.

15 And the four angels were loosed, which were prepared for an hour, and a day, and a month, and a year, for to slay the third part of men.

16 And the number of the army of the horsemen were two hundred thousand thousand: and I heard the number of them.

17 And thus I saw the horses in the vision, and them that sat on them, having breastplates of fire, and of jacinth, and brimstone: and the heads of the horses were as the heads of lions; and out of their mouths issued fire and smoke and brimstone.

18 By these three was the third part of men killed, by the fire, and by the smoke, and by the brimstone, which issued out of their mouths.

19 For their power is in their mouth, and in their tails: for their tails were like unto serpents, and had heads, and with them they do hurt.

20 And the rest of the men which were not killed by these plagues yet repented not of the works of their hands, that they should not worship devils, and idols of gold, and silver, and brass, and stone, and of wood: which neither can see, nor hear, nor walk:

21 Neither repented they of their murders, nor of their sorceries, nor of their fornication, nor of their thefts.

The fifth and sixth trumpet belong together, as is plainly indicated in the text. As we have already remarked, they are separated from the former four trumpets by the plain indication that they are all "woe trumpets." Already before the fifth trumpet sounded, its coming was announced by the eagle which was flying in mid-heaven and which threatened a three-fold woe. And in the twelfth verse of this chapter we are reminded of this fact in the words, "One woe is past; and, behold, there come two woes more hereafter." Besides, there is also difference in contents between the first four trumpets and the last three which is undeniable. The difference consists in this, that the first four all relate to the visible universe outside of man, though influencing the history of man and of nations, while the last three refer directly to the world of man. At the same time it may be remarked that as "woe trumpets" they are more vehement in their element of judgment than the former.

A World Steeped In Iniquity

As to the sixth trumpet, it is of importance that we notice, in the first place, what is the condition of the civilized world at this time. There can be little question about the fact that this sixth trumpet will find its realization more completely in the period of the last hour in the narrower sense of the word, that is, in the period which immediately precedes the time of the last judgment and of the final coming of the Lord. And what is the condition of society at this period? There are two indications in the text which inform us about this state.

In the first place, the close of our text indicates that it is a state of sin and gross iniquity in which the sixth trumpet finds the world. We read in verses 20 and 21: "And the rest of the men which were not killed by these plagues yet repented not of the works of their hands, that they should not worship devils, and idols of gold, and silver, and brass, and stone, and of wood: which neither can see, nor hear, nor walk: Neither repented they of their murders, nor of their sorceries, nor of their fornication, nor of their thefts." Of course, that they did not repent of these sins after the plague had been upon the world and one-third of men had been killed certainly indicates that they did commit these sins even before the plague came, and that this condition of society and of the world in general is the cause and the occasion for the blowing of the sixth trumpet.

Notice about this condition, first of all, that it is characteristic of a general violation of the entire law. Of course, this is not meant in the sense that we all and always fall in respect to all the commandments of God; but it is meant in a very special sense of the word. The times of Noah and of Sodom and Gomorrah have returned once more at this period to the world. And what the Lord predicted in regard to the resemblance between these Old Testament periods and the period preceding His second coming has now become realized with this sixth trumpet. The picture of the world here given is indeed a very evil one. In the first place, we are told that the people are worshipping devils; that is, they are acknowledging and placing their confidence in and seeking help and comfort in the spirits of evil who have fallen away from God originally with the prince of darkness. Do not say that this is impossible and inconceivable. For, in the first place, let me remind you of the fact that the sinful world as such is always serving Satan, and that he is their king and leader. And in the second place, remember, as we have stated in the last chapter, the world is actually surrendering itself to those spiritual hosts of wickedness that are in aerial places, against which the people of God are admonished to put on the whole armor of God. And in the third place, take a look in the world, and see whether all such things as Spiritualism, Theosophy, and all kinds of occult and abominable movements and sects are not the literal fulfillment already of this statement that people are worshipping devils. It is their influence that is felt, to which people freely yield. It is their will that is accomplished. It is the worship of devils that is not so far from being literally realized even today. In the second place, we are told that idolatry, the worship of silver and gold and brass and wood and stone, also once more is placed on the foreground. It may very well be that the heathen world in the future will have such an influence on the so-called Christian world that also this will be literally fulfilled. But even besides this possibility, is it not true that the service of Mammon, practical materialism, reliance upon silver and gold, the things of the world, as well as the worship of man, is essentially the same idolatry in a little different form than is here mentioned?

Small wonder, then, that where the first table of the law is thus violated, and men follow the worship of devils, also the second table is entirely trampled under foot. We read of this society that murders and sorceries and fornication and thefts abound. This is not meant as an exception, but as a rather general condition. Men have become murderers. They kill self and others. They have become sorcerers, which indicates, according to the original, that they employ all kinds of poisonous drugs for various purposes. They indulge in fornication, and commit adultery, and satisfy their greed for material things by becoming thieves and robbers on a large scale. Lawlessness, greed, treachery, adulterous lusts and passions, – all the evil passions of men reign supreme at this period.

In a word, there is a general degradation, and the world is steeped in iniquity, — an entirely different picture here than that which is presented by the philosophers of the world of today, and, in fact, of all times. O, no, the world is not growing worse; it is gradually improving. Such is the gospel that is preached rather generally today. And the time will come when mankind along the lines of gradual development shall have reached the heights of its ambition and the climax of its development. Sin and transgression shall be abolished, and justice and peace and happiness shall reign supreme. But the Word of God tells us a far different story. As was already pointed out, the Lord compares the times of the end to the times which immediately preceded the flood and the destruction of the cities of the plain. And if you ask Paul what the Spirit told him about these latter days, then he will tell you: "This know also, that in the last days perilous times shall come. For men shall be lovers of their own selves, covetous, boasters, proud, blasphemers, disobedient to parents, unthankful, unholy, Without natural affection, truce-breakers, false accusers, incontinent, fierce, despisers of those that are good, Traitors, heady, highminded, lovers of pleasures more than lovers of God; Having a form of godliness, but denying the power thereof: from such turn away," (II Timothy 3:1-5). To be sure, this is not a very attractive picture. But remember that it is the Word of God that assures us of all this. And I would rather adhere to the Word of God, which is always true and safe, than to follow the wisdom of men.

I find still another indication of the general and grievous wickedness of the world of that period in the first part of this passage. We read that a voice is heard from the horns of the golden altar which is before God, saying to the angel that had the sixth trumpet that he should go to the river Euphrates, in order to loose the four angels that were bound in that region.

The altar which is here referred to is evidently the same as the one that is mentioned in Chapter 8, verse 3. Also there we read of an altar in connection with the prayers of the saints which were offered together with the incense to God Almighty. Also that altar was a golden one, and also that altar stood before the throne of God and of the Lamb. And the idea of atonement, on the basis of which the prayers of the saints could be offered to God, was pre-eminent in that connection. Here we read that a voice proceeds from the horns of the altar. Both the altar of burnt offering and the altar of incense had horns, four in number. What is the idea of these horns? In Exodus 30:10 we read: "And Aaron shall make an atonement upon the horns of it once in a year with the blood of the sin offering of atonements: once in the year shall he make atonement upon it throughout your generations: it is most holy unto the Lord." And thus we find it more than once in Scripture. The horns were the most sacred part of the altar. Upon them was sprinkled the blood of atonement. And therefore, we are safe in saying that they stood above all for the idea that the blood of atonement was shed.

And now what do we notice? We notice that it is from these same horns, representative of the blood of atonement, that a voice proceeds, calling for a terrible judgment upon the world. It is the voice of the blood of the Lamb that cries for this judgment. And with a view to the wicked world, it indicates that the time has come when the world has trampled under foot and despised the blood of the Savior. It is that blood that now cries for revenge. It has therefore become plain that the world rejects the Christ and despises the blood of atonement. Whatever form of godliness they may have now and have had in the past, they have always stubbornly refused to acknowledge that there is salvation only in the blood of Christ. And now it is this blood that must be revenged and that cries: "Loose the four angels that are bound in the great river Euphrates."

A Terrible Plague

If we would find an answer to the question as to what sort of plague this sixth trumpet brings upon the world, and as to how it is historically realized, we must undoubtedly direct our attention, first of all, to the horses that are pictured in the vision and to their riders.

John receives a vision of an awful and terrible-looking host of cavalry, two hundred million in number and with fearful description. And it is clear that this infernal troop of cavalry is the symbol of the plague that is to come. They form the agents that must accomplish it. True, we read that the four angels that are bound at the great river Euphrates are let loose at the determined hour and day and month and year, in order to kill the third part of men. And from this statement we might receive the impression that they, and not the cavalry, were the direct agents for this destruction. But farther on in the text we read differently. There we find that the plague is realized by the fire and the smoke and the brimstone that proceeds out of the mouth of the infernal horses. And the picture is evidently this, that the angels who are bound at the great river Euphrates exert their influence, as soon as they are allowed, as soon as they are set loose, to set free this tremendous army of horsemen, in order that they may realize the plague. It is, therefore, in the first place, to these horsemen that we have to direct our attention, in order to find the character of the plague.

And then we may undoubtedly say that they are not real horses. That this is true needs no proof. Their description is such that real horses are out of the question. They are horses with heads as of lions and with serpents' tails. And these tails have heads. And with these tails these horses hurt. In a word, we have here a combination of the horse and the lion and the serpent such as makes it impossible to think of real horses. Besides, we read of them that out of their mouths proceed fire and smoke and brimstone, which also certainly is not true of real horses. And it is through this fire and smoke and brimstone that the plagues, through which one-third part of men are killed, are realized. Nor are they symbols of real cavalry as such. Again, this is contrary to the description that is given of them, especially the fact that they bring the plagues with the fire and smoke and brimstone which proceed out of their mouths. Nor are there any indications in the text that we must understand these horses as symbols of evil spirits. Also this is rather impossible. Of the locusts we read that they came out of the abyss and that an evil angel was their king. Nothing of the kind is mentioned in this passage. Besides, we found that the effect of the locusts was spiritual, since they might not kill men, which is in harmony with the nature of demons. But the effect of this plague is physical, as is indicated by the text when it informs us that a third part of men must be killed. Hence, all that we can say from the outset is this, that these horses and their riders are the symbols of tremendous forces of destruction. With this general statement is in harmony their fierce appearance, as well as the fact that fire and smoke and brimstone proceed out of their mouths. And with this also agrees the fact that they kill a third part of men.

But what destruction is meant here? In order to find an answer to this question we must study the appearance of these horses and their riders. Essential to this is, first of all, the fire and the smoke and the brimstone. They represent the three plagues. We read in verse 18: "By these three was the third part of men killed, by the fire, and by the smoke, and by the brimstone, which issued out of their mouths." We find, therefore, that three plagues are coming over mankind, – plagues which find their symbols in fire and smoke and brimstone, and which are therefore as closely allied as these three symbols.

Of what is the fire a symbol in the Bible? We find that it symbolizes anger (Psalms 39:3; 57:4; 78:21, etc.), jealousy (Psalm 79:5; Ezekiel 36:5; Zephaniah 1:18), vengeance (Deuteronomy 32:22; Judges 12:1, etc.). And since the passions of anger, of jealousy, and of vengeance in the unholy sense of the word, as evidently they must be taken in the words of our passage, are the root cause of war, we find that fire is also taken time and again in Scripture as the symbol of war. Jeremiah, referring to war, prophesied that Jehovah shall kindle a fire against Jerusalem (Jeremiah 17:27; 21:14). And he prophesies that He shall kindle a fire against Babylon, again referring to war (Jeremiah 15:32). In Lamentations 4:11 we read: "The Lord kindled a fire in Zion, and it hath devoured the foundations thereof." And in Amos 1:4 we are told: "But I will send a fire into the house of Hazael, which shall devour the palaces of Benhadad." If you add to this that the first color of the breastplates of these monstrous horsemen is also that of fire, and add to this that the chief appearance of these monsters is that of the horse, which, as we have seen before, is the symbol of battle and irresistible onslaught, and add to this, thirdly, that the second or red horse, as we have seen in connection with the first four seals, is also the symbol of war, then I dare say the implication is plain that the plague of the sixth trumpet, by which one-third of men are killed, certainly refers to war.

The second symbol that is used in connection with the sixth trumpet is that of smoke. Again we must turn to Scripture in order to find the meaning of it. Of course, first of all, we must take it in connection with the first symbol. It is related to the first. The fire is first; but also the smoke proceeds from the same source, namely, out of the mouths of the lions. And then I would say that the smoke, in connection with the fire, is the symbol of the desolation and destruction, and for that reason of the scarcity and famine, which follow in the wake of war. And this is but its natural result. This too is corroborated by other parts of Scripture. In Isaiah 34:10 we find a description of the desolation that shall come upon Egypt in the words: "The smoke thereof shall go up forever." If the red of the fire is symbolic of the heated passions of war, the blackness of the smoke is indicative of the desolation and hunger that follow war. Thus we find in Lamentations 4:8 that those who shall perish with hunger are described in the following words: "Their visage is blacker than a coal."

And again, in the same Lamentations of the prophet we read that he complains: "Our skin was black like an oven because of the terrible famine." The blackness of the smoke, therefore, is the symbol of the desolation following war. It is indicative of scarcity and famine and of destruction in general. This is corroborated further by the second color in the breastplates of these monsters, corresponding to the smoke that proceeds out of the mouths of the lions. And it is corroborated also by the second main feature of these monster-animals, which is that of the lion, a picture of ravening hunger that can devour anything. Again it is corroborated by the third horse in the first four seals, which is the black horse, and which, as we have seen before, is the symbol of scarcity and want. Hence, also here we are safe in saying that the picture refers rather strikingly to desolation and destruction, to want and famine, as they follow in the wake of war.

The third symbol, finally, which is representative of this particular plague is the brimstone, or sulphur, that proceeds out of the mouths of these monsters. Also here we may remark that this last plague must again have some connection with the former two, and, in fact, that there must be some kind of causal relationship between them and this particular plague. Hence, the suggestion is not far-fetched at all that we have here the picture of all kinds of pestilences as they naturally follow in the wake of war and desolation and hunger. This suggestion is confirmed, in the first place, by the nature of the sulphur, which suggests poisoning because of its gasses. But also in the Word of God we find the same meaning. Rather generally we find sulphur as a symbol of desolation in Deuteronomy 29:23, where the desolation that shall come over the land of Israel is described as follows: "The whole land thereof is brimstone, and salt, and a burning, that it is not sown, nor beareth, nor any grass groweth therein." But more clearly we find a description of this in Ezekiel 38:22: "And I will plead against him with pestilence and with blood; and I will rain upon him, and upon his bands, and upon the many people that were with him, an overflowing rain, and great hailstones, fire, and brimstone." This is prophesied in connection with Gog and Magog, and therefore in a somewhat similar connection as in our passage of Revelation. Most naturally in this passage of Ezekiel the brimstone stands as a symbol of the pestilence. Again I find this corroborated by the third color in the breastplate of this cavalry, which is also that of brimstone. Confirmed it is, also, by the last feature in the appearance of these monsters, namely, that of the sneaky and subtle serpent, which attacks unawares, so that no one notices him, like the pestilence. These serpents are found in the tails of the horses. And lastly, I find this corroborated by the last horse in the first four seals. That last horse presents the same color as the brimstone, namely, that of a pale green. And the name of that last horse is Death, mowing away one-fourth part of men by all kinds of means, also by the pestilence. And therefore I feel rather safe in maintaining that in this last plague we have the symbol of the noisome pestilence. All these taken together, as they are symbolized by the fire and the smoke and the brimstone, as well as by the horse and the lion and the serpent, as they show their resemblance to the second, third, and fourth horses of the first four seals, lead us to the conclusion that the plagues here pictured are those of war and famine and pestilence. These three cannot be separated. The one follows from the other. And in their inner connection they are here pictured as being together one awful monster, with the shape of a horse, a lion's head, and the tail of a serpent, while from these monsters proceed the fire and the smoke and the brimstone. Upon this wicked world, steeped in sin, an awful war shall break forth, carrying hunger and desolation and pestilence in its wake.

But, so we ask further: what is the special nature of this war, and what is its special occasion? For that this is not a war like other wars, but different in its nature and scope, is plainly indicated in the fact that by these three one-third of men are killed. That is, as we have explained, more than in any other, ordinary war are killed. Ordinarily only one-fourth of men are killed by war and hunger and all kinds of diseases. But at the time of this war this will be increased to one-third. And therefore we have here a war of special proportions at least.

In order to understand this, let me call your attention to the fact that in the history of the world, with its wars and progress, the main occurrences have been played on a very small part of the world's stage. From Israel this history proceeded to Assyria, from Assyria to Babylonia, from Babylonia to Persia, from Persia to Greece, from Greece to Rome, from the Roman Empire to the nations of Europe and America. Always following a westerly direction, the history of the world has limited itself to only some of the nations of the world. And still there is a large part of men that have never yet played a part in its history although in late years they already appear on its stage. There is the yellow race, which evidently is just beginning to wake up to an important extent. And there are the nations that are living at the four corners of the earth, outside of the pale of civilization, and which in Scripture are known as Gog and Magog. If this relation is clear, then you are prepared to understand our contention that here in the sixth trumpet we have the first indication of the waking up of these other nations. For our text pictures to us, according to our deepest conviction, a war which is caused by the inroads of these numberless nations into the so-called civilized and Christian nations.

In proof of this contention I point, in the first place, to the mention that is here made of the great river Euphrates. The Euphrates is one of the greatest rivers in western Asia. But the question is here: what is the significance, and why is it mentioned in this connection?

I find that Scripture pictures this river as the eastern boundary of the land promised to the children of Israel in Genesis 15:18. There we read that Abraham received the promise: "Unto thy seed have I given this land, from the river of Egypt unto the great river, the river Euphrates." And again, in Deuteronomy 1:7 we read that the children of Israel received the command: "Turn you, and take your journey, and go to the mount of the Amorites, and unto all the places nigh thereunto, in the plain, in the hills, and in the vale, and in the south, and by the sea side, to the land of the Canaanites, and unto Lebanon, unto the great river, the river Euphrates." The same we read in Deuteronomy 11:24 and in Joshua 1:4. We find that this promise was realized in the time of Solomon, for of him we read that he ruled over all the kingdoms from the river (that is, Euphrates) unto the land of the Philistines (I Kings 4:21). It was upon that river that Babylon was situated, according to Scripture. And it is in that river that the book that prophesied the destruction of Babylon, written by Jeremiah, was sunk. And therefore I find that the river Euphrates is the ideal and real boundary-line between the outward kingdom of God and the kingdom of darkness, and therefore the symbol of the boundary-line between the Christian and the heathen nations, between the so-called civilized world and Gog and Magog.

It is at this river that the four angels are bound. The purpose of these four angels is evidently to seduce the nations of Gog and Magog, and inspire them to war with the Christian world. But they are bound. It is the decree of the Almighty, and therefore the will of Christ, that has bound them, so that they cannot influence these nations as yet. For they are bound unto the exact year and month and day and hour. That hour is evidently historically determined by the completion of the preaching of the gospel also to these nations, and, on the other hand, by the fulness of the measure of iniquity of the so-called Christian nations. That hour has now come, according to the passage. For the blood of atonement cried from between the horns of the altar, and the four angels who are bound at the great river Euphrates are let loose. These four angels, whose very number indicates that we are to have a world war as we never saw before, when they are liberated, now turn themselves upon the nations of the east and seduce them to do battle against the Christian world. Hence, when they are let loose, the woes of war and famine and desolation and pestilence flood the world, rising from the east and coming from the direction of the Euphrates upon the entire world.

Finally, this entire view is corroborated by the character of the sixth vial. There is a plain correspondence, as we shall see when we are discussing this vial, between the six trumpets and the six vials which are yet to follow. And the sixth vial, which corresponds to this sixth trumpet, informs us: "And the sixth angel poured out his vial upon the great river Euphrates; and the water thereof was dried up, that the way of the kings of the east might be prepared." Here it is plainly told us what it will finally mean when the river Euphrates is dried up, when it shall no more serve as a boundary-line between the nations of the so-called Christian world and Gog and Magog. Then the kings of the east shall come and flood the whole Christian world, and the end of destruction is near.

In brief, therefore, we have here the picture of a war that is still to come, in which not only the Christian but also the heathen world shall be involved, and the outcome of which shall be that one-third of men, that is, more than ever before, shall be killed. Faint indications of this we have in history when the nations of the east at the time of the destruction of the Roman Empire rise against it and flood Europe. And more definite indications of this war that is prophesied in the Book of Revelation we have in our own time. Nevertheless, the full realization also of this trumpet is still in the future. Also this second woe we must still expect.

The World Left Hopelessly Hardened

We read in the text: "And they repented not." We might think that such severe judgments would break the hearts of these idolaters and murderers and thieves. One-third of men are killed; and no doubt also the rest of men are touched and hurt by the famine and especially by the pestilence. Think of the desolation and the woe and the sorrow and the grief and the suffering this sixth trumpet will cause for the remaining two-thirds that are still alive! All the more we would think that they should repent because it has been so plainly foretold in Scripture that these things come, and come as a revenge of the blood of Christ which is trampled under foot and a judgment upon the iniquity of the world. But no, they repented not. They are hardened. Even as Pharaoh repented not when plague after plague so plainly came from the hand of Jehovah, but continued till his judgment was complete, so also the wicked world at the end of time will not repent until their destruction is finished. We must expect also this feature. You must expect disappointment if you imagine that judgment will do what the gospel could not accomplish. In the midst of judgment the hearts will become more hardened and embittered, and people will continue in their sins. Their end will be in the pool that burneth with fire and brimstone.

Hence, the great lesson for the people of God contained in this particular passage is this: turn away from such! Have nothing to do with the world that tramples under foot the blood of Christ, except in as far as you are called to be the light of the world and to spread the testimony of the gospel. Have no communion with their idolatry and murders and thefts and fornication. Then it may be that the bitterness of the world will seek revenge upon you for a time. It may be that you will have to bear their contempt, their hatred, and their persecution. Nevertheless, there is no danger whatsoever. The people of God are sealed. And therefore you should not fear those that can kill the body and cannot touch the soul. But much rather fear Him who ruleth over all and who can condemn both soul and body in hell.

Be not afraid! In the world ye shall have tribulation, saith the Lord; but be of good cheer, I have overcome the world. In the darkest night the eternal morning of glory shall surely dawn, and the faithful shall receive the crown of glory.

Chapter XXIII

An Interlude

(Revelation 10:1-7)

1 And I saw another mighty angel come down from heaven, clothed with a cloud: and a rainbow was upon his head, and his face was as it were the sun, and his feet as pillars of fire:

2 And he had in his hand a little book open: and he set his right foot upon the sea, and his left foot on the earth,

3 And cried with a loud voice, as when a lion roareth: and when he cried, seven thunders uttered their voices.

4 And when the seven thunders had uttered their voices, I was about to write: and I heard a voice from heaven saying unto me, Seal up those things which the seven thunders uttered, and write them not.

5 And the angel which I saw stand upon the sea and upon the earth lifted up his hand to heaven,

6 And sware by him that liveth for ever and ever, who created heaven, and the things that therein are, and the earth, and the things that therein are, and the sea, and the things which are therein, that there should be time no longer:

7 But in the days of the voice of the seventh angel, when he shall begin to sound, the mystery of God should be finished, as he hath declared to his servants the prophets.

It is plain even from a superficial reading of the text that in this part of the Book of Revelation a new portion is introduced in the form of an interlude.

Perhaps it is well that at this point we recall once more the general scheme of the Book of Revelation, so that we may not lose sight of the general significance and may gain a clear view of the whole. The book, as we have pointed out repeatedly, is covered by the seven seals which are broken by the Lion of Judah's tribe. When these seven seals shall all have been broken, and all that they reveal shall have been realized, the plan of God with a view to the completion of the kingdom shall also be completely fulfilled. But these seven seals do not maintain their form as seals, as we have also remarked several times. On the contrary, the seventh seal becomes revealed to us under the aspect of the seven trumpets, six of which we have now discussed. And the seventh trumpet again does not reveal itself in the form of a trumpet, but becomes manifest as the seven vials of wrath. Seven seals, seven trumpets, seven vials, — such is the general plan of the book we are attempting to explain. And as to the relation between these seven seals and trumpets and vials, we also have remarked more than once that they are not strictly contemporaneous, neither entirely successive, so that the one seal always follows the other in strict succession or so that even the trumpets strictly follow in time upon the seals. But, as we have seen, they are both contemporaneous and successive. On the one hand, they are contemporaneous, so that in principle the vials begin at the same time that the seals are broken and are realized throughout the history of the present dispensation, side by side and at the same time. But on the other hand, they are also successive, so that there is an increase in the element of judgment. And as we study them, we feel that we are gradually led on to the time of the coming of our Lord Jesus Christ.

If with this in mind we now look back and once more glance over the material we have thus far discussed, the meaning and the truth of this interpretation will be rather clear. In connection with the first six seals we saw that the first four picture to us in general the history of the present dispensation with a view to the bringing of the kingdom of God from the four-fold point of view of the effect of the preaching of the gospel, of the influence of war, of social contrast and scarcity, and of death. The fifth seal revealed already an advance over the fourth in that at its breaking we heard the cry of the blood of those who were killed for the sake of Christ, calling for the day of judgment, while the sixth seal carried us face to face with the great day of judgment in that it revealed unto us the shakeup of the physical universe and the amazement and confusion of the wicked world. The same feature we discovered in connection with the six trumpets we have been discussing thus far. In themselves the trumpets are already an advance over the seals in that they speak of one-third, just a little increase in judgment every time. But also the relation between the six trumpets mutually is such that there is a gradual increase till again the sixth trumpet brings us immediately before the time of the coming of Christ Jesus. The first four trumpets, we saw, revealed the destruction upon the world of nature. The fifth trumpet brought an additional army of the Evil One into play upon the stage of the world. And the sixth trumpet spoke of the letting loose of the four angels who are bound by the river Euphrates, thus giving them the opportunity to influence the nations of Gog and Magog and causing that terrible plague of universal war and famine and pestilence, symbolized in the fire and the smoke and the brimstone.

To one more feature we must call your attention, namely, to that of the interludes, or episodes, portions which do not belong to the revelation of the seals or the trumpets or vials, but are thrown in between, and that too, for a definite purpose. One of these we already discussed in connection with the seventh chapter of the book. In that episode we found that in answer to the question, who shall stand, the Lord replies by revealing that His people are sealed and that they shall become heirs of the great and glorious salvation that is promised unto them. And the purpose of that interlude was naturally to comfort and strengthen the people of God in the midst of tribulation and days of judgment.

This same feature we meet once more in the chapter we are now discussing. Also here we have an interlude. The tenth chapter does not introduce as yet the blowing of the seventh trumpet. This is plain from the fifteenth verse of the eleventh chapter, where we find the definite indication that the seventh angel sounds. And on the other hand, this tenth chapter no more belongs to the sixth trumpet or to the second woe. For although the fourteenth verse of the next chapter would leave that impression, and actually proves this according to some interpreters, yet it is plain that this is not a mere continuation of the sixth trumpet. For, first of all, another angel appears. Secondly, the point of view of John is changed from the heavens to the earth. And, thirdly, this tenth chapter no more speaks of woe and judgment directly, but of something different. Hence, we regard this chapter again as an interlude. Just as there was such an episode between the opening of the sixth and the seventh seals, so also here we have an interlude between the blowing of the sixth and of the seventh trumpets.

The Identity Of The Mighty Angel

John introduces this chapter by informing us that he saw another strong angel come down from heaven. From this it is evident that the point of view in the vision is again changed. For the fact that John beholds the angel come down from heaven clearly shows that in the vision he is again upon the earth. Chapter 4, verse 1, spoke of a door opened in heaven and of a voice beckoning John to come up hither. Many interpreters have explained that portion as being indicative of the church's being called to heaven before the time of the great tribulation. Here I wish to remark that consistency would compel these interpreters to admit that here John is again upon the earth, and that therefore the church has also come down again. All of this is, of course, absurd. It is not the church, nor the person of the apostle John that was called to heaven in the fourth chapter, but only John as he appears in the vision. And therefore, not the church, neither John comes down from heaven, but only the viewpoint of the vision is changed in the words of our text.

As to the identity of the angel who here comes down from heaven, I wish to remark from the outset that I fully agree with those interpreters who find in the appearance of this angel none less than the figure of Jesus Christ in glory Himself. True, it has been remarked that there is no direct mention of Him and that the text speaks of an angel, and that the manner in which John addresses Him would suggest that it was not the Savior Himself, but a mere glorious angel. But all these objections count but little in the face of the description that here is given of this angel, of its similarity in many respects with the description given in the first chapter of this book, and also of the resemblance of this entire scene offered in the twelfth chapter of the Book of Daniel.

First of all, then, let us attend to the description which is given of this angel in the text. We are told of Him that He is arrayed in a cloud. And the cloud, as we have had occasion to remark before, is the symbol of divine majesty, especially of that divine majesty as it is coming for judgment. And who can read this description of the angel's being arrayed in a cloud without thinking of the so often repeated assertion that Christ shall come with the clouds of heaven to judge the quick and the dead? In the second place, we read that a rainbow was upon His head. In other words, the rainbow is His crown. A rainbow we found thus far only above the throne of God Almighty in heaven. It is the symbol of the grace and the faithfulness of God in keeping His covenant, especially with a view to all creation. And therefore also this detail of the description could hardly be fitted in with the picture of a common angel. It makes us think of the Angel of the Covenant, of Jesus Christ Himself. In the third place, we read that His face was as the sun, and therefore is so glorious and majestic that it is impossible to look upon. And, in the fourth place, we read that His feet were like pillars of fire. And, as we have seen before, the fire in Scripture indicates war and judgment. Here it indicates the war of the Almighty upon the wicked world. But this judgment upon the wicked world, still more emphasized by the fact that it is the **feet** that appear under this symbol, cannot be attributed to anyone else in the world than our Lord Jesus Christ Himself. And therefore, the description itself already causes us to think immediately of the Lord, and of no one else.

Secondly, let us consider the similarity between this description and that in the first chapter of the book. There, so we found, we certainly have a picture of the mighty Lord Jesus. For He was the one that was dead and is alive, and lives forevermore, and holds the key of death and of hades. And how was He described there? First of all, He came in the form of the Son of man. The description here in Chapter 10 indicates the same form. For although the text speaks of an angel, nevertheless the details of the hands and feet and face plainly picture the form of a Son of man. And, in the second place, notice that there He was described as having eyes of flames of fire and that His face was as the sun shineth in his strength. So also here, in Chapter 10, we read that His face was as the sun. In the third place, notice that there, in Chapter 1, we read that His feet were as burnished brass, indicating that they were like fire. So also here, in Chapter 10, we read in a somewhat different symbol that His feet were like pillars of fire. The chief difference between the description in our passage and that in the first chapter is that there He wears the long priestly garb, while of it we read nothing in the words of our text. But this difference is, as we shall see, in harmony with the entire occasion of the appearance of this angel. In this vision the Lord does not mean to reveal Himself as priest; and therefore the priestly garb is lacking. But if we consider the similarity in both descriptions, there can be but little doubt that here, as in Chapter 1, we have a vision of the glorified Lord, Jesus Christ.

Thirdly, we cannot help noticing a striking resemblance between this passage and the last part of the Book of Daniel. We read there that at the river Hiddekel a man appeared unto Daniel, clothed in linen. His "loins were girded with fine gold of Uphaz: His body also was like the beryl, and his face as the appearance of lightning, and his eyes as lamps of fire, and his arms and his feet like in colour to polished brass, and the voice of his words like the voice of a multitude," (Daniel 10:5, 6). That in this passage we have a description of Christ in His glory there can be no doubt. But what is of special interest is that of this man clothed in linen we read that as he stood above the river he lifted up his hands to heaven and sware by Him that liveth forever and ever that it shall be for a time and times and a half time (Daniel 12:7). There He performs somewhat the same act that is ascribed to Him in the words of our passage. There, in the passage from Daniel, He swears that the time is appointed, and that after the appointed time His words shall surely be fulfilled. Here, in the passage of Revelation, He swears that the time of the end is approaching, that there shall be no delay any more. And therefore, if in that portion we have a description of the Christ, as undoubtedly we do have, then there can be no doubt that here too we have the same Son of Man performing a similar act.

But, so we ask, how, in what capacity, does the Lord here appear to us? And also then there can be no doubt but that we see the Lord in glory as the King-Judge, and that with the emphasis on His being the Judge of heaven and earth.

That He appears as the King is indicated, in the first place, by the general glory of His appearance. His face shineth as the sun, and the rainbow is His crown, while the feet are pillars of fire. In the second place, this is indicated also by what He does. He places His feet on the earth and on the sea, by which He indicates that all is in subjection to Him, as we hope to see presently. He is the King, to Whom all power is given in heaven and on earth.

But it is especially the appearance of the Judge which is very prominent. The brightness of His face, the raiment of the cloud, and especially the fiery feet, ready to consume the enemies of His kingdom, all reveal to us that here the Lord appears especially as the Judge of heaven and earth, come to wreak vengeance upon all the host of His enemies. And this is emphasized all the more by the fact that there is no mention of the priestly garb of reconciliation. The time for the priestly work of reconciliation is drawing to an end. At any rate, the purpose of this appearance is not to reveal the Christ in that particular capacity of reconciliation. The interlude is especially connected with the last part of the preceding chapter, and it is at the same time preparing for what is still to come. In the last part of Chapter 9 we found that in spite of all the judgments that had already come upon the world, yet they did not repent, but continued in their sin of devil-worship, idolatry, murder, fornication, and theft, continued to trample under foot the blood of reconciliation that cried against them. The purpose of this vision, therefore, is not to reveal the Christ in His atoning power, as the Priest, but exclusively as the almighty Judge Who is on the verge of wreaking final vengeance upon the world of sin and corruption. The entire purpose of this vision is to announce that judgment, terrible and final judgment, shall presently and speedily come upon the world, and that the enemies of the kingdom are about to be destroyed. But although this is true, there is no reason to fear: for still He carries the rainbow, the symbol of the grace of God with regard to His creation and to all His people. It is through these final judgments that creation shall be completely redeemed, that the covenant shall be realized and perfected, and that all the world shall be subjected to the Triune God in glory. When all the judgments of this mighty King shall be realized, so the rainbow informs us, then shall also the new heavens and the new earth, in which righteousness shall dwell, be completed. In conclusion, therefore, we may say that the appearance of this angel reveals to us the Christ, reveals Him to us as the King-Judge, reveals to us that judgment is to come upon the world speedily, but reveals also at the same time that through these judgments the kingdom of our God shall be permanently established and perfected in all creation.

The Action Of The Mighty Angel

With this interpretation of the description of the angel is also in harmony the act which He performs. We read of this mighty angel that He set His right foot upon the sea and His left foot upon the earth. We must not belittle the interpretation of this passage by saying, as some of the historical interpreters have it, that the earth is the Roman Empire and that the sea is the peoples of that time. For there is nothing that indicates anything of the kind in the words of our text. No, but the earth and the sea are here to be taken as symbolic of all the world and of all that it contains. It indicates the sea and all its creatures and powers, as well as the dry land and all its inhabitants and wealth. It is symbolic of the kingdom as we have pictured it to you more than once, as God originally created it, the kingdom of the world, over which He placed man as His viceroy. That kingdom of the world, the earth and the sea and all their fulness, was surrendered into the power of the devil through the sin of man. But upon that kingdom the Lord, this mighty angel, now sets His feet as pillars of fire.

This indicates, first of all, that this King has all things subjected under Him. The placing of one's feet upon anything is symbolic of subjection and possession. In Joshua 10:24 we read that Joshua calls the chiefs of his army together and bids them place their feet upon the necks of the five kings who have tried to escape in the cave, but which cave became their prison. And then we read that Joshua pledges that Jehovah shall thus do unto all their enemies, against whom they are fighting to conquer the land. In other words, Jehovah shall subdue their enemies and put them in complete subjection. Still more clearly, we have the direct statement in Psalm 110:1: "The Lord said unto my Lord, Sit thou at my right hand, until I make thine enemies thy footstool." Again, the idea of absolute subjection is expressed here. Thus also we read in I Corinthians 15:25: "For he must reign till he hath put all enemies under his feet." And in Ephesians 1:22 we read: "And hath put all things under his feet." When this mighty angel, therefore, places his feet upon the earth and upon the sea, upon all the world, He thereby expresses plainly that, in the first place, He is their Lord and possessor. To Him belong the heaven and the earth, also in this present dispensation. He is their rightful Sovereign. But still more, He also expresses symbolically that all the world is actually subject unto Him. It may not seem so. It may seem as if the power of sin is lord and possessor in actual fact. The truth, nevertheless, is different. Christ has His feet upon the earth and upon the sea, and He has all things under His absolute control. With majestic calm He may descend out of heaven; and without any fear that He shall be opposed, He may indeed place His feet upon all things. For all things are subject unto Him even now.

But although this is true, fact is also that His dominion is still disputed and that the prince of this world still rises in rebellion against Him. And thus it shall actually appear more and more. As the judgments of Christ shall come over this world, it shall appear more and more plainly as if the power of evil is actually reigning and ruling supreme. But when that fifth trumpet shall sound and the special army of Satan out of the abyss shall be let loose and men shall follow their sinful inclinations and ambitions to the full, it shall seem as if the power of sin actually reigns and as if hell has free play on the stage of human history. When that sixth trumpet shall blow and the four angels at the river Euphrates shall instigate the nations of Gog and Magog and thus cause a universal war, it shall again appear as if the devil does as he pleases and as if hell reigns sovereignly over all the world, especially since all the while men do not repent of their wickedness but continue to defy the blood of atonement. And yet this shall not actually be the case. And therefore we must notice, in the second place, that the Lord holds His feet of fire upon the wicked world, thereby indicating that not only does He possess and control all things, but also that through it all He is executing His judgments upon the world of rebellion against Him.

But He does more. The Lord does not come only to perform a symbolic act and thereby to assure His people that He is in control and that presently He shall come for judgment upon the wicked world. But He also gives a most solemn assurance. He makes an oath. Lifting His right hand to heaven, — for in the left hand He held the book, — He swears by the name of God, in order thereby to add to the certainty and the truth of the statement which He makes. He calls God "him that liveth for ever, and ever, who created heaven, and the things that therein are, and the earth, and the things that therein are, and the sea, and the things that therein are." In the first place, therefore, He swears by the Eternal One, thereby assuring His people that as long as the name of God endures, — and this is, of course, for ever, — the truth of His statement shall also stand and shall certainly be fulfilled. In the second place, however, He also swears by the Creator of all, Who is at the same time the sovereign possessor of all things unto all eternity. He, the Almighty Sovereign of the heavens and of the earth, stands for the truth and the certainty of this statement.

Proper this oath certainly is. For the contents of this statement are closely related to its form. The main idea of it is that the mystery of God shall be realized. The mystery of God in this case is nothing less than the ultimate outcome of the entire plan of God as it was contained in the book with its seven seals. At this stage six seals have already been broken, and six trumpets are already blown. But the mystery of God has not yet been fulfilled. It is still waiting. Of that mystery His servants the prophets had already spoken: for they had repeatedly made mention of the great day of the Lord, of the dominion of the Lord God Almighty, of the new heavens and the new earth. But still the world is as before. Still the wicked world exists. Still the blood of the witnesses of Christ flows as ever. Still the world serves its idols and demons, and commits the most terrible sins. But now the time is near.

For the Lord says, "There shall be no more time." This does not mean that presently eternity shall set in, — although this is true in itself, — but that there shall be no more delay. For this "no more time" must evidently be taken in direct contrast with what follows. There shall be no more time;

but in the days of the voice of the seventh angel, when he is about to sound, shall the mystery of God be finished. The meaning is: presently the seventh trumpet shall sound, and there shall be no more delay at that time. The time for delay is drawing to a close. They have been chastised, and they repented not. They have trampled under foot the blood of atonement. The measure of their iniquity is full. There shall be no more delay. And when that seventh trumpet shall sound, then shall the entire plan of God be finished. The world of sin shall have been judged. The enemy of God shall have been destroyed. The kingdom shall have been established in glory. And the people of God shall have entered into their eternal inheritance, beautiful and fair, where they shall glorify their God forevermore.

The Accompanying Seven Thunders

A moment we must call your attention to the strange event which accompanies this outcry of the Lion of Judah's tribe. As this mighty angel cries with a voice as of a roaring lion, which makes us think of the voice of many waters and of the Lion Who stood as the Lamb that was slain, John hears at the same time the voice of seven thunders.

Three things we may notice in regard to these seven thunders.

In the first place, we must remember that the thunder in the Word of God, and especially also in the Book of Revelation, is indicative of judgment, the judgment of God. In Psalm 18:13, in the midst of that wonderful description of Jehovah's coming against the enemies of His servant David to destroy them, we read: "The Lord also thundered in the heavens, and the Highest gave His voice." As you will recall in connection with the prayers of the saints which are offered upon the altar of gold before the throne, we read that the answer to these prayers came in the form of thunders and voices and an earthquake. Whether John refers to these same thunders, so that we must think here of the specific judgments which shall come in answer to the prayers of the saints, or whether he has in mind other seven thunders, we know not. Certain it is that he speaks of a definite, well-known number of thunders. For he does not say "seven thunders" but uses the definite article, "**The** seven thunders uttered their voices." They are, therefore, symbols of judgments upon the wicked world. And as such they well fit in with this entire passage. The mighty angel, the Lord Jesus Christ, in this portion sets His feet as pillars of fire upon the entire dominion to express that He is about to subdue and destroy all His enemies. At the same time He swears that there shall be no more delay, but that presently the mystery of God shall be fulfilled. And therefore, even as the entire scene speaks of a speedy judgment, so also these thunders are symbols of the same thing.

In the second place, we may notice their number, which also is in harmony with this scene, as well as with the form of the entire book. In harmony with this portion it is, for it tells us of a finished mystery of God; and that is exactly indicated by the number **seven**. Seven is the number of the completed kingdom, as we have had occasion to remark before. And therefore the inference is perfectly legitimate, that these seven thunders are the symbols of judgments which must come for the completion and for the final perfection of the kingdom of God. And in harmony with the entire book this number seven is: for the book is based on this number throughout. There are seven churches, seven seals, seven trumpets, and seven vials. And when all of these seven are realized, the kingdom has come.

In the third place, we may also notice that these thunders speak, that they utter their voices. And they speak in plain human language, — so plain that John is immediately ready to write down what they speak. And the inference is again that they revealed in plain and direct language just what judgments would come upon the world till the completion of the kingdom.

Many are the conjectures as to the contents of the speech of these seven thunders. And the question has often been asked, and answered in many different ways: what did these thunders say, and what did they reveal of the mystery of God? There are those who assure us that here the devil appeared as an angel of light and that he imitated the Lord, that he tried to deceive John and have him write down as belonging to the mystery of the kingdom what was nothing but a lie of Satan. And hence, John, when he is about to write down what they said, receives the command to seal up their revelation and to write them not. There are others who assure us that the seven thunders contained the oracles of all the prophets who had spoken of the coming of the kingdom. Still others have it that they revealed the blessed mystery of the kingdom in its completion and spoke of the glory of the new world. Others have it that they revealed merely the sad contents of the little book without the sweet element which John tasted when he swallowed it. There are even interpreters who have been bold enough to find in them the symbols of the seven crusades for the

Holy Land. All these, and other conjectures, have been made. But all of
them, and as many as there still may be made in the future, are absolutely
wrong, for the simple reason that Scripture does not tell us anything about
the contents of the speech of these thunders. It tells us that they were
thunders and therefore symbols of judgment. It tells us too that there were
seven thunders, and therefore symbols of the judgment which must come
for the completion of the kingdom. It tells us that they spoke in plain
human language, so that John could just write down what was dictated to
him. But for the rest, it is simply presumptuous to ask exactly what they
spoke, for the simple reason that the command came to John not to write,
but to seal up what he heard. The only answer possible, therefore, is that it
was not the Lord's will that the voices of these seven thunders should be
revealed.

But then we come to another question: has then this portion no
significance at all? If the contents of these seven thunders might not be
revealed, why then did they speak at all, and why is it revealed to us that
they did speak? Why did not John simply proceed with that which we may
know, instead of first telling us that something was revealed to him which
must remain sealed to us forever?

I find the answer to this question in this, that the seven thunders spoke
directly and in plain language of the judgments to come, perhaps so plainly
that we could all follow them in the history of the world and know
exactly what was happening and how far we had proceeded on the way of
that history, so that not only the church, enlightened by the Spirit, but
even the world, without faith, could feel that these things were clearly
being realized. But that is not the purpose of the Book of Revelation. In
this book the history of the world is not outlined before us, so that we can
plainly recognize period after period that God's program is being realized.
But according to the first chapter, the things revealed are "signified." That
means that they come to us in symbolic garb. And because of this
symbolic garb it is possible that the church, under the influence of the
Holy Spirit, can recognize the coming Christ, while the world, which
tramples under foot the blood of Christ, is blind for this truth. Just as
Jesus spoke in parables with the avowed purpose that His people might
understand, but that the blind and deaf might not see nor hear and
understand, so it is also in the Book of Revelation. The mystery of God
must surely be revealed, but only in such a way that the church may
receive the proper comfort at the proper time, while its contents remain

hidden for the world of sin. Hence, as we shall see in the next chapter, it is not in this form that John may receive the revelation of the mystery of God, but in a far different form. The contents of the seven thunders, therefore, as such must forever remain hidden. And he who would understand the mystery of God must labor with its revelation under the guiding influence of the Holy Spirit.

The Comfort Of The Mighty Angel's Appearance

And now the final question: what is the purpose of this part of the interlude?

In general, we may say that it aims at the peace and the comfort of the people of God in times of persecution and tribulation. Thus it was with the episode in Chapter 7. There we were told how, in the midst of the severest trials and tribulations, the people of Christ are sealed by the Spirit, so that they need not be afraid, while the glory that was pictured there before their eyes might incite them to be faithful even unto the end. So also here the passage is rich in comfort for the people of Christ Jesus, — a comfort which they surely need.

Just imagine the condition. Already terrible things have been revealed. In the days of the fifth trumpet, when that infernal army of locusts shall be liberated to seduce men, there shall be an increase in sin and iniquity; and a wave of transgression shall sweep the sinful world that shall end in the gloomiest pessimism. Do not think that this wave of iniquity shall touch only the avowedly wicked world. It shall sweep over the established church, and many in the church shall follow in the way of the world. That this is true you may behold in our own day. Thus also in the days of the sixth trumpet, when the four angels who are bound at the river Euphrates are let loose, there shall follow terrible days. All the world shall be at war and in misery, and it shall seem as if the coming of the kingdom were more remote than ever. It shall appear as if the forces of hell are reigning supreme. Iniquity as never before, the worship of devils and idolatry, murders, and thefts, and sorceries, and fornication shall abound. And the world shall not repent. They shall be days of extreme tribulation, days in which the faithful must stand strong and firm, in which many even out of the church shall fall away into the world.

And what do you imagine shall be the spiritual condition of the people of God in those days? Of course, they shall undoubtedly receive special strength and grace; for otherwise they would never be able to stand. Yet even so, I think that in those days the condition of the people of God shall often be that of gloom and doubt. Does it after all not seem, so they will think, that the cause of Christ in this world is a lost cause when iniquity abounds, when judgment is not followed by repentance, and when even many of the church shall fall away? It also shall be often a condition of fear and anxiety and small faith. Also they fear tribulation. Also against their nature it is to suffer and to be subjected to reproach and shame. Yet these shall come in those days, and are coming now more and more. And the result will be that they will sometimes lose sight of their King and His revelation, and experience moments of fear and doubt and anxiety. But it shall also be a condition of longing for the completion of all things and for the final coming of the Lord. When faith is strong and fears are dispelled, this faith shall in those days reveal itself especially as hope and longing for the coming of the kingdom and of the King in His glory. And the prayer of the Bride shall become more and more urgent in the midst of judgment and tribulation, "Come, Lord Jesus, yea, come quickly."

And now note how comforting for such conditions is the revelation of the powerful Lord in this passage. It assures us once more that the Lord is possessor, and that He is the only Lord of all, and that in reality all things are subjected unto Him. When it should seem different, nevertheless it is true that He only rules over all. He has His feet upon the earth and upon the sea, and all things are in subjection. Nothing happens against His will. And Satan and hell and the wicked world cannot stir if He does not will them to move. In the second place, it tells us that He rules as Judge, and that all these things are directly realized through Him. If it would seem to us that the kingdom is more remote than ever and that iniquity and trouble, yea, that the forces of hell prevail, never you fear; but fasten your eyes upon that mighty Lord with feet as pillars of fire. And then you may know that war and famine and pestilence and tribulation come from Him alone. It tells you by the rainbow that in the midst of mighty judgments He will not forget His covenant, but through it all realize it. And finally, in the· midst of these judgments and tribulation your hearts go out with longing for the end of it all. And then you know that the hour is near. Fasten your eye upon that mighty figure of the Judge with His feet upon all the world and with His right hand lifted to heaven, swearing by Him that liveth forever and ever that there shall be no more delay.

"Behold, I come, and come quickly." That, above all, is the message that comes to us from this revelation of the powerful Lord in the midst of judgments and tribulations.

And therefore this vision ought, in the first place, to dispel all the fears and doubts and anxieties of the people of God, no matter how things may develop. But, in the second place, it ought to strike terror in the hearts of those who still love iniquity and who with the world indulge in their sin. It may seem as if His coming is far off. Long may seem the delay. Nevertheless He comes quickly. And the times in which we live declare more than ever that He sware by Him that liveth forever that there shall be no more delay.

Chapter XXIV
The Little Book
(Revelation 10:8-11)

8 And the voice which I heard from heaven spake unto me again, and said, Go and take the little book which is open in the hand of the angel which standeth upon the sea and upon the earth.

9 And I went unto the angel, and said unto him, Give me the little book. And he said unto me, Take it, and eat it up; and it shall make thy belly bitter, but it shall be in thy mouth sweet as honey.

10 And I took the little book out of the angel's hand, and ate it up; and it was in my mouth sweet as honey: and as soon as I had eaten it, my belly was bitter.

11 And he said unto me, Thou must prophesy again before many peoples, and nations, and tongues, and kings.

After all that was said in connection with the previous passage, this portion ought not to be difficult to understand in its purpose and significance. You will remember that in this entire chapter we have an interlude, a portion which has no immediate connection with the seven trumpets, but which has been thrown in for a certain definite purpose. The first part of this chapter answered many of the questions which might arise in the hearts of the people of God in the midst of the judgments and tribulations which have already been revealed in the first part of the book and which are still to be shown when the seventh angel shall blow his trumpet. In that passage we are assured that Christ holds the reins, and that although many tribulations may come upon the people of God, He shall nevertheless come, and come quickly, and establish His everlasting kingdom forever. And therefore that first part of the chapter was full of comfort for God's people.

One part of that portion connects itself immediately with the passage which we are now called to discuss. I refer, of course, to the little book which is in the hand of the angel who stands upon the earth and the sea. That little book we have as yet not discussed. All that we have said about

it is the unique occurrence of the voice of the seven thunders, which told
us that in that form John might not receive the revelation of the mystery
of the kingdom of God. But our present passage informs us in what form
he may receive it, and how he must be a prophet in the midst of the world
of the things which are still to be revealed. If the first part of the chapter
was for the comfort of the people of God and fixed their eyes upon the
mighty King of kings, this part is for their instruction and warns them
beforehand what they must do with the revelation of the future which
John receives. For in the hand of the angel there is a little book. That little
book must not merely be read and copied by the true prophet, but it must
be eaten. And only after it has thus been appropriated do we read that
John is prepared to be a prophet and to prophesy again to many peoples,
and nations, and tongues, and kings.

The Meaning Of The Little Book

Again I must call your attention to the fact which I have mentioned
more than once, namely, that the Book of Revelation itself determines
rather plainly whether anything is to be understood in the symbolical or in
the literal sense of the word. Disregard of this truth has led many
interpreters of the book into paths of error. And therefore we must
maintain it and point to it whenever we have the opportunity. We cannot
draw one line and say that all that is revealed in the book must be taken in
the symbolical sense: for then we become guilty of allegorizing and
spiritualizing in the wrong sense of the word. Nor can we say that all that
is revealed in this book must be taken in the literal sense: for then we
arrive at absurdities and impossibilities. But we must let the book itself
decide whether anything is meant symbolically or literally. That is also the
case with our present passage. It is more than evident that this entire scene
is not meant in the literal sense of the word. Then, if that were the case,
we would have to assume that there was actually a book in the hand of the
angel, printed in heaven, and that John actually, not in the vision,
approached the angel, took that little book out of his hand, and swallowed
it. Of course, that is both an impossibility and an absurdity. An
impossibility it is, for John could not swallow a book. And if it is
maintained that this is a miraculous swallowing of the book and that with
God all things are possible, we add that it is also an absurdity. For books
are not to be swallowed, but to be read. And one does not derive any
benefit from swallowing a book, but from appropriating its contents by

reading it. Hence, it needs no special indication to make us draw the conclusion immediately that here we have symbolism, not reality, and that John swallows the book in the vision, not apart from the vision. And the question before us is: what is the meaning of this symbolic scene?

To determine this we must, first of all, answer the question: what is the meaning of the little book itself? What is this little book in the hand of the angel, which is swallowed by John?

And then we wish to say at the outset that we do not agree with those interpreters who maintain that this book is the same as the one mentioned in Chapter 5, verse 1, namely, the book with its seven seals. In support of this contention we mention, in the first place, that this is a **little** book; the book with its seven seals was simply a book. In the second place, we must remember that the book with its seven seals was closed and sealed; this book, as it is expressly mentioned, was open. In the third place, as we have stated, that book was not merely a copy of the decree of God with a view to the bringing of the kingdom; but it was the symbol of the decree itself. When that book is opened, and seal after seal is loosed, the decree of God is realized. It cannot be maintained that that book is given to John in order that he should swallow it. And, finally, the book of the seven seals is the property and can be the possession only of the Lamb that was slain. As we noticed in that connection, there was not one who was worthy to open the book and to receive it out of the hand of Him Who sitteth upon the throne. Only the Lamb could take it and break the seals. Hence, it is simply out of the question that this could be the same book. For here it is offered to John, and he thoroughly appropriates the same.

But although this is true, it must also be maintained that this little book stands closely related to that book of the seven seals. In the first place, this might be surmised because also this book is found in the hand of the mighty angel, Who, as we have explained, is no one else than the Lord Jesus Christ Himself, the Lamb that was slain. And, in the second place, we notice that when John eats this little book, the effect of it is that he must prophesy again before many peoples, and nations, and tongues, and kings. That other book decided the fate of the peoples and nations and tongues and kings. It was the decree itself regarding them, and that with a view to the bringing of the kingdom of God. This little book makes John a prophet with regard to many peoples and nations and tongues and kings. The conclusion is that this little book reveals to John something from the book with its seven seals. It is a copy, a partial copy, of that book, – a copy in human form, so that John and the church can understand it. It is a **partial** copy, in the first place, because the full decree of God is infinite and cannot be completely revealed. Many things that are in the book of the seven seals naturally must remain a mystery to us. But partial it is also, in the second place, because much that is contained in the book of the seven seals has already been revealed to John at this stage.

We would say, therefore, that this little book, open in the hand of the angel, is the symbol of all that John still has to prophesy. He did prophesy already in the preceding portion. All that he has prophesied thus far has been revealed and has already been discussed by us. But according to verse 11, he must prophesy again. Still more is to be revealed to John and to the church. Of still more John is to be witness in the midst of the world. And this entire book is the symbol of all that John still must witness in regard to the future of the kingdom of God. And the scene that is pictured to us in the words of our passage shows how John must become prepared to be a prophet to the utmost: a prophet who not merely reveals things, who not merely informs the church and the world of some things with regard to the future, but who himself can be a living witness in the midst of a wicked world.

The Contents Of The Little Book

That this special preparation on the part of John was necessary at this stage will become evident if we consider briefly what this book contains. What is its message? What are the tidings it brings to the church and concerning the world?

As we shall understand, this little book contains the message of the seventh trumpet. Six seals have already been opened, and six trumpets have already been blown before it is deemed necessary that John receives this special preparation. All these six seals and six trumpets revealed the process of history with a view to the completion of the kingdom of God. They revealed that the kingdom would come and be completely realized, on the one hand, by the preaching of the gospel to all nations, but on the other hand, also by means of the judgments of war and famine and pestilence and various visitations upon the world and upon the physical universe. One more trumpet is to be blown. And then, as the mighty angel has sworn, the mystery of God shall have been fulfilled.

What is to be revealed to John in the future, therefore, is the process of things with a view to their consummation. How shall the kingdom come, and what will be the course of history that will destroy the power and the kingdom of darkness and establish the glorious kingdom of God and His Christ? Shall it be a gradual victory of the power of the gospel? Shall the influence of the gospel gradually spread, so that at the end, at the time of the close of history, all nations shall have embraced the Christ at His coming? How shall these things be? It is to those questions that, in the succeeding chapters, John receives the answer. It is of these truths that he must prophesy also in the future in the midst of the world. And it is for the prophesying of these things that a special preparation is required and symbolically pictured in the words of our passage.

If we glance over the rest of the book and notice what things John must still prophesy concerning many peoples and nations and tongues and kings, we soon surmise why indeed he was in need of this special preparation. For it is not a pleasing message, it is not a message of peace and gradual development which he brings. But it is a message of judgment and battle and destruction and vengeance. He speaks of the fate of the holy city and of the temple and of the two witnesses who are killed in the city and taken to heaven on account of the testimony which they give. He speaks of an awful conflict between the woman who brings forth the manchild and the dragon who attempts to destroy the child but fails. He speaks of the beast which comes out of the sea and the beast out of the earth, and of the terrible things that they do in the earth. He speaks of the development and power of Antichrist and his war upon the people of God, of tribulation and oppression for the sake of the cause of Christ and His kingdom. He makes mention of Babylon, the great harlot, describes her greatness among the nations of the world, but also pictures her final destruction. He pictures the effect of the outpouring of the seven vials of wrath and of the complete drying up of the great river, so that the nations rise for war against Zion. He speaks of the binding, but also of the loosing, of the devil and of all that follows. And only after all this has happened, and all these terrible things have been predicted, he pictures the heavenly Jerusalem coming down out of heaven, and the new heavens and the new earth in which righteousness shall dwell.

In a word, the message which John the prophet must still bring is a tremendous, a terrible message. It is not a message which concerns but part of the world and of creation, but which is as wide in its significance as creation itself and which involves many peoples and nations and tongues, which involves with special mention kings, the great and powerful of the earth. It is, moreover, a message which is awful in its significance for all who do not really belong to the people of the kingdom, a message which does not speak of peace, but very definitely conveys the truth, "There is no peace for the wicked, saith my God." No peace till the end of the world, no peace as long as Satan and his kingdom of darkness still exist and wage war against the kingdom of the Lord may be expected. It is a message of judgment and affliction and tribulation and vengeance, a message of persecution and sacrifice even for the people of God, a message which will separate the spirits definitely. And only through all these things, awful and dark for the world, it finally appears as a message of joy for all who love the day of our Lord Jesus Christ. And of that universal, tremendous, awful, but also joyous message John must be witness, a living witness, together with all the ministers, and, finally, together with all the church of God. And therefore he must be prepared; and not only he, but the ministers and the church of God must be prepared. And the way of sound and thorough preparation is indicated in the rest of the text.

The Eating Of The Little Book

What must John do with the book?

He tells us that he heard the same voice from heaven which he heard before. It is the voice which had spoken to him when he heard the voice of the seven thunders and when he was about to write down what they spoke. It is therefore a voice which directs him in this entire scene of preparation. First it warns him not to write down what the seven thunders spoke. These seven thunders, as I surmise, spoke very plainly. But John cannot become prepared truly by simply writing down what they said. He must not merely be informed as to the truth of the future, but something else must take place. And therefore this directing voice he now hears again. And it instructs him to approach the angel who stands upon the sea and upon the earth and who holds the little book in his left hand and to ask for the book. And as John does so, and asks the angel to give him the book, the latter instructs him further as to what he must do with it. The book is open, and therefore it can simply be read. But he must not read the book, but must do something else with it. The book is open, and it contains the revelation of the future, no doubt. And therefore John might simply copy it and inform the church of its contents. But he must not copy it. No, he must do nothing less than take the book and eat it, swallow it, and thus make it part of himself.

Once more, in order to understand this scene and its significance we must bear in mind that here we have the symbolical signification of the preparation of John and every true witness of Christ in the world as a prophet. John must be a prophet. He must be a living witness of the truth of God. He must bear the truth of God into the world and speak of tremendous things in which the church and the whole world, in which nations and kings, are involved. And the message he must bring is not one that will be sweet to the taste of the world, but one of woe and judgment. Hence, the message which he must deliver will meet with hatred and opposition in the world. And, of course, the same will be true of the prophet who bears this testimony. The bearer of this woeful message must not expect that all will accept the message unconditionally or stand for its contents. On the contrary, it will be contradicted and opposed. It will be opposed by the wicked world and the power of the Antichrist, that persecutes the church and that hates the truth and will speak of "Peace, peace," when there is no peace. It will be opposed, however, also by the church as it exists in the present dispensation. For many there are in that church who do not truly belong to Christ and His kingdom and who will hate and deny and oppose the message of tribulation and judgment. Also they will shout, "Peace, peace," though there is no peace, and though there cannot possibly be peace. Nay, still stronger: it will sometimes be opposed by the true people of God, who do not always see and understand that in this world the church militant must expect tribulation and judgment in order that the kingdom may come.

It requires spiritual courage, the courage of faith, therefore, to be a prophet of this message. For in spite of all the opposition, the prophet, the bearer of this truth, must insist: "Not a message of peace can I bring, but a message of war and trouble, unto the end of the world." And in order that in spite of this opposition the prophet of this message may stand firm, he receives the command to take and eat the book of this prophecy.

We have a scene similar to this recorded in the Book of Ezekiel, where the preparation of that prophet for his message is told us. In Ezekiel 2:8 to 3:3 we read: "But thou, son of man, hear what I say unto thee; Be not thou rebellious like that rebellious house: open thy mouth, and eat that I give thee. And when I looked, behold, an hand was sent unto me; and, lo, a roll of a book was therein; And he spread it before me; and it was written within and without: and there was written therein lamentations, and mourning, and woe. Moreover he said unto me, Son of man, eat that thou findest; eat this roll, and go speak unto the house of Israel. So I opened my mouth, and he caused me to eat the roll. And he said unto me, Son of man, cause thy belly to eat, and fill thy bowels with this roll that I give thee. Then did I eat it; and it was in my mouth as honey for sweetness."

From this passage it is plain:

1) That it speaks of Ezekiel's preparation as a prophet. He must first eat the roll and fill his bowels with it; then he must go and speak to the house of Israel.

2) That he also must not bring a pleasant message, but a message of woe and mourning and lamentation, and therefore of judgment upon the house of Israel.

3) That the house of Israel is a rebellious and stiffnecked people, so that he must expect opposition and persecution when he comes with the message of woe over them. And naturally, this is a reason that the prophet may become discouraged and afraid.

4) That for that very reason he must eat the book and fill his bowels with it, so that the message may become part of his very system.

If in the light of this Old Testament passage we turn once more to the text we are discussing, all will be plain. The revelation of the future, the message which John must bring, may not remain outside of him, so that he indeed is acquainted with its contents but for the rest is not influenced by it. That would have been the case had he merely quoted what the seven thunders spoke. He would have understood what the future would be, but it would not have controlled him. That would also have been the case had he merely read the little book or copied it. Its contents would still have remained outside of him and would not have influenced his heart and mind and entire life; but he would not have been a true prophet, a living witness, who would stand for the truth in the midst of the world and who would uphold its testimony in spite of opposition and suffering and tribulation. And then he would easily have been silenced by the world of sin and by the hatred against the truth. And therefore the truth must be thoroughly appropriated by the prophet. John must eat the book. He must digest it. He must fill his bowels with it. He must take it into his very system. It must become part of his flesh and blood, of his soul and spirit. It must transform him, change him, make a different man of him, and so strengthen him to bear the testimony which he must give in the midst of the world.

Or, to speak in terms of reality, John must assimilate the contents of this prophecy unto himself. He must understand it, labor with it, believe it, be convinced of its truth and also of the supreme significance of that truth. He must love it and embrace it. Nay, still stronger: the truth of this prophecy must take hold of him. He must first take it to himself and eat it, appropriate it by faith. And after he has thus assimilated the contents of the book, he must come under its power and influence, so that the truth of this prophecy so impresses and dominates him that he can never believe anything else, that he can never say anything else, that he must speak about it, and that he can never be silenced, but boldly testify of all that it reveals in opposition to the world of wickedness and in spite of all that world might do to silence the testimony of the prophet. This is the meaning of the entire passage.

This is the meaning of the passage for John himself.

However, this was not merely revealed for John, so that the passage would have no significance for us at the present time. On the contrary, in the broader sense of the word the church of Christ is the prophet, the living witness of the name of Christ and of His truth in the midst of the world. And in that broader sense, the passage undoubtedly contains a lesson for us all. It teaches us what we must do with the testimony of the Word of God in general, but especially with the testimony of the Book of Revelation. We can study the book and listen to its interpretation from more than one point of view and also from more than one motive. Perhaps we find some intellectual enjoyment in its interpretation. Perhaps we find our curiosity somewhat satisfied. Perhaps, however, we do not appropriate it at all. But all this is not sufficient, and that for the simple reason that the message of the book also demands a positive stand. This is always the case with the testimony of the Word of God. But it is such especially with respect to the book we are now discussing. The question is whether you **believe** all these things.

When that book speaks of the development of the world of sin and iniquity, how it will fight to the last against Christ and His kingdom, the question is: do you actually take these things to be the truth? When the book speaks of the apostate church and pictures that it will ultimately have an alliance with Antichrist, the question is: do you believe that it will be thus? When the book speaks of wars and judgments and tribulations, will you accept that through them all Christ brings His kingdom and that His kingdom will not and cannot come in any other way? If so, the book of this prophecy will determine your stand over against the world. You cannot understand and believe and love the truth of this book and at the same time cry along with the false philosophy of the world. And if the world continues to deny the truth and to trample under foot the blood of Christ and in spite of it maintains that the glorious kingdom of blessing and righteousness will come and dawn upon the world by gradual development, then you will oppose that world, condemn it uncompromisingly, because that blessed kingdom stands against the Christless philosophy of the world and testifies of woe and mourning and lamentation.

But then, you understand, it is not sufficient merely to listen to the sound of this book. Then you must eat it, appropriate it. It must become part of your entire system and control your life, so that you know of only one life, the life of the kingdom of God.

The Effect Of The Little Book

At first sight we would probably think that it was strange that this little book had such an effect upon John. The angel that gives him the book warns him that it will be sweet in his mouth, but bitter in his belly. And thus John actually experiences the effect of his eating of the book.

This phenomenon is generally explained by the different parts of the contents of the book. True, thus interpreters have it, the little book speaks of woe and mourning and lamentation, of bitter things. But it also speaks of joy and peace and everlasting life, of the new heavens and the new earth, of the heavenly Jerusalem that cometh down to stay forever. In a word, the contents of the book are bitter, but also sweet. Thus John experiences it. The book tastes sweet to his mouth, as sweet as honey. But afterwards he realizes the bitter element; it is bitter in his belly.

Yet this interpretation does not satisfy, for various reasons. If that was the truth, then John naturally would taste both the bitter and the sweet from the beginning. If the contents of the book are the cause of it all, then there is no reason to believe that he would taste only the sweet in his mouth and only the bitter in his belly; but then he would notice both elements from the very start. And if it is argued that it is very well possible that one follows the other, I should think that the bitter element would naturally come first. For not the heavenly Jerusalem and the kingdom of peace are first in the experience of the Christian, but the tribulations and judgments are first while the heavenly Jerusalem follows them.

It seems to us, therefore, that a different explanation must be preferred. Now it is an obvious fact that the Word of God is more than once presented in Scripture as being sweet to the mouth of the believers. The psalmist sings of this in Psalm 119:103, when he says: "How sweet are thy words unto my taste; yea, sweeter than honey to my mouth." And again, in Psalm 19:10 the ordinances of Jehovah are spoken of as "sweeter also than honey and the honeycomb." So also in this case John received the revelation of the Word of God. And to the mouth of the believer the Word of God is sweet, never to the unbeliever. To him that Word is nauseating from the beginning. His taste is corrupt. The Word does not even appeal to him, and therefore he does not even swallow the book, but spews it out. But in the case of the believer it is quite different. He has been changed by the grace of God. He has received a new taste, the taste of faith. And to that taste of faith the Word of God appeals, always appeals, so that he takes it and eats it whenever that Word is given him. But does this mean that this same Word has no bitter after-effects when it reaches the spiritual digestive organs? By no means; the process of assimilation and digestion is often a painful one, not because that Word is deceiving and different from what it is promised to be, but because the power of sin is still in our hearts and minds. Now the Word has a battle against the influence of the flesh and the lusts thereof. And this battle of the Word, however sweet it was when taken and swallowed by faith, is a painful one. It causes bitterness and struggle till the medicine of the Word of God has done its work and transformed us.

This is especially the case with the word of this prophecy, of the prophecy as we have it in the Book of Revelation. Surely, the book speaks of redemption and of salvation, of heavenly glory and a new creation, of highest joy and eternal life. But the book speaks of this only after it has pictured the battle of faithful witnessing, of self-denial and suffering. It holds before our eyes the glory of the future, but only at the end of a dark and terrible road to travel. It is the road of battle for the kingdom of God. It is the road of persecution and mockery on the part of the world. It is the road alongside of which you may read the notice, "He that shall save his life shall lose it, but he that shall lose his life for my sake shall save it." And that is hard. That is not according to the flesh. That causes inward pain and battle. And thence is the bitterness of the book when it begins to work its work of transformation.

May that also be the result on our part. May the study of this little book in the future have this effect, that it is indeed sweet to our taste because it is the Word of God, sweeter than honey to the taste of faith, so that we do not rebel but swallow it, eat it, and hide it in our inmost heart. But may it also have this result, that when it begins its work of transformation, the truth of the book may at first seem painful as it mortifies the old man, and more and more leave nothing but one desire, that the kingdom of God may come. That should be the effect of our assimilating this little book of prophecy.

Chapter XXV

The Measuring Of The Temple

(Revelation 11:1, 2)

1 And there was given me a reed like unto a rod: and the angel stood, saying, Rise, and measure the temple of God, and the altar, and them that worship therein.
2 But the court which is without the temple leave out, and measure it not; for it is given unto the Gentiles: and the holy city shall they tread under foot forty and two months.

The eleventh chapter of the Book of Revelation is one of the most important chapters of the entire book. It is not a chapter easy to be understood in its full significance, and yet it is of the utmost importance that we do understand the meaning of it as clearly as possible. If we understand this chapter not only as such but also in its relation to the sequel of the entire book, we will have less difficulty to grasp the significance of the rest of the book. But misunderstanding of the chapter which we must now discuss leads us in the wrong direction with regard to practically all that follows.

We have in this portion a general picture of the church as she exists in the present dispensation, a general description of the line of development which must be expected in the future, a general outline of the great battle the church will be called upon to fight throughout this dispensation, but especially toward the end. And at the same time we have in this chapter a brief indication of how the church in special times will receive special grace and strength and how she shall finally be delivered even before the time of the end. All the great truths which the Lord Jesus Christ has already predicted in His discourses about His second coming, — the development and struggle, the great tribulation of the church, but also the shortening of the days for the sake of the elect, — are pictured to us here in a very general outline. And therefore we may rightly say that here we have a general description of what will be presented to us in detail in the rest of the book. It is not as such a revelation of the seventh trumpet; yet it is closely connected with that trumpet. And in the rest of the book we must expect to find many an individual picture taken from the same period that is already described in the chapter we are now considering. In the future we shall understand the relation of this chapter to the rest of the book better than we are able to grasp the connection at this point. But this brief warning we have to sound so that we may the more pay attention to what the Spirit saith unto the churches, set ourselves to make prayerful study also of this part of the book of comfort, and set ourselves to give heed to the warnings issued in the preceding chapter, namely, that we must eat, that we must thoroughly appropriate, the contents of the little book, so that they may determine our entire life.

The Temple

Concerning the text under discussion at present there need be no misunderstanding whatsoever. John is called in the vision to do something. A reed, a measuring rod, is given him; and the commission is given him that with this reed he must proceed to the holy city, Jerusalem, and measure the temple.

It may be said from the outset that although he is called to measure the temple only, distinction is made between three different areas. In the first place, the text makes mention of the temple as such, the sanctuary proper, the building of the temple, along with its holy and most holy places and the altar and the people who congregate there for worship. In the second place, mention is made of the outer court, the open space which surrounds the temple building proper in distinction from the temple as such. And, in the third place, the text speaks of a still wider area, namely, the holy city, which shall be surrendered, together with the outer court, to the Gentiles, to be trodden under foot forty and two months. Three areas, therefore, are spoken of. The widest is the holy city itself. Within that is the narrower space of the outer court. And again, within that outer court is the still more limited space of the temple proper. And with regard to these three John is commissioned to measure the temple and the altar and those that worship therein, while he must not measure the outer court, nor, of course, the holy city. And he is told that only the temple will remain undefiled, but that the outer court and the holy city will be surrendered, or rather, is surrendered by this measuring to the power and the mercy of the Gentiles. This rather general picture of the text must, in the first place, be clearly understood; and from it we must draw our conclusion with regard to the explanation.

So far, then, there is no difficulty, and there can be no difference of opinion. But a different story it becomes when we ask the further question: how must we conceive of this part of the book? Must we take it all in the literal sense of the word, so that the temple means the holy place and most holy place as they once stood in Jerusalem, the outer court refers literally to the space surrounding the temple, and the holy city is literally the capital of the holy land as it once stood in all its glory but was made a miserable heap of ruins in the year 70 A.D.? It is then that interpreters begin to differ. And it is the choice at this point which will determine our entire view of the chapter, and, in fact, largely of the entire book in its sequel.

There are many interpreters who maintain that we must take this all in the literal sense of the word. Many maintain that at this period the church is already in heaven and has nothing to do with the tribulation of this present time any more. At the call from heaven to John to "come up hither," the church has followed the apostle and therefore has nothing to do any more with matters mundane, but rejoices in her salvation. And because this is the case, the possibility that by temple in this case the church might be indicated is ruled out from the beginning. No, the text pictures to us merely the condition of the latter days. Jerusalem is again to be built. The temple is to be restored. The Jews shall again worship in that temple in connection with the altars of incense and of burnt offering. And the old Jewish glory shall for a time shine forth once more. Only, they shall not be unmolested. On the contrary, the Antichrist shall come and shall claim a large part of this territory. He shall capture the holy city and shall lay siege to the temple. He shall take possession of the outer court, and he shall defile this part of the possession of the holy people. Only the sanctuary proper shall not be delivered into his power. From that sanctuary proper the witnesses shall appear and testify of the name of their great King till the enemy shall overpower them. In a word, what we have in our text must be taken in the most literal sense of the word. Jerusalem is the holy city; the outer court is the court of the temple; the temple is the Old Testament sanctuary restored; and the people who worship there are Jews; and the nations shall literally trample under foot the holy city and the court.

We cannot possibly agree with this interpretation, and our reasons are the following. In the first place, the idea that the church at this period and before the great tribulation is already in heaven rests upon the very slender and far-fetched and mistaken evidence that John in the vision is "called thither" in Chapter 4, verse 1. This cannot stand for a moment, as we have seen before. For John remained on the earth. And if he represents the church, the church necessarily remains on earth with him. In the second place, we must remember that the Book of Revelation is given for the church and her comfort. The Lord told the church that she must expect tribulation such as never was before. And knowing her need of comfort, He gave her this book that she might stand in the time of trouble. But if this portion merely pertains to the Jews as such, as a nation, and if the church is already in heaven, it stands to reason that the church has nothing to do with the rest of the book whatsoever. It can derive neither instruction nor comfort from it. In the third place, — and this is a far weightier reason, — I find in the entire New Testament, outside then of this particular portion, no mention made of the temple and of Jerusalem in the literal sense of the word. I find abundant warnings to assure the people of the New Testament dispensation that the temple in Jerusalem has served its purpose and that they must not turn again to sacrifice and ceremony. But nowhere do I find any indication that we must expect once more a literal holy city and a literal temple. Hence, if this passage speaks of such a temple, it is the only passage in the New Testament which speaks of such things.

Still more, if this part speaks of a literal temple, I must come to the conclusion that the rest of the New Testament is positively misleading. For, in the first place, we must remember that Christ Himself speaks of the destruction of Jerusalem and of the temple, but never with a word does He speak of the restoration of either or both. Paul repeatedly speaks of the New Testament church as the temple of God, the spiritual temple of the new dispensation. In I Corinthians 3:16 he asks the question, "Know ye not that ye are the temple of God?" thus referring to the church of Christ at Corinth. And in II Corinthians 6:16, with a literal reference to a passage from the Old Testament, he writes: "For ye are the temple of the living God; as God hath said, I will dwell in them, and walk in them; and I will be their God, and they shall be my people."

Again, in his Epistle to the Ephesians, which is based on the very idea that the church, as the body of Christ, is the temple of God, he says, 2:20-22: "And are built upon the foundation of the apostles and prophets,

Jesus Christ himself being the chief cornerstone; In whom all the building fitly framed together groweth unto an holy temple in the Lord: In whom ye also are builded together for an habitation of God through the Spirit." The same is true with regard to the New Testament presentation of Jerusalem. The holy city in the literal sense of the word is never mentioned. But Paul refers to Jerusalem that is above, which is the mother of us all (Galatians 4:25, 26). And in the Epistle to the Hebrews we find that the author speaks of the believers of the New Testament day when he says: "But ye are come unto mount Sion, and unto the city of the living God, the heavenly Jerusalem," (Heb. 12:22). It is, therefore, beyond all dispute that the New Testament speaks of a temple and of a Jerusalem different from that city and that building with which we become acquainted in the Old Testament.

If, therefore, we are inclined to take these terms in the symbolical sense, and refuse to take them literally, we do so with the entire New Testament backing us.

This might not be permissible if the case were thus, that either this portion or other portions in the Book of Revelation indicated that John speaks of the literal temple and the literal city whenever he mentions them. But also this is not the case. On the contrary, even in this very book the temple and Jerusalem are symbolic of something far different. In Chapter 3, verse 12, we read the promise to the church of Thyatira: "Him that overcometh will I make a pillar in the temple of my God, and he shall go no more out: and I will write upon him the name of my God, and the name of the city of my God, which is new Jerusalem, which cometh down out of heaven from my God." Needless to say, neither a literal pillar nor a literal temple nor a literal city are meant. And in Revelation 21:2, 10, 22 we read: "And I John saw the holy city, new Jerusalem, coming down from God out of heaven, prepared as a bride adorned for her husband. And he carried me away in the spirit to a great and high mountain, and shewed me that great city, the holy Jerusalem, descending out of heaven from God. And I saw no temple therein: for the Lord God Almighty and the Lamb are the temple of it."

In the face of all these indications in the New Testament, we dare not assume that without any special mention John would speak of a literal temple and a literal city in the words of our text. But in the light of Scripture we maintain that there is but one possible explanation, namely, that here we have the same symbolic language as elsewhere, and that therefore we must take this passage in the figurative sense of the word. True, many will speak of passages in the Old Testament which seem to prophesy a restoration of the old temple and altar and all its ceremonies. And especially are men fond of pointing to the last chapters of the Book of Ezekiel in order to maintain this point. Of course, we cannot now discuss these portions in detail. But, in the first place, I remind you of the simple rule that in the interpretation of Scripture the Old Testament must be explained in the light of the New. And, in the second place, if the objection is raised that one dare not explain the detailed description of the temple in Ezekiel in the symbolical sense, then I would refer you to the detailed description of Jerusalem in the last chapters of the Book of Revelation, and ask whether you ever hesitate to understand this all in the figurative sense of the word. Once more, therefore, I maintain that the text does not speak of a literal temple and city, but of that temple and of that Jerusalem in the figurative sense of the word that is repeatedly mentioned in the New Testament.

In order to understand the words of our text we must first of all remember that throughout the history of the world a holy city and temple are in the making, — not a city in the literal sense of the word, but a city of which our city is but a vague symbol or type, a city of God. With us a city is constituted of a group of dwellingplaces, sometimes surrounded by a wall or by forts to keep out the enemy. It is simply a habitation or a dwellingplace for men in social communion. So the city of God, which is in the process of completion throughout the history of the world, is the dwellingplace of God Most High. And instead of the dwellingplaces of wood and stone, in this city the people of God constitute the habitations, and in them God dwells in Christ Jesus. Needless to say, this city is the church of Christ, in which God lives and abides in Christ Jesus our Lord.

But now we must consider three stages in the process of completion of this spiritual temple or of this holy city of our God. In the first place, we must have before us the stage of perfection, when that city shall have been perfected and completed. It is pictured to us in the last chapter of this Book of Revelation in highly symbolic language as coming down out of heaven from our God. We shall discuss this in detail when we reach that passage. But here we must note one peculiarity which is mentioned with special emphasis in that connection, namely, that in that city there is no temple, for the Lord God and the Lamb are the temple thereof. Now the question is: what does that mean? Why is there no temple in this city?

And the answer is also very evident: in the state of perfection the city and the temple are one, they are completely identified. As long as there is a temple in a city, it shows that God does not yet dwell in the entire city, but merely in that particular house which is called the temple. There He lives in separation from the rest of the city. To be sure, He dwells in the city, but not in the entire city. He does not fill the city. That shall be no more the case in the state of perfection. When the holy city shall have been completed, there shall be no special dwellingplace of God in the city, for the simple reason that He shall dwell in the entire city, that is, in the heart of every citizen. You do not have to enter the city and ask, "Where is the house of God?" For the city itself is God's dwellingplace, and the temple and the city have become identical. That is the ideal. That state must be reached. And all history must serve to bring that city of God to completion.

But that city has not yet reached its state of perfection in this dispensation. And therefore we must place ourselves, in the second place, before the question: how does that city exist here upon earth? How does it reveal itself?

And then there is a difference between the old and the new dispensation. In the old dispensation that city existed typically in Jerusalem, the capital of the land of Canaan. It was the type of the eternal habitation, the eternal holy city. For that reason it is called more than once "the city of God" (Psalms 46:4; 48:1; Isaiah 60:14). It is called "the city of the great king" (Psalm 48:1; Matthew 4:5); "the city of truth" (Zechariah 8:3); "the city of righteousness" (Isaiah 1:26); "the faithful city" (Isaiah 1:21, 26); "the holy city" (Nehemiah 11:1; Isaiah 48:2); "the throne of the Lord" (Jeremiah 3:17). It is very plain that these appellations are not given to the city because of any inherent truth and holiness and faithfulness. For then, indeed, these names are but poorly chosen. Spiritually, our chapter informs us, the city is also called Sodom and Egypt. And in the prophets of the Old Testament we read time and again that they denounce the city in the name of the Lord because of its unrighteousness and unholiness, its shedding of blood and its adultery, its idolatry and abominations. It is in that city also where our Lord is crucified. But it is called holy, the faithful, the righteous city, the throne of the Lord, and the city of God, for no other reason than that it was a type of the heavenly Jerusalem and that the Lord dwelt there.

But we must remember that Jerusalem was but a very imperfect type. It is rather a type of the spiritual city of God in the present dispensation than of that city in its state of final perfection. For in Jerusalem there was a temple. God did not dwell in all the city. His presence did not fill the city, but He dwelt in a particular house. If you entered Jerusalem as a stranger, you would not immediately be aware of the presence of God, but you would naturally ask, "Where does the Lord dwell in this city?" And the answer would naturally be: "In the temple, on Mt. Moriah."

But even here we must once more distinguish. If we imagine that we approach the temple at the time when the Lord was on earth, — the form of the temple which John undoubtedly had in mind, the temple of Herod, since John never knew any other, — then we must not imagine that the Lord dwelt in all that was called the temple. On the contrary, entering this temple from the right, as worshippers were wont to do, we would find ourselves first of all in a wide, open space, a large square, seven hundred fifty feet each way, — the court of the temple. It was called the court of the Gentiles, for the reason that it was open to all, Jew and Gentile, and one need not enter here for the purpose of worshipping. It is in the midst of this court, the court of the Gentiles, or the outer court, that the temple building proper stood in all its splendor, the sanctuary of Jehovah, with its court of the women, its court of the priests and of Israel, its holy and most holy place, its altars and its throng of worshippers. There was the place for real worship. There was the altar of burnt offering, as well as the altar of incense. There were the chests, or trumpets, where the worshippers might drop their gifts to the Lord. There was the place of atonement and of the worship of our God. We must distinguish, therefore, between three things:

1) Jerusalem was as a whole the city of God, known as such over the earth, the city of God in contrast with the city of Babylon.

2) But in this holy city the Lord dwelt in a special place, the temple on Mt. Zion.

3) And even in that temple we must again distinguish between the outer court and the sanctuary proper, in which latter the Lord dwelt in the literal sense of the word.

But now all this outward show has disappeared in the new dispensation. The temple and the holy city still exist, but no more as a city and a temple built of wood and stone. There is no more such a temple. There is no more such a city. There is no more such an altar built with hands. But the temple is the church, or, in the broader sense, the temple and Jerusalem constitute the church of the living God. And Christ Jesus is our altar of atonement and reconciliation in that city of our God.

But, — and this is exactly what we must remember with regard to the New Testament church, — although the outward form of wood and stone is no more, the distinction between Jerusalem, the outer court, and the temple proper still exists and holds good. And it is on the basis of that truth that we must explain the words of our text. Jerusalem in its broadest sense is the representation of the New Testament manifestation of the entire church, of all Christianity, of all who are baptized, of the entire Christian world, of all nominal Christians. Just as all the citizens of Jerusalem were nominally inhabitants of the city of God in the old dispensation, so also all the so-called Christians belong nominally to the church of God, the spiritual Jerusalem of the new dispensation.

But within this great city of the Christian world one must distinguish between three different classes. In the first place, in this nominally Christian world there is the false church, the church that has openly cast away her Christian garment, that has openly renounced the great truths of sin and guilt, of atonement and redemption, of the divinity of Christ, and the vicarious atonement and sacrifice of our Lord. This false church still calls itself Christian, yea, what is more, still calls itself a church. It lays stress even on Christianity in our time, and it demands that the church shall be up and doing, shall perform all kinds of Christian labors and shall redeem all humanity. It cries out that the church must bring the kingdom of God. But it denies the Christ as the Savior of His people, and thereby denies its own character as church of Christ Jesus. It is the false church, the church that still insists that it is a church, but that has openly cast aside even the semblance of the church of Christ. It is Jerusalem sacrificing to Moloch, filled with abomination, the city of God serving the devil. In the second place, there is also in the New Testament church the outer court. It represents the show-church, that part of Jerusalem which outwardly pretends to belong to the true church, subscribes to its confession, feigns to believe in the great truths of atonement and redemption, but is inwardly hypocritical. They are the tares among the wheat. They go with God's people to His temple for worship, but they never enter the spiritual sanctuary of the fellowship of God. They remain in the outer court. Also they are in the church, as our Lord Himself has so plainly indicated in His parable of the tares. And, finally, there are the real, spiritual people of God, the invisible church, the body of Christ, the real temple and sanctuary proper, where God dwells, and where the people worship at the altar of Christ in spirit and in truth. They are represented by the temple which John must measure. Three distinctions, therefore, there were in Old Jerusalem: the city of Jerusalem proper, the outer court, and finally the temple. So there are also three distinctions in the spiritual Jerusalem of the New Testament day: the Christian world, or the false church; the show-church; and the true church of God, the spiritual people of the Lord. It is to these that our text refers plainly.

The Measuring And Its Meaning

But now we must still answer the question: what is the meaning of what John is commissioned to do?

We read that a reed is given unto him and that the reed looked like a rod. Now a reed is merely a measuring instrument, a stick to measure the dimensions of something. But evidently the purpose is not that John shall ascertain the size of Jerusalem and of the outer court, nor of the temple. But it is said with special mention that the reed looked like a rod. Now the rod is in Scripture a symbol of royal dominion and power. It is equivalent to a royal scepter, with this difference, that the rod at the same time symbolizes physical power to execute authority. Thus we read in Psalm 2:9: "Thou shalt break them with a rod of iron." And again, in Revelation 2:26, 27 we read: "And he that overcometh,...to him will I give power over the nations; And he shall rule them with a rod of iron." And therefore, the idea that is implied in this measuring is not merely that of ascertaining the size, but also that of dominion and authority. He must measure indeed, and therefore answer the question, "How large?" And, in the second place, he must measure, touch with a rod, and therefore use the symbol of dominion. And thus we conclude that by this measuring John must answer the question: how large is the real, spiritual dominion of the Lord Jesus in the holy city as it appears in this dispensation?

And then we find that this act of measuring results at the same time in separation. If John had proceeded on his own account, he would probably have measured all of Jerusalem and claimed the whole city for the Lord Jesus Christ. Or, if he would not have done this, he would at least have laid the rod of dominion over the outer court and claimed that all that was within belonged to the Lord of all. But he is directed differently. He must not measure Jerusalem; he must not measure the outer court. But he must simply confine himself to the temple proper, to the sanctuary building that stands within the court. That part of the temple where the altar is, and the true worshippers, must be touched as belonging to the dominion of Christ. All the rest cannot be claimed. And therefore, if the question is asked, "What is the size of Christ's true, spiritual dominion here upon earth?" the answer is: the size of the temple building proper, and that only. And if the question is asked again, "How many are the spiritual subjects of Christ in this dispensation?" the answer is again: as many as worship within the sanctuary of God at the altar of reconciliation. But one more thing we must notice. While the temple is thus separated from Jerusalem and even from the outer court, the court and the city are identified. For so we read: the outer court, together with the city, shall be given to the Gentiles to be trampled under foot. The court, which seems so closely connected with the temple, is separated from it and is identified with the city and is surrendered to the Gentiles.

If now we turn away from the symbolism and ask ourselves the question, "What is the meaning of all this?" the answer is ready. We are taught here in symbolic language not only what is the essential condition of the church in the new dispensation, but also what shall be its outward manifestation towards the end, at the coming of our Lord Jesus Christ.

As we have seen, in the church in the broader sense of the word are false Christians. There is the false church, which even denies the real Christ. In the church are, in the second place, the outward worshippers, the hypocrites, who do not spiritually belong to the church. And, finally, in the church are the real people of God. All this is pictured to us in the words of our text. By commissioning John to measure with his rod of dominion, the Lord reminds us that we must not expect that all Christianity belongs to Christ in the real sense of the word, that not even all the seeming, outward Christians, the show-Christians, belong to His dominion, and that many of whom we believe that they belong to the spiritual body of Christ will not enter in. That, in the first place. But still more is indicated here. Although essentially both the false Christians and the hypocrites always are separated from God's people, always are enemies of Christ, always defile with their presence the holy city and trample it under foot, yet the time shall come when they shall do so openly. It is now the time of the seventh trumpet. And those who still profess to be Christians, but are not, whether they have been hypocrites, of whom we thought they were faithful, or whether they were openly deniers of the

Christ though coming with a show of outward Christianity and good works, they shall reveal themselves as enemies of the true church and of Christ. Also this is indicated in these words. The hypocrites shall identify themselves with the open unbelievers; and all together shall form the enemy of the church, which shall trample the holy city under foot.

As to the forty-two months that are mentioned in our text, I shall have occasion to refer to this again. Let it be sufficient now to call your attention to the fact that forty-two months, twelve hundred sixty days, a time and times and a half a time, mentioned by Daniel, – three and a half years, – are all the same. And if we ask what period is represented by these forty-two months or twelve hundred sixty days, then I think we find the key to this explanation in the twelfth chapter of this book, where we are told that the church is in the wilderness twelve hundred sixty days. There it is very plain that the church is in the wilderness from the time of the exaltation of Christ to the time of His return in the clouds. And therefore twelve hundred sixty days are symbolic of the entire period of the present dispensation. This is also true of the forty-two months. All during this dispensation the church shall conceal in its bosom the false church and the show-church. All through this dispensation, as John already tells us in his epistles, the Antichrist shall be there in principle, only with this difference, that toward the end he shall openly reveal himself and intentionally trample under foot the holy city, as secretly he had done all the time. So it is also in the seventh chapter of the Book of Daniel, where we are told that the time of the fourth beast shall be time, times, and a half, or three and a half times. And if we remember that seven is the period of the completion of God's plan with regard to His kingdom, covering the entire period from the creation of the world to the final restoration of all things, remember that three and a half is half of seven, we shall all the more clearly understand that it is the time indicated between the first and second coming of Christ that is here meant. And as far as the forty-two is concerned, we will notice that it is employed every time of the power of the Antichrist, both here and in Chapter 13. The time he has is indicated by the number forty-two. Seven is the number of completion of the kingdom of God. Six is the number of the beast, the number of man. Six times seven indicates that the power of evil shall attempt to destroy the kingdom of God, and thus finish his work. But at the same time it indicates that he shall fail. He shall come to the six times seven, but he shall not reach the seven times seven. His work shall be a failure. He shall not succeed in destroying the kingdom of God and in establishing his own kingdom.

This is at the same time the great lesson of this portion of the Book of Revelation. The text tells us that there are in the bosom of Christianity the false church, the show-church, and the true church. Hence, we must never expect that all Christianity is Israel in the true sense of the word. In the end many shall fall away openly and shall identify themselves with the false church, from which Antichrist shall come. But at the same time, the true children of God must not be afraid, neither be amazed. If they should find that in the end many should fall away from the church, from the holy city, nay, from the temple proper, and add themselves to Antichrist, they must not fear. For all these things must needs come to pass. Christ rules! The power of Antichrist can come only to the number forty-two. Seven times seven it cannot reach. And, as we shall see, before the darkest darkness of night Christ shall take His church to heaven, and the temple of God shall be perfected in eternal glory.

Chapter XXVI
The Identity Of The Two Witnesses
(Revelation 11:3, 4)

3 And I will give power unto my two witnesses, and they
shall prophesy a thousand two hundred and threescore
days, clothed in sackcloth.
4 These are the two olive trees, and the two candlesticks
standing before the God of the earth.

The portion of the Book of Revelation which we are now discussing
speaks of the famous two witnesses. Of these the chapter tells us who they
are, what they must do, who rises against them, and what finally becomes
of them. In connection with the verses now under discussion, we must
answer the first question: who are these two witnesses. Our answer to this
question is important: for it determines, to an extent, our answer to the
other questions about these witnesses.

Various Theories As To Their Identity

The text says: "And I will give power unto my two witnesses, and they
shall prophesy a thousand two hundred and threescore days." There can
be little question but that it is Christ Who is here speaking. In the first
place, the close connection of this chapter with the preceding, where the
mighty angel with his feet on the earth and on the sea was the speaker,
leads us to this conclusion. But above all, the fact that the voice speaks not
of two witnesses, but definitely of "**my** two witnesses" makes it plain
beyond a possibility of error that the Christ is speaking. And the meaning
of the peculiar Hebraistic construction of the text is: "I will give that my
two witnesses shall prophesy a thousand two hundred and threescore days.
I will give unto my two witnesses all that they need so that they may not
keep silence, but witness for me and my cause in the midst of the world
which has no knowledge of me and of my cause."

Numerous are the answers given to the question as to the identity of
these two witnesses. In fact, you can hardly conceive of a question with a

greater variety of answers than this. All the ingenuity of man has sometimes been brought into play in order to find an answer to this question. Now it must undoubtedly be admitted that this is one of the most difficult questions in the Apocalypse, and that it behooves us to start out with the confession that without the aid of the entire Word of God and the enlightening power of the Holy Spirit we shall never be able to find certainty and satisfaction in regard to it. But on the other hand, our faith that the Book of Revelation must be explained by the rest of the Word of God and that the Holy Spirit will indeed enlighten our minds if we will diligently seek aid from Him is also in this case by no means disappointing. It will be well that we pause for a moment to find out what answers have been given to the question by different interpreters throughout the history of the church.

There are, in the first place, a number of interpreters who take this chapter to refer to the literal destruction of Jerusalem, but then as being an ideal picture of the judgment in the last days. But we do not have to pause very long to discuss this interpretation, seeing that it is an established fact that at the time when John received this revelation Jerusalem and the temple were already destroyed. Nor can one easily understand how this could be a picture of the destruction of Jerusalem in the year 70 A.D., since nothing that is depicted in the chapter before us was realized at that time. Not only a tenth part of the city was destroyed, but the whole of it. Nor was it thus, that only the city and the outer court were trampled under foot; but the temple proper was destroyed as well. Besides, where in this time do we find even an approximation to the two witnesses who are here mentioned in that awful destruction. And therefore we may safely conclude that this interpretation is surely not the true one.

On the other hand, there have been a large number of interpreters who have found in this chapter a reference to the period preceding the Protestant Reformation. The two witnesses are the Bible, the Old and New Testaments. The thousand two hundred and threescore days must be taken in the prophetical sense of the word, a day standing for a year, and therefore referring to a period of twelve hundred sixty years. And this period is found to be realized in the years of struggle preceding the Reformation. Jerusalem is the city of God, but represented by papal Rome. For a long time the witnesses of the Old and New Testament sound their testimony against the gradually growing corruption of the Roman Catholic Church, but it is all in vain. The corruption grows and develops, till finally it reaches its climax a few years before the Reformation. The testimony is actually silenced for a time, and the two witnesses are killed. In the year 1513 a papal bull is issued which apparently finishes all opposition to the Romish Church and silences every voice of truth. But three and a half days, that is, exactly three years and a half later, in the fall of 1517 Luther nails his theses to the church of Wittenberg; and the witnesses are raised from the dead, while, at the same time, they are taken to heaven, that is, placed in a sphere of safety, so that the enemy can silence them no more. This interpretation naturally finds its origin in the reformers, who had to fight such a hard battle and were so bitterly oppressed and persecuted by the power of the Roman Catholic Church. It is the favorite explanation of all who see in the pope the Antichrist and in the Roman Catholic Church his power.

Now we must not be too hasty in condemning this view. There is undoubtedly an element of truth in it. Throughout the history of this dispensation, as we know from the Word of God, Antichrist exists. Already John tells his contemporaries that Antichrist is in the world. He is not a power that arises all of a sudden while it has not been in the world before, but a power that always is in the world, always opposes the church and the development of the kingdom, always sneaks behind the heel of the seed of the woman, and gradually develops in power, till in the latter days it shall display a power as never before manifested. And so we may safely admit that in the days of the Reformation the pope and the papacy was one of the manifestations of the beast of the abyss at that time. The Roman Catholic Church was indeed the false church of the time, and those who stood openly for the truth indeed were the two witnesses at that period. But the error of this interpretation is exactly that it limits itself to that one period. It is not true that the pope is the only manifestation of the Antichrist. Nor is it true that he finds his power only in the Roman Catholic Church. This is indeed a dangerous view to maintain. Also now the Antichrist is in the world. Yet it must not be maintained that he appears most vividly in the Roman Catholic Church of today. Also the false church is in the world. Yet we would deceive ourselves and please the devil if, to find it, we would merely look at the Romish Church. And therefore, although there is an element of truth in such an interpretation, nevertheless its limitation to one period of the history of this dispensation is at the same time its condemnation.

The early church fathers and also many interpreters of today who follow them explain the two witnesses as referring to Enoch and Elijah, who shall return to earth in the literal sense of the word. Those who hold this view maintain that the text speaks very definitely of two individuals, persons, not indefinitely to be spiritualized into either powers or institutions. Christ says very definitely "my two witnesses," and therefore speaks of witnesses which He already has, of witnesses who are well-known and who shall come to earth to bear testimony of His name. And no two known individuals of Scripture better fit the requirements than Enoch and Elijah. The Scriptural references on which this interpretation is based are found both in the Old and in the New Testament. In the prophecy of Malachi, 4:5, we read: "Behold, I will send you Elijah the prophet, before the coming of the great and dreadful day of the Lord." And in the New Testament we find repeated reference to Elijah and his coming. The people of Israel, the scribes especially, clearly expected his return. And in Matthew 17:10, 11 we read that the disciples come to the Lord with the question, "Why then say the scribes that Elias must first come?" And the Lord answered: "Elias truly shall first come, and restore all things." And therefore it would seem plain that Scripture actually teaches a literal return of Elijah to the earth and that in this portion we have that return pictured to us. True, we do not read of the return of Enoch. But, in the first place, there are many sources outside of Scripture that express the expectation of the return of Enoch as well. And, in the second place, there is but one person who in the days of the old dispensation was like Elijah and shows all the characteristics of these two witnesses. Both Enoch and Elijah were witnesses in a time of general apostasy. Both Enoch and Elijah spoke of judgment and evidently did terrible things. Both Enoch and Elijah escaped death and were taken into heaven. And so these interpreters have it that both these great witnesses will return to the earth bodily, that they will once more witness of the name of the Most High in a time of great apostasy, that they, however, shall finally be killed by Antichrist, shall be raised from the dead, and shall ascend to heaven,—all in the literal sense of the word.

Again I would say that there is an element of truth also in this interpretation. I think that in Enoch and Elijah we have clear types of these two witnesses and what shall happen to them. But the mistake also in this interpretation is exactly that it is limited to these men in the literal sense of the word. This limitation makes the interpretation, in the first place, in the highest degree improbable. For I cannot imagine that Enoch and Elijah, who have not only been taken to heaven, but who have also been translated and who are now in glory, shall once more return in corruptible bodies to this earth of corruption, testify and suffer and be killed, and then rise again and go to heaven. But, in the second place, this limitation makes it to be in conflict with Scripture. True, the Lord says that Elijah cometh, but we must not forget that in this same portion He also says: "But I say unto you, That Elias is come already, and they knew him not, but have done unto him whatsoever they listed. Likewise shall also the Son of man suffer of them." And the clear remark is added: "Then the disciples understood that he spake unto them of John the Baptist." And in the eleventh chapter of the same gospel Jesus says with reference to John the Baptist: "For this is he, of whom it is written, Behold, I send my messenger before thy face, who shall prepare thy way before thee." And again, "And if ye will receive it, this is Elias which was for to come." If we take into account these Scriptural references, clear in themselves, we have no difficulty. Then we shall no longer maintain the strange notion that in the literal sense of the word Enoch and Elijah shall return; but we shall understand that these men, and especially Elijah, were types. They were powerful witnesses themselves, in the first place. In John the Baptist Elijah returns again as a powerful witness to the people. And so also it must be expected that again such witnesses shall come, according to our chapter, who shall sound their testimony before a perverted generation. Also in this interpretation, therefore, there is an element of truth. Not, indeed, as if these two prophets of the old dispensation shall return literally, but in the sense that Enoch and Elijah, and, in fact, Noah and Moses and many others, must be taken as types of the witnesses who are mentioned in the words of our text.

The Key To Their Identification

There are still other interpretations. But these are the most important. And we rather turn to the text, to see whether it can be ascertained with a reasonable amount of certainty who are meant by these two witnesses.

We then remind you of our explanation of the first two verses, in the first place. Jerusalem stands for Christendom in the broadest sense of the word. Outside of the court and the temple it symbolizes the false church, that part of Christianity which still claims to belong to it, but in the meantime tramples under foot the blood of Christ and denies the great truths of atonement and redemption in the blood of the Savior. The outer court stands for the show-church, or the hypocrites, who indeed enter the temple in the outward sense but never worship in spirit and in truth. These two essentially belong together. And the temple proper stands for the true church of Jesus Christ. It is in that condition, and during the period when the church is in that condition, that the two witnesses give their testimony, that is, during this entire dispensation, as we have seen. It is, therefore, a testimony which arises from the true church, from the midst of the true, spiritual children of God. It is a testimony which must serve two purposes, no doubt. It must testify against the wickedness of the false church and the show-church, a testimony which preaches hell and damnation to all who do not believe in Jesus Christ as the King and Redeemer. And, at the same time, it is a testimony which must serve to strengthen the true believers. And that the time of their testimony, although being of the same length as the forty-two months and the three and a half years, is nevertheless expressed in terms of **days**, twelve hundred sixty days, shows that it is a continual testimony which they give.

Hence, from the context we gather the following. First of all, the testimony for which we must look is a continual testimony all through this dispensation, from the exaltation of Christ to His second coming. It is during this period that the false and the show-church, as well as the true church, exist. It is during this same period that the testimony of these witnesses is heard. It is a testimony which is naturally heard from the true church of Christ: not from the city at large, not from the outer court, but from the temple building proper. It is a testimony of repentance and sin against the false church and the show-church. And these witnesses are preachers of repentance, as is at the same time indicated by their being girded with sackcloth. It is a testimony for the truth of Christ and for the strengthening of the true believers.

But we must now turn to the fourth verse of the chapter, for there, evidently, we have the key to the entire explanation. There we read: "These are the two olive trees, and the two candlesticks standing before the God of the earth." The plain reference here is to Zechariah 4. For there we read in the fourteenth verse, in answer to the question of the prophet concerning the identity of the two olive trees: "These are the two anointed ones, that stand by the Lord of the whole earth." Here, therefore, is the key. The two witnesses are the two olive trees and also the candlesticks there mentioned, so the text tells us. Hence, the answer to the question as to who are the two olive trees and the candlesticks in

Zechariah 4 is at the same time the correct answer to the question who are meant by the two witnesses.

Zechariah the prophet receives a vision. He beholds in the vision a candlestick with seven lamps. Above the candlestick he sees a golden bowl, or reservoir, filled with oil. This bowl of oil above the candlestick is connected with the lamps by means of seven pipes, through which they are supplied with oil from the bowl in order to give light. He beholds, further, on each side of the bowl an olive tree. These olive trees are again connected with the bowl above the candlestick, so that from them the oil continually pours into the bowl, and from the bowl into the lamps. That is the vision: a candlestick receiving its oil from a bowl above it, which in turn receives its oil from the two olive trees.

Their Identity

What is the meaning of this vision? Also that is given in the chapter.

The general meaning is a message to Zerubbabel: "Not by might, nor by power, but by my Spirit, saith the Lord." After the captivity Zerubbabel must be instrumental in the rebuilding of the temple. But in this work he meets with opposition from the imperial or world power. He can make no headway. And now this vision tends to instruct Zerubbabel that by the Spirit of the Lord the opposition of the world power shall be brought to nought, the temple rebuilt, and the kingdom of God restored. Still more in general, the meaning of the vision is that although the Lord employs human instruments, nevertheless the completion of His kingdom is not the work of human hands, but of His own Spirit. If the candlesticks are to give light, the bowl and the olive trees and the pipes are necessary indeed; but what would they be without the oil? And so it is with the church and the kingdom of God. The church as such and the servants of the Lord and the means of grace are all necessary. But what would they be without the Holy Spirit? They could not shed light of their testimony in the church and the world.

But now we must still further ask the question: what is the meaning of the details of the vision? What is meant by the candlestick, and what by the olive trees?

We need not be left in the dark as to the answer to this question. The candlestick in the temple and tabernacle was symbolic of the people of God as shining, with their knowledge of God and their testimony, in the midst of a world of darkness. That was Israel of the old dispensation. And so in the new dispensation it is symbolic of the church of Christ letting its light shine in the midst of the world of darkness and unbelief. The church is a light, a testimony of the truth of God. That this is true is clearly proved by the first chapter of this Book of Revelation, where the seven golden candlesticks are the seven churches.

But who are the two olive trees? In Zechariah 4:14 we read that they were the two anointed ones, standing before the Lord of the whole earth. From this we learn, in the first place, that they are servants of God. They stand before the Lord of the whole earth. They are, therefore, ready to serve. And that they stand before the Lord of the whole earth also implies that they are especially the ones who are ready to serve the Lord before the whole world with their testimony in word and deed. But, in the second place, we learn that they are **anointed** servants of the Lord. They are therefore officially called and ordained for service. They are divine media through which the people of God receive the blessings of God's grace, especially the blessing of the knowledge of God, so that they may let their light shine. In the Old Testament there were but two who were thus officially anointed to be servants in the theocracy, namely, the king and the priest. And there is for that reason no question among interpreters generally but that by the two olive trees, in the first place, Zerubbabel the prince and Joshua the high priest are meant. But, in the second place, a general reference is made to the royal and priestly office in Israel. And in the words of our text, therefore, the olive trees are evidently none other but the divinely ordained and called true ministers of the Word, who must serve as media to supply the church with light.

If in this light we turn once more to the words of our text, the whole is convincingly clear. The two witnesses, as our text has it, are not only the two olive trees of Zechariah 4; nor are they only the two candlesticks; but they are both. John identifies them. The olive trees and the candlesticks cannot be separated. They belong together, and together they are the two witnesses of Christ in the world. That John speaks of the **two** witnesses is also plain. It is not because two individuals are meant, but it is simply because the entire reference of the text is to the two witnesses of Zechariah 4. And the Lord means to say: "Just as in the Old Testament I had two witnesses, just as then I had my people as a shining light and testimony in the world in my people Israel and the servants I appointed over them, so also in the new dispensation, during the forty-two months that the false church and the show church shall exist and defile the sanctuary, I shall have my two witnesses who shall bear testimony before all the world." The candlesticks and the olive trees in Zechariah 4 are none other than the people of God as lights shining in the world together with the divinely anointed and appointed servants of God. So also in our portion we conclude, on the basis of Scripture, that the candlesticks and the olive trees together are the church of Christ throughout this dispensation, together with the divinely ordained servants of the Word, the true ministers of the gospel, who must serve the Lord as media to supply the congregation with light.

If we understand this, the whole is rather clear. We have in the words of our text, in the first place, again a word of comfort and warning. A word of warning: for not all is Israel that is called Israel, and not all is Christendom that calls itself by that name. On the contrary, by far the widest area is left out when God's people are measured. There is a large mass of so-called Christians who laugh at the truths of Christianity and of Scripture, who renounce the Christ, and who crucify Him anew. In the second place, there are in the visible church proper the hypocrites, scattered and hidden among the true people of God, — dangerous people, who really belong to the enemy, who shall ultimately openly unite with the power of the Antichrist, but who cannot be detected. And the question might well be asked by God's people: but is not the whole cause of God a lost cause? If that is the condition of the church, shall there be a true church in the future? Who shall stand? And our text gives us the assurance that throughout this dispensation the two witnesses shall stand. The church shall let its light shine in the midst of the world and in the midst of the apostate church. The Lord shall keep His church even to the end of the world as a shining light. Still more. Not only the candlestick, but also the two olive trees shall remain. The Lord shall not leave His church without its faithful servants. These faithful servants, in the first place, shall instruct the congregation in the full truth of the Word and thus shall serve as media to supply the congregation with the oil of knowledge necessary to let their light shine. But, in the second place, it shall be especially through them that the church shall testify. The church and the servants of God belong together. The servants are the mouthpiece of the church. They shall above all testify and witness in the midst of the world and in the midst of the apostate church. They shall testify against the wickedness of that apostate Christendom and testify for the name of Christ; testify also against the hypocrisy of the hypocrites and the false church.

This condition is to develop in extreme features toward the end of the world. Apostasy shall increase. Jerusalem shall turn once more wicked. False Christianity shall become more openly false. Days of persecution shall arise. The show church shall unite itself with the false church in the days of persecution. But still the candlestick shall shine. Many shall fall away, according to the words of our Lord. Many also of the servants of God shall become unfaithful. But always Christ shall have the two witnesses, His church and His servants,—yea, to the end of the world. And the more the lines are sharply drawn and the greater the apostasy becomes and the more clearly Antichrist develops, the louder and the more clearly and the more definitely the testimony of the faithful church, with its faithful ministers, shall resound throughout the world.

If we bear this in mind, we shall also understand that there have been many types in history of these two witnesses. Types of these were men like Enoch and Noah and Moses and Elijah. Types of these also were Zerubbabel and Joshua. And types of these were the martyrs of the early church, as well as of the church of the Reformation together with the faithful servants of their time. Huss and Wyclif and Luther and Calvin represent these faithful witnesses. Types of these witnesses at the final stage of history are the churches and the servants who sound the trumpet today and who will know of nothing but Christ and Him crucified. And through them all we have the realization of the comfort expressed in our portion: "I will give my two witnesses, throughout this dispensation, that they may prophesy. The candlestick shall shine; the olive trees shall supply with oil, all the days of this dispensation, even until the end of the world."

But at the same time we have in our text a word of admonition and calling, a word to the church as such. She must be a witness of Christ. She must let her light shine boldly, fearlessly, testifying against the apostasy of the age with all her might and main. Not according to the imagination of man, but according to the light of the Word of God must she live and speak. Regardless of what the world may say, we must witness. Regardless how beautiful the world may look and however sweet the world may speak of Christ and Christianity, the great question that must always again be asked: do you believe in Christ, the Son of the living God, in the blood of atonement and the redemptive value of the blood of Christ Jesus? If not, the world stands condemned by our testimony. For it, and it alone, is the truth. In the second place, a word of admonition is in order with regard to the relation of the church to its ministers. They are the olive trees. They must enlighten the minds of the congregation with the light of God. The congregation must receive this light. Do not be satisfied with a little siren-song of gospel that cannot establish you in the faith, but be eager to receive the whole Word of God. For you will need its full, abundant light. And, in the third place, a word of warning and admonition to the servants of God in the church: they are the olive trees. They must bring the light of the Word and nothing else. They, first of all and above all, must stand and be faithful. They shall have a hard time in the day of judgment if it should be proved that they have given the congregation stones for bread and serpents for eggs. Many have been the false prophets of all times. Many are the false prophets today. Fearful wrath and condemnation, no doubt, there will be in store for those who have pretended to preach the truth of God and have filled the pipes of the bowl with the darkness of hell.

Chapter XXVII

Witnessing, Slain, And Glorified

(Revelation 11:5-13)

5 And if any man will hurt them, fire proceedeth out of their mouth, and devoureth their enemies: and if any man will hurt them, he must in this manner be killed.
6 These have power to shut heaven, that it rain not in the days of their prophecy: and have power over waters to turn them to blood, and to smite the earth with all plagues, as often as they will.
7 And when they shall have finished their testimony, the beast that ascendeth out of the bottomless pit shall make war against them, and shall overcome them, and kill them.
8 And their dead bodies shall lie in the street of the great city, which spiritually is called Sodom and Egypt, where also our Lord was crucified.
9 And they of the people and kindreds and tongues and nations shall see their dead bodies three days and an half, and shall not suffer their dead bodies to be put in graves.
10 And they that dwell upon the earth shall rejoice over them, and make merry, and shall send gifts one to another; because these two prophets tormented them that dwelt on the earth.
11 And after three days and an half the Spirit of life from God entered into them, and they stood upon their feet; and great fear fell upon them which saw them.
12 And they heard a great voice from heaven saying unto them, Come up hither. And they ascended up to heaven in a cloud; and their enemies beheld them.
13 And the same hour was there a great earthquake, and the tenth part of the city fell, and in the earthquake were slain of men seven thousand: and the remnant were affrighted, and gave glory to the God of heaven.

It seems to me that in the words of our text quoted above we have a very strong corroboration of the conclusion which we reached thus far in regard to the two witnesses. In our first discourse on Revelation 11 we reached the conclusion that Jerusalem and temple and worshippers must not be taken literally, but in the symbolical sense of the word. Jerusalem in its all-comprehensive sense stands for the new dispensation, that is, for Christianity in its broadest and most inclusive sense. The city outside of the temple and the court is used as being typical of the false church, representing the masses of Christianity which still have the seal of the covenant on their forehead and which perhaps would deem it a shame if they were not baptized. But they have renounced the real essence of Christendom, the blood of atonement. The outer court, we found, must be understood to symbolize the show church, the church outside of the real sanctuary but outwardly belonging to the real people of God, that is, therefore, the hypocrites. And, finally, the temple building proper is symbolic of the real, spiritual body of Christ, the elect of God, who certainly shall be saved. We found, further, that the ultimate outcome of this three-fold form of Christendom will be that the show church identifies itself with the false church, and together they shall trample under foot the holy city all through this dispensation, but especially toward the end.

Now I said that in the words which we are about to discuss I find a very strong corroboration of what I have explained in regard to the two witnesses. What is here said cannot be taken as referring to two single persons, for the simple reason that they are pictured in universal features, as having a universal influence, noted by all the world, and as being the object also of universal hatred and contempt. And their death appears also as an object of universal joy. Neither Enoch nor Elijah created such a stir as these two witnesses. Nor is it conceivable that two single human beings in a single city would cause so much commotion. No, only when we conceive of these two witnesses as the candlesticks and the olive trees, according to Scripture, shall we be able to understand and appreciate to the full all that is told us in the text we are now discussing. And we note immediately, of course, that this passage still speaks of the two witnesses.

The Activity And Power Of The Two Witnesses

If we inquire into the purpose and task of these two witnesses, the answer is ready, as we have already explained. They must bear testimony of the truth and of the name of Jesus Christ. The church with its ministry is placed as a testimony in the world. That is the sole calling of the church. That this is true is plain from the fact that they are called witnesses. A silent witness is impossible. They must speak, therefore.

This is evident, further, from the fact that they are called prophets and that they must prophesy. This does not mean necessarily and merely that they must speak concerning the future. Surely, also that is the case. The church of Christ must also bear testimony in the world concerning the future, especially in times when the world lives for the present and strives after ideals which are only for the present. The church has a solemn calling to speak on the basis of prophecy of the future that is coming, of the judgment that will befall the unrighteous and the glory that shall be revealed in the children of God. But that does not exhaust their calling as prophets. A prophet is simply a person who speaks for someone else. Just as Aaron is called Moses' prophet in Scripture, so the prophets in general are persons who speak for someone else. And thus the church is called to witness of Christ; and the prophet of Christ speaks for Christ, on His authority and in His name. This is indicated, finally, by the symbolism of a candlestick and of the olive trees. Also this is in harmony with the thought that the church must be a testimony in the world, a witness of the truth. The purpose of a candlestick is that it may give light; and the two olive trees which supply the light, the media through which the church receives its light, serve no other purpose. They must themselves be witnesses in the world and be mouthpieces of the church. But at the same time they must witness for the church before the people of God, so that they receive more light to shine for the Lord of the whole earth. Hence, if you ask what the two witnesses do, and what is their calling, the simple answer is: they witness and bear testimony of the Christ and of His truth.

As to the contents of their message, they find their commission in the Word of their God. They stand before the Lord of the whole earth. They are servants of the Lord of the whole earth. They belong to God's party. As such, therefore, they will speak nothing but that which their Lord has commissioned them to speak. Centrally, they speak of Christ and His atoning blood. That blood is the witness of the righteousness and holiness of God, but at the same time of His mercy and redeeming grace. That blood is the witness to the glory of God in the midst of a world of sin. Of it they speak. They emphasize, therefore, that there is no hope in man, but only in the blood of the Redeemer. In it there is life and bliss. They openly condemn all efforts to seek salvation outside of that atoning blood, and they will know nothing of man or of a world that can save itself.

The name of Christ they bear, and that in two ways. In the first place, they bear that name to fields where never it was mentioned before, all nations. In their missionary efforts they carry the sound of that name into all the world and before every tribe and tongue. But, in the second place, also in the midst of the world in which they live do they testify. In the midst of Jerusalem, in the midst of the false church, as well as in the midst of the show church, do they bear witness. When the false church would attack the truth and trample under foot the blood of Christ, these two witnesses, the church and the servants of God in the church, stand upon the basis of God's infallible Word and defend it over against the enemy. When that world indulges in sin and iniquity more and more, they speak of judgment and of wrath to come, and openly express that there is no hope for them. In a word, they display the glory of God's name in Jesus Christ our Lord in the midst of the world, outside of Jerusalem that it may be extended, and in Jerusalem itself against those who trample the truth under foot.

It is in harmony with this essential calling of the two witnesses that we read of them how they kill those that oppose them and try to hurt them. We read: "And if any man will hurt them, fire proceedeth out of their mouth, and devoureth their enemies: and if any man will hurt them, he must in this manner be killed." This may sound strange at first. It is indeed because of such expressions as these that many interpreters do not know what to do with these two witnesses of Christ. Surely, they say, this cannot mean the church: for the simple reason that she never had this power, nor ever will have it. Hence, they must be altogether two unique human beings, who can kill their enemies at will.

But let us investigate.

In the first place, it may be remarked that these two witnesses do not kill those who rise against them and who wish to do them hurt in the literal sense of the word. If that were the case, no one would be able to touch them and to kill them. Yet the power of the beast rises against them and takes away their lives. And the fire that proceedeth out of their mouth is not of any avail against this. In the second place, let us consider that they kill with the fire that proceedeth out of their mouth. This is emphatically stated. Twice in the text it is said that this is the way in which these witnesses kill. They do not kill by the sword those who try to do them hurt, but simply by the fire that proceedeth out of their mouth. It is as if the Lord were afraid that this part of it should be misunderstood, so emphatically does He state this. Not by the sword, nor by the strength of their arm, but by the fire that comes out of their mouths are the opponents who try to do them hurt killed.

To understand this we must, in the first place, ask ourselves the question: what does it mean to hurt these two witnesses? How can the church possibly be hurt? Do you hurt them by persecution and tribulation? If that were the case, the word "hurt" in the text must be taken in the physical sense of the word. Then the meaning is: if any man try to cause them suffering, pain, persecution, affliction, if any man in that way try to kill them... And then it is also plain that the latter part of this sentence must also be taken in the same literal sense of the word, and that these witnesses kill their enemies and take their lives away. But that is evidently not the case. You do not hurt the church by persecution. You do not hurt the people of God by doing them physical harm. You cannot even hurt them by taking away their lives and killing them. No, in that sense these witnesses are willing to lose their lives. They have learned of their Lord that they need not fear those who can kill the body but who cannot kill the soul. And therefore, these two witnesses can never be hurt in the physical sense of the word. Indeed, you may persecute them, you may put them into prison, you may torture them on the rack, you may even kill them and burn their bodies; but by doing so you have not hurt them in the least. To hurt these two witnesses you must get at their spiritual existence. You must fight with them spiritually. You must make them waver in their testimony. You must lead them to deny the Christ, to renounce the truth, to be silent in regard to the Word of their Lord. Then indeed you hurt them. But if that is attempted, so the text has it, fire proceedeth out of the mouth of these witnesses, and in this manner the opponents are killed. That is, their efforts are put to nought, so that they cannot do them harm.

In the second place, we must now turn to Scripture in order to find the meaning of this fire that proceedeth out of their mouths. We must not think here of the fire which came down from heaven on the captains and their fifties who wished to do Elijah harm. For that fire came from heaven, not out of the mouth of Elijah. But we must think of the word in the prophecy of Jeremiah 5:14: "Wherefore thus saith the Lord God of hosts, Because ye speak this word, behold, I will make my words in thy mouth fire, and this people wood, and it shall devour them." The people of Israel wished to do Jeremiah harm by opposing and gainsaying his prophecy and making it of none effect. And because of this, the words of Jeremiah shall be like fire, and the people as wood. Their opposition shall not stand. It shall not hurt the prophet as such. And the same is true here. The two prophets shall meet with opposition. The enemy from the false church shall try to hurt them. They shall try to make them renounce the truth. They shall attempt to gainsay their words and to make them of none effect. But all the time these opponents shall meet with the fire that proceedeth out of the mouth of the witnesses. Not their own word, but the Word of God is in their mouth. And before that Word the enemy shall not be able to stand, but be completely defeated. In this manner they fight the battle, in harmony with their character as witnesses, in harmony also with the spiritual battle they fight, with the Word of God as their weapon. And in this they are invulnerable!

Still more strange, it has been thought, is the power with which those two witnesses are invested. We read of them that they have power to shut the heaven, that it rain not in the days of their prophecy; power to turn the waters into blood, and to smite the earth with every plague, whenever they deem fit.

First, there is a plain reference to Elijah and Moses and what they did in these words. When the glory of the God of Israel was at stake, the prophet turned the water into blood, that God's people might be delivered. And again, when the glory of Jehovah was trampled under foot by Israel itself, the prophet kneeled down in the wilds of Gilead and prayed that it might not rain; and it rained not. Through the agency of these witnesses and for the sake of the true people of God and the glory of Jehovah these plagues were brought upon the land. And the plain meaning is that even as these prophets had this power, even as they could shut the heavens and turn the waters into blood, so also these two witnesses of the new dispensation have this same power to strike the earth with every plague whenever they so desire. It will not do to change the meaning of the words by trying to spiritualize them. This has often been attempted. Just because these expressions seem so strange, at first sight, that interpreters would hardly dare to maintain them in their literal meaning and apply them to the church, they have attempted to spiritualize these words and found here a reference to the key-power of the church. They have received the power to shut the kingdom of God and to turn the waters of the truth to blood, so that they be a curse rather than a blessing, a savor of death unto death. But this is not the sense of the passage. The text speaks of a literal heaven and a literal rain of literal waters and of literal plagues with which the earth will be visited. And there is nothing that indicates that we must look for a different meaning behind these words. And therefore we must accept them as they stand. Just as the historical incidents which are here cited are also literal, so also the power of these witnesses is to be taken in the literal sense of the word.

Nor must we hesitate for a moment to maintain that this power is really given to the church and especially to its official ministry. There is indeed nothing strange and nothing new in this. Moses and Elijah had this power. The early church had this power. We read of many wonderful things of the early church. They revealed a power which they had received through the Holy Spirit which did not become revealed in the later history of the church. Besides, there is nothing strange, nothing surprising, in this assertion of the text. Christ told His people before He left that they would do still greater things than He if they believed in Him. He told them that faith was sufficient to remove mountains. Of course, they do not perform these things in their own strength. They have not this power of themselves. In themselves they have nothing, no power whatsoever. But they have it all in Christ. Christ is their head, and they are in Him. The church is organically connected with Christ. And Christ has all power in heaven and on earth. Christ certainly has power to shut the heaven, and will. He has power undoubtedly to turn the waters into blood. He has the power to strike the earth with every plague conceivable. And therefore, there is nothing strange in the assertion that His people have that same power.

But how, in what way, do they have that power? In order to understand this at all we must, in the first place, remember that the people of God always have this power, but that it is not always equally manifest that they have it. The judgments on earth, the plagues of war and famine and pestilence, and all the terrible things which must still take place in the future, as pictured in this Book of Revelation, are there for the completion of the kingdom, and for the salvation of the people of God, and for their sake. It is for their sake that the earth is visited with all kinds of plagues. Still more: it is not only for their sake, but it is also upon their prayers that these plagues come. The people of God may not always be equally conscious of this, but fact is that the judgments come on the earth as an answer to their prayers. When the prayers of the saints are offered upon the altar in heaven, the result is voices and thunders and an earthquake, caused by the fire taken from the same altar. In that connection we have explained that this means nothing else than that the prayers of the saints

are answered by judgments from heaven. Just as heaven was shut because
of the prayer of Elijah, so the judgments on the earth in the new
dispensation come in answer to the prayers of the saints. They pray, "Thy
kingdom come." That kingdom must come through tribulation and
through all kinds of plagues and calamities; and the saints know it. And
the more they become conscious of this, the more they also pray for the
coming of the kingdom, even through their prayers now as well as in the
times of old. We do not have to stop here. Though the church and their
servants really have that power and also use it, it is not always actually
plain that this is the case. On the one hand, it is not always equally
manifest before their own consciousness that their prayers really do bring
judgments upon the earth. And, in the second place, the world certainly is
not conscious of that fact. But also this shall change again. When the world
increases in wickedness and iniquity, when the blood of Christ is trampled
under foot more and more, and when the people of God towards the end
shall be subjected to tribulation because of the wicked world, when they
shall have gained a clearer insight into the word of prophecy and
understand that it is through judgment and plagues that the kingdom must
come and be completed, they shall also once more deliberately pray for
these plagues on the wicked world.

Do not think that this is strange. You do not think it strange that Moses
brought the plagues on the land of Egypt, do you? You do not criticize
Elijah for praying that it might not rain for three years and six months, do
you? Well, then, the lines shall be drawn just as sharply once more. It shall
become very plain to all the people of God through their faithful servants
that the world departs from God and His precepts. It shall become very
evident that the blood of Christ and the name of the Most High is
trampled under foot. And in those times they shall employ the power
which they have in Christ Jesus consciously and deliberately, just as Elijah
kneeled down in the wilds of Gilead and prayed that God might withhold
His blessings from the apostate people, so the people of God shall know
the time in the future when they shall consciously refuse to pray for
blessings on the wicked world, and that they shall beseech the God of
hosts for plagues and judgment, that His kingdom may come. And it shall
become plain to all the world, even as it was plain to Ahab in the case of
Elijah, that it is the two witnesses who bring these plagues.

The Opponent And Defeat Of The Witnesses

If this is plainly understood, we shall have no difficulty to understand the rest of the text. It is perfectly plain, in the first place, why the beast which rises up out of the abyss comes against these witnesses. We read: "And when they shall have finished their testimony, the beast that ascendeth out of the bottomless pit shall make war against them, and shall overcome them, and kill them."

On the one hand, you may notice that although the beast has never been mentioned before in the Book of Revelation, yet the plain presupposition is that he is well-known by the church. It is **the** beast. The reference is evidently to the seventh chapter of Daniel, where this beast has been pictured. There we find the picture of the fourth beast, more terrible than the preceding, with ten horns. And from among the ten horns rises another little horn, who destroys three of them, and who becomes more terrible than all the rest, speaking blasphemous things against the Most High, and warring with the saints of God. From this we learn the following. In the first place, the beast that is here mentioned is not the same as the dragon that is mentioned in Chapter 12. He is indeed closely connected with that dragon, but he is not to be identified with him. Nor is it the same as the prince of the locusts that rose up from the abyss. For it is a beast, an earthly form, while that was a spirit. In the second place, here we have the first mention of the Antichrist, the little horn of the seventh chapter of Daniel. Thirdly, this Antichrist rises out of the abyss, that is, he finds his spiritual origin there, although he will appear in human form. Just as we may say that believers are hid with Christ in God, that their walk is in heaven, so also Antichrist is hid with Satan in hell and has his origin in the abyss. Fourthly, it is to be understood that this power of Antichrist exists all through this dispensation. He does not just rise out of the abyss at the moment that the witnesses have finished their testimony, but he was already in the world in John's time. The fourth beast also exists before the little horn arises. But just as the power of the fourth beast in Daniel culminated in the little horn, so also this power of Antichrist shall culminate and finally rise against the people of the kingdom of God. For the rest, we need not discuss this beast in detail in this connection. As I have said, this chapter pictures the general history of the church with a view to the end in broad outlines; and individual pictures of it will be given us in subsequent chapters. Then we shall also have ample opportunity to discuss this beast, the Antichrist, in detail in connection with the thirteenth, seventeenth, and nineteenth chapters of this book. Sufficient it is, therefore, in this connection that we now understand that the Antichrist, though existing all through this dispensation and revealing himself in weaker form in special periods, shall toward the end be allowed to gather his strength and make war against the saints of the Most High.

To one element in the text, however, I must still call your attention. And that is to the statement that this beast shall rise against the two witnesses after they have finished their testimony. Paul also tells us that there is a power which holds the Antichrist so that he cannot appear before the God-ordained time. He cannot manifest himself as yet in his full power. And the power which holds him back is undoubtedly the Spirit of God, working out the decree of God, namely, that the power of Antichrist may not come to its full manifestation until the prophecy of the church shall have become finished. This implies two things. In the first place, as we gather from other parts of the Word of God, it implies that the gospel must have been preached to all nations. This does not mean that the gospel must have come to every individual, but that it must have been spread over the whole earth and come within reach of all. But, in the second place, it also means that this testimony against the wicked world and against the false church must have been finished. The measure of iniquity must be full. The world must hear the testimony of the church, must hear it repeatedly, must become conscious of its sin, must know it and reject the Christ of God willingly and deliberately. Then the testimony shall have been finished. And then it may be silenced, and it shall be silenced by the power of Antichrist himself.

For we read in the text that Antichrist shall rise against the witnesses and overcome them and kill them. This is a very pregnant and brief statement of the time of the last and terrible tribulation that shall come over the church of God. Antichrist shall prevail at last. He shall overcome the church. He shall persecute the saints of the Most High. That does not mean that he shall kill all the people of God individually. For we do not receive that impression from other parts of Holy Writ. We receive the definite information that also at the time of the end, with the second coming of the Lord for the deliverance of His people, there shall be living saints who shall be changed in the twinkling of an eye, at the last trump. But it does mean, in the first place, that it shall be a time of general and terrible persecution for the faithful people of God. The acts and testimony of the witnesses have aroused the anger of the Antichrist. Their testimony is now finished. Antichrist comes to silence it. And he succeeds. I imagine that he will succeed in two ways. In the first place, I do not doubt but that he will persecute the people of God in the literal sense of the word. He shall put them in prison and deprive them of their liberty and property. He shall kill some of them, especially some of the ministers and faithful servants. But, in the second place, the true church of God shall be declared dead. They shall be cast out of society. They shall be considered outlaws. They shall be left no standing room on earth. They shall be allowed to buy or sell no more unless they bear the mark of the beast. And literally they shall be forbidden to worship. It shall be a victory for the beast, and the church shall be heard of no more. The testimony, the prayers, the powers, and the actions of the two witnesses shall have been silenced and removed. The Antichrist shall reign supreme.

Thus we can at the same time understand what it means that their dead bodies shall lie in the streets of Jerusalem, the great city, which is spiritually called Sodom and Egypt. This cannot mean that two dead bodies shall lie in the literal sense of the word in the literal streets of Jerusalem. For it is inconceivable how in that sense all nations and tongues and tribes should look upon these two dead bodies. The text itself clearly shows again that something else is meant. Jerusalem is false Christianity, the false church, now united with the show church of hypocrites, trampling under foot the holy city and rejoicing over their victory over the church of God. The church still exists in their midst, but she is now dead. She has been declared dead. She has been silenced. And she is the object of greatest contempt all over the world. "Ye shall be hated of all nations" has now become literally true. And just as the lying unburied in the street was symbolic of greatest contempt and deepest shame, so the church, silenced in her testimony, perfectly overcome, exists in the midst of Christendom as an object of extreme contempt and shame. Her power is gone. Her influence is no more. Her prayers are silenced. She cannot pray for plagues any more. She has been annihilated as far as her manifestation in the world is concerned. And all the world rejoices because she is dead. They rejoice and make merry, they send gifts to one another, only because the church which spoke of blood and judgment has been overpowered.

The Reappearance And Glorification Of The Witnesses

However, this is not the end of these two witnesses. On the contrary, we read in the text: "And after three days and an half the spirit of life

from God entered into them, and they stood upon their feet; and great
fear fell upon them which saw them. And they heard a great voice from
heaven saying unto them, Come up hither. And they ascended up to
heaven in a cloud; and their enemies beheld them."

Let me call your attention, in the first place, to the fact that the
tribulation is to last three days and a half. This implies, first of all, that the
time of the Antichrist shall be cut short. He shall not be able to finish his
work, but shall be allowed only half a week. He shall not accomplish his
purpose. Just as the time of this entire dispensation in general is indicated
by three and one-half years, or by time, times, and a half, so also the time
of the end stands in the same sign. The power of Antichrist in its
culmination of the little horn of the beast that cometh up out of the abyss
shall be cut short. But it means, in the second place, that the days shall be
shortened for the elects' sake. This the Lord has promised definitely, and
it is plainly indicated here. At the end of the three days and a half the days
of tribulation for the people of God shall be ended. But the time of the
end is not there as yet.

I do not know how I can make this more plain than by referring you
again to Daniel. In the ninth chapter of that prophecy the prophet reveals
to us the vision of the seventy weeks. Let me call your attention to the
following facts, on the basis of this vision. First, that the seventy weeks as
a whole indicate the period from Daniel to the end of time, when iniquity
shall be finished. Secondly, that this period from the time of Daniel to the
end of all time is divided into three smaller periods. The first consists of
seven weeks, and reaches to the first coming of Christ. The second consists
of sixty-two weeks, and reaches unto the time of the culmination of
Antichrist, the twelve hundred and sixty days of the two witnesses, the
building up of Jerusalem in the new dispensation. At the end of the
sixty-two weeks we read that Christ shall be cut off and shall have nothing,
which means the same as what is indicated in our text when it says that
the witnesses are lying dead in the streets of Jerusalem. Thirdly, there is
still one week left. That is the week of Antichrist, the week in which he
shall reign supreme. But also in Daniel this week is cut in half. For in the
midst of the week he shall have accomplished his work against the church,
so that even the sacrifice and oblation has ceased.

So also in our text that last period, the last week, shall be cut in half.
The first part of that week is the time of the great tribulation. But after
the time of the great tribulation, after the church has been dead and her

testimony has ceased for some time, Christ shall cause a certain revival. A spirit of life entered into them from God, and they stood upon their feet once more. A voice comes from heaven, and calls them up thither, and they ascend into heaven in a cloud. At the same time an earthquake, a terrible earthquake, is felt, which destroys a large part of the city, but which undoubtedly at the same time accompanies the resurrection of the saints. And the church has been delivered. In other words, before the time of the end, while the Antichrist and the Gog and Magog are still on earth, the church shall be taken away from her shame and persecution and terrible suffering. The living saints shall be changed. Those who have died shall be raised. And the church of Christ shall be glorified. The days have been shortened for the elects' sake.

In regard to the power of the Antichrist that still remains behind, the text tells us that one tenth of its power is destroyed. That is evidently the meaning of the destruction which is caused by the earthquake. One tenth of the city is destroyed, and seven thousand people are killed. Ten is, as we have remarked before, the symbolic number which indicates the power that is given to the Antichrist by the decree of God. He has ten horns, has dominion over ten kingdoms, − all of which indicates that he has just as much power as God allows him. But now one tenth of his dominion is destroyed. Jerusalem at large, the holy city, which is spiritually called Sodom and Egypt, has, of course, developed into the power of the Antichrist and has served him in the culmination of his power. One tenth of that power is now taken away, that is, just as much as is in harmony with his existence. To take one tenth of his power and his dominion away simply means that he is definitely curtailed, so that he will not be able to maintain himself as Antichrist. And this is for a purpose. For a time they acknowledge the glory of God, just as Nebuchadnezzar would when he was witness of the power and glory of God. To a definite conversion it does not come. The time for conversion is now past. It is only a time for judgment. For the witness of the Word has been taken away, and the church is already in heaven. Terrible things shall still take place. Battles shall be fought between Antichrist and Gog and Magog, and the church shall be no more in tribulation. The time of her tribulation is past, and with Christ she reigns in glory, till she shall return with Him to judgment.

This, then, is the general picture we receive from this chapter and from other parts of Scripture. The true church, endowed with power and light from on high, will witness of the truth and of Christ throughout this dispensation. When the testimony is finished, the Antichrist will be allowed to develop and persecute the church. The time of the great tribulation shall follow, of which Scripture has warned us so frequently. But that time of great tribulation is to be cut short. At the darkest hour Christ shall deliver His church. History shall be continued for a while, with Antichrist and Gog and Magog as the inhabitants of the earth, till Christ shall come to judge with His church and shall establish His glorious kingdom forevermore. Now we are still in the twelve hundred and sixty days. We must still witness. Perhaps the days of tribulation will come soon. It seems as if we are fast becoming prepared for these days. But still the testimony is not finished. Still, therefore, it is the calling of the church and its ministry to witness. And the purpose of this picture is to spur us on to be faithful even unto the end, that no one may take our crown. And on the other hand, the people of God may be comforted by the fact that Christ shall not leave them alone, but that even the days shall be shortened for the elects' sake.

Chapter XXVIII

The Blowing Of The Seventh Trumpet

(Revelation 11:14-19)

14 The second woe is past; and, behold, the third woe cometh quickly.

15 And the seventh angel sounded; and there were great voices in heaven, saying, The kingdoms of this world are become the kingdoms of our Lord, and of his Christ; and he shall reign for ever and ever.

16 And the four and twenty elders, which sat before God on their seats, fell upon their faces, and worshipped God,

17 Saying, We give thee thanks, O Lord God Almighty, which art, and wast, and art to come; because thou hast taken to thee thy great power, and hast reigned.

18 And the nations were angry, and thy wrath is come, and the time of the dead, that they should be judged, and that thou shouldest give reward unto thy servants the prophets, and to the saints, and them that fear thy name, small and great; and shouldest destroy them which destroy the earth.

19 And the temple of God was opened in heaven, and there was seen in his temple the ark of his testament; and there were lightnings, and voices, and thunderings, and an earthquake, and great hail.

In order to gain a true understanding of this part of the Book of Revelation it is of the utmost importance that we bear in mind the general character of the chapter in which it occurs. We have said that in this chapter we have a picture of the general course of history, of the history of the church in the midst of the world in the present dispensation, and that too, with a view to the end. It really covers the entire history. From that point of view, the Book of Revelation might have closed with this chapter. But we must remember that it is only a general picture, a picture which gives us very general outlines; and the details of that picture shall be presented to us in the chapters that follow. It might be called the general program that is to be worked out in the succeeding chapters, or, if you please, the general index of the book from here on.

In it we found a general characterization of the condition of the church in this world. The temple was measured; and we found that the distinction was made between the holy city at large, the outer court, and the real holy place with its worshippers, — a distinction which we found to be applicable to the condition of the church in the new dispensation. There is always a Christendom in the general sense of the word, including all who belong to nominal Christianity in the outward sense, all who have been baptized in the name of the Triune God. But within this largest circle of Christianity there is, in the first place, the false church, which does no more adhere to the Christ, but tramples the blood of atonement under foot. And, in the second place, within the same sphere of Christianity in general there is also the show church, which enters with the true people of God in the sanctuary, but which does not worship with them in spirit and in truth. And, finally, there is the true church, the body of the true believers, who are implanted into Christ by a true and living faith. And this distinction will become more plain, will be emphasized, toward the time of the end in such a way that the show church of hypocrites will fall away and identify themselves with the false church, the enemies of Christ, and ultimately ally themselves with the power of Antichrist.

We found in this chapter a general picture of the calling and work of the true church in the midst of the world. They must be and are witnesses for Christ. They are the two witnesses. The believers, the church and its ministers, the servants of God, will witness throughout this dispensation, even to the time of the end. They prophesy not only in the midst of the world that does not know the Christ and the gospel, but prophesy also against the wickedness of the false church, in the midst of which they exist as a living testimony. We found that over against these enemies their word becomes a fire, consuming the enemy, so that he cannot prevail against them in the spiritual sense. We found that these two witnesses perform wonders; even as Elijah and Moses of old, they shut the heaven with their spiritual power, turn the waters into blood, and have power to strike the earth with every plague. You will remember how we explained that all of this must be taken in the most literal sense of the word, as applying to the church of the new dispensation.

Finally, we found in this chapter a general indication of the final rise of the Antichrist, the beast which comes up out of the abyss. He oppresses

the church. He persecutes the believers who witness against him and who
perform these wonders. He kills some of them undoubtedly, and succeeds
in declaring the entire church of Christ dead, so that their testimony is
silenced and they are the object of greatest scorn and contempt, as is
expressed in the figure of their bodies lying unburied in the streets of
Jerusalem for three days and a half. But we also find a general picture of
the final victory, or rather, of the ultimate deliverance of the church. The
days are shortened for their sake. They are raised, changed, and taken to
heaven even before the time of the end and before the seventh trumpet
will play the greatest havoc with the enemies of Christ and His kingdom.
And now it is in that same general sense of the word that in the passage we
are about to discuss we meet with the picture of the seventh trumpet.

The Victory Brought By The Seventh Trumpet

In the fourteenth verse of this chapter, the first verse of the passage we
are now discussing, we read: "The second woe is past; and, behold, the
third woe cometh quickly." This fact has led many interpreters to believe
that all that is told us in Chapter 9, verse 12, to Chapter 11, verse 13,
belongs to the second woe. You will remember that the eagle which flew
in mid-heaven announced a three-fold woe, evidently corresponding with
the three last trumpets. These last three trumpets, therefore, may very
appropriately be called the woe-trumpets. Now it is very evident from the
text that the first woe, or the fifth trumpet, simply includes the plague of
the locusts. All are agreed in this respect. But there is difference of opinion
with regard to the second woe, or the sixth trumpet. There are interpreters
who maintain that it includes all that is told us in Chapter 9, verse 12, to
Chapter 11, verse 13, as I said above. According to this view, it includes
the setting at liberty of the four angels who are bound at the great river
Euphrates and all the deadly destruction caused by this. It includes, in the
second place, all that is told us in Chapter 10 of the angel who stands on
the sea and on the land and of the open book which John must swallow.
And it includes, in the third place, all we have thus far discussed of the
eleventh chapter: the measuring of the temple, the witnessing of the two
prophets, the rise of the Antichrist, and the deliverance of the church.

But as we have already indicated in our discussion, we cannot agree
with this, and that for the simple reason that there is nothing woeful in
Chapter 10 and in Chapter 11, verses 1 to 13, for the world. The
woe-trumpets evidently mean to cause woe not to the church, but to the

world. And from this point of view the last-mentioned portion cannot be classed together with Chapter 9, verses 13 to 21, which speaks of the sixth trumpet. And therefore, our conception is that the second woe is recorded in Chapter 9, verses 13 to 21, where the sixth trumpet ends. Then in Chapter 10 we have an interlude, assuring the people of God that the mighty Christ shall surely bring the kingdom and perfect it. And in the eleventh chapter we have a general picture of what will be described in detail in future chapters in connection with the seventh trumpet, or the third woe.

That seventh trumpet, or third woe, John now announces and pictures in general terms. And therefore, immediately before this seventh trumpet he announces that the third woe cometh quickly.

It is of the utmost importance for the future understanding of the Book of Revelation that you have a clear view of the question in what connection this seventh trumpet is here mentioned, and how it occurs. Let it be definitely understood that in this passage we have no detailed description of the effects of the seventh trumpet, but merely a general proleptical vision of it. The last part of the chapter bears the same character as the entire portion which preceded. As we have said, in the preceding we had only general pictures: a picture of the church, her testimony, her struggle, the Antichrist, Babylon, and the relation between all these. In future chapters this will be worked out in detail. We must not be surprised if we read of the church again, even though in this chapter we saw her already going up to heaven. We must not be surprised if in future chapters we shall read again of the false church, of Babylon, of Antichrist, and of the intrigues against the church. All that follows describes in detail what is here mentioned in general. And the same is true of the seventh trumpet. We are told here that it blows, and in general terms the voices in heaven and the elders tell us what is the effect of this seventh trumpet. That trumpet finishes all. You will remember that there are seven seals, and that the last seal reveals itself as seven trumpets. When therefore the seventh trumpet shall have had its effect, all shall have been completed, and the mystery of God shall have been finished. Babylon shall have fallen, and Antichrist shall have been judged. Gog and Magog shall have been destroyed. The devil and all his host shall have been cast into the pool that burns with fire and sulphur. The new heavens and the new earth shall have been realized, and Christ shall have delivered His kingdom to the Father. The seventh trumpet shall finish all things, and carries us into eternity.

Now in our portion we have the picture of the effect of the seventh trumpet, but not in detail. We are not told here of the fall of Babylon and of the last mighty attempt of Antichrist to gain control, of the final defeat of the devil. Nor have we a real description of the resurrection of the dead and of the judgment, of the coming down out of heaven of the heavenly Jerusalem, and the realization of the kingdom. All this will be described in the future. We shall therefore also meet with the seventh trumpet again, when it shall dissolve itself into the seven vials of wrath. But in our portion we have a proleptical vision, revealing in a few sentences the entire effect of that seventh trumpet. A general statement is given of the effect of this trumpet as viewed from heaven.

We are told in the text that at the blowing of the seventh trumpet great voices were heard in heaven. Many attempts have been made to identify these voices and to answer the question whose they are. But the text does not tell us; nor is this of any account to us. There are indeed many possibilities. In future portions of the book, in connection with the carrying out of the plan of God, especially in connection with the realization of the seventh trumpet, we read of voices which speak and cry and sing. When the dragon is cast down to the earth, we read that a great voice speaks in heaven, making mention of the salvation of God's people and of woe to the earth (12:10). Chapter 14 makes mention of various voices. It speaks of the voice of the one hundred forty-four thousand who sing with the voice of many waters, of great thunder, with a voice of harpers. It makes mention of the voice of the angel flying in mid-heaven and proclaiming eternal good tidings to them that dwell on the earth. It speaks of a second angel announcing the fall of Babylon the great; of a third announcing woe to them that worship the beast and his image; of a voice pronouncing a beatitude upon the dead that die in the Lord. Chapter 15 speaks of a multitude that stands by the sea of glass and sings the song of Moses and of the Lamb. Chapter 16 tells us of a voice that proceeds from the temple and speaks to the angels who hold the seven bowls of wrath. Many and various voices are mentioned in connection with the realization of the mystery of God. As the time approaches that the kingdom shall be completed, the voices in heaven multiply. We receive the impression that heaven is watching and waiting for a long time. An occasional voice is heard now and then; but in the end it becomes plain that God Almighty is to have the victory, and heaven appears teeming with life and rebounding with songs and outcries and voices that rejoice and take part in the carrying out of the plan of the Almighty. And therefore we need not be surprised that our text describes in a few sentences the effect of the seventh trumpet, and speaks of great voices that cause themselves to be heard.

Of more importance it is to us to know what these voices say. The text says that they shout: "The kingdom of the world is become the kingdom of our Lord and of his Christ; and he shall reign for ever and ever." In our version we read of **kingdoms**, in the plural. This would leave the impression that the reference was to the various kingdoms and empires in the political sense of the word that exist upon the earth. But the original does not speak of **kingdoms**, in the plural, but simply of the **kingdom**. And the idea is that the sovereign rule over the world has completely fallen to God Almighty and His Christ. We might therefore paraphrase: "God and His Christ have gained the sovereign rule over the world as a whole." That world was originally made to be a kingdom as an organic whole. And now, at the end, when the seventh trumpet blows, God has with and through His Anointed, His Christ, gained the actual sovereign dominion over all the world. We feel that these voices speak proleptically. At the moment when the seventh trumpet sounds they speak as if the effect of it had already been accomplished, and in one sentence they tell us that God and His Christ have assumed the sovereign rule over all the world.

Two questions arise in our mind when we listen to these voices. In the first place, the question arises: in what sense does God become sovereign over all the world at the end of time, when the seventh trumpet is finished? Is He not sovereign, and is His Christ not actually sovereign, all through this dispensation? And, in the second place, what is the relation between the sovereignty of God Almighty and that of His Christ at the finishing of the seventh trumpet? Shall they reign side by side, or shall there be subordination?

In answer to the first question, it must be said that God is indeed sovereign all through the history of the world. There is nothing, there is no creature, that can thwart His will; and all are in subjection to Him. Even the devil and all his host and all the wicked world can after all do nothing against Him, even though they so imagine in the wickedness of their heart. But although in this sense He is sovereign, absolutely sovereign, yet it is not true that His sovereignty is undisputed. Even though we tremble at the thought, it is true nevertheless that the devil conceived of the plan of becoming sovereign instead of the Most High, and that he has employed other angels and man to realize this plan of his own sovereignty. And therefore, he, together with his agencies, the host of the devils from the abyss and Babylon and Antichrist on earth, rise in rebellion against the Sovereign of heaven and earth. There is, therefore, a battle being carried on in this world for the possession of the whole world as kingdom between God and His Anointed, the Christ, and the devil and his anointed, the Antichrist. God's sovereignty is disputed. The devil wars against God, to wrest His sovereignty from Him. And the full and complete sovereignty of God Almighty shall not appear before these rebels have been subdued, before these enemies have been destroyed, and God and His Christ reign in undisputed sovereignty forever. This destruction of the enemy, this final subjection of all that rebel against God, the seventh trumpet shall bring about. By this seventh trumpet Babylon shall be brought to its ruin, Antichrist shall be destroyed, Gog and Magog shall be annihilated and punished, the new Jerusalem shall be realized, and God shall spread His tabernacle over all. And now these voices, at the sound of the last trumpet, see the realization of all this. They speak as if the trumpet is already finished, as if the enemies have already been destroyed. And therefore they now shout: "The sovereignty of the world has become the sovereignty of our God and of His Anointed for ever and ever."

As to the second question, we must remember that the plan of God is that the kingdom of the world shall be a kingdom of man under God. Man is made king of the world in obedience to God Almighty as Sovereign. He is made viceroy. But man rebelled. The first man went with his power and royal glory and subjected himself to the prince of darkness with his kingdom. And now God has sent His second man, the Anointed, the man Jesus Christ. He is to take man's place. He is the Servant of God, the head of the covenant which is to be realized, the King of the new creation. But He is to take the place of man. Now He reigns at the right hand of God and carries out the decree of God with a view to the coming kingdom. He breaks the seals. He causes the trumpets to blow. He sends the vials of wrath. For He alone was worthy to receive the book out of the hand of Him Who sitteth upon the throne. But in the end, when all is completed and the seventh trumpet shall have finished its work, He shall subject Himself too, according to the apostle Paul in I Corinthians 15, and shall reign over all the works of God forever and ever, but under God as His Sovereign. In Christ, the Anointed of God, the new creation shall lie at the foot of its Maker and give Him glory.

What a glory that shall be! The enemies of God and of His church are destroyed. The people of God are delivered. All creation is lying at the feet of the Sovereign forever and ever. There will be no more war or disturbance. There will be no more sin. There will never be a second fall of angels and men. But into ages of ages God, the Supreme Ruler, reigns over all; and we shall reign with Christ forever over the works of His hands.

The Joy In Heaven At The Seventh Trumpet

But there is not only the voice of these mighty ones which is heard, but also the voice of the four and twenty elders who shout in this connection. Who they are we have explained in a different connection. We will not go into detail again. Be it sufficient to say that they are the representatives of the church of all ages, both of the old and of the new dispensation.

We read of them that at the voice of the seventh trumpet they fell upon their faces and worshipped God. This is in complete harmony with the contents of the great voice which has just spoken. The latter had announced that God and His Christ had assumed the full sovereignty of the world, and that forever and ever. In harmony with this the twenty-four elders fall upon their faces and worship. The sovereignty that had been announced by the voices is here, in the first place, acknowledged. They not only come down from their thrones. They not only kneel down before the Almighty. But they bow down, fall down in the dust on their faces, thus expressing that they are overwhelmed by the revelation of the sovereignty of God. O, surely, they knew that He was sovereign. They were aware of His great power. They felt assured that He would overcome His enemies to the last. But the reality of it is still so overwhelming that they all of a sudden fall down and bow with their faces in the dust. And they also place themselves on the same standpoint of that first great voice. Also they see the fulfillment, the full carrying out, of all that is implied in the seventh trumpet. And standing on that ground, from whence they see the complete carrying out of the mystery of God, seeing how all is fulfilled, they are overwhelmed with the reality of the things that have happened. And they fall down and worship.

So shall reality far surpass our boldest expectation. Now we are children of God. Now we have a revelation of the things that are to be, of the power of God and of His Christ that is to be revealed in the future, of the glory of the children of God that is to be revealed in them. Now we can speak, nay, stammer, about these things in imperfection; and joy fills our hearts when we speak of them. Now we fall down in humble worship and thanks whenever we obtain a glimpse of the glory of God's power and grace that is to be manifested; but it has not yet been revealed what we shall be. If these glorified elders, who at least know far more of the glory that is to be expected than we in the church militant, fall down at the blowing of the seventh trumpet, when they see all things realized, how much more will reality surpass our expectation while we are still in the period in which we are saved by hope.

That these elders actually do place themselves on this standpoint of the complete fulfillment of the seventh trumpet and of the entire mystery of God is evident too from what they say. We read that they give thanks to God Almighty, "which art, and wast." In our version there is also added: "and art to come." But this is a mistake. In the original we merely read: "which art, and wast." He has come already in the fulfillment of the seventh trumpet. And therefore they now do not make the addition which was made in a former connection, and they give thanks to God for the fact that God has now actually assumed His great power: "We give thee thanks, O Lord God Almighty, which art, and wast, because thou hast taken to thee thy great power, and hast reigned."

Surely, they knew His great power; but now He has fully revealed it and taken it on. And this great power He has revealed in a two-fold way. He has revealed it in His wrath against the enemies of His kingdom, in the first place: "And the nations were angry, and thy wrath is come, and the time of the dead, that they should be judged....and that thou shouldest destroy them which destroy the earth." Proleptically, once more, the elders have seen how, during the time of the seventh trumpet, the enemy made a last attempt, how they through all the history of this world warred against the holy city and trampled it under foot, how they allied themselves against God and His Christ and purposed to destroy His Zion. But He Who was in the heavens laughed them to scorn. He has come to destroy them with the breath of His mouth. His power revealed itself against their power, and they were completely defeated. The devil, Antichrist, Babylon, Gog and Magog, all the enemies of the kingdom and the King have been destroyed. They that oppressed the people of God are no more. God has revealed His power and now reigns forevermore. The representatives of the church triumphant give Him thanks and worship because He has revealed His great power.

But, in the second place, He has also revealed His power and the grace shown to His people, the oppressed and faithful: "And the time came to give the reward to thy servants, the prophets, and to the saints, and to them that fear thy name, the small and the great." Again, proleptically the elders see how all is accomplished. That same judgment which cast the enemies of the kingdom into the pool that burns with fire and sulphur brought the reward to the faithful. They see the new heavens and the new earth realized by the seventh trumpet. They see how God's temple is with men and how He spreads His tabernacle over them all. In that new creation they see the mighty prophets who have witnessed in the old dispensation and who have shed their lifeblood for the testimony of God. In that new creation they behold the saints of the new dispensation, they who have performed special service in the church of God. In that new creation they see the general mass of God's people, they who fear His name. And to be sure that they are not misunderstood they add: "the small and the great." Not only the prophets and the special servants, not only Abel and Enoch and Noah and Abraham and Israel and Moses and all the heroes of faith, not only the great saints of the new dispensation, the giants of faith, who shone like the stars already on earth, but also the small are among them. Those who were among the common of God's people, the little ones, the weak and the timid, but faithful children of God who feared His name, — they all have their reward, and not one is forgotten. Is it a wonder that at the sight of this the elders fall on their faces and worship and give thanks?

The Judgments On Earth Brought By The Seventh Trumpet

But this seventh trumpet is here shown also from the viewpoint of the earth. We read in vs. 19: "And the temple of God was opened in heaven, and there was seen in his temple the ark of his testament: and there were lightnings, and voices, and thunderings, and an earthquake, and great hail." The meaning of this is rather evident. It shows the seventh trumpet in general from the viewpoint of the earth at this time. For the fact that the heaven is opened and that the temple of God is seen plainly reveals that the viewpoint is on earth. And it tells us, in general, that the opening of the temple in heaven and the appearance of the ark of God's covenant spells woe and judgment to the inhabitants of the earth, as symbolized in the lightnings and voices and thunders and the earthquake and great hail. Let us consider these different elements for a moment.

The temple of God in Jerusalem was made after the pattern of the heavenly temple, as it was shown to Moses on the mount. The idea of the temple is that of a dwellingplace of God. The temple was the house of God. It was the place where God dwelt in the holy place. But to this must be added that it was a limited place, where God dwelt in distinction from the world in general, in distinction, too, from the holy city at large. It speaks of the fact that in the world at large, as long as it is the kingdom of darkness, God, the Holy One, cannot take up His abode. But that distinction is only temporal. God shall not remain in His temple in distinction from the world. On the contrary, in the end that distinction shall be wiped away. God shall come forth from His holy temple in heaven, and He shall make of all the world His dwellingplace. That shall be realized in the blowing of this seventh trumpet. And for that reason we here see the temple of God which is in heaven opened, symbolizing that the Holy One issues forth to make of all the world His dwelling. Somewhat the same idea is expressed in the appearance of the ark. Naturally, when the temple is opened, the ark is seen. For the ark stood in the most holy place. It was in a most specific sense the symbol of the presence of God. It is called the throne of God in Scripture. It stood in the immediate presence of God, as symbolized in the cloud, and on its mercy seat the blood of atonement was sprinkled once a year. It contained the law of the covenant as well as the manna and the rod of Aaron. And therefore it is the symbol of God in His covenant greatness issuing His law to His people and blessing them with all the blessings of the covenant in the blood of atonement. That ark now appears. It tells us that the time is come that the law of God's covenant shall appear and issue forth over all the earth, that the full realization of that covenant is come, and that God shall have His throne in all the world.

But naturally, when the Holy One issues forth to make of all the world His temple, and when He is about to issue His law and realize to the full His holy covenant, this must be accompanied by the final destruction of His enemies. In the world into which the Holy One now issues forth, the enemy still reigns, and wickedness prevails. And before He can make of that world His temple, these enemies must be destroyed. Judgments must necessarily follow the opening of the temple, judgments which will defeat the enemy and make of the world a fit temple of the Almighty. And so we actually find it. Judgments issue forth out of that open temple, as we shall see in the future. Out of that temple comes the angel with the sharp sickle (14:17). Out of that temple come the seven angels that carry the seven bowls of wrath, ready to pour them over the earth (Chapter 15, ff.). Out of that temple comes the command to empty the vials which will bring the judgment of God over the enemies (16:1). And out of that temple comes the voice that announces that all is finished after the seven vials of wrath have been poured out (17:1). The opening of the temple spells judgment to purify the world and make it the temple of the Lord. And for that same reason we read also in the words of our text that the opening of the temple is followed by lightnings and voices and thunders and an earthquake and great hail, — all of them symbols of judgments which are about to strike the earth. What these judgments are we must see in due time. It is not told us here in detail.

But notice that also the seventh trumpet is full of comfort to the faithful, while at the same time filled with threats and woe to those who oppose the kingdom of our God. When that seventh trumpet shall have been finally revealed, we shall stand in our reward, small and great, the mighty and the weak, as many as fear the name of our God. It shall do the people of God no harm, but will bring their complete salvation. On the other hand, the wicked, those who love not God and His precepts, who despise His covenant and trample under foot the blood of Christ, may also surely know that not one of God's words shall fall to the earth. It shall all be realized. The glory of God's children shall bring woe and judgment to them. And their end shall be in the pool that burns with fire and brimstone.

Chapter XXIX

The Two Signs In Heaven

(Revelation 12:1-6)

1 And there appeared a great wonder in heaven; a woman clothed with the sun, and the moon under her feet, and upon her head a crown of twelve stars:
2 And she being with child cried, travailing in birth, and pained to be delivered.
3 And there appeared another wonder in heaven; and behold a great red dragon, having seven heads and ten horns, and seven crowns upon his heads.
4 And his tail drew the third part of the stars of heaven, and did cast them to the earth: and the dragon stood before the woman which was ready to be delivered, for to devour her child as soon as it was born.
5 And she brought forth a man child, who was to rule all nations with a rod of iron: and her child was caught up unto God, and to his throne.
6 And the woman fled into the wilderness, where she hath a place prepared of God, that they should feed her there a thousand two hundred and threescore days.

As we have remarked more than once, the eleventh chapter of the Book of Revelation reveals to us an outline of the general history of the church in this dispensation, and that with a view especially to her final struggle and ultimate victory and the condemnation of her enemies. It pictures the church in her actual condition as false church and show church and true church. It tells us in general of the calling and work of the church in the present dispensation in the picture of the two witnesses in sackcloth. It shows us the church in her battle against Antichrist, in her apparent defeat and shame, but also in her final glorification and victory.

The same chapter, so we noticed, also gave us a general, proleptical view of the seventh trumpet and its accomplishment. It did not reveal to us the detailed work and effect of that trumpet, but merely gave us a general glimpse of it. It showed us the seventh trumpet from the point of view of

411

the great voices which shouted in heaven and which proclaimed that now the kingdom of the world had become the kingdom of our Lord and of His Christ. Besides, the seventh trumpet was brought to our attention from the viewpoint of the elders, representatives of the church triumphant, who fell down on their faces and worshipped and thanked God Almighty. They thanked Him because He had revealed and assumed His great power. He revealed that power in the destruction of the enemies who came in wrath against Zion and against the Anointed of God. But He revealed that power also in the reward which He gave to His servants the prophets and to the saints and all those who feared His name, the small and the great. And, finally, we saw that seventh trumpet once more from the point of view of the earth. The inhabitants of the earth might see the temple in heaven opened and the ark of the covenant in the temple, — something that signified, as we showed, that God is about to proceed out of His temple into all creation as the Holy One, to make of all the world His temple and to realize His covenant and make His law of effect over the length and breadth of the earth. And this opening of the temple and issuing forth of the Holy One to make of all the world His temple was necessarily followed by judgments upon the wicked world, which loves not God and tramples under foot the blood of Christ.

We must remind you once more of the fact that in the future chapters you may expect individual pictures of the general facts revealed in Chapter 11. In the chapter we are about to discuss we find a revelation of the real spiritual agency which is back of the opposition and enmity against the church. In Chapter 11 we noticed that there was a bitter enmity against the church, an enmity finally revealed in Antichrist, who came out of the abyss. But the question arises: what is that power? Whence comes this bitter enmity? Where is its origin? And our chapter gives us to understand that the great battle of the world is after all not simply one between the church and the world, that it is not even one principally between Christ and Antichrist, but that in last instance it is one between God and the devil. And we cannot understand the situation unless we grasp and appreciate this fact. And since in the future the book will more fully reveal the power of opposition which rises against the church of God on earth, we must first have an insight into the spiritual powers that are back of this bitter force of opposition. This spiritual power behind the enmity against the church is pictured in the chapter before us and is introduced in the passage we are now discussing, which speaks of the two signs in heaven.

The Woman And The Dragon

John beholds, according to our text, two great wonders, or signs, in heaven. In the first verse of our text he mentions one of them, when he says: "And a great sign was seen in heaven." And in the third verse he makes mention of a second sign: "And there was seen another sign in heaven."

What John sees, then, is signs, or wonders. And by saying this he indicates at the same time that in the chapter before us we must not expect a literal description of something real, but symbolism, and that the passage must be explained accordingly, namely, in the symbolical sense of the word. If he had not told us, the contents of the chapter might have been sufficient indication that it must be explained in this sense. But now we know all the more certainly that here we have no literal description, but the presentation of some reality in symbolical language. A sign is something which has no significance and no reality in itself, but which is indicative of something else and which has meaning only as it stands connected with the reality which it symbolizes. And also in this connection I wish to call your attention to the fact that the Book of Revelation explains itself in regard to its symbolism. There is no one who makes the mistake of taking this chapter in the literal sense, so that the woman is a woman clothed with the real and literal sun and with the real moon under her feet. There is no one who interprets the dragon literally, as a dragon in heaven with seven heads and ten horns and a tail that draws a third part of the literal stars. Here we have symbolism, and every reader of the chapter knows that it is nothing else than symbolism.

The first wonder, or sign (we prefer the translation "sign" rather than "wonder", as also the Revised Version does), which John beholds in heaven is that of a woman. She is, on the one hand, of great and glorious appearance: for she is arrayed with the sun. In what way we must conceive of this concretely, so that we can form a picture of it in our minds, we know not. Nor does it matter, if we only remember that the sun in all its glory of light must serve to deck and adorn the woman, serve her as apparel. Under her feet she has the moon, and on her head she has a crown of twelve stars. In general we may say, therefore, that this woman as to her appearance is mighty and glorious, of so great importance that even the heavenly bodies of light must serve to add to her splendor. Even as a woman in beauty and significance is far above the apparel she wears, even as the clothing she wears must only serve to bring out the beauty of a woman, so this woman is far above the sun and moon and stars of heaven. And these must serve to bring out the beauty and significance of the woman. On the other hand, it must also be said that with all her glory she has not yet reached the purpose of her existence and is not perfectly happy and blessed. For she is described as being pregnant and in pain and travail of birth. She lives in the expectation of motherhood and evidently is about to be delivered. A woman, therefore, of high station in life, of great importance, exalted above the heavenly bodies of light, but a woman also at the same time in distress and in helpless condition, — such is the woman that is described by John.

The second sign which is seen in heaven forms a terrible contrast with this glorious, yet helpless, woman. It is a dragon. And a dragon in Scripture seems to indicate not one of God's own created animals in its natural appearance, but rather a monster. It is an animal departing considerably from the usual type in size and shape and number of limbs, an animal that is greatly deformed, as it exists only in the imagination of man. Such a monster is here pictured. Its main feature is that of a serpent. For in the ninth verse of this chapter the great dragon is called the old serpent. And therefore we do best to picture him as a great serpent. But it is a serpent of strange appearance. In the first place, it is of a red color, the color of blood and war and destruction. In the second place, it is a serpent of tremendous proportions, as is indicated, in the first place, by the fact that the text calls him a great dragon, but, in the second place, also becomes plain from the fact that with his tail he can draw a third part of the stars of heaven and cast them down to the earth. It is, therefore, a great and powerful and bloodthirsty monster in the main form of a serpent that is here pictured to us. And that it is a real monster of very unnatural appearance is plain from the fact that, in distinction from all other serpents, this one has seven heads and ten horns. The question as to the relative position of the seven heads and ten horns is certainly irrelevant. Attempts have been made to make a picture of this great dragon with his seven heads and ten horns, some placing two horns on three of the heads, others placing the horns all on one head, and still others preferring to have three of the horns between the fifth and the sixth heads of the dragon. But John tells us nothing about their relative position, and hence we have nothing to do with it. A still further peculiarity of the dragon is that on each of his heads he carries a diadem, a royal crown; and therefore he is also a dragon with royal power and authority. And, as has already been said, with one stroke of his tail he carries away the third part of the stars of heaven, and therefore reveals great power. It is a monstrous serpent of prodigious dimensions, of terrible power, with royal authority, of hideous appearance, and with a bloodthirsty and destructive nature.

Now if we ask the question: what is the identity of this woman and the identity of this dragon, and what are the things signified by these signs? it is perhaps advisable to start with the dragon.

In the first place, it may be said that from his very appearance we already infer that he signifies some tremendous and evil power. In the second place, to approach his identity more definitely, we recall that already in paradise we have met with a serpent, and that there the serpent was none other than the devil in person. But above all do we find little difficulty in finding the identity of this dragon for the simple reason that our chapter tells us in plain words that it is the devil. For in the ninth verse of this chapter we read: "And the great dragon was cast out, that old serpent, called the Devil, and Satan, which deceiveth the whole world." It is therefore beyond all doubt that in this dragon we have a picture of the devil in person.

But the question still remains: why is he pictured in this manner in our text? What do the individual features of this great dragon stand for? Why is it that the sign of the devil is very appropriately this terrible dragon?

And then we call your attention, in the first place, to the fact that he is pictured as a monster, that is, as a being with an altogether unnatural and deformed appearance in nature. And such is the devil. The devil is indeed a monster. Not that God had made him a monster: God made of him a glorious and powerful creature. But with his great and glorious power he fell away from God, rose in rebellion against the Almighty, with that power still stands in opposition against the God who made him, and thus he made a caricature, a terrible monster of himself. The serpent may be the fittest symbol of the devil because of its subtlety and shrewdness. But the mere serpent does not picture the devil adequately. He must be symbolized as a monster serpent. God never made a serpent with seven heads and ten horns. The serpent as God made him has but one head and no horns at all. And thus it is with the devil. God never made a devil. The devil is self-made as devil, as an evil power. And since he deformed himself in his attempt to exalt himself, he has become a hideous monster. You understand, of course, that all this is under the power and providence of God. But nevertheless, God did not make the devil as devil. In the second place, let us consider that also the greatness of the dragon is an appropriate sign of the devil. God made of Satan a great creature among the angels. Perhaps we may say that he was the greatest of all the angels, great in power and glory. And this greatness the devil has not lost by his fall. On the contrary, he retained it. Only, that same greatness wherewith he was to glorify his Creator he now employs against Him as a real monster. In the third place, we must take into consideration the color of the dragon. He is red. And red is the color of blood, of war and destruction and murder, — again, a fit symbol of the devil, for he is the murderer from the beginning, according to Scripture.

In the fourth place, our attention is especially called to the seven crowned heads and the ten horns which he possesses. The numbers **seven** and **ten**, as we have explained repeatedly, are symbolical numbers. They do not refer to ten kingdoms, or ten kings, or to seven kings literally; but they denote the authority and power of this dragon, the devil. Seven, as well as ten, is a complete number. They therefore both indicate completeness. But as we have explained before, seven is a holy number in this respect, that it generally is used to denote the completion of the kingdom of God and its fulness, while ten is the number that denotes the measure of time or space or power as it is allotted and limited to any creature by God's decree. A divinely limited measure of something is indicated by the number ten. Further, it needs no proof that the crowned head is the symbol of royalty and of kingly power and authority. Seven crowned heads, therefore, would symbolically indicate the authority and royal power of the kingdom of God. And therefore, as to the appearance of this dragon we would draw the conclusion that the devil is king in the kingdom of God, for he possesses the seven crowned heads.

But we must be careful with the interpretation of this dragon. For remember: he is a deceiver. And therefore we must rather explain the ten horns first, before we draw our conclusion as to his real power. The horn is the symbol of might and strength and power in Scripture. And that this dragon has ten horns indicates, therefore, that the devil has just exactly as much power as God has allowed him, — no more and no less. It indicates that the power of the devil is limited by the sovereign decree of God Almighty and that the devil can do no more, no less, than that which God has decreed for him and which God wills him to do. But how must it then be explained that at the same time the devil seems to have the complete authority in the kingdom of God, as indicated in the seven crowned heads?

We would explain it simply in this way. The devil is the deceiver. And by
these seven crowns you must not be deceived. God did not put them on
his head. He put them on himself. They are not real crowns either. They
are not made in heaven, whence all authority issues forth; but they are
made in hell. And therefore they are no good; they are counterfeit. The
truth is that the devil is a pretender, an impostor, an intruder, a usurper.
He intrudes into the kingdom of God. He usurped the power of the
kingdom, and he put on his own seven crowns and tries to give his
kingdom the aspect of the kingdom of God by these seven crowns. But the
reality of the situation is that he has ten horns. He has God-limited power,
and with this God-limited power he will never be able to maintain his
seven crowns and his royal appearance. On the contrary, after he has done
all that was permitted him to do, God will take those crowns away, crush
those seven heads, break the horns, and cast the miserable dragon into
eternal hell.

What may be meant by his drawing of the stars of heaven with his tail?
This seems to be plain in itself. The stars in this connection must, of
course, not be taken in the literal sense, no more than the entire portion.
In this connection the inference is plain that they indicate the fellow
angels of the devil. In Job the angels are called the morning-stars. And
indeed this application is very appropriate for these spiritual inhabitants of
the sphere of eternal light. And the devil himself has been such a
morning-star, — perhaps, as we have said before, the greatest and most
glorious among them all. And although the passage in Isaiah 14:12 cannot
literally be applied to Satan, yet the language in which this metaphor
against the king of Babylon is used, is such that the latter is evidently a
type of the devil. And therefore also the devil may fittingly be called
Lucifer, the day or morning-star. This morning-star, as we know, rebelled
against God Almighty. But he was not alone. He instigated a general
rebellion in the heaven of heavens. He seduced others of his fellow angels
to rise with him and exalt themselves against the Most High. And it is this
feature that is pictured of the devil most probably in the fourth verse of
this chapter. He dragged the third part, that is, in this sense, a great many,
yet not a majority, of his fellow angels with him in his fall from heaven.
And they together with him were cast down from their exalted place.

In conclusion, therefore, we may say that in this dragon we have a sign
of the devil as the powerful, bloodthirsty murderer from the beginning,
the impostor and intruder into God's kingdom, the deceiver, who tries to

appear as the king of the world but whose power is limited by God
Almighty and whose ultimate defeat is certain, the rebel, who in his
rebellion succeeded to drag along with himself a host of his fellow angels,
who sank with him into perdition.

Now who is represented by the woman in the chapter?

This question is not difficult to answer. Almost immediately we
recognize in her the church of the living God in Christ Jesus. In the first
place, this is true because we meet here with the same period of time
which was mentioned in the preceding chapter in regard to the two
witnesses. Those two witnesses, symbols of the church with her anointed
servants, witnessed in the world, clothed in sackcloth, for a period of
twelve hundred and sixty days. And thus we find of this woman, after she
is delivered of her child, that she is in the wilderness for that same period
of time, that is, twelve hundred sixty days. The inference is very strong,
therefore, that this woman is essentially the same body as was symbolized
in the two witnesses, that is, therefore, the church of God. But, in the
second place, we find a still stronger indication of this truth in the fact
that this woman brings forth the man child who is to rule all nations with
a rod of iron. This last clause, in connection with the second Psalm and
with Revelation 2:27, leaves no doubt that the man child is the Christ, the
King of Zion. In Psalm 2:9 we read of this Christ: "Thou shalt break them
with a rod of iron; thou shalt dash them in pieces like a potter's vessel."
And in Revelation 2:27 we read that the promise is given to him that
overcometh that he shall rule all nations with a rod of iron; and then the
addition is given concerning the Christ, "as I also have received of my
Father." There is no question about it, therefore, that the man child
brought forth by this woman is the Christ. But then there can be no
question about it either that the woman is none other than the church of
God, the woman, namely, as is conceived of in Genesis 3:15, to whom the
great seed was promised. Christ is man. Although He is the Son of God, He
is man and He is of man. He issues from humanity, but not from humanity
as it is under the power of Satan, but rather from the people of God,
from the church of the living God, from Israel. He is the Son of David.
That this woman is the church of God is further suggested by her crown of
twelve stars: for twelve is the number of the church in this dispensation, as we have observed before. And, finally, it is suggested
by the very fact that she is a woman: for the church appears
throughout Scripture as a woman, as the bride adorned for her

husband. The woman, therefore, is the picture of the church. But also here the question must be answered: how does that church appear in the words of our text? And then we must call your attention to the fact that here we have evidently a picture of the church in the old dispensation. Before the woman is delivered and proceeds into the wilderness (that is, therefore, the woman as she appears as a sign in heaven), she represents the church of the old dispensation. This is plain from the fact that her man child is not yet born. The woman therefore represents the church before the birth of Christ, the church as she is essentially glorious and queen of the heavens, but as she still is in expectation of her man child who is to deliver her and at the same time become her Bridegroom.

Now you must not make the mistake of thinking that this woman represents the mother of Jesus, or that at least it represents merely Israel. That has often been inferred from the fact that she is already in pain to be delivered and that she expects her son momentarily. But the woman represents the church throughout the entire dispensation of the Old Testament. That entire church lived continually in the expectation that the Messiah would be born and would be born soon. Even Eve imagined that in Cain the promise was realized, and therefore she called him "acquired." Enoch prophesied of His coming for judgment. Abraham longed to see His day. Jacob foretold of His entrance into the world. Moses spoke of the coming of a great prophet. The prophets of Israel spoke of His birth, even indicating time and place. And Simeon could not die before he had seen the Hope of Israel. And the very expression in our text reminds us of the prophecy of Isaiah concerning Him: "For unto us a child is born, unto us a son is given; and the government shall be upon his shoulders," (Isaiah 9:6). And therefore, the entire church of the old dispensation, from paradise onward, presents the picture of this woman, travailing in pain and longing and expecting to bring forth the man child.

Their Attitude And Struggle

Now we must still consider the attitude of the dragon towards the woman and the conflict that ensues between the two. The text tells us that the woman stands in her glory, but also in her helplessness, and that the dragon stands before her. He is evidently watching her, and at the same time barring her way to escape. With intent watchfulness the dragon guards this woman and studies her every movement. And his purpose in doing so is most devilish indeed. It is not the woman as such who is his aim, but rather the child whom she is to bring forth. If only that woman did not expect to bring forth that man child, he would care little about her and about her glory. But that man child is evidently of extreme importance to him. And therefore he watches the woman, in order that as soon as the child sees the light of the world he may kill and devour him. But we read that the child is born and is caught up in heaven to God. The child, therefore, escapes him. The devil cannot reach his purpose. He fails. The old deceiver is deceived. And it may be expected that in his rage and fury he will now cast himself upon the woman, in order to devour her at all events. But the woman escapes by fleeing into the wilderness, where she has a place prepared by God and where she is nourished a thousand two hundred and threescore days.

The meaning of all this is not dark.

After all we have discussed, it is plain that the church of the old dispensation is laboring in pain to bring forth the Christ. It is also evident that that church of the old dispensation lives in continual expectation that the man child who is to rule the nations with a rod of iron shall be born. She has reason to expect this, for God Himself has promised the church this seed. In Genesis 3:15 we read the well-known words: "And I will put enmity between thee and the woman, and between thy seed and her seed; it shall bruise thy head, and thou shalt bruise his heel." Such was the promise. And therefore, the church lived in expectation of this seed of the woman from that very moment forth.

But also the devil lived in that expectation. He was right there when that promise was made. Nay, still stronger, the promise was addressed to him. It was a promise given in the form of a challenge to the devil that he would suffer defeat. And therefore, also the devil expected the Messiah. I dare say even, in the face of the fact that the devil understood the situation far better than either Adam or Eve, understood also the significance of this seed of the woman better than our first parents, – he clearly had caught on to the significance of that word of the Almighty. And he knows that if the seed of the woman is born, and if that seed of the woman accomplishes his purpose, he, the devil, will be deprived of his power and of his royal diadems, and his heads will be crushed; and therefore he watches the church of the old dispensation closely. His aim is all the time to crush that seed of the woman, either by preventing that it ever be born or by devouring it as soon as it sees the light of the world.

But with all his watchfulness he fails. Christ is born and gains the victory and is taken to heaven in glory and leaves the devil behind in furious rage. True, the church still remains behind. She is in the wilderness, that is, practically excluded from outward glory and dominion. The devil still reigns in the world and still has his seven diadems. But also in this period of the new dispensation the church is safely kept and nourished in the place which she has prepared for her by God Almighty Himself.

Such is the meaning of the text. It simply reveals how the devil throughout the old dispensation exerts himself to kill the seed of the woman and to prevent the victory of Christ. It is not difficult to trace this struggle throughout the old dispensation. It is to be seen already in the murder of Abel. No doubt the devil made the same mistake at first as did Adam and Eve. They thought that the Christ would be born immediately. At first Eve imagined that her firstborn was the promised seed; and therefore she called him Cain, that is, "I have begotten a man of God." But as the two boys, Cain and Abel, grew up, they must all have realized that Cain was not the man, since he was godless. And the same difference between the two boys must also have been the cause that the hope and expectation was gradually referred from Cain to Abel. The devil must have made the mistake of thinking that Abel was the promised seed; and hence, through Cain he kills him. But Seth is born, and the seed of the woman in the spiritual sense multiplies in the line of Seth. The devil begins to realize that his problem is not so simple. And therefore, standing in front of the woman, he employs different methods. He tries to gain the victory by the process of amalgamation, and the sons of God marry the daughters of men, so that the whole world is well-nigh deprived of the spiritual seed of the woman. But again God interferes through the flood, and He saves the seed of the woman in the family of Noah.

And thus it continues all through the history of the old dispensation. At the building of the tower of Babel the devil tries to make his own stronghold against the seed of the woman and to establish his own kingdom. At the time of Abraham, he only is left, practically, of the seed of the woman. In Egypt the devil tries to extinguish the seed of the woman by oppressing Israel. In the desert he brings them to apostasy. In Canaan he sends enemies against them till they finally are led into captivity. And after the captivity he makes life hard for them. At the time of Antiochus Epiphanes the daily sacrifice is taken away, and the seed of the woman is killed on a large scale.

But in spite of it all, the Great Seed appears. Christ is born. And the angels loudly proclaim that the glory is God's in the highest. Also Satan is now certain that He is the Christ, and therefore he directs all his efforts against Him. How this Christ will crush him and gain the victory is not plain to him, no more than it was to Israel of that time. And therefore he applies two different methods to devour this seed. First of all, he makes the attempt to subject Him spiritually, and he offers Him all the kingdoms of the world if only He will fall down and worship him, that is, Satan, knowing that if this promised seed will only do this, the devil will maintain his royal crowns and sovereignty. He tries this repeatedly in the life of Christ. But when he fails, he rouses the enemies of Christ against Him, so that they finally kill Him. I imagine that the devil was foolish enough, at least for some time, to hope that in His death he had killed the seed of the woman. But it was but for a short time. For that Seed, suffering on the cross, at the moment of His death cried out with a loud voice, "Father, into thy hands do I commend my spirit." That Seed rises from death and the grave and is taken to heaven, to sit at the right hand of God in everlasting glory, now working till the kingdom of the world shall lie at the feet of the Almighty. That the devil had not thought this is very evident. That victory lay in the way of suffering, exaltation through humiliation, life through death. And that he after all prepared his own defeat by killing this Seed of the woman, this he had not clearly before his mind. The deceiver is deceived! He has deceived himself. And he stays behind, as we hope to see in the future, filled with fury and rage against the woman who brought forth the man child.

Such is the meaning of the text. The battle of the world is a battle of the devil against God. Not between the world and the church in last instance, not even between Antichrist and Christ, is that battle. They all are agents. Christ is the anointed agent of God to fight, with His people, the battle against the devil. Antichrist, as we hope to see, is the agent of Satan, to fight his battles against God and His church.

What a tremendous idea is expressed here! We, as the covenant people, as being of God's party in the midst of the world, fight the battle of Jehovah against the old serpent, the devil. There is magic joy in the very idea that the Lord will use us as instruments in His hand, nay, as His living people, to fight against the old dragon. In the second place, let us also note that God Almighty has always been victorious in the past, and that the devil with all his attempts to prevent the birth of the Great Seed has simply effected his own defeat. So it will be in the future. God will always be victorious, of course. Not yet has the devil given up the attempt to gain dominion over the kingdom of God. But the voices in heaven have already sung of it, and the elders have acknowledged it, that the kingdom of the world has become the kingdom of our Lord and of His Christ.

Behold, He cometh! And His reward is with Him. Let us therefore be faithful and true to His name even unto the end.

Chapter XXX
War In Heaven

(Revelation 12:7-12)

7 And there was war in heaven: Michael and his angels fought against the dragon; and the dragon fought and his angels,
8 And prevailed not; neither was their place found any more in heaven.
9 And the great dragon was cast out, that old serpent, called the Devil, and Satan, which deceiveth the whole world: he was cast out into the earth, and his angels were cast out with him.
10 And I heard a loud voice saying in heaven, Now is come salvation, and strength, and the kingdom of our God, and the power of his Christ: for the accuser of our brethren is cast down, which accused them before our God day and night.
11 And they overcame him by the blood of the Lamb, and by the word of their testimony; and they loved not their lives unto the death.
12 Therefore rejoice, ye heavens, and ye that dwell in them. Woe to the inhabiters of the earth and of the sea! for the devil is come down unto you, having great wrath, because he knoweth that he hath but a short time.

I think that in the portion quoted above we have a parallel, and, in a way a continuation, of the first part of Chapter 12. You will remember that we have taken the position that in Chapter 12 we have a description of the spiritual agencies which are back of the power which rises out of the abyss and which exalts itself against the two witnesses, against the church of Christ, in this dispensation. In the first portion of this chapter we found a description of the two signs in heaven; and we discussed the identity of each sign, as well as their mutual relation and the attitude of the second against the first. As to the first sign, we found no difficulty in recognizing in it the symbol of the church upon earth. We found that in the sign of the woman with child we have the symbol especially of the church in the old dispensation, before Christ was born. The second sign is that of the great red dragon, which, as we interpreted, and as is literally expressed in the chapter, is none other than the devil himself. The devil stands before the woman throughout the old dispensation in an inimical attitude for the purpose of devouring her child as soon as it has been born. However, his efforts are vain. Christ is born, performs His work, and is exalted to highest glory at the right hand of the Almighty. Now parallel with this effort of the dragon against the woman runs the incident recorded in the words of our text and which speaks of the battle of the spirits in heaven.

The Combatants In This War

If the preceding portion depicted a battle of the devil against the church of the old dispensation to prevent the realization of the promise given in paradise, the present passage speaks of another war, also waged by the devil, but this time fought in person by him and by his angels, this time fought in heaven instead of upon earth, this time fought against his fellow angels who remained faithful to God at the time when the devil and his angels fell away.

We must conceive of this battle as being very real. There is no mention here of signs and symbols. There is absolutely nothing in the text which indicates that we must explain this portion in the allegorical fashion, as has been done in various ways. I take it, therefore, that we have here the record of a real battle in the real heaven. It is not a battle in aerial places, as some would have it, so that the idea would be that Michael and his angels are on the offensive, come down to fight with the devil and his host; but it is a battle in heaven, in the abode of the good and holy angels, before the very countenance of God. And I take it that the devil and his host are on the offensive and that they are challenging the holy angels to fight a spiritual war with them. A real battle, therefore, it is.

But it is well that we remember from the outset that all real battles are not fought with material weapons. It is not necessary to have sabre and bayonet or to bring forth cannon and gun in order to fight this battle. This battle has often been pictured poetically. But such a battle is inconceivable between the opposing sides that are here pictured. And we would lose the point in question altogether if we would thus picture to our minds the battle that is here described. No, this battle is a purely spiritual battle. It is fought not with material but with spiritual weapons, with weapons of intellect and shrewdness and subtlety, with the spiritual weapons of law and righteousness. For the combatants in this war are spirits pure and simple. They are, moreover, immortal spirits, at least in the sense that they have no body and that therefore they cannot die the physical death. They have no flesh and blood, so that they cannot be wounded physically. It is a war between angels, a real and fierce battle indeed, but nevertheless a purely spiritual one, fought with spiritual means, and therefore also with a purely spiritual outcome.

On the one hand, so we read in the text, stand Michael and his holy angels. It is not the Christ, as some interpreters would have it, appealing especially to his name and greatness. True, his name means "who is like God." But Christ was not merely like God, but very God Himself, the Person of the Son of God. True, he is described as very great and powerful. But are there not powerful and mighty angels that are mentioned by name in Scripture? True, he fights against the opponent of Christ. But is it so peculiar that the angels stand on the very side of Christ and fight His battles against the devil and his host? Hence, we must not interpret this as referring to the Christ, but to a mighty angel. Especially is this clear from Daniel 10, where Michael is mentioned by name. And you will find at a careful reading that he is clearly distinguished from the Christ.

Who is this Michael?

We find him mentioned once more in the New Testament besides in the portion of our text. Jude, verse 9, speaks of him as Michael, the archangel, who was "contending with the devil" and disputed with him about the body of Moses. Little it matters at this point what the dispute really implied. But we learn from this portion in regard to Michael:

1) That he is an archangel. How many of these archangels there are we know not. A Jewish tradition has it that there were seven. Of course, this is not impossible; but it is nevertheless without Scriptural basis. Sufficient it is to know that Michael is an archangel. He is a chief, one of the chiefs, of the angels, and therefore occupies a great and exalted place in heaven. He is clothed with great power and authority, no doubt.

2) That he contends with the devil, the enemy of God, just as in the words of our text.

3) That he fights in behalf of one of the great among God's people.

In the Old Testament we find him mentioned in Daniel 10:13. There we find that Michael contends with an evil prince for influence with the king of Persia, and that again in behalf of the people of God. The meaning evidently is that an evil spirit tries to influence the king of Persia against the people of Israel. But Michael comes and fights with this evil spirit and prevails. In verse 21 of the same chapter in Daniel, Michael is mentioned again: and there he is directly called the prince of the people of God. And, finally, in Daniel 12:1 we read: "And at that time shall Michael stand up, the great prince which standeth for the children of thy people: and there shall be a time of trouble, such as never was since there was a nation even to that same time." Also here we find that Michael is great, and that he is a prince among the angels, and that he stands for the people of God and in their defense in a time of great trouble, when they are evidently in great danger.

Hence, taking into consideration at the same time the words of our text, we may draw the conclusion that Michael is a great angel, a chief and prince among his fellow angels. Originally he perhaps had his equal as to power and authority only in the devil. For we read in Jude that this great Michael, acknowledging the original power and authority of the devil, did not dare to curse and blaspheme him, but left it to God. A great angel, clothed with much authority, set perhaps, as we gather also from our text, over many angels, is especially appointed by God to fight against the devil and to lead his angels against him. And he is at the same time the great guardian and combatant on the side of the people of God in time of trouble. And therefore we may surmise from the outset that as Michael, also according to the words of our text, fights with the devil, the people of God must be involved. He does not fight alone, but has his angels with him. As we have indicated already, this does not necessarily mean that all the good angels fight on the side of Michael, but merely that he is chief of a certain number of angels in heaven and that now he leads his army of good angels against the devil and his host.

For the latter is the opposing side. The dragon and his angels are fighting here with Michael and his angels. We need not dwell very long upon their identity and power. We have seen that the devil is a most powerful monster, bloodthirsty and fierce, with terrible hatred in his bosom against the man child, as the great opponent of God and His kingdom, who has usurped the power of the kingdom but who is limited in his power by the decree of God. At present we need not pay any more attention to him. He is here called the old serpent, the devil, the old deceiver, and Satan. And no doubt these names are here given him with a special purpose. But the meaning of these we shall learn later, as well as the purpose for which they are given to him in this connection. He comes with his angels. No doubt he has a large army of them, as we have learned from the preceding portion: he dragged along in his fall from God a third of the angels in heaven. And though I do not think that he has all these evil spirits at his own disposal at any time, nevertheless we may well imagine that he is there with a large and powerful army, to give battle to Michael and his angels. Such, then, are the combatants in this war. It is a spiritual war between the mightiest among the mighty of God's spiritual creatures: those who fell away from Him and hate Him and strive after His authority, on the one hand; and those who remained obedient and subject to God and who therefore fight His battles, on the other.

The Time Of This Warfare

It will be of importance to ascertain, in the second place, the time of this battle. For this will help us to determine the significance and the object of this war to a large extent. As we have said in the beginning, we understand this portion as running parallel with the preceding, so that the time of the devil's opposition against the woman and the time of this battle coincide. The scene differs, the stage of the one being upon earth, of the other in heaven; but the time is the same.

We must therefore not think of a spiritual battle in heaven before Satan entered into paradise to deceive man. It is true that at a superficial reading we may receive the impression that this is the battle referred to and that we are here taught that when Satan and his angels rebelled against God, the Lord employed the good and holy angels to expel them from heaven. It is also true that some have interpreted this passage in that sense, and that especially poetic imagination is fond of drawing this picture in this connection. Then it should seem as if the text were really explained. It is a battle in heaven, and therefore it was fought when Satan was still there. It is a battle the result of which is that the place of the devil is found no more in heaven, exactly corresponding with what we know of the rebellion of Satan before he came to the earth. And, in the third place, the devil and his angels are cast down to the earth, again explaining his work in paradise and ever since. Nevertheless this explanation is soon proven to be impossible if we only study the text once more. The great voice in heaven tells us of more results of this spiritual battle. It tells us that now the salvation and the power of the kingdom of God have come, that the authority of Christ has appeared, — things which surely could not be said immediately after the first rebellion of Satan and his angels. There was as yet no salvation. There was as yet no manifestation of the authority of Christ. But there is more. The devil is here called "accuser of our brethren." And by "brethren" is here meant the saved in Christ Jesus evidently. It is in that capacity evidently that he fought this spiritual battle. It is also in that capacity that he was defeated. For the joy in heaven is caused especially by the fact that the accuser of the brethren as such is cast down. The same great voice speaks of the fact that there were saved in Christ who have overcome through the blood of the Lamb and the testimony which they gave. All this gives us an entirely different impression. The time during which this battle is fought is not before the entrance of the devil into paradise: for at this time there are already saved in Christ Jesus, brethren who fight through the blood of the Lamb and who overcome, who have loved not their lives even unto death. And at this time the devil already appears as the accuser of the brethren, who accuses them before the countenance of God day and night.

On the other hand, it cannot be the time of the end that is here referred to. Thus other interpreters have it. There are some who maintain that the woman referred to in the first part of this chapter is the visible church and that the man child whom this woman is about to bring forth is the church invisible, the real spiritual children of God. Their birth is their final glorification. When all the children of God shall have been gathered into glory, the visible church, as pictured in the sign of the woman, shall have finished her giving birth to the church invisible; and the latter shall be caught up in glory to God's throne. But now, after the final glorification of these real spiritual people of God has taken place in the end of time, the devil makes a last and bold attack upon them, in order to draw them down to hell. And in this last attack they are defended by Michael and his holy angels. In itself this were possible, were it not against the plain indication of the text. First of all, it is against the simple meaning of the text to make of the man child the church invisible instead of the Christ. Such an explanation leads us into all kinds of difficulties from which we cannot extricate ourselves. But besides, when the birth of the man child in the sense of the church invisible shall have been completed, there shall be no more people of God upon earth. Or, to speak plainly, if the giving birth to the man child represents the visible church giving birth to the invisible in her final glorification, then it is plain that when this birth is finished and all the people of God shall have been caught up to the throne of God, there shall be no more children of God in the church militant upon earth. Yet we read that after this battle is finished there is still the woman, there is still the church of God upon earth. For the devil persecutes her in his wrath. And not only is it true that there is still a church of God on earth, but there are also faithful children of God who keep the commandments of God and who hold the testimony, verse 17. All this makes it sufficiently plain that this battle is not fought at the time of the end, when all the people of God shall already have been taken up into glory. And therefore also this interpretation must evidently be discarded.

Finally, we also discard the interpretation which has it that this battle is fought immediately after the exaltation of Christ. This interpretation imagines that in this chapter we have a strictly chronological order of events. First the devil stands watching the people of God to devour the great seed they are to bring forth. Then, when the child is born, and he fails to crush it, and it is caught up to the throne of God in heaven, the devil immediately after the exaltation of Christ also attempts to ascend to heaven, in order that he may attack the glorified Christ in heaven. But aside from the fact that we read nowhere of such an attack upon Christ in heaven, in which He was defended by Michael and his angels, it certainly must be evident that this is also against the plain indication of the text. Not the Christ, but the brethren are the immediate object of this attack of Satan. And as we shall presently see, he appears here especially as the accuser of the brethren, who is overcome by them because of the blood of the Lamb and the word of their testimony. And therefore also this interpretation cannot be maintained.

There is but one possibility left. That possibility, which is fully warranted by the text itself and which satisfies all the elements, is that our text gives us a picture of a battle fought in heaven between the devil and his host and Michael and his angels **all through the old dispensation.** At the same time that the devil carries on a war upon earth and watches the church, in order to devour the Christ as soon as He is born, or even to prevent His birth, he also wages war in heaven with the spiritual powers that remain standing. All during this time there were brethren of whom the devil appears as the accuser. All through this dispensation there were those who loved not their life unto the death. It is, therefore, a battle fought all during this time. It is a battle, however, which must necessarily end, as we shall see, with the manifestation of Christ's glory and victory and His completed work, so that the battle is won through the blood of the Lamb. And if we take this view, we can also explain how the devil, after having suffered defeat in this spiritual battle in heaven, still can come down to the earth to persecute the rest of the seed of the woman. For these others are the faithful of the New Testament day. And therefore, as to the time of this war, we would hold that it began immediately after the death of Abel, that it continued all through the time of the Old Testament, and that it was finished contemporaneously with the exaltation of Jesus Christ.

The Immediate Object Of This Warfare

I think that this interpretation will become all the more acceptable if we for a moment consider what might be the object of the devil in making this attack in heaven upon Michael and his angels.

Was it his object to drag down these mighty ones, even as once he did with one third of the stars of heaven? Did he aim at the fall of Michael and his angels? This does not seem likely from the outset. For, in the first place, the fact that Michael is here defending and battling with the devil as the one who stands for the children of God's people and who once fought with the devil for the body of Moses immediately makes us think that also here he is fighting not in his own defense, but in behalf of the people of God. The people of God are the object of the wrath of the devil. And Michael is sent, is appointed, to defend them. Besides, in the record of the great voice, which evidently sings of the victory of this spiritual battle, there is not even mention made of either Michael or of his angels. They do not sing of victory because they have been delivered from danger, but because of the deliverance and the victory of the brethren. And therefore, it is not likely that Satan's object in this attack is the angels themselves, against whom he is fighting, but rather the people of God of the old dispensation in as far as they have already entered into glory.

This, therefore, is our interpretation. We think that all through the Old Testament days there was a battle fought in heaven for the souls of those who entered into glory before the suffering and exaltation of Christ, — a battle which was the logical concomitant of the battle the devil was fighting against the church to prevent the coming of the Great Seed. Just as certain as the devil was in his fight to prevent the coming of the Messiah, just as determined he had to be to fight this spiritual battle in heaven for the souls of the saved ones of the old dispensation. And therefore, once more, our explanation is that the devil fights a battle in heaven all through the days of the Old Testament for the possession of the souls who already had entered into glory from the days of Abel on, and that in this attack he is opposed by Michael and his angels, who stand for the children of God's people.

That this is but logical is clear. Christ had not yet come. And that meant that historically speaking the debt of the sinner had not yet been paid. Historically the sins of Abel and Enoch and Noah, the patriarchs, the prophets, had not yet been atoned for. And therefore, historically they died as sinners. Historically Christ had not yet crushed the head of the serpent, had not yet assumed dominion. Historically speaking, the devil still was sovereign, and all the world lay at his feet because of the sin of man, all during the time of the old dispensation. True, in God's counsel it was different. In God's counsel it was established. In that counsel Christ had been appointed head and mediator of His people, and all His people had been given to Him. In that counsel not only the people who should be born on earth after His own appearance, suffering, and exaltation, but also those who were born before this had been given to Christ. Also Abel and Enoch and Noah and Abraham and Isaac and Jacob and all the saved in Christ of the Old Testament were given to this head of the covenant. They were in Him. And because God's counsel is absolutely sure, therefore these men of the Old Testament did not have to wait for their salvation till all was finished. But being justified in the decree from all eternity, they entered into glory before the Savior had actually come and paid for their sins.

But Satan did not figure with this counsel of God. Nor could he imagine how certain that counsel of the Almighty was. He could not know that all these men were justified from all eternity for the simple reason that in the counsel of God they were given to Christ. On the contrary, it was against that counsel, in as far as he knew it, that he fought the battle on earth. Satan actually must have had the hope in his devilish heart that he could so thwart the purpose of the Almighty that the Christ would never be born, would never pay for the sins of the people of God, would never enter into everlasting glory with them. And therefore, according to Satan's view of the matter, all these saints of the Old Testament entered into glory as sinners upon whom he had a righteous claim, as sinners who deserved to go to hell because their sins had not yet been atoned for. God acted according to His counsel, however; and that counsel was certain as to its fulfillment. But Satan took the historical view of the matter, and maintained that all these souls who entered into glory belonged rightfully to him, that they had sinned against the Almighty, that they according to His own sentence were condemned to death, and that therefore they might not be in heaven. And thus we imagine that the devil goes to heaven to accuse the brethren.

Now we also understand the text. Now we understand why he is called the old serpent, the devil, that is, the slanderer and accuser, why he is called Satan, the old deceiver. He slanders the saints of the Old Testament before God. He lies about them. He says that they have no right to enter into glory because they are condemned sinners. He accuses them by lying and slandering, and at the same time he slanders the name and the righteousness of God Who takes sinners into everlasting glory.

Thus we can also understand the nature of the battle to a certain extent. The devil comes to fight for the souls of Abel and Enoch and Noah and Abraham and Isaac and Jacob, and of Moses and Samuel and of all the prophets, and of all those who had the promise and who lived and died by faith, endured the shame and mockery and persecution of the world in the old dispensation, and loved not their lives unto the death. And God sends Michael against him, to guard these souls and to defend the righteousness of God and the right of the saints to glory. The devil claims that they are sinners; Michael retorts that they are righteous. The devil maintains that they have sinned in paradise in Adam, and that they have sinned all their lives, and that therefore according to the righteousness of God they must be lost, they must go to hell. Michael replies that God Almighty has declared them righteous and that His Word alone is sovereign. The devil maintains that they are not righteous since they themselves have never paid for their sins and no mediator has yet appeared. Michael answers that God has revealed that He would send the Great Seed to perform this work of salvation and that to Him all these saints have been given. The devil finally assures Michael that he is fighting a great war on earth and that he will surely prevent the coming of this man child, or, if he comes, will certainly devour him. Michael's answer is that God is mighty to fulfill all His Word and to crush the head of the serpent. And thus this spiritual battle continues all through the old dispensation. The battle here pictured is a battle for the possession of the saints of Christ who have died and entered into glory during the time of the old dispensation, who have not loved their lives unto death, who have clung to the word of their testimony, and who were accused day and night before the countenance of

Almighty God by the devil, that old serpent, who deceives the whole world and who slanders the people of God from age to age, day and night.

The Outcome Of The Warfare

Thus we can also understand that this battle must end with the historical realization of the salvation of Christ. When Christ comes, suffers, pays for the sins of His people, ascends to heaven, and is glorified, the contest is decided in favor of Michael and his angels. It is become plain, so plain that even the devil cannot contradict it, that the saints of the Old Testament had a right to glory on the basis of the future expiation of their sins and guilt. And therefore the conflict must end here. The devil is defeated. He cannot continue. Michael can now point to facts. He can now point to the finished work of Christ and overwhelmingly convince the devil that he fights a vain battle and that God was righteous in saving the saints of the old dispensation.

Then we can also understand why in the song of victory, sung immediately after this battle is finished, no mention is made of the angels, but only of the brethren who were accused but who had gained the victory through the blood of the Lamb and their faith in Him. Then we can understand why this great voice sings, "Now is come the salvation and the power and the kingdom of our God, and the authority of his Christ." It is the death-blow to Satan. It seems to me that Michael and all his angels shout this at the same time in the ears of Satan at the moment when Christ enters into His exaltation. Now is come, that is, now has appeared, now has been revealed, the salvation and the power and the kingdom of our God, and the authority of His Christ. All was still hidden in the Old Testament day. It had not yet been historically revealed. And therefore there was room for argument on the part of the devil, and he could wage this war. But now has come the realization of the whole thing. Satan, you must go; you have no argument left. These saints of the Old Testament day belong to Christ, and they have a right to His inheritance. For their sins have been atoned by Him. Your defeat is accomplished. The accuser of the brethren in that sense of the word is cast down. For the shout of victory which the apostle uses in this same connection may now be heard: "Who shall lay anything to the charge of God's elect?" The result of the war, therefore, is that Michael and his angels have the spiritual victory in this battle for the saints of the Old Testament.

There is, however, a second result. And that is that the devil will now direct all his efforts toward the persecution of the church militant. He has been cast down, and he cannot fight the battle for the church triumphant any more. And therefore that same voice shouts: "Woe to the inhabiters of the earth and of the sea! for the devil is come down unto you, having great wrath, because he knoweth that he hath but a short time." What he does in this short time against the church militant we must see in the future. There is, however, one comforting thought with which I may close this discussion. It is this, that in the fight against the devil we have the company of Michael and his mighty angels. Not only in the old dispensation, but also in the new, and especially at the time of the end and in great trouble, he is the prince who standeth for the children of God's people. The Lord is our King. Directly He fights for us. And millions of His angels, with mighty Michael at the head, He sends to our protection. To be sure, the defeat, the final defeat, of the devil is certain. Stand, therefore, and overcome through the Lamb and the word of the testimony.

Chapter XXXI

The Conflict Between The Woman And The Dragon

(Revelation 12:13-17)

13 And when the dragon saw that he was cast unto the earth, he persecuted the woman which brought forth the man child.

14 And to the woman were given two wings of a great eagle, that she might fly into the wilderness, into her place, where she is nourished for a time, and times, and half a time, from the face of the serpent.

15 And the serpent cast out of his mouth water as a flood after the woman, that he might cause her to be carried away of the flood.

16 And the earth helped the woman, and the earth opened her mouth, and swallowed up the flood which the dragon cast out of his mouth.

17 And the dragon was wroth with the woman, and went to make war with the remnant of her seed, which keep the commandments of God, and have the testimony of Jesus Christ.

The beginning of this passage calls to our mind what immediately precedes: "And when the dragon saw that he was cast unto the earth..." We will remember that these words refer to the battle which was fought in heaven, as pictured in the words immediately preceding those of the present passage. We found that this war was a battle between spirits. For that very reason we also drew the conclusion that it was indeed a very real war, but nevertheless one which must not in all respects be compared to the battles fought among men. It was not fought with sword and cannon, and it did not leave the battlefield strewn with wounded and killed. But it was a spiritual battle, fought with spiritual weapons of intellect and argumentation, of righteousness and law, a war which could only end in the casting away from the battlefield of one of the opposing parties.

Michael, so we found, was the general on one side. He is not to be identified, so we found, with the Christ; but Scripture pictures him to us

436

as an angel who is a prince over other angels, and whose special task it is to fight the battle against Satan in behalf of the people of God. This is also true of the passage we studied in the last chapter. In this instance he was fighting against the devil, the old serpent, the great red dragon and opponent of God.

As to the time of this battle, we concluded that it would not have been the time before the entrance of sin into paradise, and therefore could not refer to the first rebellion of Satan and his angels in heaven, for the simple reason that the text calls him the accuser of the brethren and that also in other ways it indicates that already during the time of this battle there were people of God, saved in Christ Jesus, upon the earth, saints who loved not their lives even unto death. Nor is it the time of the end in the strictest sense of the word that is referred to in the preceding passage. For even after this war has been fought, there are still saved of God who have the testimony of Jesus and keep the commandments of God on earth, which certainly could not be the case were the war that is here fought one that must be placed after the glorification of the saints in Christ. We concluded, therefore, that it is a war which is fought all during the time of the old dispensation. Only in the old dispensation there are brethren on earth that love not their lives even unto death, as is so beautifully recorded in the eleventh chapter of the Epistle to the Hebrews. It is a war fought between Michael and his angels and the devil and his angels all during the time of the old dispensation, and that too, for the prize of the saints who had died and had been glorified in heaven in the days of the old dispensation.

Thus understood, all is clear. Then we understand that the devil had to fight this war just as well as the battle to prevent the coming of the Great Seed was fought by him on earth. For Christ had not yet come. And the devil, on the one hand trying to prevent His first coming, on the other hand claimed that the dead who died before He had come and before their sins were atoned belonged to him and had no right to glory. Then we could also understand why the devil is called the deceiver and the accuser of the brethren, the slanderer of God's people. For all during this period he must have slandered the people of God who had died in the days of the Old Testament and accused them of their sins before the countenance of God. And then, finally, we also understand that when the man child is brought forth and caught up to God's throne in glory, the battle between the spirits in heaven must come to an end, and the devil must be defeated.

For it was exactly through the suffering and exaltation of the Lord Jesus Christ, the man child, that Michael and his angels were placed in the right as they defended the right of the Old Testament saints to their glory in heaven. And the result was, on the one hand, that the devil and his angels were cast out from heaven, so that he can no more carry on this war there; but at the same time the result.is that he is cast down to the earth, so that he will pay all his evil attention to the church in the world. Here our text begins, and it speaks of the tremendous conflict between the woman and the dragon.

The Woman In The Wilderness

We must call attention, in the first place, to the fact that in the words of this passage we have a continuation of the symbolism which we met with in verses 1 to 6. Here we have no plain reality, but a symbolical representation of the things that are mentioned here. That was not the case in verses 7 to 12. In that passage there was nothing to indicate symbolism; and therefore without any difficulty we took it as plain reality, as a real war fought between real beings with a real purpose and with real results. Literally we explain that portion. But that is not the case here. There is no one who takes this woman for a real woman. Nor are there any interpreters who understand the dragon as a real animal, or the stream which he casts out of his mouth as a real stream, or the wings which the woman receives as real wings. In so far there is no difficulty.

But in spite of this, it is necessary that we remind you of the fact that here we have no literal presentation of facts, but rather an allegory, which does not allow of literal interpretation. For although all agree that this is not a real woman with real eagle's wings, and that the dragon mentioned here is not a real dragon, and that the stream of water he casts out after the woman is not a real stream of water, yet there are interpreters who make the mistake of singling out that wilderness and of maintaining that it, at all events, must be taken in a literal sense of the word. The woman, so they say, is at this time evidently in Jerusalem, the Old Testament holy city. And as she is attacked by the enemy, she flees into a literal wilderness somewhere in the vicinity, where she is hidden twelve hundred sixty days, even as at the time of the destruction of Jerusalem the disciples fled to Pella. Now this is violating one of the most fundamental rules of interpretation, and especially of the interpretation of the Apocalypse. And we must guard against it. There is no right to single out one element in an allegorical representation of things and to take it in the literal sense. And therefore it is well that we remember from the outset and bear in mind throughout our interpretation of this passage that here we have a continuation of the symbolism we met with in the first portion of this chapter.

In the second place, it may also be said that the symbolical representation as such is very clear. There is no difficulty in obtaining a picture of it in our minds. The woman who has brought forth the man child, — of whom we have lost sight for a moment because of the record of the war in heaven that intervened, — is still on earth. And as is plain from the seventeenth verse of this chapter, she brings forth still other children. For that verse speaks of the rest of her seed, that keep the commandments of God and have the testimony of Jesus Christ. The dragon now comes down to the earth. He has failed in every respect thus far. He failed to prevent the birth of the man child, and he failed to devour it when once it was born. And he also failed to gain his point in the war which he fought with Michael and his angels in heaven for the possession of the saints of the old dispensation. And because of this absolute failure, on the one hand, and because of the fact that he also realizes that he cannot continue to fight indefinitely and that his time henceforth is short, he is filled with raging fury. And thus he comes down to the earth for the purpose of persecuting the woman who brought forth the man child. But the woman receives wings of a great eagle. Already in the sixth verse we read that the woman fled into the wilderness, where she had a place prepared of God. But now we are told once more, and definitely, that she received wings of a great eagle and that with them she flees into the wilderness. The idea is clear. She cannot outrun the dragon. If she comes into contact with him, she cannot stand in the battle. And therefore there is but one place of escape, and that is the wilderness. There the dragon cannot live, for there is nothing for him to feed on. There the woman is nourished in a miraculous way, and there she is hid from the face of the serpent. And at the same time, there is but one way of escape, and that is through the air. And therefore it is in perfect harmony with the symbolism of the entire passage that the woman received wings, and that she flees away from the face of the serpent into the wilderness. The serpent pursues her up to the very edge of the desert, but cannot follow farther. And therefore in his rage he casts a stream after her, not to drown her exactly, but evidently to carry her away and out of the wilderness, so that he may be able to approach her. But the earth opens her mouth and swallows up the stream, which again is in perfect harmony with the idea of the arid desert, where the water easily disappears. And finally, the dragon, seeing that also now his efforts are vain and that all his attempts to destroy the woman meet with failure, turns to her individual children, in order that at any rate he may destroy them. Thus is the symbolism.

In the third place, there are also some elements in the symbolism which we understand immediately and with which we have met before and which we do not have to interpret again. The woman, so we have learned, is the church. In the first part of the chapter we have become acquainted with her. But there is a little difference between the woman as she appeared in the first part of this chapter and as she appears in the present passage. In the first passage she was still travailing to bring forth the man child; and therefore she represented the church of the old dispensation. There she was the symbol of the people of God, of the church, as the mother of Christ. But here she appears after she has brought forth the Christ, and therefore in the new dispensation, as the mother of the New Testament believers, the rest of her seed. In parentheses, we may notice that also here the Word of God teaches us the essential unity of the church of all ages. It is the same woman all the time, representing the same church, only in different dispensations. And therefore it will not harmonize with Scripture to maintain that there was an essential difference between the church of the Old and of the New Testament days. But this in passing. The second element in the symbolism with which we are acquainted is that of the dragon. He is the devil. He is the great opponent of God. And we must remember that as the opponent of God his great and only purpose is to prevent the establishment of the kingdom of God and to maintain his own sovereignty. It is for that purpose that he battled against the woman in the Old Testament, to prevent the birth of her man child. It is for that same purpose that he went to heaven to question the right of the Old Testament saints to enter into glory. And it is again for that same purpose that he now attacks the woman as we meet her in our present passage. The devil does not care for the woman as such. He does not care for her seed as such. But he knows that she must be instrumental in the completion of the kingdom of God and in the realization of God's counsel, and therefore fights her to the last ditch.

The Attack Of The Devil

This last thought brings us to the next question: why does the devil persecute the woman after she has brought forth the man child? Why does the devil still persecute the church after she has given birth to the Christ? Was it merely a streak of vengeance that led him to do so? That is sometimes the impression that is received from the symbolism in the text. The dragon, so the idea often is, has failed twice in his attempts to thwart the plan of God. He failed to devour the man child, and he also failed in his war in heaven to bring down the saints of the old dispensation to hell. And now he is just raving mad. The woman really has served her purpose, and she is of no account to him any more. But in spite of that fact, and in spite of the fact that the dragon well knows that he is defeated and that his attack upon the woman will not help him even if he should succeed to destroy her, he just means to wreak vengeance and to empty his raving madness and fury upon the head of the poor woman.

But we might know from the very outset that this is not the case. The devil is not a mad fool. He certainly is a fool, and he also is mad. But he is not a mad fool in this sense, that he does things that have nothing to do with the plan of God Almighty. And you may depend on it, if the woman after she has brought forth the man child was of no account any more, the devil would not trouble himself about her. He has but one purpose, and he lives from but one principle. It is the purpose and the principle of opposition against God Almighty. This principle he never denies. And whatever has nothing to do with that principle he leaves severely alone. That is already plain in the individual lives of the people of God on earth and in the church. If you are of no account to the coming of God's kingdom and are in no way related to the glory of God, the devil does not trouble his head about you. It is only when he begins to surmise that you also are one of the followers of Christ and that you confess Him that he begins his action against you. Thus it is also with the woman. The very fact that the dragon in raving madness indeed turns against the woman, to persecute her, already causes us to surmise that she is still of great importance to the kingdom of God and the fulfillment of His plans.

Nor need we search very long to find the answer to this question. What is the motive of the devil in persecuting the woman even after she has brought forth the man child? This woman, as we have had occasion to notice before, is the church, the visible church as she exists on earth. In the former passage we noticed how she appeared as the mother of the

Savior, of the King in the kingdom. The church brings forth the Christ. Christ is the great seed of the woman. He is the Son of Mary, out of the house of David, of the tribe of Judah, born from Israel, out of the loins of Abraham, in the line of Shem and Seth, and finally born from Eve as the spiritual mother of the holy seed. But this is not all. The church as she exists in the present dispensation is not only the mother of Christ, the great seed. But she is also the mother of us all. She is the mother of the true, spiritual children of God. As such it may be said that the church visible, as a visible institution on earth, brings forth the church invisible, true believers, from age to age. The church is the mother of the true children of the kingdom. These are born from her, are baptized by her, are nourished through her, receive their strength and life and all the blessings of God's covenant in her bosom. And it is as such, evidently, that the church appears in the words that we are now discussing. For as we have maintained already, the passage makes mention of the rest of her seed, of her spiritual children. She is the mother of all the true children of God, of all the subjects in the kingdom that is to be established in the future. That is her great importance.

Now the devil knows this.

He knew from the beginning that the Great Seed which this woman is to bring forth is the all-important factor in the entire war which he wages. If he can prevent His coming or devour Him as soon as He is born, he does not have to trouble himself about the rest of her seed. And therefore all his efforts are directed toward that end in the old dispensation. And because he is so certain that he will succeed in that battle against the woman and surely prevent the birth of the Great Seed, he also thinks it strange and without justice that all the saints who are born and die before the coming of Christ go into glory. But he has failed.

And now he knows too that the church still exists. He knows that even as that same woman has not only brought forth the Great Seed, but was also the mother of Abel and Enoch and Noah and the patriarchs and Moses and all the prophets and all the faithful believers of the old dispensation, so she will continue to bring forth seed in the new dispensation. Also in the New Testament day she will have children. She will bring forth children of the kingdom who will fight the battle of the kingdom here below and who will enter into the glorious kingdom hereafter. And since he cannot fight directly against the King of the kingdom any more, Who is caught up to the throne of God, and since he cannot go to heaven any more to dispute about the right of the glorified saints, he will persecute the woman and try to destroy her at all events, before she has brought forth many more children who will serve as subjects of the kingdom that is to be established. And therefore he goes and persecutes her.

Now the text tells us that when the dragon comes to persecute the woman, two wings of an eagle are given to her, in order that she might fly into the wilderness. The question as to the meaning of the eagle's wings, as if they could be interpreted to mean work and prayer, or anything else, is certainly irrelevant. The figure has perhaps been obtained from Exodus 19:4, where we read that Jehovah says: "Ye have seen what I did unto the Egyptians, and how I bare you on eagle's wings and brought you unto myself." And the idea is evidently that God Himself provides the church with means to escape the fury of the devil.

Different, however, it is with the idea of the wilderness. Also this has been obtained from the episode of the people of Israel's history in the desert. Even as there God delivered His people from the fury of the world-power in Egypt by bringing them into the wilderness, so also now He brings His people into the wilderness to escape the rage of the devil. But the difference is that in Israel's case it was a real wilderness into which they were led, while evidently in this case the figure is employed to represent something different. And the question is: what is the meaning of this wilderness into which God enables the church to fly in the new dispensation in order that she might escape the wrath and persecution of the devil?

It has been said that the wilderness is here used to depict the want and deprivation which the people of God must suffer in the world. They are the despised of the world; and there are not many noble and mighty among them. They must suffer all kinds of persecutions and deprivations in the world. And therefore that world is a real wilderness to them. And, of course, this is true in itself. But it is not the meaning of the text. For, in the first place, the church is driven into this wilderness after the birth of Christ and after His exaltation. But it cannot be said that the being subjected to want and deprivation of all kinds is peculiar to the people of God in the new dispensation only. Also the long list of witnesses mentioned in Hebrews 11 could tell you of them. And therefore, this cannot be meant. In the second place, it is difficult to see how this could possibly be a means of hiding them from the face of the devil, so that he could not attack them. Yet this is evidently the purpose of it all. The woman received these wings to fly into the wilderness in order that she might be able to escape the wrath of the devil, and so be safe. And, in the third place, the wilderness is a place prepared for her by God, where she does not suffer want and deprivation, but is nourished by God for a time, and times, and half a time, or twelve hundred sixty days. And therefore, that cannot be the meaning of the term **wilderness** in our present passage.

We would rather adhere to the symbolism, and derive the meaning from the representation itself. In the literal and natural sense of the word the wilderness, or desert, is a place in the world, but not of the world. It may lie right in the midst of the world, yet it is absolutely separated from the life of the world. There is no plant life, no vegetation to speak of, no animal life, no human life; there are no houses, no cities, no rivers and streams. It is a place in the midst of the world, yet separated from the world. If one is in the wilderness, he is separated from the life of the world.

If we adhere to this meaning, the explanation of the symbolism cannot be difficult. It reminds us of the words of the Savior, "In the world, yet not of the world." And it tells us that the visible church in the new dispensation is an institution separate in every respect from the world-power as such. It exists, indeed, in the world; but it exists as a separate institution. That is not true of her children individually. They live right in the midst of the world, and they live the life of the world, even though they are spiritually separated from that life, and live it from the principle of the kingdom of God. But that is true of the church.

The church as such is a separate institution in the world. She has her own King. And as an institution the church does not recognize any other ruler. No earthly king has any dominion over her. There is no worldly ruler, be he king or president or dictator, who can exercise dominion over the church as the mother of her spiritual children. Only Christ is King. From this it follows that the church has its own laws. There may be laws established and ordained by the worldly ruler regarding the existence of the church in this world, regarding her buildings and property, etc.; but the church in this world, in regard to her real existence and life, acknowledges no other power, no other sovereignty, than that of Christ. No world-power, no emperor, or king, or president, can formulate her creed. She does so herself, in obedience to Christ her King. No world-power can regulate her worship, can compose her hymns and her forms, can dictate how she must pray and what she must preach. No world-power can tell her how and when and why she must censure her members and exercise discipline over them. The church as an institute is a separate institution. She has her own King, her own laws, her own life. She does not mingle in politics as such. She may instruct her children how to behave in regard to the powers that be; but she herself does not mingle in the politics of the world. She has no armies. She does not fight with the sword. Again, she may instruct her children that even in regard to the battles of the world they must be subject to the authorities, and obedient; but she herself, as an institute and as the mother of her spiritual children, does not take part in the battles of the world. She lives in separation. Even as the children of Israel in the desert lived in separation from the world-power in Egypt, and even as they received their own laws from their own King in that wilderness, so also the church of the New Testament is in the wilderness with regard to the world and its power and its life. The church does not do business. The church does not mingle with the affairs of this world. She owns no property for its own sake. She has no factories. She has no army or navy. She fights her own battles and does her own work. The church as an institution is separate from the life of the world. She has received a God-prepared place in the wilderness.

Only in this sense can we see, in the first place, that this condition commenced actually in the new dispensation and with the exaltation of Christ. In the old dispensation, among Israel, church and state were intertwined in the theocracy. Israel was the people of God. Israel was the church. They were not identical, but they were inseparably combined. For that reason the people of God also could have an earthly king, could fight the battles of Jehovah with bow and sword, could have an earthly country of their own, could have possessions and do business as a people of God. With the new dispensation this is changed. The church does no more live in a certain land, but is spread all over the world and among all nations. One and the same church, with the same King, with essentially the same faith, with the same life, now exists among all the nations of the earth. And as the most general confession has it, "I believe an holy catholic church." But at the same time, and for that very reason, the church is now in the wilderness. It is separated from the world-power. It does not acknowledge any other authority for her life as such than the authority of Jesus Christ.

But, in the second place, it is also very plain that this is exactly her safety in the present dispensation. The world-power is and remains on the earth, earthy. It has a temporal purpose, and ultimately shall unite, as we shall see, to make war against the Christ and His kingdom. If the church did not live as a separate institution, living her own life, acknowledging her own King, regulating her own affairs, making her own laws, establishing her own forms of belief, and controlling her own worship, she would be gone, and would ultimately unite with the power that rises against the Christ and His kingdom. No matter whether this would realize itself in one or in the other, whether the church would have dominion over the powers of the world and over the affairs of the world, — as the Romish Church would have it, — or whether the power of the world would exercise authority over the church of Christ as an institution in the midst of the world, the same result would necessarily follow, namely, the destruction of the church as the mother of the faithful subjects of the kingdom of Christ. The church is in the wilderness of this world, separated from the power of the world, and must needs be in that wilderness for her own safety.

The measure of time here indicated need not detain us very long. It is plain from the context that time, times, and half a time is the same period as the twelve hundred sixty days mentioned in the first portion of this chapter. This leads us to the conclusion that time, times, and half a time indicates three and one-half symbolic years. One symbolic year, and two symbolic years, and half a symbolic year. One symbolic year is calculated to be three hundred sixty days, which, multiplied by three and one-half, gives us the twelve hundred sixty days. And again, this is evidently the same period as the forty-two months of the two witnesses. For, taking a symbolic month to contain thirty days, forty and two months would again give us twelve hundred sixty days, or three and one-half years. All these indications of time refer, therefore, to the time of the new dispensation, from the exaltation of Christ to the very end, as has become plain before.

Only, the three and a half times indicate this period, in the first place, from the point of view that the history of the world is divided, as it were, into two halves, because of the coming of Christ. If seven is the symbolic number indicating the completion of all that God does in time, and therefore also indicating the complete period of the history of the present world, both before and after Christ, then it is plain that three and one-half must indicate the period of one dispensation, in this case that of the dispensation after the coming and exaltation of Christ Jesus. And, in the second place, this number also indicates that the period of the church's being in the wilderness shall be cut short. The days shall be shortened for the elects' sake. But whatever this number, which also occurs in Daniel, may indicate, certain it is from a comparison of the different places in which it occurs, that it points to the entire period of the new dispensation, even to the end. In this entire period the church has to suffer from the attacks of the dragon. In this entire period God has prepared her a place in the wilderness in separation from the powers of the world, and that too, to her own safety.

The Devil's Failure

That this is actually so is also plain if we study for a moment the manner in which the dragon attacks this woman in the wilderness, and how he fails.

Symbolically the text indicates this by saying that the dragon, when he saw that he could not pursue her into the wilderness, cast a stream of water after the woman, in order that she might be carried away with the flood. Evidently this does not mean that the devil makes an attempt directly to destroy the woman while she is in the wilderness. On the contrary, especially the original gives us reason to believe that the purpose is different. He knows that he cannot approach the woman in her isolation in the desert. He cannot touch her. She must remain there. He must leave her alone. Hence, he casts a stream of water after her, that she might be borne up by that flood and be carried out of the wilderness. Especially the word used here in the original gives us that very idea. He does not mean to drown her: that would be impossible. But he means to lift her from her isolation. And therefore he casts a stream after her, in order that she might be carried away by the stream, and thus be borne into the world from which she fled.

Understood in that sense, the meaning is not difficult to grasp. The devil realizes that in the isolation of the church as an institution from the powers of this world lies her strength, and that as long as the church remains in this state of separation he cannot do anything against her. And therefore he makes the attempt to establish an alliance, to unite the church and the world. He tries to carry the church into the world and either offer her the dominion over the powers that be or subject her to the powers of the world. Then he may be sure that her strength is gone. Then he is certain that she will also bring up her spiritual children as subjects of the kingdom of the world, which is his kingdom. Then he is certain that the kingdom of the Christ shall at least be deprived of its subjects in the new dispensation. Clearly you may see this attempt. Now the devil tries to subject the church as an institution to the powers of the world, and establish a state church, as in various countries of Europe has been and still is the case. In that case the worldly rulers are at the same time the rulers of the church, and they establish its creeds and forms of worship and confessions. The church is ruled by the worldly power. Now he tries to gain his point along the way of offering the church dominion over the powers of the world, as in the time of Constantine the Great, and ever since, in the Romish Church.

But the devil always failed. That does not mean that he never saw results. He surely did. Church after church was affected by this stream of water he spits after the woman. Now the church is actually subject to the state; now she has absolute sway over the powers of the world. And every time she lost her true character. But it never succeeded completely. The woman always remained in her isolation. And even today, although the tendency is once more to bring the church into the service and the subjection of the worldly power, and although the church has a hard fight to remain in her God-appointed place in the wilderness, nevertheless in many places the church stands as a separate institution; and also in our own land the separation of church and state is still constitutionally established. And therefore, the devil fails in principle. And our text tells us that he **will** fail. Surely, also in the future many a church will be carried away, and her subjection and unification with the worldly power will be one of the factors in her apostasy. But nevertheless, the church shall always stand, shall always remain as an institution and as a separate institution, shall always bring forth and nourish her spiritual children, till the last one of God's elect shall have been gathered into the glory of the kingdom.

The Devil's Turning To The Rest Of Her Seed

If we have understood the text correctly thus far, it is not difficult to understand the last verse of this passage, where we read that the dragon, being enraged with the woman and yet realizing his impotency to destroy her as such, goes to make war with the rest of her seed, who keep the commandments of God and have the testimony of Jesus Christ.

At first sight we may think that this is a somewhat strange expression. Is the church after all not the sum-total of all her seed? And how, then, must we conceive of this idea that the devil, after he has failed to destroy the church as such, can still turn to her children, to the rest of her seed?

This is not difficult to understand, however. The woman represents the church as such, the church as a visible institution in the world. And as such she is the mother of the true spiritual children of God. At first the devil makes the attempt to destroy the church as an institution by making her part of his own kingdom and by uniting her with the power of the world. But when this fails, he turns to the individual believers, in order that he may persecute and destroy them and bring them to apostasy. These individual members move about in the world. In every sphere of life they claim that they must live according to the principles of the Word of God, that they must keep His commandments, and that they must proclaim that Jesus Christ is King over all. And so they attempt to realize these principles in the midst of the world. They have been brought up in the commandments of God by their mother, the church; and they have learned to embrace and keep the testimony of Jesus. And therefore, in every sphere of life, in the home and in society and in the state, wherever they go and whatever they do, they keep these commandments and refuse to live from the principles of the world. They come into contact with the world, and therefore the devil can approach them. He can employ that world to make life hard for them, in order that by his persecution he may bring them to destruction. It is not told us in this chapter how the devil attempts to accomplish this. The following chapter pictures to us this tremendous attempt in detail; for there we have the description of the power of the Antichrist.

Let us now close this particular passage with the application of the text. In the first place, the church is in the wilderness. Neither must she attempt to rule over the powers of the world or to mingle with the affairs of the world, nor must she subject herself to these powers. Christ is King, and no other beside Him, over the church. There are many rulers in the world; there is but one King in the church. In the second place, love the church as your spiritual mother. More than once we find this presentation of the church in relation to her members. She exists for your spiritual care and nourishment, that through her you might be strengthened with the bread of life, and that too, through the preaching of the Word and the administration of the sacraments. In the third place, walk as her faithful children in the midst of the world. Keep the commandments of God and hold the testimony of Jesus. And finally, be assured that all the attempts of the devil shall surely fail. He shall fail in his attempts to destroy the church as such. She shall remain, and the gates of hell shall not prevail against her. And if you must experience the wrath of the great red dragon as her individual children, never you fear: Christ has overcome the world!

Chapter XXXII

The Power Of The Antichrist

(Revelation 13:1-10)

1 And I stood upon the sand of the sea, and saw a beast rise up out of the sea, having seven heads and ten horns, and upon his horns ten crowns, and upon his heads the name of blasphemy.

2 And the beast which I saw was like unto a leopard, and his feet were as the feet of a bear, and his mouth as the mouth of a lion: and the dragon gave him his power, and his seat, and great authority.

3 And I saw one of his heads as it were wounded to death; and his deadly wound was healed: and all the world wondered after the beast.

4 And they worshipped the dragon which gave power unto the beast: and they worshipped the beast, saying, Who is like unto the beast? who is able to make war with him?

5 And there was given unto him a mouth speaking great things and blasphemies; and power was given unto him to continue forty and two months.

6 And he opened his mouth in blasphemy against God, to blaspheme his name, and his tabernacle, and them that dwell in heaven.

7 And it was given unto him to make war with the saints, and to overcome them: and power was given him over all kindreds, and tongues, and nations.

8 And all that dwell upon the earth shall worship him, whose names are not written in the book of life of the Lamb slain from the foundation of the world.

9 If any man have an ear, let him hear.

10 He that leadeth into captivity shall go into captivity: he that killeth with the sword must be killed by the sword. Here is the patience and the faith of the saints.

I need not give a long introduction to show the connection between the present passage and the preceding text. Already we have studied three attempts of the devil to frustrate God's plan with a view to establishing His kingdom. First we saw how the devil attempted to oppose the plan of God

451

with a view to the birth of Christ, and how he failed. Secondly, we noticed that contemporaneously with the first war on earth the devil also carried on a war with the angels in heaven for the possession of the saints of the old dispensation, and how he was defeated. Thirdly, we saw that the devil attempted to amalgamate the power of the church and the power of the world; and again he failed, at least in this respect, that the church as such is not destroyed by him. And finally, we just mentioned that the devil determined at least to make war with the rest of the seed of the woman, that is, of the church, — with the individual believers on earth. And we already mentioned the fact that in this thirteenth chapter we would be told in what manner the dragon makes this war with the saints, and principally with the God of heaven and earth and with His Anointed, Jesus Christ our Lord.

In short, it may be said that the devil in this last attempt to oppose God's plan simply realizes his own kingdom, or attempts to realize it, and boldly sets it up. The first attempts were rather negative in nature, always aiming at the destruction of God's kingdom first of all. But this last attempt really consists in this, that the devil now ignores all that has been done by God Almighty, ignores that Christ has come and is King, ignores that the church exists and that there is already a kingdom of Christ in principle established in the world, and simply proceeds to realize and establish his own kingdom before Christ has an opportunity (speaking from the devil's point of view, of course) to do so.

We have in this chapter a complete picture of the antichristian power and kingdom and its king. There is, as far as I know, no controversy about this truth. And therefore we proceed from the assumption that this may be regarded as an established fact. He gives us a picture of Antichrist. That it is deemed of greatest importance that we should understand the picture is clearly proved by the solemn conclusion of the text: "If any man have an ear, let him hear." If we have no ear, it is, of course, quite a different question. But if by the grace of God our ear has been opened, and we may have a spiritual understanding of what God has revealed to us, let us hear, that we may be instructed from the Word of our God, and from it derive light and strength to stand in the evil day.

The Description Of The Beast Out Of The Sea

Let us then call your attention, in the first place, to the description of this beast as it is given in the text. John beholds how out of the sea rises a frightful monster. Very naturally it is described in the text, just as John must have beheld it in his vision. What he saw first he describes first. Naturally the horns appeared first of all; and John tells us that it was a beast with ten horns. Naturally also the heads followed; and John continues to inform us that the monster had seven heads. He further notices as details in the description that the ten horns had ten crowns, royal diadems, and that on the heads there were names of blasphemy written. And finally, he is able to give a general description of this dreadful monster; and he informs us that its general appearance was like that of a leopard, while its feet were like those of a bear, and its mouth a lion's mouth. And as a detail, which at first he probably did not notice, but which he observed upon closer examination, he remarks that one of the heads appeared to have been smitten in the past with a death-stroke, but that the stroke now was healed.

Let us investigate into the meaning of this highly symbolic picture. For that here again we have symbolism needs no further argument. The text itself indicates this more than plainly. The sea is the birthplace, the source, the origin, of this beast. In this case there is little doubt that it must be taken in the sense of peoples and nations and tongues as they live on earth under the power and principle of sin. We read of the sea in that sense more than once in Scripture. Isaiah says in Chapter 57, verse 20: "But the wicked are like the troubled sea, when it cannot rest, whose waters cast up mire and dirt." In Daniel 7:2, 3 we read: "Behold, the four winds of the heaven strove upon the great sea. And four great beasts came up from the sea, diverse one from another." And the entire context shows very plainly that nothing else can be meant than the troubled sea of nations. Indeed, a very fit symbol it is, too. The peoples and nations of the earth as they are under the power and principle of sin and as they develop according to this principle are indeed like unto the troubled sea, war-swept, revolution-swept, plague- and famine-swept as they are. And that this same sea of nations and peoples is meant in the words of our text is clearly proved by Revelation 17:15, where the same beast, together with the harlot, is described once more, now with a view to its final destruction, and where the angel interprets: "The waters which thou sawest, where the whore sitteth, are peoples, and multitudes, and nations, and tongues." And therefore we arrive at this conclusion, that the beast finds its origin, its source, its birthplace, from among the peoples and nations and tongues of the earth as they develop under the principle and power of sin. The picture is that this sea of nations is swept and in uproar, rages and foams, till finally this beast comes up as a result.

In the second place, looking at the beast proper, let us notice, first of all, that it is a beast, and that too, a wild beast, a monster, just as the dragon was a monster. We may be more or less familiar with this figure; and in this case the Word of God gives us the unmistakable key to its interpretation. In Daniel we also read of beasts, especially of four. And in Daniel the interpretation is given by the guiding angel who directs the prophet. And this angel interprets the figure of the beast as referring both to kingdoms and kings. In Daniel 7:17 we read: "These great beasts, which are four, are four kings, which shall arise out of the earth." And in verse 23 of the same chapter: "Thus he said, The fourth beast shall be the fourth kingdom upon earth." Evidently, therefore, the figure of the beast represents a great political world-power, together with its government as its head.

There has been a great controversy all through the ages of the new dispensation about the question whether this beast, or the Antichrist, is a person or a power or a system or a kingdom. But it seems to me that this controversy is not necessary. Daniel tells us that the beast is both, the kingdom and the king. Or to speak just a little more generally, it represents both the world-power and its government. And I would say that this beast neither represents merely a person, who in personal power and by personal strength without any aid conquers and subdues and controls the whole world and all that it contains; nor only a kingdom or dominion, without its head and government; but it represents both. And not only do we find it so in Daniel, but it stands to reason and lies in the very nature of the case. A king is powerless without his kingdom. And a kingdom without a king is inconceivable. The two are inseparable. And therefore, we come to the conclusion that this beast is the symbol of a political government as we know it, — I care not whether you are thinking now of a kingdom, or empire, or republic, or a worldly dominion, — as it naturally culminates and is represented by its head. Again, I care not whether you conceive of this head as a king, or emperor, or president, or even as a group or body of persons.

Let us call your attention, further, to the fact that this world-power as described in our passage is a consummation and culmination of all that has gone before and of all separate kingdoms which might possibly exist or have existed. It is well that we have our attention called to this feature.

For it is one of the main features of our text.

This power as it is here pictured does not merely consist of one nation and one people. But it combines within itself all the kingdoms and empires and republics of the world; and at the same time it constitutes a combination and accumulation of all the power of all the empires and kingdoms and republics of the past. This is plain, in the first place, from the various beasts that are represented in this one beast. First of all, we may notice that they are all wild beasts, and therefore destructive in their nature. In ordinary circumstances they would not form a unity, but rather exist to their mutual destruction. But, in the second place, it cannot escape our attention that in this wild beast we have a combination of the beasts pictured to us in Daniel 7. There also we read of the beast like a lion, and like a bear, and like a leopard, and of a fourth beast, not accurately described, but terrible. And there these beasts constitute four separate kingdoms, the fourth of which finally blends into the vision of the Antichrist in the little horn rising among the ten. Here, then, we have a combination of all these. The kingdoms of the world, ordinarily like wild animals, existing to their mutual destruction, have succeeded in forming a unity. And even as the spirit of the one beast is in all the beasts, — the lion and the bear and the leopard, — and, on the other hand, the spirits and powers of these various beasts have combined in the one, so the world-kingdom which is represented by this beast is one which combines in itself all the power and glory and ambitions and spirit of all the kingdoms which have aimed at world-power in the past and that do aim at it at the present time.

Secondly, this is also more or less symbolized in the ten horns and seven heads. Although we do not interpret these ten horns as representing ten different kingdoms or the seven heads as seven different kings, yet the general idea is expressed that this beast represents a combination of all the kingdoms of the world. Hence also the resemblance of this beast with the dragon. It is the incarnation of the dragon, who possesses all the kingdoms of the world. The dragon has ten horns and seven heads; so has this beast. And the idea is clearly that the devil, to whom the kingdoms of the world belong, who could say to the Christ, "Fall down and worship me, and I will give thee all the kingdoms of the world," now has succeeded in combining all his kingdoms under one head and inspiring them all with the same principle. The only difference is that he does not succeed in giving to his kingdom the complete and perfect aspect of the kingdom of God. Ten is the number of the world-kingdom. Seven is the number of the kingdom of God. For a long time the dragon wore his seven crowns on his seven heads. But now his authority and strength are both represented by the number ten. And though it is true that he still has seven heads, no one can mistake them for heads of the kingdom of Christ: for names of blasphemy are written upon them.

Finally, that this is a world-power including all the existing powers of the whole earth is also plain from the fact that the head of this power has authority over all peoples and nations and tribes and tongues, vs. 7. And therefore we come to this conclusion so far: the beast represents a consummation of all the world-powers that have been in the past. It combines within itself all the power of these dominions, all the glory of them, all the ambitions of them, all their aspirations and aims and accomplishments. And, in the second place, it is itself a combination, a confederation, of all nations and peoples and tongues and tribes which may exist at that time under one head and under one government.

If we understand this, we shall also be able to comprehend the significant detail of the scar which this beast has in one of its heads. We read: "And I saw one of his heads as it were wounded to death; and his deadly wound was healed."

This does not refer to the fall of the Roman Empire, or to the fall of the Grecian Empire, or to the fall of the Babylonian or the Egyptian Empire, or, in fact, to the fall of any particular empire or to all of them combined. It is true that many attempts have been made to realize this great world-power in the past. Babylon made the attempt; Persia also made the attempt; Greece was filled with the same aspirations; and Rome advanced a good way to its establishment. It is also true that all failed, and that they were smitten unto death. But there are two things which lead us to the consideration that the fall of any or of all these empires together cannot be meant by this death-stroke. In the first place, the death-stroke here meant was healed; but the death-stroke of these empires was final. And, in the second place, these empires in the past consisted of the domination of one nation over all the rest of the world, and not of a combination of them all, as is indicated in this beast.

Hence, there is but one thing in past history which can be indicated by this scar on one of the heads of the beast. It is the attempt in the days of mighty Nimrod and the building of the tower of Babel to establish a universal world-power. Also then it was to be a combination, rather than the dominion of one individual or group. They planned to form a mighty federation, a mighty league, with a common center in the city and tower, with common aims and purposes. But then it received the death-stroke for a time. That death-stroke consisted in the confusion of tongues and the consequent separation into nations with their national differences and aspirations and the resulting wars and strifes. But that death-stroke is now healed. After many an individual power has made the attempt to gain the world-power and to obtain control of the whole earth, the nations have finally come to the conclusion that the way of combination is the only way. National differences have been overcome; national aspirations have now been combined into the aspiration of all. No more world wars, no more strife and competition, but a great world-wide empire, including all nations and comprehending them all under one head, has now been realized. The death-stroke has been healed, and what was prevented in the days of Nimrod now is accomplished.

The Power Of The First Beast

Let us now attend to the power of the beast.

Let me say, first of all, that the power of this beast originated in the dragon, the old serpent, the devil: "And the dragon gave him his power, and his seat, and great authority." In regard to this, we may remark, in the first place, that the dragon's power and authority itself is limited. He bears the number ten, and his kingdom bears that same number. And that number refers to God's own sovereign decree. It is well that we bear this in mind, for it is to our comfort. It assures us from the outset that the power and authority of this kingdom of the beast, however great, is not unlimited, and that Christ, Who has all power, is mightier than the Antichrist.

But the fact remains that the dragon is permitted to give his power and authority and throne to the beast. He has now realized what he failed to establish when he tempted Christ. He also made the offer to Christ. You see, the devil is a spirit; and as such he cannot establish an earthly throne in person. He must have some human agent or agents who will take the position. He wants to establish a world-kingdom. But he cannot rule over that world in person. He must have human beings, or a human being, to be his vice-regent. That is why he offered the position to Christ. He thought Christ was powerful and able, capable of filling the place. But there was one condition to be fulfilled: this great vice-regent of the devil had to worship and fall down before him, otherwise the devil would lose the very dominion he sought. He himself must remain lord. And this condition Christ refused to fulfill, for the simple reason that He was the anointed Vice-regent, not of the devil, but of God. But now the devil has found someone. I think we must conceive of this in such a manner that in general the power of the devil is vested in the entire dominion that is pictured in the beast. For the authority and power is given to the beast as a whole. But, in the second place, we must also maintain that this power and authority will be concentrated in the governing head of this world-power. It makes no difference now whether this governing head is a person or a group of persons, a sort of central committee, which rules the whole world. At this stage of history this is difficult to say. But the fact is that in the future there will be the full realization of a great world-power, combining in itself all powers of the earth, with a government which has all the authority of the dragon, the old serpent, the devil. That world-power in general, and that governing head in particular, we may therefore fitly describe as the very incarnation of the devil.

In the second place, the text tells us that this Antichrist, this central government, in combination with its kingdom will do great things. Do not make a mistake here. You must not imagine that the whole world will groan under the yoke of Antichrist and long to be delivered from it. That is perhaps what the devil tries to tell us, in order that we should not recognize the power of Antichrist when it is established. It will be just the opposite. This Antichrist will be attractive and inspiring. The whole world will be fond of his regime. The whole world will live in the conviction that this is just the thing. There will be a splendid time for the world. It will be a time of peace, all nations having been combined into one great whole. There will be no more rising of nation against nation. It will be a time of wonderful accomplishments. This central person or government will have all things under its control. It will control the powers of nature. It will control science and philosophy. It will control religion and worship. It will control commerce and industry. It will control all that this world possesses in hidden talents and powers. And the promise given to man in the beginning, that he would have dominion over all things, will be realized.

I imagine that in that kingdom or world-power you will be able to scan the heavens: for the air shall have been conquered. Perhaps we shall even be able to visit other planets in the universe, as is already attempted in this present time. In that kingdom you will be able to fathom the depths of the sea. In that kingdom you will be able to speak with its remotest inhabitant. There shall be no poor, no miserable from a worldly point of view; but all the powers of creation, come to full development under the direction and under the control of the central head, shall be at our command. In a word, it will be a splendid kingdom, and the realization of all that the world desires will there be had. No, not a heavy yoke on groaning subjects is that of the Antichrist, but a most beautiful kingdom, with peace and splendor and riches and plenty and harmony and great developments. And the whole earth will wonder after the beast. All the inhabitants will admire that state of things, and they will say, "Who is like unto this great government, and who is able now to war with us?" And in pure gratitude they will worship him and worship the devil.

That this must be so follows from the fact that this kingdom is universal in its scope. In the first place it is universal because there shall be no nations that are outside and that therefore can make war: "And there was given him authority over every tribe and people and tongue and nation." All nations freely and willingly obey the one government. That one government has its own laws, which hold for all the nations of the world. It has its own police force and its own representatives, who have authority in every clime and over every nation. And perhaps it will succeed even in establishing one language. At any rate, all the nations are now one nation. There is no more competition; there is no more difference and war. It is a peaceful kingdom.

In the second place, universal that kingdom is because all things will be under the control of its central government. If I may just run ahead for a moment, the rest of the chapter tells us that this central government has the power over buying and selling, so that you cannot buy the necessities of life and cannot do business and live along in society unless you are allowed to do so by the beast. It must be a government, therefore, which not only has complete control over all the inhabitants of the historic world, but also controls all things connected with their life and existence in this kingdom. Commerce and industry will be completely in the power of the central government. Natural resources and railroads and air roads and waterways and other roads, coal and iron and grain and vegetables, telegraph and telephone, radio and television, and all things will be in the power of this central government. Schools and universities and churches will be under its jurisdiction. It will tell you what to believe and how to

worship, for it will want one science and one religion and one worship. It
has power to command you to worship the beast and its image. And
therefore, once more we come to the conclusion, based on the words of
this passage and also on other parts of Scripture: the one final
manifestation of Antichrist will be that of a great and universal
world-power which will include all nations. That universal kingdom will
have a central government which will have authority over all nations and
over all things. That central government will control all things in the
world, and will be admired and worshipped by all the inhabitants of the
whole earth.

The Spiritual Character Of The First Beast

I say: by all. But that is not quite true. There is one class of people who
will refuse to put their trust in this great power and to worship the beast.
And that class of people is especially described as those whose names have
been written in the book of life of the Lamb. In short, the people of God
will still be on earth. There will be elect of the Most High, covenant
people, on earth. And they will refuse to worship the beast.

And this brings us to our third question: what is the spiritual character
of this great and splendid world-power?

The answer to this question is that it is anti-God and anti-Christ. It is
anti-saints and anti- the kingdom of God. That this is so might be surmised
from the fact that this world-power received its power from the dragon,
the old serpent. He, as we have said before, has but one principle; and
from that principle he lives. It is the principle of opposition against God.
He has but one aim, and that is to thrust the Almighty from His throne,
deprive Him of His sovereignty, and to be God instead of Him. And he,
therefore, is the author and accomplisher of this power. And that he gives
it his power and throne and authority would be sufficient to conclude that
his kingdom and dominion is anti-God and anti-Christ in character.

But this is also plain from other portions of the text. In the first place,
let me call your attention to the fact that this beast has names of
blasphemy inscribed upon his seven heads, that he received a mouth
speaking great things and blasphemies, and that he actually opens his
mouth to blaspheme the name of God and of His tabernacle, namely,
those that dwell in heaven. To blaspheme the name of God is to deny His
name, His sovereignty, His power, and all His virtues. Nebuchadnezzar was
blaspheming when he said in the pride of his heart that he himself was the

author of mighty Babylon. And so this kingdom and its head will blaspheme the name of the Most High. It will deny that God and His Christ have anything to do with that world-kingdom, and it will maintain that all that is in the world is the result of the power of man and the manifestation of his glory. In a word, it will try to expel the very name and authority of the Almighty from His own works. And the same it will do with the saints who have already gone into glory. It will deny that there is such a thing as glory in the hereafter. It will refuse to speak of it, and it will not tolerate to have it mentioned. It will banish their very remembrance. All that is connected with God and His name and His worship it will not tolerate.

Secondly, I would call your attention to the fact that this power is its own god. They worship the beast: "And all that dwell on the earth shall worship him." That is, again, in general all the inhabitants of the earth shall at that time worship the existing state of things, and centrally also the government which is at the head. They will put all their trust in the antichristian beast. They will expect the very necessities of life from him. They will turn to him in trouble. They shall worship and admire him and give divine honor and praise to him in gratitude of heart. They shall worship the beast and its image, and through it all they shall worship the dragon.

Must I prove that this is the realization of all that has been pictured to us in the Scriptures concerning Antichrist? If so, let me first call your attention to still another feature. They shall make war with the saints. There are still saints on earth. And they shall be witnesses. They shall refuse to submit to the power of Antichrist. Not that they shall fight with the sword and rise in political rebellion. No, not that; but they shall refuse to worship the beast, and they shall uphold the sovereignty of the Almighty and of His Christ in those days. They shall refuse to change their religion and their worship and their testimony. And they shall maintain that not Antichrist, but Christ is King. And therefore they shall be hated. Then shall be fully realized what Christ said, "Ye shall be hated of all nations." Antichrist shall make war with them and overcome them. They shall be hard days, — days so hard that the elect would not hold out if the days were not shortened. Days of persecution they are. We shall learn more about them in future discussions. Let it now be sufficient to prove that this world-power is anti-God and anti-Christ and anti-kingdom and anti-saints.

Thus Antichrist in his final consummation is pictured to us everywhere in the Word of God. In Daniel 4:25 we read of him: "And he shall speak great words against the most High, and shall wear out the saints of the most High, and think to change times and law; and they shall be given into his hand until a time and times and the dividing of time." And in Daniel 8:23-25: "And in the latter time of their kingdom, when the transgressors are come to the full, a king of fierce countenance, and understanding dark sentences, shall stand up. And his power shall be mighty, but not by his own power: and he shall destroy wonderfully, and shall prosper, and practise, and shall destroy the mighty and the holy people. And through his policy also he shall cause craft to prosper in his hand; and he shall magnify himself in his heart, and by peace he shall destroy many; he shall also stand up against the Prince of princes; but he shall be broken without hand." Or, still stronger, in Daniel 11:36 we read: "And the king shall do according to his will; and he shall exalt himself, and magnify himself above every god, and shall speak marvellous things against the God of gods, and shall prosper till the indignation be accomplished: for that that is determined shall be done." Or, to quote no more, turn to the New Testament and read what Paul says in II Thessalonians 2:3-4: "Let no man deceive you by any means: for that day shall not come, except there come a falling away first, and that man of sin be revealed, the son of perdition; Who opposeth and exalteth himself above all that is called God, or that is worshipped; so that he as God sitteth in the temple of God, shewing himself that he is God." And again, in vs. 9 of the same chapter: "Even him, whose coming is after the working of Satan with all power and signs and lying wonders, And with all deceivableness of unrighteousness in them that perish." Surely, there is no doubt about the fact that all these passages wonderfully harmonize with all that we learned about the beast that cometh up out of the sea, and that this beast is the antichristian power in its final and full consummation, and that it will consist of a wicked and universal world-power, with a central government, doing wonderful things, but rising against the Most High and against Christ and His people.

The Identity Of The Beast Out Of The Sea

Finally, we probably may ask for the historical realization of this passage.

Let me say, in the first place, that according to all Scripture that power as such is in the world already, and has been in the world all through this dispensation, as the power of Antichrist. The mystery of iniquity is already working, Paul warns. And John, writing to the Christians of his time, says: "Everyone that confesseth not that Jesus Christ is come in the flesh is not of God: and this is the spirit of Antichrist, whereof ye have heard that it should come, and even now already is it in the world," (I John 4:3). And thus, as I have also explained before, I take the period indicated in the text. Time is given to the power represented in the beast of forty and two months. In this period of his making or continuing his power I include all that has gone before, all the attempts that have been made to establish this world-power in opposition to Christ and His kingdom in the entire period of the new dispensation. It may very well be this forty and two months, of which we read more than once, now in the form of twelve hundred sixty days, now in the form of three and a half years, or times, now in the form of forty and two months, will in the future also have another meaning which we cannot now determine. But certain it is that it first of all points to this entire dispensation. For in this entire dispensation the power of iniquity and the spirit of Antichrist is already in the world. In this entire period the two witnesses give their prophecy. In this entire period the church is in the wilderness of her separation. In this entire period the beast that rises up out of the abyss and that culminates in this beast that is pictured to us in the present chapter is present. And therefore, let no man beguile you also in this respect. He is in the world already. He works in the world. He has made many bold attempts already to reach his culmination. And his final manifestation will be but the consummation of a long process of development.

But on the other hand, let me also warn you not to make the mistake of finding him already in his full manifestation and power. Never yet has there been a power such as is pictured here. Never yet was there a universal world-power that had free sway over every nation and people and tribe and tongue. Never yet was there a nation whom all the peoples worshipped, never was there a kingdom or dominion that had power over all the forces and resources of creation, so that no one could even buy or sell in any part of the world except by the grace of this antichristian power. And this also applies to the present. Let no one beguile you. This antichristian power is not yet in its full reality. No single nation represents it. The world-power will not be realized by sword or cannon, so that there would be a tyrannical government lording it over a groaning lot of subjects. But it will be a kingdom or government established by common consent and agreement, in which all admire and worship the beast. And again, the war this government or dominion will wage is not against any world kingdom, but against the saints of the Most High who refuse to worship the beast. And such a power does not yet exist.

In the third place, let me also warn you that the time is at hand. We know not how soon, but soon it will be. All the signs of the times point to such a tremendous power, such a league of the nations that has control over all things, to such a unity of all religion, in which man is exalted and the Christ of the Scriptures is blasphemed and His blood trampled under foot. And therefore I would say: the time is at hand! Watch therefore! Let no one beguile you; but watch!

Finally, if you ask why this complete picture of the Antichrist is given us in Scripture, my answer is: in order that we might clearly recognize it when it is revealed. And what then must we do when we see it is come? Must we oppose it, must we fight it with the sword? That, of course, is completely impossible. It will come. It must come. And to oppose its coming is entirely vain. Its coming is irresistible. And the battle is not one of the sword. But as the text has it, he that is for captivity, into captivity he goeth; and if any man shall kill with the sword, with the sword he must be killed. No, we cannot oppose the power of Antichrist by main force. When that world-power comes and reigns supreme, we shall be submissive to the last, as far as God and our conscience permit. But here is the patience and the faith of the saints, that in all these times they remain faithful, and refuse to deny the Christ. They wait for the day of His coming. May God give us grace to be found faithful at all times, and watching and praying, so that no one may take our crown.

Chapter XXXIII
The Beast Out Of The Earth
(Revelation 13:11-18)

11 And I beheld another beast coming up out of the earth; and he had two horns like a lamb, and he spake as a dragon.
12 And he exerciseth all the power of the first beast before him, and causeth the earth and them which dwell therein to worship the first beast, whose deadly wound was healed.
13 And he doeth great wonders, so that he maketh fire come down from heaven on the earth in the sight of men,
14 And deceiveth them that dwell on the earth, by the means of those miracles which he had power to do in the sight of the beast; saying to them that dwell on the earth, that they should make an image to the beast, which had the wound by a sword, and did live.
15 And he had power to give life unto the image of the beast, that the image of the beast should both speak, and cause that as many as would not worship the image of the beast should be killed.
16 And he causeth all, both small and great, rich and poor, free and bond, to receive a mark in their right hand, or in their foreheads:
17 And that no man might buy or sell, save he that had the mark, or the name of the beast, or the number of his name.
18 Here is wisdom. Let him that hath understanding count the number of the beast: for it is the number of a man; and his number is Six hundred threescore and six.

We have discussed the first beast, which came up out of the sea and which combined within itself the appearance of a leopard, a bear, and a lion, which had the ten horns and the seven heads. We came to the conclusion, in the first place, that this beast is the symbol of a great political world-power, as is evident from the passages in the Book of Daniel which refer to similar beasts. We found that it is not merely a king or emperor or government that is here pictured, but that the beast

465

represents the entire power, the government and its dominion, and that they belong together inseparably. We also found that this world-power is universal in its sway. It has dominion over all nations and tongues and tribes, and that, not by main force, but by free alliance of all the nations together. For they all wonder after the beast, think him great, admire him, and subject themselves to him willingly, offering him even their worship. But universal this kingdom also is, we saw, because it has absolute sway over all things in its kingdom, over industry and commerce, over science and art, over religion and philosophy, and over all the powers and talents of creation.

As to its spiritual character, we found that this kingdom is anti-God and anti-Christ, anti-kingdom and anti-saints. This was plain from the fact that the beast received his power and throne from the dragon, the old serpent, the devil, the incurable opponent of the Most High and of His Christ. This is clear also from the fact that he bears names of blasphemy on his seven heads, that he has a mouth to blaspheme, and that he opens that mouth actually to blaspheme the Most High and the saints of Christ in His tabernacle. This is clear, in the third place, from the fact that he kills and persecutes the saints who refuse to worship the beast. And, finally, this is evident from the fact that he himself allows himself to be worshipped as God instead of the Most High. Thus the kingdom of man under Satan is complete. It is a kingdom which has sway over all the universe, over all men, over all the powers of creation, a kingdom in the which man worships his own work and in the which the devil is lord supreme.

As to the historical realization, we pointed out that it is already in the world as to its spiritual principle, and that it is in the making all during the history of the present dispensation, revealing itself more or less boldly at different stages of history. In the second place, we warned that you must not imagine that it has already reached its full manifestation and that Revelation 13 has already been fully realized. But, in the third place, we also pointed out that for him who has understanding and who can at all read the signs of the times, it is plain that the time is at hand and that all things develop very fast in the direction of this fascinating world-kingdom.

Now the text speaks of a second beast. And to prevent any misunderstanding at all, let me say from the outset that there is a definite relation between the first and the second beast. We must not have the impression that in the first part of the chapter Antichrist was pictured in its full manifestation, and that now in the second part we have the representation of something quite different. But much rather we must maintain that in the entire thirteenth chapter of Revelation we have the picture of Antichrist. The two beasts together form the picture of the full and complete antichristian power. But the first beast pictures it in its political aspect; the second beast deals with its religious and moral and scientific forces. The first beast tells us that this kingdom has sway over all men and over all things; the second beast rather explains to us how this first beast exercises his authority.

The Meaning Of The Second Beast

It is clear from a glance at the text that the symbolism of the first part is simply continued. In the preceding part of the chapter we found the picture of a beast rising up out of the sea, with seven heads and ten horns, and appearing like a leopard, a bear, and a lion, all in one. In that first part of the chapter we found things that were really unintelligible without the second. And therefore, to complete the picture we must really insert the picture of the second beast into that of the first.

The full symbolism is as follows. The first beast is followed by a second, who rises up out of the earth. He is less formidable in appearance. Nor is his origin in the stormy sea, but from the more quiet and more stable earth. He looks like a lamb, it seems, for he has horns as of a lamb. But when he speaks, he reminds one of the awful red dragon. He stands in a very definite relation to the first beast. Repeatedly this is indicated in the text. He exercises all his authority in the sight of, in the presence of, in behalf of, as servant of the first beast. All that he does he does in the presence of the first beast. And therefore, the purpose of this second beast lies in the service of the first. And this soon becomes apparent. For the second beast causes the inhabitants of the world to wonder after the first, admire him, and worship him. This second beast makes man build an image of the first beast, in order to worship the beast through his image. This second beast causes all the worshippers of the beast to receive a sign which distinguishes them from those who refuse to worship the first beast, in order that they may be killed. This second beast is, therefore, as it were, the actual power of the first; and the first works and exercises his power through the second. The first beast could not exist and could not exercise his authority and would not be worshipped without the work of the second beast. And the second beast would have no reason to exist and to work, were it not for the fact that this first beast must reach its full power.

What now does this second beast represent?

It is plain from what we have said that it cannot represent a second kingdom. True, in Daniel, as we have said, the beasts are symbols of kings together with their kingdoms. And also here we have the picture of a beast. But let me call your attention to the fact, in the first place, that this second beast makes a radically different impression from the first and from the beasts that are pictured in Daniel 7. There we have the wild animal, — leopard and bear and lion, and all combined into one. But here we have an entirely different picture. This beast evidently makes one think of a lamb, first of all. He has horns like those of a lamb, though he speaks like the dragon. In the second place, let me call your attention to the fact that evidently his power is quite different from that of a king. A king commands, makes laws, and thus exercises authority. But this beast, although it exercises authority, even the same as that of the first beast, does not exercise his power by commands, but evidently by persuasion. He speaks. And what this speaking of the second beast implies may become plain from the repeated indications in the text concerning the manner of his work. We read that he makes the earth and its inhabitants worship the beast, that he deceives man by the great signs and wonders which he performs, that he says to them who dwell on the earth that they should make an image. He causes all who worship the beast to receive a sign.

Hence, we receive the clear impression that the beast here mentioned does not work like the first beast, but that he is of a different character. He comes by speaking and doing great signs and wonders. He comes therefore with the persuasion of a prophet. He does not force, but convince. He does not command and issue laws, but he wins the hearts of men. And if we add to this that we read repeatedly that this second beast works in the sight of and in the presence of the first beast and that he does all he can for the power and maintenance of the first beast, it is plain that this second beast represents some power in the kingdom, some tremendous influence in that great, universal kingdom which we have pictured to you according to the first part of the chapter, through which the hearts and minds of men are influenced and bewitched and charmed, so that they worship the beast and admire him and submit themselves gladly.

What power, then, does this second beast represent? We will find no difficulty in identifying him. Scripture itself tells us. In the nineteenth chapter of the Book of Revelation we find that this same beast is referred to. And there we read, vs. 20: "And the beast was taken, and with him the false prophet that wrought miracles before him, with which he deceived them that had received the mark of the beast, and them that worshipped his image. These both were cast alive into a lake of fire that burneth with brimstone." And in Revelation 20:10 we find mention of him once more: "And the devil that deceived them was cast into the lake of fire and brimstone, where the beast and the false prophet are." The identity is unmistakable. The beast that is mentioned in these passages is evidently the first beast; and the false prophet is none other than this second beast, with the two lamb's horns, who speaks as the dragon. And therefore we come to the conclusion that this second beast is called the false prophet.

What is a prophet? We must banish from our minds the popular conception that a prophet is chiefly a man who foretells the future. True, a prophet also foretells the future; but that is not his only work. We find from Scripture that a prophet is characteristically a person who speaks for someone else. Aaron is called the prophet of Moses when they two together go to Pharaoh, and Aaron expresses the message instead of and for Moses. So are the prophets of God among Israel. They are men who speak for God and bring His message, who appeal to the minds and hearts of men, of Israel, in behalf of Jehovah and His covenant and cause. They teach and speak and reveal the will of God and try to persuade men that they may embrace Jehovah's cause.

Now this second beast is also a prophet: he speaks for someone else. He tries to influence the minds of men, to persuade them, to gain them for the cause of him in whose interest he speaks. But he is a false prophet. He does not preach the truth. He speaks the lie. He persuades men and teaches them, and by doing so deceives them, so that they believe the lie. And if we compare this with what we find in the words of the passage we are now discussing, we shall find that this is actually his character. In the first place, his very appearance is deceiving. He looks like a lamb; and one would receive the impression, therefore, that he is in some way affiliated with Christ, the great Prophet, and that the words he speaks are the words of Christ. But he speaks like the dragon, that is, he derives the contents of his prophecy and teaching not from Christ, but from the devil, from hell itself. He is a prophet. He speaks for someone else. But the one for whom he speaks is the first beast, who exercises all the authority of the devil and received it from him. In his presence and in behalf of him he speaks and exercises his authority. In his sight and in his behalf he does his great signs and wonders. For him he persuades men to establish an entire worship, and erect an image. And he causes that all who refuse the image are killed. In a word, this prophet is the exact opposite of what Elijah was among Israel. Elijah stood before Jehovah; this prophet stands for the opponent of Jehovah. Elijah spoke the truth of God; this prophet speaks the lie of the dragon. Elijah persuaded men to break down the image of Baal and serve and worship the true God; this prophet persuades men to forsake Jehovah and make an image for the first beast and the dragon. Elijah persuaded men to kill the priests of Baal; this prophet persuades men to kill the saints of the Most High.

How must we conceive of the realization of the second beast in history?

In order to answer this question I would say, in the first place, that the beast as a whole does not represent a single person, a single individual. I know, there are interpreters who urge this very strongly; but it is not necessary to maintain this, nor is it very probably the interpretation. We found in explanation of the first beast that it did not simply refer to an individual king or emperor or governor, but just as much to the kingdom or world-power under the sway of that government. And the same must be borne in mind here. I do not think it impossible that in the future some great philosopher will arise who will dominate almost any intellectual movement of his time, so that all others follow him. But this beast does not represent a single individual, but rather all the power of false philosophy and science and religion combined.

In the future all science and philosophy and all religion shall be united into one science and one philosophy and one religion. There shall be no more difference of opinion. Just as politically the world shall be one, so it shall be one intellectually and religiously. They shall all have the same ideas about things. They shall all admire the same science. They shall all have the same religion. There will be a new religion. Already we hear of it in our own time. And that new religion shall embrace all things; it shall be universal. All creeds and all denominations and all sects shall be blended and united into one, so that there shall be no more strife and ecclesiastical contention. It shall have a universal creed, laying down the precepts and principles for every sphere of life. It shall lay down rules for our individual life, just as the Christian religion. It shall lay down the principles for our home life, just as the Christian religion does. It shall reveal principles for the life of society and for the life of nations. It shall lay down the rules for religious life in particular, tell all men how they must worship and what they must worship. It shall be a new system of thought and religion, with a new creed, universal in its scope, and, at the same time, with a new god. That new god will be the beast, the great world-power, whom all shall admire and worship and for whom all shall erect an image, in order that they may worship the same.

Thus it is also plain that the first beast has need of the second. The universal world-power, being based upon the unity and voluntary submission of all, has need of the power of false prophecy, of this universal science and religion. For the moment men shall begin to differ principally in regard to their religion and worship the disintegration of the world-power shall have begun. The second beast must serve the first, is indispensable to the first. The world-power has need of false science and philosophy and religion to maintain his authority and the integrity and unity of his kingdom.

The Activity Of The Second Beast

If we understand this, it is not very difficult to comprehend the action of the second beast.

In the first place, we read in the text that he doeth great things, signs and wonders, and that it is exactly through these that he succeeds in gaining men for his cause and deceiving them. Naturally a prophet must do signs and wonders. These must establish his prophetic authority, the truth of the things he speaks. Thus it was with Moses before Pharaoh, and at the same time with the magi of the king. They performed signs and wonders to impress the authority with which they appeared. Thus it was with Elijah on Carmel, with Christ as a prophet, with the appearance of the apostles in the midst of the heathen world. They all performed signs and wonders in order that these might corroborate the truth of their message. Thus it is also in the antichristian world-power. This second beast performs signs and wonders. So it was foretold already by Daniel the prophet. The Antichrist will perform marvellous things. So it is prophesied by Christ Himself: "For there shall arise false Christs and false prophets, and shall shew great signs and wonders; insomuch that, if it were possible, they shall deceive the very elect," (Matthew 24:24).

So it was also foretold by the apostle Paul, who predicted that the man of sin should manifest himself in great signs and wonders. And thus we find it in the words of our text. The second beast, the false prophet, the power of this false philosophy and science and religion, shall do things which will astonish the world and which will cause all men to flock to him, to listen to his prophecy, and to worship the beast.

What shall this power do? There are interpreters who take it all in the literal sense of the word and who claim that this second beast represents a person who will actually perform miracles. We are not inclined that way. All that is necessary is to assume that this great power will do things that will corroborate his teachings, and thus establish the universal kingdom. He will not only talk, but he will show that he can do things in harmony with the message he brings. He will apply his science and philosophy and show that man is extremely powerful. He will bring fire from heaven. Why not? Through the power of electricity man has already done great things. In the future he may actually be able to extract the fire from the clouds of heaven and bring it down in the sight of all men. He will provide men with all the commodities and all the conveniences and pleasures modern science can invent, so that they can fly through the air without danger, speak with their fellow men in the remotest corner of this great kingdom without trouble, enter into the bowels of the earth and plow through the depth of the sea. It is that false philosophy that will discover all the powers of creation and bring them into use, so that all men shall wonder at the great things it does. And wondering at its action, they shall follow him and believe his message and obey his command.

This is evidently the sole, ultimate purpose of these signs and wonders, that men may believe and follow the beast. For we read in the words of our text that by these he so deceives men that they make an image of the beast. Notice that this false prophet does not make the image, but that under his influence, as he speaks for the beast and performs signs and wonders in his name, men make such an image. This image is, of course, a representation of the beast itself, so that whosoever worships the image worships the beast, and he who worships the beast worships the dragon.

Exactly of what this image shall consist we do not know at present. The idea of an image through which the world-power is worshipped is nothing strange. The emperors of the Roman Empire had such images made, through which they were worshipped as gods. And to come to more recent times, in the French Revolution we well know how images of the great leaders of that revolution were made and worshipped, how men paid religious worship to the images of liberty, equality, and fraternity that were made, and how in the Notre Dame of Paris the goddess of reason was actually worshipped by the great of France. And therefore, there would be nothing strange if in these latter days there would be once more such idol-worship in the literal sense of the word. At all events, some sign, some ensign, some device, representing this universal world-power will be conceived of and made and distributed all through the dominion of Antichrist, that they may pay divine honor to it and worship the beast. Before that emblem of the universal world-power all men shall bow down.

Still greater things this false prophet is allowed to perform. He gives to that image a spirit, a breath of life. Also this cannot be definitely explained with a view to its realization. How this universal idol shall speak, I know not. But that is of minor importance. We know the purpose of it all. The text tells us that this image is given a breath of life in order that it may speak and that those who do not worship the image may be killed. There are still saints of the Most High on earth; the remnant of the seed of the woman is still there. They are not yet taken to heaven. And they, of course, refuse to go along with all this beautiful and worldwide movement. They refuse to adopt the philosophy of the second beast. They refuse to wonder at its great signs. They refuse to adopt its religion. They refuse to worship the beast and the dragon. And therefore they cannot be tolerated. They must be discovered, so that this great universal kingdom may be rid of them. And therefore an image must be made, some universal ensign. And that universal ensign must be displayed everywhere. Wherever you turn you can see it in this kingdom of the Antichrist, and all humbly bow down before it or in some way pay it divine honor. But the saints of the Most High refuse to worship the idol. And thus it speaks. The universal insignia is the means through which it becomes evident who do not worship the beast, so that they may be killed. Distinction, separation, must now be made between the seed of the woman and the followers and worshippers of the beast. And this universal idol must serve as the means through which the distinction is realized.

In close connection with this idea is the idea of the sign. When, by means of the image, distinction is made between the followers of the beast and those who refuse to worship him, the faithful followers receive a sign. Of little importance it is for us at present to determine exactly in what this sign shall consist. It may be that the kingdom shall literally provide for some brand or badge or button which the beast's faithful followers shall be allowed to wear and with which they shall be allowed to appear in modern society. In our age of badges and buttons this idea is not far-fetched. But it also may be that this is all symbolism, to denote that there shall be a visible difference in the manifestation of the followers of the beast and the followers of Christ.

Certain it is that the difference shall be there and that the difference shall be very plain. The false prophet, the power of false science and philosophy and religion, shall see to it that the distinction is very public and evident to all, so that only his followers may share in the blessings of this great kingdom. Just as only the followers of Christ, baptized in His name and confessing Him faithfully, shall share in the blessings of the kingdom Christ will establish, so also the followers of the beast only shall reap the benefits of this universal world-kingdom. The rest, who do not wear the mark of the beast, shall be excluded, shall be boycotted in every respect. They shall not be able to buy or to sell. Of course, all things are under the control of the first beast, of this great and universal world-power. The very necessities of life are in his power. And he can surely allow or prevent buying and selling according to his good pleasure. The saints of Christ, who do not worship the image, who refuse to receive the mark of the beast, shall not be able to do business, shall not be able to live along with that great society, shall not be able to buy the necessities of life. They shall be outcasts, mocked at, held in derision, thrust aside, ousted from society, and killed. Those shall be terrible days. More terrible shall they be than any form of persecution the children of God have ever experienced. There shall be no place for them on earth. They shall be left without a helper on earth. So terrible shall those days be that, in the first place, many shall fall who appeared to be children of the Most High, and that, in the second place, the very elect would not be able to resist, were it not for the fact that the days are shortened.

The Number Of The Beast

Finally, we must still discuss the name of this great beast which all its worshippers bear on their foreheads or in their right hand. We read: "Here is wisdom. Let him that hath understanding count the number of the beast: for it is the number of a man; and his number is Six hundred threescore and six."

Many and varied are the interpretations given of this number; and we shall not tire your attention by enumerating them all. A very favorite interpretation is that which is given by an old church father, Irenaeus, and accepted by many of our own time. The interpretation is as follows. The letters of the Greek alphabet were used as numbers. If this is taken as the basis of the interpretation, we find that the letters in the word **Lateinos**, or Latin, together give us the number 666. And therefore the name of the beast as it is spelled by this number is "Latin," and denotes the kingdom of the Latins, or of the Roman Empire. But even this interpretation we cannot possibly accept as true. For, in the first place, however ingenious it may be, it is nevertheless more or less arbitrary. On this basis I can also construe other names which are just as suitable, which also amount to the number 666, but which simply are formed by a different arrangement of the same letters. But, in the second place, notice that our text does not say, "Here is a riddle; let him that is bright solve it," but plainly states: "Here is wisdom. Let him that hath understanding count the number of the beast." And therefore we must have something different. And, in the third place, we should not lose sight of the fact that the numbers in Revelation have symbolical significance and that they stand also in this case for a higher spiritual reality.

Let us then notice, in the first place, that the mark of the beast, the number of his name, the number of the beast, and the name of the beast all denote identically the same thing. The beast has a name. And the name in Scripture always denotes character and being. The name of this beast has been impressed upon his followers, so that also they may be distinguished as his subjects. And that name is the same as is expressed in the number Six hundred sixty-six. Now what is the meaning of this number?

Six is the number of the creature in all its fulness. In six days God created the world; and in six days creation was completed. The fulness of creation has come to realization in six days. But the full week is not expressed in the six, but in the number seven. The seventh day is the day of consecration and adoration of God, on which the creature was to lift himself from the sphere of the mundane and consecrate himself to the Creator. On the seventh day man was to bring the glory of all God's work to Him. It was hallowed. But the seven is lacking in the six. And therefore it speaks of the fulness of creation and all the powers of creation, but without God and without the service and glory of God. The world with all its fulness, with all its powers, but without God, under the influence of sin, − that is the symbolism of the number six. Ten, as we have had occasion to notice more than once, is the number that denotes a complete measure of anything according to the decree of God, whether it be a measure of time, or power, or development, or anything else. Now notice that Six hundred sixty-six is six, plus ten times six, plus ten times ten times six. Ten times six would denote the world and all its fulness, without God, developed according to the measure of God's plan. And ten times ten times six denotes that same development in the highest degree, coming to its fullest consummation.

The idea, therefore, is not so difficult. God has created a world, in order that this world should glorify Him and be consecrated to Him. But that world tore itself loose from Him, refused to glorify Him; and man now developed the kingdom of the world without God. God allows that kingdom of the world to develop to its full extent. Although man has fallen away from Him, He nevertheless allows him to exercise dominion over the earthly creation and to bring to light all the hidden powers and talents of creation to their fullest degree. And that kingdom we have in this antichristian beast. These beasts represent the highest development of the sovereignty of man apart from God, developing all the powers of creation without God and under the devil. It is the climax of development of the Man of Sin. It is the kingdom of man, of the creature, without God, without the seven. And therefore his number is Six hundred sixty-six, the number of man indeed.

Such, I feel persuaded, is the meaning of this chapter.

If we have spiritual understanding, we must count the number of the beast. You may see him rise before your very eyes in the world of today. Hence, we must watch and pray, that we may not fall into temptation. We must be faithful unto the end. But it is not our calling to resist the coming of the beast: for that is impossible. You cannot prevent his coming. But what we must do is watch. Here is the patience of the saints. Here is wisdom. We must know how he will come, that we may recognize his coming and be faithful even unto the end. God grant that we may be found watching in that day, so that we may not be allured by all the beauty and fascination and Christian appearance and strength and stability of that world-kingdom and by the signs and wonders of the false prophet, but that we may remain faithful even unto the very end, so that no one may take our crown.

Chapter XXXIV

The Lamb On Mount Zion

(Revelation 14:1-5)

1 And I looked, and, lo, a Lamb stood on the mount Sion, and with him an hundred forty and four thousand, having his Father's name written in their foreheads.

2 And I heard a voice from heaven, as the voice of many waters, and as the voice of a great thunder: and I heard the voice of harpers harping with their harps:

3 And they sung as it were a new song before the throne, and before the four beasts, and the elders: and no man could learn that song but the hundred and forty and four thousand, which were redeemed from the earth.

4 These are they which were not defiled with women; for they are virgins. These are they which follow the Lamb whithersoever he goeth. These were redeemed from among men, being the firstfruits unto God and to the Lamb.

5 And in their mouth was found no guile: for they are without fault before the throne of God.

The Book of Revelation is full of happy and striking contrasts which cannot but keep alive one's interest even from a natural point of view. This phenomenon is but natural and can easily be explained from the subject matter itself. Revelation deals with the mightiest contrast that ever existed, the contrast between the kingdom of light and the kingdom of darkness, principally between God and the devil; and it shows the opposition and enmity of the devil against God, and the power and authority of the Almighty maintaining itself over against this enmity of the dragon in actual conflict. It is the prophetic record of the great battle of the ages on the part of the devil against the Almighty for the possession of the kingdoms of the world. And for that reason it is but natural that time and again we meet with tremendous contrasts in this book. We meet with the contrast between the dragon and the woman, between the dragon and the Lamb, between the Lamb and the beast, between the Christ and the Antichrist, between the church and the world.

For the same reason we have also found repeatedly that a dark and frightfully horrible picture was immediately followed by one of light and joy and glory. Thus we found it, for instance, in Chapter 7. In Chapter 6 we studied the picture of the time immediately before the last judgment at the opening of the sixth seal. Dark and terrible that picture was indeed. Heaven and earth were shaken, and the foundations of all existence seemed to be removed. Earthquakes and thunders and darkness were the signs that accompanied this terrible incident. And the great and small of the world hid themselves and cried to the rocks and mountains to cover them. And the question was asked, in near despair: "Who shall stand?" But that dark picture was followed immediately by the joyous one in Chapter 7, where we read of the one hundred forty-four thousand who were sealed and secure in the midst of tribulation, and of the innumerable multitude before the throne in glory. The same contrast exists between Chapters 9 and 10. In the ninth chapter we studied the fifth and sixth trumpets, the first and second woes. There we read of the terrible locusts out of the abyss and how they tortured men, and of the awful horsemen sent by the angels who were let loose at the Euphrates, who killed one-third of men. And also that horrible picture is followed by a hopeful and joyous one in Chapter 10, where we read of the mighty angel standing with his feet on the earth and the sea and swearing by Him that liveth forever and ever that there should be no more delay.

The same phenomenon is met with once more in our chapter. In Chapter 13 we found the picture of the world-power, of Antichrist, of the Man of Sin in the full development of his power and authority. We found that it was a universal kingdom, having sway over all nations and over all things in the universe. We found that all the people followed this beast, were delighted over him, worshipped him because of the instigation of the power of false prophecy as pictured in the second beast. We found that an image was erected for the beast, so that by means of this image it might become plain who would worship the beast and who would not. We found, further, that to all who worshipped the beast a sign was given, and that only those who received this sign and could show this sign are participants of the blessings of this kingdom, all the rest being excluded, so that the people of God could neither buy nor sell, could not procure wherewith to clothe or feed themselves. In short, it was a horrible picture of hell and Satan and Antichrist in all their power, a picture of affliction and tribulation for the people of God. And now in the chapter before us we have once more a picture of the opposite side, a picture of the power that opposes this world-kingdom and its king, and therefore at the same time a picture of joy and salvation and glory for God's people. That is characteristic of the entire chapter, and that is also the purpose of the picture we are now studying in the present passage.

The Purpose Of The Vision

Let us once more take note of the very evident fact that in this portion we have a continuation of the symbolism begun in Chapter 13. The fact that this has been overlooked has led to the gravest errors in the interpretation of this chapter and especially of the portion we are now discussing. It has led many interpreters to read this portion, wholly or in part, as if we merely had a historical record of the future in this chapter. They read then as if John said: "Then, at that time, shall Jesus appear on Mt. Sion, and He shall gather all His people in glory round about Him, in order to save them to the full and wreak vengeance upon the enemy." And naturally in that case the mistake is also made to take Mt. Sion in the literal sense of the word and to maintain that in the days of Antichrist Jesus shall appear on Mt. Sion as the defender of His people and the opponent of the beast. And thus we come into conflict with the general revelation of Scripture, which assures us time and again that the Lord shall come on the clouds of heaven in the day of judgment. In that case also the angels in heaven are taken in the most literal sense of the word; and it is maintained that in the day of Antichrist angels shall send a warning, a last warning, to the people on earth, in order to bring them to the fear of Jehovah's name and to proclaim to them the impending judgment. And again, by doing so we come into conflict with the entire trend of Scripture, which teaches us that Moses and the prophets are sufficient, and that if people refuse to believe them, even the dead rising from the grave would have no effect whatever upon them. From the literal point of view we can never understand this passage, nor from the point of view that confuses the literal and symbolical interpretations.

It must be clear to us, therefore, that John does not write history, that he does not even directly prophesy in the sense of foretelling future events, but that he speaks in highly symbolic language. After the dark vision of the beast and his kingdom he now receives a bright vision of the Lamb and His people. And all is symbolism. That this is true is plain from the context. In the preceding chapter we had symbolism pure and simple.

No one mistook the beast for a real beast, the horns for real horns, the heads for real heads. No one misunderstood the picture there. And this is also true of the picture in the present passage. What right have we to change the method of interpretation all of a sudden, without any indication in the text. On the contrary, also the text brings us to the same conclusion. In the first place, John does not begin to say, "**Then** shall Christ appear on Mt. Sion." But he merely states that he saw the Lamb on Mt. Sion with His people. The two visions, of Chapter 13 and the present chapter, belong together. John by no means conveys the idea that the Lamb was not on Mt. Sion when the beast established his kingdom, but far rather that He was there all the time. In all the confusion of the nations during this entire period when Antichrist seemingly reigns supreme, the Lamb is on Mt. Sion, calm and majestic, surrounded by His people, the one hundred forty-four thousand. John sees another vision, but a vision that belongs to the one of Chapter 13 and that is its counter-part. This is plain also from the very language employed. Christ is denoted as the Lamb, which, however familiar, is nevertheless symbolic language. His people are described as the one hundred forty-four thousand, as those who are not defiled with women; for they are virgins. And a wonderful song is heard from heaven, which they alone can learn. In short, the entire passage gives us immediately the impression that here we have once more symbolism in the highest sense of the word, and that as such it must be interpreted.

It may be well, before we explain this beautiful picture in detail, to ascertain the purpose of the whole. Why is this picture here inserted?

In the first place, let us remark that it cannot escape our attention what a tremendous contrast this portion forms with the preceding vision of the beast. The reference to that chapter by way of contrast is very evident. There we have the picture of the beast lording it supremely over all; here we have the vision of the Lamb on Mt. Sion, standing majestic and in authority as the King and protector of His people. There we have the vision especially of the thousands and millions who worship the beast and his image; here we have the picture of the one hundred forty-four thousand who belong to the Lamb. There we found that the followers of the beast and his worshippers receive his sign on their right hand or on their foreheads; here we find that also the people of the Lamb have a sign, the name of the Lamb and of the Father. There we learned how only the followers of the beast were supreme and blest and happy, controlling the entire world; here we learn that only the one hundred forty-four thousand can learn the song of glory and of joy which is heard from heaven. There we found that the followers of the Lamb were threatened with destruction and woe, so that they could not buy or sell; the present picture is full of woe and destruction to the followers of the beast and Babylon. In a word, the same condition of things, the same state of affairs is described. In both visions we read of the beast and the Lamb. In both visions we read of the worshipping of both. But the difference is that in Chapter 13 we find the cause of the Lamb and His people apparently lost, while in this chapter we find Him as the victor. In Chapter 13 we found the people of God in distress; here we find them in security and in all glory. In a word, in Chapter 13 the kingdom of Antichrist is described from its own point of view, and therefore as victorious; in this chapter the entire state of things is viewed in the light of heaven and of God's decree, and the Lamb therefore is victorious after all.

The contrast reminds us of Elisha and his servant at Dothan. The Syrians were provoked by the work of the prophet, and therefore were seeking his soul. And in the morning, as the servant of Elisha woke up in Dothan, he found that the city was surrounded by foes on all sides, and that escape was impossible. The servant of the prophet, looking at this whole affair from the natural point of view, is perplexed, is in distress. He despairs and looks upon his master as a lost man. But the prophet prays that the eyes of his servant may be opened, so that he may be able to see the entire situation in its full reality. And now the servant beholds that on their side is a mightier host than on the side of the enemy. The whole mountain is filled with chariots and horses of fire round about them. So is the relation here. Antichrist is supreme. He lords it over all the world and over all things. It seems as if nothing can check his power and authority. The devil has finally gained the victory. The people of God are in distress. From the natural point of view, from the point of view of visible things, it would seem as if the cause of the Lamb and His people were a lost cause. But there is another side, a spiritual side, to this entire economy of things. And when the light of heaven falls on the scene, and the eyes of the people of God through faith are opened, they see that the Lamb is standing on Mt. Sion in calm majesty, and that His people are safe in His protection. The kingdom of Antichrist, — so the vision tells us, — apparently so safe and secure, is doomed to destruction. For the Lamb stands on Mt. Sion ready to consume His enemies. The people of God, — so the vision tells us, — apparently in distress and defeat, shall have the victory. For they are

with the victorious Lamb, and follow Him whithersoever He goeth.
Chapter 14 sheds the light of heaven upon the kingdom of Antichrist.

A Symbol Of Power And Authority

If this is clear, it will not be difficult to understand the meaning of this
entire picture in detail.

With the Lamb we are already acquainted, and we need not determine
His identity at all. He is the Christ, and especially from the point of view
of having accomplished the will of the Father to inherit the kingdom.
Christ is the Anointed of God. And it is the will of the Father to give Him
the kingdom of the whole world. But in order to receive the kingdom He
had to redeem it by His blood and fulfill the will of the Triune God. In
that capacity He stands here, as the Lamb, and, as we know from other
passages, as the Lamb that was slain. There is no controversy about the
identity of the Lamb.

But different it is with regard to Mt. Sion. Interpreters differ widely
when they come to explain this figure. As we have already mentioned,
there are some who take it in the literal sense of the word, not as a symbol
but as the literal Mt. Sion in Jerusalem, and then explain that Christ during
the days of Antichrist shall stand on that mount. But the symbolic nature
of the entire passage, as we have already observed, is against this
interpretation. It will not do to separate one element from all the rest and
to explain it in the literal sense of the word. There are others who
maintain that Sion is heavenly Jerusalem. But this is impossible because of
the context. We read that as the Lamb stands with His people on Mt. Sion,
a voice is heard from heaven, clearly indicating that Mt. Sion is on earth.
Still others claim that Mt. Sion is the symbol of the church invisible on
earth. And this is perfectly allowable as such, for Mt. Sion appears in
Scripture as the church of Christ. Only the contents of this passage are all
against this interpretation. If Mt. Sion is the church, what then must we
make of the one hundred forty-four thousand? They are evidently the
church of the living God in Christ Jesus our Lord. But if they are, then Mt.
Sion cannot mean the same thing. And therefore, we feel compelled to
discard all these interpretations and to look for something else.

Mt. Sion in the literal sense was originally the hill in the city of
Jerusalem on which was built the stronghold, the citadel, of the city. It
was this citadel that was captured from the Jebusites by David and that
became the stronghold of David. Later that same name was often applied

to the temple-hill, on which Jehovah dwelt among His people. And again, it is not infrequently referred to as including the entire city of Jerusalem, the city of God. And therefore, in the symbolical sense of the word we may say that Sion implies two things. In the first place, it is the center of God's power, the stronghold from which Jehovah rules over and defends His people. And, in the second place, it is also the hill of His presence, on which He dwells among His people.

Yet we will never be able to explain this symbolism if we take the Lamb and Mt. Sion separately and explain them individually first, in order then to bring them together. On the contrary, the Lamb standing on Mt. Sion constitutes one symbol; and they must be taken together, as belonging together from the very outset. And then it is our conviction that the expression must be explained in the light of Psalm 2:1-9, a psalm which is so often referred to in the Book of Revelation, but never more plainly than in Chapters 13 and 14. If we turn to this psalm, we will find that verses 1-3 give us the exact picture, in a few brief expressions, of Revelation 13. We read: "Why do the heathen rage, and the people imagine a vain thing? The kings of the earth set themselves, and the rulers take counsel together, against the Lord, and against his anointed, saying, Let us break their bands asunder, and cast away their cords from us." Could you find a more exact picture of what is told us in Revelation 13? There we found that all the kingdoms of the earth had combined and conspired together, and that with the definite purpose of rebellion against God and against His Christ. The nations we found raging with madness to establish their kingdom, in which the devil is worshipped and Jehovah is thrust from His throne. And those same facts are described in Psalm 2. But let us continue. Verse 4 reveals to us the attitude of God Almighty over against these raging nations and peoples. What does Jehovah think about this condition? Is He frightened? Does He now admit His defeat and acknowledge that He must surrender His kingdom? Not at all. We read: "He that sitteth in the heavens shall laugh: the Lord shall have them in derision." When Antichrist shall rage and establish his kingdom and apparently will have the victory and realize his kingdom, God Almighty shall laugh. The whole thing appears so utterly foolish to Him that He laughs about it. That man could conceive of the possibility of establishing a kingdom in which the devil should be supreme is such a piece of folly to God in heaven that He derides them from heaven and mocks at the whole deviltry of the dragon. It is a vain thing which they imagine. The whole plan of the raging nations shall collapse and prove to be without reality. And why? Simply because of His own eternal plan and counsel. The Lord God Almighty made His counsel. And that eternal counsel of the Almighty does not call for the permanent existence of such a kingdom of Satan, but for its destruction. And for that reason the psalm continues to reveal that plan of God Almighty. In verses 5 to 9 we read: "Then shall he speak unto them in his wrath, and vex them in his sore displeasure. Yet have I set my king upon my holy hill of Zion. I will declare the decree: the Lord hath said unto me, Thou art my Son; this day have I begotten thee. Ask of me, and I shall give thee the heathen for thine inheritance, and the uttermost parts of the earth for thy possession. Thou shalt break them with a rod of iron; thou shalt dash them in pieces like a potter's vessel." Because God had anointed Christ, and not the devil, over His holy hill, the stronghold of the kingdom, the latter shall never succeed; but his kingdom shall fall. And therefore, it is from that psalm that we learn the meaning of the expression "the Lamb on mount Zion." It implies that God's decree shall stand and that no raging nations shall ever frustrate His plan. It implies that God's decree calls for a kingdom under Christ, the Lamb, the Anointed of God, and that this Lamb actually stands in authority over the nations at all times. It implies that the entire deviltry of Antichrist shall be destroyed and that the Holy One of Zion shall break them in pieces.

If this is clear, the whole vision of John and its purpose are also clear. The question might arise, as we look at that mighty kingdom of Antichrist: is not this after all the kingdom which shall abide forever, — this mighty kingdom, beautiful and strong, lording it over all the world and finding its highest purpose in the worship of the beast and the devil? If that is so, is not then the cause of Christ a lost cause, and have not the people of God then hoped in Him in vain? These questions are answered in our vision of the Lamb on Mount Zion. No, that entire kingdom of the world is bound to fall and to be destroyed. Why? Because the Lamb still stands on Mount Zion. To the natural eye He is not visible; the spiritual eye of faith sees Him plainly. The Lamb, not the devil, is the King of this world. The Lamb, not the beast, shall have the victory. The devil, not the Lamb, shall be defeated and destroyed. Because the Lamb is the Anointed One and therefore has the certain decree of God back of Him, He shall surely have the victory. And therefore the people of God, when all things seem against them and when Antichrist rages in all his fury, need never despair. Lift up your eyes to heaven, and behold the Lamb on Mount Zion. His is the victory!

A Picture Of Glory And Victory

If this picture of the power of the Lamb over against the Antichrist is clear, we will also understand that the rest of our text shows us the effect of this power of our mighty King upon His own people.

The Lamb is not alone. He has His people with Him, the one hundred forty-four thousand. We have met with this number before, in Chapter 7; and we do not, therefore, have to explain the meaning of it again. At that time we called your attention to the fact that they were not Israelites in the literal sense of the word. The present passage corroborates this. There can be no question that in both cases the number has the same meaning. If in the former case they were Jews, they must also be Jews here. But then you obtain the strange explanation, which some actually hold, that the saints who will be on earth at the time of Antichrist will all be from the seed of Abraham in the literal sense of the word. And that is, evidently, not the case. We maintain, therefore, that the one hundred forty-four thousand represent the number of the elect who are on the earth at any moment of the world's history. There are always one hundred forty-four thousand people of God on earth: the number of God's elect. In the present passage they denote the people of God on earth at the time of the antichristian power. What, then, is the meaning of this number in this connection? Why are they mentioned here? Simply to show that not one of the elect is missing. They are all with the Lamb on Mount Zion. They have all remained faithful. They have all followed the Lamb whithersoever He leadeth them even in the time of tribulation. It might perhaps be expected that some of God's people would be missing, that some would have abandoned the attempt to follow the Lamb. The times were hard; the suffering for Christ's sake was very severe. They could not buy or sell. They had no place left on the earth. They were hated of all nations. Perhaps some of them yielded to the demand of Antichrist, forsook the Lamb, and bowed before the beast. But no: all the one hundred forty-four thousand are still with the Lamb. Not one is lacking. All God's people are saved through the power of the Lamb in spite of the raging fury of Antichrist.

In what respect have they remained untouched? Have they been protected by the power of the Lamb in the physical sense of the word?

Have they not been in prison? Have they not been in suffering and death? We know better. They have suffered hunger and nakedness because of their faithful refusal to worship the beast. They were killed all the day long. But this does not hurt them. They have a spiritual existence and life. The question is not whether they were hurt physically, but whether they had any spiritual want. The great question for the people of God in the world is not whether or not they must suffer the suffering for Christ's sake because of their faithfulness, but whether they shall remain faithful in the midst of tribulation. And, behold, that is the case with these one hundred forty-four thousand! All have remained with the Lamb. All have chosen His side. All have faithfully followed Him even in tribulation and distress.

Still more: they remained pure. The text says: "These are they which were not defiled with women; for they are virgins." You understand, of course, that these words must not be taken in the literal sense any more than the rest of the text, as if celibacy were advocated here and as if the unmarried state were given preference above the married. This certainly is not the case. But we must remember that fornication in Scripture is the symbol of spiritual fornication. In that sense Esau was a fornicator because he despised God's covenant. In that sense Israel of the old dispensation is very often pictured in the Old Testament as an adulterous woman, whoring after other gods and departing from the service of Jehovah their covenant God. Being defiled in the physical sense of the word, therefore, is symbolic of violation of the covenant of Jehovah. In this sense, then, these one hundred forty-four thousand have not becomed defiled. All the world was committing fornication in the spiritual sense. All went awhoring after the beast. And all the evil world demanded of these one hundred forty-four thousand to commit fornication as they did. They had threatened them with expulsion from the world if they would not worship the beast. But these had not heeded this call and had ignored the threat of the beast. They had remained faithful to their covenant God. The same is expressed in the words, "they are without blemish." They have not been stained by the defilement of the world. Yea, still more clearly: in their mouth was found no lie. All the kingdom of Antichrist was filled with, was based upon, the lie that the beast must be worshipped and that the dragon was king. But they had adhered to the truth and had maintained boldly and without fear: Christ is King, and the Almighty God is sovereign of heaven and earth. Thus they had remained faithful all through the reign of Antichrist. The people of God need not fear. For when that terrible time shall come, they shall remain with the powerful Lamb on Mount Zion and follow Him whithersoever He goeth.

But why do the people of God remain faithful even in the midst of most terrible suffering and persecution for Christ's sake? Is it in their own strength? Is it because of their own natural faithful character perhaps?

By no means! In the first place, let me call your attention to the sign they bear on their forehead. Even as the wicked have the sign of the beast, so these have the name of the Lamb and of the Father. What does that mean? It simply implies in this connection that the Father and the Lamb have marked them as their own. And therefore, by this name of the Lamb and of the Father we are reminded of God's eternal counsel. From all eternity God Almighty has chosen them and graven them in the palms of His hands. And in all eternity the Father has given His people to His Son, that He might redeem them to the full. No one, therefore, is able to pluck them out of the Lamb's and out of the Father's hand. The Lamb had purchased them with His own blood from the world and from among men; and they belong to Him with body and soul, for time and eternity. Shall Antichrist then prevail against them? Shall he persuade them to worship the beast? No, never! The counsel of Almighty God must first be broken, and it must first be evident that the precious blood of the Lamb was shed in vain, before this can ever happen. And that, of course, is absolutely impossible. Standing therefore in the power of the Almighty, conscious of this power by faith, redeemed by the blood of the Lamb, they cannot perish; and Antichrist has nothing in them. Firstfruits they must be unto God and the Lamb. And no more than God will give His glory to another, no more could these one hundred forty-four thousand of the Lamb be lost, whom the Almighty has formed for Himself that they should show forth His praise.

Finally, let us also notice that this power of God and of the Lamb enabled them to sing even in the midst of the battle, and sing of joy and victory. From heaven swells a song, strong as the voice of many waters, rolling through the air and through heaven like the voice of mighty thunder, yet carried along on the breeze in the sweet melody of harpers harping on their harps.

What is this song? It is the song of the church triumphant in heaven, the song of the saints who have been in tribulation who have been redeemed, — the song of Abel and Enoch and Noah and Abraham and Isaac and Jacob and Moses and Elijah and all the prophets and witnesses of the old dispensation. It is the song of the apostles and the martyrs, of the cloud of witnesses. This song swells the breeze till it reaches the ears of these suffering one hundred forty-four thousand who are still in the heat of their spiritual battle. It is the song of the innumerable multitude that has gone in before them, that already are apparelled in their white robes and wear the palm branches. They hunger no more, neither do they thirst any more, neither doth the sun strike upon them, nor any heat. The Lamb is their shepherd, and God is their guide and wipes away all tears from their eyes. And this glorified throng, this church triumphant, sings in forceful melody: "Salvation belongeth unto our God, and unto the Lamb." It is the song of joy and victory. Behold, it reaches the ears of these one hundred forty-four thousand who are still in tribulation but with the Lamb on Mount Zion.

And what happens? Does it fill their hearts with sorrow because they are still in trouble and distress? Does it cause them to despair of their own glory? Does it sound like sarcasm in their ears perhaps? Ah, no: they understand it. They can realize already that this song is theirs. They can apply it to themselves. Surely, they are still in trouble and tribulation, and their suffering is severe. They still hunger and thirst, and the heat of the sun strikes them day by day. But conscious of the fact that they stand on the side of the powerful Lamb, conscious of the fact that they bear the name of the Father and of the Lamb on their foreheads, conscious of the fact that they have been purchased to be first fruits unto the Father and unto the Lamb, they are sure of victory. Antichrist may rage and make life extremely hard for them. His time is but short. Christ shall have the victory. And they know it. And in that consciousness they can learn this song of victory. In the midst of tribulation they too can sing it. And in joy of heart and to the amazement of the world, which cannot understand this song and which can never learn it, they chime in with the song of the glorified saints in heaven: "Salvation belongeth unto our God and to the Lamb forever."

Such is the truth of the passage we just discussed. Shall the saints endure tribulation? They surely shall. Shall they not worship the beast and fall for the power of Antichrist? They surely shall not. On the contrary, they shall glorify God and His power, so that the world shall stand amazed. And in the midst of apparent defeat they shall sing the song of victory. How glorious to be of God's party in the world! But, on the other hand, how terrible to stand on the side of the beast! For his kingdom is doomed to destruction. May God ever give us abundant grace to stand on the side of the Lamb on Mount Zion. For there, and there alone, is victory and life.

Chapter XXXV

The Angels And The Voice

(Revelation 14:6-13)

6 And I saw another angel fly in the midst of heaven, having the everlasting gospel to preach unto them that dwell on the earth, and to every nation, and kindred, and tongue, and people,

7 Saying with a loud voice, Fear God, and give glory to him; for the hour of his judgment is come: and worship him that made heaven, and earth, and the sea, and the fountains of waters.

8 And there followed another angel, saying, Babylon is fallen, is fallen, that great city, because she made all nations drink of the wine of the wrath of her fornication.

9 And the third angel followed them, saying with a loud voice, If any man worship the beast and his image, and receive his mark in his forehead, or in his hand,

10 The same shall drink of the wine of the wrath of God, which is poured out without mixture into the cup of his indignation; and he shall be tormented with fire and brimstone in the presence of the holy angels, and in the presence of the Lamb:

11 And the smoke of their torment ascendeth up for ever and ever: and they have no rest day nor night, who worship the beast and his image, and whosoever receiveth the mark of his name.

12 Here is the patience of the saints: here are they that keep the commandments of God, and the faith of Jesus.

13 And I heard a voice from heaven saying unto me, Write, Blessed are the dead which die in the Lord from henceforth: Yea, saith the Spirit, that they may rest from their labours; and their works do follow them.

We must continually bear in mind that Chapters 13 and 14 of the Book of Revelation belong together. As we said in connection with the passage discussed in the preceding chapter, we shall never obtain a complete and true picture of the kingdom of Antichrist from the thirteenth chapter

490

only. Chapter 14 must be taken in connection with it. In the thirteenth chapter we found indeed that the whole kingdom and reign of Antichrist was pictured to us both from its political and from its religious point of view. It was a kingdom in which all the works of God were developed to the full, but in which they were all devoted to the devil and the glory of the beast. It was a kingdom in which only they that worshipped the beast could participate in the blessings of the kingdom, and in which the faithful in Christ Jesus were pushed to the wall, so that they could neither buy nor sell. And therefore it seemed rather hopeless for the people of God, who put their trust in Christ Jesus their Lord. But for that very reason it will not do to consider Chapter 13 as a complete picture of the kingdom of Antichrist. No, Chapter 14 belongs with it. And if in Chapter 13 we found the picture of the antichristian power and kingdom from its own point of view, apparently victorious, from the point of view of things visible, here, in Chapter 14, we find a picture of that same kingdom from the point of view of God Almighty. And hence, we find it as being doomed to destruction. If in Chapter 13 we found the people of Jesus apparently lost and without hope, in this chapter we find that they enter into glory and that the people of the beast shall be drunken with the wrath of God forever and ever.

The Lamb, so we found in the preceding passage of this chapter, was standing on Mount Zion. There was no difference of opinion about the identity of the Lamb, representing, of course, Christ Jesus as the servant of God, having fulfilled all things. And as to the figure of Mount Zion, we explained that it must be taken as a whole, and that the expression, "the Lamb on Mount Zion," denotes just one, single idea. Explaining it in connection with Psalm 2, we found that it denotes how God in heaven laughs about the output and power of Antichrist because He has anointed His Son and given to Him the kingdoms of the world. Because of that fact Antichrist must suffer defeat, and the kingdom of Christ must be victorious.

In the same light we also viewed the one hundred forty-four thousand who were standing with the Lamb on Mount Zion. As to the meaning of the one hundred forty-four thousand, we said that they represented God's people, the complete number of God's elect on earth during the time of the antichristian reign. And the great significance of this number in this connection, we found, was that they were all there and that not one is lacking. In the power of the Lamb they all stand; and they remain faithful to the end, even in the midst of the suffering and tribulation of the last times. We found that they remained pure and free from the defilement of the antichristian kingdom and that they did not worship the beast; but following the Lamb whithersoever He leadeth them, they remain faithful even unto the end. We found that the secret of their faithfulness must be sought in the name they bear on their foreheads, denoting that they belong to the Father and to the Lamb and that they have been redeemed by the precious blood of Christ Jesus. And we found, finally, that because they were conscious of their being loved from eternity and of their being redeemed by the Lamb, they could learn the song of victory in the midst of tribulation and could chime in with the church triumphant in heaven, "Salvation belongeth unto our God and unto the Lamb for ever and ever."

The relation between the first portion of the chapter and the passage we are now discussing is evident. Also in the present passage the light of heaven is shed upon the established kingdom of the beast. In the first part of the chapter we are told that God maintained His power and that He has anointed His King over Zion forever. In this portion, however, we have an indication of the manner in which that Lamb will maintain His authority and power over the kingdom of darkness.

God's Eternal Demand Maintained

Once more I must warn you against a literal conception and interpretation of the text. There are many who all of a sudden forget that they have to do with symbolism and that in our text we have to do with a vision when they come to this portion of the book. And then they read as if the text said: "Then shall an angel fly in mid-heaven and shall preach the gospel once more to every creature." And yet that is certainly not the meaning. John tells us that he sees a vision. And in that vision he first beholds the beasts representing Antichrist coming out of the earth and out of the sea. And, in the second place, he tells us how he sees the Lamb standing on Mount Zion, surrounded by His people. And now once more, he beholds three angels and hears one voice. And therefore also this part still belongs to the vision. As such it must be explained. If we bear this in mind, we will not reach the absurd conclusion that in this portion Scripture teaches us that in the end of time angels will proclaim the gospel of Christ in order to sound a last warning to all nations. That certainly is not the meaning. In fact, this entire portion is not written for the people of the beast at all, but to comfort the people of God and of the Lamb.

Hence, the text does not mean that an angel shall preach the gospel in the end of time as a last warning. We have no literalism, but symbolism, a vision, in the words of our text. The contents of the symbolism is that an angel flies in mid-heaven and shouts to all the earth, to all nations and tongues and tribes, that they shall fear and worship God. Thus it is in the vision. And the question is: what is the significance of this?

There are many who maintain that here we have a symbol of the preaching of the true gospel of Jesus Christ. The angel and his voice represents the call of the gospel to all nations. Among these there are again some who find in Rome the Antichrist, and who therefore find the fulfillment of this vision in the rise and work of Martin Luther. Immediately before the days of Martin Luther, so they say, the power of Rome was supreme. And therefore Chapter 13 is really fulfilled in the dominance of the papacy. And when Martin Luther rose and recovered the Word from the dust of the cloister and preached that Word to all nations, the fulfillment of the prophecy of this angel was seen. Others claim that here we have no reference to the time of the Reformation, but rather to the time of the judgment, to the end of time. And they are undoubtedly more correct. This entire vision has reference to the time of the end. And according to these interpreters, this portion symbolizes the fact that in the end the gospel will be preached to all men, so that it may cover the earth.

But none of these interpretations fits the contents of our text. In regard to the first it may be said that the Romish papacy may be a type of Babylon, but it was certainly not the final manifestation of Antichrist pictured in Chapter 13. It was only a very partial realization of that power. And therefore, our portion, which evidently refers to the said Antichrist, cannot refer to Martin Luther. And again, as to the second interpretation, that in those latter days there will be a special preaching of the gospel, I would maintain that in those days the preaching of the gospel has well-nigh finished its course. There is no place for it, at least not in the kingdom of Antichrist. That kingdom is not characterized by heathen darkness, in which the light of the gospel never shone. On the contrary, Antichrist shall rise from the midst of the Christian world. It shall be well-acquainted with the gospel. It shall know the truth. But it shall deliberately depart from the truth. The sin against the Holy Spirit shall be a general phenomenon in that kingdom. And therefore there is no hope, and there is no gospel. But, in the third place, against all such interpretations stands the plain indication of the text that this angel does not preach the gospel of Christ Jesus at all. He does not come with the message of salvation. He does not preach Christ. He does not urge men, "Be reconciled to God." Not at all. Interpreters have been deceived by the word "good tidings," or "gospel." Just because we read that this angel proclaimed eternal good tidings, they draw the conclusion that he was preaching the gospel of Jesus Christ to all men once more. But that is not the case. The good tidings of this angel have nothing to do with the gospel of Jesus Christ and salvation. For, in the first place, let us notice that he preached an eternal gospel; and the gospel of Jesus is not eternal. God does not eternally proclaim that gospel. He does not eternally come with the call to accept Him and believe in His name. That gospel to all men covers but a very brief period of history. And therefore, the gospel of Christ cannot be meant. Still more clear this becomes if we read the contents. It merely states a demand. It does not speak of salvation. It does not mention the name of Christ. It does not tell the old story at all. It simply comes with the demand to all people and nations: "Fear God, and give him glory, and worship him." And therefore we must discard all these interpretations.

In order to understand the words of our text you must grasp the whole situation once more. Antichrist is supreme. Just imagine that you, as a child of God, live in those days. Antichrist has set up his kingdom. He rules over all the world, and all the world admires him and his kingdom. That antichristian reign will be characterized by apostasy from the living God. God and His truth shall be denied, and the blood of Jesus shall be trampled under foot. The devil and the beast shall be the object of worship. On every street and corner, in every shop and store you meet with the image of the beast; and universally men bow before him. Everywhere you meet with men who bear the sign of the beast on their forehead and on their right hand. You, as a people of God, shall not be able to buy or sell; and they shall push you to the wall. There is no refuge, it seems, and the suffering is awful. It is a world of tribulation, and the blasphemy against God's name is seemingly unpunished.

What now will be the question arising in your mind? It will be this: shall God allow all this? Shall He let the glory of His name be trampled under foot, and shall He let His saints be unrevenged? That all depends: if God will let go His eternal claim, namely, that the creature shall worship Him, and worship Him alone, and fear and glorify His name, He shall let these things go, and there is no end in sight. If God has changed His mind, if our covenant God can renounce His eternal claim, namely, that He only should receive the glory, then indeed the case is hopeless. Then He shall do nothing. Then He shall not arise to crush this awful power and to save His own people. Then we are the covenant people of a God Who has surrendered the glory of His own name. But that is not the case. No, the Lamb stands on Mount Zion. And because the Lamb, the Anointed of God, stands in the place of His power, God will not let go His demand. And therefore, to every nation and tribe and tongue comes the demand: "Fear God, and give glory to him; for the hour of his judgment is come: and worship him that made heaven, and earth, and the sea, and the fountains of waters."

From this point of view all is plain. The meaning of these words can now be understood. The angel sounds the eternal gospel. It is the gospel that God is sovereign, the gospel that God is supreme. It is the gospel that all creation must fear Him, and Him alone, and that He will judge all who refuse to worship Him. It is the gospel that He alone is worthy of worship since He made all things and therefore is the sole sovereign of them all. That demand is as eternal as God's own decree, and it will last forever. That gospel God will never change. For unto all eternity, even in the new heavens and the new earth, it will still be the gospel. That demand is now placed over against the wicked kingdom of Antichrist. There, in that kingdom, they worship the beast; there they give glory to Satan, and they fear Antichrist. There they say, "Antichrist has made all things. Who is like unto the beast, and who can war with him?" There they cast God's glory in the dust and trample His precepts under foot. But even over against this state of things God maintains His claim: "Fear Me, and give Me glory. For the hour of My judgment is come. And worship Me: for I have made the heavens and the earth, the sea, and the fountains of waters." Then also the whole significance of the scene is clear. This sounds like gospel in the ears of God's people. Even though it may seem as if God has relinquished His eternal claim, they may depend on it that He shall vindicate it to the end and that He shall reveal His wrath to the kingdom of Antichrist. It does not mean that in the future this message shall actually go forth. It does not mean that an angel shall bring it. But it does mean that the people of God may depend on it: God shall maintain His glory and claim. And because the Almighty maintains that claim, the kingdom of darkness must be destroyed.

The Gospel Of Babylon's Fall

If this is clear, then the rest is not difficult to understand. The first angel announced that God maintains His eternal claim over against the power and the kingdom of Antichrist. And the second and third angels announce the destruction and punishment which must naturally follow where this eternal demand of the Almighty is not obeyed. In that eternal gospel which the first angel in the vision preached we have the deepest ground, the supreme reason, for the judgment of Antichrist and his kingdom. Just because God is sovereign and maintains His claim to be feared and worshipped and glorified by all creatures, and because, in direct opposition to this claim of the Almighty, stands the kingdom of Antichrist, trampling that glory under foot and worshipping the beast, the latter must be judged and destroyed. Already the first angel announced that the hour of God's judgment is come. The second angel prophesies of that judgment and speaks as if Babylon is fallen already. And the third angel announces the terrible punishment which will be inflicted upon those who worship the beast and his image.

It is here that we meet with the term **Babylon**. "Fallen, fallen is Babylon the great, who hath made all the nations to drink of the wine of her fornication," so the first angel shouts through mid-heaven. As to this name **Babylon**, we may remark, in the first place, that this is not the place to explain it in detail. Naturally not: the angel merely makes a pre-announcement of its destruction. He is prophesying. And prophesying, he sees the objects of his prophecy so vividly that it appears to him that Babylon is fallen already. In a future portion of the Book of Revelation we read of the fall of this Babylon in detail, and then is the time to explain it. And therefore, here we merely must understand the general idea.

There are different interpretations of this Babylon. There are some who make it the apostate church pure and simple, without anything else, while others claim that it denotes not the apostate church but the center of the political world-power. It seems to us that neither is quite correct, and that for the simple reason that the apostate church and the power of the world in the future will be perfectly one: one in life and view, one in hope and doctrine, one in purpose and aspiration, one in power and attainment. And for that reason apostate Christianity, or the apostate church, must not be separated from the power of the beast.

In our portion it is evident that the entire power of Antichrist is denoted by the name **Babylon**. It rather denotes the heart of the antichristian kingdom, just as Jerusalem was the heart of Canaan and of the theocracy of Israel. And as to the name, we remember that Babel, or Babylon, is originally the name of the city of mighty Nimrod. When the peoples came together and made the attempt to establish the world-power and maintain themselves, they also tried to build a city and a great tower. That city is the city of Babel, or Babylon. And therefore this name reminds one of the wound which the beast had received and which was healed. Babylon in Scripture stands for the great opponent of the people of God, the center of the world-power that oppresses God's saints. By Babylon the children of Jerusalem were made captive. In Babylon they suffered in captivity, far from the holy land. There they sang in lonely exile, yearning for the land of their covenant God: "O daughter of Babylon, who art to be destroyed; happy shall he be, that rewardeth thee as thou hast served us. Happy shall he be, that taketh and dasheth thy little ones against the stones."

Of Babylon's fall in the literal as well as in the symbolical sense of the word the prophets of old had spoken. Babylon stands for all that opposes and oppresses the people of God's kingdom. So here it denotes in one term the rule and dominion of Antichrist. That kingdom has made the nations drunk with the wine of her fornication. It has through its false prophet led all the tribes of the earth to blaspheme the name of Jehovah and to worship the beast. It has oppressed the people of God and made it that they could neither buy nor sell. Its destruction and judgment is the hope of the people of God. For its destruction they pray. For its judgment they long. And they can sing it with the people of God of old: "Happy is he that taketh and dasheth thy little ones against a rock." And now, behold, the fall of that great and powerful Babylon is announced. That kingdom of Babylon seemed permanent and impregnable. But the Lord had appointed His Holy One over Zion. And the angel announces the fall of the great city with a certainty that leaves no doubt and that looks upon the whole scene as if it were already accomplished: "Fallen, fallen is Babylon, the great, that had made all nations to drink of the wine of her fornication." Again, it is to the comfort of the people of God that this vision is seen. For in the fall of Babylon they see their own victory and the victory of Christ.

A third angel comes upon the scene and announces the judgment upon the individual worshippers of the beast. Here upon earth it seemed as if they were supreme and as if they could oppress the people of God with impunity. They lived like lords and participated in all the blessings of creation. And often the people of God were perhaps inclined to complain with Asaph that there is no knowledge with the Most High. They themselves, who served the Lord and followed Him wheresoever He goeth, — they themselves suffered want and tribulation, were in pain and distress every day. But the wicked and unbelievers, the worshippers of the beast, prospered and knew of no suffering. And therefore the people of God are given a glimpse of their end. Even as Asaph of old went into the sanctuary and considered their latter end, so also the people of God who live at the time of Antichrist receive a vision of the end and of these worshippers of the beast in their eternal estate. Their eternal punishment is described in vivid terms. The torment of hell is pictured as God has prepared it for them.

Let us notice, in the first place, that this torment is both internal and external. Everyone that worshippeth the beast, so the text reads, and receiveth a mark on his forehead or upon his hand, he shall also drink of the wine of the wrath of God which is prepared unmixed in the cup of His anger. Evidently these words refer to the spiritual and internal suffering of the ungodly. The "wine of the wrath of God" is evidently a figure. The meaning is that these worshippers of the beast shall receive a wine to drink, the spirit, or alcoholic contents, of which is the wrath of God. Even as natural wine affects the spirit of man, so shall the wine of the wrath of God affect the worshippers of the beast. By drinking this wine the worshipper of the beast shall receive the wrath of God as a burning fire within his soul, so that this wrath of God burns him from within, troubles him, leaves him no rest day or night. It shall be spiritual torment night and day. Even as the greatest happiness and the most profound peace consists of communion with the God of grace and love, so the most terrible suffering shall be that which is caused by the consciousness of the wrath of the Almighty. It shall be unmixed, that is, undiluted. Never shall the worshipper of the beast in eternity receive one glimpse of God's love. Here upon earth he received the things of the world, and God let His sun shine upon the wicked and the good alike. But when the measure of iniquity shall once be full, they shall receive nothing but the wine of the wrath of God unmixed.

But it shall also be an external suffering. They shall exist body and soul, and therefore they shall suffer as such. With fire and brimstone they shall be tormented, and that forever. Little are we able to describe the terribleness of hell. No more than we can fully describe the bliss of the new heaven and the new earth, no more can we describe the state of the damned in hell. But we may be sure that these symbols of fire and brimstone stand for grave realities. Worse than all the suffering of the earth, worse than all the agony that may be seen upon the battlefield of the world, shall be the suffering of those who worship the beast and his image. And, in the third place, that suffering shall be everlasting. Their smoke goeth up forever and ever. God is vindicating His righteousness and glory in the wicked who are prepared unto the day of destruction.

The Patience Of The Saints Justified

Wonderfully strange, at first sight, stands the sentence: "Here is the patience of the saints, that keep the commandments of God and the faith of Jesus." And yet, if only these words are read in their proper light, the whole is plain. The idea is that because the saints see the end of their enemies, see it and believe it, that Babylon is fallen and that the worshippers of the beast are doomed to everlasting punishment, they can be so patient.

What is their patience? It has been described in a portion of Chapter 13. It was they that did not kill by the sword. It was they that did not lead into captivity. In other words, that patience consists in this, that in all the tribulation and suffering in the reign of Antichrist, they were calmly, serenely submissive. They did not try to gain control of things. They did not employ main force. They were patient. Even though they could not buy or sell, they did not use the sword to obtain what they wanted. Their suffering did not persuade them to deny their God and their Lord, did not seduce them from the way of God's covenant. One word, one nod, one bow might suffice, perhaps, to gain for them the favor of the power of Antichrist and would supply them with the necessities of life abundantly. But they refused. Patiently they bore the cross and followed the Lamb whithersoever He led them. And that patience is explained. Why were they so patient? Why could they bear the suffering? Why could they submit without rising in rebellion and employing main force? Simply for the same reason that Asaph became patient when he regarded their latter end in the sanctuary of his God. They knew that their enemies could not escape their reward, and that in the day of the Lord they would be judged in righteousness. And hence, they left it all to their Lord, mindful of the warning of Scripture that vengeance belongeth unto Him.

But this is not all. The scene does not close with the announcement of destruction upon the enemies and upon the kingdom that follows the beast; but it also pictures the great and glorious victory of believers, who do the will of God and die in the Lord. For after the angels have retired and sounded their voice, another voice is heard from heaven, we do not know of whom. He commands John with special emphasis to write: "Blessed are the dead which die in the Lord from henceforth. Yea, saith the Spirit, that they may rest from their labours; and their works do follow them."

These words have been often misunderstood, and preached at many a funeral. They have been wrongly interpreted. It was thought generally that here we have a proof of the fact that the soul is blessed immediately after death. "From henceforth" would then mean: from the time they depart from this earth, immediately after physical death. Of course, this is true in itself: the dead shall be blessed, shall rest from their labors immediately after death. But it is not true that this word refers to that truth. In the first place, we might remark that in that case it would be very ambiguously expressed. Instead of "from henceforth" an expression like "from death on," or "immediately after death," would have been much clearer. In the second place, — and this is a far weightier objection, — we read that their works do follow them, evidently referring to the day when each one shall be judged according to his works. And this cannot be said of the soul immediately after death. And therefore, that explanation does not hold. On the other hand, there are interpreters who limit the blessedness of those who are mentioned here to the saints who die during the time of Antichrist or in some other period. They limit the expression "that die in the Lord." But also this is not to be done. It simply says that the dead who die in the Lord shall be blessed henceforth. And that does not allow of any arbitrary limitation.

In order to obtain a clear view of the meaning of these last words we must remember that the entire portion places itself upon the standpoint of the very last. That is plain, for instance, from the voice of the three angels. The first one announces that the hour of God's judgment is come. The second one announces that Babylon is already fallen. The third one announces that the worshippers of the beast are to be sent to everlasting torment. On that same standpoint also the voice that is here speaking evidently places itself. It speaks, therefore, not of the bliss of the soul which it shall enjoy immediately after death, but rather after all is past. Henceforth, that is, from the time that the voice speaks, after all the battles are fought, after Babylon is fallen, after the wicked are sent to hell, when the judgment day is past, — henceforth shall be blessed those who die in the Lord. And therefore, not merely the dead who die during the time of Antichrist, but the dead of all ages shall be blessed from that time forth and forevermore. Are they then not blessed before that time? Surely, they are. They have entered into life, and they are free from the tribulation of this present time the moment they pass away from the scene of battle of the church militant. But their bliss is not perfect. Their body is still in the grave. And all the brethren have not been gathered in. But henceforth, that is, from the point of view of the angel who speaks, when time shall be no more and when eternity shall dawn, then shall be fully blessed all the saints who die in the Lord. Just because they died in the Lord, just because they belong to Him and because He has paid for all their sins, they shall enter into everlasting glory.

But there is still more.

Surely, all the saints shall die and be blessed in the Lord. It is not because of their works, but because of the work of Christ Jesus that they shall enter into the eternal kingdom. And therefore the bliss shall be general. But shall there be no distinction? Surely, there shall be. All shall be perfectly blessed. But not all shall reach the same state of glory.

In the covenant God has prepared some of His people to do great things, to be special witnesses of His name, to fight the kingdom of darkness in a special way. And just because God has prepared some of His children for special works, so that they do more than others and suffer more than others and bear the brunt of the battle more than others, they also shall have a special place in glory. They were in suffering more than others. They were despised more than others. They were in tribulation in a special sense of the word. God prepared Elijah to do great things. But he also fought more than all the prophets of his time. God prepared His prophets, like Isaiah and Jeremiah, for special work. But they also went through special suffering and tribulation. God prepared the apostles and the martyrs to be faithful in a special sense of the word. And they suffered more than others. And so it.shall be at the time of Antichrist. Not all are equally strong among the children of God. Not all are equally fit to testify and bear the brunt of the battle. It is not because they themselves are less faithful; not as if the stronger would have any power of their own. No, God has prepared them, and even prepared their works, also their special works. But what now shall become of these? Shall they all be lost? Shall in the day of judgment all these works dwindle away in the general bliss of God's people? Of course not; their works shall follow them. And these works shall be rewarded. All shall enter into bliss: for Christ died for them, and they all die in the Lord. But all shall not attain to the same state of glory. There shall be distinction and difference. And those whom God prepared to do more work than others and to suffer more than others may thank the Lord God for this great privilege. For their works shall follow them also in the new creation.

What a difference! By the light shed from heaven upon the scene of Antichrist the scene has changed completely. First the beast seemed to be supreme, and Babylon permanently established forever; now the Lamb appears as the King over Zion. First the kingdom of the Holy One seemed to be a lost cause; now the kingdom of the beast is doomed to destruction. First the people of God seemed to be hopelessly lost; now the worshippers of the beast are sent to everlasting torment. First the worshippers of the beast seemed to be in control of all things and participated in the blessings of the kingdom; now the followers of the Lamb inherit everlasting bliss, and serve God and the Lamb day and night forevermore. Surely, the saints may indeed be patient. For all things are theirs, because they are Christ's, and Christ is God's.

Chapter XXXVI

The Harvest And The Vintage

(Revelation 14:14-20)

14 And I looked, and behold a white cloud, and upon the cloud one sat like unto the Son of man, having on his head a golden crown, and in his hand a sharp sickle.

15 And another angel came out of the temple, crying with a loud voice to him that sat on the cloud, Thrust in thy sickle, and reap: for the time is come for thee to reap; for the harvest of the earth is ripe.

16 And he that sat on the cloud thrust in his sickle on the earth; and the earth was reaped.

17 And another angel came out of the temple which is in heaven, he also having a sharp sickle.

18 And another angel came out from the altar, which had power over fire; and cried with a loud cry to him that had the sharp sickle, saying, Thrust in thy sharp sickle, and gather the clusters of the vine of the earth; for her grapes are fully ripe.

19 And the angel thrust in his sickle into the earth, and gathered the vine of the earth, and cast it into the great winepress of the wrath of God.

20 And the winepress was trodden without the city, and blood came out of the winepress, even unto the horse bridles, by the space of a thousand and six hundred furlongs.

When we read these words, we are, of course, immediately reminded of the fact that this constitutes the close of the vision which was begun in Chapter 13. Taking Chapters 13 and 14 together, we found that they could not be separated; but they form one vision, a vision of the kingdom of Antichrist in its highest stage of development, and that both from the worldly point of view and from the point of view of heaven, of God and His Anointed.

The first vision, that of the beast with his seven heads and ten horns, pictured to us the kingdom of Antichrist from the political point of view and informed us that the kingdom would be universal, established by the voluntary consent of all nations and peoples and tribes of the earth. The central power of this kingdom has sway over all peoples and, at the same time, over all things, so that all are dependent upon the beast. And, in the second place, it pictured to us that final kingdom as being anti-Christ, anti-God, anti-kingdom, and anti-saints. All worship the beast. All admire this tremendous kingdom. But for the people of God there is no standing-room on the earth.

This last feature of the kingdom of Antichrist was pictured to us especially in the vision of the second beast, with his two horns like a lamb's and speech like the dragon. He, so we found, was a picture of the false prophet, of the influence of false philosophy and false religion. And we found that this beast succeeded in uniting the whole world under his creed. They all put stock in the words of this beast. He made them make an image. He gave them a sign. And only the worshippers of the beast and his image, who had the sign, could participate in the blessings of the kingdom of Antichrist, the rest not being able to buy or sell.

The third vision was that of the Lamb on Mount Zion, which, so we found, began to shed an entirely new light upon the scene of worldly power and iniquity and oppression and idolatry. If it seemed as if the kingdom of Antichrist was actually supreme and everlasting, this vision tells us a different story. It tells us that God Almighty never anointed the beast or the dragon to rule, but that He has His own King over Zion and that this King surely shall have control over all things. It tells us for that very reason that God in the heavens sits and laughs about all the efforts of the beast and Satan, and that God's people are perfectly safe. The one hundred forty-four thousand are all there, and not one is lacking.

The fourth vision was that of angels flying in mid-heaven, each delivering his message for the kingdom of Antichrist, and of a voice speaking of joy to those who die in the Lord. The first angel announced, to the comfort of God's people, that God did not renounce His claim, but demanded as ever that every creature should bow before Him and worship Him as the God of heaven and earth. The second and third angels follow up this claim of the Almighty by announcing destruction upon the kingdom that rose against His sovereignty and upon the individual worshippers of the beast and his image. And, in conclusion, the voice spoke of joy and glory and rest for those who were subjected to tribulation and persecution in this dispensation because they refused to worship the beast.

Now we are at the close of the vision. The words of the passage quoted above take us to the end of time. Just as evidently the opening of the sixth seal in Chapter 6 took us to the close of all human history, so also does the passage we are about to discuss, though from a slightly different point of view and with fuller development of detail. Nevertheless, also what is recorded in these words will again be spoken of in future chapters. And the fall of Babylon, the great harlot, and the treading of the nations in the winepress of the wrath of God will all be developed and pictured to us in future chapters with greater vividness and in greater detail. And therefore, in our present chapter we must discuss in a general way the harvest and the vintage, or the end of the world.

The Harvester

It does not need a lengthy discussion to convince us that the harvester in this case, or at least he who supervises the reaping of the earth, is none other than Jesus Christ our Lord. We read: "And I looked, and behold a white cloud, and upon the cloud one sat like unto the Son of man, having on his head a golden crown, and in his hand a sharp sickle." We are acquainted with the expression "one like unto the Son of man." We are so well acquainted with this expression that we can never fail to recognize Him Who bears this name. It is always used of Christ. It was the name with which Christ loved to call Himself. It denotes His all-overshadowing glory as the human servant of God. When John sees the vision of the seven golden candlesticks, he tells us that he also saw "in the midst of the candlesticks one like unto a Son of man." And we know immediately who He is. In Daniel 7:13 we read of the same person: "I saw in the night visions, and, behold, one like the Son of man came with the clouds of heaven, and came to the Ancient of days, and they brought him near before him." And therefore, there is no possibility of mistaking the identity of this person who holds the sharp sickle. He is the Son of Man, the Christ, the Servant of Jehovah, the Lamb Who was slain, the King of Zion anointed by the Almighty to have dominion over all. Besides, also His sitting on the white cloud would lead us to the same conclusion. To come with the clouds has already become a standing expression, and it denotes an honor which is bestowed only upon Christ Jesus. Before the high priest, Jesus already had witnessed: "Hereafter shall ye see the Son of man sitting on the right hand of power, and coming in the clouds of heaven," (Matthew 26:64). And also in the first part of this Book of Revelation the warning note was heard: "Behold, he cometh with clouds; and every eye shall see him," (Revelation 1:7). Hence, both of these expressions, "the Son of man" and "sitting on a white cloud," establish it beyond a shadow of doubt that here we have again a vision of Christ.

But how, in what capacity does He appear?

In the first place, it is plain that He reveals Himself here as King. He is the Lamb on Mount Zion and has been anointed by God to be king over all, and that forever. He must rule. He has gained His kingdom by obedience even unto the death of the cross and now has received a name which is above every name. As such He now appears. His appearance spells evil and destruction to the beast and his dominion. For that beast has attempted to gain the kingdom over all. All the dominion over which the beast apparently holds power belongs to this Son of Man on the cloud. That He appears here, therefore, while Antichrist rages, certainly can only mean destruction for the usurper. But, at the same time, the appearance of the Son of man on the white cloud also means deliverance for His people who have been oppressed and persecuted by the antichristian power. He comes as King. He comes to claim His own. He comes to destroy His enemies, and He comes to save His people. That this is true is also plain from the fact that He sits on the white cloud. To come with the clouds always denotes that this Son of Man is coming for judgment. We have become accustomed to this expression; and as soon as we hear or read of it, we think, and rightly so, of Christ coming as Judge. The purity of the white cloud indicates that He will judge in righteousness and destroy the unrighteous. And the same idea of judgment is indicated by the sickle. He has come to cut down, for the sickle is sharp and is whetted to do the work. Hence, the Lord appears in this connection as the King-Judge.

But He is not alone.

In fact, we receive the impression that He merely supervises and that the work of reaping proper is left to the angels, His servants. That is also the impression we receive from other parts of Scripture. In Matthew 13:39 Christ explains, at the close of the parable of the tares among the wheat: "The reapers are the angels." And in Matthew 24:31 we read: "And he shall send his angels with a great sound of a trumpet, and they shall gather together his elect from the four winds, from one end of heaven to the other." Thus the text here also speaks of the angels as the servants of the

Son of Man. At least one of them comes out of the temple, and therefore out of the immediate presence of the Holy One; one of the angels who stand before God acts as the reaper in this scene. Two other angels act as messengers, and both proclaim that the time is ripe and that it is the exact hour for the harvest of the earth to be gathered in. One of them carries the command directly from God; and he announces to the Son of Man that it is time to reap and that the hour is come for harvesting.

This is not without significance. In the first place, we are given to understand that this is an important hour. The harvest must be gathered, but not before it is fully ripe. It is a very significant hour indeed. All must be finished. And the Savior tells us that only God knows of this hour. Even He, as the Christ, does not know it. For thus He tells us, Matthew 24:36: "But of that day and hour knoweth no man, no, not the angels of heaven, but my Father only." And this He says in answer to the question of His disciples concerning the end of the world. It is entirely in harmony with this idea that in the vision the angel comes out of the temple of God and announces that the hour has now come and that the reaping of the harvest may begin.

The second angel brings a similar message to the angel who must gather the vintage, the clusters of the vine of the earth. He comes out from the altar and has power over fire. Although, therefore, he brings a similar message as that of the first angel, his message must be considered from a different viewpoint. With the altar from which the angel proceeds we have become acquainted before. In the sixth chapter we read of it; and there we heard how the cry for vengeance proceeded from under it, pressed from the souls of those who had been slain for the Word of God. And then they received the answer that they would have to wait a little while, till also their brethren would have been slain for the same cause. Hence, the angel who proceeds from the altar with the message to reap tells us that now all God's people have been oppressed and have suffered from Antichrist and that the time of vengeance has come. Also in the eighth chapter we read of this same altar, upon which the angels minister unto the prayers of the saints which are followed by judgments on the earth. The same idea, therefore, is again expressed here. The time of judgment, the time that the prayers of all the saints shall be heard, has now come. Hence, it is also said that this angel has power over fire, a symbol of the same truth, namely, that the reaping which is to be done is judgment and vengeance. We arrive, therefore, at this conclusion: first, that the harvest is symbolic of judgment and vengeance; and, secondly, that the reapers or harvesters are Christ and His servants, His angels.

The Order Of The Harvest And The Vintage

Thus far all is rather simple and clear.

But a more difficult question we approach when we attempt to explain the harvest as such.

In order to understand the meaning of this harvest and vintage, it is well to bear in mind that here there is no mention of the judgment proper, that is, of the public judgment before the throne of God, by which everyone will be rewarded according to his works. This impression might easily be received from the vision of the Son of Man on the great white cloud. But this is not the case. We must not confuse things. There is a difference between the final judgment and the end of this dispensation. And it is only of the latter that this passage speaks. The world is to come to an end. History will reach a certain climax. The question is: how shall history reach its termination? How must we picture to ourselves the end of all history? You understand, of course, that it certainly is not proper to picture to ourselves this end of the world and of all history by a sudden appearance of Christ at any arbitrary moment to destroy His enemies and to deliver His church. That may be easy to imagine, but that is not in harmony with Scripture. What we must attempt to answer is the question: how shall the general course of history be so as to lead to a climax and end? This question is, in a general way, answered in the words of our text. How shall these things be? How must I conceive of the general course of the history of this world that it must necessarily lead to the final catastrophe and to the coming of Christ? That this is, indeed, the idea of the text is plain from the figure of the harvest. In the parable of the tares among the wheat the Lord explains that "the harvest is the end of the world." But it stands to reason that the harvest must be ripe before that end can come. The end cannot come at any arbitrary moment. Hence, the question must be answered: what is the course of the history of the world so as to lead necessarily to the end?

Besides, we must not entertain the false notion that the "day of the Lord" and the end of the world shall come in one moment, or even in one day. Such is often the conception we have of that "day of the Lord." History shall continue very regularly and normally, and there will be nothing special or extraordinary in that history of the world until of a sudden Christ comes; then all will be ended, all in one moment, in the twinkling of an eye as it were. But this is evidently not the case. The harvest, the end of the world implies big things and great events. Some time may very well elapse before the harvest is finished. And the question is: in that period of the harvest of the world what will be the order of events? How must we conceive of the end of the world? Of course, this would be an idle and vain question if Scripture did not reveal anything about this. But now it is different. The Bible certainly does reveal to us something about the order of events in this great day of the Lord. And also the passage now under discussion gives us at least a general indication of the order of the events which shall then take place.

First of all, I would say that our text gives us reason to believe that the elect of God, the church of Christ, will be taken up just before the end. I do not mean from the point of view of time, but rather that of order.

There is in our text a reference to a wheat harvest and a vintage, the gathering of grain and the cutting off of the clusters of the vine of the earth. Now there are interpreters who maintain that both these visions refer to the reaping of the wicked, to the worshippers of the beast and his image, and that there is no mention here at all of the removal of God's children from the earth. Naturally, many are forced to adopt this interpretation for the simple reason that they have caused the church to go to heaven at a much earlier period. But these interpreters fail to explain to us why the Lord in that case gives us two visions of such an entirely different nature. The first vision merely speaks of the reaping, but the second immediately leaves the impression of being a harvest of a different nature. In connection with it we read of the altar and of the angel who has power over fire, of the winepress of the wrath of God, and of the blood that reaches up to the horses' bridles. In a word, the first harvest leaves no impression of judgment and vengeance while the second does. Interpreters who refuse to make a distinction fail to explain the fact that we have nevertheless two visions of a different nature.

Besides, what we read elsewhere in Scripture gives us reason to maintain that in our text we have a reference to the gathering of God's people and of the wicked both. The wheat harvest generally is a symbol which refers to the gathering of God's people. In Luke 3:17 we hear John the Baptist testify of Jesus: "Whose fan is in his hand, and he will throughly purge his floor, and will gather the wheat into his garner." True, the figure may be taken as referring to both God's people and the wicked, seeing that there is chaff among the wheat and that the tares have grown up among it. But the purpose of the wheat harvest is nevertheless the gathering of the wheat, not the gathering of the tares or of the chaff. And the gathering of the wheat is a symbol of the removal of God's people from the earth. So also the harvest of the wicked is more than once referred to in the Word of God as the cutting of the grapes and the gathering of them in the winepress, to be pressed and trodden. In Joel 3:13 we read: "Put ye in the sickle, for the harvest is ripe: come, get you down; for the press is full, the vats overflow; for their wickedness is great." And in Isaiah 63:3 we have the vision of the man who cometh from Edom, with blood-stained garments from Bozrah, — a passage of Scripture which is so often erroneously quoted as referring to the suffering Servant of Jehovah. There we read: "I have trodden the winepress alone; and of the people there was none with me: for I will tread them in mine anger, and trample them in my fury; and their blood shall be sprinkled upon my garments." Evidently in both these passages we have a picture of the end of the wicked in the symbol of the winepress of the wrath of God. And therefore we may regard it as established that also in our text the distinction is made, and that in the first vision we have a picture of the removal of God's people from the earth, in the second a symbol of the end of the wicked power of Antichrist.

Secondly, we may remark that also this portion teaches us that the people of God shall be removed first. Their removal is mentioned first: the wheat harvest shall be gathered first of all. And although the fact that it is mentioned first in the vision does not at all establish beyond a doubt that thus it shall be in reality, other parts of the Word of God give us the same impression. In Chapter 11 of the Book of Revelation we found that the two witnesses, representing the church, after their three days of shame and suffering, when they were as outcasts in the world, were called up to heaven and ascended thither. And in Matthew 24:22 the Lord says: "And except those days should be shortened, there should no flesh be saved: but for the elect's sake those days shall be shortened." Also this word gives us the same impression. Not history shall be shortened; but for the elect the days shall be shortened. That is, they shall be taken away first of all. Besides, this is practically in the nature of the case. The removal of the wicked shall be a scene of general destruction and upheaval. It shall be a scene in which the people of God may not participate for the simple reason that it is the manifestation of the wrath of God. Hence, they must be removed first. And so the order in which these two visions are given us is supported by other passages of the Word of God. The first harvest is the removal of the people of God. They shall be gathered by the holy angels from the four winds, and they shall leave the scene of their suffering and affliction to enter into glory.

To this, finally, may be added that also the events which are mentioned in Scripture as being typical of the harvest of the latter days corroborate this view. God sends the flood to destroy the wicked world; but that destruction of the world may not strike His own people. And therefore the destruction does not come till Noah and his people are separated in the ark. God means to destroy Sodom and Gomorrah. But again, there are people of God in that city. And the destruction that shall lay the city in ruins may not destroy the people of Jehovah. Hence, the destruction does not begin till Lot is led outside. So it shall be also in the time of the end. Two shall be in bed: the one shall be taken, and the other left. God's people must first be removed; and after they have been removed, the destruction of the wicked, the harvest of the grapes, may proceed.

We obtain therefore this conception of the future, that there shall be a period, — not very long, in fact, — but nevertheless a period in which there will be no more people of God in the earth. And it is this period which is utilized to end the existence of the wicked upon the earth. That this is meant by the vision of the vintage we have already shown. Let us notice in connection with the words of the passage we are now discussing that the reaping of the grapes is symbolic of the gathering of the nations into one place. The clusters of the earth, the various nations and peoples, must be cut, in order that they may be gathered into one place. Notice, in the second place, that the place where they are gathered is the winepress of the wrath of God, a place designated as being outside of the city. And notice, in the third place, that from this juncture the scene changes into one of battle and bloodshed. The grapes are pressed; and as they are pressed, blood comes out, so much that it reaches to the bridles of the horses, and that for sixteen hundred stadia, or furlongs. It is, therefore, a tremendous battle that is here pictured. The nations shall finally be gathered for battle, and such a battle as the world has never seen before shall be fought. The winepress of the wrath of God shall be trodden in that place.

The Reality Of The Harvest And Vintage

But the question is: how can we picture this in reality?

You will remember our explanation of Jerusalem and the temple in connection with Chapter 11. Then we said that the city of Jerusalem at large stood for nominal Christendom in its widest sense, that the outer court stood for the show-church, or the hypocrites in the church, and that only the holy place represented the true people of God. Now what has happened? Jerusalem, as nominal Christianity, still exists. The Christian world is still there, in distinction from heathendom. But it has become the kingdom of Antichrist. Jerusalem is Babylon, the center of the power which opposes the kingdom of God.

We must clearly grasp the situation. At the end of time nominal Christianity shall be antichristian. Jerusalem in the outward sense shall be Babylon in character. Still more, the people of God have been removed. The holy place is no more. And therefore, all that is left is outward Christianity, which is in reality the antichristian kingdom. That antichristian power is for a time lording it over all nations. The kingdom of Antichrist is universal. It is also supreme over those other nations which do not belong to the outward Christian world, the nations of heathendom, called Gog and Magog in Scripture. For a time all is well. Gog and Magog, the heathen nations, are ruled over by the outward Christian world, which is in reality antichristian, or outward Jerusalem, which is in reality Babylon. These nations are as yet not aroused, but they never become an integral part of that universal kingdom. They never embrace its cause. They never truly adopt its religion. They remain heathen. And therefore they stand diametrically opposed to the Christian world. For them the kingdom of Antichrist is still Christianity. And what has already become Babylon is still Jerusalem in the estimation of those nations. That is the situation. There is one universal kingdom. And in that one universal kingdom there is peace for a time, complete peace. But there are two elements in that kingdom nevertheless. In the first place, there is the element of the Christian world, of the civilized nations that have become antichristian. But, in the second place, there is also the element of the heathen nations, as, for instance, China and Japan and all that refuse to embrace the cause of Christianity. And they never become an integral part in the kingdom of Antichrist.

Now what shall happen in the future? Gog and Magog shall finally be aroused against the Christian nations in the outward sense. You must clearly understand the situation. There are no true Christians any more. No, they have been taken away from the earth. But outward Christianity, outward Jerusalem, still exists for a short time. And that outward Christianity, that nominal Jerusalem, which is in reality Antichrist and Babylon, shall be looked upon by these heathen nations as Christianity itself and as the real Jerusalem. And they shall be aroused. They shall say: "Let us go up to Jerusalem. Let us break loose from the bondage of the Christian nations and destroy them." They think that they strike at the people of Christ, which they hate. And they shall come against them. And thus the greatest, bloodiest battle of history shall ensue, although, I repeat, all this shall last but a little time in the history of the end. Antichrist shall prepare himself for the battle, shall beat the plowshares again into swords, and shall gather his armies. All the kingdom of Antichrist, all Babylon, shall gather together for the great battle. In their estimation this battle will be the last. It will wipe out heathendom. And the nations of heathendom will do the same. They shall gather their armies and prepare for the battle. And the place where they shall meet will be the winepress of the wrath of the Most High. It will be outside of the city, outside of nominal Jerusalem, outside of Babylon, outside of the Christian world, perhaps in the literal sense of the word. Terrible will be the bloodshed in that battle. In fact, the nations shall destroy one another, and the wrath of God shall tread upon them till they are destroyed completely. For the blood shall form a stream which denotes the completeness of their destruction. It will reach to the horses' bridles and will be sixteen hundred furlongs in length. Sixteen hundred evidently denotes the lifeblood of the world in its completeness. Four is the number of the world. Ten is the number of completeness. Sixteen hundred is forty times forty, and therefore denotes the lifeblood of the whole world. At the same time, the scene already pictured in the sixth trumpet shall be realized. It shall be a day of thick darkness. The sun shall be darkened, and the moon shall be changed into blood. Earthquakes and thunder shall add horror, till the entire power of Antichrist and Gog and Magog is actually destroyed.

Let me call your attention to the fact that this is in harmony with the Word of God in general. Isaiah pictures to us the same scene in Chapter 34 of his prophecy. There we read: "Come near, ye nations, to hear; and hearken, ye people: let the earth hear, and all that is therein; the world, and all things that come forth of it. For the indignation of the Lord is upon all nations, and his fury upon all their armies: he hath utterly destroyed them, he hath delivered them to the slaughter. Their slain also shall be cast out, and their stink shall come up out of their carcases, and the mountains shall be melted with their blood. And all the host of heaven shall be dissolved, and the heavens shall be rolled together as a scroll: and all their host shall fall down, as the leaf falleth off from the vine, and as a falling fig from the fig tree. For my sword shall be bathed in heaven: behold, it shall come down upon Idumea, and upon the people of my curse, to judgment. The sword of the Lord is filled with blood, it is made fat with fatness, and with the blood of lambs and goats, with the fat of the kidneys of rams: for the Lord hath a sacrifice in Bozrah, and a great slaughter in the land of Idumea. And the unicorns shall come down with them, and the bullocks with the bulls; and their land shall be soaked with blood, and their dust made fat with fatness."

Or a still more vivid picture and graphic description of the last great battle is given in Joel 3:9-17: "Proclaim ye this among the Gentiles; Prepare war, wake up the mighty men, let all the men of war draw near; let them come up: Beat your plowshares into swords, and your pruninghooks into spears: let the weak say, I am strong. Assemble yourselves, and come, all ye heathen, and gather yourselves together round about: thither cause thy mighty ones to come down, O Lord. Let the heathen be wakened, and come up to the valley of Jehoshaphat: for there will I sit to judge all the heathen round about. Put ye in the sickle, for the harvest is ripe: come, get you down; for the press is full, the vats overflow: for their wickedness is great. Multitudes, multitudes in the valley of decision: for the day of the Lord is near in the valley of decision. The sun and the moon shall be darkened, and the stars shall withdraw their shining. The Lord also shall roar out of Zion, and utter his voice from Jerusalem; and the heavens and the earth shall shake: but the Lord will be the hope of his people, and the strength of the children of Israel. So shall ye know that I am the Lord your God dwelling in Zion, my holy mountain: then shall Jerusalem be holy, and there shall no strangers pass through her any more."

The Time Of These Events

Such shall be the order of events.

When shall all these things be?

Of course, no one knows the day and the hour. But nevertheless it may be said that the picture of the harvest is significant in this respect: it tells us that the harvest must be ripe and that all history must pass through its own necessary process before these things shall be. The church must have been completed. The gospel must have been preached to all men. And the wickedness of the wicked must be full. History must finish its course. And therefore it teaches us that we must not look out of the window in the expectation that these things shall come tomorrow, or even today. They shall not. First must be the man of sin. The antichristian kingdom must come to complete manifestation. Then must the people of God be oppressed and pushed to the wall, and live as outcasts upon the earth. Then must Gog and Magog be aroused from its sleep and contemplate the great war against the power of Antichrist. And then all things shall come as we are told in Scripture. Christ shall remove His people. He shall stir up the nations against one another. It shall be an awful day. But the people of God shall then be on earth no more.

But once more: these things shall not happen tomorrow. They may happen quickly. We are making history fast. Let, then, our eye be fixed on the promise. And let us not be afraid. Christ is our King, and He rules now and forever. And He that sits in the heavens shall laugh. At the last battle of Jehovah He shall gather them all together and tread them in the great winepress of His wrath.

Let no one, then, take our crown; but may we be found faithful even unto the end.

Chapter XXXVII
The Song Of Moses And Of The Lamb

(Revelation 15:1-8)

1 And I saw another sign in heaven, great and marvellous, seven angels having the seven last plagues; for in them is filled up the wrath of God.

2 And I saw as it were a sea of glass mingled with fire: and them that had gotten the victory over the beast, and over his image, and over his mark, and over the number of his name, stand on the sea of glass, having the harps of God.

3 And they sing the song of Moses the servant of God, and the song of the Lamb, saying, Great and marvellous are thy works, Lord God Almighty; just and true are thy ways, thou King of saints.

4 Who shall not fear thee, O Lord, and glorify thy name? for thou only art holy: for all nations shall come and worship before thee; for thy judgments are made manifest.

5 And after that I looked, and, behold, the temple of the tabernacle of the testimony in heaven was opened:

6 And the seven angels came out of the temple, having the seven plagues, clothed in pure and white linen, and having their breasts girded with golden girdles.

7 And one of the four beasts gave unto the seven angels seven golden vials full of the wrath of God, who liveth for ever and ever.

8 And the temple was filled with smoke from the glory of God, and from his power; and no man was able to enter into the temple, till the seven plagues of the seven angels were fulfilled.

You will remember, no doubt, that in connection with our interpretation of Chapter 11 we called your attention to the fact that in that passage things were revealed only in general outline, while they were to be explained in detail in future chapters. If in that light you consider the passage we are now called to discuss, you will have no difficulty finding its counterpart in Chapter 11. Chapter 11 spoke of the two witnesses who were oppressed and persecuted and cast out by Antichrist, but caught up to God in heaven. And after the witnesses were caught up, we read of the sounding of the seven trumpets, the voices which sing in heaven, and the opening of the temple of God which is in heaven, followed by signs of great judgment upon the earth. Evidently this passage is now worked out in detail, not only in the present chapter but also in future chapters. Already we have studied the rise of Antichrist and his power. We have received an insight into his nature and work. And we have seen how he would persecute the church which refuses to worship the beast and his image. We have also become acquainted with the attitude of God over against this power of Antichrist, and seen that in the end He would redeem and fully deliver His church and destroy the wicked antichristian kingdom. Now then, the destruction of Antichrist is worked out in greater detail in the chapters following. In Chapters 15 and 16 we have a vision of the seven vials of the wrath of God as poured out on the earth by the seven angels. These two chapters belong together, and they are related in such a way that our present chapter serves as an introduction to Chapter 16, while in the latter the actual pouring out of the seven vials is pictured.

Of course, here we are reminded of the general plan of the Book of Revelation. There are seven seals. And when all of these seven seals are opened, the wrath of God and of the Lamb against the kingdom of Antichrist will be finished. But these seven seals do not maintain their character as seals throughout. The seventh seal reveals itself as seven trumpets, and the seventh trumpet as seven vials. We must remember, as we have repeatedly stated, that it is not in harmony with the contents to take these seals and trumpets as being strictly successive, nor as being entirely contemporaneous. Taking them as a whole, they are both successive and contemporaneous. In principle there is nothing new in the seven vials. Only there is progress again, so that the destruction, which was more complete in the seven trumpets than in the seven seals, is now entirely complete in the seven vials; and the wrath of God is finished in them. Let us therefore now, first of all, discuss the passage of Chapter 15, which speaks of the song of Moses and of the Lamb.

The Occasion Of The Song

The first verse of the chapter announces the general theme of its contents. John tells us: "And I saw another sign in heaven, great and marvellous, seven angels having the seven last plagues; for in them is filled up the wrath of God." John speaks here of another sign in contrast with the signs he has seen before. The sign of the woman arrayed with the sun and with the moon under her feet; the sign of the beast with the seven heads and ten horns; and the other sign, of the two-horned beast; the sign of the angels flying in mid-heaven and of the Lamb on Mount Zion; of the Holy One coming to reap, being seated on the white cloud, — all these signs John has already seen. And now he beholds another sign.

That sign which he now beholds is great and marvellous. It is, in other words, awe-inspiring and wonderful. And no wonder: for the sign which he now beholds is of the greatest importance. It cannot be looked upon without having the effect of filling our hearts with an overflowing emotion of wonder and joy. John beholds seven angels. And although, no doubt, the sight of these seven angels standing side by side is already astounding, — for they are glorious and beautiful, shining in their appearance, pure and bright, — yet their purpose and message is still more awful. These are the angels who have the seven last plagues, John tells us. Just in general he tells us here that they have the seven plagues. Evidently they do not have these seven plagues of themselves. No, angels are also creatures: and they have no power except it be given them from above. But the power of these seven plagues is given them, and they now hold this power.

They possess the power of pouring out these plagues and evidently destroying the earth. For the destruction implied in these plagues is complete. The text tells us that in these plagues is finished the wrath of God. Evidently that does not mean that with these seven plagues the final judgment has already come upon all nations before the throne of God. Still less does it imply that when these seven plagues shall have been finished, the subjects of the kingdom of Antichrist shall have received all their punishment. No, in that sense the wrath of God is not finished in these plagues. That wrath of God is infinite, as His majesty is infinite. If that infinite majesty is attacked, it is simply the demand of the law that the creature thus attacking that infinite majesty also be subject to infinite wrath and death eternal. And therefore, the wrath of God in that sense of the word is not fulfilled in these seven plagues. But with a view to time the wrath of God is now finished. Even as in the vision of the harvest we called your attention to the fact that in it we were given a vision not of the last and final judgment of all before the throne of God, but simply of the end of time, of the finishing of the wrath of God with a view to this sinful and wicked world, thus it is also here. When these angels shall have sent the seven plagues which they have, the wrath of God shall have been finished in so far that there shall be no power on earth any more which shall provoke His wrath. The wicked world shall be no more. Antichrist and his kingdom shall have been completely destroyed. The end of this dispensation shall have come. And therefore, with a view to this significance John might well speak of the greatness and marvellousness of this sign of the seven angels who were about to realize all these things.

However, John does not merely behold their general presence and appearance on the scene of his vision. He also is privileged to describe some of the details concerning them.

In the first place, he tells us of their origin, informs us whence they come as angels of the wrath of God. For he tells us: "And after that I looked, and, behold, the temple of the tabernacle of the testimony in heaven was opened: And the seven angels came out of the temple, having the seven plagues." Also in Chapter 11 we came into contact with the same idea. In connection with the seventh trumpet we there read: "And the temple of God was opened in heaven, and there was seen in his temple the ark of his testament." And then the significant expression was added: "and there were lightnings, and voices, and thunderings, and an earthquake, and great hail." And there we explained that the symbol evidently meant that when God is about to make of all the earth His temple, judgments of destruction are sure to follow. Thus it is also here. The temple is His holy place, His dwelling, in the narrower sense of the word. But now that temple is still in heaven, is limited, therefore. Surely, He also dwells in this dispensation in the hearts of His people. But, in the first place, it must not be forgotten that at this stage there shall be no more people of God on the earth; and, in the second place, that God shall make of all creation His city and His dwellingplace. He therefore shall break forth from His holy place which is in heaven. He shall break forth as the Holy One. He shall break forth with His testimony, His law, in order to establish His righteousness in all the earth. And when He thus issues forth from His holy place for the purpose of making of all the earth His temple, when He thus issues forth in the fire of His holiness, the result cannot but be that all sin and wickedness is bound to meet with destruction and distress. Only He does not issue forth personally. No, the seven angels come out of His temple, out of the temple of God which is in heaven. They must reveal themselves as angels of wrath, which spell woe to the wicked world.

In the second place, John is able to describe their appearance. They are seven in number, which symbolizes what John has already mentioned in the first verse, namely, that in their plagues the wrath of God shall be finished, and, at the same time, that by the work of these angels the kingdom of God shall finally be completed. Seven is the symbol of the completion of the kingdom. And for that reason there were seven seals and seven trumpets. Only, in case of the seven seals and also in the case of the seven trumpets the work ceased with the sixth; and after the sixth had been fulfilled, the scene was allowed to change. The wrath of God, therefore, had not yet been finished. But now it is different. Not six angels shall pour out their vials, but all seven. And when all of these seven shall have done their work, the kingdom of God shall have come to its completion, and all the power of opposition shall have been broken down. They appear bright and pure and beautiful, arrayed with precious stones, pure and bright. A golden girdle, which reminds us of the royal priesthood of the King of kings, is about their breasts. They are, as it were, over-poured with the glory of the holiness of God, Whose wrath they now represent. With a reflection of the glory of the Holy One, from Whose presence they issue forth, they now enter upon their work.

In the third place, John describes how they receive their vials of wrath from the creatures, from one of the four. There is a beautiful symbolism in the vials, or bowls, of wrath. Each of them receives a vial. And that vial is filled with the wrath of God, that is, with His holiness in relation to the world of sin. And as each pours His vial upon the wicked world, that wrath of God becomes a powerful force of destruction. And as far as the fact is concerned that in the vision they receive that vial from one of the four creatures, he tells us in beautiful symbolism that all creation is concerned in the work which these angels are to perform. The four living creatures, who represent all animate creation in its state of perfection, are concerned in the work of these angels. They are privileged to hand them the vials of the wrath of God.

And thus they stand, these angels, ready to finish their work, just waiting for the command. It is therefore indeed a sign, great and marvellous. It is one of the most wonderful periods in all the history of the world. It is the eve of the realization of all things, the eve of that moment when God shall appear in all the power of His holiness, when His Word shall appear to be the truth also over the wicked world, when His name shall appear glorious and victorious over all things. It is the eve of that greatest of all events, for which the hearts of all God's people long and yearn, for which the souls beneath the altar cry day and night without rest. It is the eve of that event when Christ shall appear as the Lamb Who hath been slain, as the victorious King of kings, as the Mighty One Who has power over all things, as the Anointed One over Zion, His holy place. It is the eve of that event which shall show the futility of all the works of the devil and shall forevermore do away with the kingdom of darkness. It is the most momentous period in the history of the world, the eve of the realization of all God's counsel. And it is on the eve of this greatest of all events that we hear the song of those who stand at the crystal sea, singing the song of Moses and of the Lamb. It is that event, which they already see, which they celebrate in their song.

The Singers

John says: "And I saw as it were a sea of glass mingled with fire: and them that had gotten the victory over the beast, and over his image, and over his mark, and over the number of his name, stand on the sea of glass, having the harps of God. And they sing the song of Moses the servant of God, and the song of the Lamb."

We ask: who are these singers at the sea of glass?

In the first place, we learn of them that they are those who come off victorious from the beast and his image and the number of his name. In the most literal sense of the word, therefore, they are those who have lived at the time of the final manifestation of the antichristian kingdom. When the Antichrist reigned supreme and all the world wondered after the beast, when he established his universal emblem and gave to all men a sign, they lived on the earth. They were in tribulation. They were those who refused to worship the beast. They were those who could neither buy nor sell, who could not live in the midst of society, who were the outcasts in the streets of Jerusalem, which is spiritually Sodom and Gomorrah, where also our Lord was crucified. They, therefore, have fought a fierce battle. But in their battle they were sustained by the faith in Jesus and by His testimony, and they remained faithful. Outcasts in the earth for the name of Jesus, they looked forward to the day of their final victory. Exiles and refugees, without a place to stand, they nevertheless refused to worship the beast; and they remained faithful even to the end. Now they stand by the glass sea, and at the eve of their final victory, already glorified themselves but awaiting the final destruction of their enemy; and they sing the song of victory.

But is this multitude then limited to a small number of the people of God who have lived at the time of Antichrist?

We do not think so.

Truly, they have been in the thickest of the battle. It was for them to live at the time of Antichrist in all his power and fulness. The honor and privilege to live at that time was in store for them. For thus it is in reality: it will be a time of special privilege for the people of God to live at the time of Antichrist. It is much rather a cause of longing and yearning, than of fear and trembling, for the people of God to live at that time. Is not a soldier in the battle honored by being in the thickest of the battle? And shall not the soldier of the kingdom of Christ by faith deem it an honor to be in the thickest of the fight against the power of Antichrist and to show that he fears nothing even though he be hated of all men and of all nations? And therefore, it is a special honor to be deemed worthy to live at that time. God shall have His strongest children, His best forces, in the world at that last period. And therefore, to belong to those picked forces of Christ in the world at the time of Antichrist shall be the greatest honor conceivable. For that same reason I have no doubt but that there shall be a special place in store for them in the new heaven and the new earth, — a place which they alone can occupy. I have no doubt but that they are the leaders in the chorus which is here singing at the sea of glass.

Nevertheless, I do not think that this number is limited to them. For, in the first place, as we have said before, in principle the Antichrist and his power are in the world from the very beginning. Not merely in the end, but also at the time of the apostles he was already in the world, denying that Jesus is the Christ. Still more: not merely in the new dispensation, but also in the old that same power was already in the world, trying to realize itself and opposing the kingdom that was to come. It was already in the time of Elijah, in the time of Moses, in the time of Abraham, in the time of Nimrod, that he attempted to establish his kingdom. It was at the time of Enoch, who testified of the coming of the Lord against it, and even at the time of Abel, who clung to the truth and became a martyr. And therefore, it may be said indeed that in principle the people of God fight the same battle all through the ages, even though this battle shall rage most severely in the time of the full manifestation of the antichristian kingdom. Abel fought that same battle. Enoch fought the battle. Noah fought the battle. All the witnesses and prophets of the Old Testament fought that same battle. All the martyrs of the new dispensation also fought that same battle. Only, that one great battle becomes most severe at the time when Antichrist shall reveal himself in all his power. And, in the third place, subjectively it may also be said that all the saints of the old, as well as of the new dispensation, hoped and longed for the coming of that day of which these victorious ones sing. It was the hope of Israel. It was the keynote in the prophecies of the old dispensation. Enoch already spoke of it against the wicked world of his day. And the souls under the altar cry for it day and night. All the history of the world looks forward to this day. Is it conceivable, then, that only a small part of the people of God are standing here at the sea of glass, now God is about to reveal His righteousness and power over the antichristian enemy, to sing this song of victory? No, we do not believe this. All the saints, all those who have been faithful, from Abel to the last witness, in the kingdom of God on earth shall stand there at the sea of glass to join the victorious crowd in singing their song of Moses and of the Lamb. And as we shall see presently, this is supported by the fact that the song which they sing is that of Moses and of the Lamb, combining therefore the Old and the New Testament in one.

They stand by the sea of glass. We have met with this sea of glass, shining like crystal, earlier, in the fourth chapter of this book. You remember how there it was pictured as being part of the dispensation of perfection which is to displace this dispensation of sin. Especially did it symbolize the truth that in the new creation the glory of God shall be reflected in all His works. Well, here we meet with the sea of glass once more, though from a slightly different point of view. It tells us, in the first place, that these singers are no more on earth. In the days when the seven vials shall be poured out and destruction shall be completed, God shall have His people with Him. It is the church in glory. And the sea of glass is here mingled with fire because it reflects the wrath of God as He shall presently reveal it over the wicked world and for the salvation and glory of His people.

And thus the entire scene reminds us of the children of Israel standing at the border of the Red Sea, looking back upon that sea which had become the sea of wrath for the enemies, but at the same time the sea of their own salvation. Even as the children of Israel stood by the sea, reflecting the wrath of God, so stand these victorious ones by the sea of glass mingled with fire. Even as that sea in the case of Israel had become the cause of destruction for the enemies of God, so also this sea of glass symbolizes the reflection of God's wrath which will destroy the Antichrist and his kingdom. Even as in the case of Israel the same sea that was instrumental in destroying the power of opposition was their own salvation, so also shall these victorious ones enter into their full inheritance if God shall have caused the vials of His wrath to be poured out over the wicked world. And even as the children of Israel at the Red Sea sang of victory, so do these victorious ones exalt the arm and the righteousness of the Lord, the God of their salvation.

The Song

Let us, then, for a few moments pay attention to their song.

In the first place, it may not escape our attention that they sing their song on harps of God. That is, God Himself had given them their instruments of music. He is the author of their harps. He is at the same time the author of their song. Never would they have sung this song were it not for the grace of God. Never would they have remained faithful unless God through Jesus Christ had sustained them by His grace. Never would they, therefore, have been able to sing this song, were it not that God Himself had formed them to be His people. They have harps of God.

In the second place, it may draw our attention that their song is designated as being the song of Moses and of the Lamb. Evidently this does not imply that this multitude is singing two songs, one of Moses and another of the Lamb, but that the same song is at the same time the song of Moses and the song of the Lamb. Once more, it points to the fact that history repeats itself, and that one phase of history in Scripture is typical of the other, so that it may be said that Israel of the old dispensation already sang the song of the Lamb, and vice versa, that the people of the Lamb of the new dispensation also sing the song of Moses. Old and new dispensations shall be one. There is no break, no difference between them in glory. They form one multitude, and they sing one song. And that one song, sung by one multitude, is the song of Moses and of the Lamb. And therefore, also here the miserable world-conception of those who postulate an eternal difference and separation between Jew and Gentile is condemned. Jew and Gentile, one in Christ, sing the same song, the song of Moses and of the Lamb.

As to the meaning of this expression, it cannot be difficult to understand it. As we have already indicated, the whole vision plainly refers to the passage through the Red Sea by the children of Israel, which constituted their final deliverance from Egypt. They had been oppressed by the mighty arm of Pharaoh, but by a still mightier arm they had been delivered. But the enemy pursued them and aimed at their destruction. At the Red Sea arrives the critical moment. Through that sea God causes His people to pass in safety, but by the same instrumentality He destroys the enemy. Just as the flood was both a means of salvation for God's people and a means of destruction for the wicked world, so was the Red Sea the means whereby God saved Israel and at the same time destroyed the pursuing enemy. And as the enemy is destroyed and the people are safe on the other shore, Moses composes this song of victory, in the which he exalts the arm of Jehovah, sings of joy over the destruction of Pharaoh and his host and because of the salvation of God's people, (cf. Exodus 15). Now this entire incident is typical of Christ and His salvation. Moses as the mediator of the Old Testament is the type of Christ, the Mediator of the new dispensation. Even as Moses, so Christ leads His people out of the house of the bondage of sin. Even as Moses and his people, so Christ and His people are the object of the pursuing wrath of the enemy. But even as Moses, so also Christ leads His people safely through the waters of separation and of wrath, strikes those waters of the wrath of God, so that they become at the same time a means of salvation for His people and a means of destruction for the enemy.

Now then, at this moment the people of Christ stand at the sea of glass, all delivered from sin and from the oppression of the enemy. And they see how God will pour out His wrath upon the enemy. Yea, they already see that wrath poured out and the enemy destroyed. They place themselves upon the standpoint of the completed and full wrath of God. And therefore, their condition is now exactly like that of the children of Israel after they had passed through the Red Sea and had seen the destruction of their oppressors. And for that same reason they now sing the same song, exalting the power of Jehovah, the salvation of His people, and the wrath visited upon the wicked power of opposition. Truly, the song of Moses is the song of the Lamb. Even as Moses taught his people to sing his song, so the Lamb taught His people to sing this song. And essentially they are alike, sing of the same theme, the one being merely a type of the other.

What then do they sing? "Great and marvellous are thy works, Lord God Almighty; just and true are thy ways, thou King of saints. Who shall not fear, O Lord, and glorify thy name? for thou only art holy: for all nations shall come and worship before thee; for thy judgments are made manifest."

Let us briefly note the main features of this song. In the first place, it cannot escape our attention that there is nothing in this song of man, but that it is from beginning to end an exaltation of the greatness and power and glory of God. It is God's greatness, God's truth, God's righteousness, God's holiness, that is here celebrated. In the second place, it must draw our attention that from the very contents of the song it becomes plain that these singers already live by sight, not by faith. Here upon earth we also glorify God's greatness and His power and righteousness and truth and holiness. But it is a glorification by faith, which is an evidence of things unseen. These attributes of God Almighty have not yet been fully revealed. But now it is different. God's greatness is now clearly manifested in all His works. His truth and righteousness is now distinctly displayed in all His ways. His holiness has been revealed. It has all been realized. In this dispensation it seemed that the devil and the Antichrist were mighty, were true, and, in fact, were righteous, and that God would not have the victory, but suffer defeat. Long was the period of longsuffering. And often the people of God asked with the poet of old, "Is there no knowledge with the Almighty?" But when the vials of God's wrath shall have been poured out, it shall be publicly manifest, and that before all the world, that God Almighty sits in heaven and laughs and realizes all His counsel in spite of the workings of Satan and his servants. His truth and His righteousness and His power and holiness shall then be revealed.

In the third place, we may notice, too, that these multitudes also sing of the final fulfillment of all prophecy, namely, of this, that now all nations should fear Him and glorify His name. It seemed for a time as if all nations should glorify and fear the Antichrist. But now it is all different. They who feared Antichrist were not the nations; they were the branches of the nations which were to be cut off and cast into outer darkness. The nations have been preserved, and they are in this multitude, represented by it. Presently the new heavens and the new earth shall appear in glory, and then all nations shall fear and glorify the mighty acts and name of the Lord God Almighty forever and ever.

We too, while we are still in this world, may indeed sing this song of Moses and of the Lamb, though not yet in perfection. We are still in the world. And in the world we are still in the midst of battle. But by the grace of God we can listen to the song of the redeemed, and learn it, and look forward to the day when we all shall stand by the sea of glass, delivered from sin and oppression, delivered from the enemy that always surrounds us, free to serve and glorify the God of our salvation, in order to sing the song of Moses and of the Lamb. May our faith cause us to look forward in hope and teach us to sing this song of victory in the midst of the present battle.

Chapter XXXVIII
The First Four Vials
(Revelation 16:1-9)

1 And I heard a great voice out of the temple saying to the seven angels, Go your ways, and pour out the vials of the wrath of God upon the earth.

2 And the first went, and poured out his vial upon the earth; and there fell a noisome and grievous sore upon the men which had the mark of the beast, and upon them which worshipped his image.

3 And the second angel poured out his vial upon the sea; and it became as the blood of a dead man: and every living soul died in the sea.

4 And the third angel poured out his vial upon the rivers and fountains of waters; and they became blood.

5 And I heard the angel of the waters say, Thou art righteous, O Lord, which art, and wast, and shalt be, because thou hast judged thus.

6 For they have shed the blood of saints and prophets, and thou hast given them blood to drink; for they are worthy.

7 And I heard another out of the altar say, Even so, Lord God Almighty, true and righteous are thy judgments.

8 And the fourth angel poured out his vial upon the sun; and power was given unto him to scorch men with fire.

9 And men were scorched with great heat, and blasphemed the name of God, which hath power over these plagues: and they repented not to give him glory.

It will now be plain that Chapters 15 and 16 belong together, and that Chapter 15 constitutes a mighty prelude to the events pictured in the sixteenth chapter of the Book of Revelation. There we found mention of the song of Moses and of the Lamb. We found that this song was sung at the occasion of the eve of the pouring out of the seven last plagues. Seven angels stand in battle array, ready to receive the command out of the temple to go and pour out the last of the plagues of God. They are

528

brilliantly arrayed with costly, precious stones; and there is a reflection of the holiness of God in their very appearance. They have come forth out of the temple of God, which is filled with the smoke of His holiness, ready to fill all the earth and to reveal itself as wrath over the ungodly and oppressors of His people. And in their hands they hold seven vials, or bowls, filled with the wrath of God. When these shall have been poured out, God's wrath shall have been spent, and all is finished. This is indicated by the number seven, symbolic of completeness with a view to the coming of the kingdom in this dispensation. But this was also directly stated by John when he says that in these is finished the wrath of God. And this does not mean that the wrath of God is finished in these seven plagues with a view to eternity, but that this dispensation shall have been finished. The power which opposes the kingdom of God shall forever have been destroyed, and the way is open for the descent of the city of our God upon the new earth.

We found, in the second place, that these singers are described as those who have not worshipped the beast and his image, but who have been victorious. First of all, by those who are mentioned in this section are indicated those who have lived in the time of the greatest and most powerful manifestation of Antichrist. They have fought the battle at its very climax. They were deemed worthy to belong to the picked, or selected, forces of Christ. They are also undoubtedly worthy of receiving double honor and of being capable of occupying a special place in the new temple of God. But they are not the only ones. For, in the first place, the power of Antichrist rages throughout the ages, be it not in that form and with that power as it shall be revealed in the last time. In the second place, and for that reason, the battle is in principle the same throughout the ages, not only in the new dispensation but even in the old. And therefore God's people of all ages fight in principle against the beast. And finally, the subjective longing of all the children of God is for this day of the Lord, in which He may destroy the enemies and establish His kingdom in glory forever. And therefore, all believers here stand at the crystal sea, which is symbolic of the glory and holiness of God, now reflecting the wrath of the Almighty, and of which the Red Sea was a type.

In the third place, we had our attention called to the song itself. It was the song of Moses and of the Lamb. We found that this does not indicate two songs, but only one. It is the one song, and also the one multitude that sings this song, the song of Moses being typical of and essentially the same as the song of the Lamb. And we found in it but another indication that in eternity there shall not be two forces and two kinds of people of God, but one multitude, singing one and the same song, the song of Moses and of the Lamb. Moses is the type of Christ. He is the mediator of the old dispensation. He led his people out of bondage; so did Christ. He was pursued by the enemy; so are Christ and His people pursued by the enemy of God's kingdom. He led his people through the sea of salvation and of wrath at the same time, that is, the Red Sea; so does Christ finally cause His people to be delivered through the sea of the wrath of God that completely destroys the enemy and that is symbolized in the sea of glass. Moses, finally, taught his people to sing a song of deliverance and glory and triumph; so does Christ teach His people to sing of victory, to the glory of God. It is a song all of God, a song extolling the glory and holiness, the righteousness and the truth and justice of God as having become manifest in all His works and ways.

Now the command goes forth to the angels to pour out the bowls into the earth. Even though the angels have already received their vials of wrath, they must still wait for the command from the temple. For everything proceeds orderly even in the pouring out of the wrath of God, and only at the exact moment may God's judgment begin. And therefore we are now called to discuss the seven last vials of the wrath of God. Four of these are mentioned in the passage we are now discussing.

The General Character Of The First Four Vials

In regard to the general character of these first four vials, or bowls, I want to call your attention, first of all, to the fact that we must not fall into the rut of false spiritualization and allegorization of the text. As with many portions of the Book of Revelation, so also with this part, this has been done by many.

There are those who allegorize practically every element of the text and give it a spiritual meaning. When the text speaks of the earth, it has a different significance than the literal meaning. When it speaks of the sore boils, it means something spiritual. When it speaks of the sea, it refers to the sea of nations. And the rivers and fountains of water are spiritual rivers and spiritual fountains. When we read that the first vial is poured out upon the earth and causes a sore boil on those that worshipped the beast and his image, there are interpreters who inform us that this is a spiritual boil, a sore of the mind and of the heart, caused by the dissatisfaction which naturally follows all the service of idols, the sad disenchantment of all idolaters. Or, according to others, who can follow the Book of Revelation and trace it page after page in the history of mankind in chronological order, it refers to the sore of infidelity which had been festering for a long time, but which ripened under the influence of such men as Paine, Voltaire, and Rousseau, and finally broke out in the terrible French Revolution. Or it is made to mean the corruption of the church just before the Reformation. The second angel pours out his vial into the sea, which means, of course, naval battles, coloring the sea red with the blood of the slain, turning the ocean into blood. And then it is made to refer especially to the naval battles which were fought between Protestant England and the Catholic countries of the continent between 1793 and 1815, resulting in the defeat of the Catholic naval powers and the victory of the Protestant one. Or, since the sea is the symbol of nations and tongues and tribes, the second vial is interpreted as referring in general to the disintegration of the papal power and the shaking off of the yoke of the pope by many kings and powers in Europe. The third angel pours out his vial upon the rivers and fountains of waters. And interpreters tell us in all seriousness and sincerity that we have here a prophecy of the victory of Napoleon in the regions of the Alps over the enemy at the very rivers of Switzerland, turning its rivers into blood by the many slain ones, his victorious entry into Rome, and the subjection of the pope. Or, it represents the corruption of the sources of life and thought in the spiritual sense of the word. And so, finally, the fourth vial is interpreted in different ways. It is poured out upon the sun. That sun is Napoleon, who receives power to scorch the nations of Europe by his military genius and becomes a veritable plague to all peoples of the continent. Or it is Christ, scorching those who reject His name with the fire of His wrath.

Such, and other interpretations, have been given of these first four vials. But we cannot agree with this method of interpretation of the Book of Revelation.

In the first place, as we have remarked time and again, we must not take anything in the spiritual sense unless the book plainly indicates this. That the beast who rises out of the earth is not a real animal, but something extraordinary, to be interpreted in the symbolical sense of the word, is something which needs no argument. Everyone admits that this is so. Its appearance, as well as all that he does, plainly indicates this. That the harvest in Chapter 14 is not a real harvest of grain and grapes is also beyond dispute. The book indicates very clearly when we must think of symbolism and spiritualization. But surely that is not the case here. Our text speaks of the pouring out of the vials upon the earth, into the sea, and into the rivers and fountains of waters without anything else. It tells us that the fourth angel pours his vial upon the sun, and that the effect is that the sun increases terribly in heat, so that it scorches men. And there is absolutely no indication that we must or may interpret them in the spiritual sense. If nevertheless we attempt to do so without any indication and guide from the text, the question immediately arises as to which interpretation is the correct one. Are the rivers and fountains of waters springs of life and thought? Is the sore boil a symbol of the corruption of the church? Or is it the sore boil of infidelity? Is the sun Napoleon, or Christ, or perhaps something else? And who will answer these questions? The result is that we leave the book and its interpretation in despair, deeply dissatisfied and quite convinced that we have not hit upon the right interpretation, leaving it to the future perhaps, — perhaps even to eternity, — to unveil the hidden depths that here are concealed from our eye. So much as to the false allegorization of the text. As to the historical interpretation, we have partly the same objection. Who will tell us exactly what period of history is represented by each plague? Is it the period of the Reformation? Or is it that of the French Revolution?

In the second place, it is entirely against the plain indication of the significance of the seven vials themselves. For we are plainly told that in these the wrath of God is finished. Each of these seven vials must pour out the wrath of God upon a certain sphere. And although the wrath of God is not finished to the full in each of them separately, yet it is certainly complete with a view to the sphere in which it is poured out. But what completion is there in the naval battles of 1793 to 1815? Did that color the entire sea, so that every living creature in it died? Or were they perhaps the last naval battles that were ever fought, so that the sea is never colored again? History of a later date reveals to us a radically different picture. If the sore boil that breaks out with the first vial is the sore of infidelity breaking out in the French Revolution, is it true then that there were never such vials poured out again? Was it the last of its kind? Was the wrath of God finished in that sphere? And if the third vial represents the battles of Napoleon fought over the rivers of Switzerland, is it true that these were the last battles of the kind? And did not God pour out these vials repeatedly in history? If the sun is Napoleon, are there then not many of these suns in later history? Indeed, such interpretations of the Word of God can hardly be taken seriously; and they lead us to hopeless confusion.

We maintain, therefore, that the first four vials refer to natural phenomena, — natural not in the sense that they shall not be extraordinary in measure and scope, for they surely shall be. But they are natural in this sense, that they all affect a sphere of nature. In other words, we take this portion in the literal sense of the word.

Of course, there is symbolism in the picture. John beholds a vision. And in one vision he beholds mighty things, things which will perhaps take years to be accomplished and completed. The vial is naturally symbolic. No one of us will imagine that in the end of time it will be possible that God pours His wrath into seven vials in the literal sense of the word and has them poured out upon the wicked world. Wrath is not a substance, and therefore cannot be poured out. There is no one who does not understand this.

But for the rest, we may safely take the portion in as literal a sense as possible and as referring to phenomena in nature. In the first place, we may never forget that it is necessary that by the seven last plagues creation is affected. The earth and the sea, the rivers and fountains of waters, yea, even the sun in its effect upon the earth, belong to the kingdom which God originally created with man as its head. And even though man became a subject of the kingdom of Satan, he yet knew in part how to subject the powers of the world to be subject unto his ends. And therefore, also that world must be subjected to the plagues of God. In the second place, as we have pointed out before, it is on that creation, on the earth and the sea and the rivers and fountains of water, that man is absolutely dependent. It is through them that God reaches man. It is through all kinds of agencies that God reaches the health of man and sends unto him sickness and disease. It is through affecting the atmosphere and the heat of the sun that God sends scarcity and famine. And thus God controls the history of the world also through affecting the various spheres of nature. In the third place, this is a plain indication of the text. First of all, let us notice that there are four of these vials. Do not say that we have arbitrarily separated them from the rest: for that is not the case. It is very plain that there is a difference between the first four and the rest. The first four all relate to different spheres of nature: the earth, the sea, the rivers and fountains of waters, the sun in the heavens are all affected by these first four vials. And they all form a part of nature. But the fifth vial is poured out upon the throne of the beast. The sixth prepares the battle of Armageddon. And the seventh is indeed poured out in the air, but is universal in its effect. And therefore we have here a group of four. Four is the number of the world as creation. And it is creation that is here immediately affected. Then, as we have said before, there is absolutely no reason to take the terms **earth** and **sea , rivers and fountains of waters**, and **sun** in a symbolic sense, since there is nothing in the text that warrants such an interpretation. And, finally, there is an unmistakable correspondence between the first four vials and the first four trumpets. The first trumpet affects the earth; so does the first vial. The second trumpet affects the sea; so does the second vial. The third trumpet affects the rivers and fountains of waters; so does the third vial. The fourth trumpet affects the heavenly luminaries; so does the fourth vial. And since, as we proved at that time, the first four trumpets all relate to phenomena in nature, so it is also the case with the first four vials. And therefore, once more: the earth is the earth, the sea is the sea, the rivers and fountains of waters are exactly as indicated, and the sun is the heavenly luminary as we know it. The first four vials, therefore, represent the plagues of God in nature; and then, of course, these various spheres of nature as they affect in turn the world of man.

In the second place, we may also notice that these plagues this time are universal in their character. There is no exception. There is no escape from them. This is one of the characteristic distinctions between the vials and the trumpets.

Notice, in general, that there is progress in the succession of the seals and the trumpets and the vials. In connection with the seals we found that there was mention of one-fourth. And one-fourth, we found, indicates the regular rate of death and destruction upon the earth. Always one-fourth of men die. Always one-fourth of the crops is destroyed. Always one-fourth of the ships are lost. Always there is one-fourth of darkening of the sun, resulting in loss of crops. In the trumpets, however, we found that the one-fourth is changed to one-third, indicating that God at stated times and to control the history of the world and of the nations sends just a little more than the ordinary death-rate and destruction of crops, thus influencing the history of nations and of the world in general. But in the vials there is no mention of a fraction whatever. All of the earth is affected by the first vial. The entire sea is changed into blood by the second. All the rivers and fountains of water are poisoned by the third. And the sun scorches terribly and evidently affects the whole earth. This is also indicated in the difference between the symbols used. The trumpets indicated by their loud resounding that the judgment of God is very near and heavy. But the vials are completely emptied. God has emptied His wrath into the vials, and they again are emptied upon the earth. And therefore the wrath of God in these vials is complete.

Further, we may also notice that these plagues differ from those symbolized in the trumpets in that they do not affect the saints. The plagues of the trumpets naturally also were plagues for the children of the Most High. They were still on earth; and they suffered from the famine and sickness as well as the children of wrath, even though these plagues could not touch them as children of God. But the vials touch only the children of wrath, the worshippers of the beast. And I know of but one reason, namely, this, that the church has been taken away. At the beginning of these signs they have been taken up into glory, and they do not have to suffer because of these universal plagues. Even as in the plagues of Egypt the children of Israel were at first also affected, but with the latter plagues they were exempted, so in these vial-plagues the children of God do not suffer with the children of wrath for the simple reason that they have been taken up into glory.

Hence, we come to the conclusion that the plagues of these first four vials are plagues affecting nature in its various spheres; that they are universal in their character, leaving no exception; and that only the worshippers of the beast are troubled by them. This also indicates that these vials are poured out almost at the very end of time.

The Individual Significance Of The First Four Vials

If now we try to explain these four vials in their individual significance, we may say, first of all, that it behooves us to be careful. The history of these vials belongs entirely to the remote future. True, in principle we find the four vials upon earth all through this dispensation. They are also in the trumpets, and even in the seals. But in their universal character they have not yet been realized. They belong to the future. And therefore we shall do well not to go beyond the text in this respect. We must not go into detail and try to explain exactly how God shall work in those days, through what agencies He shall bring about the changes in nature, exactly what is meant by the sore on the men who worshipped the beast, by the blood into which the sea and the rivers are turned. All these questions we would not be able to answer with any reasonable amount of certainty. But what we must do is obtain the general idea of each vial, ascertain its effect upon man and upon the kingdom of Antichrist which still exists in those days. And then we shall be satisfied that the Lord has also here given us a clear revelation of the future.

The first vial is poured out upon the earth. If we may at all compare the trumpets with the vials, as must be inferred from their resemblance, we find that by the earth is meant the dry land in distinction from the sea and the rivers, and that too, the dry land and all that it contains. The earth brings forth the substance with which man must prolong his life. On its crops he depends for health and strength, yea, for very life itself. And so we found in connection with the first trumpet that it destroyed the crops, the trees, and the grass for one-third. The earth, therefore, must be taken in the sense of its being the habitation of men, upon which man is dependent for very life. From the earth he derives his food and substance. From that earth he obtains his gold and silver. From the earth he derives his fuel wherewith to protect himself against the cold of winter. In a word, from that earth he derives all the necessities, as well as the luxuries, of life. It is from this same point of view that we must consider the earth here. And then the effect of the first vial is such that man does not die, but that he is stricken with disease. The earth upon which man depends for life and health is affected so that terrible and universal disease breaks out. The text speaks of sores, which may indeed be taken in the literal sense of the word, but which I would rather take as indicating disease in general. A universal disease breaks out. Everybody is suffering from it because the earth is, as it were, poisoned with the wrath of God. The crops do grow indeed, but they are filled with God's wrath. They supply no health and strength, but poison men, so that sores break out on their bodies and so that they are stricken universally with all kinds of disease. Medical science stands aghast and dumbfounded. For even the drugs and medicines which might otherwise be employed must be obtained from the same earth; and therefore they offer no alleviation from suffering. Universal sickness prevails. No more one-third, but all men are stricken. It has become a world of universal misery.

The second vial affects the sea. Also here there is correspondence between the vials and the trumpets. The second trumpet turned one-third part of the sea into blood, destroyed one-third part of the living creatures and one-third part of the ships. But now the whole sea is turned into a pool of rottenness. Also here we do not have to ask how and through what agencies the Lord will bring this about. This is of little importance. The main fact is clear: the sea is turned into a rotten pool, into blood as of a dead man. This means, in the first place, that the sea as a source of other necessities for man has become worthless. For every living thing in the sea is now dead. Man, who cannot find on the earth what he needs, may turn to the sea to feed himself with the creatures that are in it. But this is now cut off. The earth being poisonous, the sea offers nothing to relieve the suffering. In the second place, we may depend on it that this rotten pool of ocean and sea makes life unbearable and spreads the disease and pestilences still more rapidly. And, in the third place, the sea is no more a means of communication between nation and nation. Commerce is now at a stand-still. All the beautiful castles of the sea which man has built and with which he travels around the earth are now lying still in their harbors, or they perish in the rotten sea. The sea, that mighty treasure to man, has lost its value. It no more offers him any aid or comfort.

Still more, the waters and the rivers are also affected. If man in his distress only might turn to these waters for help and feed on its living creatures, drink from its fountains, he might perhaps find some relief. But this is not the case. Also these are influenced and filled with the wrath of God. Again, exactly in what way we do not know. This is certain, however, that they afford man no pleasant and refreshing drink any more. Most likely all this will come upon the earth gradually, rather than suddenly, although it will be but a short time before the end. All the comforts and necessities of life are taken away from man. For certain it is that he does not immediately die. But all spheres of nature are affected. By the third vial the rivers and fountains of waters are turned into blood as the sea and the ocean. And they add to the universal suffering of man.

And, finally, the sun is affected. The fourth vial is turned empty upon the sun. It is not darkened. That will be still later. But now it is increased in heat to such an extent that it scorches men by its heat. Naturally, it does not only affect men, but also the crops and the cattle of the meadows and the beasts of the field. In short, it has become a terrible world to live in. The earth poisoned and bringing disease! The sea and the waters rot and afford no help! The sun scorches with its terrible heat! Nowhere in all creation is there help or comfort. The whole world is now filled with the wrath of God!

The Combined Effect Of The First Four Vials

In order to understand the combined effect of these seven vials we must first of all recall the actual condition of affairs at this time. Antichrist has established his universal kingdom, a kingdom uniting all nations and having sway over all things in the world. As we have said before, that kingdom shall from a worldly point of view be a glorious kingdom. There shall be great development of human power and talents. There shall be peace and plenty in every way. There shall be joy and luxury. All the world shall be in subjection unto that kingdom of Antichrist. And they shall know how to use all things in creation. It shall be chiefly because of the blessings of that kingdom that it shall be able to establish and maintain itself. It is because of the outward prosperity and because of the wonderful things the beast performs that the whole world wonders after him. But it is a kingdom under Satan and against God and His Christ. God's children, who refuse to worship the beast, may not participate in the blessings of that marvellous kingdom. God is not acknowledged. The beast is supreme. The people of God may not buy or sell.

Now if we view the first four vials in this light, it is very plain what is their significance.

In the first place, through them God makes plain that He after all is the One Who sells things in the world. Antichrist acted as if he were supreme. But after all, he was dependent upon God Almighty. Antichrist acted as if he could sovereignly determine who were to buy and sell and enjoy the blessings of the kingdom of earth and sea and river and sun. But now God comes to show that He is sovereign. And He determines that none who worship the beast shall be able to buy or sell, to enjoy the blessings in His creation. He takes everything away from them. He takes the earth away from them, the crops and the rain, the food and the clothing. Just as Antichrist in his godlessness had done to God's people, so God now does to Antichrist. And all of a sudden all things become manifestly a curse. And therefore, in the first place, there is just revenge in these four vials. We find an indication of this in the voice of the angel who pours out the third vial. He says: "Righteous art thou, who art, and who wast, thou Holy One, because thou didst thus judge: For they poured out the blood of the saints and prophets, and blood thou hast given them to drink; for they are worthy." The implication is, of course, that in this third plague God metes out unto Antichrist as he has meted unto His people. And that is not only true of the third plague, but of all of them. A short while ago the people of God were outcasts, so that they could neither buy nor sell. Now God shows that He is powerful and supreme, and that the people of Antichrist cannot procure in all creation wherewith to feed and clothe themselves. It is an act of just revenge. It is for the same reason that the souls beneath the altar also are satisfied. For the voice comes from the altar, saying, "Yea, Lord God Almighty, true and righteous are thy judgments." Once more, therefore, the first four vials constitute a just revenge upon the subjects of the beast, who worship his image.

But there is more. The combined effect of these plagues is also that it causes the kingdom of Antichrist to be disintegrated and that it prepares for the great battle which is still to be fought, the battle of Armageddon. You understand that the factor which combined the kingdom was its outward prosperity and its outward peace. Men wondered after the beast because they were blessed under his reign with earthly things. But now the power and the glory of the beast are of a sudden gone; and the time is at hand that Gog and Magog shall break loose and prepare for battle against the center of the antichristian kingdom, to break it to pieces.

Finally, we should not forget that these plagues harden the heart of the individual subjects of the kingdom. We would perhaps imagine that such severe judgments as these would soften the hearts and would cause them to give glory to God and repent in dust and ashes. But just the reverse is the case. Man blasphemes God Who has power over these plagues. The implication seems to be that they realize that the God of creation sends them these plagues. Yet they do not repent. On the contrary, they blaspheme and rise still more in rebellion in the midst of all their suffering. A terrible and solemn lesson this is. It teaches us clearly that absolutely nothing but the grace of God will break the sinner. If the grace of God does not enter our hearts and the Word of His gospel does not call us to His covenant, judgments will only have the effect that men harden their hearts.

What a glorious comfort in these four vials! Here is the patience of the saints. As certain as Christ is King, just as certain it is that these judgments shall come. And therefore the saints can afford to be patient. Vengeance belongeth unto the Lord. And He shall surely come to justify Himself and all His people and to prepare the earth for His glorious kingdom.

Chapter XXXIX

The Battle Of Armageddon

(Revelation 16:10-21)

10 And the fifth angel poured out his vial upon the seat of the beast; and his kingdom was full of darkness; and they gnawed their tongues for pain,

11 And blasphemed the God of heaven because of their pains and their sores, and repented not of their deeds.

12 And the sixth angel poured out his vial upon the great river Euphrates; and the water thereof was dried up, that the way of the kings of the east might be prepared.

13 And I saw three unclean spirits like frogs come out of the mouth of the dragon, and out of the mouth of the beast, and out of the mouth of the false prophet.

14 For they are the spirits of devils, working miracles, which go forth unto the kings of the earth and of the whole world, to gather them to the battle of that great day of God Almighty.

15 Behold, I come as a thief. Blessed is he that watcheth, and keepeth his garments, lest he walk naked, and they see his shame.

16 And he gathered them together into a place called in the Hebrew tongue Armageddon.

17 And the seventh angel poured out his vial into the air; and there came a great voice out of the temple of heaven, from the throne, saying, It is done.

18 And there were voices, and thunders, and lightnings; and there was a great earthquake, such as was not since men were upon the earth, so mighty an earthquake, and so great.

19 And the great city was divided into three parts, and the cities of the nations fell: and great Babylon came in remembrance before God, to give unto her the cup of the wine of the fierceness of his wrath.

20 And every island fled away, and the mountains were not found.

21 And there fell upon men a great hail out of heaven, every stone about the weight of a talent: and men blasphemed God because of the plague of the hail; for the plague thereof was exceeding great.

540

Again the words of our text lead us to the very end of this dispensation. That this is so a most superficial reading of the text will show. It speaks of the battle of the great day of God Almighty. It speaks of the downfall of Babylon the Great and of her remembrance before the countenance of the Lord God Almighty; of a terrible shakeup of the heavens and of the earth, so that islands flee away and the mountains are found no more; and it speaks of a last and crushing hail, through which evidently the battle of Armageddon is finished. It is the end of time. It is the close of this entire dispensation.

Repeatedly we have stood at the termination of history as we made study of the Book of Revelation. In Chapter 6:12-17, where the sixth seal is pictured to us, we also found that all the universe was shaken and that it was the great day of the wrath of God and of His Christ. Again, in Chapter 11, the chapter which speaks of the two witnesses, we saw the temple opened at the blowing of the seventh trumpet, and signs of great judgments following, the judgments of the final battle of Christ against His opponents. In Chapter 14 we also received a picture of the end of time in the vision of the great and final harvest and of the vintage. And also there we found that the end was terrible, a treading of the nations in the winepress of the wrath of God.

And now again we stand before the same period of time, the very close of history. And again it is a bloody battle and terrible judgments from heaven that are pictured to us here. Those who dream of a great millennium of peace, who imagine that the kingdom of Christ will gradually have the victory over the kingdom of darkness without any great disturbance and upheaval, certainly find but very little support in the Word of our God and none at all in the Book of Revelation. The wicked shall not gradually be won, but they shall be destroyed. Judgments are in store for them. And these judgments shall not gradually diminish in force, but rather increase and become more terrible. The end of time shall not be peace but war, terrible war, war such as the world has not seen before, war in which all the nations of the earth shall participate and in which.Christ shall have the victory.

That end and that victory is pictured here in the words of our text more clearly than ever before. There is progress in respect to clearness and vividness of revelation and description as we proceed. And in our text the end is already definitely pictured as a great battle. It is not as if that end is already pictured here in all its detail. No, in succeeding chapters we shall find a detailed description of some of the main scenes that are pictured here in general. The fall of Babylon, the coming of the King on the white horse for battle, the loosening of Satan with a view to the nations, – all these things will be reviewed before our vision once more before we get the vision of the New Jerusalem which is to come down out of heaven from God. But here we have nevertheless the picture of the end. For in the seven vials which the seven angels pour out the wrath of God is finished.

Events Leading To This Battle

We must make no mistake as to the time element in these seven vials of wrath. If we do, we shall never be able to understand the whole. Especially must we warn you once more not to consider these seven vials as being strictly successive. It is not thus, that the first of these seven vials must be finished before the second is poured out, that the third must wait till the second has had its effect, the fourth for the fulfillment of the third, etc. Much rather must we conceive of these seven vials as being upon the earth at the same time, so that all their misery together finally combines into one great effect. It may be that the one precedes the other in its coming. And especially is it very well possible, nay, even probable, that the first four vials shall be witnessed before the others. But for the rest we may not refer them to seven different periods in the history of man and of the world.

Nor must we, on the other hand, conceive of them as bearing no relation to one another. That is generally not the way in which God works in the history of the world; and that will not be the case in the period of the end. No, also at that time one thing will bring on the other, till all the world is steeped in misery and pain and agony. The first four vials evidently belong together from this point of view, and they form one definite group. They are the plagues of God in nature. That they have a combined effect is very plain. The earth and the sea and the rivers and the fountains of water are poisoned with the wrath of God; and the sun is so inflamed by it that it scorches men with its heat. All these plagues together cause sickness and want, hunger and thirst and great suffering, so that they have their influence upon the kingdom of Antichrist. I conceive of these plagues as coming on gradually, and not all of a sudden, so that one moment man enjoys life and the other moment he is lost in the depth of misery. No, they come rather gradually. It shall hardly be noticeable perhaps that anything special is coming upon the world. But gradually the earth shall become more and more poisoned, the sea shall show itself more and more as a rotten pool, the fountains of water shall afford no more relief and refreshment, and the sun shall become more and more intolerably hot, so that it scorches men. Gradually the kingdom of Antichrist, which was such a glorious kingdom, shall lose control of its blessings. And gradually its downfall shall be prepared. And so I also imagine that during this period gradually the fifth vial shall be realized, which shall darken the kingdom of the beast.

We read that the fifth vial is poured out upon the throne of the beast. The beast here is evidently Antichrist. And the throne of the beast stands for the seat of his authority and power to rule. The throne is always a symbol of royal power and authority. The king on his throne issues the laws for his kingdom, executes judgment, and expresses sentences. The king on his throne is obeyed and honored by all his subjects. The king on his throne is the symbol of royal power. When a king is dethroned, he has lost his royal dominion. Thus it is here. Antichrist was enthroned by all the nations of the world. He had a great and glorious dominion. All the nations of the world bow down to him and acknowledge him. They willingly pay him homage. They admire him. They wonder after him. They glorify him. They worship him. People put their trust in him as they do in a god. They expect everything from him. They deem nothing too wonderful for him. They look upon him as their god; and everywhere they make images of him, and worship the image of the beast. The beast, therefore, had a glorious dominion. And it seemed indeed as if the last millennium of peace and bliss had come under his rule upon the world of man. He had control over all things, − control over commerce and industry, control over science and art, control over philosophy and religion. And for all these different spheres he freely issued his laws. And those who refused to obey them he banished from the kingdom, made them social outcasts, so that they could occupy no position, find no job, could neither buy nor sell, were miserable and poor. That is implied in the throne, in the dominion and royal authority and power of the beast.

But now the fifth vial is poured out upon that throne. And the result is, so our text tells us, that his dominion is darkened. There are some interpreters who have it that "dominion" here must be taken in the sense of territory, the kingdom as the territory over which the beast rules. And then the darkness is to be taken as a darkness in nature. But I do not think so. In the first place, this is little to be harmonized with the scorching heat of the sun, which shall continue, no doubt, also at this time. But besides, the entire contents of this fifth vial is against this interpretation. The meaning evidently is that the dominion of the beast is darkened, his glory wanes, his authority is questioned, his power ceases to be, his appearance ceases to inspire with awe and confidence. People and nations lose their trust in the beast. They used to worship him; they now begin to doubt his divinity. They used to shout, "Who can make war with the beast?" They now are not so sure of his unconquerable power and his unconquerable nature. They used to admire him. They now withhold their admiration. A sort of political unrest is noticeable in the dominion of the beast, so that the power of his kingdom is darkened.

This is, in the first place, in harmony with the correspondence between the fifth vial and the fifth trumpet. That trumpet spoke of the fierce locusts which rose out of the abyss, the result of which was a terrible, agonizing pessimism, so that men sought death and could not find it. The same is the case here. People had put all their trust in the antichristian kingdom and power. In that kingdom there was plenty and peace and blessing. And they deemed nothing too wonderful for Man to perform. They worshipped the beast and his image. They put their trust in him. But now they lose the object of their hope. They lose their god. The domain of the beast is darkened, and the nations gradually lose their trust in the only object of their hope. For years and years they had hoped for this kingdom. For years and years they had struggled for its establishment. And for a time it seemed possible to reach happiness and bliss without the God of heaven and without His Christ. But now all is vain. Also this hope they lose, but not in order to turn to the true God in repentance. No, they blaspheme the God of heaven. And therefore they are now without any object in which they can put their trust. They are now literally without God in the world. And hence, their despair, their complete hopelessness is coming on as the kingdom is darkened and the authority of what they looked upon as their god is questioned. They gnaw their tongues because of their trouble and their pain and their despair.

In the second place, this is also entirely in harmony with the effect of the first four vials. As we have said before, the first four vials prepare the way for the last three. They constitute the plagues in nature which deprive the Antichrist and his kingdom of their material blessings. Instead of plenty and blessing there is now suffering and want and hunger and thirst and sickness. And since the people admired the beast especially because of the material blessings that were connected with his reign, it is but natural that his dominion gradually wanes as the plagues in nature become more and more severe. And therefore, the fifth plague brings disturbance over the reign of Antichrist. People are in despair and pain, partly because of the plagues in the nature, partly because they have lost and are losing their only god. And they blaspheme the God of heaven Who hath power over these plagues.

How The Nations Are Gathered For This Battle

Exactly to what extent this darkening of the throne of the beast will be and just what shall take place at that time is not told us. But clear it seems to be that the Christian nations, which, of course, are the antichristian nations proper, are affected first of all. Perhaps we must picture the relation thus, that in course of time one of the Christian, or civilized, nations has gained control and predominance over the other nations of the antichristian confederacy, so that there the throne of the beast, the government of the kingdom, is seated. Then it is possible that the rest of the civilized nations, especially under the influence of the plagues which come in the first four vials, rise against this throne of the beast and free themselves from antichristian dominion, thus darkening the throne of the beast. In the future we shall read more about this. Now it is plain that the dominion of the antichristian kingdom has lost its hold, first of all, upon the nominally Christian nations, which are the nations of Antichrist proper.

But it is not only these that are affected. On the contrary, there are still the other nations, the nations that live outside of the sphere of Christianity in its outward sense, the nations that live at the four corners of the earth, Gog and Magog. By these are meant all those nations that have never played a part in the history of the world, the millions and millions of Chinese and Japanese, and the inhabitants of India and Africa and Australia. Always they have lived outside of the pale of history proper, and never have they played any appreciable part in that history of the world. When we speak of the history of the world, we refer to the history of but very few nations. And since the coming of Christ, we refer to the nations that have come under the influence of Christianity. The only nations that might possibly form an exception in this respect are the Mohammedans. But for the rest, all the pagan world has had no part in the history of man and of the world. Also these nations have belonged to the antichristian kingdom outwardly. They have naturally somewhat shared in its prosperity, and have at the same time subjected themselves outwardly. But they never formed an integral part of the dominion, and on the whole they simply followed their pagan customs and religions. They lived in separation and isolation, more or less. But the time shall come, so Scripture tells us more than once, when also these nations shall take a definite stand and rise up against God Almighty and His Anointed for battle, in order that they and their gods may have dominion of the world. And that time has come with the sixth and seventh vials.

The sixth vial is poured out on the great river Euphrates, so the text tells us. Also here we may notice the correspondence between the sixth trumpet and the sixth vial. When the sixth trumpet sounded, the four angels who were bound at the great river Euphrates were liberated, and they gathered the army of monstrous warriors from the east to battle against the nations of Christendom. Then one-third of the men were killed. But now we have the sixth vial. And that sixth vial is poured out on the great river, the river Euphrates. But this time it is completely dried up, and that for the purpose that the way might be prepared for the kings who come from the sun-rising, or from the east.

It is not necessary to explain again in detail what is the meaning of the great river Euphrates, since this was done in connection with the sixth trumpet. Let me then remind you of the fact that in the literal sense the river Euphrates, flowing through Mesopotamia and Chaldea for hundreds of miles, wide and deep, and emptying itself in the Persian Gulf, – that this river in the old dispensation formed the boundary line between the nation of Israel and the heathen nations, the boundary line, therefore, between the people of God in the outward sense of the word and the nations of heathendom. As such it is a fit symbol of the boundary line between the Christian nations and the heathen nations in the new dispensation, the line of demarcation and separation between Christendom and Gog and Magog. At this time, when Christendom shall be Antichristendom, it will naturally be the boundary line between Antichrist and the nations that live on the four corners of the earth. Some take it that with this sixth vial the river Euphrates shall be literally dried up, so that the nations may pass through it. Of course, there is nothing against such an explanation. It is very well possible for God to do so if it pleases Him. No one can doubt this. But this is not very likely the explanation. Evidently we again must think of symbolism in connection with the sixth vial. If the nations wish to gather for battle, a river would surely not keep them from it, even if it is never dried up. And therefore, the drying up of the river merely refers to the removal of all obstacles from the external point of view. There shall come a time when these nations on the four corners of the earth shall be capable of meeting the armies of the civilized world. They shall gradually be prepared, till all external obstacles shall have been removed.

At the same time, however, there is a spiritual agency at work among these nations. We read: "And I saw three unclean spirits like frogs come out of the mouth of the dragon, and out of the mouth of the beast, and out of the mouth of the false prophet. For they are spirits of devils, working miracles."

Many attempts have been made to ascertain definitely what these three evil and unclean spirits might signify. And often they have had personal application. But naturally the very question is irrelevant, is at least impossible to be answered definitely from the text. And therefore the answers which have been suggested are naturally absurd. All we can do is follow the text and gather from it the information that it affords.

In the first place, it tells us that the unclean spirits proceed from the mouth of the infernal trinity, – the dragon, the beast, and the false prophet. The dragon, you recognize, is the devil, the old serpent, who is after all the real king over the kingdom of Antichrist. The beast is the monster with its ten horns and seven heads, Antichrist from its political aspect. And the false prophet is the same as the second beast, who has the two horns, as a lamb, but speaks like the dragon. And we may also remember that the relation between these three is such that the beast, or Antichrist, is the representative of the dragon upon the earth, exists for him and works for him, and that the false prophet in turn labors and deceives the nations in behalf of the beast and its image. The Christian nations have been deceived by their work. They make an image for the beast, and worship him. They are filled with enmity against God and His Christ and His saints. But the nations that live at the four corners of the earth are not so easily converted. They do not understand this establishment of the kingdom of Antichrist. They are heathen. They serve their idols. They cannot erect the image of the beast and fall down before it. And therefore the infernal trinity work together to convert the whole world for Antichristendom. Just as it is the task of Christianity to preach the gospel to all nations, so that they all may bow before the God of heaven and His Christ, so the dragon and the beast and the false prophet cannot rest before all the nations of the earth have come under the influence of their antichristian principles. The principles of that kingdom must be spread. They must be disseminated among the Gentiles. They must be preached far and wide over the whole world, so that finally all the world shall have been won for Antichrist. It is to my mind this antichristian missionary work which is symbolized in these unclean spirits proceeding out of the mouth of the infernal trinity. They are unclean spirits, demons in nature, naturally, for they preach opposition against God and His Christ. They spread and sow the seed of infidelity and conscious opposition against Almighty God and His people. They go forth unto the kings of the whole earth, our text tells us, evidently referring to the kings who rule at the four corners of the earth. Everywhere they preach their infernal doctrine, that the whole world may be civilized in the antichristian sense of the word. But God also uses evil spirits to reach His purpose. For the text tells us that in very fact they gather the nations for the great day of the war of God Almighty. Of course, that is not the dragon's purpose. His purpose was to gain these nations for his own kingdom. But through these evil spirits the Almighty gains His own purpose. For Christ rules the world, and rules all things for the completion of His kingdom.

What then is the relation of things?

At the same time that these evil spirits sow the seeds of hatred against Christ and against God Almighty and against His people in the hearts of all the nations outside of the pale of Christianity, the throne of the beast is darkened, and the terrible plagues, from which also Gog and Magog suffer, are upon the earth. As I have suggested before, I imagine that the darkening of the throne of the beast will consist of an uprising in the antichristian world itself among the nominally Christian nations against the central government of Antichrist. But at the same time the nations that live at the four corners of the earth shall fully wake up. They shall look upon these nominally Christian nations, that fight against the throne of the beast, as being true Christendom, against which their hearts have been filled with hatred by the three unclean spirits. They shall come up for war against the civilized nations. They shall gather their armies, and so shall the nations of Europe and America. All the world shall fly to arms.

And all the nations of the world shall gather for battle, so our text tells us, at the place which is called Armageddon. Armageddon literally means

"Mount Megiddo." Historically and geographically it is the mount situated on the great plain of Esdraelon in Issachar, near the famous valley of Jezreel. It was one of the great battle fields of Canaan. It was on that field that Josiah, the God-fearing king of Judah, was slain when he went to war against Pharaoh-Necho, king of Egypt, II Kings 23:29-30. It was there too that Ahaziah, king of Judah, fleeing together with Joram before the face of Jehu, was killed. But in connection with the words of our text it must be taken in a different significance. It was on the battlefield of Megiddo that Deborah and Barak had their great victory over the Canaanites who had opposed the people of God. Of it Deborah sings: "The kings came and fought, then fought the kings of Canaan in Taanach by the waters of Megiddo." Judges 5:19. And it is undoubtedly in the light of that historical event that the field is mentioned in this connection. Whether the last battle of the nations shall be literally fought in that neighborhood, which is very well possible, or not, fact is that the symbolical significance of the battlefield of Megiddo is such that it represents the defeat of the enemies of the kingdom of God. The unclean spirits, therefore, although their purpose is far different, gather the armies of the nations on the battlefield of their final defeat by Christ and His saints. The devil is ultimately but an instrument in the hand of God to work his own destruction. And all things must work together in such a way that the plan of the Almighty is carried out to the full.

The Outcome Of This Battle

There, then, are the nations gathered. It is the last battle which shall ever be fought on earth. It is the battle which shall finish all. It is the battle which shall lead to the destruction of all the enemies of God and of His Anointed. Terrible is the bloodshed that shall then be witnessed. And the nations shall destroy one another. They are in the great winepress of the wrath of God.

But still more: as they are battling, the seventh vial is poured out into the air, and a voice is heard, "It is finished." The voice proceeds from the temple of heaven, from the throne. It is no doubt the voice of Christ that is here heard. Once before He used these very words, when the battle was finished in principle on the bloody cross. Then He fought the battle as the suffering Servant, and finished it. But since then He has been exalted. And as the exalted Son of Man He continued the work throughout the ages of the new dispensation. The book with its seven seals is given Him, in order that He might have all power in heaven and on earth. Seal after seal has been broken. Trumpet after trumpet has been blown. Vial after vial has been poured out. All history has been controlled by Him from year to year and from stage to stage, till the last vial is poured out and the last scene is to take place on the stage of history, the scene which will prepare the earth for the descent of the New Jerusalem. It is finished.

The last vial is poured out. As the nations are gathered in the winepress of the wrath of God, battling one another to death, the very atmosphere is filled with the wrath of God. The devils, who find their abode in that air, are defeated forever. And nature is angry with terrible convulsions. There are terrific lightnings and thunders and voices. The sun is darkened, and the moon appears blood red. A great and terrible earthquake cracks the earth, so that Babylon is split and destroyed and the cities of the nations are wiped out, — an earthquake as never before, as long as man lived on earth. And to finish all, great hail falls from heaven, making the destruction complete. Every hailstone weighs a talent, that is, approximately one hundred pounds. Just imagine the scene. It is the great day of the wrath of God. All the nations are gathered. They fight and rage, wild with the despair of their forlorn kingdom. They are at each other's throats in fury, filled with the wrath of God. Darkness prevails. The moon by night looks like blood. Tremendous hailstones begin to fall, crushing them to death. An earthquake destroys their cities. Mountains are rooted out of their place. The very surface of the earth is changing. Islands flee away. And in the midst of this universal destruction, from which no one shall escape, are heard the cursings and blasphemies of a wicked race, rebellious to the very last. No indeed, there is no repentance except through the grace of God. God is fully justified in this last scene of human history. Sin is rebellion, hatred against the God of heaven!

Strikingly, this is the fulfillment of what was prophesied by Ezekiel in Old Testament symbolism. In Ezekiel we read: "And the word of the Lord came unto me, saying, Son of man, set thy face against Gog, the land of Magog, the chief prince of Meshech and Tubal, and prophesy against him, And say, Thus saith the Lord God; Behold, I am against thee, O Gog, the chief prince of Meshech and Tubal: And I will turn thee back, and put hooks into thy jaws, and I will bring thee forth, and all thine army, horses and horsemen, all of them clothed with all sorts of armour, even a great company with bucklers and shields, all of them handling swords: Persia, Ethiopia, and Libya with them; all of them with shield and helmet:

Gomer, and all his bands; the house of Togarmah of the north quarters, and all his bands: and many people with thee.... It shall also come to pass, that at the same time shall things come into thy mind, and thou shalt think an evil thought: And thou shalt say, I will go up to the land of unwalled villages; I will go to them that are at rest, that dwell safely, all of them dwelling without walls, and having neither bars nor gates, To take a spoil, and to take a prey; to turn thine hand upon the desolate places that are now inhabited, and upon the people that are gathered out of the nations, which have gotten cattle and goods, that dwell in the midst of the land.... And it shall come to pass at the same time when Gog shall come against the land of Israel, saith the Lord God, that my fury shall come up in my face. For in my jealousy and in the fire of my wrath have I spoken, Surely in that day there shall be a great shaking in the land of Israel; So that the fishes of the sea, and the fowls of the heaven, and the beasts of the field, and all creeping things that creep upon the earth, and all the men that are upon the face of the earth, shall shake at my presence, and the mountains shall be thrown down, and the steep places shall fall, and every wall shall fall to the ground. And I will call for a sword against him throughout all my mountains, saith the Lord God: every man's sword shall be against his brother. And I will plead against him with pestilence and with blood; and I will rain upon him, and upon his bands, and upon the many people that are with him, an overflowing rain, and great hailstones, fire, and brimstone," (Ezekiel 38:1-6, 10-12, 18-22).

Thus shall the evil intentions of the nations and of the beast and of the dragon be turned against themselves.

In that last battle the people of God shall have no part. They shall have been taken away. A beautiful indication is given us once more of this truth in the fifteenth verse of this chapter, where the Lord so wonderfully warns: "Behold, I come as a thief. Blessed is he that watcheth, and keepeth his garments, lest he walk naked, and they see his shame." The Lord will come as a thief, unexpectedly, unawares, with His judgments, but also to take His people away from the earth. He shall come and go, and no one shall have noticed that He shall have been. The nations shall continue to rage and to blaspheme the God of heaven; but the church of God shall be upon earth no more. Therefore the chapter is a warning to watch, to look for the coming of the Lord, when all these things shall come to pass. We are making history fast, especially in the last years. And therefore, we must keep our garments clean, watch out for the defilement of Antichrist, refuse to have anything to do with him, watch as children of light, expecting the day of our Lord Jesus Christ, so that we may be faithful even unto the end; and no one shall take our crown.

Chapter XL

Babylon, The Bride Of Antichrist

(Revelation 17:1-6)

1 And there came one of the seven angels which had the seven vials, and talked with me, saying unto me, Come hither; I will shew unto thee the judgment of the great whore that sitteth upon many waters:
2 With whom the kings of the earth have committed fornication, and the inhabitants of the earth have been made drunk with the wine of her fornication.
3 So he carried me away in the spirit into the wilderness: and I saw a woman sit upon a scarlet coloured beast, full of names of blasphemy, having seven heads and ten horns.
4 And the woman was arrayed in purple and scarlet colour, and decked with gold and precious stones and pearls, having a golden cup in her hand full of abominations and filthiness of her fornication:
5 And upon her forehead was a name written, MYSTERY, BABYLON THE GREAT, THE MOTHER OF HARLOTS AND ABOMINATIONS OF THE EARTH.
6 And I saw the woman drunken with the blood of the saints, and with the blood of the martyrs of Jesus: and when I saw her, I wondered with great admiration.

Chapters 17 and 18 of the Book of Revelation present us with a description of the great harlot and of her fall.

It is of the utmost significance that we obtain as clear a conception of this picture, of the appearance and the essential character of this harlot, as possible. In the first place, this is necessary for the clear and definite understanding of the rest of the Book of Revelation. But, in the second place, this clear conception of Babylon and her essential significance is also necessary for a practical reason. The voice comes to the people of God in the eighteenth chapter, "Come out of her, my people, that ye be not partakers of her sins, and that ye receive not of her plagues," a voice which ultimately may signify an irresistible, effectual call into everlasting glory, the final deliverance of the church of Christ, when the days shall be shortened, but which undoubtedly bears the practical significance that the people of God may never have fellowship with this Babylon in the world. And in order to go out of her and refuse to have fellowship with her we must be able to discern her also among the many movements of our own day. Hence, the clear understanding of the character and manifestation of Babylon, the great harlot, is of extreme practical importance.

At the same time, however, we may as well confess that this is one of the most difficult passages of the entire Book of Revelation to understand, a passage which for that very reason has found many interpreters and has been favored with as many different interpretations. By far the most efficient method would be that of treating the entire portion in just one chapter, so that you might immediately have a clear conception of the whole. But because of the abundance of material, this is a practical impossibility. We cannot treat Chapters 17 and 18 in one chapter. And therefore we shall have to divide our material, and gradually explain these two chapters, carefully reviewing what we had before, in the former exposition of this book, so that finally we may obtain a clear conception of the whole. And therefore we start with verses 1 to 6 of Chapter 17.

The Problem Of Interpretation

By way of introduction, I must still caution you against the possibility of introducing an imaginary and false time element into these two chapters which speak of the fall of Babylon. We are so naturally and easily inclined to picture to our mind the events that are recorded and the realization of the various prophecies in this book as occurring in the same order in which they are revealed in the Book of Revelation. More than once we have warned you against such a conception of the book which we are discussing. But the same caution is called for again in this particular connection. You must not picture the course of events thus, that what is revealed in Chapters 17 and 18 chronologically follows the events pictured in Chapter 16: for this is evidently not the case. As we have remarked in the previous chapter, after Chapter 16 there is no history any more. All has been finished. The seven vials have been poured out. Antichrist has been at battle with Gog and Magog on Armageddon, and they have been in the winepress of the wrath of God. History, therefore, has come to an end. There is no Babylon any more. For also of its destruction we read in connection with the seven vials. Nor shall she ever receive a chance to develop herself anew. For this very evident reason, which must be plain to all, it is an impossibility to conceive of the events pictured in the two chapters we must now discuss as chronologically following those pictured in Chapter 16. There is but one possibility; and that is to conceive of these two chapters as presenting a more detailed picture of something which we have already been told in broad outline before. In fact, we are presented with a detailed portraiture of Babylon and her fall, of the battle of Armageddon, of the last attempt of Satan to deceive the nations which are called Gog and Magog in Scripture and which live at the four corners of the earth, and, finally, of the beautiful New Jerusalem which comes down from heaven from God Almighty.

Of Babylon and her destruction we have read before. Essentially we have met her in Chapter 11, where she still appears as the outward holy city, but where her very name is designated as being identical with that of Sodom and Gomorrah, where the Lord was crucified. Jerusalem no doubt appears in that chapter as the city which essentially is Babylonian in character and persecutes the witnesses of Jesus. Again, we read of her destruction already in Chapter 14, verse 8, where it is announced by the angel as imminent when he cries, "Babylon is fallen, is fallen, that great city, because she made all nations drink of the wine of the wrath of her fornication." And in our previous discourse, in connection with the pouring out of the seventh vial, we also met with her destruction. For there it was said: "And the great city was divided into three parts, and the cities of the nations fell: and great Babylon came in remembrance before God, to give unto her the cup of the wine of the fierceness of his wrath." It is, of course, that same Babylon of which we meet a description rather in detail in the words of the present chapter and of the passage we are discussing now.

In the second place, it may be interesting to review some of the interpretations which have been presented of this great harlot. In doing so we shall find that interpreters generally have struggled to overcome the difficulty that this Babylon is pictured both as a woman and as a city, but have but ill succeeded in interpreting it.

There are interpretations which have it that this Babylon is nothing else than the city of Rome as it existed at the time of John, — the mighty capital of the powerful Roman Empire at that time, the city which indeed became guilty of the blood of many of the children of God who held the testimony of Jesus. This interpretation they base on verse 9, where we read that the seven heads of the beast on which the harlot sitteth are seven mountains on which the woman sitteth. The city of Rome is famous for its being built on seven hills. And these are indicated in the verse that we just cited. There are others who claim that in this woman we must see the power of the papacy as finding its center in the papal see, and therefore, again in the city of Rome. The Romish Church especially through the papacy rules over the kings of the earth. She spoke words of blasphemy indeed, and made kings and nations drunk with the wine of her spiritual fornications. She persecuted the church and the saints of Christ Jesus, and her hands are red with the blood of the saints. In all these respects she surely answers the description given of her in the text. And therefore, we must surely think of the Roman Catholic Church of all ages, according to these interpretations. Still others find in this Babylon nothing but a picture of the false church as she has apostatized from Jesus Christ and from the truth of the Word of God and become a servant of Satan and Antichrist: the counterfeit church, or counterfeit Christianity in general. And there are even those who find in Babylon the picture of the world-city as we know it today, so that London and Paris and New York and Chicago and many other large towns are individual examples of this general picture that is called Babylon in our passage. These world-cities, so they say, are the great centers of religion and philosophy, of science and art, of commerce and industry. And they have their influence for evil felt all over the known world. Thus they present the picture of the harlot who commits fornication with all the nations of the earth.

All these interpretations struggle, evidently, to harmonize the presentation of the woman-harlot with that of the prosperous city as indicated in the text. But it seems to me that none of these interpretations succeeds entirely. It certainly will not do simply to explain that Babylon is the city of Rome. For, in the first place, it is not true that the text in verse 9 warrants that conclusion. For, first of all, it may not escape our attention that the text further interprets these seven mountains as being seven kings. And besides, Rome was built, if at all, not on seven mountains, but simply on seven hills. But besides, this interpretation evidently leaves the symbolism of the woman, by which evidently the church is indicated, altogether out of sight. Babylon is a city, surely; but it is also a woman. And the two must in some way be harmonized. For the same reason it cannot indicate simply the counterfeit church, whether it is the papal Rome or the false church in general. For she is not merely the church, but also the city, and is very definitely pictured as a city which is the center of commerce and industry and science and art, admired by all the great of the world. Chapter 18 can never be explained on this basis. And therefore, both of these elements we must continually bear in mind. And whether we shall at all gain a conception of Babylon the great will depend upon our being able to harmonize the idea of the woman and the idea of the city.

The Pretentious Appearance Of The Whore

First of all, then, let us study her pretentious appearance as the woman. Evidently the text makes a distinction between her outward appearance and her essential character, a distinction which comes down to this, that she appears as a woman, but that her essential character, as expressed in her mysterious name, is that of a city, named Babylon.

One of the seven angels who had the seven vials and poured them out on the earth, so John tells us, spoke to him and led him into a wilderness, in order that he might see and understand the mystery of the great harlot and witness her judgment. The wilderness in this case may be taken as the proper abode of this woman. It must not be connected with the wilderness into which the church fled after the exaltation of Christ. The wilderness is a picture of the desolation caused by sin, and as such the proper abode for all that exalts itself against the living God and loves unrighteousness. At the same time, this wilderness, I take it, is already prophetic of the judgment this harlot, beautifully arrayed, may expect. In that wilderness, then, John beholds a woman seated on a scarlet colored beast, with seven heads and ten horns, and full of names of blasphemy. To this beast we shall not pay attention just now, seeing that he is explained in the next portion of this chapter. The woman now draws our attention. She is richly and beautifully arrayed with all that is glittering and luxurious in the world, being decked with precious stones and pearls and arrayed in purple and scarlet, while holding in her hand a golden cup. She certainly makes the impression of being rich and powerful, enveloped in a halo of worldly glory. The beast carries her, and is evidently controlled by her. And on her forehead she bears a name, MYSTERY, BABYLON THE GREAT, THE MOTHER OF HARLOTS AND ABOMINATIONS OF THE EARTH. Such is the picture. And we are told that John was amazed and wondered with great wonder at the sight of her.

If you ask who this woman is, it may be observed, in the first place, that the woman in Scripture is continually the symbol of the church of God and of God's covenant people in the external sense of the word.

Surely, essentially only the true spiritual people of God are His bride, are the wife of Jehovah, those who stand on the basis of faithfulness in covenant relation to their God. Nevertheless, also the church as she appears in the present dispensation is compared to a woman, a married woman, the wife of Jehovah.

In the Old Testament we find this picture time and again, that Israel as a nation, the covenant people in the outward sense, are called Jehovah's wife. He has married her, and she stands in relation of a covenant to Him, pledged to be faithful to her husband. In the Song of Solomon we find throughout that the entire symbolism of the book is based on this very idea, that the church is the bride of Christ. And in the New Testament we meet with this same relation repeatedly. The apostle Paul writes to the church in Ephesus: "Husbands, love your wives, even as Christ also loved the church, and gave himself for it; That he might sanctify and cleanse it with the washing of water by the word, That he might present it to himself a glorious church, not having spot, or wrinkle, or any such thing; but that it should be holy and without blemish." And after he has spoken of this relation between man and wife in the succeeding verses, he concludes, "This is a great mystery: but I speak concerning Christ and the church," (Ephesians 5:25-32).

In the nineteenth chapter of this same Book of Revelation we find the great multitude in glory singing at the eve of the marriage supper of the Lamb: "Let us be glad and rejoice, and give honour to him: for the marriage of the Lamb is come, and his wife hath made herself ready. And to her was granted that she should be arrayed in fine linen, clean and white: for the fine linen is the righteousness of saints," (Revelation 19:7, 8). And in the twenty-first chapter of the Book of Revelation the same idea is expressed: "And there came unto me one of the seven angels which had the seven vials full of the seven last plagues, and talked with me, saying, Come hither, I will shew thee the bride, the Lamb's wife," (Revelation 21:9). And very strikingly, also here the bride, the wife of the Lamb, is a city. For the passage continues, vs. 10: "And he carried me away in the spirit to a great and high mountain, and shewed me that great city, the holy Jerusalem, descending out of heaven from God." Also there the church is the bride, but at the same time a city. Or let me remind you of the picture which was given in Chapter 12 of this book. Also there the church was presented as a woman, clothed with the sun, and the moon under her feet. Also there the woman was a mother, just as she is here.

Only, in that connection she appears as the mother of the Great Seed and the mother of believers. And therefore, we first of all reach the conclusion that this woman is the church as she appears on earth. It may cause a little astonishment; but also John was astonished. It is when we bear in mind this fact that we can understand why John was astonished with such great amazement. He had seen this woman as the church before. Her general features were still the same. Only she is now allied with the scarlet colored beast that carries her: and that is the cause undoubtedly of John's astonishment and wonder. The woman is the church in her historical appearance on earth.

But to this we must hasten to add that this harlot is not a portraiture of the true church, but of the false, the counterfeit church, which has apostatized from her true husband and is now committing fornication with the enemy. For in the text she is called the great harlot with whom the kings of the earth committed fornication; and they that dwell on the earth were made drunken with the wine of her fornication. In the golden cup which she holds in her hand and which is the symbol of her deceitful abominations there is nothing but the unclean things of her fornication. In a word, she is a harlot.

And what is a harlot? In the general sense of the word, the harlot is a woman who sells that which is her characteristic honor and glory and lives in dissipation, a woman without honor, who lives in most intimate relation and intercourse with men outside of the sacred bond of marriage. But in Scripture, and especially in this connection, a harlot is something more: it is generally the woman who has been married, who has sworn faith and love in all things to her rightful husband once, but has shamefully forsaken him in order to whore after other men, strangers. She is the unfaithful, the deceitful woman, who breaks the most sacred pledge. And spiritually, fornication and harlotry in Scripture indicate the breaking of the covenant, the departure from the ways of Jehovah and the service of other gods. As such it appears time and again in the Old Testament. In Ezekiel 16:8-22 we read of Israel as the wife of Jehovah, prepared and blessed by Him, but whoring after other gods: "Now when I passed by thee, and looked upon thee, behold, thy time was the time of love; and I spread my skirt over thee, and covered thy nakedness: yea, I sware unto thee, and entered into a covenant with thee, saith the Lord God, and thou becamest mine. Then washed I thee with water; yea, I throughly washed away thy blood from thee, and I anointed thee with oil. I clothed thee also with broidered work, and shod thee with badgers' skin, and I girded thee about with fine linen, and I covered thee with silk. I decked thee also with ornaments, and I put bracelets upon thy hands, and a chain on thy neck. And I put a jewel on thy forehead, and earrings in thine ears, and a beautiful crown upon thine head. Thus wast thou decked with gold and silver; and thy raiment was of fine linen, and silk, and broidered work; thou didst eat fine flour, and honey, and oil: and thou wast exceeding beautiful, and thou didst prosper into a kingdom. And thy renown went forth among the heathen for thy beauty: for it was perfect through my comeliness, which I had put upon thee, saith the Lord God. But thou didst trust in thine own beauty, and playedst the harlot because of thy renown, and pouredst out thy fornications on every one that passed by; his it was. And of thy garments thou didst take, and deckedst thy high places with divers colours, and playedst the harlot thereupon: the like things shall not come, neither shall it be so. Thou hast also taken thy fair jewels of my gold and of my silver, which I had given thee, and madest to thyself images of men, and didst commit whoredom with them, And tookest thy broidered garments, and coveredst them: and thou hast set mine oil and mine incense before them. My meat also which I gave thee, fine flour, and oil, and honey, wherewith I fed thee, thou hast even set it before them for a sweet savour: and thus it was saith the Lord God. Moreover thou hast taken thy sons and thy daughters, whom thou hast borne unto me, and these hast thou sacrificed unto them to be devoured. Is this of thy whoredoms a small matter, That thou hast slain my children, and delivered them to cause them to pass through the fire for them? And in all thine abominations and thy whoredoms thou hast not remembered the days of thy youth, when thou wast naked and bare, and wast polluted in thy blood." A complete picture you have in this passage of the spiritual harlot, the covenant people of God in the outward sense, blessed with all the blessings of the covenant, but employing them in the service of strange gods and departing from the ways of Jehovah, their rightful husband. The same truth lies at the basis of the prophecy of Hosea, where the prophet receives the command that he must take unto himself a wife of whoredoms and children of whoredoms, in order to symbolize the harlotry of Israel, the covenant people of Jehovah. And therefore, in the spiritual sense a harlot is one who has belonged to Jehovah in the external sense of the word, was in covenant relation with Him, was blessed by Him, but deceitfully has broken her pledge and now sacrifices her honor unto other gods.

In the words of our text, therefore, we have a picture of the harlot church, the false church, the counterfeit church. For even as the devil aims at establishing a counterfeit kingdom, so he also establishes a counterfeit church. Naturally! We have told you before that he uses all the institutions which God has placed on earth in this dispensation for the maintenance and establishment of his kingdom, that he employs them all for his own purpose and for the propagation of his own principle. The same is true of the church. Also the church as an institution in this dispensation, designed to be the army of the kingdom,— also that church the devil shrewdly employs in his service. And the result is that a counterfeit church, the harlot church, is established. The true church is the spiritual bride of Christ, ingrafted into Him by a true faith, and through Him stands in covenant relation with the Lord Jehovah. But that counterfeit church is the church which still bears the name of church, still appears as the church in the world, still claims or pretends to be the church, outwardly also looks like the church, has its ministers and sacraments, the preaching of the Word and teaching, and all kinds of institutions and societies besides, but employs all the blessings she has outwardly received in the service of Antichrist, and not in the service of Jehovah. Her ministers preach for Antichrist. The officebearers work for Antichrist. Publicly she displays all the signs of Antichrist, and all her members she educates to work for the dragon and his kingdom. She enjoys the favor and the good will of the world, of the great and the mighty and the strong and the rich in the world. And they bless and deck her with all kinds of precious jewels and gold. She becomes great and powerful. And the more she labors in the interest of the antichristian kingdom, the more she will enjoy the favor of the dragon: for she is nothing but his harlot, and allows herself to be the instrument of Antichrist.

That this is true is plain from the description that is given of her in the text. For she is called the harlot, and is described as one who commits fornication with the great of the earth and with all that dwell in the world. That this is true is plain also from the fact that she is sitting on the scarlet beast with his seven heads and ten horns, evidently implying that she is borne by the power of Antichrist, and, at the same time, controls that power with her fascinating fornications. That this is true, finally, is also plain from the fact that of her the terrible sentence is expressed that she is fairly drunken with the blood of the saints. Surely, this woman is the church as she appears on earth; but it is the false church, rapidly developing in our own time. It is the church that has abandoned the truth of the Word of God, that laughs about the truth of the atonement of Christ and tramples under foot the blood of the new covenant. Every pledge with her Lord and covenant God she has broken. And even those who do remain faithful she kills in her hatred.

Her Mystic Character

But this is not all. For this woman, representing the counterfeit or false church, is also represented to us as a city. We read that this woman bears a name on her forehead, "MYSTERY, BABYLON THE GREAT, THE MOTHER OF THE HARLOTS AND OF THE ABOMINATIONS OF THE EARTH."

In regard to this name, let us observe, in the first place, that the name in Scripture is always expressive of one's real being. And therefore, we learn that the real being of this woman is that of a city, and specifically of Babylon. In the second place, note that in this case the name is called "Mystery." A mystery is that which is concealed, which is hidden from view, which does not reveal itself on the surface. So it is here: not so much because the woman bears the name of a city, — for that might be very well expected of her, as we shall see, — but because the name of that city is Babylon. We would not expect the name of this Babylon, no more than we would expect her to be seated on this scarlet colored beast. She appears as the church. If we were bidden to guess the name of this woman as she appears, we would say her name is Church, Christianity, the Covenant People. Or, if we would guess her name as to her essential and future character, we would say, "This is Jerusalem, the Holy City, the bride of Christ." But this is not the case. This woman appears as the church; but she is the false church. She bears the appearance of Jerusalem, the Holy City, the bride of Christ; but in essence she is nothing but Babylon. That is her real nature.

As to the significance of the name as such, we can be brief. Babylon stands in Scripture for all that opposes the kingdom of God. It stands for the initiation of the kingdom of Antichrist in remotest past times under the mighty Nimrod. And if God had not prevented it by the confusion of speech, she would have succeeded then already in establishing the outward kingdom of Antichrist. She is the capital of the kingdom of oppression for

the people of God, which always stood inimical over against the kingdom
of God even in the Old Testament. In a word, Babylon is a name which
suggests a center of the kingdom of the dragon. And therefore, this
woman, which is a harlot church and the mother and propagator of all
spiritual harlotry, — this woman is essentially the center of the
antichristian world power, and shall in the future reveal herself as such.

Strange this may seem at first sight. Yet, at a second consideration this
is but perfectly natural. The figure of the woman changes ultimately into
that of a great city which controls the affairs of the world and is a center
of all the movements and science and art and literature and commerce and
industry in all the earth. In a word, the figure of this woman, of this
harlot-church, changes into that of the city which shall be the center and
the chief power in the antichristian kingdom.

But, as I say, this need not surprise us in the least. The same is true of
the true church. She ultimately appears as the New Jerusalem, that comes
down out of heaven from God. The church that is in this dispensation, the
woman, the bride of Christ, is at the same time destined to be the power in
control ultimately of the new heaven and of the new earth, destined to
reign with Christ forever in the glorious city, the New Jerusalem. The real,
the mystical character of the church is that of a city, the glorious city that
shall be the center of the new creation, of the kingdom of Christ in glory.
The same now is true of the false church. She appears as the woman; in
reality she is also a city. This false church, with all her harlotry and power,
shall ultimately reveal herself as **the power** in the kingdom of Antichrist.
Essentially she is one with Antichrist. Gradually she shall reveal her
character more clearly. Gradually her bridal alliance with the opponent of
Christ shall be brought to light. And when once the beast shall reign
supreme for a time and shall actually have succeeded in establishing his
glorious kingdom, it will be that false Christianity, the harlot-church, that
shall be the center of its dominion.

Her Historical Realization

If you ask how this shall be historically realized, the answer in our time,
it seems to me, cannot be so very difficult. According to the apostle Paul,
before the Man of Sin can reveal himself, a great apostasy must take place,
apostasy from the true church. That is, the false church will openly reveal
herself as such, will openly separate herself from all that calls itself after
the true and living Christ, not so much in name, but in very fact. The

church shall deny the Christ, shall trample under foot the blood of Christ, shall invent a religion, a Christianity, of its own, and thus shall become a mighty, apostate church, calling itself Christianity, and in reality being related to the kingdom of Antichrist. That mighty, apostate church shall naturally embrace all that calls itself Christendom but is not. It shall embrace and control all the so-called Christian world and ultimately be perfectly identified with the kingdom of Antichrist. It is not at all inconceivable, it is indeed in perfect harmony with the picture given in the text, that this apostate Christendom shall erect a center in some great world-city, a literal city, with all the modern conveniences and products of science and art conceivable. A city, it shall be, which is a center in every respect, a city of science and philosophy and religion, a city which is the center of the antichristian kingdom, thoroughly imbued with the harlotry of the apostate church. Literally the woman shall thus merge into a kingdom, with the city whose name is mystically Babylon in the center. And Christianity shall have become antichristianity to the core.

That movement is in the air today. It presses itself forward at every corner and from various angles. The church must do away with all creeds and doctrine, so we hear today. And I have no doubt but she will do so, nay, even to a large extent has done so already. And having done away with all doctrine, she must labor for her own reconstruction and for the reconstruction of the entire world. She must unite. Denominationalism must have an end. All churches of all kinds of creeds and doctrines and different shades of belief must become literally one. Catholic and Protestant, Jew and Gentile, – all must unite in the one great purpose, the reconstruction of the world. This world must become a suitable place to live in for all men. The blessings of this world must become the blessings of all.

And therefore the word that is so warningly spoken to the true church I will sound in your ears, namely: "Come out of her, my people, and have no fellowship with her sins." The great amalgamation movement that is in the air today is not of Christ and not of the true church, but is of the dragon and of Antichrist. And to go along with it will mean a loss of the truth, a loss of all that is sacred and dear, a loss of the Christ Himself. Stand, therefore, and watch, that ye may have no fellowship with the sins of Babylon.

Chapter XLI

The Mystery Of The Beast

(Revelation 17:7-14)

7 And the angel said unto me, Wherefore didst thou marvel? I will tell thee the mystery of the woman, and of the beast that carrieth her, which hath the seven heads and ten horns.

8 The beast that thou sawest was, and is not; and shall ascend out of the bottomless pit, and go into perdition: and they that dwell on the earth shall wonder, whose names were not written in the book of life from the foundation of the world, when they behold the beast that was, and is not, and yet is.

9 And here is the mind which hath wisdom. The seven heads are seven mountains, on which the woman sitteth.

10 And there are seven kings: five are fallen, and one is, and the other is not yet come; and when he cometh, he must continue a short space.

11 And the beast that was, and is not, even he is the eighth, and is of the seven, and goeth into perdition.

12 And the ten horns which thou sawest are ten kings, which have received no kingdom as yet; but receive power as kings one hour with the beast.

13 These have one mind, and shall give their power and strength unto the beast.

14 These shall make war with the Lamb, and the Lamb shall overcome them: for he is Lord of lords, and King of kings: and they that are with him are called, and chosen, and faithful.

Let us, first of all, have a little review.

Babylon's picture we have tried to draw in the preceding. In all the various attempts and interpretations which have been made to make the symbol of Babylon intelligible to the minds of God's people we found the noticeable struggle to harmonize and unify in one picture the symbol of Babylon as a woman and as a city. And we also discovered that exactly in this respect they failed to a large extent. Yet we concluded that it is essential to bring about this harmony. For evidently the text pictures Babylon to us under both of these aspects. The symbol of the woman evidently indicates her historic appearance, while that of the city designates her essential and mystical character. For her name, which is Babylon, the name of a city, is Mystery. Her essential character is concealed behind the historical appearance of the woman.

As woman, Babylon is symbol of the church, in the first place, as all Scripture plainly indicates. The church, the people of God, the covenant people, appear time and again in Holy Writ under the symbol of a married woman. In the Old Testament, Israel is the wife of Jehovah, pledged to Him in sacred bond of marriage in all faith and truth. And in the New Testament, the church is the bride of Christ. Especially in the Book of Revelation, so we found, she appears time and again as the bride of Christ, appears again and again as a woman and mother both. In the twelfth chapter of this book we meet with a rather elaborate description of the church symbolized as a woman. And as the church she appears as the perfected bride of the Lamb, without spot or wrinkle. And therefore, the symbol of the woman as such is, on the basis of Scripture, nothing else than the people of God, the church of Christ, pledged to Him in faith and truth in all things.

But we found, in the second place, that this woman is a harlot, and as such representative not of the true but of the apostate church. A harlot in Scripture is a married woman who has forsaken her rightful husband, has become unfaithful, and whores after other men, who are strangers. And so is the false, or the apostate church. Committing spiritual fornication, she bears the name of church. She stands outwardly in covenant relation to the God of salvation. She enjoys all the spiritual blessings of that relation to God. But essentially she has broken the pledge of faith and truth and separated herself from the covenant God, in order to ally herself with the powers of the world and the kingdom of Antichrist. She has all the outward appearance of the church, with ministry and officebearers, with the outward signs of the Word and the sacraments. She is busy in all kinds of nominally Christian work, and has perhaps more organizations than any other local church on earth. But she denies the truth, forsakes her God and Savior, tramples under foot the blood of the new covenant. In a word, Babylon, as the harlot woman, is the apostate church in this dispensation.

Finally, we found that at first consideration it may seem strange that this woman also appears as a city. But at second thought we found that after all this is not strange whatever, if only the analogy of the true church is kept in view. Also the true church is finally pictured to us as a city, as the New Jerusalem, coming down out of heaven from God, destined to rule centrally over all the works of God in the new creation. And the same is true of the false church. In every sense of the word the work of Satan is the parallel with the works of God. Even as the ultimate purpose of God is to establish His own kingdom in glory, so the purpose of the devil is to establish his own kingdom through the power of Antichrist. And even as in God's plan the church is, as it were, the army of the kingdom on earth, but is destined to rule over the works of God in the new kingdom that is to come, so also Satan established his own counterfeit church, in order that also she may develop into a city and ultimately have control over all things in the antichristian kingdom. That city, that center of the antichristian kingdom, that shall cap the climax of apostate Christianity, shall be Babylon in character although she shall continue to claim to be the true Jerusalem. And therefore the warning voice came to us from above: "Go ye out of her, my people, that ye may have no fellowship with her sins."

And now we must make a little study of the beast that carries the woman and with which she is evidently closely allied.

The Character Of The Beast

As to the character and identity of this beast, we need not be in doubt very long. In fact, in the light of what we have discussed in the past, we have already recognized this beast as the same as the one that was pictured to us in Chapters 11 and 13. It is the antichristian world-power especially from its political point of view. It is the attempt of the devil to establish his own kingdom through the agencies of the powers that have been instituted for this present sinful world and dispensation.

That this is true is clear, in the first place, from the fact that the general description here and in Chapter 13 is the same. You will remember that in that chapter we were told of the beast who rose up out of the sea and which manifested itself as having seven heads and ten horns. So also this beast that is described in our present passage and that is carrying the woman is possessed of seven heads and ten horns. In the second place, it may be noticed that this beast has the same origin as the one pictured in Chapter 11. True, in Chapter 13 he is pictured as coming out of the sea, which symbolized the tempestuous ocean of the nations and tribes and tongues of the earth, swept on by war and revolution, while here he is pictured as coming up out of the abyss. But this is not necessarily conflicting. We must remember, in the first place, that in Chapter 11 this same beast, which is there pictured in his antagonism and hatred against the two witnesses of Jesus Christ and in his war against them, is pictured as coming up out of the abyss, just as in the passage before us. There can be no doubt about the identity of the two. The same beast is pictured all the while, in Chapters 11 and 17 as 'coming up out of the abyss, and in Chapter 13 as rising out of the sea of war and revolution-swept nations. And the difference is simply this, that in the one case he is pictured as to the idea and spiritual character. Spiritually this beast finds his origin in the abyss, in the kingdom of darkness, in the mind of the devil; and therefore he is pictured as rising up out of the abyss. But the devil realizes his kingdom, this antichristian beast, through the agency of men and in the course of history; and for that reason he is also pictured as coming up out of the sea. In both, therefore, it is the same beast. But in the one case he is pictured as being the ultimate historic result of all the uprisings and developments of the kingdoms and nations of the world, while in the other he is pictured to us in his essential and spiritual origin, namely, in the wicked mind of Satan himself.

In the third place, we immediately recognize this beast as identical with the one we have studied before because evidently his relation to the inhabitants of the earth is the same, both in regard to the saints and to the followers of Antichrist. In Chapter 13 we read that all the dwellers of the earth wondered after the beast, were surprised at his wonderful appearance, admired and worshipped him. Thus in our text we read that the inhabitants of the earth wondered at the appearance of this beast, especially in view of the fact that he was, and is not, and yet is. In Chapter 13 we read, however, that those whose names were written in the book of life of the Lamb were an exception to this rule, since they did not worship the beast, neither his image. And so do we read in our chapter that those who worship the beast are limited as to their number to those whose names are not written in the book of life from before the foundation of the world. And, finally, in Chapter 13 we read that the saints who refused to worship the beast and his image and to receive the sign of the beast on their forehead or hand were bitterly hated and maliciously persecuted, so that they could neither buy nor sell. Here we read that those who give their power to the beast are all of one mind, also in their war against the Lamb and against the called and chosen and faithful of Jesus Christ.

In general, therefore, there can be no question about the fact that here we have again a picture of the final manifestation of Antichrist, the highest development of all the power of the world, the greatest feat of the devil, the terrible and glorious kingdom that shall come in the future to make war with the Lamb and His people. It is the picture of that great, universal kingdom that shall have sway over all the nations of the world for a time and have control over all things, but that shall be the opposition kingdom against the kingdom of Jesus Christ and shall make life unbearable for the saints of Jesus.

But although the identity of this beast with the one that is mentioned in Chapter 13 is established beyond any possible doubt, yet it must not be overlooked that in our chapter he is described from a different point of view and with a different purpose. That may be regarded as plain from the simple fact that we have here once more a description of the same beast, and that rather elaborately. If the vision in this chapter were not for a different purpose and in order to show the beast from a different point of view, it would have been sufficient for the angel to explain to John that this was the same beast as the one he saw before rising up out of the sea. This, however, he does not do; but, on the contrary, he adds various details in the interpretation which have not been mentioned before. In the second place, this is plain from these details themselves. We read of this beast that "he was, and is not, and is about to come up out of the abyss," and that "he was, and is not, and shall be," and the equally mysterious words, "The beast that was, and is not, is himself also the eighth, and is of the seven." So we read in this text a detailed explanation of the historic significance of the seven heads and the ten horns. Of the seven heads we read that they are seven mountains and seven kings, of which five are fallen, one still is, and the seventh is still to come in the future, while the beast as a whole is himself an eighth kingdom, or king, and is of the seven. And of the ten horns we also read that they are ten kings who have not yet received their power, but who shall receive authority in the future and shall give their power to the beast, all being of one mind with the beast. All these apparently mysterious details are added to the information we receive in Chapter 13. And hence, it is plain that the purpose of this description is different from that in the former chapter.

That difference, it seems to me, consists in this, that in Chapter 13 the purpose was simply to picture the terrible opposition of the beast against the kingdom of the Anointed of God, while in our chapter this opposition recedes into the background. The purpose of our chapter is, in connection with Chapters 18 and 19, to reveal the historical development of the antichristian power, as well as its final defeat and descent into destruction, as are mentioned three times in the words of our present passage.

And then it is our conviction that in the heads we receive a picture of the various individual manifestations of the antichristian world-power in the history of the world, while in the ten horns we have a picture of the final formation of this power, when all the kings of the earth shall unite, being of one mind, to give their power to the beast. We must remember that in principle the beast, representing the antichristian power of the world, exists throughout the history of the world, particularly in the new dispensation. It existed in Daniel's time in the form of the Babylonian Empire; and Daniel prophesies of different forms of that same world-power that are to manifest themselves as principally opposed to the people of God. He speaks of the Persian, of the Grecian, of the Syrian and Roman power that is still to come in the future, each of which are temporary manifestations of the world-power in history, so clearly even that in Antiochus Epiphanes we may find a clear type of Antichrist in person. At any rate, the world-power as such always exists, and, characteristically, is always opposed to the people of God. Instead of being satisfied to occupy their God-ordained position in the world, they aim at absolute control and at the establishment of one grand kingdom, in which man shall be his own god. The result is that there are various successive manifestations of the world-power, and that the latter passes through different stages of development. At the same time, we must remember that none of these realizes the entire beast. None of them succeeds to establish the universal kingdom for which they strive. On the contrary, they all fail; and in so far they do not fulfill the symbol of the beast in its entirety. And, in the third place, we must also remember that this universal kingdom shall nevertheless be realized in the future, and that this complete realization of the beast shall form the ultimate outcome, the historical product, of all that have gone before.

If, therefore, you would have a full picture of this beast, of the antichristian world-power, you must not merely think of the final manifestation, but just as well of the historic process through which the beast has passed. And it is this complete picture of the beast which is drawn before our eyes in the words of our present passage. The seven heads, then, represent different stages of development through which this beast has passed in the various kingdoms which existed before its complete manifestation, while the ten horns reveal to us the final formation, or league of kings, which shall be of one mind and completely realize the ideal of the beast for a short time. And, for the same reason, we are called to study this picture of the beast, first of all, in its historical appearance, and, in the second place, from the point of view of its ultimate formation.

The Historical Development Of The Beast

As to its historical development, we must, first of all, call your attention to the apparently dark expression that the beast was, and is not, and yet shall come up out of the abyss. Three times this is repeated in the text; and therefore it will be of importance that we understand the significance of this expression.

In the first place, it must be clear to us that this is asserted of the beast as a whole. We must make a distinction between the beast in principle and the beast in its completion manifestation. And we must remember that the beast never entirely disappears from the scene of history. He is always there in some form. Even in John's time the angel interprets that one of the heads is, exists, so that also then the beast appeared in one of his heads. But the beast does not always appear in his proper and full manifestation. He does not appear in his full and complete aspect. And therefore it is of the beast as a whole that the text says that "he was, and is not, and comes up out of the abyss," or again, that "he was, and is not, and shall be."

Many have been the interpretations that have been given of this mysterious expression. It seems to us that it makes us think immediately of what we read in Chapter 13 about the death-stroke that was healed. You will remember that in that chapter we had a picture of the full manifestation of the world-power of the beast in its ultimate formation and appearance. And of that final manifestation of the beast it was said that it had been wounded to death, but that the wound was healed. At that time we referred to the kingdom of mighty Nimrod, which also aimed at universal world-power, but which was distinct from all the forms of the world-power which succeeded it in this particular, that it consisted rather of a confederation of all the different tribes and peoples which existed at the time, rather than of the dominion and aggrandizement of one particular nation at the expense of the rest. They all spoke one language. They all were of one mind. They all combined in one purpose, to establish the kingdom of the world and exalt themselves against God Almighty. But by the separation and confusion of their language and counsel that mighty dominion had received its death-stroke, a stroke, however, which shall be healed in the future, when that same world-power shall appear in the same form once more, as a great and powerful federation, as a league of nations that shall be of one mind.

If we recall this, it seems to me the interpretation of the seemingly mysterious words, "the beast that was, and is not, and shall come out of the abyss," cannot be difficult. The beast did exist also in its proper form at the time of the building of the tower of Babel. Then a great and mighty federation must have been formed, for they were already building their central city and tower. Then they were of one mind and purpose. Then the beast revealed himself in his proper form. And therefore, in that sense the angel can say, "The beast that was...." It was in the dominion of ancient Babel and mighty Nimrod. But in that sense the angel also could truly say, "It is not..." Surely, there was a mighty world-power at the time. The Roman Empire had sway over practically all the world. It had succeeded by the strength of its legions and by its mighty organizing power to extend its dominion over all the important countries of Europe and Africa and Asia. It was a world-power which might be called universal. But it is not true of the Roman power that it resembled the ancient federation of Nimrod. For in the Roman Empire they were not all of one mind. It merely consisted of one mighty nation which had subdued a number of others and for that reason ruled the world. And therefore, however mighty the Roman Empire may have been, it was a strength of force, not of purpose. They were one, not because they were of one mind, but because they were suppressed by one single nation. And therefore, in John's time the beast was not. But the same beast shall again appear in the future. Again the nations of the earth shall unite, shall be of one mind, shall all give their power to the beast, and by a great league, or federation, shall succeed in establishing a universal world-power, having sway over all things.

In the second place, we must pay attention to the seven heads, indicating seven different manifestations of the world-power in history. As we have remarked, the picture of the beast in our text places before us the historic development of the world-power, as well as its final formation. And the former is symbolized in the heads. That this is the case is plain from the language of the angels. He tells us about these heads that one is, that five have fallen, and that one is not yet, evidently pointing to succession. The ten horns evidently indicate a number of world-powers existing all at the same time; but there is succession, – past, present, and future, – in the number of heads.

Now what does the angel tell us about these heads? In the first place, he tells us that the seven heads are seven mountains. He adds that they are seven mountains on which the woman sitteth. But for the present we can leave this out of consideration, and discuss the relation of the woman to this beast in a future discourse. We now take the interpretation of the seven heads as such. They are seven mountains. As I have remarked before, there are interpreters who take it that these seven mountains refer to the seven hills of Rome. The city of Rome was built on seven hills; and so the woman, which was the city of Rome, was sitting on the seven hills of the Roman capital. But that this interpretation is not correct may be plain, in the first place, from the fact that the text speaks of mountains, while the hills of Rome were mere mole hills, not for a moment to be called mountains. But in the second place, the angel indicates that mountains must be taken in the figurative sense of the word: for he adds, "and they are seven kings." Not merely, "And there are seven kings," as some would translate, but specifically referring to the seven heads of the beast, "And they (namely, the heads, the mountains) are seven kings." Now surely, the hills of Rome are not at the same time the kings of Rome: and therefore, this interpretation will not hold. They stand for strong and conspicuous kingdoms, just as a mountain stands for a conspicuous elevation of the earth's surface, elevating itself above even the smaller elevations and hills which may appear next to it. Thus, a mountain is symbolic of a mighty empire or kingdom. More than once it appears thus in Scripture. In Psalm 30:7 we hear David sing of his kingdom: "Lord, by thy favour thou hast made my mountain to stand strong." In Jeremiah 51:25 we read that the prophet spells destruction upon the mighty kingdom of Babylon when he says: "Behold, I am against thee, O destroying mountain, saith the Lord, which destroyest all the earth: and I will stretch out mine hand upon thee, and roll thee down from the rocks, and will make thee a burnt mountain." In Daniel 2:35 we read that the stone which is cut loose and symbolizes the kingdom of God will develop into a great mountain, filling all the earth. And again, in Zechariah 4:7 we read in respect to the world-power that opposes the rebuilding of the temple: "Who art thou, O great mountain? before Zerubbabel thou shalt become a plain." And therefore, it is nothing strange to meet with the figure of a mountain as indicating a king and a kingdom. And as far as the objection is concerned that in this case the angel interprets one symbolism by another, that of the heads by that of the mountains, if the latter must not be taken in the literal sense of the word, this is sufficiently explained by the fact that the heads do not symbolize **any** world-power, — not Moab and Edom and Samaria, — but specifically, great and mighty, conspicuous kingdoms and kings, which may be compared to mountains in their high and powerful exaltation. And therefore, the heads refer to seven mighty dominions.

In this light it is not difficult to understand the rest of the angel's explanation of the mystery of the beast. He says: "Five are fallen, one is, the other is not yet come." Taking our starting-point at the one that is, we can make no mistake about it. It is, of course, the one that existed at the time of John's exile on Patmos, namely, the mighty Roman Empire, with its sway over practically all the world. Figuring back from that mighty empire to the five that are fallen, we obtain the result that before the Roman Empire the Graeco-Macedonian Empire held sway over all the world, especially in the time of Alexander the Great. Before that great Macedonian empire, it was the power of the Medo-Persian kingdom that was supreme. It was preceded by the tremendous and glorious world-power of Babylonia, having its representative king in Nebuchadnezzar. Before the last, the Assyrian Empire was supremely powerful under Sennacherib. And again, before the Assyrian Empire we have the royal power of Egypt, as pictured in Scripture. Thus we obtain the following five: Egypt, Assyria, Babylonia, Persia, and Greece. All these are mentioned in Scripture. And besides, all of them were conspicuous also in their opposition to the kingdom of Israel. Besides, four of these six are mentioned in the image of Nebuchadnezzar's dream, namely, Babylonia, Persia, Greece, and Rome, — the golden, silver, brass, and iron elements of the image. And therefore, there can be little doubt but that the angel, prophesying from the viewpoint of John's own time, refers to the power of the Roman Empire as the head that **is** at that period, and to the five representative powers of the world which have just been mentioned as the ones that have fallen already.

The seventh is not yet, so the angel continues. And when he comes, he must continue a little while. That seventh power has not yet been today. Ever since the final downfall of the Roman Empire in the year 476, the history of Europe has been a struggle between the various nations of the continent. True, there have been powerful empires; but never has any succeeded in obtaining undisputed control of the universal power of the world. And since the discovery of a new continent, this has become all the more impossible. It is very plain from history that God wills not that any one nation shall gain the complete control over the others, in order thus to realize the kingdom of Antichrist. No, evidently that kingdom shall be established in an entirely different way, as already has been discussed before and as also is indicated in the words of our passage in an unmistakable manner.

The Ultimate Formation Of The Beast

How then shall the final formation of the beast come to its realization? In order to understand this, we must, in the first place, understand the expression that there shall still be a seventh powerful kingdom which has not yet been. For a time it was thought by some, – and personally, we have been inclined to think, – that Germany might become that seventh head. But evidently that is not the way in which God has it. Germany's aim was extension of her own power and the Germanizing of the world; and that was not the purpose of the Almighty. No, but a mighty nation is still to appear, it seems, in an entirely different light. For if we take in connection with this picture of the seven heads the symbolism of the ten horns, and read that they are all of one mind and shall give their power to the beast, we receive the impression that the future realization of the kingdom of Antichrist shall rather be by way of confederation than by way of conquest.

Taking these two statements together, then, it seems that we are justified in drawing the following picture. The text speaks of a seventh mighty power which is still in the future. It had not yet received its dominion at that time. But there can be no question about the fact that it shall receive its dominion. For a short while it shall show its power as a separate power. For it must continue a little while in the midst of all the other kingdoms or powers which may exist together with it. But after this little while is finished, whatever may be the history of it, the other powers, indicated by the ten horns, shall give their power to the beast together with that seventh head, thus forming the great, final confederation, or league, that shall constitute the ultimate form of the antichristian world-power. It shall be a league formed of the seventh head together with the ten horns. And then we can also understand the expression, apparently so difficult to grasp, "The beast that was, and is not, even he is the eighth, and is of the seven." That is, the beast in its entirety, as a confederation of world-powers, all being of one mind and one purpose, and all giving their power to the beast, — that one great league is, in the first place, as such an eighth power. It is distinct from all the seven heads separately, for they formed no confederation. It is the old kingdom of Nimrod over again in modern form. First, therefore, come the seven great powers, but the seventh culminating in the final manifestation of the antichristian world-power, which as such shall be the eighth. And, in the second place, that great, final world-power is of the seven in the sense that it is the culmination and the consummation of all history, the climax of the history of these seven powers, the combination of all that Egypt and Assyria, Babylonia and Persia, Greece and Rome, and all the powers which followed have ever stood for and realized. It shall be the ultimate product of all the aims of the powers of the world.

To recapitulate in brief, therefore, there are to be eight world-powers in all. Six have been, in Egypt, Assyria, Babylonia, Persia, Greece, and Rome. The seventh is not yet, or, if it is today, it has not yet become plainly manifest. Its existence shall be peculiar in this respect, that it shall aim at the unification and combination of all the powers that exist at this time. And this shall lead to the final league of nations to realize the kingdom of Antichrist.

The Sure Defeat Of The Beast

Spiritually, our text plainly characterizes this league, this final realization of the beast, as standing in direct antagonism against the Lamb and His people. For our text tells us that these confederate kings shall make war with the Lamb.

Of course, they shall not fight Him in body: for the Lamb is exalted in heaven. But they shall attack all who stand for the Lamb in this dispensation. They shall fight the Lamb by fighting His Word, His worship, His name, His blood, His cause, His kingdom, His people. They shall deny the truth of His revelation. They shall refuse to believe His Word. They shall refuse to accept His authority. They shall not worship Him as King of kings and Lord of lords; and they shall instead worship the beast, deify their own power, and set up the image of the beast. And so they shall also fight His people.

Notice how beautifully and significantly these people of the Lamb are designated in our text. They are the called, the chosen, the faithful. Because of their own effectual, irresistible calling they are also faithful. It is because Christ has called them that they consciously belong to Him. And it is because they are the chosen of God that the Lord has called them. Objectively, their faithfulness rests in the eternal counsel of God. They shall be faithful even unto death because the Lord Jehovah has chosen them to be His people. And subjectively, their faithfulness is assured in the irresistible calling of Christ Jesus, which can never be changed. And therefore the people of God shall be faithful also in those days. They may not be able to buy or sell, as it is expressed in a preceding chapter; but they shall faithfully cling to the name of Jesus because Jehovah of Hosts has chosen them, and because they have been called by the Spirit of Christ irresistibly. Hence, in the midst of tribulation, persecuted and pressed from all sides, as social outcasts in the world, they shall maintain, "The Lord Jehovah is our God, and Christ alone is King."

And they shall not be ashamed!

Three times we are assured in the words of our passage that the victory shall be ours. In the first place, we read in verse 8 that the beast shall come up out of the abyss, but shall go into destruction. The same expression we read in verse 11. And, finally, we read in verse 14 that the Lamb shall overcome them. How, in what way, we are told in a later connection. Now we are simply told the fact that also this final attempt of the devil shall fail. And at the same time we are informed as to the reason why: the Lamb is Lord of lords and King of kings. That explains it all. He stands on Mount Zion as the great victor, as the Anointed of God, destined to rule over the kingdoms of the world. And when all these kingdoms, though striving to establish the kingdom of opposition, shall have served the purpose of Jesus Christ, He shall consume them by the breath of His mouth, establish the new heaven and the new earth, the kingdom of His people, and reign in glory over them forevermore. And therefore, the picture is rather clear, especially with a view to the times in which we now live.

Watch, therefore, and cling to the name of Jesus; and have no fellowship with the great sin of Babylon, namely, to be carried by the beast. For then you shall have no fellowship with her judgment. And be comforted with this thought: the Lord is King of kings and Lord of lords! Our Lord is mightier than they all! The victory is assured!

Chapter XLII
The Judgment Of The Harlot
(Revelation 17:15-18)

15 And he saith unto me, The waters which thou sawest, where the whore sitteth, are peoples, and multitudes, and nations, and tongues.

16 And the ten horns which thou sawest upon the beast, these shall hate the whore, and shall make her desolate and naked, and shall eat her flesh, and burn her with fire.

17 For God hath put in their hearts to fulfil his will, and to agree, and give their kingdom unto the beast, until the words of God shall be fulfilled.

18 And the woman which thou sawest is that great city, which reigneth over the kings of the earth.

The harlot and the beast with the seven heads and ten horns we have now discussed. What remains to be considered is the relation between them and the judgment of the harlot as these are pictured in the entire chapter, and more particularly in the words of our present passage.

The woman as such, so we found, is the symbol, first of all, of the church in this dispensation, the wife of Jehovah, the bride of Christ. But the woman pictured in the words of our passage is a harlot, and therefore a woman who has forsaken her rightful husband and who lives in most intimate, but illegal, relationship with strangers, who are not her husband. And as such, the woman is symbolic of the apostate church, which has forsaken her rightful husband, Jesus Christ, has fallen away from the truth, and now surrenders herself as an institution to the service of the world and of Antichrist. But still more, this woman is also the figure of a great city which is to have dominion over the world and over the kings of the earth. And we found that even as the true church is destined to develop into a city, the New Jerusalem, which is to come down from heaven, so also the apostate, or false, church is to develop into a city, a great center, which is representative of her real character and at the same time the embodiment and center of the antichristian kingdom.

The beast, so we found, is the same as the one which was pictured to us in Chapter 13 and which was already mentioned in the eleventh chapter of this book. Plain this was, so we found, from its description as the beast with its seven heads and ten horns, as well as from its origin as the beast that rises up out of the abyss, and finally, too, from his relation to the inhabitants of the world and the saints of Christ. The former admire this beast and wonder after him; the latter stand in opposition to him and refuse to bow before him as their rightful king. It is, therefore, the world-power from its political aspect, as it shall finally give rise to the antichristian kingdom and all that it implies.

Only, we also found that the point of view is different, and that we learn different details of this antichristian kingdom in the words of the passage we were discussing before. And we came to the conclusion that this beast is here pictured both in his historical development and in his final formation. His historical development is evidently pictured to us in the seven heads which represent, according to the interpretation of the angel, seven different manifestations of the antichristian world-power in the history of the world, one of which existed in the time of John, five of which had already risen and vanished before that time, and one of which is still to come. And we found that if we started from the safe assumption, that the one which is was the Roman Empire in all its glory, as it existed in John's time, the five that had already fallen could be none other than the Egyptian, Assyrian, Babylonian, Persian, and Grecian empires, which had successively existed before that time, and all of which had already perished. And we found, too, that it is a striking characteristic of the period of this dispensation after the downfall of the Roman Empire in 476 that not one great empire has succeeded in obtaining and holding sway over all the world, something that became well-nigh an impossibility after the discovery and settlement of the new world had become an accomplished fact. The seventh power has not yet revealed itself in its full manifestation, but must still be revealed. And in the ten horns we have the picture of ten minor powers that shall exist simultaneously with the seventh head, exist side by side for a short time, but ultimately shall give their power to the beast. That is, with the seventh head, under its leadership, they shall come to one great confederation of nations, thus realizing the beast that was in Nimrod's time, never was again, but again shall be in the future. That world-power shall stand antithetically against Christ and His people, shall make war against Him, but shall be overcome by Him and by the called and chosen and faithful, who shall reign with Christ in the New Jerusalem.

The Picture Of Her Harlotry

In the present passage we find the judgment of the harlot. I think the general meaning of the words of our passage is so plain that after all we have discussed, it is scarcely necessary to give any direct and special explanation. In brief, they tell us that the ten kings and the beast, who committed fornication with the harlot for a long time and who made the best of her for their own interests and lust, — that these shall finally bitterly hate the harlot and destroy her very appearance, kill her, eat her flesh, and burn her with fire. And the text explains that this they do because God has given it in their hearts to do so and to perform His will, come to one mind, the mind of the beast, and destroy the harlot they first loved. And it is only after the angel has spoken of the destruction of the harlot as such that he explains the symbol of the woman once more as the great city, which hath dominion over the kings of the earth. And in the next chapter the destruction of the city is pictured to us.

Just as we have learned to distinguish, therefore, between the woman as the harlot-church and the woman as the mystic city, so we shall also have to distinguish between these two in their end. And the order of events will evidently be thus, that the apostate church as a separate church institution will be done away with first of all, so that the church shall no more exist, and that then exactly this destruction of the church apostate shall lead to the final unification of all so-called religion, and culminate in the religion of the beast, without any church as such, but with Babylon, the great city, for its leading center. I think this order of events stands beyond all doubt, and is exactly as the text describes it to us, and therefore as such really needs no explanation. Yet we must make an attempt, in the light of what we see in the history of the world today, somewhat to explain the possibility of this order, and try to picture to ourselves how things are to develop, as far as we are permitted to see. And in order to obtain a clear understanding of these things we must try to explain what is really meant by the harlotry of the church with the beast.

And then it will be necessary, first of all, that we obtain a clear picture of the realities that are symbolized by the woman, as well as by the beast.

The woman, we must remember, in her outward appearance is the instituted church of Christ on earth. Outwardly she is nothing but the church in her entire appearance in the world. In every respect she looks like the true church externally. She calls herself church of Christ. She has her church edifices, just as the true church. In those sanctuaries the congregation gathers, at least on every sabbath, for worship. As you enter, you find that on the pulpit lies the Word of God, the Scriptures, just as it is in the true church. There is no difference. Behind the pulpit stands the regularly ordained minister of the Word. Regardless now of what use there is made of that Bible on the pulpit, regardless too of how the minister accomplishes his task of administering the Word, fact is that outwardly there is no difference. The Bible on the pulpit and the minister of that Bible behind it, pretending to administer the Word of God to the congregation, and that congregation too, in outward appearance look like the true church. They sing and pray, confess, and listen to the preaching of the Word. And as they go, they receive the benediction in the name of God. Regardless, again, of the nature of their worship, they evidently gather for the worship of God in their sanctuary. Yea, you will find that not only the Word but also the sacraments are administered. The members of the church are baptized; and occasionally they gather around the table of communion solemnly to celebrate the supper of the Lord. We may have our scruples as to the significance attached to these things. Fact is, nevertheless, that the sacraments as well as the Word are administered, just as well as in the true church of Christ. In a word, the harlot woman represents the church, the church of Christ, with the Word and the sacraments, as she comes to manifestation here upon earth. The woman is the church as we know her. Just as well as any real harlot outwardly looks just like any other woman, so also does the harlot-church look like the true church of Christ on earth in her entire appearance.

The same we must remember of the beast. In itself, the beast as pictured in the words of our passage is nothing wrong. It is simply the regular state with its regular, instituted government, as we all believe in the legality and necessity of its existence in this dispensation. This is very plain from the heads. They are seven kings, and they constitute seven manifestations of different states and governments. As such there was nothing wrong with them. God wills that they shall be there. God has Himself instituted government for this dispensation, just as well as He has established and instituted the church. It makes no difference now what form of government is meant. It does not make a particle of difference for our purpose whether the governments referred to were empires or monarchies or republics. Fact is that they are regularly instituted governments, with their heads and officers, with their power and authority, with their laws and maintenance of these laws, with their armies and navies. So also the ten horns inform us: they shall be ten kings, or ten governments, in the world. And therefore, also these represent nothing but regularly instituted, orderly, God-willed governments, institutions of God in the world.

Outwardly, therefore, as to the form of this woman and of this beast there is nothing wrong. The woman represents the church as an institution of God; and the beast with all his heads and horns represents worldly government as God has willed that it should exist. Regardless now of their degenerate character, there is as such nothing wrong in either of them. They are both institutions of God. They both have their work and their purpose in the world. And without neither could this dispensation continue.

But the purpose of our chapter is undoubtedly to picture these two in a most wonderful combination, in a most intimate union. And it is exactly the nature of this union, or confederacy, between the instituted church and the instituted government which makes of the woman the harlot and of the beast the antichristian kingdom.

This is symbolically portrayed in the fact that the woman is sitting on the beast, – a most intimate relation and combination of the two. The church and the worldly state have allied themselves, in the first place. The one supports the other, and the other directs and aids the one. Where the one goes, the other follows. For the beast carries the woman, which at least also seems to imply that after all the beast employs the woman for his own purpose and carries her whithersoever he will, though, in turn, he is the strength and support of the woman, and she owes it to the beast that she is decked with jewels and precious stones and arrayed in purple. However this may be, the fact that the woman is riding or sitting upon the beast means to show intimate union between church and worldly government, shows that they have united in character, united in purpose, united in aim and effort, and that together they strive to realize a common aim. The church stands here in an illegal, wrong relation to the power of the world, is employed by the latter, fulfills its purpose, and therefore loses her true character.

This idea is emphasized by the fact that the woman is directly called the harlot. She is the harlot in a two-fold sense. In the first place, she is that because she allows herself to be the whore of the kings of the world, with which the great of the world can do as they please, on the which they can satisfy all their desire. But, in the second place, she is also the great whore because she is the mother of abominations, and makes all the inhabitants of the world drunken with the wine of her fornications. And therefore we obtain the two-fold picture that, on the one hand, the instituted church allows herself to be employed by the world-power, and, on the other hand, she leads all the individual inhabitants of the earth to follow her in this and to serve the purpose of the beast.

In What Her Harlotry Consists

But even thus we cannot be satisfied, but must ask the concrete question: in what does this harlotry of the church consist? What is the illegality of the relation between the two? And then it will be necessary to determine, in the first place, what would be the right relation and what is the character and purpose of each, the church and the state, in the world? Just as you must determine the nature of literal harlotry by first determining the proper relation of man and woman, so also we must come to a true understanding of the harlotry of the church with the worldly power by ascertaining, first of all, what is the right relation between the two.

What is the state? What is instituted government, according to the Word of God? Of this we find a very clear description in Romans 13:1-4: "Let every soul be subject unto the higher powers. For there is no power but of God: the powers that be are ordained of God. Whosoever therefore resisteth the power, resisteth the ordinance of God: and they that resist shall receive to themselves damnation. For rulers are not a terror to good works, but to the evil. Wilt thou then not be afraid of the power? do that which is good, and thou shalt have praise of the same: For he is the minister of God to thee for good. But if thou do that which is evil, be afraid; for he beareth not the sword in vain: for he is the minister of God, a revenger to execute wrath upon him that doeth evil." Hence, it is plain that:

1) The state is an institution of God. It is ordained by Him to bear the sword power, to punish evil-doers and to protect the good.

2) The state is a temporal institution, to maintain law and order in the midst of a corrupt world.

3) The God-given instrument it employs is not spiritual but material:

the power of the sword and all that this implies. It is not the power of a certain common grace, but the power of the sword. That, in our view, is the purpose of government. And that is the Scriptural conception. To it we are in subjection, of course. And for conscience' sake the Christian can never become a rebel or even a traitor in time of war or of peace, unless that state, that government, should demand of him that he would act contrary to the will of God.

What, however, is the church?

It is an entirely different institution. It is the manifestation of the body of Christ on earth and represents the authority of Christ in the world. It is the result, the product, the manifestation of the grace of God through Jesus Christ. Through the church it becomes possible for the people of God to manifest themselves as the body of Christ, worship and glorify their God and King, and reveal His glory in the midst of the world. Its purpose is two-fold. In the first place, it is the establishment and upbuilding of the saints in Christ Jesus, so that they may come to a fuller and clearer knowledge and stronger faith concerning the grace that is in Christ. And, in the second place, it is the propagation of the gospel of the kingdom in every land. Its task, therefore, is definitely circumscribed. She does not receive her instructions from the worldly power. The latter cannot tell her what to believe and to confess and how to worship. It has no authority to define the contents of the message which she must bring in the church and in all the world. In all this she acknowledges no other authority than that of Jesus Christ and the Word of her God. She is different from the state in that she employs no earthly or physical power, but only the spiritual instrument of the Word and the reliance on the work of the Holy Spirit. Moreover, she is eternal, not destined to disappear, but to exist forever when her King shall come to deliver her. And her task is not to make the world better, but simply to aim at the rooting out of sin and its power through the Word and the Spirit. And the relation between her and the state is essentially such that the worldly power exists for her sake, namely, to make the development of the people of God possible in the world.

Each, therefore, has its own sphere. The church represents the power of the eternal kingdom, can be satisfied with nothing less than the complete deliverance from sin, and looks for the eternal kingdom of God to come. The instituted government, however, represents a temporal power, is ordained in order to handle the sword and to punish the evil-doer, to protect the righteous, and to maintain order until God shall have completed His own, eternal kingdom.

Now when does the wrong relation ensue between the two? And when does the worldly power become the beast, and the church the harlot?

This comes about when, in the first place, the state, the power of the world, presumes to represent the development of the kingdom of Christ, and thus claims to be essentially the eternal kingdom itself. In that case it will deny its original character, refuse to be satisfied with being a punishing power upon evil and a maintainer of public order, and will strive for world-wide power, in order that through her agency the world may become the kingdom of God. It will conceive of the possibility of rooting out evil and establishing real righteousness and peace by main power, by the power of the law and by the action of the sword. And it will tell you that this is the kingdom of Christ which was to come. Of course, you understand that this is not true and that this never can be. The state does not exist on the basis of the atoning blood of Christ directly. It is not destined to be eternal. It is not purposed to become the main and eternal kingdom. Its purpose is temporal, not eternal. Its power is auxiliary, not chief. And therefore, as soon as the state through its power aims at establishing the eternal kingdom, a kingdom of righteousness and peace and justice, without the spiritual means of the Word and the blood of Christ, it becomes the antichristian kingdom. It becomes the beast.

Naturally, with that aim the children of God, the true church, will come into conflict. For the latter will deny that it is the purpose of the state to develop into the eternal kingdom of God and will maintain that this can only lead to the establishment of the show-kingdom of Antichrist. But this will only lead to persecution on the part of the world-power. That world-power will try to get control of all things, of art and science and commerce and industry, but also of religion and worship, and ultimately dictate what god we shall worship and how we must worship him. There you have the antichristian beast.

And the church becomes the harlot, the apostate church, when she becomes of one mind with the beast. Negatively, she will begin by admitting that the blood of Christ is not necessary for the establishment of the kingdom of God. She will deny that the Holy Spirit only can truly make children of the kingdom. She will abandon the name of Jesus and the Word of God, and seek her hope in this dispensation and in this world. Positively, she will help in forming that great state for which also the world-power strives. She will offer her full services to the state, give her most hearty support to any movement that comes along, and be busy in the things of this world instead of in the things of the eternal kingdom of Christ. Concretely speaking, she will no more preach on sin and total depravity. She will no more teach the necessity of personal regeneration and the atoning blood of Christ, but be full of messages which pertain only to this world. She will preach on the great topics of war and peace, on the betterment of humanity through all kinds of legislation, on prohibition and woman suffrage, on hygiene and health ordinances, on wages and labor, on business and industry. And she will try to picture before the minds of her members how through all these things the great and glorious kingdom of God shall come in the earth. Thus she has abandoned her true, her spiritual, her eternal character, and become the great harlot.

The Utter Destruction Of The Harlot

Now then, what shall become of this harlot, in the first place? What shall be the end of her harlotry? Simply this, that she shall ultimately cease to exist as a separate institution.

She shall be great and glorious for a time. She shall score great victories evidently. For, in the first place, the text tells us that she is sitting upon many waters. Twice this is mentioned in the text. Already in our passage the angel explains that this symbol refers to peoples and nations and tongues and multitudes. Of course, this is not in conflict with her being seated on the beast. For the beast evidently comprises many peoples. And therefore by sitting on the beast the harlot naturally sits on many peoples. But in this figure, as well as in the statement that she has made the inhabitants of the earth drunken with the wine of her fornications, the idea is expressed that she influences and fascinates the minds of many, of a great multitude. She preaches a religion that can be adopted by the world; and therefore her victory is great. And, in the second place, she scores great victories from the side of the world-power. It is no doubt through the power of the beast that she is decked with pearls and arrayed in purple and that she is great and glorious. For a time she is victorious as an institution, enjoys the favor of the world, and succeeds in persecuting the true saints of Christ, who refuse the join her harlotry. It is after all through her influence that the true church is ultimately a castaway, an object of shame and mockery.

But this is not her end. The text plainly tells us that the same kings and the same beast whose favorite pet she was with all her harlotries will hate her and despise her and utterly destroy her, eat her flesh and burn her. Notice, in the first place, that there is something perfectly natural in this. Just as the whoremongers in a natural and literal sense ultimately hate the harlot who has been instrumental in the satisfaction of their lust, so also these kings and these beasts, when the apostate church as an institution shall have fulfilled all their desire, shall hate her and become envious and jealous of her power and glory. After all, what is the use and the place of the church as an institution when the vague and general religion of Antichrist shall prevail? What is the use of an established form of worship in an established church? Just as the church as an institution shall disappear when the kingdom of glory of our Lord shall have been completed, so also shall the institution of the false church disappear when her work is finished and she has been instrumental in preparing the religion of Antichrist. At any rate, the church shall be abolished. That is clear from the text. Not her apostate spirit shall be destroyed, but her body, her manifestation, shall come to an end. It makes no difference to us now how this shall be realized. Certain it is that the beast shall do away with the institution of the church that has served his purpose. And then shall the kingdom be realized. Then all shall be blended, and the institution even of the church shall be no more. The very shadow of Christ shall have been obliterated from the earth. And all that remains in the world is the world-power, the antichristian kingdom. The woman as to her form shall have disappeared. But essentially her apostate spirit shall be realized in the worship of the image of the beast. And that same woman, spiritually realized in the kingdom of Antichrist from its religious point of view, shall reappear in Babylon, the great center of the world-power that is to come. From there she shall rule over the hearts and minds of great and small and of the inhabitants of the world. The appearance of the harlot has vanished. She now exists centrally as the great city, Babylon, the capital of the kingdom of Antichrist.

Two remarks we wish to make in application. In the first place, notice that God controls all these developments through Jesus Christ. It is God, so we read, Who gives it into the heart of these kings and of the beast to hate the harlot and to come to oneness of mind. God, then, controls all things. Christ reigns! There is nothing to fear! When the institution of the apostate church shall be abolished, the same shall be true of the true church. Public worship then for us belongs to the past. It shall be the reign of the Man of Sin. But never fear: God reigns! He has given it in the heart of the kings to hate the harlot. His will must be done; and all things work together for good to them that love Him. In the second place, the repetition of the practical admonition is also now in order: "Go ye out of her, my people, and have no fellowship with her sins, that ye may not partake of her judgment." Even as the institution of the harlot church, so shall Babylon also fall. And only the New Jerusalem shall ultimately prevail. Watch, therefore, that ye fall not into temptation.

Chapter XLIII

The Fall Of Babylon

(Revelation 18)

1 And after these things I saw another angel come down from heaven, having great power; and the earth was lightened with his glory.

2 And he cried mightily with a strong voice, saying, Babylon the great is fallen, is fallen, and is become the habitation of devils, and the hold of every foul spirit, and a cage of every unclean and hateful bird.

3 For all nations have drunk of the wine of the wrath of her fornication, and the kings of the earth have committed fornication with her, and the merchants of the earth are waxed rich through the abundance of her delicacies.

4 And I heard another voice from heaven, saying, Come out of her, my people, that ye be not partakers of her sins, and that ye receive not of her plagues.

5 For her sins have reached unto heaven, and God hath remembered her iniquities.

6 Reward her even as she rewarded you, and double unto her double according to her works: in the cup which she hath filled fill to her double.

7 How much she hath glorified herself, and lived deliciously, so much torment and sorrow give her: for she saith in her heart, I sit a queen, and am no widow, and shall see no sorrow.

8 Therefore shall her plagues come in one day, death, and mourning, and famine; and she shall be utterly burned with fire: for strong is the Lord God who judgeth her.

9 And the kings of the earth, who have committed fornication and lived deliciously with her, shall bewail her, and lament for her, when they shall see the smoke of her burning,

10 Standing afar off for the fear of her torment, saying, Alas, alas that great city Babylon, that mighty city! for in one hour is thy judgment come.

11 And the merchants of the earth shall weep and mourn over her; for no man buyeth their merchandise any more;

12 The merchandise of gold, and silver, and precious stones, and of pearls, and fine linen, and purple, and silk, and scarlet, and all thyine wood, and all manner vessels of ivory, and all manner vessels of most precious wood, and of brass, and iron, and marble,

13 And cinnamon, and odours, and ointments, and frankincense, and wine, and oil, and fine flour, and wheat, and beasts, and sheep, and horses, and chariots, and slaves, and souls of men.

14 And the fruits that thy soul lusted after are departed from thee, and all things which were dainty and goodly are departed from thee, and thou shalt find them no more at all.

15 The merchants of these things, which were made rich by her, shall stand afar off for the fear of her torment, weeping and wailing,

16 And saying, Alas, alas that great city, that was clothed in fine linen, and purple, and scarlet, and decked with gold, and precious stones, and pearls!

17 For in one hour so great riches is come to nought. And every shipmaster, and all the company in ships, and sailors, and as many as trade by sea, stood afar off,

18 And cried when they saw the smoke of her burning, saying, What city is like unto this great city!

19 And they cast dust on their heads, and cried, weeping and wailing, saying, Alas, alas that great city, wherein were made rich all that had ships in the sea by reason of her costliness! for in one hour is she made desolate.

20 Rejoice over her, thou heaven, and ye holy apostles and prophets; for God hath avenged you on her.

21 And a mighty angel took up a stone like a great millstone, and cast it into the sea, saying, Thus with violence shall that great city Babylon be thrown down, and shall be found no more at all.

22 And the voice of harpers, and musicians, and of pipers, and trumpeters, shall be heard no more at all in thee; and no craftsman, of whatsoever craft he be, shall be found any more in thee; and the sound of a millstone shall be heard no more at all in thee;

23 And the light of a candle shall shine no more at all in thee; and the voice of the bridegroom and of the bride shall be heard no more at all in thee: for thy merchants were the great men of the earth; for by thy sorceries were all nations deceived.

24 And in her was found the blood of prophets, and of saints, and of all that were slain upon the earth.

We have devoted considerable time to the discussion of Babylon the Great, the Mystery, the Mother of Harlots and Abominations of the Earth. First we discussed Babylon as such. We found that she is both a woman-harlot and a city. As woman she is no doubt a symbol of the church on earth as an institution for the building up of the saints and for the propagation of the gospel of the kingdom. As harlot, however, she is the apostate church, who has denied her true character, forsaken her rightful husband, Jesus Christ, and surrendered herself to be employed as an instrument of the world-power and of Antichrist. And as a city her essential character is revealed. For even as the true church of Christ shall ultimately reveal itself as the New Jerusalem, so the counterfeit church shall reveal itself as the counterfeit Jerusalem, that is, Babylon.

Secondly, we also discussed the beast on whom the woman-harlot was found sitting. And we found that in it a picture is presented to our view of the world-power in its historical development as well as in its ultimate formation. Seven kingdoms shall come before the world-power, as the eighth, shall be able to come to its realization and consummation. With the seventh all the then-existing kings shall combine their power; and they all shall give it to the beast, that is, the kingdom of Antichrist. That beast shall make war with the Christ and His saints, but shall be overthrown by them; and Christ shall have the victory.

In the third place, we discussed the judgment of the great whore, the harlot-woman. We found that her harlotry consisted in an illegal relation in which she, as church, stands to the world-power. She is called to be the manifestation of the body of Christ in the world, and she gives herself to be the body of the beast. She is called to build the saints in the most holy faith, and she makes all the inhabitants of the earth drunk with the wine of her fornications. She is called to be the army of an eternal kingdom, based on the atoning blood of the Savior; and she labors for the establishment of a temporal kingdom of Antichrist which has no part with the blood of Christ Jesus and is doomed to destruction. She is called to employ the spiritual means of the Word and of the sacraments; and instead she abandons the truth of the Word of God and seeks refuge in outward means and external instruments to establish the promised kingdom. She is the harlot, the apostate woman, who labors for the beast instead of for the kingdom of Christ. And we found also that her judgment as harlot is certain: she will ultimately disappear as an institution, because her very lovers shall hate her. The kings who committed fornication with her shall aim at her destruction. The very appearance of the church in this dispensation shall be annoying, nauseating, to them; and therefore they shall obliterate her from the face of the earth. Then the woman as harlot shall exist no more. The instituted church has come to the end of her existence. But she shall reappear as a city whose mystical name is Babylon. For in Babylon, the center and heart of the antichristian kingdom, the spirit of that same woman who once appeared as the apostate church shall reign supreme.

In the chapter we are now approaching, Chapter 18, however, the destruction of that great city is portrayed in highly descriptive and symbolic language. It is not advisable to divide the chapter: for evidently all the material found here belongs together, elaborates upon one and the same theme, concentrates itself around the same central thought. And that central thought of the chapter is the fall of Babylon. And therefore this we must now discuss.

Babylon's Greatness

It cannot escape our attention that purposely the text gives us once more a description of Babylon, this time of her existence as a city. Even as in the end we are presented with an elaborate description of the New Jerusalem, its beauty and glory and blessedness, so we are also given a picture of the highest attainment of the world-power and of the apostate church as it is pictured in the city of Babylon. But the difference is that while Jerusalem's description is connected with her final and absolute glory and victory over all enemies, the elaborate description of Babylon is connected with its ultimate destruction. But in order to understand the significance of the downfall of Babylon, it will be necessary that we obtain a glimpse of her real importance, of her greatness and riches, of her influence and control of all the matters of the world. It makes no difference whether we accept the view that Babylon shall be a real city, or whether we are inclined to believe that this element belongs to the symbolism of the picture, certain it remains that in the fall of Babylon we meet with the fall of all human labor and attainment, the fall of the entire structure of the antichristian kingdom.

In the first place, then, Babylon is plainly pictured as the center of the antichristian kingdom from a royal and legislative point of view. In the pride of her heart she exclaims to herself: "I sit a queen, and shall see no sorrow!" She sits, therefore, upon many waters as a queen. Babylon is the

royal city. From Babylon goes forth the law over many nations and
tongues and tribes and multitudes. There is the judicial wisdom of the
kingdom. From there the laws are issued. There resides the executive
power. If I may for a moment accept that the head of that kingdom shall
be a person, the very culmination of the antichristian principle, he lives in
Babylon, and from Babylon he reigns. There is the power which controls
all things, which keeps order, which regulates commerce and industry,
which regulates science and art and religion, which establishes the form of
worship for the beast. This is also plain from the repeated expression that
"the kings of the earth committed fornication with her and lived
deliciously with her." Babylon was the glory of the kings of the earth,
their stronghold and center. In Babylon the ten kings of the earth, of the
great alliance with the beast, came together to make their plans for the
advancement of their cause and kingdom and for their war against the
Christ and against His saints. In a word, Babylon appears as the royal
center, as the throne of Antichrist. She is the center of all law and rule for
the entire world; and all the world obeys her will. Without Babylon the
antichristian kingdom is inconceivable, even as Germany is inconceivable
without Berlin, France without Paris, England without London. She is of
central significance for all the kingdom.

In the second place, we may also notice that Babylon is pictured in the
text as being the heart and center of all the commerce in the world, the
home of industry and art. Not merely a city among others is Babylon, but
the city, the only city that is a center of business and industry and art and
science, from whence these are controlled over the entire world and
without which the life of industry and commerce is gone. Such a city is
Babylon, according to the chapter we are now discussing. This is plain
from the description of the weeping and wailing merchants, who stand afar
off and are pictured as beholding her destruction with fear and anguish.
Babylon is the merchant of this world. She sells every conceivable article;
and if she cannot sell, all the commerce and business of the world is at a
standstill. Babylon sells gold and silver and precious stones and pearls. She
is the only money-market in the world. Babylon sells fine linen and purple
and scarlet, matters of necessity and luxury. Babylon controls the sale of
all the products of industry. She it is who sells vessels of thyine wood, of
ivory, and most precious wood, of brass and iron, and marble. On her
market we find the products of all parts of the world: the spices of
tropical zones, the wine and the oil of more moderate climate, cinnamon

and incense and ointment and frankincense, — these all must be bought within her walls. Babylon controls all the necessities of life. For they are her merchants who have a monopoly of fine flour and wheat, of cattle and sheep and horses and chariots. Yea, Babylon controls the power of universal labor. For her merchants sell the bodies and souls of men. Babylon controls the luxuries of the world. For she is decked with purple and gold; and the luscious fruits and dainty things are found within her borders. Still more, Babylon also controls every craft. For the angel who symbolizes the fall of Babylon by casting a large stone into the sea announces that no craftsman, of whatsoever craft, shall be found any more in her, and that the sound of the millstone is silenced within her walls forever. She is the mother of music and fine arts, of pipers and trumpeters, of the invention of many a thing of convenience and luxury. She is the center of joy, the mistress of life, in the kingdom of Antichrist. Without her there is no commerce: for the merchants shall wail because no one can buy their merchandise any more after the destruction of Babylon. Without her there is neither art nor science nor industry conceivable. She is, in one word, the heart and center of the business and life of all the world.

In the third place, she is pictured as a luxurious and wicked city. The kings of the earth commit fornication with her, and the merchants of the earth wax rich by the power of her wantonness, vs. 3. Luscious fruits and dainty things, whatever is nice and pleasant to the taste, are found in her, vs. 14. She is arrayed in fine linen and purple and scarlet and decked with gold and precious stones and pearls, vs. 16. Within her walls is heard the voice of harpers and minstrels, of flute-players and trumpeters, the joyful voice of the bridegroom and the bride, vss. 22, 23. She is, therefore, a city filled to overflowing with joy and abundance. There is the culmination of all that human ingenuity could possibly invent for the joy and bliss and ease and comfort of man. There is no cry of the suffering. There is no groan of the poor. There is no complaint of the wronged. There is the gathering of all the blessings of science and art and industry. There is equality and justice and brotherhood. There is found the climax of man's attainment, the realization of the number **Six hundred sixty-six.**

But there is also found the very height of iniquity and godlessness. Of her we read that her sins have reached to heaven, and they have risen mountain-high, so that she deceived all the nations of the earth with her sorceries, and that the blood of prophets and saints and of all who have been slain upon the earth is flowing through her streets. Her antitype, therefore, is Sodom and Gomorrah, the wicked center of godlessness and luxury of old. Also there was luxury and splendor and riches and no want. But also there the voice of their iniquity cried to Jehovah Sabaoth, so that He remembered their sins. In the pride of her wantonness and the rottenness of her luxurious living she blasphemes the name of Jehovah. She arose in wanton rebellion against the Almighty, fought against the Lamb and against His saints, and proudly manifests the emblem of the image of the beast. She is also world-controlling in her wicked luxury and godlessness.

Babylon's Fall

As to the fall of this great metropolitan city, we may remark, first of all, that the manner of it is not definitely described in the chapter.

In the first place, we may notice that this is generally the case when pictures concerning the end are held before us in the Word of God. We usually are not told in detail just exactly how the end shall be. We are informed that Christ shall come, and that He shall come with the clouds; but we are not told the details of that coming. We must be content with the facts. We are told that God's people shall be delivered and that they shall have no part with the very final judgment of the world; but exactly how this shall take place is hidden behind the veil of symbolism. We must be satisfied with the facts. The New Jerusalem is to come down from heaven and shall have dominion over the new heaven and the new earth; but also this greatest of all events is clothed in the garb of highest symbolism, and the manner is left in the dark.

The same is true of Babylon. We are told that she shall come to her final destruction. As we have remarked in a former connection, we are also told in general outlines that the devil shall be the cause of his own destruction, — a fact which has repeatedly become plain in history and which lies in the nature of the case. He shall rouse the nations against his own kingdom, not indeed for that purpose, but to war against Jehovah. But in the meantime he shall fulfill God's own counsel, and he shall work for his own destruction. But exactly how the devil shall do this we are not informed. Most natural it is, indeed, to assume that the satanic influence of Antichrist in the world of the nations which live at the four corners of the earth shall ultimately have the result that they rise in enmity against the world of Christendom, which is really the Antichristendom of the beast; and, thinking that they shall strike at the Lamb and His people, they shall destroy the beast. For that same reason I would take the address in verses 6 and 7 as meant not for God's people, but rather for the nations which must execute God's wrath upon Babylon. Outwardly the text would seem to contradict this statement. For we read: "Reward her even as she rewarded you," which evidently would be addressed to the people of God. But in the original this impression is not given. We simply read: "Render unto her even as she rendered, and double unto her double according to her works: in the cup which she mingled mingle unto her double. How much soever she glorified herself and waxed wanton, so much give unto her of torment and mourning." It is true, the nations which execute this wrath of God upon Babylon will have an entirely different purpose in mind. Their purpose will undoubtedly be to strike at the power of the Lamb and His people. And this very purpose becomes their sin and their guilt. But the fact remains that through this God executes His own will and counsel, even as through the pride and self-exaltation of Jehu, for which he was afterward rebuked and punished, God sent His punishment upon the house of Ahab.

However this may be, Babylon shall fall. That is the certainty of our text and of our chapter.

This is pictured twice. In the first place, it is announced by the strong and powerful angel with great authority who comes down from heaven and shouts, "Fallen, fallen is Babylon the great." The certainty of her fall is indicated in the perfect tense. The angel speaks as if the city is fallen already, even though evidently that fall is still anticipated, to indicate that her doom is certain. And again, the certainty of her doom is also expressed in the repetition of the word "fallen." Babylon shall surely fall. The certainty of that fall is so great, and the fall is so imminent, that it is as though it had already taken place. And, in the second place, we are told of this fall of Babylon symbolically in the picture of the angel who comes down from heaven and, taking up a great millstone, casts it into the sea, explaining, "Thus with violence shall that great city Babylon be thrown down, and shall be found no more at all." And therefore we receive the information that the fall of Babylon is certain, as well as that it shall be sudden and complete and that it shall be found no more at all.

The last consideration leads us to the second thought on the fall of Babylon, namely, that it shall evidently be complete and final. It shall be the last of Babylon and her antichristian power. She shall never be rebuilt. Her utter desolation is directly pictured in the words of the mighty angel, vs. 2: "Babylon the great is fallen, is fallen, and is become the habitation of devils, and the hold of every foul spirit, and a cage of every unclean and hateful bird." So the prophet Isaiah had pictured the fall of Babylon before, a fall which was partially fulfilled in the destruction of literal Babylon, but which shall reach its complete realization in the fall of the great antichristian power: "And Babylon, the glory of kingdoms, the beauty of the Chaldees' excellency, shall be as when God overthrew Sodom and Gomorrah. It shall never be inhabited, neither shall it be dwelt in from generation to generation: neither shall the Arabian pitch tent there; neither shall the shepherds make their fold there. But wild beasts of the desert shall lie there; and their houses shall be full of doleful creatures; and owls shall dwell there, and satyrs shall dance there. And the wild beasts of the islands shall cry in their desolate houses, and dragons in their pleasant palaces: and her time is near to come, and her days shall not be prolonged," (Isaiah 13:19-22). The same is indicated in verse 8 of our chapter, where we read: "Therefore shall her plagues come in one day, death, and mourning, and famine; and she shall be utterly burned with fire: for strong is the Lord God who judgeth her." And, lastly, this is pictured once again in verses 22 and 23 of our chapter, where the angel announces her future condition: "And the voice of harpers, and musicians, and of pipers, and trumpeters, shall be heard no more at all in thee; and no craftsman, of whatsoever craft he be, shall be found any more in thee; and the sound of a millstone shall be heard no more at all in thee; And the light of a candle shall shine no more at all in thee; and the voice of the bridegroom and of the bride shall be heard no more at all in thee."

In a word, it is a picture of utter desolation that is drawn before our eyes. Instead of the splendor of her appearance, she now shows the appearance of a hole of demons and evil spirits and wild and unclean beasts. Instead of the joyful light and illumination of her festive streets, there is now absolute darkness: for even the light of a candle shall shine no more. Instead of the bustle of machinery, the joyful sound of music, the glad voice of bride and bridegroom, there is now a doleful and gloomy silence. Babylon is turned into a region of death and destruction. All her glory is gone in one hour, and that forever. It is the final and complete judgment upon Babylon. She has committed fornication with the kings and princes of the world. She has made the nations drunk with the wine of her fornication. She has deceived them all with her sorceries. In her was found the blood of all the saints and prophets. She has made war with the

Lamb throughout the ages. Her iniquity rises to heaven. Therefore, in one hour is her final and complete destruction come. God judges her rightly: according to what she has done she is rewarded.

This leads us to our third observation on the fall of Babylon as such, namely, the time of her destruction. The chapter itself does not indicate any time. It simply tells us of the destruction. But, in the first place, it may be remarked that the very completeness and finality of her destruction already makes us think that this is one of the scenes of the last days, when all who have exalted themselves against Him shall be destroyed by the appearance of the Mighty One. And from Chapter 16, verse 19, we learned that this destruction of Babylon falls within the events which constitute the realization of the seventh vial. Driven by God's own counsel, the devil shall have bewitched the nations to war against the Lamb. And at the outpouring of the sixth vial, Euphrates shall be dried up and the way of the kings of the east prepared. The thrones of the kings of the beast shall be darkness, indicating that there shall be internal unrest within the kingdom of Antichrist itself before the great day of Armageddon comes. They shall strike at the center of the antichristian dominion first of all, and she shall be overcome. All these things constitute the tremendous events which must take place at the end of time. And it is at that very last that also Babylon shall be destroyed, that she shall fall and her sins shall be remembered in the sight of God.

Babylon's Fall And The World

As to the significance of this fall of Babylon for the world in general, we may be brief. Her fall simply means the fall of the entire antichristian kingdom. This is already clear from the very nature of the case. Babylon is pictured as the very center of antichristian power. She is pictured as the throne and heart of the kingdom. Without her, as we mentioned, there is no commerce and no industry, no business, no science, no art, no philosophy, no riches, and no pleasure and joy. In a word, the entire structure of the kingdom rested on Babylon as its cornerstone. And therefore, when she falls, the kingdom falls. It is all done with her greatness and her joy, her riches and her abundance, her pleasure and luxury. The power of Antichrist is completely broken through the fall of Babylon.

This is also indicated symbolically by the weeping and wailing of the kings of the earth and the merchants and the shipmasters and sailors. First of all, the kings are mentioned. They are pictured as standing afar off and weeping over the fall of Babylon. These princes of the earth had all their power concentrated in Babylon. The fall of that city is their fall. It is the end of all world power. It is the end of kings and princes and of all rulers of the earth. Then the merchants, the great businessmen and corporations of the world, are mentioned. They had all their riches in Babylon, – their gold and their silver and precious stones, and all the articles of their merchandise. They also stand weeping for the reason that no one from now on can buy their merchandise any more. It is the end of materialism, the end of the god of this world, the end of all greed and lust and gain, the end of that power that would buy from and sell to only those who had the mark of the beast. And, finally, the people who work for these merchants, the shipmasters and sailors, who depended on Babylon for a job, are also pictured as bewailing the fall of the great city. And therefore, it is very plain that the fall of Babylon implies the downfall of that entire beautiful structure of the dragon which was pictured in Chapter 13 as having dominion over all things and over all the nations of the world. With Babylon, so Chapter 16, verse 19 tells us, all the cities of the nations fall together. And therefore, whether we take it that Babylon shall be a real center, or whether we look upon her as the symbolic center of Antichristendom, certain it is that her fall is the last of Antichrist.

Babylon's Fall And God's People

Finally, in regard to the relation of the people of God to Babylon and its fall, we must observe, in the first place, that they are admonished to separate from Babylon. No doubt this is first of all meant in the spiritual sense of the word. A voice comes to them, "Come out of her, my people, that ye be not partakers of her sins." Literally they shall not be able to separate themselves from Babylon, for she is everywhere. Even if in her final manifestation she shall reveal herself as a literal city, which is not at all impossible, the fact remains that she will be sitting upon many waters and that her sway and influence is felt all over the world, yea, that she is present in every city, in all business and commerce, and in every shop and store. If she would literally separate from Babylon, the church would have to go out of the world. And therefore, a spiritual separation is meant, in the first place. And this is plainly indicated by the words "that ye may have no fellowship with her sins." The people of God must know Babylon. They must see her true character. They must realize that her hope is outside of Christ, that her hope is altogether in this world, that she is antichristian and serves the devil, that she tramples under foot the blood of Christ. However beautiful and Christian she may appear, they must discern her true nature and refuse to have fellowship with her. And instead, they must with might and main cling to the Word of God and the testimony of Jesus. They must maintain that Christ is King and that His kingdom will be an everlasting kingdom in glory.

But although this is true, nevertheless I do not doubt that also a literal separation is implied in these words. I imagine, as we have had occasion to notice before, that before the last judgment shall be inflicted upon wicked Babylon, the voice mentioned here will go forth with power; and the people of God shall be taken away from the world. Not, indeed, as if a long period would intervene between the removal of the last of God's children and the end of the world; but they shall be removed. The voice will become powerful, will become irresistible, and will call powerfully the faithful and chosen from the midst of the arena of strife and tribulation to be with Christ in glory forever. How this is to be performed the text does not tell us; but that it is to be done is very clear. And the purpose of this removal of the children of God is plainly indicated in the words "and that ye receive not of her plagues." They shall not partake of her judgment. Before the final punishment is inflicted on Babylon, the children of God shall be no more in the world.

In the second place, the judgment on Babylon and on the antichristian kingdom in general will be a cause of great joy to all them that love the appearance of our Lord Jesus Christ. In the text this is indicated, as also in the next chapter. A voice shouts: "Rejoice over her, thou heaven, and ye holy apostles and prophets; for God hath avenged you on her," (vs. 20). No wonder! It is in Babylon that the blood of all the saints is found: for she is the culmination and highest realization of the power of opposition in the world of all ages. It was in Babylon that these saints were in tribulation, that they were made a laughing-stock because of their antiquated ideas and other-worldly hopes. It was Babylon that laughed at them when they testified of Jesus and of the hope that was in them, when they refused to believe in all the hopes and expectations of the world, refused to help along in the building up of the world. In a word, the apostles and prophets and the saints were always the mockery and laughingstock, looked upon as fools and idiots who knew not how to value things at their right estimation. And therefore, they must be set right; and it must become apparent that they were right and true. Even as for a long time they laughed at Noah and his message and his building of the ark, so also the world for ages laughed at all the people of God and their message and the building of their ark of hope in Christ Jesus. But even as Noah was justified when the world of wickedness was destroyed, so also shall the saints and the apostles and prophets be publicly justified when this world and all the vainglorious harlotries of this world shall be destroyed and its calamity shall come in one day.

Rejoice, therefore, ye saints, even in anticipation! Have no fellowship with the sins of Babylon! For the New Jerusalem alone shall stand and have the victory forever! But Babylon and all its abominations shall fall and be desolate forever!

Chapter XLIV
The Voice Of Joy

(Revelation 19:1-5)

1 And after these things I heard a great voice of much people in heaven, saying, Alleluia; Salvation, and glory, and honour, and power, unto the Lord our God:
2 For true and righteous are his judgments: for he hath judged the great whore, which did corrupt the earth with her fornication, and hath avenged the blood of his servants at her hand.
3 And again they said, Alleluia. And her smoke rose up for ever and ever.
4 And the four and twenty elders and the four beasts fell down and worshipped God that sat on the throne, saying, Amen; Alleluia.
5 And a voice came out of the throne, saying, Praise our God, all ye his servants, and ye that fear him, both small and great.

From one particular point of view the scene of the end has now been pictured in detail; and along just one line we have reached the very end of history. Babylon, as we saw, was the ultimate outcome of the line of false religion, of apostasy from the living God, of faith in the lie of Satan, "Ye shall not surely die, but ye shall be like God." The principle of this lie is that it rebels against the living God and tries to work out its own salvation and come to the establishment of its own kingdom, without God and without Jesus Christ. And the development of this lie in the new dispensation is that the apostate church commits fornication with the powers of the world, aids them in their efforts to establish that one and final, powerful kingdom, which shall exalt itself against the living God and do wondrous things. That church as an institute shall be done away with by the very powers which courted her favor, so that her spirit and principle shall ultimately embody itself in the great city which bears her name, Babylon. But as we saw in the preceding chapter, also this great city shall be destroyed, and that by the power of God through Jesus Christ.

602

As we studied the ultimate downfall of this Babylon, we had at the same time a most beautiful opportunity to obtain a glimpse of her real character, as it becomes manifest from all that is said of her in the eighteenth chapter of Revelation. We found that in every respect Babylon appears as a great world-center, as a city of worldwide significance. She is pictured as a center of world power, and all the kings and the great of the earth commit fornication with her. She is pictured as a center of commerce, and she has control over every article sold on the world's market. She is portrayed, too, as a center of industry and art and science: for every craftsman and artist finds his home in Babylon. But above all, she is presented as the great center of the luxury and dissipation, and, in close connection with this, as the embodiment of the wickedness of the earth. Her sin rises up to heaven; and in her is found all the blood of the saints and apostles and prophets who have died because of the Word of God and the testimony of Jesus. And hence, her doom and punishment is inevitable. She falls!

Concerning her fall specifically, we found that the manner of it is not revealed to us, but that it appears to be sudden and complete and final. Babylon becomes a hold of demons; and after her fall she is utterly desolate, never to be rebuilt. We found, too, that this fall of Babylon is the fall of the entire antichristian power, that because of her greatness and worldwide significance it is plain that without her the world-power cannot exist. It is, therefore, completely destroyed. That is true for the very reason that the kings of the world and the merchants and sailors and shipmasters and all classes of people weep and wail over her destruction. And, finally, we found that the people of God are admonished to separate themselves from Babylon, – an exhortation which implies, no doubt, in the first place, that the children of the kingdom must separate themselves spiritually from the wicked city, so that they have no fellowship with her sins. But, in the second place, it becomes a powerful and irresistible call, taking the people of the Savior to glory immediately before the very last and final punishment of Babylon.

In the chapter now under discussion, we have a different scene, a scene of joy and exultation.

The Joyful Multitude In Heaven

We may observe, in the first place, that in this chapter we meet once more one of those remarkable contrasts of which the Book of Revelation is full, and, in fact, which are numerous throughout the Word of God. The same event leaves different impressions and arouses radically different sentiments in different people. When the Savior is born and there is joy in heaven and the angels come down to shout of the glad tidings for the earth, the shepherds of Bethlehem in joyful expectation direct their way to the manger of Bethlehem, and even the wise men from the distant east follow the star of the King with keenest interest and deepest concern; but, on the other hand, you find that Herod is deeply worried about this event and makes the treacherous attempt to remove the Babe from the earth before it can rise to glory; and the scribes and Pharisees, the wise men of the nation, evidently meet it with stoical indifference. At the cross, which for a moment appears to the bystanders as the last and complete defeat of the Man of Galilee, you may note Mary and John and the women who used to follow Jesus filled with astonishment and sorrow because of the things that happen; but there is also the exultant joy of the leaders, of the scribes and Pharisees, − a joy aroused by the same event as was the grief of the disciples. At the resurrection morning the disciples joyfully meet one another with the exultant greeting, "The Lord is risen indeed!" And their hearts are filled with a new-born hope. But the same fact of the resurrection caused the enemies to flee in dismay and filled the hearts of the leaders with devilish apprehension. Thus the illustrations might be multiplied. The same events, connected somehow with the kingdom of our Lord Jesus Christ and its coming, are the cause of fear and sorrow to some, of joy and gladness to others.

Thus it was with Babylon, the great city. For some time it had been the cause of dismay and fear and terror to the people of God. For Babylon embodied all the principles which they hated, and, therefore, became the cause of their persecution and tribulation. But the great of the earth committed fornication with her, and the masses in general were wondering at her glory and filled with joy because of the greatness of her power. But now the scene has changed. Babylon is fallen. And even as her glory was the joy of the world and the grief of the children of the kingdom, so also her downfall causes a two-fold sentiment to come to manifestation. But this time the joy is of God's people, and the grief is expressed by the children of unbelief.

Let us notice concerning these singers, in the first place, that they are in heaven. "After these things," so John informs us, "I heard a great voice of much people in heaven."

The scene of this chapter, therefore, connects itself with that of the preceding. It takes place after what has been recorded in Chapter 18; in fact, what is described here is occasioned by what is told us in Chapter 18. And the scene here described takes place in heaven. Heaven and earth are still separated. In fact, I imagine that there never was a moment in the history of the world that the gap between heaven and earth was so wide as at this present moment. Because of sin a breach was made between heaven, the dwelling-place of the Holy One and all His holy servants and of the saints who have gone before, and the earth, condemned and cursed because of the entrance of sin. Originally this was not so. There was harmony and unity between heaven and earth, a harmony which was purposed to grow and increase till all the world, heaven and earth, had become the glorious kingdom of our God in perfection. But sin made the breach, a breach which was scarcely visible in paradise, but which becomes wider and wider as history develops, until, at the time of Babylon's culmination and destruction, it has reached its climax. The man of sin has developed to his last stage. The iniquity of Babylon cried unto heaven, cried to Jehovah Sabaoth; and at this moment all that is left upon earth is a mass of misery and desolation. Children of God there are no more upon the earth.

The picture presents us with a scene of misery and desolation, wept over and bewailed by the great and merchants and all the people of the world. It is a picture of sorrow and grief. The kings of the earth express their grief. The merchants wail and weep over the loss of Babylon. And the shipmasters and sailors stand afar off to shed their tears of grief over Babylon's desolation. But it is a sorrow of the world. They are sorry not because the iniquity of the city called for the punishment of the Almighty. They are sorry not because they so greatly sinned and provoked the wrath of the Most High. But they are sorry because of material loss and because they cannot now continue to engage in wanton rebellion against the Most High and enjoy the pleasures of sin. It is the sorrow of the world. They are tears of sin and selfishness, not of true repentance, which are shed by the world over the destruction of Babylon. But however this may be, fact is that all the inhabitants of the earth are pictured as in misery because of the destruction of the great and glorious city.

But in heaven there is an entirely different scene. The very same event which causes so much misery and sorrow on earth among the people of the world fills the heavens with joy and causes them to rebound with a fourfold **hallelujah**, to the glory of Him who sitteth upon the throne. A tremendous contrast, therefore, is caused by the fall of Babylon, a contrast which finds its principle in the attitude of men to the Lamb. On earth were the followers of the dragon, the subjects of the beast, the worshippers of his image, who expected their all from him and his reign. And therefore they are disappointed at the desolation of the great city. But in heaven are the Lamb and His one hundred forty-four thousand and the holy angels, they that serve and love and fear the Lord and His name and look for the kingdom of God and His righteousness in perfection. They naturally are filled with joy because the destruction of the great city is their glory and victory. The joy is in heaven.

In the second place, we may ask the question: who are these who sing at the destruction of Babylon?

Must we think here of a particular class of people, as some venture to guess? Must we separate the people of God in heaven? Must we say that they are only those who have suffered directly from Babylon at the time of her culmination and greatest glory, the saints who were on earth at that time? I do not think that we are warranted at all in so interpreting the scene. True, it must be confessed that not all have been in contact with Babylon in her clearest and most blatant manifestation. Not all have suffered from her in an equal degree. But the fact remains that in principle Babylon always existed and that she has always been the enemy of the people of God. Besides, it is simply a monstrous and inconceivable assumption to suppose that part of the people of God should sing the praise of the Almighty while others would be profoundly silent in connection with the fall of Babylon. If it is true in regard to the suffering of this dispensation that all the members suffer where one member is in tribulation, it is equally true that in the state of glory all shall rejoice even though not all have been in equally close contact with the cause of this joy personally.

Besides, in the preceding chapter we read, in the first place, that Babylon is to blame for all the suffering of the children of God and that in her is found the blood of all the saints, of all who have been slain upon the earth. And, in the second place, we find that the call comes to all, the apostles and prophets and saints, to rejoice over the fall of Babylon, vs. 20. The song of this multitude in heaven is undoubtedly the response to that voice. Still more, the text is careful to mention all the people of God and, in fact, all the animate creation, as participants in this joy over fallen Babylon. In a very general way John tells us, in the first place, that he heard a tremendous voice, as of a great multitude, in heaven without specifically stating who belongs to this multitude. Even if he had not informed us further, we would not have the right to limit their number to any particular class. But he does speak more specifically too. He tells us that the twenty-four elders, − representatives, as we know, of the entire church, both of the old and of the new dispensation, − fall down and worship God and join in with the **hallelujah** that rebounds through the heavens. And not only they, but the four living creatures, − representative of the glorified creature delivered from the bondage of corruption, − worship Him that sitteth upon the throne. And finally, the voice comes from the throne, calling upon all the servants who fear the Lord, both small and great, to call upon the name of Jehovah in exultant praise.

The text, therefore, rather leaves the impression that this multitude embraces all the saints and even all the inhabitants of the heavens, and, still more widely, embraces all the animate creation, which sees in the destruction of Babylon its own restoration and deliverance. Abel and Noah, Abraham and Isaac and Jacob, Moses and Joshua, all the patriarchs and prophets and saints of the old dispensation, and all the apostles and martyrs and saints of the New Testament day join in with this song and give praise to God Almighty and unto the Lamb. And as they sing, the angels respond in songs of joy and gladness, and all creation as it is represented in the picture of the glorified economy in heaven worship and praise and sing their **hallelujahs** to the glory of the Most High God.

The Song Which Is Sung

As to the song, we may remark, in the first place, that the glory of God is very emphatically the main theme of the entire praise that flows from the lips of this tremendous multitude. It is noteworthy that four times the shout of praise, "Hallelujah," is repeated by them; that the voice from the throne has but one message, "Give praise unto our God;" that the multitude sings, "Salvation, and glory, and honour, and power belong unto our God;" and, finally, that the four and twenty elders and the four living creatures fall down to worship repeating the "Hallelujah, Amen" of the saints and the holy angels. There is in this song nothing of man, nothing of the creature; it is all of God and His glory that all the creatures sing. And the purpose of all God's plans and works is certainly plainly reached when Babylon is destroyed. For He receives praise and adoration from all His creation, and His name is glorified.

Hallelujah is a word which occurs nowhere else in Revelation, and, in fact, nowhere else in the entire New Testament. Here it occurs four times in practically the same song. In the Old Testament it occurs very frequently, especially in the Psalms. It is a Hebrew word. The first part of it, **hallelu,** means "praise ye," while the second part of this compound noun is an abbreviation of Jehovah, the covenant name of God. And therefore, the entire word simply means, "Praise ye Jehovah; praise our covenant God."

The reason for this praise of Jehovah is further set forth in the following sentence of the song of the multitude: "Salvation, and glory, and power belong unto our God." It is because the salvation and glory and power belong to God that He must be praised. All these three attributes of God, all these three ascriptions of praise, must be taken in their most comprehensive sense. Salvation belongs unto our God, that is, salvation to its fullest extent. This multitude stands at the close of history. Babylon is already destroyed, and the power of Antichrist is broken. All things are ready for the coming of the new heaven and the new earth and the complete glorification of all God's saints and of all God's creation. The multitude naturally looks on salvation from this comprehensive point of view, salvation of body and soul, salvation of man and the whole world, the complete salvation and restoration and glorification of that entire kingdom which God created at the beginning, which for a time seemed to be in the hands of the devil, but which is redeemed by the Lamb. That salvation is of our God. It came from Him. He is the planner and the author of that salvation. He is the finisher of that salvation. He it is Who must receive all the glory. And from the depth of their heart all the saints who have been redeemed now shout and sing, "Salvation is of our God! Hence, to Him belongeth the glory." God's glory is the effulgence, the radiation, of His glorious being. In all His works, His name, the wonders of His revelation, the works of His hands, here especially the glory of God as it became evident in the work of salvation, more particularly in the destruction of Babylon, — in all this is manifested the radiation of God's glorious being. The same is true of His power. It is His mighty strength, over against which no enemy can stand, the power of His omnipotence, before which all the powers on earth and in hell are brought to nought.

But we must not forget that in these very words which ascribe salvation and glory and power to the Most High there is implied a silent contrast, which must, however, be very consciously before the minds of these singers. They undoubtedly mean to say too: "Salvation and glory and power belong not to the gods of the world, but to our God."

The world also has its gods. And for a time it seemed as if these gods were powerful and glorious enough to save the world from its misery and to establish the glorious kingdom of peace and justice without God and without the Lamb. In Babylon, the city of the great beast and of the dragon, there was joy and happiness and riches and luxury. There accumulated the tremendous wealth of the world. There shone the power of the world. There was heard the voice of the harper and the trumpeter, the voice of the bride and the bridegroom. It was a picture of joy and happiness and greatness and power. And it seemed as if the dragon finally had succeeded to make the world his glorious kingdom. It seemed as if salvation belonged to him. For only those who were of him and worshipped his image could partake of the blessings of that kingdom. It seemed as if all the glory of the world belonged to the dragon. For in fact all the inhabitants of the world wondered after the beast; and those who refused could find no place of safety in the world. It seemed as if all the power belonged to him: for all the kings of the world had added their power unto the beast, and the faithful worshippers of the Lamb were helpless and defenseless. And therefore, for some time it had seemed actually as if the hope of the people of God was idle and as if not their God, but the gods of the world were the authors of salvation, to whom belonged glory and power. And it was only by faith, as an evidence of things unseen and as the substance of things hoped for, that the faithful witnesses of Jesus Christ had maintained all the time that unto their God belonged salvation through the Lamb and that unto Him all glory and honor and power must be ascribed.

But now it is all so different. Gone is the power and the splendor and the glory of Babylon. The boasting of the dragon and of the beast has come to an end. Babylon is destroyed. The kingdom of Antichrist is no more. The historic proof has finally been given that salvation and glory and power did not belong unto the gods of this world, did not belong unto the beast, did not belong to the dragon, not unto all the world-powers, not unto the power of Antichrist, but unto God. On earth there is desolation and weeping and wailing because of the fall of the great city which once was the hope and the pride of the world. But in heaven are the Lamb and all His people and all the glorious angels, the entire glorious economy of the New Jerusalem that is presently to descend from heaven to earth. And therefore, that entire throng, in jubilant joy because of the victory of their God, breaks out in song. And in emphatic contrast with the gods of the world and their absolute failure to establish salvation and reveal their power, they sing, "Salvation and glory and power belong unto our God." Hence, the multitude sings, "Hallelujah, praise Jehovah." Hence, the twenty-four elders and the four living creatures bow down in reverent worship. Hence, all the servants of the Lord who fear His name, both small and great, are urged to sing praise unto the God Who has revealed His power and glory and His wonderful salvation.

It is, then, not in the abstract that they sing of God's glory, but in connection with the revelation of that glory in the specific incident of the destruction of Babylon. The joy of the world is the grief of God's children; the grief of the world is the joy of the children of the kingdom.

Not, indeed, as if the children of the kingdom should rejoice with a sinful joy over the suffering and agony of the dwellers in Babylon; but they rejoice in the righteous judgment of God. Babylon was for them the embodiment of rebellion and transgression against the God Whose name they loved. It is the city whose iniquity cries unto the heavens. There God's name was trampled under foot, and His righteousness and glory was despised. There the Savior of the world was mocked at and crucified, and His name was defiled. There the truth of God was denied, and the worship of God forbidden. There the people of God were persecuted and cast into severest tribulation. In a word, all that was connected with God, with their God and His name, was hooted at and despised and mocked and trodden under foot. The glory of God's name was covered up by the iniquitous rebellion of Babylon. But now the glory of that name has appeared. It has appeared in the judgment of Babylon, the great whore. It has appeared that God is righteous and just and powerful and glorious. And therefore, they sing in joy over the destruction of Babylon. Babylon hated God and His Christ: and therefore they hate Babylon. And hence, they cannot but exult in her weeping and wailing and desolation: "For true and righteous are his judgments: for he hath judged the great whore, which did corrupt the earth with her fornication." She it was that caused all the earth to depart from the living God and to rise in rebellion against Him. She it was that corrupted the whole earth with her harlotry. Her destruction is the destruction of the entire system of black iniquity inaugurated in paradise by the devil. And therefore, even as the whole earth justly rejoices in the eternal damnation of the devil, that prince of darkness, and no one can pity that embodiment of hellish iniquity in his suffering, so all the people of our God rejoice at the desolation of Babylon and all that her name implies and can have no pity with her hellish sorrow.

Finally, this multitude sings with joy over the destruction of Babylon because her destruction, besides being the justification of God, the theodicy, is at the same time the justification of all God's people.

With the opening of the fifth seal we saw how the souls under the altar cried to God Almighty for vengeance because their blood had been shed for the testimony of Jesus. Then it was told them that they should wait yet a little while and have patience until also the rest of their brethren had died and been killed by the power of Babylon. Since that time centuries have elapsed. And in those centuries the brethren have suffered and have been persecuted and put in prison and brought to the scaffold and to the stake; and the power of Antichrist has been triumphant in her wanton iniquity and godlessness and cruelty against the saints of the Most High. Streams of blood have flowed since that time. But now the time of judgment has come. It has become evident that the testimony of Jesus and the Word of God is true forevermore and that the cry of His people came into the ears of Jehovah Sabaoth: "He hath avenged the blood of his servants at her hand." And once more, therefore, they sing and praise and shout for joy. For Babylon is fallen; and God is glorified and justified in her destruction; and they have been avenged for all the suffering and tribulation they endured at her hand. Small and great join in with the song of those who fear the name of God. For Babylon is fallen, fallen forever. For her smoke riseth forever and ever, and never shall the power of rebellion and iniquity arise again.

Once more, if we enter into the sanctuary of our God and notice the end both of Babylon and of God's people, can there be much doubt in our hearts as to the side we choose, by the grace of God, to take in this world? Heed, therefore, the call of your God, and go out from her; have nothing to do with the sins of Babylon, that ye may not partake of her judgments. Let us join in with the chorus of the multitude and of the elders and of the living creatures, and respond to the voice that goeth forth from the throne with the four-fold, "Hallelujah, Amen! Yea, Amen forevermore!"

Chapter XLV

The Marriage Of The Lamb

(Revelation 19:6-10)

6 And I heard as it were the voice of a great multitude, and as the voice of many waters, and as the voice of mighty thunderings, saying, Alleluia: for the Lord God omnipotent reigneth.

7 Let us be glad and rejoice, and give honour to him: for the marriage of the Lamb is come, and his wife hath made herself ready.

8 And to her was granted that she should be arrayed in fine linen, clean and white: for the fine linen is the righteousness of saints.

9 And he saith unto me, Write, Blessed are they which are called unto the marriage supper of the Lamb. And he saith unto me, These are the true sayings of God.

10 And I fell at his feet to worship him. And he said unto me, See thou do it not: I am thy fellowservant, and of thy brethren that have the testimony of Jesus: worship God: for the testimony of Jesus is the spirit of prophecy.

In this passage we have a new vision, the vision of the marriage of the Lamb, which is at the same time the conclusion of a series of visions which were shown and explained to the apostle by one and the same angel.

That this passage is the concluding portion of a larger section and of an entire series of visions is plain especially from verses 9 and 10. There we read of an angel who talked with John, giving him the assurance that "these are the true sayings of God." This angel is designated as "he," presupposing that he has been mentioned before. And if we look for this earlier mention, we discover it already in Chapter 17:1. He is "one of the seven angels which had the seven vials," who began to talk with John and to shew him the judgment of the great whore, the harlot-woman who is also the city of Babylon. He is mentioned again in verse 7 of the same chapter, where he is recorded as explaining to John the mystery of the woman and of the beast that carries her. And in Chapter 17:15 this same angel is referred to as "he." Hence, this passage must be understood as telling us of one vision which belongs to and concludes a series of visions, all of which are shown to John and explained by one of the seven angels who had the seven vials. In this series, on the one hand, we find the picture of Babylon, the great world-power, in the history of its development and in its ultimate formation, along with the prophecy and vision of Babylon's final destruction. And, on the other hand, we find in this series the contrasting picture of the beatification of the people of God. This second, positive part begins with the song of the multitude in heaven in Chapter 19, verses 1-5; and the present vision of the marriage of the Lamb follows upon that vision and concludes the entire section.

That the passage now under discussion is very closely related to the immediately preceding portion is evident from the fact that the same note of joy and praise to God is heard in both passages. In the former passage the four-fold "Hallelujah" is directly connected with the judgment of the great whore. Here the rejoicing is over the omnipotent reign of the Lord God as connected with the marriage of the Lamb. And the vision concludes with the statement of the beatitude of those who are called to the marriage supper of the Lamb, the assurance concerning the truth of "these sayings," and the refusal of the angel to be worshipped by John.

The Bridegroom

The vision is introduced by "the voice as it were of a great multitude." John hears a great and mighty voice, as of a great multitude, and as of many waters, and of mighty thunderings, saying, "Alleluia: for the Lord God omnipotent reigneth." It is evident that all are in heaven. The vision does not take place on the earth, as some would have it, but in heaven. Nor is it a vision which takes place in this present time, but in the beginning of the everlasting day. And the multitude is here presented as uniting in praise and joy to the Lord God omnipotent, Who reigns, on account of the marriage of the Lamb in heavenly glory. Their sound is as the sound of many waters and as the voice of mighty thunderings, roaring and reverberating through the heavens. It is as though John exhausts himself to give expression to the mighty and overwhelming impression which the vision makes upon him.

First of all, this great multitude express praise to God Almighty in the same form as in the first part of this chapter, "Alleluia: for the Lord God omnipotent reigneth." Undoubtedly this praise is still connected with the fact of His victory over Babylon. The idea is that the power of opposition has been broken and destroyed, and now God is revealed as sovereign, as King absolute. God's sovereignty and omnipotent reign and power are, of course, always evident in the history of the world. But here the reference is undoubtedly to the fact that this sovereignty and power of God have become revealed in the judgment of the harlot-woman, Babylon. That judgment means that His kingdom has now come. He is revealed as being King alone. For a time that power and sovereignty had been disputed by the prince of darkness; and it even seemed for a time that the powers of opposition had succeeded in enforcing their challenge of God's sovereignty when they had established their mighty and glorious world-kingdom without God and without Jesus Christ. But now the power that disputed and challenged God's sovereignty has been completely destroyed. Babylon is fallen, completely and finally; and the judgment of the great whore has been accomplished. Christ has subdued all under Him and has delivered the kingdom unto the Father. This is the viewpoint in the vision. And for this reason the vision begins with the ascription of praise once more to the Lord God omnipotent, the King.

Not only does the great multitude express praise to God, however; but it also expresses joy and gladness, "Let us be glad and rejoice, and give honour to him." The reason is, evidently, that they know that after the completion of the kingdom the marriage of the Lamb takes place. The destruction of the anti-christian world-power means the completion of the kingdom of God. And the completion of the kingdom means that the marriage of the Lamb shall take place. And this marriage of the Lamb is now celebrated in this vision with great joy. At the same time, John hears the multitude once again ascribing honor to God. For God, Who is the only omnipotent one, and Who is the author of the destruction of great Babylon and therefore the author of the mighty and victorious kingdom which has now been achieved, is therefore also the author of the great salvation which is realized in the marriage of the Lamb. Hence, all honor is to be ascribed to Him alone. Thus, with glad shouting of rejoicing and with loud ascriptions of honor and praise to God, this multitude, as it were, rushes to the wedding to be present as guests.

We may notice that there are two distinct elements in the vision, that of the marriage as such and that of the marriage supper, or feast. Neither one of these is described in the text as being witnessed by John himself; but they are pictured by him in terms of the words of the multitude and of the angel. The multitude is pictured, first of all, as saying: "For the marriage of the Lamb is come, and his wife hath made herself ready." Then the bride of the Lamb is described, also in the words of the multitude: "And to her was granted that she should be arrayed in fine linen, clean and white: for the fine linen is the righteousness of saints." And, finally, the marriage supper is introduced into the picture in the angel's words of beatitude which John is specifically instructed to write, "Blessed are they which are called to the marriage supper of the Lamb."

Once again we must be careful to remember that we are dealing here with a vision, with a picture which is highly symbolic. We cannot take the language of this passage literally without falling into all kinds of absurdities, as will become evident in our subsequent discussion of the various elements in this vision. What we have here is a highly symbolic picture of the wedding, or marriage, of the Lamb. And in that picture there are several elements, namely, the bridegroom, the bride, the wedding, and the marriage supper of the Lamb. Each of these elements we must try to understand.

The Bridegroom is the Lamb, our Lord Jesus Christ, according to the vision.

This figure of the Bridegroom is a familiar one in Scripture. He appears, for example, in the Old Testament in the highly descriptive language of Psalm 45:6-9: "Thy throne, O God, is for ever and ever: the sceptre of thy kingdom is a right sceptre. Thou lovest righteousness, and hatest wickedness: therefore God, thy God, hath anointed thee with the oil of gladness above thy fellows. All thy garments smell of myrrh, and aloes, and cassia, out of the ivory palaces, whereby they have made thee glad. Kings' daughters were among thy honourable women: upon thy right hand did stand the queen in gold of Ophir." Also according to the testimony of John the Baptist, Christ is the Bridegroom, John 3:28, 29: "Ye yourselves bear me witness, that I said, I am not the Christ, but that I am sent before him. He that hath the bride is the bridegroom: but the friend of the bridegroom, which standeth and heareth him, rejoiceth greatly because of the bridegroom's voice: this my joy therefore is fulfilled." In the parable of the wise and the foolish virgins, Matthew 25:1-13, the Lord Jesus undoubtedly refers to Himself, the Son of Man, as the Bridegroom for whose coming the five foolish virgins were not ready. And, finally, when in Ephesians 5 the apostle writes about the calling of husbands to love their wives, he refers ultimately to the marriage of Christ and His church: "This is a great mystery: but I speak concerning Christ and the church," (verse 32).

Here, however, the Bridegroom is specifically referred to as the Lamb. The marriage of the Lamb is come. Very often in the Book of Revelation He is called not only the Lamb, but the "Lamb standing as though he hath been slain." That this wedding is here referred to as the marriage of the Lamb points very evidently to the Bridegroom, our Lord Jesus Christ, in the work and power and efficacy of His atonement. And that atonement is the central revelation of the love of God in Christ for His people. The emphasis, therefore, is upon the great love of the Bridegroom for His bride. Christ, the Bridegroom, loved the church, His bride, and gave Himself for her, Ephesians 5:25. He loved His bride even unto death, yea, the death of the cross. He purchased her with His own precious blood.

The Bride

Also the bride of the Lamb, the Lamb's wife, appears as a significant element in the vision. She is described as having made herself ready; and of her it is said that "to her was granted that she should be arrayed in fine linen, clean and white: for the fine linen is the righteousness of saints."

There are various interpretations as to the identity of the bride. Some interpreters attempt to explain this entire vision as taking place **before** the final coming of the Lord. According to them, it takes place in the "rapture" and the "first resurrection," before the final translation into glory and before the days of Antichrist and of the great tribulation. These same interpreters deny that the scene of this marriage is heaven, but explain that it takes place neither in heaven nor on earth, but in the air. And they also severely limit the identity of the bride to a very small fraction of the saints. Others also would limit the identity of the bride of the Lamb to part of the saints, but on a different basis. They wish to take the vision literally. And then they point to the distinction between the wedding proper and the marriage supper, and maintain that some are evidently the bride of the Lamb while others are guests at the marriage supper. This distinction they explain as meaning that there will be differences in glory. Some of the saints will be the bride of the Lamb. The greatest saints will live in most intimate communion with the Savior, and they will constitute the Lamb's wife. Other saints shall also enter into glory, and they shall participate in the gladness and rejoicing of the saints in glory that is pictured in this vision. But they will not be of the number of the greatest saints. They will inherit heavenly glory and its bliss as servants and attendants in this wedding of the Lamb. They shall have a part; but that part will be a lesser part, comparable to that of guests at the marriage supper.

It is our conviction, however, that by the bride of the Lamb is meant the entire church. All the saints, both of the old and of the new dispensation, and that as one church, constitute the Lamb's bride.

In the first place, as we have already pointed out, the scene of this vision is very definitely heaven, not the air; and as to the time, this vision conducts us to the very end of this dispensation, to the last day. Babylon has already fallen and been destroyed. And before the judgment of the great whore, the last of the saints had been taken out of the world, irresistibly called out of Babylon and its plagues. We are in this vision at the time of the end, at the dawn of the everlasting day, and in heaven. Secondly, it is the presentation of the entire Word of God that the church, both of the old and of the new dispensation, is one, and that this church, comprised of all the saints, is the bride of Christ. Christ is the Bridegroom of the church, not of only a part of the church, Ephesians 5:32. This is also the presentation of this passage in Revelation 19. For the fine linen with which the bride is clothed is the righteousness of saints, not the special righteousness of a few saints. The Lamb's wife, therefore, is the saints.

Moreover, we should bear in mind that this marriage of the Lamb is essential to heavenly glory. Surely, there shall be different degrees of glory in heaven. Nor is the presentation of the text in conflict with this difference in degrees. But we must remember that whatever difference there will be as to degrees of glory for the saints, such difference will be within the framework of the union of the entire church with Christ. For the union with Christ as such, here pictured in the symbolism of the marriage, is not a matter of degree. On the contrary, the union with Christ is essential to heavenly glory. That we shall be forever and perfectly united with Christ, and through Christ to God, is, in fact, the very essence of heaven. Heaven would not be heaven and would not be glorious without that union. Hence, that union must needs involve all the saints.

As to the presentation of the text that there is one bride and many guests, we remind you that the picture of the text is not literal, but highly symbolic. If only we bear this in mind, and do not attempt to press a literal interpretation upon this vision, we can also understand this element.

Then we can understand that the bride and the guests are one and the same, but that in the figure of the bride the church is presented as a whole, as a unity, in her marriage with Christ, while the members of the church considered individually are the guests at the feast which the Father has prepared for His Son, the Lamb.

For all these reasons, then, we must insist that the bride is not to be limited to the saints of the new dispensation, and then not even all of them. But the bride of the Lamb is the whole church, comprised of all the saints of all ages, but that church considered as one whole, while the guests at the supper are the members of the church considered individually.

This bride of the Lamb is clothed in fine linen, clean and white. The text itself explains that this fine, white linen is "the righteousness of saints." This righteousness is, first of all, the fundamental righteousness of the saints in the blood of Christ, the Lamb. It is their legal righteousness, the righteousness of their state, according to which the perfect righteousness of Christ is imputed to them. It is the righteousness which is theirs through the very fact that the Lamb was slain and laid down His life for them, and thus purchased them to be His bride. But the reference is also to the righteousness of the saints in the spiritual, ethical sense of the word, or, if you will, to the holiness of the bride. She has kept her garments clean and unspotted from the pollutions of the world, of Babylon. She has heeded the call to come out of Babylon and not to be partaker of Babylon's sins. Hence, the church, the bride of the Lamb, appears here as clothed in garments of justification and sanctification, the pure and white linen of the righteousness of Christ. Moreover, in the vision she appears as having made herself ready. This cannot mean, of course, that the church has justified and sanctified herself, as if her righteousness were of her own accomplishment. On the contrary, the text even emphasizes that these garments of fine linen with which she is clothed are a matter of grace: "And to her was granted that she should be arrayed in fine linen, clean and white." But by faith and in love, and with a view to meeting her Bridegroom, through grace, the bride has prepared herself, has put on the garments provided by the Lamb Himself, and kept herself unspotted from the world.

She is ready for her marriage to the Lamb.

The Marriage

The symbolism of marriage occurs very often in Scripture, both in the

Old and in the New Testament. Sometimes the marriage bond portrays the covenant relation between God and His people; sometimes the picture of marriage is used to describe the union between Christ and His church. Here, as we have already noted, the latter is the case. The marriage of the Lamb is come, and His wife hath made herself ready. All things, therefore, are in readiness for this wedding.

As to the idea of marriage, it is an intimate union of fellowship of nature, of life, and of love between husband and wife. And here in our text it is such a union in the spiritual sense between Christ and His church. There is a union of nature between Christ and His church. Christ imparts His nature to the church, through His Spirit, so that the church, the bride, is like Him, that is, conformed to the image of God's Son. Secondly, there is fellowship of life between Christ and His bride. Christ's life is the life of the church. The same Spirit dwells in Him as the head and in His people as the members of His body. And through that Spirit Christ imparts His own incorruptible, heavenly, glorious, resurrection life to the entire church. And, thirdly, there is a communion of love between Christ and His church, based upon the communion of nature and of life. Even as His church is like Him and has His life, so He loves His church. And that love of Christ, which is always first, finds response in the heart and life of the bride, who is like Him; and the church loves Him.

Now what is pictured in the vision of our text is the final and heavenly union of Christ and His church in everlasting and perfect glory. It is not, as some would have it, a new period of prosperity for the church on earth that is pictured here. No, it is nothing else than the final and perfect consummation of the union between Christ and His church, the final salvation. When the entire church shall be perfected in glory and shall be perfectly like Him, perfectly united with Him spiritually, and when in perfect heavenly glory, body and soul, they shall be with Him forever, then is the marriage of the Lamb. This presupposes, of course, too, that then the communion of the saints shall be perfected. The bride is one. And the bliss of the church and her perfect enjoyment of that union with Christ cannot and shall not be completed before all the members of that church are literally united. Then the bride shall appear in the perfection of righteousness, clothed in pure and white linen, prepared as a bride for her husband; and then Christ shall take unto Himself His bride forever.

Such, in brief, is the presentation of the vision.

Now, indeed, that union of Christ and His church exists already essentially. Even as it is true in our earthly marriages, which are ideally a reflection of the marriage of Christ and His church, that the communion of nature and of life and of love exists already before husband and wife are united in marriage, so it is with the Lord and His church. That union already exists essentially. But here and now that union is not perfect. There are all kinds of imperfections and separations between the Bridegroom and His bride. Partly this is due to sin. Partly this is due to the imperfection of things earthy. Partly this is due to the fact that in this present dispensation the great whore has not yet been judged: the bride and the great whore live, as it were, in the same house yet. But for all these reasons the bride is not yet ready, and the Lamb is not yet ready to take her to Himself. All the elect are not yet called and saved. There is separation as yet between the church militant and the church triumphant. Besides, for various reasons there is separation between different parts of the church militant. Moreover, prior to that final day neither the church militant nor that part of the church which is already in heaven is glorified as to the body.

But now, — such is the picture of this vision, — the bride is all glorified and united. And the union between Christ and His church is perfected. There is no more separation and no more reason for separation. The bride, the entire church shall forever be with the Lord. Publicly the Lamb takes His bride. The kingdom is prepared: for a bridegroom must have a proper house where he can make his home with his bride. He is ready to lead His bride into that kingdom at this very moment. And before all the world (a wedding is a public affair!) Christ presents His church to the Father without spot or wrinkle and takes her as His bride, to bestow upon her all the blessings of His love in His perfect and glorious kingdom.

The Supper

The last element in this vision of the marriage of the Lamb is that of the supper. Plainly this is a distinct element, different from the marriage itself. The same angel who talks with John at the very beginning of this entire series of visions now instructs John: "Write, Blessed are they which are called unto the marriage supper of the Lamb." Here, too, as with the marriage itself, John does not directly record a vision of this marriage supper, but rather is given knowledge of this supper and its blessedness this time through the speech of the angel.

Those who are called to this marriage supper of the Lamb are not some special guests, other than the church. They are the same as the wife of the Lamb, but now considered as individual believers, members of the church. We must notice also that they are **called** to this marriage supper. This is the calling of God Himself, the efficacious calling. All that are called, all the elect, all the glorified saints take part in this supper. Here that calling is viewed especially from the viewpoint of its blessedness: "Blessed are they which are called..." And John is especially instructed to write this, the reason being that the saints in the midst of the world, especially as they must suffer at the hand of the antichristian world-power for the testimony of Jesus and for the Word of God, may be reminded and assured of the hope of their calling. That same power of the calling which for a time involves them in suffering for Christ's sake is nevertheless blessed: for the end, the goal, of that calling is the blessedness and joy of the marriage supper of the Lamb. Well may the saints keep in view this hope of their calling!

For the special emphasis of the symbolism of the marriage supper is upon the fact that the marriage of the Lamb is a joyous occasion. If we may follow the parallel of such a marriage supper as it is presented elsewhere in Scripture, then the picture is that the Father prepares the feast, is the host at this supper, bids the guests. Christ and His bride are forever united in Father's home and Father's kingdom. And in celebration of their marriage, Father prepares this feast. Christ and His bride are the guests of honor at this feast; and all the individual members of the church are those who share in this occasion of great joy. Only, we must remember that this feast is not a passing event; and its joy is not only for a moment. But it is everlasting. Eternally the saints will rejoice in the fact that now they have been perfectly united in life, in nature, and in love to Christ, the Bridegroom. This blessed covenant fellowship is also the significance of the marriage supper. At that supper the guests eat and drink together, with the Lamb and with the Father, in intimate communion of friendship. Through Christ we shall eternally have perfect covenant fellowship with God, shall know Him as we are known, love as we are loved, behold God's beauty, dwell in His house, and walk with Him and talk with Him. The Word of the Lord shall be perfectly realized: "I in them, and thou in me, that they may be made perfect in one," (John 17:23). Blessed indeed, therefore, are they who are called to the marriage supper of the Lamb!

At the conclusion of the vision the angel instructs John pointedly: "These are the true sayings of God." These sayings to which the angel refers do not only include the sayings concerning the marriage and the marriage supper of the Lamb and concerning the joy of the saints who are now united with Christ; but they refer to the entire vision, or series of visions, which begins in Chapter 17 and extends to Chapter 19, verse 10. All that is revealed concerning Babylon and concerning Babylon's destruction and concerning the rejoicing of the redeemed multitude over the judgment of the great whore and concerning the joyous marriage of the Lamb, — all these are the true sayings, the real words, of God. And the words of God are infallibly true; they can never lie. We can surely rely on those words of God in life and in death. For as surely as they are true, so surely also shall they come to pass. The angel makes a special point of this. This certainly does not imply that other words, apart from this vision, are less true. Not at all: all the words of God are true. But here this is emphasized. And this emphasis has its reason in the purpose of comforting and reassuring the people of God in the midst of the tribulation and suffering which are their portion in Babylon. Their lot may be very severe; and the way may seem very dark. It may appear that the powers of darkness triumph completely, and that the cause of Christ is utterly defeated. But the words of God are true. The marriage of the Lamb is surely coming! The great whore shall certainly be judged, and Babylon and all the enemies of Christ and His people shall be destroyed. Blessed are they which are called unto the marriage supper of the Lamb!

John is evidently deeply impressed. For we read that he fell at the feet of the angel and wanted to worship him. From the last statement of the angel the apostle probably concluded that it was Christ Himself speaking to him, and therefore he falls down to worship. But immediately the angel corrects him. He assures John that he is not divine and that he is not the Christ, but that he is only a fellowservant of John and of all the saints, and that God alone must be worshipped. No creature, no matter how glorious and no matter how important, even how divine, his message is, may be worshipped; only God is the proper object of our adoration and worship.

And then the angel concludes by stressing that he has "the testimony of Jesus," and that this "testimony of Jesus is the spirit of prophecy." His testimony, therefore, is about Jesus. It is the testimony which speaks of the coming of Jesus in glory and of the salvation of the saints. Moreover, this testimony of Jesus is the "spirit of prophecy." The meaning is that this testimony is also **from** Jesus. That prophecy is the Word of God, the true sayings of God, to which the angel has already referred. And they are prophecy not only in the sense of predicting the future, but in the sense that all the salvation of the saints is declared in this prophecy, and that in the name of God Himself. All that God has ever promised for His people, both for the present and for the future, is implied in the words of the angel. This testimony about and from Jesus is the spirit of prophecy, therefore. That is, the entire testimony concerning Christ and concerning the salvation of the people of God is wrought by the Spirit, the Spirit of God Who is given to Christ and through Christ to His people, and Who declares all the words of God. By this Spirit the angel can deliver the true sayings of God. And while the angel is not divine, but a fellowservant of John and of all the saints, nevertheless his word is divine: for it is the testimony of Jesus, which is the Spirit of prophecy. And all the saints and fellowservants of this angel receive this testimony of Jesus, and will therefore also embrace the words of the angel as the true sayings of God.

In conclusion, let us face this question: what is our preparation? Is it a preparation for Babylon's lot? Or is it a preparation for the everlasting union with Christ and the Father in the marriage of the Lamb? For remember: the bride of the Lamb makes herself ready! Longing to be with the Bridegroom, through grace she keeps herself unspotted from the corruptions of Babylon, in order that in the day of Christ she may appear in the pure and white linen of the righteousness of the saints, prepared as the bride adorned for the Bridegroom. Hence, mindful of the blessed hope that is ours according to the true sayings of God Himself, let us purify ourselves even as He is pure!

Chapter XLVI

The Final Victory Of The Lamb Over Antichrist

(Revelation 19:11-21)

11 And I saw heaven opened, and behold a white horse; and he that sat upon him was called Faithful and True, and in righteousness he doth judge and make war.

12 His eyes were as a flame of fire, and on his head were many crowns; and he had a name written, that no man knew, but he himself.

13 And he was clothed with a vesture dipped in blood: and his name is called The Word of God.

14 And the armies which were in heaven followed him upon white horses, clothed in fine linen, white and clean.

15 And out of his mouth goeth a sharp sword, that with it he should smite the nations: and he shall rule them with a rod of iron: and he treadeth the winepress of the fierceness and wrath of Almighty God.

16 And he hath on his vesture and on his thigh a name written, KING OF KINGS, AND LORD OF LORDS.

17 And I saw an angel standing in the sun; and he cried with a loud voice, saying to all the fowls that fly in the midst of heaven, Come and gather yourselves together unto the supper of the great God;

18 That ye may eat the flesh of kings, and the flesh of captains, and the flesh of mighty men, and the flesh of horses, and of them that sit on them, and the flesh of all men, both free and bond, both small and great.

19 And I saw the beast, and the kings of the earth, and their armies, gathered together to make war against him that sat on the horse, and against his army.

20 And the beast was taken, and with him the false prophet that wrought miracles before him, with which he deceived them that had received the mark of the beast, and them that worshipped his image. These both were cast alive into a lake of fire burning with brimstone.

21 And the remnant were slain with the sword of him that sat upon the horse, which sword proceeded out of his mouth: and all the fowls were filled with their flesh.

Once more we must caution you against the view that the events which are described in the words of the present passage historically follow those of the preceding verses. As I have said before, there are many interpreters who entertain this view. First there is the destruction of Babylon, the great city; then the supper and the marriage of the Lamb follow immediately upon the destruction of the great harlot in time; and then follows the battle of Armageddon. According to this view, then, the marriage and supper of the Lamb is a special event that will be terminated by the battle of Armageddon. This is, however, not our view; and I do not believe that this interpretation is tenable. As I have said before, the picture of the marriage and of the marriage supper symbolize the same thing; and they both signify the final and complete union of the church of all ages with Christ. It is a picture of eternity, or, if you please, a picture of the inauguration of eternity. In connection with that view, we stated that Chapter 17, verse 1, to Chapter 19, verse 10, belong together and constitute one vision. The words of the angel who is evidently the medium in revealing these things to John, "These are the true words of God," did not merely refer to the marriage and the marriage supper, but to the entire vision in these chapters, from Chapter 17 on; and they constitute the close of the vision. It was a vision which pictured to us the destruction of the false church, but also the glory of the true church, — a vision which is based upon and finished with this contrast. And in our text a new chapter really ought to have been begun, for the simple reason that it introduces a new vision, as is plain from the very introduction, "And I saw the heaven opened."

Let us, therefore, briefly review the entire context. In Chapter 16 we were given a picture of the seventh vial, which was characterized by the fact that it finished all things. Naturally, when that last vial is poured out, there is nothing left any more; history is finished. The Book of Revelation might have been closed there, except for the picture of the new heavens and earth and the New Jerusalem coming down from God out of heaven. With this seventh vial Babylon is destroyed, the battle of Armageddon is fought, Antichrist is consumed, and Gog and Magog are judged. The whole picture of that seventh vial is very plainly the picture of the end. After that nothing remains any more of history. And therefore it is plain that the chronological order cannot be maintained as the true one. What now is the case? In the rest of the book we are given separate pictures of the end of various agencies and powers which are destroyed by the seventh vial.

First of all, we are given a picture of the harlot, the false church, and her end in the great city. Then in our text we are given a detailed picture of the end of Antichrist and the false prophet and the victory of the Lord over them. In the next chapter the vision pictures the history of Gog and Magog and of the devil. And finally, after the judgment is pictured, we see a picture of the new heavens and earth, especially of the New Jerusalem that comes down from God out of heaven. And when this is all finished, the book closes with an epilogue. All these things belong to the seventh vial. They all carry us to the end. They are all closely connected; but they simply are detailed pictures of the same scene and the same time.

Our vision, then, that is, the vision in the words of the present text, carries us to that end, and pictures the battle of Armageddon, as a comparison with previous passages will immediately show. Of this battle we receive a brief announcement in Chapter 14, verses 17 to 20, where we were told of the great vintage and the picture was given us of the treading of the winepress of the wrath of God, enveloping a vision of a tremendous battle, so that the blood even reaches to the very bridles of the horses. Further, we found the preparation of this battle pictured to us in the emptying of the sixth vial, when the great river Euphrates was dried up, and the evil spirits proceeded out of the mouth of the dragon and of the beast and of the false prophet, in order to gather the people together for the great battle of God Almighty; and thus the nations were gathered together for battle on the field of Armageddon. Finally, we also received a picture of this battle itself in the pouring out of the seventh vial, when all is finished and great hail falls upon the terrible battlefield. It is of this same battle that we receive a more detailed picture in the passage we are now discussing, especially with a view to the victory of Christ and the judgment of Antichrist and of the false prophet.

The Army Of The Enemy

Also in regard to this portion of Revelation there are interpreters who delight to understand the entire passage in the literal sense of the word. They refuse to see any symbolism in the whole scene. What we have here, according to them, is the literal description of the coming of Jesus and the literal picture of the attempt of the nations under Antichrist to strike at Him and to subdue Him. He shall come exactly as pictured, seated on a real white horse, or at least the real appearance of one, with a real diadem on His head, and with garments sprinkled with blood. In a word, He shall come exactly as described in the text, according to this view. The saints also shall follow Him from heaven, as described, being seated on white horses, riding behind their great Captain to meet the enemy. But in the same way we must also take the order of the text and understand the purpose of the nations under Antichrist to be no other than to fight against and overcome the Lamb and the glory of His coming. There are interpreters who take the most extreme delight in that concrete picture. The Antichrist also knows that Jesus is coming. And therefore he hurriedly musters his forces in the valley of Armageddon, in order to strike down the living and glorified King as soon as He sets His feet on the earth. For the text says that they are gathered together for the purpose of making war against the Christ and His people.

However, this is not our view at all. Mark well, this is not because we think anything is too great and too wonderful for the Lord to accomplish, as some of these literal interpreters love to accuse us; but it is simply because, in the first place, the text tells you that again you have a symbolical representation of things, and, in the second place, because there is nothing so wonderful in that literal interpretation of what is meant to be symbolism. Let us notice, in the first place, that John once more sees a vision. He does not directly prophesy, but he plainly informs us that he receives a vision: he "saw heaven opened;" he "saw the angel standing in the sun;" he "saw the beast, and the kings of the earth, and their armies, gathered together." He saw this all. It is therefore a vision. And the entire form in which the vision is presented shows very clearly that it is symbolism. If nothing else, the portion which describes the angel standing in the sun and the portion which tells us of the supper of God prepared for the ravenous birds of the air should be sufficient to emphasize the truth of this conception, that is, the truth of the conception that here we have symbolism. Surely, we too believe that here we have a picture of the final return of Jesus Christ. But the picture is clothed in the form of symbolism that must be interpreted.

Especially the view that the nations of the earth under Antichrist must be conceived of as being purposely assembled here for the purpose of fighting against Christ when He comes from heaven in His final appearance in glory must be condemned. First of all, let us notice that it is against the Word of God. The Scriptures never leave the impression that all the world shall, as it were, expect the coming of Christ. Nor do they leave the impression that the people of the world shall be bold enough to strike at

Him or assemble for battle against the Christ in His second coming. On the contrary, we are given to understand that the world does not believe in the coming of Jesus. They marry and are given in marriage and merrily live along from day to day, even in the midst of the terrible visitations of God on the earth. And they never expect that the end will come. So it was in the days before the flood and in the days of the destruction of the wicked cities of the plain. Those times are typical of these latter days. In the second place, history of the present day corroborates this presentation of Scripture. There is nothing from which the world as such weans away more and more than from the idea of a second advent of the great King. And even now, in the midst of the visitations of God on the whole earth, people are blind to the fact and repent not. In the third place, it is simply absurd to suppose that even if they did expect the coming of Christ towards the very last of time, they would have the courage to gather their armies in order to fight against Him Who shall come in glory. No, the nations of the earth shall be filled with consternation and fear, so that they shall never conceive of battling with Him Who cometh in glory.

In order to obtain a clear conception of the entire scene that is here presented, we will do well to picture it before us in the historic order. We must understand that John does not do this. When his eyes open upon the scene, things are all prepared for the final struggle. The armies of the nations already have gathered in the valley of Armageddon for the last battle; and the heavens are open already, from the which issues forth the Lamb with His heavenly host following Him. And the angel standing in the sun calls to the birds that fly in midheaven to gather themselves together for the supper of God. The entire scene presents itself as a painting appears before our eyes. Now John describes what he saw in that prophetic vision. And he does so, not picturing every object in the order in which it actually appears on the scene, but rather speaking first of all of what is most obtrusive and striking. In this scene the great King on the white horse, issuing forth from the open heaven, draws his attention first of all. Naturally, this is the most glorious, the chief element in the entire vision. And therefore, Him he mentions and describes, first of all. Next he has his attention fixed on the wonderful scene of the angel in the sun and his message. And last of all, he notices that the armies have been gathered for battle in the field of Armageddon.

But we must not make the mistake of thinking that this is in reality the order in which these various powers appear on the scene. Then, if that were the case, the fact would be that the powers of the world expected and saw Christ in His coming and hurriedly gathered their hosts to battle against Him. But, as we have said already, this is absurd. That cannot be the order.

On the contrary, we must understand that the armies of the nations have gathered in Armageddon first of all. This is clear from Chapter 16. Let us recall this for a moment. The infernal trinity, — the dragon, the beast, and the false prophet, — have sent their missionaries into all the world, to the nations of Gog and Magog, the nations that live on the four corners of the earth, the heathen nations, in order to gain them for their cause and make of the whole world a kingdom of Antichrist, (vs. 13). The result is, however, that under their influence these nations are aroused to battle against Antichrist, upon whom they look as being true Christianity. As I have said before, they think that they war against Christendom; but in reality they muster their forces against the powers of Antichristendom. Thus the armies of the whole world are gathered for battle. It is merely a tremendous war that has broken out, a war far more universal than we have witnessed in the recent past. A war it is in which the outwardly Christian world will be pitted against the heathen world. The intention of the heathen is to strike at Christendom, at Christ and His people. And to do this they have been aroused by the spirit of Antichrist. Outwardly, then, this war shall appear like any other war. They do not expect Christ from heaven. Nothing of the kind can even be supposed here. The people of God on earth have been oppressed by Antichrist. And now the heathen imagine that they strike at those same people of Christ. That is their sin. In principle they intend to fight against Christ and His people. In principle they have always done this. But that Christ personally is to appear on this last battle-scene is far from their minds. But this is the last battle. What they did not expect at all happens. Christ comes personally with His saints from heaven in order to give battle to Antichrist and to Gog and Magog both and to consume them by the breath of His mouth.

Hence, if we ask when Christ shall come for the second time, the answer of our text is that He shall come on the scene of one of the most tremendous battles that has ever been fought in the history of the world. Not when all is peace and the whole world is gained for the Savior and for His kingdom, but, on the contrary, when the people of God have been removed from the scene and all the nations of the earth have gathered for the great war, the Son of Man shall appear in glory to have the final victory over all His enemies. For the same reason I have no faith in the realization of a final and lasting peace in the world, no matter how beautiful this may seem from a natural point of view. Already the world begins once more to preach its idealism. And although one of the most disastrous wars the world has witnessed has just come to its close, the humanistic idealists assure us nevertheless that this will be the last war, and that after peace has been officially declared there shall be no war any more. But is this possible? Shall there be peace in a world which refuses to bow before the Almighty God? Shall there be peace in a world at war with the Holy One? Shall there be outward peace without the inward peace of reconciliation through the blood of Jesus Christ? No, positively not! It is impossible. Is it, – and this is the weightiest of all, – is it in harmony with the Word of God to expect a final and lasting peace on earth in this dispensation? Not at all: the Word of God tells us that we must expect war to the end. The final coming of Christ shall be to appear on the scene of one of the most terrible and universal battlefields ever seen in history.

The Appearance Of The Victor

For Christ appears on the scene. As the nations, rising in rebellion against the Christ but not at all expecting to see Him in person, are gathered on the field of Armageddon, of a sudden He appears. In glory He is arrayed, followed by a long train of attendants. He appears in every detail as a victorious warrior and as a righteous judge.

For, in the first place, He is seated on a white horse. In a former connection we have called your attention to the fact that the horse is preeminently the animal for battle, the war steed, irrepressible in his onslaught, undaunted in courage. The Lord, therefore, comes for war. He does not come on the colt of an ass, but on a horse. When He comes again, – and He shall come surely, – it shall not be as the Man of Galilee, proceeding through the country doing good, meek and lowly, to save the lost sheep; but it shall be to offer battle to all who have opposed Him. On the horse He comes. And we also have said before that white is the color of victory. The white of the horse indicates that He comes not only to fight, but to gain the victory. That is the meaning of the color white throughout Scripture, as we have said in a former connection. He will meet His enemies as the great victor, Whose victory is assured. This is also plain, in the second place, from His personal appearance. His eyes are like a flame of fire. With them He penetrates the darkness and the deepest corner of iniquity; and nothing remains hid before the Lamb when He comes for judgment. Upon the wicked world He comes. And He evidently comes to reign and to judge. And besides, these flaming eyes picture to us the holy wrath that burns in His bosom at this moment, now that the measure of iniquity is filled. On His head He wears many diadems, royal crowns, symbolic of victories won in the past. This is not the first time that He has won the battle. Spiritually He already has overcome sin, the devil, and his whole dominion. And therefore, many crowns that formerly belonged to the enemy He has already placed on His own head. The battle of Armageddon is only the grand climax of the holy war this captain has fought throughout the ages. The same idea is indicated by the fact that His garments are already sprinkled with blood. This does not refer to His former suffering: for the garb He wears is the garment of battle and of victory. But it symbolically indicates that the Man from Edom, with sprinkled garments as from Bozrah, has judged many an enemy before, all through the history of the world, while now the final scene has come, in which He shall tread the winepress of the wrath of God for the last time. And, finally, this is also indicated by the sharp sword that proceeds out of His mouth. He shall surely not deign to fight as the princes and great of the earth fight, with their swords and spears in hand. No, as also is indicated in other parts of the Word of God, He shall simply consume the enemy by the Word of His mouth. His Word is His sword. For it is a word of power. By it the enemies are defeated. By it they are judged. By it their punishment is executed to the full. And therefore, He is now come as He was pictured long ago in Psalm 2, for the purpose of ruling the nations with a rod of iron and to tread the winepress of God all alone.

That it is really the Lamb, our Lord Jesus Christ, Who here comes to battle is raised beyond all doubt by the names which are given Him here.

He is called, first of all, the Faithful and True. Of course, He is **the** Faithful One as He now comes on the clouds of heaven according to His Word. All the saints have been looking for that coming. The coming of the Lord was the object of their hope. If He should not come, all their hope would be vain. For then their trials and tribulations have been in vain, and their every hope would come to nought. Of that coming all the prophets had prophesied ever since the time of Enoch. But that coming seemingly tarried. Century after century elapses, and generation after generation passes away. Dark and troublesome times ensued. And yet the Lord did not come. His church suffered persecution because they held the testimony and the Word of God. They were poor and despised. And the souls under the altar increased from year to year. Yet He did not come. Is He then not the Faithful One? Most surely He is: in His final appearance He shall prove to be what all the prophets of the Old Testament and the apostles of the New Testament have told us that He was. Faithful He is, and He shall surely avenge His ,people quickly. But He also is True. In distinction from the powers that oppose Him, He is the true Prophet and the true King. Antichrist claimed that he was the Christ, the prophet and the king of the whole world. He was the Christ, so they claimed. Many false Christs arose in His absence, according to His Word. But He is the True One, the fulfillment of all prophecy, the Christ. He is to come in glory, according to His own promise.

Still more, He is to come as The Word of God. Especially in this name do we recognize our Lord and our Savior: The Word, which denotes Him as the eternal Son of God, the express image of the Father, God of God, the manifestation of God's power and glory. As such He appears. He appears in the glory of His Godhead, though also as the man Jesus Christ.

For besides this name, The Word of God, He still has another name, which no one knows but Himself. It is a name peculiar to Him alone. It is His Mediator's name, the name which exalts Him above every name that is named in heaven and on earth, among the creatures in the sea and on the land. The Mediator's glory is all His own. No one shares it. Not even His brethren can bear that name. And therefore He also appears here with that name in all the glory of His Mediatorship. As such He is the KING OF KINGS, AND LORD OF LORDS. Many a king and lord has appeared on the scene of history in His absence. Kings and lords have refused to bow before His sovereignty; and they have aimed at nothing short of the possession and control of the whole world. And the very incarnation and climax of all these worldly lords and kings is there in the form of Antichrist on the field of Armageddon. But now He appears. And He appears as KING OF KINGS, AND LORD OF LORDS. And His very appearance and names indicate that it shall go ill with the lords of the world, who have refused to recognize His authority of the Word of God.

But He is not alone. We read that the armies that are in heaven follow Him. Who are they? Some have it that they are angels; and I have no doubt but that also the holy angels shall appear with Jesus on the scene of His final coming and victory. But it is not to be maintained that these are the only ones. Yea, it is not even to be defended that they are especially

The Final Victory Of The Lamb Over Antichrist   633

mentioned in this instance. The way they are described informs us differently.

In the first place, like their Captain Who leads them, they also are mounted on white horses. And therefore, there is a certain similarity between them and their great King. But especially the fact that they are pictured as being clothed in fine linen, white and pure, makes us think that this army is not constituted of the angels in heaven, but much rather of the saints who are with Christ. For this garment of fine linen, white and pure, denotes that they have been washed in the blood of the Lamb, as well as that they have been faithful to their King and performed righteous acts. They are garments which have been given them of grace. And this is not applicable to the angels, but only to the saints of Christ.

Nor is there anything new or strange in the idea that Christ shall come accompanied by His saints. Already to the faithful in Sardis the Lord had promised: "They shall walk with me in white: for they are worthy," (Rev. 3:4). And more particularly, unto those that overcame of the church of Thyatira the Lord had given the assurance, "And he that overcometh, and keepeth my works unto the end, to him will I give power over the nations: And he shall rule them with a rod of iron; as the vessels of a potter shall they be broken to shivers: even as I received of my Father," (Rev. 2:26, 27). Specifically, therefore, the promise is given to the saints of Christ that they shall share in His honor. And that this ruling of the nations with a rod of iron does not refer to a fancied millennium of a thousand years in which Christ shall exercise earthly dominion over imperfect nations is plain from the fact that in the text Christ is represented as coming to rule the nations with a rod of iron now, in the field of Armageddon. In I Corinthians 6:2, 3 the holy apostle writes to the congregation of Corinth: "Know ye not that the saints shall judge the world? Know ye not that we shall judge angels?" There is absolutely nothing new in the idea that the saints shall come with Jesus to judge the nations gathered for battle against Him. Exactly how this shall be we know not. But a little of it we can understand if we bear in mind, as I have stated before, that the transformation of the living saints and the removal of the church from the earth shall take place immediately before the coming of Christ and the turmoil of the battle of Armageddon.

The Outcome Of The Battle

Thus, then, the contending armies in this last battle are pictured:

Antichrist and Gog and Magog, assembled for this final struggle and principally fighting against Christ and His people, on the one side; Christ and His armies, coming from heaven in glory and unexpectedly appearing on the scene of battle, on the other side. The world-power is now face to face with the reality of all its aspirations, and they shall have a chance to meet the King Whom they have always opposed in person.

What shall the outcome be? The question is absurd.

The victory of the One Who is mounted on the white horse is first of all announced by the angel who stands in the sun. That he stands in the sun is symbolic of his task. He is to call all the fowls of the heaven together and partake of the supper of the great God. The meaning of this passage is plain. It symbolizes the complete victory of Him Who sits on the white horse and the shameful defeat of the enemy. As we know from the Old Testament, to give one's flesh to the birds of heaven for meat is expressive of the most complete defeat and shameful subjection of the enemy conceivable. So here, the Lord is to have the victory, complete and final victory. And the birds of heaven are called together to partake of the flesh of the vanquished hosts of the enemy.

But also in actual fact the victory is assured, and the victory is pictured as belonging only to Him Who sits on the white horse. We read, first of all, of the beast and the false prophet that they are cast alive into the lake of fire. There is no question of the fact that they are here represented as very concrete and individual persons. But this does not necessarily indicate that there shall be but one person who is the Antichrist and another individual who is the false prophet. It denotes rather, in the first place, that here we have the end of all the deviltry and rebellion and antichristian power. Without any form of trial they are destroyed forever. From the lake of fire there is no return. But besides, among this host of the Antichrist there are leaders and followers. The great and the powerful and the wise of this world lead, and the great masses follow them and their power and counsel. So also in this case: no doubt there is a difference indicated in our text between those who led and deceived the whole world, — the preachers and the great and the wise and the giants of thought and science, — and those who followed, the masses of the earth who wondered after the tremendous system of the antichristian power. This difference also becomes plain in their punishment. Even as there shall be degrees of glory, so there shall be various shades of punishment. Not all have sinned in like degree, and not all shall be punished with like measure. The leaders are cast alive into hell; but the rest are killed there and then, to await the final day of judgment, with the sword that proceeds out of the mouth of Him Who cometh.

And thus we have arrived once more at the very end of all history. It is at this moment that all the powers of iniquity are vanquished. At this moment it is that Antichrist and all his host perish, that the heavens and the earth are set afire in order to make room for the new heavens and the new earth that are to come. It is the end of this dispensation, to be followed by nothing else than the eternal glory in the new creation. Nothing shall take place in history after this. This must be kept in mind, now and in the future. In the second place, let us also not forget that here we have the climax and a clear picture of the climax of the coming of our Lord in glory.

Behold, He cometh with the clouds; and every eye shall see Him! Here we see no continuing city. Let us be ready for His coming, when the continuing city shall be created in the new heavens and the new earth.

Chapter XLVII

The Binding Of Satan With A View To Gog And Magog

(Revelation 20:1-10)

1 And I saw an angel come down from heaven, having the key of the bottomless pit and a great chain in his hand.

2 And he laid hold on the dragon, that old serpent, which is the Devil, and Satan, and bound him a thousand years,

3 And cast him into the bottomless pit, and shut him up, and set a seal upon him, that he should deceive the nations no more, till the thousand years should be fulfilled: and after that he must be loosed a little season.

4 And I saw thrones, and they sat upon them, and judgment was given unto them: and I saw the souls of them that were beheaded for the witness of Jesus, and for the word of God, and which had not worshipped the beast, neither his image, neither had received his mark upon their foreheads, or in their hands; and they lived and reigned with Christ a thousand years.

5 But the rest of the dead lived not again until the thousand years were finished. This is the first resurrection.

6 Blessed and holy is he that hath part in the first resurrection: on such the second death hath no power, but they shall be priests of God and of Christ, and shall reign with him a thousand years.

7 And when the thousand years are expired, Satan shall be loosed out of prison,

8 And shall go out to deceive the nations which are in the four quarters of the earth, Gog and Magog, to gather them together to battle: the number of whom is as the sand of the sea.

9 And they went up on the breadth of the earth, and compassed the camp of the saints about, and the beloved city: and fire came down from God out of heaven, and devoured them.

10 And the devil that deceived them was cast into the lake of fire and brimstone, where the beast and the false prophet are, and shall be tormented day and night for ever and ever.

Introductory Remarks

Before we enter into the interpretation of these verses, we wish to make a few preliminary remarks.

First of all, it should be observed that Scripture knows of only one coming of the Lord; and this coming marks the end of the world, and that too, by way of a universal catastrophe, as well as the inauguration of the world to come, the new heavens and the new earth.

This observation precludes the view of the premillenarians, who speak of two comings of Christ. The one is called the rapture, the other the revelation. The former will take place some time before the great tribulation, the latter after that tribulation. At the former will take place the resurrection of the just and the change of those believers who are faithful and look for His coming; the latter will witness the resurrection of the tribulation-saints and the inauguration of the millennium. In the rapture the Lord will come **for** His saints, to take them with Him in the air; in the revelation He will come **with** His saints, destroy Antichrist, and with His people reign over the nations. But even in both these comings the end of the world is not realized. They will mark the end of this "age;" but they inaugurate another age, that of the millennium. Only after the millennium is the last enemy, death, destroyed and eternity, or "the ages of ages," ushered in. When, therefore, the premillenarians speak of the coming of the Lord, they have in mind especially the "rapture" and the "first resurrection." This may be expected momentarily, may come at any time. The blessedness of that rapture is that those who are deemed worthy of it shall escape the great tribulation under Antichrist and have part in the marriage supper of the Lamb.

We cannot possibly agree with this view, nor with the premillenarian interpretation of Scripture generally and of Revelation 20:1-10 specifically.

First of all, it is an essential element in this view that it is based upon an erroneous interpretation of the Old Testament, which leads to a separation of Israel and the church, as if they were two separate peoples. The former, Israel, is the kingdom people; the latter, the church, is the body of Christ. A correct interpretation of the Old Testament in the light of the New will lead to the conclusion that Israel and the church are not two peoples, but one.

Then too, the view of the two comings, the rapture and the revelation, is based on a wrong interpretation of several passages of Holy Writ. An

outstanding example of this wrong interpretation is that of the passage in I
Thessalonians 4:16 and 17: "For the Lord himself shall descend from
heaven with a shout, and with the voice of the archangel, and with the
trump of God: and the dead in Christ shall rise first: Then we which are
alive and remain shall be caught up together with them in the clouds, to
meet the Lord in the air: and so shall we ever be with the Lord." It is
claimed that this passage of Scripture plainly teaches what the premillen-
nialist terms "the first resurrection," that is, the resurrection of the just in
distinction from the resurrection of the wicked, which is supposed to take
place after the millennium. Further, it is claimed that the word used in vs.
17, "to meet," means, according to the original, "a going forth in order to
return with." The meaning accordingly is that we shall be caught up with
Christ in the air in order to return with Him later.

But all this is quite arbitrary, and certainly is not the correct
interpretation of the text in I Thessalonians 4. As to this "first
resurrection," anyone who reads the text without prejudice, without
millennially colored glasses, can readily see that it makes no distinction
between the dead in Christ who shall be raised first and the dead outside
of Christ who shall be raised later. But the distinction is between the **dead**
in Christ, that is, those who have died before His coming, and the **living** in
Christ, that is, those believers who shall be alive at the parousia. The
resurrection of the former shall occur before the change of the latter. That
is the meaning of the text. And so they shall meet the Lord together in the
air. And the interpretation given of the word "to meet" as if it should
imply the idea of a returning with Christ is a pure invention. The Greek
term does not even remotely suggest this notion. Nor does the rest of the
passage harmonize with the premillennial conception of the rapture. The
text quite clearly refers to a public and universally announced coming of
the Lord. The Lord shall descend from heaven with a shout, with the voice
of the archangel, and with the trump of God. If this means anything at all,
it certainly means that there will be nothing private or secret about this
coming, but it will be loudly proclaimed to all the world. But according to
the millennial view, this will be a coming only for the church, only for the
faithful believers. The world will not even notice this private coming of the
Lord, except that certain persons will suddenly be strangely missed. And
while the millennial view emphasizes that there will be a return from this
rapture and that it will last only during the years of the great tribulation in

the world, the text, on the contrary, emphasizes that it will be **forever**: "And so shall we ever be with the Lord."

Then too, the idea that believers must look forward to their final redemption through the coming of the Lord **before the great tribulation** is contrary to all the current teaching of Holy Writ, which not only warns us to expect tribulation, but also, rather than exhorting us to rejoice in the idea of escaping it, emphasizes that we shall consider it a great honor and privilege to suffer with Christ. To suffer in behalf of Christ is given us of grace, Phil 1:29. The millennium hope of escaping the tribulation is not spiritual, but carnal. And it is as dangerous as it is false, because it fills its followers with a false hope which will leave them unprepared in the evil day.

In the fourth place, the Bible throughout clearly connects with the one and only coming of the Lord the end of this world, the final salvation of the whole church, the last judgment, and the creation of the new heavens and the new earth. Consider, for instance, Matthew 24:29-31: "Immediately after the tribulation of those days shall the sun be darkened, and the moon shall not give her light, and the stars shall fall from heaven, and the powers of the heavens shall be shaken: And then shall appear the sign of the Son of man in heaven: and then shall all the tribes of the earth mourn, and they shall see the Son of man coming in the clouds of heaven with power and great glory. And he shall send his angels with a great sound of a trumpet, and they shall gather together his elect from the four winds, from one end of heaven to the other." And thus, in Matthew 25:31, ff., we read: "When the Son of man shall come in his glory, and all the holy angels with him, then shall he sit upon the throne of his glory: And before him shall be gathered all nations: and he shall separate them one from another, as a shepherd divideth his sheep from the goats." And once more, consider the Lord's own interpretation of the parable of the tares: "The harvest is the end of the world; and the reapers are the angels. As therefore the tares are gathered and burned in the fire, so shall it be in the end of this world. The Son of man shall send forth his angels, and they shall gather out of his kingdom all things that offend, and them which do iniquity; And shall cast them into a furnace of fire: there shall be wailing and gnashing of teeth. Then shall the righteous shine forth as the sun in the kingdom of their Father," (Matt. 13:39-43).

Finally, this view is based on an interpretation of the Book of Revelation which is neither in accord with the highly apocalyptic contents of the whole book nor with the evidently symbolic presentation of Chapter 20 itself. It is quite impossible to read this twentieth chapter of the Book of Revelation as if it recorded a simple historical event which will take place some time in the future, an event which will follow in time upon what was revealed in Chapter 19 of the same book. Such an interpretation is quite impossible.

These are the preliminary remarks which I wanted to make before entering into the interpretation of the text itself. And this is certainly evident, that Scripture teaches not all kinds of different comings of the Lord, but only one coming.

The Binding Of Satan

And now we will interpret the text itself.

John writes that he "saw an angel come down from heaven, having the key of the bottomless pit and a great chain in his hand. And he laid hold on the dragon, that old serpent, which is the Devil, and Satan, and bound him a thousand years. And cast him into the bottomless pit, and shut him up, and set a seal upon him, that he should deceive the nations no more, till the thousand years should be fulfilled; and after that he must be loosed for a little season."

It is very evident that in these words the Seer of Patmos describes not what he saw happening historically, but what he beheld in a vision. A strictly literal interpretation of the text, therefore, is not in harmony with the nature of the passage. Nor is it possible. No one thinks of the possibility of a literal interpretation when in Revelation 13:1 the prophet tells us that "he stood upon the sand of the sea and saw a beast rise up out of the sea, having seven heads and ten horns, and upon his horns ten crowns, and upon his heads the name of blasphemy." It is understood without difficulty that all this was seen by John in a vision. And the same is true of the entire passage of the Book of Revelation which we are now discussing. It is not contradicting, but a correct interpretation of Scripture when we say that John did not **actually** see an angel come down with a great chain in his hand and the key of the bottomless pit, and that he did not **actually** see that the devil was bound and shut up in the bottomless pit, but that he saw all this as it was represented to him **in a vision.**

Neither must a vision be interpreted as if it were a mere and direct foretelling of events as they shall actually happen. It would not be interpreting but doing violence to Scripture and also to this particular passage of Scripture if we should paraphrase these verses in the following fashion: "Then shall an angel come down from heaven with the key of the bottomless pit and a great chain in his hand. And he shall lay hold on the dragon, that old serpent, which is the Devil, and Satan, and shall bind him a thousand years." Such a paraphrasing of the text completely disregards the fact that the passage speaks of a vision. The question is rather: what is the central idea of the vision? What fact does John here behold as being realized before his eyes? And the answer to this question is readily given: that the devil is bound by a divine decree, so that he is prevented from accomplishing his purpose. The angel coming down from God to carry out this decree, the key of the bottomless pit, the great chain, the shutting and the sealing, — all these may be regarded as belonging to the form of the vision only. But they all serve to emphasize the fact that Satan is bound by the divine decree securely and effectively, so that during the period of his confinement he cannot carry out his evil purposes.

We must also understand, for a correct interpretation of this widely discussed part of the Book of Revelation, that it is extremely important that we conceive of it in its true light, that is, merely as another apocalyptic picture of some phase of the "day of the Lord." Any attempt to carry into this prophecy the time element and interpret it as if the events here foretold follow in time upon those referred to in Chapter 19:11-21, must fail. In 19:17, ff., we have the picture of the destruction of all nations. Yet here we still meet with those very nations that live on the four corners of the earth. This can be understood only if we take the stand that in Revelation 20:1-10 a new aspect of the same "day of the Lord," other phases of which have been pictured before, is presented here. This particular vision presents to us the aspect of the judgment upon Gog and Magog, together with an explanation of the fact that these nations appear upon the scene last, and of the final judgment of the dragon, the devil. Hence, we may not read as if John had written, "And after this shall the devil be bound a thousand years, etc.," as all the premillennialists must needs do. But we must leave the text as it stands: "And I saw an angel come down from heaven, etc." The angel has "the key of the bottomless pit and a great chain in his hand." Evidently John beholds the angel in some human, physical form. For "the key of the bottomless pit," confer Chapter 9, verse 1. The bottomless pit is the proper temporary abode of the devil and his angels, (cf. II Peter 2:4). The key and the chain are not to be allegorized. In the picture they are just that, and nothing else. They represent the power of the angel to open and shut the pit and to bind Satan.

Before we go further, we must ask the question not only, but also very definitely answer it, whether this imprisonment of Satan, this secure confinement of the devil, must be regarded as absolute and complete, so that he is restrained in all his activity, or as relative and in part, so that the restraint placed upon him limits him in part, only in a certain direction, and dooms him to partial inactivity only.

This question is answered in the text. And the text replies to this question, without a doubt, that the restraint is partial and with a view to a certain sphere of action. For the purpose of the binding of Satan is designated in verse 3 as being "that he should deceive the nations no more." And in verse 8 we are informed still more definitely that when he shall be loosed for a little season, he "shall go out to deceive the nations which are in the four quarters of the earth, Gog and Magog, to gather them to battle: the number of whom is as the sand of the sea." If we take these two passages in connection with each other, it may be regarded as established, in the first place, that the binding of Satan is limited to certain nations which are called Gog and Magog; and, secondly, that his confinement prevents him from deceiving those nations; and, in the third place, that the deception which by his imprisonment, or the restraint that is put upon him, he is prevented from realizing is what would otherwise cause these nations to gather for battle against the camp of the saints and the beloved city.

Of Gog and Magog we read in Ezekiel 38:2, ff., and Ezekiel 39:1-16. There Gog is the prince of Rosh, Meshech and Tubal, of the land of Magog. They constitute a vast horde that descend upon Israel from the north, even from the limit of the horizon, to make a final onslaught on the people of God. But hailstones, fire, and brimstone from heaven cause their utter destruction. In the passage of Revelation which we are now discussing these same hordes are simply called Gog and Magog; and now they are described as living on the four corners of the earth and as coming on the camp of saints from every direction. Israel here is to be taken, in harmony with all Scripture, in the New Testament sense of the word. The vision of the restored Israel of which Ezekiel 38 and 39 speak has been realized in the church of the new dispensation. It is "the camp of the saints," and it is "the beloved city;" that is, Christianity in its widest sense, as it exists and develops in the new dispensation and corresponds to the nations of Israel in the Old Testament. It is represented in the text as being situated in the center of the earth. Around it, on the four quarters of the earth, that is, outside of the pale of history, are nations which remain pagan. Although also from them the elect are gathered into the church, as nations they remain distinctly heathen. Gog and Magog, therefore, are heathen nations in distinction from nominal Christendom.

We may note here that the dragon, the devil, upon which the angel lays hold, is described in all his evil powers. He represents the prince of this world, the spiritual power behind all the antichristian forces of opposition to Christ and His church, (cf. Chapter 12:3, 4). Moreover, he is described here in all his evil purposes and power of deceit. He is the old serpent, referring, of course, to the temptation in paradise. He is called the devil, that is, the liar and deceiver, mud-slinger, accuser of the brethren. And he is described, or named, as Satan, the opponent, the adversary of Christ and of the cause of God in the world. In the vision the angel overpowers the devil and securely binds him with the chain, casts him into the bottomless pit, locks the pit, and sets a seal upon him, that is, seals the pit against all violation.

The devil, therefore, is very securely bound. And he is bound with respect to these heathen nations as such in the passage we are now discussing. The passage teaches, therefore, that the devil is bound in such a way that he cannot marshal the nations of Gog and Magog to battle against the church, the beloved city, or, if you please, against the Christian nations. He may in this very period of his restraint do many things, both among the nominally Christian nations and among the peoples who are called Gog and Magog. He may go about as a roaring lion, seeking whom he may devour, as he actually does also. But he is prevented from deceiving those nations so as to gather them to battle.

The Time Of Satan's Being Bound

The period of this restraint is designated as a thousand years.

Again, it would be very arbitrary to interpret this number in its literal sense. For, in the first place, all Scripture attaches a symbolical significance to numbers, as it also does to colors and dimensions. Numbers such as one, three, four, six, seven, ten, and twelve, and their combinations and products, represent certain realities of the kingdom of God. The earthly relations are also in their numbers the picture of the heavenly and spiritual realities of God's covenant. That this is true is evident as soon as we call to mind that, for instance, in our weekly period of time there is a combination of six plus one, labor and rest, time and the eternal sabbath, the completion of the kingdom of God; or that seven in Scripture, and especially in the Book of Revelation, occurs evidently as the combination of three and four, the Triune God and the world, the perfection of God's covenant. Besides, the number twelve occurs as the product of three and four, which is evidently the number of the elect, — the reason why there are twelve tribes, twelve apostles, twelve times twelve thousand servants of God who are sealed, twelve plus twelve elders around the throne of God and of the Lamb. These numbers abound in Scripture, and more emphatically in their symbolical significance in the Book of Revelation. The whole book is based on the scheme of the number seven. There are seven seals to the book which is opened by the Lamb. The seventh seal dissolves itself into seven trumpets. And the seventh trumpet reveals itself as comprehending seven vials. There are seven golden candlesticks, even as the complete picture of the church in the world is represented by the seven churches of Asia.

But this is equally true of the number ten and its products, especially in the thousands. The days of tribulation for the church of Smyrna are ten. The number of the servants of God who are sealed is ten times ten times ten, multiplied by one hundred forty-four. The number of those who appear on Mt. Zion with the Lamb, who have His Father's name written on their foreheads, is one thousand times one hundred forty-four, (cf. Rev. 14). The antichristian beast appears with ten horns. The length and breadth and height of the New Jerusalem are twelve times a thousand furlongs. In the light of all these facts, as well as in connection with the apocalyptic character of the Book of Revelation in general, we are certainly justified in saying that it would be arbitrary to insist that the thousand years of Revelation 20 must be understood in the literal sense of the word.

Now, the number itself suggests completeness, a fulness of measure. It is a round number. All the instances in Scripture where this number occurs denote the same idea. There are ten plagues upon Egypt, indicating the fulness of the wrath of God upon Pharaoh and his people. There are ten commandments, expressing the fulness of God's ethical will for men. We feel, as it were, spontaneously that there could not be either nine or eleven commandments. There are one hundred forty-four thousand people of God according to the election of grace, i.e. ten times ten times ten times one hundred forty-four. Thus there are ten virgins, ten talents, and ten days of tribulation for the church of Smyrna. In all these instances the number ten, evidently, expresses the idea of fulness or completeness. It represents the idea of completeness determined by the will and counsel of God. Now, the number one thousand in the text is the number ten in the third power. Besides, it does not speak of days or even of hours, but of years; and therefore it suggests the idea of a long period. On all these grounds we interpret the text as indicating a long period of time, fully determined by the will and counsel of God, a period which must be fulfilled before the devil can be permitted to deceive the nations which live on the four corners of the earth.

The above interpretation is based on the text. This is fully justified by the entire character of the Book of Revelation. It is also in harmony with the line of Scripture in general. Of all this there can be no doubt.

Besides, this explanation is capable of application to history itself and to actually existing conditions in the world of today. The period of the thousand years is to be applied to this entire dispensation until the time shortly before the second coming of the Lord on the clouds of heaven. The fact that the vision in the passage we are now discussing follows the vision of the second coming of Christ mentioned in Chapter 19 cannot be adduced as an objection against this view, for the simple reason that the order of the Book of Revelation is not chronological but rather idealogical. Repeatedly the book follows the development of the world to its very end from a certain point of view in order then to resume the drawing of the same picture from a different viewpoint. Thus, for instance in Chapters 6:12-16; 11:15-19; 14:17-20; 16:17-21; 18; 19:11-21.

In the chapter we are now discussing we have the same phenomenon, now from the viewpoint of the history and end of Gog and Magog. The nations of Gog and Magog, who live on the four corners of the earth, I would identify as the peoples which in the new dispensation never played a part in the history of the world, but which in our very day are waking up. I refer to the overwhelmingly strong heathen world, the nations of China and Japan, the great and strong multitudes in India, the followers of Confucius and Buddha, of Islam and Brahmanism, the millions of Africa and of the islands of the sea. What it would mean if these nations were permitted to unite and marshal their tremendous forces against the nominally Christian nations can easily be surmised. The church would have no place in the world, no room for development. But the devil is bound with respect to them. In the old dispensation he might repeatedly deceive the nations to come against Israel. Egypt and Assyria, Babylonia and Persia, Greece and Rome, all had a controlling influence in the history of the world. In the new dispensation, however, this relation is exactly the opposite. The Christian nations are the historical powers, and Gog and Magog were hitherto apparently asleep. The prince of this world is restrained from employing these forces against the church, the beloved city, the camp of the saints. The devil is bound, as we said, in regard to the nations of Gog and Magog.

The Reign Of The Saints

And now the vision changes. For John tells us that he "saw thrones, and they sat upon them, and judgment was given unto them." This part of the picture evidently represents a people who reign, a royal people. For such is the meaning of their sitting on thrones, as well as of the statement that judgment was given unto them. For to judge is a function of royalty, implies authority to rule.

The question, however, is: who are these royal people? Directly the text does not answer this question, does not inform us who they are, nor where we must look for their thrones. But in the latter part of verse 4 John plainly describes these same people, as he continues: "And I saw the souls of them that were beheaded for the witness of Jesus and for the word of God, and which had not worshipped the beast, neither his image, neither had received his mark upon their foreheads, or in their hands; and they lived and reigned with Christ a· thousand years." That the thousand years refer to the same period as that in which the devil is bound with respect to Gog and Magog is self-evident. In that entire period these people reign with Christ. And they are saints in glory before the final resurrection, the resurrection of the body. For the expression "souls of them that were beheaded" permits no other interpretation.

The Chiliast denies this in order to be able to save his theory of an earthly millennium and of a separate resurrection of the saints. But the denial is without support in Scripture. It is rather strange that he who always would insist on a literal interpretation of Holy Writ in this case looks about for a figurative explanation. Yet so he does. It is essential to his theory of the millennium that these "souls of them that were beheaded" should be transformed into the resurrected saints in their glorified bodies. If he does not succeed in this, his interpretation of the entire passage must needs be regarded as false. Hence, he argues that in this expression we have an illustration of the figure called synecdoche, according to which a part must be taken for the whole. As we speak of so many sails, meaning ships, as we speak of a hundred head, meaning cattle, so the Scripture speaks of souls, signifying persons. All the souls that came with Jacob into Egypt were threescore and ten; in the ark few, that is, eight souls, were saved; on the day of Pentecost about three thousand souls were added to the church; and there were in all two hundred threescore and sixteen souls with Paul in the ship, (Gen. 46:27; I Peter 3:20; Acts 2:41; Acts 27:37). Hence, the Chiliast argues that we must interpret the expression "the souls of them that were beheaded" in the same figurative way, as referring to resurrected persons.

There are, however, two weighty objections against this mode of interpretation, which prove it false beyond a shadow of doubt. The first objection is that whenever the above-mentioned figure is employed, whether in our daily language and secular literature or in Holy Writ, uniformly a numeral is used in connection with it. We can speak of a hundred head and fifty sails; but we do not merely speak of head and of sails. And in all the instances quoted the Bible follows the same rule. Seventy souls came with Jacob into Egypt. Eight souls were in the ark. Three thousand souls were added to the church. Two hundred seventy-six souls were in the ship. But in Revelation 20:4 we simply read, "And I saw the souls." John does not employ the figure in this instance. And the second objection is in the addition "of them that were beheaded." What a strange way of referring to persons in the body, whether corruptible or resurrected, it would be to speak of the souls of them that were beheaded. The Chiliast must admit this. He must relinquish the attempt to save his theory of the earthly millennium by thus imposing his interpretation upon the simple and strange words of Scripture.

And surely, the statement in verse 5 that "this is the first resurrection" does not change matters whatsoever. The Chiliast indeed adduces this clause in support of his contention that verse 4 refers to risen saints. Nevertheless, he is mistaken. The text plainly says: **This** is the first resurrection." And the pronoun "this" refers back to the statement in verse 4 concerning the souls that reign with Christ. In answer to the question, therefore, what is the first resurrection, we cannot introduce our own preconceived notion; but we are bound to the text, and are therefore constrained to say: **The reign of the souls of them that were beheaded for the witness of Jesus is the first resurrection.**

Scripture speaks of the resurrection of the dead in more than one sense. It refers to regeneration in John 5:25: "Verily, verily, I say unto you, The hour is coming, and now is, when the dead shall hear the voice of the Son of God: and they that hear shall live." The same resurrection is meant in Ephesians 5:14: "Wherefore he saith, Awake, thou that sleepest, and arise from the dead, and Christ shall give thee light." In Revelation 20:5, however, the first resurrection refers to the state of the saints in glory immediately after death. They are delivered from battle and from persecution and from the suffering inflicted on them by the antichristian forces that are always in the world throughout this dispensation, and they reign with the Lord.

The expression "the first resurrection," therefore, does not refer to a separate group of saints who are raised first, in distinction from the raising of the wicked a thousand years later as the second resurrection, but to a state or degree in the resurrection of the saints. That this is the correct interpretation a comparison with the similar expression "the second death" corroborates. For "the second death" refers to the ultimate state of death in hell, (Rev. 20:14). First and second death, therefore, are different stages of death, and not different groups of dead people. But surely, this establishes beyond any reasonable doubt that the first resurrection also refers to a stage in life and glorification. If we may complete the parallel, we would say that even as the first death is physical death, so the first resurrection is the glory that follows immediately upon physical death; and even as the second death is the state of perdition of body and soul in hell, so the second resurrection is the final state of glory after the resurrection in the glory of the body. Hence, "Blessed and holy is he that hath part in the first resurrection: on such the second death hath no power, but they shall be priests of God and of Christ, and shall reign with him a thousand years."

Finally, as an objection against this interpretation the millennialist cannot adduce the first part of verse 5, "But the rest of the dead lived not again until the thousand years were finished." Certainly, the rest of the dead are the ungodly dead. And it may be frankly admitted that the form of the expression would almost invite us to complete it as follows: "Then they also shall live again." But it must be remembered that the text does not say this and that we have no authority to add to Scripture. Besides, even the millennialist would not venture to finish the expression in that fashion. For although also the wicked shall have a certain rising from their graves and receive their bodies again, it cannot be said of them that they shall "live" again. Their resurrection will be a resurrection to eternal perdition. And Scripture clearly teaches that this going forth out of the grave unto perdition will take place at the same time, as in one hour, with the resurrection of the righteous unto glory, (cf. John 5:29). So, then, the text in Revelation 20:5 can only mean that while the souls of the righteous were seen as living in glory and in power, the rest of the dead had no place in this picture at all, and did not live again. And when they do appear once more, it will be to be sent into perdition, to be cast into the lake of fire, which is the second death.

These blessed and glorified saints, then, reign with Christ. On earth they endured suffering for Christ's sake. It was given them of grace to have the testimony of Jesus and the word of God in their hearts and in their mouths. And therefore, it was given them also in the cause of Christ to suffer with Him, (cf. Phil. 1:29). For they had this testimony in the midst of an antichristian world. That the antichristian power is here described as it will manifest itself in its ultimate realization and consummation does not signify that only the saints who shall live and suffer in the last days, shortly before the coming of Christ, are included in these saints who reign with Christ. Essentially the power of Antichrist, the beast and his image, are always in the world. And always the believers have the testimony of Jesus and the Word of God. And they always refuse to worship the beast and his image, and refuse to receive his sign in their right hand or in their forehead. And therefore the entire church triumphant in heaven is meant by these reigning saints. They reign and judge the world with Christ. Now they are in glory with Him and are free from all suffering and persecution. It is a reign which commenced in heaven with the exaltation of their Lord at the right hand of God.

That the saints who overcome and endure unto the end shall reign with the Lord in glory is a common idea in Scripture. "And he that overcometh and keepeth my works unto the end, to him will I give power over the nations: And he shall rule them with a rod of iron; as the vessels of a potter shall they be broken to shivers: even as I received of my Father," (Rev. 2:26, 27). And again: "To him that overcometh will I grant to sit with me in my throne, even as I also overcame, and am set down with my Father in his throne," (Rev. 3:21).

Concerning this reign with Christ, it is evident that centrally and essentially it is a reign of the exalted Lord, to Whom is given all power in heaven and on earth, a name that is above all names. But even as the saints while they are still in this world and must suffer in the cause of Christ nevertheless have the victory and overcome and judge the world by faith in Christ, so they shall participate in His glorious reign in heaven, when they shall be completely delivered from all the power of the enemy and be with Him forever and ever. And they shall be given to know His works with regard to the final realization of the kingdom of God, even as He knows the Father's counsel and is found worthy to open the book with its seven seals. They shall perfectly know the mind of Christ, and He shall have no secrets from them. They shall concur in His judgments of the world, and thus shall partake in them. And they shall rejoice in the full realization of His perfect victory. And, finally, this reign of Christ with respect to the world is such, that almost until the very end the devil shall be bound with respect to Gog and Magog, so that he cannot deceive them and gather them for battle against the camp of the saints.

Satan Loosed To Deceive The Nations

But this is not the end. For "when the thousand years are expired, Satan shall be loosed out of his prison, and shall go out to deceive the nations which are in the four quarters of the earth, Gog and Magog, to gather them together to battle; the number of whom is as the sand of the sea. And they went up on the breadth of the earth, and compassed the camp of the saints about, the beloved city; and fire came down from God out of heaven and destroyed them. And the devil that deceived them was cast into the lake of fire and brimstone, where the beast and the false prophet are, and shall be tormented day and night for ever and ever."

What is here presented in a separate vision had partly been pictured in a different setting in preceding chapters. We may gather from Chapter 16:12-16 that this deception of the nations that live on the four quarters of the earth by the devil, to gather them together for battle, will be realized in the period of the sixth vial. This is also in harmony with the statement in Revelation 20:3 that "he must be loosed for a little season." Shortly before the end of this world this final deception of the nations shall take place.

In Chapter 16 we read this: "And the sixth angel poured out his vial upon the great river Euphrates; and the water thereof was dried up, that the way of the kings of the east might be prepared. And I saw three unclean spirits like frogs come out of the mouth of the dragon, and out of the mouth of the beast, and out of the mouth of the false prophet. For they are the spirits of devils, working miracles, which go forth unto the kings of the earth and of the whole world, to gather them to the battle of that great day of God Almighty. Behold, I come as a thief. Blessed is he that watcheth, and keepeth his garments, lest he walk naked, and they see his shame. And he gathered them together into a place called in the Hebrew tongue Armageddon." In this passage the reference is evidently to the same going forth of the devils to the nations that live on the four quarters of the earth, the kings of the whole world, to deceive them and gather them for battle. And we learn besides that this deception of the nations through the devil shall proceed immediately from the antichristian kingdom. Unclean spirits shall proceed from the center of the antichristian world, and they shall have their influence upon the nations that live on the four corners of the earth. It matters not now what is presented by these unclean spirits. They certainly signify a three-fold influence of the antichristian civilization. And the final result of this three-fold antichristian influence will be that the nations thus affected will unite their forces for war, the last war that shall ever be fought on earth.

Again, a similar presentation of the same period of history we find in Chapter 17:12-17. There mention is made of ten kings who as yet have received no kingdom, but shall receive power as kings one hour with the beast. The fact that they are kings in distinction from the antichristian power proper, as well as the fact that their dominion shall last but one hour with the beast, that is, "a little season," suggests that these ten kings are again the same as the power of Gog and Magog in Revelation 20, and as the kings of the whole world and the kings of the east that are mentioned in Revelation 16. If this is correct, then we learn from the passage in Revelation 17 that the first result of the deceptive influence of the devil through the medium of the three-fold antichristian influence will be that the heathen nations of Gog and Magog shall join into one great world-power with the central antichristian dominion. For one hour, for a little season, the world-power shall realize its greatest ambition, and a strictly universal empire shall be established, of which also the heathen but civilized nations form an integral part. However, this cannot last. For ultimately the ten kings shall hate the whore and shall make her desolate and naked and shall eat her flesh and burn her with fire, Rev. 17:16. The ultimate result, therefore, of the deception of the devil through the antichristian influences upon the heathen nations shall be that they shall be gathered for battle against the very center of the antichristian dominion.

If we combine these different elements, which undoubtedly have bearing upon the same historic event of the future, we may come to the following conception. In the nominally Christian world shall ultimately be realized the final consummation of the antichristian world-power, the power of the beast and the false prophet. It will be an empire in which shall be represented the highest ambitions of man; and they shall be realized to the utmost. From a purely humanistic viewpoint, it will be a glorious kingdom. And thoroughly humanistic it will surely be: religiously, scientifically, socially, industrially, and politically. But it will be anti-God, anti-Christ, and anti-church. The saints who refuse to receive the mark of the beast shall have no place in that kingdom. In the meantime, influences shall issue forth from that central realization of the antichristian kingdom upon the nations that live on the four corners of the earth. And these nations shall be civilized. They shall become conscious of their power. And they shall for a time join forces with the beast and the false prophet to form one great world-empire. But under the influence of the so-called mission work of the antichristian unclean spirits, they were indeed awakened out of their prolonged slumber, became conscious of their power, and quickly adopted the antichristian civilization. Nevertheless, they remained pagan in every respect. Though they give their power to the beast for one hour, for a little season, this cannot possibly last. The deception of the devil must work out till the bitter end. And they will ultimately gather as separate forces for the last war, which will be a world war in the strictest sense of the word. Looking upon the nominally Christian world, — which will in fact be antichristian, though the church will still exist in her midst, — as the real Christian nations, as the church of Christ indeed, they shall do as the nations of the old dispensation did with respect to Jerusalem, and shall say: "Let us go up to Jerusalem; let Zion be defiled; let our eye look upon Zion!" This shall be their guilt: for their purpose shall be to fight against the camp of the saints and the beloved city, against God and His Christ and against the church. But it will also be their deception. For, as in the old dispensation God used the nations in their hatred against the Holy City to chasten and destroy a Jerusalem which had actually become Sodom, so He will use the hostile spirit of the heathen nations to destroy the antichristian power and eat the flesh of the great whore. The camp of the saints they will never touch. The people of God shall look for the coming redemption, which shall then be very nigh. For it will be upon this final scene of confusion and iniquity that the Lord will appear in judgment to destroy His enemies and to deliver His saints, in order to give them the victory forever.

If we thus conceive of the end of Gog and Magog, it is needless to conclude that we are living in significant times. A humanistic modernism claims the right and title to the name of Christianity, — a religion without the Christ of the Scriptures, without the incarnation of the Son of God, without the cross, without the resurrection, a religion of this world, based on human imagination rather than on the Word of God in the Scriptures. In the meantime, the power of men develops with tremendous strides in every sphere of life. And the influence of this modern spirit is felt far outside of the Christian world. For modernism has its missionaries. The nations on the four corners of the earth are waking up. The millions upon millions in China and Japan clamor for their own place in the midst of the nations of the world. No, we do not mean to speak of the day and the hour when Christ shall come. But we do emphasize that God's people must not be deceived. They must know the times and know what Israel ought to do at all times and seasons. They must above all watch, and keep the testimony of Jesus and the Word of God; and they must steadfastly refuse to worship the beast and the image of the beast. For blessed is he that watcheth and keepeth his garments! And let us be of good cheer! For our King is given us of Israel's God. He has all power in heaven and on earth. He has a Name above all names. The victory, therefore, is His, and ours through Him. "In the world ye shall have tribulation. But be of good cheer: I have overcome the world!"

We must add a few words yet about the rest of this section. In verse 9 we read about the judgment of the nations: "And they went up on the breadth of the earth, and compassed the camp of the saints about, and the beloved city: and fire came down from God out of heaven, and devoured them."

We may note here:

a) That in this verse the prophecy contained in this section of Revelation changes again from direct prediction, as we had it in the preceding, into the form of the vision. In the vision John now beholds the nations marching up from the ends of the earth against "the beloved city."

b) That in the vision "the camp of the saints" and "the beloved city" dare not to be allegorized. They are certainly Jerusalem and the people of God encamped round about it. Only, we must remember that this is true only of the vision, and that also this part may not be read as if it were history literally foretold.

c) That therefore they violate all the rules of interpretation, who apply this prophecy in such a way that they find here a prediction that Jerusalem (the earthly capital of earthly Canaan) shall be rebuilt, that there Christ and His resurrected and glorified saints in their spiritual bodies shall live and reign a thousand years (the millennium), and that after the millennium the nations of Gog and Magog shall actually gather for battle against these glorified saints and their Lord. This interpretation errs because: 1) It violates the apocalyptic character of the whole Book of Revelation in general and of this passage in particular, and reads it as if it were literal history, although it may only be interpreted as a vision. 2) Because in the whole New Testament Jerusalem as it exists after Christ's exaltation is the church, the heavenly Jerusalem, (cf. Galatians 4:26; Hebrews 11:16; Hebrews 12:22). And this is also true in particular of the Book of Revelation, (cf. 3:12; 21:22). It is quite in accord with this to explain "the beloved city" in this passage as representing the same Jerusalem. 3) Because "the first resurrection" is not the bodily resurrection, but the glorification of the saints with Christ after death, (cf. my interpretation of verses 4 and 5). 4) Because of the absurdity of the presentation of glorified saints in their incorruptible and spiritual bodies with their glorified Lord living in an earthly, material city in a corruptible and corrupt world and being actually attacked by earthly enemies with material weapons.

d) The camp of the saints and the beloved city, therefore, certainly represent the church and the people of God. And they represent the entire church, in the whole world and even in heaven. In the first place, the church, of course, is centrally in heaven in Christ their Lord and through faith reigns with Him. And they are actually in heaven as far as the church triumphant, or the church glorified, is concerned. In the second place, they are, notwithstanding their heavenly character, in part still in this world and are represented by the church visible on earth. And, thirdly, in their widest representation in the world they are known as Christendom, that is, nominal Christianity. It is especially Gog and Magog that look upon all Christendom, no matter how apostate, as the beloved city, even as the heathen nations in the old dispensation considered earthly Jerusalem to be the city of God, no matter how apostate and how wicked it had become.

The nations of Gog and Magog in compassing about and coming to battle against Christendom in its widest sense certainly intend to destroy "the beloved city," the cause of Christ, and to make paganism supreme in the world. In this they reveal their wickedness and become ripe for the judgment. God nevertheless uses them to inflict His judgments upon the antichristian world, (cf. Isaiah 10:5, ff.). There we read: "O Assyrian, the rod of mine anger, and the staff in their hand is mine indignation. I will send him against an hypocritical nation, and against the people of my wrath will I give him a charge, to take the spoil, and to take the prey, and to tread them down like the mire of the streets. Howbeit he meaneth not so, neither doth his heart think so; but it is in his heart to destroy and cut off nations not a few. For he saith, Are not my princes altogether kings? Is not Calno as Carchemish? is not Hamath as Arpad? is not Samaria as Damascus? As my hand hath found the kingdoms of the idols, and whose graven images did excel them of Jerusalem and of Samaria; Shall I not, as I have done unto Samaria and her idols, so do to Jerusalem and her idols? Wherefore it shall come to pass, that when the Lord hath performed his whole work upon mount Zion and on Jerusalem, I will punish the fruit of the stout heart of the king of Assyria, and the glory of his high looks. For he saith, By the strength of my hand I have done it, and by my wisdom; for I am prudent: and I have removed the bounds of the people, and have robbed their treasurers, and I have put down the inhabitants like a valiant man: And my hand hath found as a nest the riches of the people: and as one gathereth eggs that are left, have I gathered all the earth; and there was none that moved the wing, or opened the mouth, or peeped. Shall the axe boast itself against him that heweth therewith? or shall the saw magnify itself against him that shaketh it? as if the rod should shake itself against them that lift it up, or as if the staff should lift up itself, as if it were no wood. Therefore shall the Lord, the Lord of hosts, send among his fat ones leanness; and under his glory he shall kindle a burning like the burning of a fire."

That fire from God out of heaven destroys them is evident and clearly stated in the text. We must also in this connection confer Chapter 16, verse 21. There we read: "And there fell upon men a great hail out of heaven, every stone about the weight of a talent: and men blasphemed

God because of the plague of the hail; for the plague thereof was exceeding great." Moreover, we can refer also to Chapter 19, verse 21: "And the remnant were slain with the sword of him that sat upon the horse, which sword proceedeth out of his mouth: and all the fowls were filled with their flesh." All these passages refer to the same end although the presentation differs. In 16:21 it is the great hail that destroys them. In 19:21 it is the sword that proceeds out of the mouth of Christ that slays them. Here it is fire from God out of heaven. The idea is that all the wicked shall be killed in that last day in order to pass through the resurrection of damnation and to appear before the judgment seat of God in Christ.

Finally, in verse 10 of this chapter we have the judgment of Satan recorded: "And the devil that deceived them was cast into the lake of fire and brimstone, where the beast and the false prophet are, and shall be tormented day and night for ever and ever."

We may note here, in the first place, that by deceiving the nations which live on the four corners of the earth Satan performs his last act of wicked deception and rebellion against the Most High, and thereby fills the measure of iniquity, thus becoming ripe for judgment. In the second place, we must also note that, like the beast and the false prophet, he is here presented as being unworthy even of any public and formal judgment. He is immediately cast into the lake of fire and brimstone, that is, into hell, (cf. 19:20). This is true not of his fellow devils, but of Satan himself, as the prince of the devils, alone, even as it is not true of the followers and worshippers of the beast and his image, but of the beast and the false prophet only. In the third place, we may also note that this punishment consists in continuous torment day and night, and that too, without end, forever and ever. Those who teach that the agents of darkness will ultimately be annihilated and who deny eternal punishment may base their view on falsely conceived humane considerations; but Scripture everywhere contradicts this doctrine. The justice of divine retribution rendered to the wicked cannot be gauged by man's finite existence, but must be viewed in the light of the terrible nature of sin as committed against the infinite majesty of the ever blessed and glorious God. In this light we can somewhat understand that Satan and all his subjects, the beast and his worshippers, shall be tormented night and day forever and ever.

Behold, He cometh! He, the mighty Lord! And His second advent shall undoubtedly be the culmination of all wonders!

Let us be prepared. Blessed and holy is he that hath part in the first resurrection. Blessed are those servants whom their Lord, when He cometh, shall find watching!

Chapter XLVIII
The Final Judgment
(Revelation 20:11-15)

11 And I saw a great white throne, and him that sat on it, from whose face the earth and the heaven fled away; and there was found no place for them.
12 And I saw the dead, small and great, stand before God; and the books were opened: and another book was opened, which is the book of life: and the dead were judged out of those things which were written in the books, according to their works.
13 And the sea gave up the dead which were in it; and death and hell delivered up the dead which were in them: and they were judged every man according to their works.
14 And death and hell were cast into the lake of fire. This is the second death.
15 And whosoever was not found written in the book of life was cast into the lake of fire.

In connection with the first ten verses of Revelation 20 we found that the position of those who would find in these verses an indication of a literal thousand-year reign of Christ on earth is untenable. Their theory is untenable because the temporal-historical view of the Book of Revelation is untenable. It is unrealistic because even a complete binding of Satan would nevertheless not do away with the sin which is in the hearts of men. Further, their view is untenable because in that case Revelation 20 would be the only place in Scripture where such a millennium were taught, while other passages contradict it. And, finally, this millennium theory is impossible because it is plainly not taught even here in Revelation 20. Satan's binding, we found, is symbolic of the restraint placed upon him with regard to Gog and Magog. The reign of the saints with Christ, we saw, refers to the souls of the saints before the bodily resurrection. And the loosing of Satan we explained as referring to the fact that he will be allowed to stir the heathen nations against Christ shortly before the time of the end.

In our present passage we have a new vision, as is evident from the introductory words, "And I saw..." We have been shown the end of history from every aspect. Various enemies have been pictured to us as overcome. Babylon is destroyed. Antichrist and the false prophet have been cast into the lake of fire. The devil has played his last part in the scene of the world's history, and the last tremendous conflict of the nations and their destruction has been pictured to us. The last enemy to be overcome is death. And in the present vision the victory over that last enemy is pictured to us, along with the last judgment, which will inaugurate the age of ages, in which history will be made no more. This vision, therefore, properly precedes the description of the New Jerusalem and the new creation in subsequent chapters.

A Judgment Over All

First of all, we must note that the judgment described in this vision is a general, a universal judgment. It is a judgment over all men, a judgment passed upon the wicked and upon the righteous at the same time. The judgment pictured here is not merely a judgment in the unfavorable, evil sense of the word, resulting in punishment only; but it is general. All are judged; and the judgment results in rewards as well as in punishments.

Naturally, this is denied by premillenarians. According to them, the saints have been raised a thousand years before this time. They have already been judged; and in their reign with Christ they have received their reward. Hence, according to the premillennial theory, what is left is nothing but the wicked; and they only are judged here and receive their punishment.

But let us note carefully that this view is contrary to the text. Notice, in the first place, that there is no exception made with respect to this judgment, but that all the dead in general are included. We read in verse 12: "And I saw the dead, small and great, stand before God." And again: "...and the dead were judged out of those things which were written in the books, according to their works." In fact, throughout the passage the dead are mentioned entirely in general and without any exception. Verse 13 speaks the same language: "And the sea gave up the dead which were in it; and death and hell delivered up the dead which were in them: and they were judged every man according to their works." The completely general nature of these expressions would certainly be misleading if only the wicked were meant. Still more, there is even positive reference to the saints in this passage. Verse 12 tells us, "...and another book was opened, which is the book of life." Also out of this book of life these dead were judged, according to the vision. And this would be neither necessary nor possible unless there were saints, as well as wicked, among these dead who are judged. Again, we read in verse 15, "And whosoever was not found written in the book of life was cast into the lake of fire." This presupposes a differentiation between those who were and those who were not found written in the book of life, and that among these dead there were also those who are written in the book of life. True enough, the reward of the saints is not pictured in the present vision, and the emphasis here is upon the punishment of the wicked. But in the following chapters that reward of the righteous is pictured in detail.

This explanation is confirmed by other passages of Scripture. In the parable of the last judgment in Matthew 25:31-46 we find the very same picture. In verse 32 it is plainly taught that both the righteous and the wicked shall appear together in the judgment: "And before him shall be gathered all nations; and he shall separate them one from another, as a shepherd divideth his sheep from the goats." And in verse 46 the Lord also refers to the wicked and the righteous: "And these shall go away into everlasting punishment: but the righteous into life eternal." And in John 5:28 and 29 the Lord Jesus plainly speaks of a general resurrection which will be followed by the final judgment: "Marvel not at this: for the hour is coming, in the which all that are in the graves shall hear his voice, And shall come forth; they that have done good, unto the resurrection of life; and they that have done evil, unto the resurrection of damnation." Certainly, a statement like this does not at all leave the impression that a thousand years shall intervene between the "resurrection of life" and the "resurrection of damnation." In fact, the text literally teaches that they shall take place in the same hour.

This, therefore, is the picture. All the dead, both wicked and righteous, all who ever lived, from Adam to the very last man that ever lived, shall appear in the final judgment. Cain and Abel, Noah and the men who perished in the flood, all the saints of the old dispensation and their enemies, Judas and Caiaphas and Pilate and Herod, the apostles and the martyrs of the early new dispensation, all the saints from Pentecost until the end, all the enemies of God's people down through the centuries, and all the heathen, – all men shall appear in that judgment. Moreover, they shall appear as they lived on earth. The dead, that is, those who have died the physical death, and that too, small and great, shall appear before the throne of judgment. "Small and great" may simply mean children and adults; but it may also refer to the different stations and positions which they occupied in this present life. Whatever the reference may be in this expression, — and there is really no reason to exclude either idea, — the point is that this description of those who appear in the judgment is derived from their earthly position and their relative differences in this present world. All shall stand before God. The powerful and the insignificant, adults and children, the kings of the earth and their subjects, masters and servants, the rich and the paupers, learned professors and the ignorant and illiterate, ministers and those who constituted their flock, — all shall appear in the judgment in their proper relations in the organism of the race.

Finally, we must notice that they shall appear in the judgment as **raised**.

In the twelfth verse we read that John "saw the dead, small and great, stand before God." Then, in the rest of verse 12 we read of the judgment. And then, in verse 13, we read of the resurrection: "And the sea gave up the dead which were in it; and death and hell (hades) delivered up the dead which were in them." The meaning is that John indeed beholds the dead, that is, he beholds them as those who passed through physical death. But from this and from the fact that the judgment is described before the resurrection we may not conclude that the judgment shall actually take place before the resurrection. This is not the order. And that it is not the order is plain from the last part of verse 13, where it is stated (after the description of the resurrection) that "they were judged every man according to their works." The order, therefore, is this, that in our text the dead before the throne of God and the judgment are described first; and then it is explained whence these dead came, namely, out of the resurrection.

But we must notice that the tremendous wonder of the resurrection is included in this vision. The end of history shall be characterized by many wonders; in fact, this is the one element which makes the events connected with the final consummation so inconceivable, so incomprehensible. Wonder shall follow upon wonder, and they all belong to the things which eye hath not seen, and ear hath not heard, and which have never arisen in the heart of man. The final, bodily resurrection is one of those wonders. It exceeds our boldest comprehension. Just ponder for a moment what shall take place, according to the description in this vision. John writes that "the sea gave up the dead which were in it; and death and hades delivered up the dead which were in them." In short, all the dead are raised. They are raised from every form of death. The vast majority, of course, are in the graves, in hades. Many of them are literally in the sea; they have gone down to a "watery grave," which, of course, was no grave. But also "death," that is, all kinds of violent death, has taken many of them. They were burnt, or they were devoured by wild beasts, or their bodies were blown to bits so that they never could be recovered and buried. One would certainly say that their bodies are irretrievably in the power of death and physical corruption. From the depths of the sea they could never be recovered. Those who died a violent death seem in many cases to have been utterly destroyed. And those in the graves have decayed and returned to the dust. Yet they shall all be recovered and raised. No essentially new bodies shall be created for them; but they shall be raised in their own individual bodies. The same bodies shall be reunited with the same souls. This is indeed a great mystery. I cannot "explain" how it is possible. In fact, I cannot even form a conception of this vast wonder and begin to comprehend all that is involved in it. It is a miracle! But the Lord is powerful! He is the omnipotent!

This, in comparison with what is earlier called "the first resurrection," shall be the second (stage of the) resurrection. It shall include all the dead, righteous and wicked. But it shall immediately be distinguished as a resurrection to glory or a resurrection unto damnation. Even though the righteous judgment of God must still be **revealed,** the state of the righteous and of the wicked is already determined. When the resurrection shall have taken place, and when all shall stand in the judgment, there can be no fear and no cause of fear for the righteous; but there can also be no hope and no reason for hope for the wicked in the hour of judgment. The latter shall be raised unto damnation, while the former shall be raised unto life and glory.

A Righteous Judge

The Judge, according to this vision, is God Himself.

John writes: "And I saw a great white throne, and him that sat on it, from whose face the earth and the heaven fled away; and there was found no place for them." The throne as it is pictured in this vision is not the same as the throne pictured in Revelation 4:2 (cf. our explanation in Chapter XI). Here it is evidently a throne of judgment. This throne is described as "great," indicating the magnitude of the judgment which is to take place: all the dead stand before it! And it is described as "white," symbolic of the glory and holiness and righteousness of the Judge, and therefore also of the perfect holiness and righteousness of the judgment which proceeds from Him.

As to the identity of Him Who sits on the throne, there have been especially two interpretations. According to some, the Judge pictured in this vision is our Lord Jesus Christ. Others, however, maintain that according to the present vision the Judge is God Himself.

Now it is certainly true that Scripture more than once speaks of the fact that we must all appear before the judgment seat of Christ and that Christ shall appear as the Judge of the whole world. Thus, we are instructed in John 5:22: "For the Father judgeth no man, but hath committed all judgment unto the Son." And again, in verse 27 of the same chapter: "And hath given him authority to execute judgment also, because he is the Son of man." In II Corinthians 5:10 we are taught directly: "For we must all appear before the judgment seat of Christ; that every one may receive the things done in his body, according to that he hath done, whether it be good or bad." Nevertheless, in the vision of our text it is less correct to say that the Judge is Christ, not God. For there is more than one indication that here it is God Whom John beholds in the vision as seated on the throne of judgment. In the first place, it is significant that though John states that he "saw a great white throne, and him that sat on it," nevertheless he offers no description of Him Whom he saw seated on the throne. At the same time, in the second place, he adds the significant fact that from the countenance of Him Who is seated on the throne the heaven and the earth flee away. His appearance itself is not described, therefore; yet that appearance is so terrible, so awesome, that the earth and the heaven fled away. And in verse 12, according to the rendering of the King James Version, we are told that the dead, small and great, stand "before God." We take the position, therefore, that the Judge in this vision is God Himself. He is the sole Judge of heaven and earth, the great, the righteous, the awful Judge.

And if, then, the question is asked as to the place of Christ in this judgment, the answer is not difficult to find. The fact that Christ is presented in Scripture as the Judge is not to be explained as though there are two judgments, one of the church by Christ and one of the world by God. As we have already pointed out, both the wicked and the righteous, all of them, must appear in the final judgment, the judgment described in our text. But the explanation lies in the fact that God judges the world in and through Christ, Who is His representative and revelation also in the hour of judgment. He is God in the human nature. And He is the revelation and representative of God in all the world. And it is through Him that also the final judgment of God will be **revelation,** revelation of the righteous judgment of God. And with respect to Christ Himself, in view of His work as the Christ and the Mediator, this is but proper. Moreover, with a view to those who are judged, we may add that this very fact, that Christ will be the revelation and representative of God in the judgment, constitutes at once a great comfort for the believers and a terror for the wicked world which always hated and opposed the cause of God's Anointed.

A Judgment According To Works

Here, as everywhere in Scripture, this judgment is pictured as taking place **according to every man's works**. Thus we read in the text: "...and the books were opened: and another book was opened, which is the book of life: and the dead were judged out of those things which were written in the books, according to their works," (vs. 12). And of this we read again in verse 13: "...and they were judged every man according to their works."

That "the books were opened" is a symbolic representation of the truth that all men must be and shall be revealed in their true ethical character, in their right moral value. All must be made manifest before the judgment seat of God in Christ. We must not ask the question in this connection: what are those books? This is not the point of the symbolism; nor is there anything in the text which would help us arrive at an answer to such a question. It may be true that subjectively the consciences and the memories of men have something to do with these "books." It may also be true from an objective point of view that creation itself, the creature, has something to do with the books. Who knows what creation shall reveal concerning men in that day? Who knows, for example, how the ground shall testify of the blood of the saints which it has swallowed down through the ages? Nevertheless, the text does not say anything specifically about this. The idea is, rather, that these books in the case of each and every man constitute a record, a record which has been written full, as it were, with all their works. And in the day of judgment that record shall be opened and shall be made known. The symbolism of the opening of the books, therefore, represents one idea; and that idea is much the same as that expressed in II Corinthians 5:10, namely, that every man and his works shall be **manifested** in that day. All men with all their works shall be manifested in their proper value and light. Our works in their proper light shall be exposed not only before God, but also before ourselves, and also before all the world.

The reason is that God must be justified when He judges. It must be revealed that God is the righteous Judge, and He must be acknowledged as such by all the judged. Moreover, it must be revealed that He always did judge a righteous judgment in all the history of the world; and this also must be acknowledged by all. In that day the judgment of the righteous Judge of heaven and earth will not be disputed. Now, indeed, in this present time, it may seem sometimes as though there is no judgment, as though the wicked sin with impunity and as though the cause of the righteous stands condemned. Now, indeed, it may even be that the righteousness of God's judgments is challenged by wicked men; and in the face of the plain judgments of God in the earth they may wickedly say, "There is no God." And it may even seem, though that is never really true, that men may ignore or dispute God's judgments with impunity. But in that day every mouth shall be stopped, and all shall acknowledge the perfect justice of God. No one shall be able to be dissatisfied with the judgment. This cannot possibly be. For this is the final judgment of the entire universe, remember. From that judgment there is no appeal; and of that judgment there is no reversal. God will stand justified in the minds and hearts of all His moral creatures. Satan and hell and all the wicked, as well as God's people and all the angels, will have to acknowledge, "His judgment is perfectly righteous." To this end the opening of the books serves. All that the moral creature has ever done, his internal as well as his external works, his thoughts and words and deeds, his deepest and secret motives and desires, and that too, in their proper relation and connection, – in connection with the time and age and country and environment in which we lived, in connection with our gifts and talents, in connection with our relation to former generations, in connection with our relation to the whole human race, – all will be made manifest in its proper value and light. And we shall be able to see clearly the proper value of "every man's work" and the relation between all our life and the judgment which is pronounced. And all shall justify God!

The question may be asked, however: if all shall be judged according to their works, what will become of God's people? They also have sinned; and they also would be condemned, would they not?

To this question the text furnishes the answer when it informs us that not only shall "the books" be opened, but also another book shall be opened, which is the book of life. The book of life is God's own record of His elect saints, the book of God's election in Christ. It contains the names of all His chosen saints. They are written in that book as redeemed by the blood of their Lord and Savior. Through that blood they were justified. By that blood they were also sanctified in Christ Jesus. This book is also opened. For when men are judged according to their works, the work of Christ for His people, in His people, and through His saints, the elect whom God hath given to Christ from before the foundation of the world, shall also be made manifest. This work of Christ for, in, and through the saints belongs to the works according to which they shall be judged. And therefore the saints can never perish in the judgment. Also God's children, therefore, shall see their sins in that day of judgment as they have never fully seen them before. Everything shall be brought into remembrance and shall be seen in its true light. They shall see the corruption and filth of their sin in that day, and they shall fully understand that even their best works were defiled by sin. They shall understand the truth of their confession that even the holiest of men has but a small beginning of the new obedience in this present life. But, thanks be unto God, we shall also understand as we have never perfectly understood before that we are in Christ. We shall see ourselves in Christ as God sees us, as perfectly righteous, as having all our sins so covered by His atoning blood that it is as though we never have had nor committed any sin. And we shall be able to appear before the judgment seat of God without terror, clothed in the perfect righteousness of Christ!

Such, then, shall be the judgment. All the works of men shall be seen in their true ethical character, our works inward and outward, our works together with their motive and purpose; and they shall be judged according to the standard of the Judge of heaven and earth, the holy law of God, and that according to perfect justice. But this judgment will take place organically. There will be distinction, distinction between the righteous and the wicked. For we must remember that this opening of the book of life has a negative significance for the wicked as well as a positive significance for the righteous. The great question shall be whether or not one's name is written in the book of life! For according to verse 12, the dead, **all** the dead, are judged out of the things which were written in the books; and those books include not only the first books mentioned in the verse, but also the book of life. And in verse 15 the negative significance of this book of life is very clear; for there we read that "whosoever was not found written in the book of life was cast into the lake of fire." The judgment, therefore, shall be passed on all organically. Some shall appear in that judgment outside of Christ, that is, in Adam only; and they shall be judged and condemned. Their names are not found written in the book of life. And all the saints shall appear in that judgment as in Christ Jesus through faith; and they shall be judged as such and justified. For their names are written in the book of life!

Finally, the fact that the judgment takes place according to works also implies that there shall be individual difference of degree in the judgment of both the righteous and the wicked. All the works of the wicked shall be judged in the true ethical character; and they shall be judged individually **according** to their individual wickedness, so that there will be difference of degree of damnation unto desolation. And also the works of the saints in Christ, the works of faith, the works of repentance, of sorrow over sin, of sanctification shall be judged, in order that it may be manifest of all the saints in general that although their own works were wicked, nevertheless the saints are perfectly righteous in Christ. But also the latter judgment shall proceed individually. Not all the saints are alike. There are also among them great and small. They shall, therefore, be individually judged as righteous; and in that judgment it shall be made manifest that there is difference of value unto glory in their works of righteousness in Christ.

What a mighty day that will be! How terrifying for the wicked! And what a glorious day for the righteous! And God in Christ shall be perfectly justified, and acknowledged by all in His perfect righteousness!

A Just Verdict

As to the outcome of this judgment, the vision points to the following elements.

In the first place, the heavens and the earth pass away. In the vision they are pictured as fleeing from the face of Him Who sat upon the throne of judgment. And it is added that "there was found no place for them." The last clause here explains the first. It tells us that the earth and the heaven so "fled away" from the face of God that they completely pass away and completely disappear. This presentation is in accord with other

parts of Scripture, as, for example, II Peter 3:10-14: "But the day of the
Lord will come as a thief in the night; in the which the heavens shall pass
away with a great noise, and the elements shall melt with fervent heat, the
earth also and the works that are therein shall be burned up. Seeing then
that all these things shall be dissolved, what manner of persons ought ye to
be in all holy conversation and godliness, Looking for and hasting unto the
coming of the day of God, wherein the heavens being on fire shall be
dissolved, and the elements shall melt with fervent heat? Nevertheless we,
according to his promise, look for new heavens and a new earth, wherein
dwelleth righteousness. Wherefore, beloved, seeing that ye look for such
things, be diligent that ye may be found of him in peace, without spot,
and blameless." The fashion of this present universe must pass away,
according to Scripture. The old heavens and the old earth will have served
their purpose at that day; and they must be consumed in the final
world-conflagration, in order to make room for the new heavens and the
new earth, in which righteousness shall dwell.

In the second place, we are told that "death and hades were cast into
the lake of fire," and that this is the "second death." Death and hades are
here personified. In reality they are powers of corruption; but here they
are being presented as if they were persons. And they are represented as
being cast into hell. They, too, will have served their purpose. Henceforth
there is no place for them any more. They have done their work, and they
are now completely overcome by Christ and consigned to their proper
place, hell. They are banished from the new creation. For, according to
I Corinthians 15:26, death is the last enemy that shall be destroyed. That
destruction is the "second death." And that second death implies eternal
desolation in hell.

To that second death, in the third place, all the wicked are consigned.
For thus we read: "And whosoever was not found written in the book of
life was cast into the lake of fire." The verdict of the righteous Judge of
heaven and earth consigns all whose names are not written in the book of
life to the place of everlasting torment, where there is weeping and
gnashing of teeth.

In conclusion, we may notice that the lot of the righteous is not
mentioned in this connection, except by implication. Their names are
written in the book of life; and therefore they are not cast into the lake of
fire. This reference is only negative. But in the next two chapters of the
Book of Revelation they are pictured as being in the tabernacle of God, in
the New Jerusalem. There is neither sorrow nor crying. And there God will
be their God forevermore!

Chapter XLIX
The Blessedness Of The New Jerusalem
(Revelation 21:1-4)

1 And I saw a new heaven and a new earth: for the first heaven and the first earth were passed away; and there was no more sea.

2 And I John saw the holy city, new Jerusalem, coming down from God out of heaven, prepared as a bride adorned for her husband.

3 And I heard a great voice out of heaven saying, Behold, the tabernacle of God is with men, and he will dwell with them, and they shall be his people, and God himself shall be with them, and be their God.

4 And God shall wipe away all tears from their eyes; and there shall be no more death, neither sorrow, nor crying, neither shall there be any more pain: for the former things are passed away.

The description of the negative and destructive work of God's program is now finished.

There was a power of opposition whose principle was hatred against God, the Almighty Sovereign of heaven and earth. That power revealed itself first in heaven, when mighty Satan rebelled against God and apostatized with his angels. That same power was introduced into the world of men when Adam committed the principal sin, and, accepting the word of the devil, rose in rebellion against God. The development and action of that power of opposition has been pictured to us in the Book of Revelation. We have been shown how **politically** this power develops into a tremendous confederacy called "the beast out of the sea," aiming at the establishment of an antichristian kingdom. It has been revealed how **scientifically and ideologically** this power develops as the power of the false prophet, "the beast out of the earth," deceiving the minds of the masses. In the picture of the great whore and of Babylon we have been shown the **ecclesiastical** development of this power of opposition into the false church, the bride of the Antichrist. How all these powers ultimately constitute the powerful kingdom of Antichrist in its final manifestation, and how even the nations of Gog and Magog are deceived to rise against Christ and His people, — all this has been pictured to us prophetically.

But that power of opposition is completely vanquished. All the judgments implied in the seals and the trumpets and the vials were occasioned by the presence of this power of opposition. And at this point in the Book of Revelation the judgment and destruction of this power of opposition is complete. Babylon is destroyed. The Antichrist and the false prophet and the devil and all who have worshipped them have their place in hell. Gog and Magog have been overcome. Death has been judged. This aspect of God's program is finished.

However, with this negative result the Book of Revelation could not end. What remains is the picture of the positive result of all the work of Christ, the description of the glorious realization of all the promises of God, the final and everlasting reward of the righteous. This is presented in Chapter 21, verse 1, to Chapter 22, verse 5. In the passage we are about to discuss we have a general statement about the final glory. It speaks of the new creation, the New Jerusalem, God's tabernacle with men, and the blessedness of the eternal economy of things.

The New Jerusalem

In order to gain some conception of the meaning of this passage we must not rivet our attention on the external aspects of the state of final glory which is described here. There is a danger that we do this. When we think of our future salvation we are inclined to call before our minds first of all a beautiful heaven or a beautiful new creation in which all the misery of the present world shall be found no more; and the inner spiritual realities of that salvation tend to recede into the background. At first glance it might seem that the text leaves the same impression. John first beholds a new heaven and a new earth. Only in the second place does he mention the New Jerusalem and the tabernacle of God with men. This might leave the impression that the new heaven and the new earth are the most important elements in the vision. But this is not correct. The central idea of that state of final glory lies in the New Jerusalem and the tabernacle of God with men as these depict the internal, spiritual relation between God and His people which is the essence of all their bliss and of all the beauty of the final state. And in the passage under discussion not what is most important is described first, but what is naturally first. Just as in Genesis 1 we read first of the formation of the heavens and the earth, of the preparation of the abode of man and beast, and last of all of the creation of man, God's covenant friend, so here we are told first of the new creation and then of the New Jerusalem and the tabernacle of God with men. The order, therefore, is perfectly natural: the New Jerusalem and the tabernacle of God with men cannot come before the new creation is complete. But it is not that new creation as such, but the New Jerusalem and the tabernacle of God which constitute the central idea of the final glory and bliss of God's people.

We read in verse 2: "And I John saw the holy city, new Jerusalem, coming down from God out of heaven, prepared as a bride adorned for her husband." John, therefore, beholds a city come down from heaven. Later this city is described in detail. But even now we must inquire into the meaning of this vision.

And then we must remember that this is a **vision,** and a vision of **heavenly things.** This should already caution us against thinking of a literal city. There are, indeed, those who maintain this and who claim that this must be taken in a literal sense. However, that is quite impossible. Against this idea is the text itself. For already in this present passage there is an indication that this New Jerusalem is the bride of the Lamb. This is also expressed in verses 9 and 10 of this same chapter: "And there came unto me one of the seven angels which had the seven vials full of the seven last plagues, and talked with me, saying, Come hither, and I will shew thee the bride, the Lamb's wife. And he carried me away in the spirit to a great and high mountain, and shewed me that great city, the holy Jerusalem, descending out of heaven from God." The presentation is that the New Jerusalem and the bride of the Lamb are identical. Now the bride of the Lamb surely is not a city in the literal sense of the word. Against this literalism is also the development of Jerusalem in Scripture. As we have pointed out before, Jerusalem is manifested in a three-fold form. First of all, it was the capital of the old land of Canaan. Secondly, it is also the church of the New Testament in the broadest sense of the word. This is also very plain from Scripture, and I do not have to quote to corroborate this idea. But, in the third place, Jerusalem is also the perfected church, the bride of the Lamb in glory. This, therefore, is the idea of the text. Jerusalem here is not a literal city, but it is the church triumphant in perfect glory.

Concerning this New Jerusalem we may note, in the first place, that it is the perfect antitype of the old Jerusalem; it is the city of God now perfected and glorified. This is plain from more than one passage of Scripture. In Galatians 4:26 we read: "But Jerusalem which is above is free, which is the mother of us all." And in Hebrews 11:10 we read: "For he (that is, Abraham) looked for a city which hath foundations, whose builder and maker is God." And in verse 16: "But now they desire a better country, that is, an heavenly: wherefore God is not ashamed to be called their God: for he hath prepared for them a city." Of this same city we read in Revelation 3:12: "Him that overcometh will I make a pillar in the temple of my God, and he shall go no more out: and I will write upon him the name of my God, and the name of the city of my God, which is new Jerusalem, which cometh down out of heaven from my God: and I will write upon him my new name."

In close connection with the preceding stands the fact that this city is called the New Jerusalem, not merely Jerusalem. What does this mean, and what is the reason for it?

In answer to this question, we point out, in the first place, that the idea of Jerusalem was that it was the city of God. The idea of a city is that it is a social community, a commonwealth, in close fellowship (in distinction from a country), and under its own government. Thus Jerusalem was the city of God. There God dwelt among His Old Testament people Israel. From there He had communion with them; from there He blessed them with all the blessings of salvation as it was foreshadowed in the old dispensation. From Jerusalem He reigned over them and protected them against the enemies who were round about them. But we must remember that the earthly Jerusalem was imperfect. It is true that God dwelt among His people; but He did not dwell **in** them. The relationship in the old dispensation was more or less external. Nor did the presence of God **fill** the city: God dwelt in the temple, particularly in the most holy place. Hence, in the old dispensation Jerusalem existed only in a typical form.

That typical form of Jerusalem was ended through the cross of our Lord Jesus Christ. In His death the old Jerusalem passed away, as is evident from the fact that the veil of the temple was rent in twain. And the New Jerusalem is not merely the old city rebuilt; but it is the realization of that old city, the fulfillment of prophecy, the hope of the Old Testament saints. It is realized, first of all, in the church of the new dispensation in principle. The church in Christ Jesus is the holy city of the new dispensation. It differs from the city in its Old Testament form, first of all, in that it is not a city of brick and stone. The believers themselves are the dwellingplace of God. In the second place, the New Jerusalem differs in that God does not merely dwell **among** His people, but **in** them. Through the Spirit of our Lord Jesus Christ God dwells in their hearts; and therefore they have spiritual communion, are spiritually blessed. The Lord reigns over them from within.

But also this New Testament form of the New Jerusalem is still imperfect. This imperfection is due to the fact, first of all, that not the entire church is filled with God's presence. There are in the midst of the church as it develops in the world in the line of continued generations unbelievers and hypocrites. Moreover, the communion between God and His people, the believers, is not perfect: for sin still reigns in their members. Perfectly God dwells only in Christ. And therefore, the New Jerusalem is realized ultimately and fully in the perfected church triumphant. That perfect church, the church triumphant, is the perfect city of God. It is the **holy** city in the full sense of the word. In it is neither unbeliever nor hypocrite. In it there is no sin and no power of evil. It is perfectly consecrated to God. As such it is also beautiful, adorned as a bride for her husband, that is, Christ. Moreover, the New Jerusalem comes down from God out of heaven. God is its author; and in its ultimate realization the New Jerusalem will perfectly reflect this divine authorship. And all that is of the earth, earthy shall be forever done away; the New Jerusalem will be perfectly heavenly, coming down from heaven to dwell on the new earth and thus to fill all the new creation.

The Tabernacle Of God

That this is actually the idea of the New Jerusalem is plainly shown by the voice from the throne which John hears, verse 3: "And I heard a great voice out of heaven saying, Behold, the tabernacle of God is with men, and he will dwell with them, and they shall be his people, and God himself shall be with them, and be their God." This is undoubtedly the principle and the cause of the blessedness of the New Jerusalem. This great voice, whose author is not mentioned here, expresses emphatically the central idea of the New Jerusalem: "Behold, the tabernacle of God is with men." This idea is further explained in what follows: "and he will dwell with them, and they shall be his people, and God himself shall be with them, and be their God." The New Jerusalem, therefore, is the city where God dwells. And the idea of the great voice from heaven is that when the New Jerusalem shall have come down from God out of heaven, the tabernacle of God shall be with men, and the communion between Him and His people shall be perfected.

The tabernacle in the Old Testament is the type of God's fellowship with His people. Typically, in the tabernacle God and His people dwelt together under one roof. The idea, therefore, of the tabernacle is fellowship, the fellowship of God's covenant. And the idea of the tabernacle of God with men in the New Jerusalem is the perfection of the fellowship of God's covenant. That covenant, with its perfect fellowship of friendship, is now fully realized. God's people are perfectly like Him. They know even as they are known. They see face to face. This is the essence of the blessedness of the city of God. The tabernacle of God with men and the city, the holy city, are now identical and co-extensive. This was not so in the old dispensation. As we have already indicated, God dwelt in the temple, or tabernacle, particularly; but His presence did not fill the city. It is not yet so in the new dispensation. Perfectly God dwells in Christ, and we in Him by faith. With us there is still sin and imperfection; and in so far the communion of God's covenant is imperfect. But in the new future the city shall be the tabernacle, and God's abode shall be with men perfectly and completely. We shall be like Him. And God shall dwell in all of us perfectly. He shall fill us, enlighten us, quicken our love, bind us to Himself with unbreakable bonds of everlasting friendship. And we shall know Him and love Him and serve Him and taste His goodness to the full.

This is also the ultimate realization of all prophecy. Thus, for instance, we read in Ezekiel 37:27: "My tabernacle also shall be with them: yea, I will be their God, and they shall be my people." And in Isaiah 25:6-8 the same is expressed: "And in this mountain shall the Lord of hosts make unto all people a feast of fat things, a feast of wines on the lees, of fat things full of marrow, of wines on the lees well refined. And he will destroy in this mountain the face of the covering cast over all people, and the veil that is spread over all nations. He will swallow up death in victory; and the Lord God will wipe away tears from off all faces; and the rebuke of his people shall he take away from off all the earth: for the Lord hath spoken it." And almost the entire sixtieth chapter of Isaiah refers to the same thing. Thus, for example, in verse 14 we read: "...and they shall call thee, The city of the Lord, The Zion of the Holy One of Israel." And in verses 18-20 the following picture of the blessedness of this city is drawn:

"Violence shall no more be heard in thy land, wasting nor destruction within thy borders; but thou shalt call thy walls Salvation, and thy gates Praise. The sun shall be no more thy light by day; neither for brightness shall the moon give light unto thee: but the Lord shall be unto thee an everlasting light, and thy God thy glory. Thy sun shall no more go down; neither shall thy moon withdraw itself: for the Lord shall be thine everlasting light, and the days of thy mourning shall be ended."

This goal of all prophecy is now reached, according to the vision. The perfection of God's covenant in Christ Jesus on the plane of the heavenly is attained. God will dwell with His people. They shall be His people in the special sense of the word, His peculiar people. And He shall be with them and be their God!

The Universal Scope Of The Final Glory

It is in connection with the central idea of the vision, that of the New Jerusalem and the tabernacle of God with men, that we must consider what is described in verse 1: "And I saw a new heaven and a new earth: for the first heaven and the first earth were passed away; and there was no more sea." The final glory, therefore, shall be universal in scope.

This new creation, too, belongs to the goal, the end, of all prophecy. Clearly already the prophecy of Isaiah speaks of this. In Isaiah 65:17 we read: "For, behold, I create new heavens and a new earth: and the former shall not be remembered, nor come into mind." Also in Isaiah 66:22 we read of this: "For as the new heavens and the new earth, which I will make, shall remain before me, saith the Lord, so shall your seed and your name remain." To this also the New Testament looks forward, as is plain from II Peter 3:13: "Nevertheless we, according to his promise, look for new heavens and a new earth, wherein dwelleth righteousness."

We may notice, in the first place, that John beholds the old creation as having passed away. The first heaven and the first earth constitute the two main parts of the original creation as mentioned in Genesis 1:1. This earth, together with all its creatures, and the heaven, including both the firmament and all the heavenly bodies and the heaven of heavens, and therefore the whole created universe, shall pass away. This does not mean that the present heaven and earth are to be annihilated. From other parts of Scripture we learn that this is not true. And besides, the works of God shall not perish. But the first heaven and the first earth are under the influence of sin and of the curse. That first creation as it developed through sin and the curse and as it has been affected by all the works of sinful men cannot serve as the proper sphere for the New Jerusalem and the tabernacle of God with men. It shall pass away. Even the creature itself, according to Romans 8, awaits the day of the manifestation of the sons of God, the day which shall also be the day of the deliverance of the creation from the bondage of corruption. But although the present creation shall pass away, it will not be annihilated. It will be destroyed by fire. But even fire does not annihilate. Rather, the passing away of the old creation and the creation of the new is to be compared to the resurrection of the body. Even as in death the old body is not annihilated, so the old creation shall not be annihilated. And even as the resurrection body is not an essentially new creation, so the renewal of the universe is not an essentially new creation, not a creation out of nothing, but a renewal. Through the passing away of the old creation all that is of sin and of the curse shall be done away, and nothing of this present world will enter into the new creation. Old things are passed away!

In this connection we may also consider the statement, "and there was no more sea." This would seem to leave the impression that there will be no more sea at all in the new creation. The Revised Version translates more literally and correctly, "and the sea is no more." The reference here is not to the sea of nations, as some have it. For although the sea sometimes has that significance in the Book of Revelation and elsewhere in Scripture, the present context forbids this interpretation. The text here refers literally to the sea, even as it refers to the heaven and the earth. The meaning of the text is not, however, that there will be no sea at all in the new creation. The reference here is rather to the old sea, even as the text speaks of the first heaven and the first earth. That old sea is no more. The sea as it was originally created, but as it came under the curse of sin and under the bondage of corruption, constitutes a barrier between nation and nation and between people and people; and as such it constitutes a dangerous element in the present creation. Hence, while there may very well be a representation of the sea in the new heavens and the new earth, that is, a new sea, the old sea will be no more. There will no more be a sea which causes separation in the new creation.

In the second place, the first heaven and the first earth shall be replaced by a creation which is radically new. As we have already remarked, this new heaven and earth will not be a creation out of nothing, but a renewal, a transformation. But it must be emphasized that the renewal shall be radical, a complete transformation. First of all, there shall be nothing of sin and the effects of sin in the new creation. There shall be no thorn and no thistle, no storm and no flood, no barren desert and burning sun, no destructive earthquake and terrible volcano. The old things are completely passed away. The creation shall be perfect, the fit abode of the perfected people of God. In the second place, all creation shall be united, and that too, in a higher unity than before. Heaven and earth and all things contained in them will be united in one, that is, Christ. Thus we read in Scripture in more than one place. In Ephesians 1:9-11 we are told: "Having made known unto us the mystery of his will, according to his good pleasure which he hath purposed in himself: That in the dispensation of the fulness of times he might gather together in one all things in Christ, both which are in heaven, and which are on earth; even in him: In whom also we have obtained an inheritance, being predestinated according to the purpose of him who worketh all things after the counsel of his own will." And in Colossians 1:12, ff., we read: "Giving thanks unto the Father, which hath made us meet to be partakers of the inheritance of the saints in light: Who hath delivered us from the power of darkness, and hath translated us into the kingdom of his dear Son: In whom we have redemption through his blood, even the forgiveness of sins." And then follows the passage which we have particularly in mind in this connection, a passage which speaks of the unity of all things in Christ: "Who is the image of the invisible God, the firstborn of every creature: For by him were all things created, that are in heaven, and that are in earth, visible and invisible, whether they be thrones, or dominions, or principalities, or powers: all things were created by him, and for him: And he is before all things, and by him all things consist. And he is the head of the body, the church: who is the beginning, the firstborn from the dead; that in all things he might have the preeminence. For it pleased the Father that in him should all fulness dwell; And, having made peace through the blood of his cross, by him to reconcile all things unto himself; by him, I say, whether they be things in earth, or things in heaven." Heaven and earth, therefore, shall be united in Christ. The New Jerusalem shall have its abode on earth, yet it shall inhabit all creation. And the whole creation shall be heavenly, made like unto the risen Lord. In that new creation all things shall be perfectly adapted to serve the resurrected and glorified church in Christ, in order that we may serve our God and enjoy the fellowship of His covenant forever and ever.

The Perfect Bliss Of The Final State

Finally, the passage tells us of the state of bliss which results from God's fellowship with His people in verse 4: "And God shall wipe away all tears from their eyes; and there shall be no more death, neither sorrow, nor crying, neither shall there be any more pain: for the former things are passed away."

We may note here, in the first place, that this description is negative. The heavenly things in themselves we cannot yet understand and imagine. Hence, they are described to us by way of comparison with the present things. In all these negative terms we are told, in effect: over there things are not as they are here and now.

The main point is that there shall be no more death. Death is completely and in all its forms and operations swallowed up in victory. Positively this indicates, of course, that when God's tabernacle shall be with men, then the saints shall live forever in glory with Christ; and they shall reign forevermore. Their life shall be perfect. Death can nevermore enter into the New Jerusalem and the new creation. And therefore, there shall be no sorrow, which means, positively speaking, that there shall be everlasting joy and gladness. There shall be no more crying, but everlasting rejoicing, with songs of gladness. There shall be no more pain, but everlasting well-being and prosperity. For all these, — sorrow, crying, pain, — are implied in and are the result of death. And when death is swallowed up in victory, and when everlasting life reigns supreme in Christ, none of these shall ever enter into the glory that shall then be revealed.

The reason given is that the former things are passed away. The "former things" are the present economy of things since the fall, since sin entered into the world. For since then we are under the curse, characterized by death and suffering and sorrow and by persecution on the part of the enemy. All these are passed away forevermore. They can never enter into the new creation in order to spoil and mar its bliss; and there shall be no fear that they shall ever enter again. They are passed away!

Hence, the final state of God's people shall be one of perfect consolation. God shall wipe away all tears from their eyes! What a beautiful and comforting expression to denote that the Lord God shall remove every cause of sorrow! What a lot of tears have been shed! Tears have been shed because of the sufferings of this present time in general; and tears have been shed because of suffering for Christ's sake. But in the final state of glory there shall be no reason for weeping forevermore. God shall comfort His people perfectly for all their suffering which they endured while they were in the present world, causing them to inherit the exceeding great reward of heavenly glory. He shall console them perfectly for all their present sorrow, filling them with joy unspeakable and full of glory. "For the sufferings of this present time are not worthy to be compared with the glory that shall be revealed in us."

And therefore we can shout with the apostle Paul in I Corinthians 15:51-57: "Behold, I shew you a mystery; We shall not all sleep, but we shall all be changed, In a moment, in the twinkling of an eye, at the last trump: for the trumpet shall sound, and the dead shall be raised incorruptible, and we shall be changed. For this corruptible must put on incorruption, and this mortal must put on immortality. So when this corruptible shall have put on incorruption, and this mortal shall have put on immortality, then shall be brought to pass the saying that is written, Death is swallowed up in victory. O death, where is thy sting? O grave, where is thy victory? The sting of death is sin; and the strength of sin is the law. But thanks be to God, which giveth us the victory through our Lord Jesus Christ."

Chapter L

True And Faithful

(Revelation 21:5-8)

5 And he that sat upon the throne said, Behold, I make all things new. And he said unto me, Write: for these words are true and faithful.
6 And he said unto me, It is done. I am Alpha and Omega, the beginning and the end. I will give unto him that is athirst of the fountain of the water of life freely.
7 He that overcometh shall inherit all things; and I will be his God, and he shall be my son.
8 But the fearful, and unbelieving, and the abominable, and murderers, and whoremongers, and sorcerers, and idolaters, and all liars, shall have their part in the lake which burneth with fire and brimstone: which is the second death.

In the preceding section we find the vision of the new heavens and the new earth and of the New Jerusalem. And in this vision John hears the words of the great voice out of heaven proclaiming, "Behold, the tabernacle of God is with men." A glance at the words of the passage we are about to discuss will tell us that there is no further vision here. Rather do we have in this passage a solemn affirmation and assurance by God Himself of the things which John had seen and heard in the vision of verses 1 to 4. The passage is characterized, except, perhaps, in verse 5-b, by the fact that in it we have direct speech, and that too, by the living God Himself. The contents are, in the first place, a statement that God makes all things new. In the second place, there is an injunction for John to write these words: for they are true and faithful. In the third place, there is a declaration that it is done, that it is come to pass, that it is all finished, and that God is the Alpha and Omega. And, in the fourth place, there is a designation of who shall and who shall not inherit these things: those who overcome, in contrast to the wicked, whose part is in the lake of fire.

The point of the passage is that the things which John has seen in the vision just recorded seem so remote, so far away and contrary to our present experience as the people of God in the midst of the world, that a special confirmation of them is necessary: these words are true and faithful! It is well worth our while, therefore, to consider this affirmation a little more in detail.

What Is True And Faithful?

The passage is introduced by the divine declaration, "Behold, I make all things new." Thus we read in verse 5: "And he that sat (ARV: "he that sitteth") on the throne said, Behold, I make all things new." And in verse 6 this is presented as actually accomplished. For there we read, "It is done," or, as the American Revised Version has it, "They are come to pass." The reference in verse 6 is to the renewal of all things which is proclaimed in the opening words of verse 5. Here, therefore, we have the primary answer to the question concerning the **contents** of the words which are true and faithful.

Evidently the declaration, "Behold, I make all things new," and, "They are come to pass," refers to the vision of verses 1 and 2. It serves to emphasize the truth that God, the sovereign Lord, is the Savior and Redeemer of all creation and that He will certainly cause all these things to come to pass.

In order to understand somewhat the significance of this solemn declaration and the necessity of it, let us remind ourselves of the tremendous import of the words, "Behold, I make all things new." God shall make all things in heaven and on earth **new!** They shall be new not merely in the sense that we can speak of something as being brand new, that is, unused. But they shall be new in character, different from the old things. There shall be a different earth and different heaven. There shall be different creatures and different relationships than there are in the present heavens and earth. The life of God's people in the new heavens and the new earth shall be altogether different and in that sense new. So different and unspeakably glorious shall all things be that we cannot even conceive of them now. According to Scripture, eye hath not seen, nor ear heard, neither have entered into the heart of man the things which God hath prepared for them that love Him. There are no adequate human terms to describe the glorious inheritance of God's people. There is no proper earthly language which can depict the real character, the unspeakable glory and beauty of that inheritance. Even as God's people are themselves become radically different from, other than, the world in which they sojourn for a time, so that future inheritance is not to be compared, except by way of contrast, in a negative way, by way of contrast to anything the eye sees and the ear hears here below, or anything that can possibly arise in the heart of man. For that inheritance is not earthy, but heavenly. And the heavenly things cannot be adequately expressed in earthy language. The new creation shall be in harmony with the glory of the resurrected Lord, the Lord from heaven. And as such it shall be wholly other than all that we ever experience in the present land of our pilgrimage; it shall be in contrast to all that the eye can see and the ear can hear and the heart can conceive in this world. Hence, as we remarked already in the preceding chapter, it is described in terms of the absence of "the former things." God shall wipe away all tears from our eyes; there shall be no more death, neither sorrow, nor crying, neither shall there be any more pain. Or, as it is described in I Peter 1:4, the inheritance is incorruptible, and undefiled, and fadeth not away.

In the second place, to the words that are true and faithful belong the words of promise which are found in this passage concerning the believers' portion and place in the new creation. The text does not merely speak objectively of the fact that God shall make all things new, but it speaks words of promise. And again, these words of promise are presented here as spoken by God Himself. Thus we read in verses 6 and 7: "I am Alpha and Omega, the beginning and the end. I will give unto him that is athirst of the fountain of the water of life freely. He that overcometh shall inherit all things; and I will be his God, and he shall be my son." In general, the promise is the promise of a blessed life in the new creation.

First of all, God's people shall inherit all things. Incidentally, whether we adopt the reading of the Authorized Version, "all things," or that of the American Revised Version, "these things," the meaning remains the same. For "these things" are the "all things" which shall be made new. There are several elements which we may notice here. In the first place, we shall **inherit** all things, that is, receive them as an inheritance. And it is characteristic of an inheritance that it is free and freely bestowed, that is, a matter of pure grace. In the second place, we may notice that this surely implies not only that all things shall be made new, but also that God's people shall be so changed as to be able to possess all things and enjoy them and use them; with all things they too shall be renewed. In the third place, we should pay special attention to the singular "he." Everyone of God's victorious children shall be an heirsof the whole world! And, finally, we may once more pay attention here to the utter inconceivability of this from the point of view of this present time. Here God's children are anything but heirs of the world; principally they are always deprived of all things. And in the days of the final manifestation of the antichristian kingdom it shall be literally true that they will have nothing; they will not be able to buy or sell. Yet in the day of our Lord Jesus Christ they shall inherit all things, and that too, in the new creation! These words are true and faithful!

The second aspect of the blessed life is that of perfect satisfaction: "I will give unto him that is athirst of the fountain of the water of life freely." This is evidently a promise to him that is athirst now, here in this world, but that shall be completely fulfilled when all things are made new.

As to the contents of this promise, we may note that it promises the water of life as a free gift of grace. And the meaning is that God will constantly supply all that is necessary to have and to enjoy eternal life. The life that is here spoken of is true, eternal life in fellowship with God. And water of life is all that is necessary to sustain and to replenish that life. It is evident that when the text here speaks of the fountain of the water of life, it uses figurative language. And the figure is not that of spiritual cleansing, which also occurs in Scripture, butsof quickening and refreshment and complete satisfaction, in which sense water occurs more than once in Holy Writ. In that sense, even as in natural life, water is essential; it is not a luxury, but a necessity. Hence, water represents that which is necessary for the sustaining and quickening and refreshment of the life of God's people, that which is necessary for them to have and to enjoy eternal life. From that point of view, it may be said, in the first place, that living water, or water of life, represents principally, and in its deeper sense, the Holy Spirit, as the Spirit of Christ, by Whom all the spiritual blessings of salvation are bestowed upon the church as a whole, and upon believers individually. He is this living water which flows constantly out of God, through Christ, into the church, (cf. Isaiah 44:3; John 7:37-39). He, the Holy Spirit as the Spirit of Christ, realizes unto us and within us all the spiritual blessings which are in Christ and which Christ obtained for us by His perfect obedience. He is the Spirit of life, the Spirit of adoption, the Spirit of truth, the Spirit of wisdom and knowledge and revelation, the Spirit of holiness and sanctification. All the spiritual blessings of knowledge and wisdom, of life and glory, of righteousness and holiness, and all other riches of grace constantly flow from Christ in the

Spirit into the church and into the believers. And by these they live and are constantly refreshed unto eternal life. And it is this stream of spiritual blessings that is symbolized by the water of life.

These blessings flow from "the fountain of the water of life." This fount ultimately is God Himself: He is the eternal fountain. But this promise is realized through our Lord Jesus Christ, so that He may properly be said to be the fount of the water of life, even as He Himself said, according to John 7:37, "If any man thirst, let him come unto me and drink." Christ, the Christ of the Scriptures, the Son of God in the flesh, Who dwelled among us, Who revealed unto us the Father and spoke the words of eternal life, Who was delivered unto death for our transgressions, and was raised the third day for our justification, Who was exalted in the highest heavens, and Who received the promise of the Holy Spirit, Who, finally, on the day of Pentecost poured out His Spirit into the church to the end that His church might ultimately be gathered together in the final day in the new heavens and the new earth, — that Christ is the open Fount of the water of life. And of that Fount all the believers shall drink and shall be refreshed and quickened unto eternal life and be perfectly satisfied forever! These words are true and faithful!

All this shall be the portion of God's people in the son-relation, according to the text: "...and I will be his God, and he shall be my son." Essentially the promise of verse 3 is repeated here, but with a difference. The difference is, in the first place, that here the promise occurs in the singular, and therefore very personally. And, in the second place, the text here speaks of sonship. He that overcometh will be God's son and heir in perfection. He will be legally God's son, with all the rights of a son and heir. But also ethically and spiritually he will be perfectly God's son, like Him, conformed to the image of God's Son, as he is constantly sustained by drinking from the fountain of the water of life.

Why Faithful And True?

With respect to all these things John receives an injunction to write: "And he said unto me (ARV: "And he saith"), Write: for these words are true and faithful." Most likely these words of verse 5 are of the interpreting angel, since they contain an injunction for John to write, while all the rest of the passage must be understood as the direct speech of God in the hearing of John in the vision.

As far as the language of the text in the original is concerned, the words

can mean either that John must write **that** these words are true and
faithful, or that John must write down these words **because** they are true
and faithful. In either case the essential meaning remains the same. And
the reference is not only to the declaration which immediately precedes
this injunction, "Behold, I make all things new." But the entire promise is
embraced, and all that is included in this passage is affirmed to be true and
faithful.

The meaning of this solemn affirmation is not difficult to ascertain.
These words are "true," that is, they are in harmony with reality. The
implication is not, of course, that these words concerning the renewal of
all things are more true than other words which are written in the Book of
Revelation and which were revealed to John. But as we have already
pointed out, from our present viewpoint the fact that God will make all
things new seems so unreal, so remote, so contrary to all our present
experience. Hence, for our sake, for the sake of God's children in the
midst of this present world, it must be emphasized that they are real and
that they will surely be realized. Just as in our everyday life someone
might tell us about an event that is fantastic and well-nigh unbelievable,
and when he detects on our faces the disinclination to accept what he says,
he will add the affirmation that what he says is certainly true, so with
respect to these things, things which eye hath not seen, nor ear heard, and
which have never arisen in the heart of man, things which are utterly
contrary to all experience, it is affirmed that all these things are certainly
true and will surely be realized just as they have been revealed to John.
And remember, it is these very things which constitute the object of the
believers' hope. That hope is not of this world; it is other-worldly. It is
fixed on things which do not belong to the sphere of this present world
and our present existence. Its object lies beyond death and beyond
corruption and beyond this present time. It belongs to the things heavenly
and abiding. It belongs to the sphere of the resurrection. Is that object
real? Or shall the believer be ashamed when he discovers that after all
those things on which he has always fixed his hope and his longing were
mere fantasy? And the answer of the Word of God is: "These words are
true!" For that reason they are also called "faithful." All these things
concern the promise of God. For the renewal of all creation is the ultimate
realization of the promise of the gospel. And as they involve the promise
of the gospel, they therefore concern God Himself. Hence, they are
faithful, that is dependable. God surely can and will fulfill them. They

shall never fail. Even as God is faithful and cannot deny Himself, so His promise is absolutely dependable. His people, therefore, may rely on these words in life and in death. And John is instructed by the interpreting angel to place special emphasis upon the truth and faithfulness of these words, so that God's people may be reassured and strengthened in their hope.

It is not difficult to discover the reason and ground for this solemn affirmation and for the injunction to John to write.

That reason lies, in the first place, in the fact that they are the words of Him Who "sitteth upon the throne." Very beautifully is this expressed in the text. In the first part of verse 5 we read: "And he that sat upon the throne said, Behold, I make all things new." And immediately thereupon the interpreting angel says to John: "Write: for these words are true and faithful." In other words, the very fact that the words concerning the renewal of all things are the words of Him Who sitteth upon the throne is the guarantee of their truth and faithfulness; and it is at once sufficient reason for John to write and to emphasize their truth and faithfulness. We are reminded in this expression of the vision of the throne of God in Revelation 4, especially verses 2 and 3, (cf. Chapter XI for an explanation of this vision). Here we are briefly reminded that these are the words of Him Whose throne is there described. A throne is the symbol of royal sovereignty and majesty, and therefore, at the same time, of the supreme power of judgment. Here the throne stands for the absolute sovereignty of heaven and earth. For He Who sits on the throne is none other than the Triune God. He is the Lord, Whose is all power and authority. Nothing, therefore, is too wonderful for Him. And nothing can possibly prevent the realization of His Word, "Behold, I make all things new." Moreover, even as God the Lord is the True and Faithful One, Who is faithful, first of all, to Himself, so that He can never deny Himself, so His Word is true and faithful. It shall certainly come to pass, and His promise shall not fail.

In the second place, the Lord announces Himself as the "Alpha and Omega, the beginning and the end." As we have already explained in connection with Revelation 1:8, alpha and omega are the first and last letters respectively of the Greek alphabet. The meaning of these symbols is further explained in the words "the beginning and the end." This Self-announcement of God serves to emphasize, therefore, that all these words are true and faithful. For His counsel shall stand, and He will do all His good pleasure. He is the Sovereign Creator of all things, the Fount out of which are all things. And in Him all things have their purpose. Even as all things are out of Him, so they also are unto Him. From the beginning He made all things with a view to the end: the alpha is connected with the omega, the one must inevitably lead to the other. And whatever lies between the alpha and the omega is through Him. He controls all things in such a way that His counsel is accomplished, His design is fulfilled, His end is reached. And that end is the "revelation of Jesus Christ," the firstborn of every creature and the first begotten of the dead, as the One in Whom all things in heaven and on earth are to be united forever. Then, in the new creation, the tabernacle of God shall be with men, and God shall be all in all, through Jesus Christ our Lord. As surely, therefore, as the end of all things must show that God is the Alpha and Omega, so surely are the words true and faithful, "Behold, I make all things new!"

It is in this light, in the third place, that we must understand the words, "It is done," or, "They are come to pass." The reference is to the things which John saw in the vision in verses 1 to 4. There John saw the new creation and the new Jerusalem. Here it is stated by the Lord God Himself, the Alpha and Omega, Who sitteth upon the throne, that they are come to pass, that the promise of God is completely realized. The victory is accomplished. It is now fully evident that God is the Alpha and Omega, the beginning and the end of all things. It is revealed that old things are passed away; behold, all things are become new. It is revealed in the death and resurrection of our Lord Jesus Christ that God the Lord is the Savior and Redeemer of His people, and the Redeemer and Renewer of all creation. For though now we see not yet all things put under Him, nevertheless we see Jesus, for the suffering of death crowned with glory and honor!

True And Faithful: For Whom?

The promise, therefore, is sure to all God's people.

Not for all are these promises.

For true and faithful are also these words, vs. 8: "But the fearful, and unbelieving, and the abominable, and murderers, and whoremongers, and sorcerers, and idolaters, and all liars, shall have their part in the lake which burneth with fire and brimstone: which is the second death."

In these words are designated those who shall not inherit all things, but whose part shall be in the lake of fire. Notice that they are classified, first of all, as the fearful. These fearful are very likely the nominal Christians, men who must be looked for in the church. They are afraid. In the world they must suffer tribulation if they belong to the people of God. But they love the world and their own life and their position. And when they are threatened with persecution and tribulation for Christ's sake, they become afraid and become unfaithful. In the second place, there are the unbelieving. They are the professed unbelievers, the hostile powers of Antichrist, who openly reject the gospel and oppose Christ. They are the abominable, that is, those who are filled with the abominations of the great whore, Revelation 17:4. Moreover, that they are filled with those abominations becomes manifest in their walk. For they walk as murderers, as whoremongers, as sorcerers, that is, as deceivers and those who trust in vanities, as idolaters, and liars, who hate the truth as it is in Jesus Christ. They have their part in the lake that burneth with fire and brimstone, which is the second death. The first death is, of course, the death of these unbelievers and sorcerers and idolaters and liars in this present life, ending with physical death. Really they are dead now. They never lived. But that death is finished when they die the physical death. And therefore, now they are in the first death. But when they shall have been cast into the lake that burns with fire and brimstone, that is, hell, they shall be in the second death. And that second death is not annihilation, but, according to all Scripture, is everlasting desolation and anguish, the dreadful experience of the wrath of God without end. These words are faithful and true! There is no peace, saith my God, to the wicked!

Positively, the promise of the water of life as a free gift of grace is for "him that is athirst." That is, it is for the spiritual man in Christ, for him that longs for God and His righteousness. For the reference is, of course, to spiritual, not to natural thirst. And this spiritual thirst implies, in the first place, that there is in a man's soul a profound consciousness of his sinful state, of his own lost condition, of his being devoid of all righteousness, and of his being full of sin and corruption in himself, so that he is damnable before God. It implies, secondly, that he deplores his sin in true repentance, that he longs for forgiveness and for deliverance from the power and the dominion of sin, longs to be clothed with righteousness. It signifies, too, that he recognizes Christ as the Fount of living water, as the fulness of righteousness and life out of which he must drink and longs to drink. He yearns for the full Christ and all the blessings of salvation, for forgiveness and righteousness, for wisdom and knowledge, for light and life eternal! To such an one, who through the grace of God is spiritually thirsty, the promise is true and faithful: God shall give him to drink from the fountain of the water of life freely. He shall be satisfied forever when God shall make all things new!

In the second place, the recipients of this blessed promise are designated as those who are victorious: "He that overcometh shall inherit all things." This is the very opposite of the fearful. The presupposition is that there is a battle to be fought, that is, the spiritual battle of faith. In that battle we must suffer for the cause of Christ. We may not all be called to sacrifice our lives upon the altar ofsfaithful confession. But we surely must all fight and endure suffering for Christ's sake. And in that battle against sin, the world, and the devil and his whole dominion, we must overcome. Not in our own strength, not by sword and cannon, but spiritually, in the power of our Lord Jesus Christ and through faith, we must overcome. And to him who thus overcomes, who by the grace of God endures to the end, the promise is: "He shall inherit all things."

Let us, therefore, not have our part with the fearful and unbelieving. For they shall have their part in the lake that burneth with fire and brimstone. Come out from among them, and be not partakers of their sins. Seek not your satisfaction in this present world, but at the Fountain of the water of life. For His Word is true and faithful, "Behold, I make all things new."

He that overcometh shall inherit all things!

And the thirsty soul shall be forever satisfied at the fountain of the water of life!

Chapter LI

The Holy City, New Jerusalem

(Revelation 21:9-27)

9 And there came unto me one of the seven angels which had the seven vials full of the seven last plagues, and talked with me, saying, Come hither, I will shew thee the bride, the Lamb's wife.

10 And he carried me away in the spirit to a great and high mountain, and shewed me that great city, the holy Jerusalem, descending out of heaven from God,

11 Having the glory of God: and her light was like unto a stone most precious, even like a jasper stone, clear as crystal;

12 And had a wall great and high, and had twelve gates, and at the gates twelve angels, and names written thereon, which are the names of the twelve tribes of the children of Israel:

13 On the east three gates; on the north three gates; on the south three gates; and on the west three gates.

14 And the wall of the city had twelve foundations, and in them the names of the twelve apostles of the Lamb.

15 And he that talked with me had a golden reed to measure the city, and the gates thereof, and the wall thereof.

16 And the city lieth foursquare, and the length is as large as the breadth: and he measured the city with the reed, twelve thousand furlongs. The length and the breadth and the height of it are equal.

17 And he measured the wall thereof, an hundred and forty and four cubits, according to the measure of a man, that is, of the angel.

18 And the building of the wall of it was of jasper: and the city was pure gold, like unto clear glass.

19 And the foundations of the wall of the city were garnished with all manner of precious stones. The first foundation was jasper; the second, sapphire; the third, a chalcedony; the fourth, an emerald;

20 The fifth, sardonyx; the sixth, sardius; the seventh, chrysolyte; the eighth, beryl; the ninth, a topaz; the tenth, a chrysoprasus; the eleventh, a jacinth; the twelfth, an amethyst.
21 And the twelve gates were twelve pearls; every several gate was of one pearl: and the street of the city was pure gold, as it were transparent glass.
22 And I saw no temple therein: for the Lord God Almighty and the Lamb are the temple of it.
23 And the city had no need of the sun, neither of the moon, to shine in it: for the glory of God did lighten it, and the Lamb is the light thereof.
24 And the nations of them which are saved shall walk in the light of it: and the kings of the earth do bring their glory and honour into it.
25 And the gates of it shall not be shut at all by day: for there shall be no night there.
26 And they shall bring the glory and honour of the nations into it.
27 And there shall in no wise enter into it any thing that defileth, neither whatsoever worketh abomination, or maketh a lie: but they which were written in the Lamb's book of life.

The Queen of Sheba had heard of Solomon's greatness and glory and wisdom. Others had tried to give her an idea of it. They had pictured it to her so vividly and strongly that she would not believe it. She determined to investigate for herself. She beholds the glory of the king. She listens to his words of wisdom. And she returns with the confession that the half had not been told her.

The same will, no doubt, be true with respect to the things described in the passage we are about to discuss.

All things are to be new in the eternal future of the kingdom of heaven and in the perfect church. We expect a new heaven and a new earth, that is, a new and entirely different state of things. Essentially this new state of things shall consist in this, that God's tabernacle shall then be with men. In detail, however, Scripture tells us very little about the rest. How shall this new state be? We know a few things of that new and perfect state which shall be characterized by God's dwelling with men. Certainly, we know that sin and suffering shall be no more. All will be holy and righteous and filled with the glory and knowledge of God. We also know that the temporal and all that is connected with it shall be no more. All that is of this present time shall be changed. In the present passage Scripture gives a symbolical picture of that new state of things, particularly of the holy city, New Jerusalem. And we can stammer a few words in explanation. But for the rest, our experience will be like that of the Queen of Sheba after she had visited Solomon, and we shall undoubtedly say: "The half was not told us."

In this section of Revelation 21 we have before us in a little more detail the description of the New Jerusalem. Already in verse 2 John saw the New Jerusalem. Now he is shown the city in detail.

The City's Appearance To John

The vision is introduced in verses 9 and 10, where we read: "And there came unto me one of the seven angels which had the seven vials full of the seven last plagues, and talked with me, saying, Come hither, I will shew thee the bride, the Lamb's wife. And he carried me away in the spirit to a great and high mountain, and shewed me that great city, the holy Jerusalem, descending out of heaven from God."

The agent who shows John the vision, therefore, is one of the seven vial-angels, one of those who had poured out the seven last plagues. This is very appropriate. It reminds us of the fact that there is a connection between those judgments and the coming of the New Jerusalem. Those judgments and the final destruction of Babylon had their positive purpose in the coming of the New Jerusalem. They must serve to prepare the way. This mediating angel says to John, "Come hither, I will shew thee the bride, the Lamb's wife." And then we read in verse 10 that he showed John "that great city, the holy Jerusalem, descending out of heaven from God." John is carried away in the spirit, and he is shown the New Jerusalem from a great and high mountain. We are warned here at once that the description of the city which follows is by no means to be interpreted as referring to a literal city. The New Jerusalem is here called "the bride, the Lamb's wife," which is, as we know, the church. And John is shown spiritual things in a vision and in signs and symbols. The mountain to which John is carried away in the spirit is a great and high mountain, in order to afford John a proper view of this colossal city. The picture is that the city is still descending out of heaven from God (cf. verse 2); and in order to have a clear and unobstructed view of it and because of its colossal size, John must be situated on this great and high mountain "in the spirit" in this vision.

John beholds a huge city, suspended in mid-heaven, descending from heaven to earth. It is the great city, the holy Jerusalem. In shape the city is a perfect cube; and in size the city is twelve thousand stadia, or furlongs, each way. The city, therefore, is in the shape of a cube which is approximately 1400 miles long, 1400 miles wide, and 1400 miles high. Imagine! Travelling at sixty miles per hour, it would require a full day and a night to go from one side of that city to the other. Or, superimposing the city on our continent, it would reach from the Atlantic Ocean to the Great Plains and from Maine to Florida. And the height is also some 1400 miles! Around the city is a wall which, though very high in itself, is not nearly as high as the city. It is 144 cubits, or approximately 220 feet, high. In the wall are twelve gates, three on each of the four sides. And at each of the gates stands an angel. Moreover, on the gates are written the names of the twelve tribes of Israel. Further, the wall has twelve foundations, evidently standing next to one another and stretching from gate to gate. And the names of the twelve apostles of the Lamb are written in the foundations.

As to its material, the city itself is pure gold, transparent in its splendor like glass. The wall is of pure jasper, a beautiful precious stone which may appear in divers colors, but which here shines like crystal and is perhaps white like the diamond. The gates in the wall are each a huge pearl, pure and lustrous. The foundations are adorned with all manner of precious stones, in which blue and green, red and white and yellow vie with one another in splendor and beauty. The first foundation is again jasper. The second is sapphire, which is a beautiful dark blue stone. The third is a chalcedony, probably an agate. The fourth is emerald, which is a beautiful green. The fifth, sardonyx, a brilliant flesh color. Then there is the sardius, a precious stone of a bright red hue (cf. Rev. 4:3). The seventh is chrysolyte, a stone of a golden, yellow luster. The eighth is beryl, like the greenness of the sea when the sun shines upon it. The ninth is topaz, which is a transparent, yellow color. The tenth is chrysoprasus, a pale, golden color. The eleventh is jacinth, a violet color. And the twelfth is amethyst, which is a purple color. And the street of the city is of pure gold, like transparent glass. The question whether there was only one street in the city or whether the term **street** is representative of all the streets is of no moment. The over all impression of this colossal city which John beholds is one of overwhelming beauty. For thus we read already in verse 11: "and her light was like unto a stone most precious, even like a jasper stone, clear as crystal."

The Identity Of The City

Now it is of the utmost importance to understand that what John beholds is not a literal city, but a symbolic and visionary city. It is, in fact, very difficult to avoid thinking of a literal city when we contemplate this passage. Yet we make a very serious mistake if we do so, a mistake which would cause us to miss the thrust of the entire passage, and one which would also involve us in impossible difficulties as far as the interpretation of this graphic and detailed description of the city is concerned.

Yet there are those who would have us think of a literal city with a literal wall and literal gates and streets, in which the saints of all ages shall dwell. Some would even locate this city permanently in mid-heaven, that is, between heaven and earth, so that other nations on earth will walk in and enjoy its light. But there is every indication in the passage itself and in the context to the contrary. In the first place, the very fact of the symbolic character of the Book of Revelation as a whole should put us on our guard against a literal understanding of a passage like this. Secondly, there is the fact that John introduces the entire passage by telling us that he was carried away in the spirit unto a great and high mountain. In other words, what we have here is a vision. And when we consider in this connection the highly symbolic nature of the passage, every thought of a literal city is ruled out. Think, for example, only of the shape and size of the city. Who can conceive of a literal city in the shape of a cube? And what kind of literal city would be the size of almost half of the United States? Besides, there are the precious stones mentioned, and the names of the twelve tribes engraved in the gates, and those of the twelve apostles written in the foundations; there are the recurring multiples of 12 and of 10, both of which numbers are used again and again in the symbolic sense in the Book of Revelation and elsewhere. All these facts are indications that here we must think not of a literal city, but of a highly symbolic city. In the fourth place, not a city suspended in mid-heaven is the everlasting habitation of the saints. But the new heaven and earth shall be their habitation. The meek shall inherit the earth, not a city in mid-air. And, above all, this literalistic interpretation is contradicted by the introduction by the angel. He says to John, "Come hither, I will shew thee the bride, the Lamb's wife." And then he proceeds to shew John, who is "in the spirit" and on "a great and high mountain," a city, "that great city, the holy Jerusalem, descending (not suspended permanently in mid-air, but in the process of coming down) out of heaven, from God." In other words, when John beholds this great city, holy Jerusalem, he is being shown "the bride, the Lamb's wife." They are the same, the latter being shown to John under the symbolism of this city.

In this same connection we should be cautioned against thinking rather idyllically and sentimentally of heaven in terms of this city. This is not infrequently done in song and in the spoken word, as though heaven, or the new creation, were a place with streets of gold and gates of pearl, where there is literally no night, etc. Now there is no question about it, in the light of Scripture, that the abode of the saints in the new creation will be exceedingly glorious. But it is not in harmony with this passage, nor with any other passage of Scripture, to think in any wise of a literal city and literal gates and streets. The sole purpose of the vision is to show us "the bride, the Lamb's wife." We must therefore constantly be on our guard against a literal conception of the things here described.

Hence, rather than thinking of a literal city, we must understand that the vision purposes to show us the church under the symbolism of this great and holy city. This is clearly in harmony with the words of the angel, "Come hither, I will shew thee the bride, the Lamb's wife." The passage considers the whole of what is here described, that is, the church, the Lamb's wife, as a city in relation to Christ. This implies, in the first place, that the church is not in this city; but this city is the church. In the second place, this city, as the bride, the Lamb's wife, stands in a most intimate relation to Christ, and through Christ to God. The relation is that of a communion of nature, a communion of life, and a communion of love, (cf. Revelation 19:6-10). Christ, therefore, is everything in this city. He fills the whole city with His life and love. And through Him the city stands in fellowship with God. And, in the third place, this implies that Christ is the Lord of this city, His bride. He is the One Whose will she delights to do; and, through Him, it is the will of God that is her delight.

This same idea is also emphasized by the names of the apostles on the foundation. This element in the vision expresses that principally the apostles constitute the foundation of the church, that foundation having been laid through the instrumentality of the apostles. But then we must remember that of that foundation Jesus Christ is the chief cornerstone, which means that Christ incarnate, crucified, raised, exalted and glorified, determines the whole foundation, and thus the whole city. In other words, again, Christ is everything in this city. In the New Jerusalem we shall always be with and in Christ consciously. This is in harmony with the teaching of Scripture in Ephesians 2:19-22: "Now therefore ye are no more strangers and foreigners, but fellow-citizens with the saints, and of the household of God; And are built upon the foundation of the apostles and prophets, Jesus Christ himself being the chief corner stone; In whom all the building fitly framed together groweth unto an holy temple in the Lord: In whom ye also are, builded together for an habitation of God through the Spirit."

Finally, we must notice in this connection that the bride and wife of the Lamb appears as a **city**. There is nothing strange about this symbolism if we remember that after all a city is not the number of houses and buildings. These are not meant here at all. They do not constitute a city. It is the living citizens, the people, who constitute the city, and that too, in the peculiar life and relation which is denoted by the term **city**. The bride of the Lamb is not one person, but consists of millions and millions. Truly, in the world at any given point in history she is a "little flock." But in the end she shall appear as an innumerable multitude. And in this vision the size of the city is proof of this.

But for what reason is the church depicted especially as a city? The purpose is to emphasize the idea of communion, the idea of a commonwealth, of a social community. This is expressed in the very idea of a city. The city, in distinction from the country, is representative of a more highly developed social life. In it the people do not live miles apart, but closely together. Hence, in the city there is human development in science and art and industry. There is close social intercourse. And it is from the cities as the great centers of civilization that the effects of this high development spread into the country round about. True, in this present world this more highly developed social life stands in the sign of sin and in the service of sin. But this does not change this basic idea of a closely knit social community which is characteristic of a city. And it is this idea which is on the foreground in the symbolism of our passage. The church, the New Jerusalem, will be the perfect society. All the saints of the old and of the new dispensation shall be one in Christ. Nothing shall divide them any more. They shall be of one life, of one principle, of one aim and purpose. In Christ they shall be one with the Triune God. And as such they shall stand in close communion with one another. Each occupying his own position, they shall serve a common purpose, namely, consecrated service of God. They shall be a holy priesthood!

The Perfection Of This City

In this connection we must pay attention to the several details of the vision which point to the perfection of this city.

This perfection is denoted, first of all, by the fact that the city is in the shape of a perfect cube. The interpreting angel measures the city, as John looks on, with a golden reed. Golden is the reed, in harmony with the glory of the city. This measuring reveals that the city is equal in length and breadth and height. Jerusalem has attained the perfection of the most holy place in the temple of the old dispensation, which was also a perfect cube. But now the entire city is such a perfect cube. The church has attained to universal perfection. It is the perfect dwelling-place of God, even as was the holy of holies typically. And its perfection embraces heaven and earth. Here we behold the climax of the work of God in the building of His church. For there is development in this work. First there is the line, represented in the rectangle of the old temple, symbolizing the church of the old dispensation as it was found in one nation. Then follows the temple of Ezekiel's prophecy, in which the square is dominant, symboliz-ing the church as it is gathered from all nations. And in the vision of our passage we find the cube, symbolizing the universal perfection of the heavenly New Jerusalem.

In the second place, we must take notice of the wall of this city. As we have seen earlier, that wall is foursquare; it is one hundred forty-four cubits high; it has twelve foundations, lying next to one another; in it are twelve gates, three on each side, with an angel stationed at each gate; and in the gates are written the names of the twelve tribes of Israel.

What may be the meaning of all this?

Certainly that wall is not for protection, and the angels do not function as guards. The wall itself is too low to serve that purpose: for what are 144 cubits in comparison with 12,000 furlongs, the height of the city? Besides, the gates of the city are never shut, according to verse 25. No, there is no need of guards and protection against possible enemies and attacks any more: for there will be no one in the new creation and no one in the New Jerusalem who will hate and attack the people of God any longer. Rather must we understand the symbolism of the wall as meaning that the city is complete and finished. All the elect are gathered and are included within that wall. And the angels standing one at each of the twelve gates, or entrances, of the city are the angels who have served in the ingathering of the citizens and who have gathered all God's elect, and them only, into the city. In this connection, the names of the twelve tribes of Israel on the gates are indicative of the identity of those who are within the gates. All Israel constitutes the glorious church of God, the glorious and holy Jerusalem. We may notice too that the idea that Israel and the church are two separate peoples is condemned in this passage. There shall not be two peoples, an earthy Jerusalem over which Christ shall rule and a heavenly people. There is only one people, and that one people is the church. The bride, the Lamb's wife is constituted the New Jerusalem; and New Jerusalem's citizens are all Israel, from Jew and Gentile.

In the third place, the perfection of Jerusalem is indicated by the symbolic numbers which occur in this vision. First of all, the number twelve prevails throughout the vision. The wall of the city is twelve times twelve cubits high. Twelve thousand furlongs is the measurement of the city. There are twelve foundations of the wall, and in them the names of the twelve apostles of the Lamb. And there are twelve gates and twelve angels and twelve tribes of Israel. The number twelve, as we have had occasion to note before, is the product of three (the number of the Trinity) and four (the number of the creature). Hence, it is the number of election, the number of God's chosen people. All have entered through the gates, and all are within those walls, and there is room for them all in that great city. But, secondly, the number ten also occurs here. For the size of the city is twelve times ten times ten times ten furlongs. This number ten emphasizes the idea of fulness, completeness, according to the decree of God. The church is complete. The fulness of the number of its citizens according to the counsel of God is circumscribed within its walls. And if in this connection, finally, we consider the colossal size of the city, we obtain the idea that this completed church, the sum total of the elect of God, is the multitude which no man can number. Such is the great city, the holy Jerusalem!

Finally, we must notice the glory of New Jerusalem's perfection.

This is expressed in several ways in the text. In the first place, our attention is called to the light of the city: "and her light was like unto a stone most precious, even like a jasper stone, clear as crystal." In the second place, we are told that the "building of the wall of it was of jasper," emphasizing once more the crystalline light of the city. And, in the third place, we are informed that the city, and also the street of it, are of pure, transparent gold. And all of this is enhanced by the description of all the precious stones in the foundations and the pearls of the gates. All these details serve to express the glory, the purity, the beauty, and the preciousness of this great and holy city. We must not attempt to allegorize every detail here: that would be in conflict with the whole idea of the vision and would involve us in hopeless difficulty. But we may notice a few details.

In the first place, we must notice that the glory of God fills the city. Thus we are informed directly in the text, verse 11: "having the glory of God." This glory of God in the city is in the vision compared to the simple white luster of the jasper stone, which in the vision of Revelation 4 is associated with "him that sat on the throne." This glory of God, like the brilliancy of the jasper, is the light of the city, very bright and very clear and very transparent. The meaning is evident. The glory of God is the radiation of God's infinite perfections and virtues. And this glory of God, the radiation of His knowledge and grace and righteousness and holiness and love and wisdom and infinite goodness, is imparted to and reflected in the glorified church.

Moreover, the manifold beauty of that one glory of God is symbolized by the precious stones, which serve to picture the beauty and the preciousness of the city, of the bride of the Lamb. But we may notice that these precious stones are found in the **foundation**, the foundation of which, as we have seen, the chief cornerstone is our Lord Jesus Christ. It is in and through our Lord Jesus Christ, therefore, that the manifold glory of God will be revealed in the entire city, the church.

This beautiful bride of the Lamb, the city of God, is precious. Of this we are reminded by the pure, transparent gold of the city. For did not the apostle Peter speak of this in I Peter 1:7: "That the trial of your faith, being much more precious than of gold that perisheth, though it be tried with fire, might be found unto praise and honour and glory at the appearance of Jesus Christ." That gold, therefore, represents the preciousness of all believers. They have been refined and beautified in the crucible of affliction. And now, at the appearance of Jesus Christ, they are found unto the praise and honor and glory of God forever!

The Life Of The New Jerusalem

In the last section of this passage, from verse 22 to verse 27, we have a further description of the perfection and glory of the New Jerusalem, but now especially from the point of view of the glory and activity of the citizens, as well as their spiritual character and perfection. Also in this part of the vision it is important to remember that we do not have here a literal city, but a description of the bride of the Lamb, the church, from the viewpoint of its being a social community. All the details must be interpreted accordingly.

First of all, we may observe that the citizens of the New Jerusalem are described both from a natural and from a spiritual viewpoint.

In verse 24 we read: "And the nations of them which are saved shall walk in the light of it: and the kings of the earth do bring their glory and honour into it." The same thought occurs in verse 26: "And they shall bring the glory and honour of the nations into it." The city, therefore, is strictly cosmopolitan. It is out of all nations. We may notice, too, that they appear here as **nations**. This certainly does not imply · that the separation of the nations shall continue in the New Jerusalem. All national separation, separation of language and interests and aims, shall disappear forever. Yet it is plain that the organic development of the race and of the various nations is of significance for the church in glory. Also in this respect history has not been in vain. Out of the one root have developed all the various branches of nations and tribes. And this development has not been for nought. The citizens of the New Jerusalem are from every nation; and the organic development of the nations serves the purpose of the multiformity of the church and the revelation of the manifold glory of God in the multitude of the redeemed from every nation and tribe and tongue.

We may notice that the passage also speaks of the kings, who bring the glory and honor of the nations into the city. The reference here certainly cannot be to kings here in this world. Whether the interpretation is that the culture and civilization of the great of this world, the fruit of the inventions and productions of this present world, shall be carried into the eternal city, or whether this is explained as meaning that in this present world the kings of the nations serve the well-being of the church, both of these interpretations are impossible. In the first place, we must remember that this world and all that is in it will be destroyed by fire. Nothing of this present world and its culture can possibly have a place in the holy city. And, in the second place, we must bear in mind that the description here is of the heavenly Jerusalem, not of the church in this present time. The meaning is rather that also in the eternal kingdom there will be great and small. There will be rulers in the New Jerusalem, as well as those who

are subject to those rulers. All shall not be the same and of the same rank.
This need not be considered strange and out of place. For one thing, this is
in harmony with what Scripture tells us of the angel world; also among the
perfect and heavenly spirits there are differences of rank and glory,
thrones and principalities and powers. Moreover, Scripture elsewhere
teaches that among the saints there shall also be differences. Of the
apostles we read that they shall sit on twelve thrones, for example.
Nevertheless, all the dominion and glory of kings and of nations shall be in
the service of the glorified Christ in the church.

Spiritually the citizens and their perfection are described both
negatively and positively. We read in verse 27: "And there shall in no wise
enter into it any thing that defileth, neither whatsoever worketh
abomination, or maketh a lie: but they which are written in the Lamb's
book of life." Nothing that defiles either the nature of the citizens or the
relation between them or the entire inheritance, nothing at all of the
defilement of sin, shall enter into the city. Nothing which worketh
abomination, that is, no spiritual adultery or whatsoever may occasion it,
shall enter into the city. And nothing which makes a lie, that is, an idol
and whatever is a denial of the only true God, shall enter into the city. On
the contrary, only they which are written in the Lamb's book of life shall
have a place there. They are the elect, those who are chosen in Christ, who
are redeemed by Him and delivered by Him from all the defilement of sin,
from all the abomination of spiritual adultery, and from all the power of
the lie. They are sanctified and cleansed and purified in the blood of the
Lamb. They are the perfect citizens of the kingdom forevermore.
Moreover, we may notice that the perfection of the New Jerusalem is
greater than that of the first paradise. For it is emphasized that that which
defiles and works abomination and makes a lie shall **in no wise** enter into
the city; that is, the very possibility of corruption is forever gone. The
reason is that the center and head of this communion of the holy city is
Christ, the Son of God in the flesh, Who died and rose again. Death hath
no more dominion over Him, and therefore no more dominion over those
who are of Him, those who are written in the Lamb's book of life.

In the second place, our attention is drawn to the heavenly glory of the
city and its citizens.

John writes: "And I saw no temple therein: for the Lord God Almighty
and the Lamb are the temple of it." The idea of the temple, as we have
seen before, is that it is the house of God, the dwellingplace of God in

fellowship with His people. In the old, earthly Jerusalem there was a special temple, a separate building, distinct from the rest of the city. Although Jerusalem as a whole was the city of God, the Lord nevertheless did not dwell in the entire city; but He had His dwelling in the city in a special house, and particularly in the holy of holies, behind the veil. Then the people would go there to worship and to sacrifice and pray and to be blessed. In that sense there shall be no temple in the New Jerusalem, no special house of God. And the reason for the absence of a special temple is given in the text: "For the Lord God Almighty and the Lamb are the temple of it." In other words, the text does not mean that the temple-idea is done away, but rather that it has come to its highest and fullest realization. There is no need, no occasion, for a special temple: for God Himself is the temple of His people in Christ. That God and the Lamb are the temple signifies that God through the Lamb is the temple. Through the Lamb God dwells with His people. Christ, through His Spirit, will perfectly and completely fill the glorified church; and through Him God shall be with us in constant and perfect fellowship. Not a special building will be His temple, but the entire spiritual building of the church, that is, the whole city, shall be His dwellingplace. Constantly and everywhere His people shall know Him as He reveals Himself to them and as He walks with them. They see God evermore and everywhere, and dwell in His blessed fellowship. And all of life will be a constant worship of God in perfection.

It is in this context that we must also consider the words of verse 23: "And the city had no need of the sun, neither of the moon, to shine in it: for the glory of God did lighten it, and the Lamb is the light thereof." This does not mean that in the new creation there will be neither sun nor moon. For the reference here is not to the new creation, but to the holy city, the bride of the Lamb, the church. Nor does the text state that there will be no sun and moon, but that the glorified church will have no **need** of it. The question is: why and for what does the city not need sun or moon? And the reason is given in the second part of the verse: "for the glory of God did lighten it, and the Lamb is the light thereof." Here, in the earthly creation, our knowledge of God is mediate. It is through earthly things. And there is only a reflection of the glory of God through the light of the sun and moon. For that kind of knowledge the light of the sun and the moon is necessary. But there we shall know and see God face to face. The glory of God, that is, the radiation of all His perfections, lightens the city, that is, the hearts and minds of the saints who constitute the city.

And this is through Christ, the Lamb, Who is the lamp in Whom that light shines. In the New Jerusalem, therefore, the saints behold the glory of God's virtues in Christ directly and immediately. They shall see Him face to face, and know Him as they are known!

Finally, the passage speaks of the activity of the citizens of the New Jerusalem.

First of all, we read that "the nations of them which are saved shall walk..." There shall be activity in the New Jerusalem. Its citizens shall not lazily loll by the river of the water of life, but shall be active. In the frequently used Scriptural expression "walk" we have a reference to this. By their walk is meant their entire life and conversation, all their activity, and that too, in relation to God. In the new creation there will be work. Indeed, there shall be no toil in order to eke out an existence or to accumulate wealth. But the citizens, each in his own place and with his definite tasks and his talents and gifts, shall be active. In eternal glory there will be constant life and constant activity, all in the service of God. For all the activity is in the light of the city; that is, all their walk and conversation is controlled and motivated by the perfect knowledge of and fellowship with God through the Lamb. And therefore, all their work will at the same time be perfect rest, the rest of God's everlasting covenant. In harmony with this is also the idea that all, the kings and the nations, bring their glory and honor into the New Jerusalem. The language and presentation are derived from the prophecies of the Old Testament (cf., for example, Isaiah 60 and Psalm 72). From that point of view, the nations are the Gentile nations who come to Jerusalem to worship and bring their treasures and offerings to the city of God. Actually, of course, the nations are not outside of Jerusalem, but included in it. And the picture of the vision is that all the honor and glory of the nations concentrates around Christ and His church, and all the fruit of their labors is consecrated to the glory of God and of the Lamb. All the activity of the New Jerusalem shall be perfect service of God!

Moreover, this activity shall be constant. This is the point of verse 25: "And the gates of it shall not be shut at all by day: for there shall be no night there." Once again we must remember that the reference is not to the new creation, but to the glorified church. Hence, we dare not draw the conclusion from this verse that there will be no representation of the glory and beauty of the night in the new creation. The idea is rather that for the glorified church there will be no night, but only constant light and constant, uninterrupted activity. In harmony with this is the idea that the gates shall not be shut. The gates of a city are shut at night, when there is fear of the enemy. But in that city the gates shall not be shut: for there is no night with its fear of the enemy, no night and its cessation of all activity, when the glory and honor of kings and nations cannot be brought into the city. There shall only be constant activity and constant fulness of life and joy.

What a great and holy city that shall be!

What a tremendous contrast there is between Babylon and its end in outer darkness and the New Jerusalem, the church, with its everlasting light and perfection and bliss and glory!

Well may we rejoice if our names are written in the Lamb's book of life! And well may we strive to keep our spiritual garments clean from everything that defileth, or that maketh abomination, or that maketh a lie! For if we are of the former, then we cannot be of the latter; and if we are of them who partake of Babylon's corruptions, then we are not of those whose names are written in the Lamb's book of life. And only they, but surely they, who are written in the Lamb's book of life shall enter into that city, where the covenant and kingdom of God shall be perfect forevermore!

Chapter LII

The Paradise Of God

(Revelation 22:1-5)

1 And he shewed me a pure river of water of life, clear as crystal, proceeding out of the throne of God and of the Lamb.
2 In the midst of the street of it, and on either side of the river, was there the tree of life, which bare twelve manner of fruits, and yielded her fruit every month: and the leaves of the tree were for the healing of the nations.
3 And there shall be no more curse: but the throne of God and of the Lamb shall be in it; and his servants shall serve him:
4 And they shall see his face; and his name shall be in their foreheads.
5 And there shall be no night there; and they need no candle, neither light of the sun; for the Lord God giveth them light: and they shall reign for ever and ever.

As a most cursory glance will show, this portion of Revelation 22 is a continuation of the vision in the preceding chapter, and it constitutes the close of the vision of the New Jerusalem. Especially in the last part of Chapter 21 our attention was drawn to the blessedness of the life of the New Jerusalem, to its glory, its light, its righteous inhabitants, and to its victory. In the passage now under discussion it is that same New Jerusalem that is described. This is evident from the fact that the text simply continues the narrative of Chapter 21. When it says, "And he shewed me..," the reference is to the same angel, one of the seven vial-angels, who had said to John in verse 9 of the preceding chapter, "Come hither, I will shew thee the bride, the Lamb's wife." In the same vein, moreover, the text continues to speak of the street of the city, which was mentioned in verse 21 of the last chapter, and of the nations and the citizens, who also appear more than once in the preceding chapter. There can be no doubt, therefore, that this is not a new and different vision, but a continuation of the description of the New Jerusalem.

However, there is a new and additional viewpoint in this section. In the former portion all was pictured under the aspect of a city, the New Jerusalem, as the antitype and fulfillment of the old city of earthly Jerusalem. Here something is added. In this section the life and blessedness of the glorified church is described under the imagery of the original garden of Eden, Paradise the First. The symbolism of the city is not abandoned, as is evident from the reference to the street of the city and to the throne of God and of the Lamb and to the nations. But into this vision of the New Jerusalem is injected the symbolism of Paradise. There was mention of this already in the letter to the church at Ephesus in Revelation 2:7: "To him that overcometh will I give to eat of the tree of life, which is in the midst of the paradise of God." And here the Paradise of God is presented as the final realization of the promise, the fulness of joy of eternal life for the church, the New Jerusalem.

Also in this passage, therefore, we must remember that this is a vision, and that in highly symbolic form the glorified church is here described. The purpose is not to describe the new creation or some specific part of the new creation. On the contrary, in the Paradise-idea and the various details, such as the river of water of life and the tree of life with its fruits and its leaves, the bride, the Lamb's wife, that is, the church, is being described. And the same caution which was mentioned in connection with the preceding vision of the New Jerusalem must be observed: we must not be tempted to think in terms of a literal river and a literal tree in a literal garden, but must try to understand the meaning of this symbolism as a description of the blessedness of the life of the glorified church.

The Idea Of The Paradise Of God

In order to understand this passage we must try first to get before us the picture that is drawn by the text. There can be no question about it, that the reference here is to Paradise. For while Paradise is not mentioned in so many words, the details, considered in the light of Scripture, certainly convey the idea of Paradise. In the garden of Eden there was a river, watering the garden; here the text speaks of the river of the water of life. In the garden there was the tree of life; so here we find the tree of life. The reference, therefore, is clearly to the Paradise-idea, which appears historically, of course, at the dawn of history, but which also occurs prophetically in the Old Testament, (cf. Genesis 2:8-17; Ezekiel 47:1-12; Zechariah 14:8).

The Paradise Of God

707

Here, as we already suggested, the idea of Paradise is, so to speak, superimposed upon the picture of the holy city, New Jerusalem. Attention is called in the passage to the street of the city. Apparently in the midst of the city and at the head of the street stands the throne of God and of the Lamb. From that throne issues forth a river, whose waters are clear as crystal, gushing forth through the midst of the street. For thus the text should be read, as the American Revised Version translates correctly: "And he showed me a river of water of life, bright as crystal, proceeding out of the throne of God and of the Lamb, in the midst of the street thereof." The river of the water of life flows through the midst of the street from the throne of God and the Lamb. Such is the picture. Moreover, on either side of the river, that is, on this side and on that side, grows the tree of life. There is, therefore, not only one tree, but many trees of the same species. The brink of the river is lined with trees. These trees yield a twelve-fold fruit, and they yield their fruit every month, that is, continually. And the leaves of the tree of life are for the healing of the nations who are earlier pictured as walking in the light of the city, the nations of them which are saved, (cf. Revelation 21:24).

In order to understand the meaning of this part of John's vision we must, first of all, look back to the original Paradise.

That original Paradise assumed the form of a beautiful garden, specially prepared as a dwelling-place for man. In connection with our present passage we need not give our attention to all the details of that first Paradise. That it was a most beautiful and pleasant place to live is clear from the description in Genesis 2. But all the details given us in Genesis which belonged only to the earthly form of Paradise are not essential now. The idea, the meaning, of it is essential and is realized in the vision of our text. That idea of Paradise is that it was a house of God, where Adam dwelled in fellowship with God. There the Lord God revealed Himself to man, and there Adam knew God and tasted His grace. There Adam served God in keeping and cultivating the garden. And there, in the fellowship of God's covenant, Adam functioned as God's prophet, priest, and king. Paradise the First was God's house for man; it was man's dwelling-place in the favor and fellowship of the Lord his God. This was its fundamental idea.

Here the future glory and blessedness of the New Jerusalem in the new heavens and the new earth is pictured as the final and highest possible realization of that earthly paradise, of the earthly tree of life, and of the original state of righteousness. Parenthetically, we may note here that if we understand this, and understand the idea of Paradise as the house of God for and with man, then it also does not seem at all strange that the idea of Paradise is introduced in the vision of the New Jerusalem. As to the two ideas, there is perfect unity in the text. For the fundamental idea of Paradise is nothing else than the tabernacle idea and the temple idea which have occurred in Revelation 21. Here we have that same idea conveyed in terms of the first Paradise.

But the question is: how must we understand all this? Do we have mere imagery here? Or does the final state of glory represent a return to the original state of righteousness? What is the meaning?

In answer to this question, we must emphasize, in the first place, that Paradise as it is pictured in Revelation 22 represents the final and perfect realization of the earthly Paradise. The first Paradise was an image of the last. But it was an image not in the sense of mere imagery, or symbolism. On the contrary, the Paradise of God in the new creation is the original and real Paradise, even though it is last in historical order. It is the ultimate and perfect realization of Paradise, and the first was only an image, a shadow, an earthly realization of that which was to come and which God purposed to realize in and through our Lord Jesus Christ. That first Paradise had to be destroyed to make room for the second Paradise, the real one. And in the New Jerusalem is the final and highest possible realization of the latter. The New Jerusalem, the Lamb's wife, the church, is the realization of the house, the dwelling-place, of God. "Behold, the tabernacle of God is with men!"

Let us understand the implications of this clearly.

In all of the preceding the picture is derived from the idea of the city of God, Jerusalem. In that connection we have pointed out more than once that throughout the ages the Lord our God is accomplishing one grand work of grace. He is building, realizing, Jerusalem, the city of God. For that reason the perfect and holy and great city, New Jerusalem, can be described in terms of the old, earthly city in the land of Canaan. But in the present passage the future glory and blessedness of God's people are described in terms of the old Paradise, before the fall. And the relationship is the same. The reason why this description is possible is that in that first Paradise we have an image, a picture of things to come. But the heavenly Paradise will not be a return to that first state of things. It is not thus, that sin spoiled the first creation and that the new heavens and the new earth and the new humanity will be the old creation over again. No, while Adam was of the earth, earthy, Christ is the Lord from heaven. And as now we bear the image of the earthy, so we shall also bear the image of the heavenly, I Corinthians 15:45-49. And thus it will be with all things in Christ. But that which was first in history was an image of things to come. The first Adam was an image of Him Who was to come. The covenant as it was realized with Adam was an image of the perfection of the covenant of grace in Christ. The temporal sabbath was an image of the everlasting rest. And the first Paradise was an image of the Paradise of God in the New Jerusalem. For that reason that first Paradise will never return. We must not picture to ourselves a literal river and a literal tree of life, no more than we must picture a literal return to the literal old Jerusalem. There shall be no return, but an advance to the perfection of the heavenly things in Christ Jesus.

In that connection, in the second place, we may point out that there is a difference between the Paradise of Revelation 22 and that of Genesis 2. The latter was a special garden in the land of Eden. The final Paradise will not feature such a special garden. The church itself shall constitute the house of God. And as far as the location of that house of God is concerned, the entire new creation is its place, Secondly, the final Paradise is not earthy, but heavenly in character, like our resurrected and heavenly Lord. And, in close connection with this, is the third difference: the final Paradise is characterized by absolute incorruptibility. For notice that while indeed the tree of life is represented here, there is no longer any tree of the knowledge of good and evil and no longer any probationary command such as was connected with that tree. And the reason is that there is no room for the tree of knowledge of good and evil any more. In Christ Jesus the church is victorious, incorruptible, immortal, heavenly!

The Life Of The Paradise Of God

In harmony with the preceding are all the details of the vision.

In the first place, John sees the river of the water of life: "And he showed me a river of water of life, bright as crystal, proceeding out of the throne of God and of the Lamb, in the midst of the street thereof," (ARV).

The text speaks of a river, that is, of a stream, of the water of life which was clear as crystal. In connection with Revelation 21:6 we have explained the idea and meaning of the water of life; and we need not explain it again at length. Here we may especially notice the element of the **river**. The river of the water of life, therefore, is symbolic of a constant flow of life, of the continuous operation of the life-giving Spirit of God in Christ which the glorified saints constantly and by a constant act on their part receive and appropriate. We are reminded of the well-known words of the Lord Jesus recorded in John 7:37-39: "In the last day, that great day of the feast, Jesus stood and cried, saying, If any man thirst, let him come unto me, and drink. He that believeth on me, as the scripture hath said, out of his belly shall flow rivers of living water. But this spake he of the Spirit, which they that believe on him should receive: for the Holy Ghost was not yet given; because that Jesus was not yet glorified." Especially in the light of this passage it is clear that this river of the water of life refers to the Spirit as the Spirit of Christ and to His continuous life-imparting operation. Or, if you will, the reference is to that stream of the blessings of grace,—the blessings of knowledge of God, righteousness, and holiness, of the favor of God, and of all that is implied in life in the true sense of the word,—a constant stream of blessings which flow to the saints through the Spirit of our Lord Jesus Christ.

In beautiful harmony with this idea of the river of the water of life are the other details mentioned in the text. First of all, the water of this river is clear as crystal, symbolizing that this life is pure and undefiled. In the second place, John beholds this river as proceeding out of the throne of God and of the Lamb. This evidently signifies that this energizing stream of pure life has its source in the God of our salvation through Christ. It is the life of God in and through Christ and through the Holy Spirit as the Spirit of Christ which flows into the New Jerusalem. And the fact that the **throne** of God and of the Lamb is mentioned as the source of this river emphasizes that this stream of life is the life of the kingdom of God as perfected in Christ. It is the life of the kingdom and its righteousness, the life of that perfect and heavenly commonwealth in which God is revealed and acknowledged as God. This life of the perfected kingdom of heaven fills the city and is received and consciously appropriated by the glorified saints. For even though here it is not specifically mentioned that the saints drink of this water, yet that is undoubtedly the implication also here. Besides, this river is represented as flowing through the midst of the street of the city, that is, as flowing through the very heart of the glorified church. And, in addition, the tree of life is pictured as growing on the banks of this river; and of this tree of life, which derives its life from the waters of this river, the saints partake. One life through one Spirit, therefore,—the life of God in Christ,—fills the entire church and all the saints.

In the second place, John sees the tree of life: "And on either side of the river was there the tree of life, which bare twelve manner of fruits, and yielded her fruit every month: and the leaves of the tree were for the healing of the nations."

The general meaning is clear. In the first Paradise the tree of life had especially a two-fold significance. First of all, that tree and its fruit had the power of giving perpetual, earthly life to man. This is clear from Genesis 3:22. Evidently the tree had the power to supply man with perpetual, earthly life, the power to perpetuate his existence, even after he had sinned, so that it was necessary to bar the way to the tree of life after the fall of Adam. In that same connection, we may notice that also the eating of that first tree of life was not a once-for-all matter, but that it would be necessary for Adam to eat of this tree continually and repeatedly. But the significance of the tree of life did not lie merely in the perpetuation of Adam's earthly existence. In the second place, it had a certain sacramental character. It was a sign and seal of God's favor, an emblem of God's covenant. It was a visible and tangible sign of that higher aspect of Adam's life which consisted in the knowledge of and fellowship with God. The tree of life was more than a mere physical means for the extension of man's physical existence. It was the tree of **life**. And life is more than mere perpetual existence. Even though Adam's life was earthy, nevertheless life also for Adam implied the favor and fellowship of God, his Creator-Lord. And if in this connection we bear in mind that the tree of life was in the midst of the garden, in the very heart of Paradise the First, we may say that according to the analogy of the temple, the tree of life constituted the most holy place. There, in the midst of the garden, where the tree of life was, dwelt God. There He met man in the wind of the day. To approach the tree of life, therefore, before the fall, was to approach God. As long as Adam could draw near to God, in order to enjoy His fellowship and communion, he could have life: not mere existence, but life in the true sense. Such was the significance of the earthly tree of life.

Now if we bear the preceding in mind, then we can clearly see the significance of the tree of life in this vision. In the first place, it symbolizes the perfected life of heavenly fellowship with God, which means that the saints constantly taste God's covenant friendship. But in the New

Jerusalem is the **reality** of the tree of life. Hence, not merely a sign of God's favor and friendship will the saints enjoy, but the full, heavenly reality of God's ever present favor. And, in the second place, the tree of life represents the perpetuation of the glorious life in the resurrection body. In our resurrection bodies we shall enjoy heavenly and immortal existence in the glory and blessedness of God's covenant friendship forever. This, as we have already noted, is in harmony with the fact that the tree of life stands on the brink of the river of the water of life. The power of the life of fellowship and friendship which resides in the tree of life proceeds from the throne of God and of the Lamb in and through the Spirit of Christ.

In connection with all this stands the fact that the tree bears twelve manner of fruit. Twelve is the number of the church, as we have seen before. Thus, there are twelve patriarchs, twelve tribes, twelve apostles, two times twelve elders, twelve times twelve thousand saints. All refers to the completeness of the perfected church in the new heavens and the new earth. Hence, that the tree bears twelve manner of fruits signifies that it bears a fulness of fruit for the entire church. Moreover, that the tree yields her fruit every month, that is, throughout the year, indicates that it bears fruit continuously. There is never any want of fruit, and therefore never any want of life and immortality, for the church. Finally, the text tells us that the leaves of the tree are for the healing of the nations. The implication cannot be that there will still be sickness to be cured in the New Jerusalem. Nor is this to be interpreted, as some would have it, that conversions will occur in the new creation. This is simply a figurative way of saying that no sickness of any kind can ever enter into the city of God and afflict the nations of them that are saved. Sickness is forever excluded from the New Jerusalem because of this power of eternal life which constantly flows from God in Christ through the Spirit into the church.

A Four-Fold Blessedness

In the remainder of this passage detail upon significant detail is added to the record of this vision, as though to emphasize that the glory and bliss of the New Jerusalem are beyond description. We ought to notice, concerning all these details, that they find their central significance in God and the Lamb. Thus we read that "the throne of God and of the Lamb shall be in it" (verse 3); that they "shall see **his face**," and that "**his name** shall be in their foreheads" (verse 4); and again, that "the Lord God giveth them light" (verse 5). All the blessedness of the eternal state concentrates in the fact that we shall be with God!

In detail, the blessedness of the Paradise of God is described here from a four-fold viewpoint.

In the first place, there will be no curse, verse 3: "And there shall be no more curse: but the throne of God and of the Lamb shall be in it; and his servants shall serve him." The curse of God is the expression and operation of God's wrath against sin, manifested in thorn and thistle, in toil and sweat, in the vanity of all things, in all kinds of suffering and sorrow and pain and death. In the New Jerusalem and in the new creation there shall be no more curse. It shall be absent. And this means, positively, that the opposite shall be true: there God's constant favor is present, manifested in joy and bliss and pleasures forevermore. The reason is that there is no room for the curse whatsoever: "but the throne of God and of the Lamb shall be in it; and his servants shall serve him." The meaning is clear. The perfected kingdom of heaven is there. God's reign of grace is finally and perfectly realized there. God reigns through Christ, the Lamb; and the service of Him by the saints, His servants, is perfect. The will of God is done by all. And where the will of God is done, there can be no curse. There can be only the perfect favor and fellowship of God.

In the second place, there will be the vision of God, verse 4: "And they shall see his face." It will be forever impossible to see God in His infinite essence. But the glorified saints shall see the face of God in the New Jerusalem. In the new creation there shall be the revelation of God in the face of Jesus Christ in the direct and highest possible sense of the word. Here we see only a reflection of that face of God through the Scriptures. We see in a glass, darkly. There, however, we shall see face to face. On the part of the saints, this will be possible because "his name shall be in their foreheads." The saints shall be like Him, as I John 3:2 tells us: "Beloved, now are we the sons of God, and it doth not yet appear what we shall be: but we know that, when he shall appear, (it is better to translate: "but we know that when it shall appear"), we shall be like him; for we shall see him as he is." This means, of course, that we shall see Christ as He is, and we shall see Him everywhere and always; and through Christ we shall see the face of God forever. This is implied in the fact that His name shall be in their foreheads. God's name is Himself in His revelation. Hence, there shall be true knowledge of Him. The minds and hearts of the saints shall be perfectly receptive for the knowledge of God as revealed in His face.

In close connection with this, in the third place, the text teaches that there will be direct knowledge of God, verse 5: "And there shall be no night there; and they need no candle, neither light of the sun; for the Lord God giveth them light." We are reminded here of the words of Revelation 21:23 and 25. Here, in this present world, all life and all knowledge is conditioned by the light of the sun, or even, as the text reminds us, by the artificial light of man, the light of a candle. Without light there is no possibility of knowledge. But there, in the new creation, there will be no need of physical or artificial light. As we said in connection with Revelation 21, the point of the text is not that there will be no natural night, or no natural sun or moon. But the latter will not be necessary as a medium of knowledge; in that sense there will be no darkness. And the reason is that the Lord God gives them light, light in the ethical, spiritual sense of the word, the light according to which we shall know and walk directly. The knowledge of God which is life eternal will be immediate and direct.

And thus, finally, the text speaks of the everlasting reign of the saints: "and they shall reign for ever and ever." With and in Christ the saints shall participate in the reign over all creatures in the new creation. A royal priesthood they shall be: they shall reign as the servants of God. All things shall serve them, that they may serve their God in Christ. Forever they shall reign! There will be no interruption, but their service and their reign shall be constant. And it will be unending. There will be no possibility of an end, no possibility of a fall any more. For all is concentrated and finally established in the throne of God and of the Lamb!

This is the hope of the saints, of them that are written in the Lamb's book of life.

Behold, He cometh!

And His promise is certain: "To him that overcometh will I give to eat of the tree of life, which is in the midst of the paradise of God."

Chapter LIII

The Epilogue

(Revelation 22:6-21)

6 And he said unto me, These sayings are faithful and true: and the Lord God of the holy prophets sent his angel to shew unto his servants the things which must shortly be done.

7 Behold, I come quickly: blessed is he that keepeth the sayings of the prophecy of this book.

8 And I John saw these things and heard them. And when I had heard and seen, I fell down to worship before the feet of the angel which shewed me these things.

9 Then saith he unto me, See thou do it not: for I am thy fellowservant, and of thy brethren the prophets, and of them which keep the sayings of this book: worship God.

10 And he saith unto me, Seal not the sayings of the prophecy of this book: for the time is at hand.

11 He that is unjust, let him be unjust still: and he which is filthy, let him be filthy still: and he that is righteous, let him be righteous still: and he that is holy, let him be holy still.

12 And, behold, I come quickly; and my reward is with me, to give every man according as his work shall be.

13 I am Alpha and Omega, the beginning and the end, the first and the last.

14 Blessed are they that do his commandments, that they may have right to the tree of life, and may enter in through the gates into the city.

15 For without are dogs, and sorcerers, and whoremongers, and murderers, and idolaters, and whosoever loveth and maketh a lie.

16 I Jesus have sent mine angel to testify unto you these things in the churches. I am the root and the offspring of David, and the bright and morning star.

17 And the Spirit and the bride say, Come. And let him that heareth say, Come. And let him that is athirst come. And whosoever will, let him take the water of life freely.

715

18 For I testify unto every man that heareth the words of the prophecy of this book, If any man shall add unto these things, God shall add unto him the plagues that are written in this book:
19 And if any man shall take away from the words of the book of this prophecy, God shall take away his part out of the book of life, and out of the holy city, and from the things which are written in this book.
20 He which testifieth these things saith, Surely I come quickly. Amen. Even so, come, Lord Jesus.
21 The grace of our Lord Jesus Christ be with you all. Amen.

As we have seen, the Book of Revelation consists, first of all, of an introduction in Chapter 1, verses 1 to 8. Secondly, there is the main body of the book. And finally, there is the close, or epilogue.

The main body of the book we have now finished. In our discussion we saw, in the first place, a picture of the church in its completeness, in its universality, and as she appears in every age, gradually degenerating into the church of Laodicea, or Babylon. Secondly, we found the vision of the Lamb standing as though it were slain before the throne of God and counted worthy to receive and to open the book with its seven seals. And then we followed the revelation contained in seal after seal as it was broken and as it was finally made manifest in the trumpets, and, in turn, in the vials. We obtained some vision of the mighty struggle which is carried on throughout the ages of the present dispensation for the completion and consummation of the kingdom of God in Jesus Christ our Lord. Mighty enemies arose against that kingdom. We obtained a view of the power of Antichrist developing throughout the ages and finally realizing itself in a tremendous world-power which is pictured as the beast out of the sea, aided by the beast arising from the earth. We learned how the church will apostatize from God and the Lamb and degenerate into an abominable harlot, who will be instrumental in the power of Antichrist. But plagues were also sent, just because of the existence of this power of opposition, — plagues of war and all kinds of social trouble, of revolution and insurrection, of famine and pestilence. And these plagues, we found, had for their purpose the detention of the powers of opposition, so that the world-power could not develop itself prematurely. But also the final destruction of that inimical power of the world and of all the enemies of Christ was revealed. In the meantime, we found that those plagues did not harm the people of God. On the contrary, they served to purify and to strengthen them. And in the midst of the tumult and tribulation of this present time, the one hundred forty-four thousand of the Lamb were sealed and kept safely. Finally, we also found how, in spite of all the counsel of the devil and of his host, the New Jerusalem descended out of the new heavens upon the new earth, and how the covenant of God was completely realized in that new world, where all the world shall lie at the bosom of God and be His kingdom, under Christ, the Anointed.

And now we have come to the close of the book. No more revelations and visions are to follow. What follows is an epilogue, a fit close and application of all that has been revealed to John and written by him. There is in this epilogue, no doubt, abundant material for many separate discourses. We shall treat it, however, as one whole. For, in the first place, it actually constitutes one whole and belongs together. And, in the second place, as we said in the beginning, it is not our purpose to develop the different points of doctrine which are implied in the book, but merely to study it with a view to the purpose for which it has been given to the church, that is, to obtain a vision of the coming Lord. Much of the detail that is found in this passage we have met with at various other points in the book; and we will not repeat. Hence, we view the rest of this twenty-second chapter, from verse 6 to the end, as an epilogue.

The Speedy Coming Of The Lord: Assured

The main subject and contents of this epilogue is undoubtedly the speedy coming of the Lord. A careful reading will show that this is actually the all-pervading idea of this passage. For it is mentioned in the text repeatedly. In verse 6 we read: "These sayings are faithful and true: and the Lord God of the holy prophets sent his angel to shew unto his servants the things which must shortly be done." These "things which must shortly be done," (or: "come to pass") are all concentrated around the coming of the Lord. Here John records once more that they **must** come to pass. That the Lord does come constitutes the consummation of the counsel of God. And that these things must come to pass shortly, or quickly, is emphasized throughout the passage. This is really an assertion, therefore, that the Lord will surely come quickly. The same is true of verse 7. Here we have a direct statement of the Lord Himself: "Behold, I come quickly." The same thought is twice more expressed in verse 12 and in verse 20: "And, behold, I come quickly." The same idea is expressed in

verse 10 from a slightly different point of view: "Seal not the sayings of
the prophecy of this book: for the time is at hand." Once more, in verse
17 we read of the response of the Spirit and of the bride, as well as of the
individual believer. And that response is again that the Lord may come
quickly: "And the Spirit and the bride say, Come. And let him that
heareth say, Come. And let him that is athirst come. And whosoever will,
let him take the water of life freely." And, finally, in verse 20 we meet
with the response from the heart of John himself in the same words: "He
which testifieth these things saith, Surely I come quickly. Amen. Even so,
come, Lord Jesus." No less than seven times, therefore, in the space of
these few verses do we meet with an indication of the coming of the Lord.
Hence, I regard this as the main topic of the epilogue.

Neither need we be surprised that it should be so.

For we have here the close of the entire book. And it is the purpose of
an epilogue, or application, to drive home the main subject of the Book of
Revelation. That chief subject of the entire book is, beyond all doubt, that
the Lord cometh quickly. The book was written that the church might not
be forgetful of that fact, might not grow weary and despondent. It was
written that the church might be able to see the coming of the Lord in the
history of the world. Hence, it was indeed meet that the chief subject of
the application, or epilogue, should be: "The Lord cometh quickly."

Now what is the meaning of this statement?

After all that we have discussed, we can realize the truth of this
statement all the more clearly. Also at the beginning the statement was
made. But then we could not conceive of all that was implied in this
coming of the Lord. Now, however, we have obtained a conception of it;
and we can realize the truth that is expressed here all the better.

Jesus is coming!

He has told us how He would come. He would come accompanied by
wars and plagues of famine and pestilence. And the nearer He would come,
the more emphatically the power of opposition would assert itself. We
have learned to see that history is actually carried out so as to point to the
coming of the Lord. And therefore we say, "He is coming!" Others may be
blind to the fact that the Lord is coming; but we say nevertheless, "He is
coming; and we see Him come!"

Besides, according to the text, He is coming **quickly**. Also this we can
now understand all the better. Nineteen hundred years have passed, and
yet He has not arrived. But we understand that He is coming speedily

nevertheless; He is coming quickly, very rapidly. He is coming as soon and as quickly as it is possible. If we will understand how rapidly Jesus is coming, we must take into consideration what must happen before His final coming. Let us use an illustration from the history of World War I, and, in fact, also from the Second World War. When Germany pressed the Allies and pressed them hard, they were for a time in desperate straits. And longingly they looked for the coming of the Americans. The Americans said, "We are coming, and we are coming quickly." But many months elapsed before they actually did come. To the Allies in their desperate condition it seemed a long time before they actually came. Yet did not the Americans come quickly? Surely, they did; and they came as fast as it was possible for them to come. But think what was implied in their coming. Many, many things had to be prepared before they could come. An army had to be drafted and trained. Money had to be raised. The army had to be equipped. The material, clothing and ammunition and weapons, had to be manufactured. Ships had to be built. In view of all this, it was absolutely true that they were coming quickly. The same may be applied to the coming of our Lord Jesus Christ. From our point of view it may seem a long time. But look! The children of God must be gathered. The whole church, gathered from all nations, must be filled: not one of the elect may be lacking. Besides, the great apostasy must take place. Antichrist and all the power of iniquity must develop. Babylon must be realized. The world-power must be formed. Surely, all these things being taken into consideration, we may certainly say, "He comes quickly." Things, especially in the last twenty-five or fifty years, are developing before our very eyes. We see Him come!

Realizing, however, that from our point of view the time may seem long, the Lord assures His church in this application repeatedly that He is actually and surely coming, that all that has been written in the book concerning His coming is absolutely true.

For thus we read in verse 6: "And he said unto me, These sayings are faithful and true: and the Lord God of the holy prophets sent his angel to shew unto his servants the things which must shortly be done." These words, according to the text, are faithful. They are faithful, that is, they shall prove to be real. They shall not disappoint those who read and believe. What is written in the book shall surely be realized. And therefore, they are not only faithful, but true. They are not mere fiction, a romance; but they are in harmony with reality. They are a revelation of the counsel of God which can never fail. And there is the most complete harmony between that counsel and these words of the Book of Revelation. In the second place, this is solemnly assured by supporting the statement that these sayings are faithful and true by the name of the Author. He is none less than the Lord God of the spirit of the prophets Who revealed these things to the churches through the medium of the angel who spoke with John. God controlled the spirit of the prophets; and He controlled also the spirit of John when he received these visions. God revealed to him the entire truth concerning the coming of the Lord and concerning His coming speedily. They were not products of a fanciful imagination, but they were the revelation of the living God. He is the Alpha and the Omega, the first and the last, the beginning and the end. He stands above all time and history. And He is the Unchangeable One. He is the cause and also the purpose of all history; and He alone absolutely controls it, even by our Lord Jesus Christ. He, the unchangeable and almighty God, is the pledge for the truth of the statement that these things will come to pass, and that they will come to pass soon, so that it is certainly true that the Lord will come quickly. Jesus, the root and offspring of David, the bright and morning star, is the chief servant of the Lord. He is the Savior, Who once shed His lifeblood for His people; the root and offspring of David, Who once came as the realization of Old Testament prophecy. He is the bright and morning star, Who Himself is therefore the light of that eternal morning and Who will surely appear as the herald of the morning, as certainly as the morning star appears in the heavens.

Shall we waver in the sight of such witnesses? The wise of the world say, "You are demented. What you are teaching is absolutely contrary to fact." The powerful of the world say, "You are a dreamer." The rich of the world say, "You are a pessimist." Whatever they say, we have the testimony of Jesus, of the almighty, everlasting, faithful Savior. Shall we exchange world-views? Never! Jesus is surely coming! He is coming quickly!

The Speedy Coming Of The Lord: Impressed

This truth, that the contents of the Book of Revelation are faithful and true, is impressed upon us, first of all, by the mention of reward and punishment. It is because of the tremendous certainty and significance of this fact that the truth of Jesus' coming is impressed upon us very seriously.

First the command comes that the book must not be sealed, but must remain open, verse 10: "And he saith unto me, Seal not the sayings of the prophecy of this book: for the time is at hand." The book, therefore, must not be closed, and the sayings of this book must never be sealed. Its contents must be transmitted to the church. And it must be expounded by the church in the midst of the world. They must read it, understand it, and testify of it.

If this is done, the result will be two-fold, as is the case with the entire Word of God. Always there are those who are saved and those who are hardened. The Word of God is always a savor of life unto life, but also a savor of death unto death. What is true of the Word of God in general is also and emphatically true of the Book of Revelation. When it is opened and expounded, there will be those who will have nothing of it, who will deny the truth of its contents. As I said before, they will say, "You dream. You are beside yourself. You are a pessimist." The sayings of this prophecy will arouse the opposition of the wicked, of those who have no hope, or whose hope is vain because it is only a hope in and of the present world. This prophecy leaves no hope for their vain dreams. Thus, it will arouse them to greater hostility and opposition, to more wickedness. But, on the other hand, it will also strengthen the faith and hope of the people of God. This, therefore, is inevitable.

What then? Must this book remain closed because it will arouse opposition, because it will reveal more wickedness on the part of some?

No, the answer is in verse 11: "He that is unjust, let him be unjust still: and he which is filthy, let him be filthy still: and he that is righteous, let him be righteous still: and he that is holy, let him be holy still." These words have been variously interpreted. Some find irony in them. But this certainly does not fit the second part of the text, concerning him that is righteous and holy. Others explain them as referring to the confirmed state of the righteous and of the wicked after the final judgment. But there is nothing in the context to suggest this. Besides, it can hardly be said that the damned in hell are confirmed in their sin and still commit iniquity. The meaning, however, is rather clear if we see these words in their close connection with the statement in verse 10 that the time is at hand and that therefore the book must not be sealed. Before the end can come, the two-fold ethical fruit, that of the root-sin of Adam and that of the righteousness in Christ, must be ripe. And this is to be attained in the continued works of iniquity of the reprobate ungodly, on the one hand;

and, on the other hand, it is to be attained in the fruits of righteousness in Christ on the part of the saints in the midst of an ungodly world. In this light we can understand the words of verse 11. This book will draw the lines. It will strengthen and emphasize the great difference between the people of God and the world. It will make the world more conscious of the great difference between its ideals and those of the people of God; it will also make the children of God more conscious of the same fact. And for the latter purpose the book may not remain closed, but must be open, so that all can hear and read and so that this two-fold effect may be achieved. For the time is at hand! The Lord cometh quickly! Let this separating process, this process of the bearing of a two-fold ethical fruit, go on without restraint, so that the fruit may become ripe, and so that the end may come!

To be sure, there is also the responsibility connected with the reading and hearing of the sayings of this book. For it is emphasized that the Lord will come with His reward, to render to every man according as his work shall be, (verse 12). Have we been more unrighteous and more filthy through the revelation of this book? We shall have no part with the tree of life, and we shall not enter into the eternal and glorious city of God. In the New Jerusalem are only those who have their robes washed, those who have by faith washed their robes in the blood of Christ. (The ARV renders verse 14 more correctly: "Blessed are they that wash their robes...") By faith they have been sanctified and cleansed from all unrighteousness and from all filth, even as by faith they have been justified and freed from all the guilt of sin. This implies too, of course, as far as the reward of the righteous is concerned, that the reward of their works is ever a reward of grace. For fundamentally the work of Christ their Lord in their behalf is the righteousness of the saints; and its imputation to them is the guarantee that they can never be condemned. It is **in His blood** that they wash their robes by faith! And they are blessed! They have a right to come to the tree of life. And they shall enter into the city through the gates. The meaning is not that there is a possibility of entering in any other way. But this expression is added in order to emphasize the fact that they enter into the city as those who are its rightful citizens. The angels of the gates open to them; and they belong to the commonwealth of Israel, the names of whose tribes are written on these gates. But in marked contrast are those who are "without," verse 15: "For without are dogs (meaning: false teachers), and sorcerers, and whoremongers, and murderers, and idolaters, and whosoever loveth and maketh a lie." They receive the just reward of their works. They are "without," that is, in outer darkness!

But there is more.

The contents of the Book of Revelation is not only impressed by this mention of reward and of punishment. It is also impressed by a dire threat to those who assume an unbelieving attitude toward the contents of this book. This we find in verses 18 and 19: "For I testify unto every man that heareth the words of the prophecy of this book, If any man shall add unto these things, God shall add unto him the plagues that are written in this book: And if any man shall take away from the words of the book of this prophecy, God shall take away his part out of the book of life, and out of the holy city, and from the things which are written in this book." In these words there is a very serious warning, a warning which is based upon and which proceeds from the truth and faithfulness of the sayings of the prophecy of this book.

Surely, what is said in these verses does not apply to the imperfect understanding of believers. After all, the words of the book remain a prophecy, with all the difficulties of interpretation contained in it. We realize clearly our own feebleness in understanding perfectly all that is implied in this prophecy. No, the words refer to a conscious attitude of unbelief. They are addressed to him that heareth the words of this prophecy, who therefore becomes acquainted with its contents. He can change the book so as to suit his own fancy and his own purpose, so that after all the kingdom of the world is confused with the kingdom of God in Christ. He can do that by adding to the book or by detracting from it. The book can indeed be so augmented and can be so abridged that the light of the truth of this prophecy is bedimmed, and so that particularly the truth that Jesus is coming is deliberately corrupted and denied.

The punishment which is threatened is, negatively, that he shall be deprived of his part in the book of life and of his part in the holy city and in all the things which are written in the book.

Of course, this must not be interpreted as if there were a falling away from grace, as though such a person at one time really had a part in these things, but later fell from grace and lost that part. All Scripture emphasizes very clearly that such a falling away is impossible. God preserves His people. And through the power of God's preservation they certainly will persevere. In actual fact, of course, no names can ever be taken out of the book of life. Nor does the person to whom these words apply truly have a part in the book of life even before his own consciousness. The Holy Spirit does not testify in his heart that he is a child of God, but witnesses, through the Word, that he is a child of the devil. He has no faith, and, therefore, no hope, that is, no expectation, no assurance, and no longing for eternal glory. Moreover, God, through His Spirit, impresses upon his mind that, seeing that he willfully distorts the sayings of this book, he must know and be conscious of the fact that he has no part in the real book of life and the real holy city. But it is possible for such an one to have a part in a book of life of his own imagination and in a holy city of his own creation. And it is possible for such an one to act and to speak as though he has a part in the book of life and the holy city while in actual fact he does not mean God's book of life and the real holy city at all, and while in actual fact he distorts and corrupts the very words of the prophecy concerning the holy city and the coming of the Lord. And it is possible to appear before men, before the church in the world, as having a part in the book of life and in the holy city. And it is possible that as far as men are concerned the name of such a person is written in the book of life. But what the text states here is another and emphatic way of saying that he who takes away from the words of the book of this prophecy has never had any part in the book of life and in the holy city. And in the end this shall be revealed. Positively, these verses teach that such a false prophet shall participate in all the plagues that are written in this book, that is, in the plagues that are threatened upon the wicked, upon the antichristian world. He is like them and of them; and he shall participate in all their plagues, to the very last, in the lake that burns with fire and brimstone. For, "Behold, he cometh!" And His reward is with Him, to render unto every man according as his work shall be. And His Word is inviolable!

The Speedy Coming Of The Lord: Kindling Response

Finally, we find in this passage a beautiful response to the prophecy of this book, and especially to the truth that Jesus is coming. This is expressed as a fact, let us notice. The text says, in the first place, that the effect of this revelation of the coming of the Lord upon the church as a whole is that she responds and eagerly says, "Come, Lord." We find this, in the first place, in verse 17: "And the Spirit and the bride say, Come. And let him that heareth say, Come. And let him that is athirst come. And whosoever will, let him take the water of life freely." And again, in verse

20 we read: "He which testifieth these things saith, Surely I come quickly. Amen. Even so, come, Lord Jesus."

In verse 17, therefore, we read that the Spirit and the bride say, "Come." And we understand, of course, that they are not to be taken separately, as if the Spirit of Christ and the bride separately express this longing for the coming of the Lord. This is impossible. The Spirit is the Spirit of the Bridegroom. That Spirit of the Bridegroom dwells in the bride, that is, in the church. Hence, it is through the Spirit that the bride says, "Come." Under the influence of this revelation the bride says, through the Spirit, "Come, Lord Jesus." Naturally! This must needs be the spontaneous response of the bride. For the bride receives a picture of the glory of the Bridegroom and of the time when she shall always be with Him. She is conscious all the more, through the prophecy of this book, of her present misery, of her tribulation which she must and does suffer in the midst of the world. She is conscious of her present separation. She is conscious of her sinfulness. And when, through the words of the book of this prophecy, she looks at the glory which shall be revealed to her, she calls out, under the influence of the Spirit of the Bridegroom, "Come; yea, come, Lord Jesus!"

This response comes from the bride as a whole. The church organically in principle always longs for the coming of the Bridegroom even though she may not always be equally conscious of this longing for the coming of the Lord. But also individual believers do not always partake in this sigh of longing. But the church responds to this promise of the coming of the Lord not only directly and in earnest prayer, but also in the preaching. Hence, through that preaching of the bride comes the admonition, or exhortation, "And let him that heareth say, Come." And again: "And let him that is athirst come." And once more: "And whosoever will (that is: whosoever longs for righteousness and life, and who therefore will), let him take of the water of life freely."

This is at the same time a test for us as a church and as individual believers. The question is: do we participate in this response? More or less, as the book was explained to us, did we say sometimes, "Come, Lord Jesus; yea, come quickly?" But, in the first place, as these words are an exhortation, we must turn away from the world and its lusts. We must look forward in hope to the blessed day when the Lord shall come. And it is only in that hope, which certainly can never fail, that we are able to say, "Come, Lord Jesus." Secondly, and in connection with this exhortation, to that individual child of God comes the glad evangel, "Take of the water of life freely." This water of life, as it flows forevermore in the New Jerusalem, is promised to us. It is for him that is athirst. There may be among God's people those who fear and doubt, who wonder whether they shall partake of the blessedness and the glory of the New Jerusalem. O, they are indeed thirsty. They long for the perfection which shall be revealed to us in the day of our Lord Jesus Christ. Nevertheless, they have nothing to bring, absolutely nothing. And therefore the exhortation and assurance is very significant: "Come, take of the water of life freely." That is, have absolutely nothing of yourselves. Have all things only in Christ Jesus. Then, indeed, you shall not only look at the water of life. You shall not only be athirst. You shall listen to this exhortation, "Let him come and drink of the water of life freely!"

Finally, we have at the close of the book a testimony of John, first of all in verses 8 and 9: "And I John saw these things and heard them. And when I had heard and seen, I fell down to worship before the feet of the angel which shewed me these things. Then saith he unto me, See thou do it not: for I am thy fellowservant, and of thy brethren the prophets, and of them which keep the sayings of this book: worship God." John evidently is so overwhelmed by the visions he had received, and especially by the vision of the New Jerusalem, that he falls down to worship. Surely, that worship was mistaken, as is explained by the angel; and the angel corrects him. But the impression is indeed comprehensible. He is overwhelmed, and he accepted all that he saw and heard by faith. And there is a final testimony of John himself when, according to verse 20, he personally responds to the repeated assurance of the Lord's quick coming in the words, "Even so, come, Lord Jesus."

If that may be the result of our discussion of the Book of Revelation, the result that we have grown in the knowledge of the glory of the coming of our Lord Jesus Christ, grown in the faith and in the hope and longing and in the strength to renounce the world, in grace to wash our robes, and to walk in the midst of the world in that hope eternal, and therefore also in sanctification of life, it will be sufficient. And we may close where the book closes, with the apostle pronouncing the blessing upon the church: "The grace of our Lord Jesus Christ be with you all. Amen."